KISS Alive Forever

The Complete Touring History

Curt Gooch & Jeff Suhs

Dedicated to Mike Wren, Elliot Swainson, JR Smalling, Mick Campise, Peter Oreckinto, Rick Munroe, Sean Delaney, Jay Barth, Mark Stinner, and the long-lost Mike McGurl—where are you?

Library of Congress Cataloging-in-Publication Data

Gooch, Curt.
    Kiss alive forever : the complete touring history / Curt Gooch & Jeff Suhs.— 1st ed.
        p.   cm.
    ISBN 0-8230-8322-5 (pbk.)
    1. Kiss (Musical group)—Performances. 2. Rock musicians—United States. I.
Suhs, Jeff. II. Title.
ML421.K57 G6 2002
782.42166'092'2—dc21
                                                    2002011724

Senior Editor: Bob Nirkind
Editor: Elizabeth Wright
Book design: Jay Anning, Thumb Print
Graphic Production: Ellen Greene
Cover photo © Ebet Roberts
Cover photo editing/research: Ros Radley
Archivists: Jeff Falk, John Daniel, and Mike Wren
Research Assistants: Joe Fields and Brian Johnson
Scans by Art Box for Graphic Arts, Oklahoma City—
    special thanks to Brian Malwick

CONTENTS

ACKNOWLEDGEMENTS

Although there are only two names on the cover of this book, hundreds of people contributed to its writing and they need to be acknowledged. We are especially indebted to the following individuals without whom this book would not have been possible: Mike Wren, Mark Cicchini at kissvidking@aol.com, Bill Kershaw from Heaven's Tapes, Tom Valentino, Steve Sils, Bill Baker, C.K. Lendt, Mike Brandvold, Jay Shanker, Martin Dean, Jacques van Gool, Melissa Stallings and Joshua Derr at *Performance* magazine, Chris & Beth White at www.kissasylum.com, and Bob Nirkind and Elizabeth Wright at Billboard Books.

The majority of research was conducted at Harold Washington Library in Chicago; Washington University Library and St. Louis Public Library in St. Louis; University of South Florida Library in Tampa; the Cleveland Public Library; and the Library of Congress. Over the course of the last six years, the research trail has taken us to the phones, computers, and doorsteps of dozens of other libraries throughout the world and we would like to offer our sincerest thanks for their assistance and tireless efforts.

While the information acquired from libraries, paperwork, and itineraries makes up the substance of this book, its color and life come from the many individuals who graciously consented to interviews or spent time discussing their memories with us. The authors' appreciation and enduring thanks go to: Bill Aucoin, Rick Munroe, Mick Campise, JR Smalling, Peter Oreckinto, Jay Barth, Mark Stinner, Rick Stuart, Sean Delaney, Eddie Solan, Eddie Balandas, Bill McManus, Chuck Elias, Pixie Esmonde, Mark Ravitz, Don Ketteler, Linda West, Steve Gansky, Jaan Uhelski, Arlene Dockett, Virginia Barrett, Ann Tonetti, Lew Linet, Joshua White, Bill Welch, Brooke Ostrander, Tony Zarrella, Ron Leejack, Joey Criscuola, Ron Johnsen, Eddie Kramer, Alice West, Tom Werman, Greg Gellar, Sol Saffian, Billy Michelle, Alan Cohen, Fritz Postlethwaite, Gary Corbett, Les Haber, John McGraw, Robert Roth, Mike Taite, Dave Bonilla, Larry Mazer, Steve Wood, Bob Kulick, Bruce Kulick, Peter Criss (1994), Ron Gitman, Ginger Bianco, Jeanie Fineberg, Paul Sub, Rick Rivets, Rik Fox, Keith West, Ken Donovan, John Montgomery, Jayne County, Lydia Criss, Ron Blanchard, Nicky Martyn, Sylvain Sylvain, Arthur Kane, John Segall, Ivan Kral, Andy Doback, Pearl E. Gates, Bob Kelleher, Jayne Grodd, Ida Langsam, Richard Nader, Vincent Calandra, Arnie Toshner, Stan Orlen, Ken Anderson, Al Ross, Danny Goldberg, Ric Aliberte, John Bestwick, Bob Brigham, Pat Morrow, Lamar Scott, Bruce Redoute, Lee Neaves, Hal Clifford, Allan Schwartzberg, Pat Rebillot, Neal Schon, Billy Squier, Richie Ranno, James Young, Tommy Shaw, Keith Nelson, Cyndi Lauper, Kevin Bacon, John Waite, Derek Sherinian, David Lee, Scott Shannon, Dex Card, Bill Starkey, John Schwanke, Frank Morgan, Paul Cangialosi, Lee Peyton, and Jeff Franklin.

The following people also made vital contributions to the book: Alan Stout, Kevin Gladden, Mike Naimoli, Bill Bartell, Tommy Sommers, Ken Sharp, Andrew Doback and everyone at Whiplash Records, Jeff Falk, Brian Johnson, Joe Fields, Pieter Brown, Jonathan Fenno, Jay Wethington, Ray deCarlo, Greg Schmitt, Dave Streicher, Keith West, Rick Rivets and all The Brats, Ken Gullic, John Ostrosky, Lydia Criss, Dale Sherman, Richard Terzieff, Ros Radley, Chuck Faust, Bob Alford and Angel, Jeff Fields, Dave Johnson, Alan Marshall, Paul Drennan, Kathy Kapralos, Gerhard Wimmer, Bill Barren, Gary Stone, Bill Mercier, Tim Turcotte, Scott Bissonette, Nico Ciccarone from www.nicostrike.com, Joop van Pelt, KISS Japan F.C., Gabriel Ravarini, Willy Salas, John Lowery, Stefan Gunnarsson, Jakob Lipczynski, Andreas Eileng, Dave Ritz, Mike Powers, Ann Tonetti, Jackie Drexler, Richie Ranno, Tom Saldamarco, Lyle Minter at the Library of Congress, Jules Belkin, Brandon Lucas, Chris Desing, Ron Albanese, Byron Fogle, Julian Gill, Linda West, Bill Starkey, Jay Smith at *Pollstar,* the entire 1995-era KAOL board especially John and Michelle Stockwell, Kathy LaBonte, Steve Schneider, Bartley Collins, and Dave Wellerstein; Jeff Schreiner, Benny Bruce, Jim Campanile, Brad Steakley, Clay Gonzales, The Cleveland KISS Army—Bryan A. Krieger, Brian Osbourne, Kevin Rahm, Don Anderson, and James Bulloch and Frank Novinec from Ringworm; Phil Elliott, Ernie Caltenback and Ron Whitmore from VA, John Lemmon, Gordon Gebert, Rick Schwinden, Gene Triplett, Ronnie "Dancin' Machine" Green, Brad Elterman, Jon Rubin, Nick Smith, Roy Teaze, Rick Reese, Mark Ouellette, Chad Lee, Mark Campbell, Alan Tate, Joe Marshall, Duane Gendreaux, David Massie, Chad Storm, Jeff Welch, Eric Brumitt, Dave Schulps, Andrew and Chris Allin, Bradley H. Fredrick, Ron Blanchard, Troy Correia, Kim Decicco, Tony Williams, Charles Randau, Joe Merante, Steven Stierwalt, Chris Armes, Steven Reeder, Deb Cascio, and A.G. Parr for New Orleans. All interior photos that appear in the book were researched and obtained by Curt Gooch.

Curt would like to make a special dedication to: Tina and Bill for always believing in me; Angela for her inspirational level of discipline; Johnnie for her love and encouragement; Ernie Curtis—the greatest of them all; the 7 Eleven on Council Rd. and Donruss for getting me started; and Dr. Derek Mask for introducing me to rock and roll and the larger world around me. Curt would also like to thank: Steve, Peter, JY, Tony Field, and Kristen Kessel for the Summer of '96; The Fosters, Jeremy/Jamie Samples from Texas, Bryan Baldwin, Marvin and Carla McQuaid, Taylor Truesdell from Rainbow Records, Holly Krieger, Kristy Renay Nichols, and last but not least Dane Smart.

Jeff would like to thank: Paul and Judy Suhs for the Love Gun 8-track and years of support, Jennifer Suhs for the shining example of perseverance, Dorothy N., Bob and Ellie and the entire Z family for finding room for one more, Glenn Doorack who was there when this started, and John Daniel who was there when it continued, and to Tina and Madeleine—first and forever.

PREFACE

Believe everything and believe nothing.

This was our approach throughout researching *KISS Alive Forever: The Complete Touring History,* which is to say that we believed every bit of information we ran across may have occurred, but doubted that it actually did happen until we could prove it.

Keeping this theory in mind, we sat down in February 1996 and began our research into KISS's performance history, talking with as many people as possible to get the accurate story from those who were there firsthand, and accumulating over 472 hours of interviews in the process. We spent hundreds of hours at libraries around the United States, including several weeks at the Library of Congress, exchanged over 4,000 correspondences with KISS fans from five different continents, and accumulated in excess of 22,000 pieces of paperwork relating to KISS's history.

As you are about to see, much of KISS's history has remained unspoken, rewritten, and even forgotten. Over the years, these factors have combined to create a history that is full of inaccuracies, inconsistencies, exaggerations, and even outright lies. Naturally, biographical works suffer when too much information is cannibalized from one source to another, or when "facts" are accepted at face value without much effort made to verify their accuracy. It's also natural to assume that historical information coming from KISS is accurate. But the truth is that the guys in the band were far too busy living their lives to sit down and archive it properly. For these reasons, we went to as many firsthand sources as possible in order to reconstruct KISS's touring history with the utmost accuracy.

The task of analyzing and reconciling this enormous archive of information was often very difficult and the results of our research frequently surprised us. In fact, there is a tremendous amount of information here that will directly conflict with what you may have read before. Do not be dissuaded; we have thoroughly researched everything you're about to read. So, while the story told within may not mirror any history of KISS with which you are familiar, we think you'll find the real story of KISS's touring history richer, more human, and perhaps even more inspiring than ever.

Enjoy.
Curt and Jeff

P.S. If you enjoy this book, you'll love our Web site; please stop by for a visit at www.kissaliveforever.com. In some respects, this is a work in progress, so if you have any questions, comments, additions, or corrections, or even a recording of a performance that is not listed as archived (no matter how poor the quality may be), please contact the authors directly at questions@kissaliveforever.com. We'd love to hear from you.

HOW TO USE THIS BOOK

This book is an archive of KISS's performances, not just their concerts. Our criteria for a "KISS performance" was that all four bandmembers be involved, that the event take place before an audience of some sort (rehearsals attended exclusively by production staff, for instance, would not qualify), and that the performance *not* be lip-synched.

The following fictional example will help clarify the format and terms used throughout the book.

APRIL 24, 1974

Northfield (Chicago), Illinois
Joseph Young Auditorium @ Parkway West High School
Headlining Acts: Black Sabbath, Golden Earring
Opening Acts: Nektar, Rush
Attendance: 3,250   Capacity: 3,250
Promoters: Sunshine Promotions, Sound 70 Concerts
Archived: Audio, Super 8mm

■ SET LIST

Deuce
Gene Simmons Bass Solo
100,000 Years
Peter Criss Drum Solo - Reprise
Black Diamond

Date: The show date is always listed in a Month/Day/Year format.

City, State: In most cases, only a city and state are listed. A country is cited for shows outside of the United States. The city listed is always the exact location of the venue, which may be in a suburb of a larger city. In the example, many people will naturally not recognize that Northfield is a suburb of Chicago, so in these cases we have included the name of the better-known city in parentheses. For foreign cities, we have attempted to list the city by its true name and not the Americanized version (Göteborg vs. Gothenburg). To avoid confusion, the country, however, is listed in its Americanized form.

Venue: Whenever possible, we have listed the venues with their full, official names.

Occasionally, a venue will be listed with an "@" sign. In those instances, the information before the @ sign is the specific site of the performance, but the site is actually part of a larger complex, campus, etc. In the example, Joseph Young Auditorium is located on the campus of Parkway West High School. In almost every case throughout the book, however, the @ sign is not part of the official venue name.

It's also important to note that many of the venues KISS has played have undergone name changes over the years. For each show, the venue name listed was the venue's name at the time of the show and may not bear any resemblance to its current name.

Headlining and Opening Acts: All other acts on the bill are always listed in order of relative "importance," which means that they are listed in *reverse* running order. Unless otherwise noted, all bands appearing on stage before KISS are listed as "opening acts," and all bands appearing after KISS have been designated as "headlining acts." In the example, the actual running order for the show would be: Rush, Nektar, KISS, Golden Earring, Black Sabbath. Technically speaking, Golden Earring may not have been a headliner and Nektar was not necessarily a true opening act, but we have listed them that way in order to simplify the information.

With regard to television or radio shows where other acts performed, we have chosen to include information on any additional acts in the body of text below the show. These acts were not considered to be opening or headlining acts, and they are not cited as such.

Attendance and Capacity: Attendance and capacity figures are complex issues.

Attendance can mean any number of things, among them:

1. The number of people who have gone through the turnstiles at the venue.

2. The number of tickets sold, which may or may not include walk-up sales on the day of the show.

3. The number of tickets sold plus comps (complimentary tickets given out to VIPs, friends of the band, radio, etc.).

Since it is impossible to determine how each promoter arrived at an attendance figure, there may be a significant difference between the reported figure and what a concertgoer recalls about the size of the crowd. In the authors' opinions, the turnstile count is the truest mea-

sure of a show's attendance and every effort has been made to acquire this information.

Capacity can also be a confusing topic.

Most people would naturally assume that the capacity for a concert is the number of people that can be accommodated in the venue. As sensible as this is, it is rare for a concert's capacity figure to reflect the total capacity for the venue.

When scheduling a concert, one of the first things a promoter does is to make a rough estimate of how many tickets the event will sell. Let's say that Sunshine Promotions feels that KISS will sell 3,250 tickets at Joseph Young Auditorium, they would then place 3,250 tickets for sale on a ticket manifest. But maybe Joseph Young Auditorium can technically hold 4,700 people. If that is the case, Sunshine Promotions can choose to release more tickets (up to and sometimes over the true venue capacity) if sales justify it, otherwise the initial ticket manifest of 3,250 will remain the "capacity" for the show.

This process of reducing the capacity for a show downward from the true venue capacity is referred to as "scaling" the event. Among other things, it allows a promoter to report a sellout—advantageous for both band and promoter—for events whose ticket manifest sells out, regardless of how large the actual venue is. This explains why you will sometimes see a sellout of 5,000 tickets in a venue that holds in excess of 15,000.

Promoter: For shows where more than one promoter is listed, there is no emphasis given to any promoter, regardless of who played the largest part in promoting the show. The promoters are simply listed as they appeared in ads.

Archived: The term "Archived" indicates that a show was recorded in some fashion. The terms used to describe how a show was archived are: Audio, Video, Film, and Super 8mm. Unless otherwise noted, all archived performances were privately recorded on the form of media listed. For shows where only a small portion of the performance was recorded, the word "Partial" will appear in front of the form of media, e.g., "Partial Video." (Please note: all shows on Super 8mm were only partially archived.) Bear in mind that our goal was to list everything that we could prove existed, not necessarily what's been circulated, and in all instances where a show is listed as archived, one or both of the authors has direct irrefutable proof that the show was archived. Also note that if a show was archived on video, it implies that audio was included as well, unless otherwise indicated. Lastly, there are many concerts where local television crews were allowed to shoot short portions of a show. These occasions are far too numerous to archive and we have chosen not to include them.

Set List: The majority of the set list information was taken from audio or video recordings of the concerts; newspaper reviews, interviews, and in some rare instances fan reports (although fan reports are duly noted within) were also used as sources. Since we have attempted to accumulate as much set list information as possible, we chose to list partial set lists where more complete information is not available.

Two items may cause some confusion:

1. For shows where a relatively small amount of set list information was missing, and the missing portions could be assumed with some certainty, we have listed the missing information in square brackets [ ] as seen in the following example.

■ SET LIST
Deuce
Strutter
C'mon and Love Me
[Hotter Than Hell]
Firehouse

If the missing songs cannot be safely assumed, we have chosen to list only the confirmed information and indicated that the set list is a "Partial Set List."

2. The placement of solos in the set list has varied over the years. If a solo is an independent piece, it is usually listed that way.

A solo existing within the framework of a song is a more complicated matter. For instance, during typical performances of "100,000 Years," Peter Criss would do a drum solo lasting several minutes, and the song would segue into and out of his solo. Unfortunately, spacing concerns make the following listing cumbersome: 100,000 Years—Peter Criss Drum Solo—100,000 Years reprise. We have chosen to list the example as:

100,000 Years
Peter Criss Drum Solo - reprise

In some cases, additional details regarding the solos/set lists are needed and in those instances any further explanation will appear at the end of the chapter's introduction.

PSYCHO CIRCUS TOUR

Number of Shows: 62
Start Date: October 31, 1998 - Los Angeles, California
End Date: January 3, 2000 - Anchorage, Alaska
Countries: Argentina; Austria; Belgium; Brazil; Canada, Czech Republic; England; Finland; France; Germany; Italy; Mexico; The Netherlands; Norway; Sweden; USA
Opening Acts: Big Wreck; Bionic; Buck Cherry; Caroline's Spine; Econoline Crush; Everclear; John Hayes Project; Junkbox; Lit; Los Villanos; Natural Born Hippies; Nickelback; Ozone Monday; PUYA; Rammstein; Smashing Pumpkins
Average Attendance: 12,826

At the beginning of each chapter is a tour summary, as seen in this example:

The Start Date and End Date listed in these summaries represent the first and last concerts included in the chapter and do *not* necessarily represent a tour's beginning or end. In some cases, we have included one-off shows in a chapter that were not technically part of the tour. Other headings, e.g., Number of Shows, Countries, etc., also reflect what is included in the chapter, not strictly what was defined by the tour.

Additionally, Average Attendance is listed as a reference point and may not be a literal average. In some cases, when tabulating Average Attendance, we have filtered out a show or group of shows that would have resulted in a misleading average. For instance, the Creatures of the Night Tour averaged only 5,313 attendees for the 56 dates in North America. However, if you incorporate the three Brazilian stadium shows at the tour's end into the calculations, the tour's average skyrockets to over 9,200. In this case, we chose to eliminate the Brazilian shows in order to arrive at a more valid attendance average.

Throughout the book are occasional references to songs being performed for the first/last time, or being added to/dropped from a set list. In all instances, these comments do not take KISS's 1995 conventions (where the band attempted many rare songs) into account. Nor do they take into account any instances where a song was included in a medley or any other partial performance.

When relevant, we have included release dates for KISS albums. Over the years, several different release dates have been published for some of the albums; we've attempted to correct this by verifying release dates at the Library of Congress (whose copyright records define the release date as the first date the material was available in commerce) and with extensive datebooks kept by coauthor Curt Gooch (1984–Present).

It should be noted that the "world premiere" or "debut" date on all music videos (1984–Present) are also from the datebooks kept by Curt Gooch. In most cases, the dates reflect the initial broadcast date on MTV. It should be noted that MTV, due to their screening and approval process, would often "world-premiere" videos 7–10 days after they had been in rotation on MuchMusic or on other national/local video shows.

Lastly, in several instances throughout there are references to "*Performance* itineraries." These refer to itineraries published in *Performance* magazine, a weekly publication (circa late 1960s through late 1990s) that focused on the entertainment touring industry and devoted more than half of each issue to itinerary listings. *Performance* shut its doors indefinitely in the late 1990s, but we were privileged enough to be allowed exclusive access to their archives in 1997. The search through their large collection of back issues from the 1970s yielded information on several KISS shows that would have otherwise been lost forever.

CHAPTER 1

RAINBOW, WICKED LESTER, AND WHAT CAME FIRST . . .

It was January 30, 1973. It was cold, 26 degrees, and the first real snowfall of the season had covered New York City. Richard Nixon was explaining why he wasn't a crook; the Dow Jones registered a meager 992.93; and cars with panicked drivers were lined up 20-deep at gas stations across the United States.

America, maybe, wasn't very sure of itself.

But inside a small club in Queens, there were four young musicians who *were* sure of themselves. And they had every right to be, because they knew they were going to be the biggest band in the world.

As it turns out, they were right.

While the first tenuous threads of KISS's story can be traced back to the late 1960s, the fabric of its strange tale did not really begin to gather until 1970.

In January of that year, future guitar pickup entrepreneur Larry DiMarzio and a New York keyboardist named Brooke Ostrander were playing out a string of gigs in a dead-end cover band named Gas, Food & Lodging. One night, DiMarzio invited fellow Richmond Community College student Gene Klein (later Simmons) to a gig. Between sets, DiMarzio, Ostrander, and bassist/songwriter Klein began to discuss working on material together and forming a band. Though DiMarzio ultimately opted to concentrate on developing guitar pickups, Klein and Ostrander hit it off immediately, and from January through May 1970 the two young musicians arranged and recorded songs in Ostrander's Garden Drive apartment in Linden, New Jersey.

The quality of the resulting recordings was poor, but Klein shopped the songs Klein and Ostrander decided to turn the collaboration into a full-fledged band, and they soon placed an ad for a lead guitarist in *The Village Voice.* Unfortunately, the ad only garnered a single response, and that was from a Queens rhythm guitarist whom Klein and Ostrander quickly dismissed.

Rather than conduct a lengthy search for a guitarist, Klein asked his friend Steve Coronel to fill the spot and Coronel agreed. Soon after, the band adopted the name Rainbow.

Upon joining, Coronel pitched the idea that they recruit Stanley Eisen (later Paul Stanley), whom he recommended on the basis of his songwriting and rhythm guitar skills. The sales pitch worked and Eisen became the band's fourth member. Eisen was an ironic choice, considering that he was the very Queens rhythm guitarist whom the band turned down in the first place. Ostrander quickly recruited drummer Joe Davidson, who completed the lineup with Klein, Coronel, and Eisen.

"We rehearsed a few times at my mother's house right in the very beginning," recalls Ostrander. "She wasn't real thrilled about having a rock band in her basement. Then we rehearsed at Steve's a few times in an apartment by the George Washington Bridge, but there were problems with some of the neighbors. That's when we decided to get the loft down on Canal Street (near Mott Street in Chinatown). We rehearsed an average of five or six nights a week. Six o'clock to midnight was our schedule."

After a short tenure, Davidson departed and was replaced by Tony Zarrella, another local drummer. Zarrella recalls: "I met Brooke at a party in Highpoint, New Jersey. He approached me and said he had a band that was rehearsing on Canal Street, and asked if I would be interested in auditioning. I told him that I'd love to but I was going to California with another group. Turns out the group never went to California, so a week later I called him and auditioned; we got along great and that's when I joined."

In the spring of 1971, Larry DiMarzio helped the quintet score their first gig, a two-set show at Richmond Community College on Staten Island. "We got tired of rehearsing every night without an audience," explains Ostrander. "We learned a few cover tunes just in case people started moaning 'play something we know.' We did a couple of Jethro Tull and Moody Blues tunes; 'Locomotive Breath' and 'Tuesday Afternoon' stick out. The attendance was fairly light to medium; it wasn't real big."

After only one gig, the band dropped the name Rainbow. "At this point, the five of us discovered there was another band called Rainbow," relates Ostrander. "We had to come up with another name, and 'Wicked Lester' literally came out of thin air. I remember thinking, 'Wicked Lester? Where did that come from?' But Gene was very excited, 'Yeah, it's a really unusual name!' I thought, 'OK. What the hell?'"

The first of Wicked Lester's two gigs took place on April 23 when the band played the Rivoli Theatre in South Fallsburg, New York. The second and final Wicked Lester show occurred one Saturday during the later part of the summer in Atlantic City. Ostrander explains, "At the time, I was teaching in New Jersey, and the director of a Jewish youth convention was the parent of one of my band students. He knew about Wicked Lester through his son, and he started making some inquiries. The next thing I know, we're playing at a convention in this huge ballroom at one of the big Atlantic City hotels. There were a couple of thousand kids. It was a

great gig. We played everything we had."

On the Monday following the gig, the band returned to their Chinatown loft to rehearse, only to discover that all of their gear had been stolen. "I remember going up the stairs, walking in, and there was nothing there," Zarrella recollects, "just a stand with a cowbell was all that was left of the drums." The equipment was never recovered.

The band was gearless and going nowhere when veteran producer Ron Johnsen entered the story. "They wanted me to come and see them play," remembers Johnsen, "but they weren't playing anywhere. I caught one of their rehearsals and they were horrible. I told them, 'Keep writing songs guys, and if you think you've got some things that are worthy, keep in touch.' After that, every other day Gene and Stan were at my door."

"Absolutely nothing was passable," remarks Johnsen on the band's material, "and they could only copy what other people were doing. There was nothing about them that was even remotely professional."

Nothing may have come of the relationship with Ron Johnsen—the chief engineer at Jimi Hendrix's Electric Lady Studios at the time— had Hendrix's manager Michael Jeffries not been in need of a band. Polydor Records had loaned Jeffries $150,000 to find and develop three bands within a 12–18 month time frame. Towards the end of that time period, Jeffries had only signed two acts and was becoming desperate to fill the third slot. He approached Johnsen for a recommendation, and Johnsen offered Wicked Lester. "I had control over Electric Lady in those days," Johnsen continues, "I was pretty much running it. When those studios were clear, I would tell them to come on in, and we'd cut tracks or do overdubs without any charge. I created a layered sound that was mostly Gene. It was all done through a lot of sound bouncing and sel-synching [a recording technique used for taping overdubs] and doing things to create multilevel sounds that give you more of a group feel."

Johnsen gave a two- or three-song tape to Jeffries, who submitted it to Polydor, where it was quickly rejected. Ron and his lawyer, Bob Casper, then continued shopping the demo to record companies with whom they had good relationships, among them MetroMedia and Elektra. "Elektra were talking about signing us," Ostrander remembers, "but they backed down. Then MetroMedia were sponsoring us for a while because they were looking at picking us up. As we got closer to closing the deal with MetroMedia, another company bought them out."

After moving out of their Chinatown loft, Wicked Lester tried various rehearsal facilities before settling on Jams Studios, located on the fourth floor at 10 East Twenty-third Street.

On February 3, 1972, Johnsen met with music publisher Billy Michelle of Famous Music and left a reel of Wicked Lester material with him. The reel quickly found its way to Tom Werman, who was the assistant to the director of artists and repertoire (A&R) at Epic Records, and a meeting was set up for February 15. Werman recalls: "Ron Johnsen brought me these work-in-progress tapes, and they sounded really good at the time. So, Epic did a master purchase. We financed the album halfway through and paid to finish it."

Later in February, following an audition for Epic Records at CBS Studios, Steve Coronel was let go, reportedly at the company's insistence. "I don't think his departure had anything to do with the record company not liking him," offers Ron Johnsen. "I think the boys had a hard time telling Steve he was fired, so we made it sound like it was the record company who demanded a strong lead guitarist. Steve was a very close friend of theirs, especially Gene. Gene may have even had tears in his eyes, but he understood that Steve was not on the same level."

Recording continued, as Johnsen notes: "We ended up making the album with five of their songs that were passable and about five or six songs which were from the Dick James Music catalog. A couple of Paul and Gene's songs were pretty great. 'She' was always a favorite song of mine, and I actually helped write the lyrics to that. Gene was talking about a girl who was no good and was a whore. I told him, 'Gene, make it positive. Make it a good thing that she's doing, not a bad thing. She's a good whore; she does favors for people that they really dig. "She's *so* good" not "She's *no* good."' He was scolding her for being a bad girl. He was so angelic about things.

"The album was huge, with horns, and multi-layers, etc. Brooke and I played tons of trumpet and sax parts. I did the orchestrations and I played brass with him, and he and I both played keyboards and did a lot of mallet-work with vibes and marimbas. Paul and Gene had no idea what they were doing, although Gene was a very articulate bass player and Paul was good at doing rhythm parts. But he was no lead guitarist."

The band's search for a capable lead guitarist was quickly narrowed down to two candidates: Ron Leejack, a local session player, and a guitarist from Queens nominated by Gene. "Gene and I were fighting to the death over these two guitar players," remembers Ostrander. "It couldn't be resolved between us. We ended up having Ron Johnsen set up an audition at Electric Lady for Epic and the lawyers. We let them choose." The audition was held on February 27, and Ron Leejack was unanimously named the victor. According to both Johnsen and Ostrander, Leejack was not initially hired to be a member of the band, but, rather, was contracted to complete guitar-work on the album. He would eventually become a full member of the group.

Gene and Paul during a 1994 visit to Wicked Lester's Chinatown rehearsal loft.

Besides Leejack, several other notable guest musicians also appeared on the album. "All the stars were around Electric Lady at that time," offers Zarrella. "Stephen Sills played on one of our tracks, and Gary U.S. Bonds sat in on one of our sessions, too, though I don't know if he really did any vocals. Ron [Johnsen] also brought in Jimmy Maelen, a famous conga player who had played with Buddy Rich."

During this time, Wicked Lester began looking for a manager. Previously, Johnsen and the band had courted Lew Linet, who resisted their offers at first, but Klein and Eisen persisted in badgering him. "I got several phone calls from both Gene and Stan," Linet relates. "They kept telling me, 'Lew, we really like you. We've got some new material. We hired this well-known guitar player Ronnie Leejack. Would you come hear us again?' So I said sure. I went back and listened and told them I'd represent them.

"At this point, Ron Johnsen told me that he was in the middle of a deal with Don Ellis, A&R Director at Epic Records. Ron had played some material for Don, and he was impressed. But there was something holding up the deal. I told him that I could jump in and make this thing happen. So, I went to Don and worked out a one-album deal with options and a nice little advance for the boys."

In addition to the money, the band was beginning to enjoy some of the other excesses of the rock and roll lifestyle, as Ron Johnsen explains: "There was some girl, Therese, that Paul and Gene met outside the studio, and she was into rock and roll and was a groupie, I guess. We were doing overdubbing in the vocal booth and the drum booth, and the guys were lining up and getting blow jobs from her. We thought it was a riot. These guys were standing in line like they were waiting for tickets. I think Tom Werman was pretty stunned, He was the guy who was in charge of keeping the expenses down." Werman adds, "It was my very first glimpse into rock and roll decadence. Gene went out for a hot dog and came back into Studio A with a hooker."

A groupie, a record contract, and an outstanding producer at a renowned studio would be enough for most aspiring rock stars. Yet something about the directionless nature of Wicked Lester drove Stan and Gene to want something greater, and they began quietly searching for it.

In early June, they approached a New York guitarist by the name of John Segall. Segall, who as Jay Jay French would go on to find success as a member of Twisted Sister, recalls: "I invited Stanley and Gene to come see me play in a church in Greenwich Village one Sunday in June [the 4th], 1972. Afterward, they walked up to me and said, 'Wow you're a really good guitar player. We have this band called Wicked Lester,

The Wicked Lester lineup circa summer 1972. From left to right: Ron Leejack, Gene Klein, Stan Eisen, Brooke Ostrander, and Tony Zarrella.

but the band looks like a bunch of hippies and we are not into that anymore.' They started talking to me about the coming of glam and said, 'We are gonna go into a Zep/Slade/glam type of thing with makeup. We've got all of these bizarre ideas.' I told them that I was aware of the glam scene and was kind of changing myself. I went and auditioned at the Twenty-third Street loft. I probably went down there [to audition] at least half a dozen times in June of '72. Then, they called me up one day and told me it wasn't working out."

Later that summer, Brooke and Gene experimented with revamping the lineup. Ostrander remembers: "That summer, Stan said he had a family issue and was gone for a few weeks. We explored my thought of using Stan as a frontman, and we started to rehearse without him. A lot of things cleaned up musically, and we were a lot tighter. But there were also a lot of missing things. We talked about the possibility of an additional guitar player. In my mind, there were musical conflicts between what Stan was playing and what Ronnie was playing. He was limiting what Ronnie could do and was kind of in the way.

"Stan didn't know anything about this until he came back, and he kind of went a little nuts over the whole thing. I told him, 'It was just an idea, and you were gone anyway. You do most of the heavier rock singing. You'd get a chance to be a Mick Jagger or Rod Stewart and run around.' He was pissed, but we were trying to

figure out how to perform this intricate studio album live."

In the interim, the album was finally mixed and completed. "We all went to Don Ellis's office to deliver the album," Linet explains, "and when we got there, Don put the tape on and listened. Afterward, he said, 'I hate it. Not only do I hate it, I'm not even going to release the record. That's the end of the story.' All this after they had paid the advance money and paid for the production! We were totally shocked.

"The next day I went up to see Don and said, 'Listen, buddy, if you don't want to release their album, do me a favor and release the group from their contract,' which he did. I called Gene and Stan and told them I couldn't rescue the deal, and I asked for their thoughts. They had come to a conclusion: 'We don't want to be this folk rock type of group. We want to be a hard, loud, four-piece rock and roll band. We want to fire the other three guys and find two more players.' So, I said, 'If that's what you feel, and you think that's going to make it work, let's do it. I'm with you.'"

During this period in their careers, Eisen and Klein began to use their familiar monikers Paul Stanley and Gene Simmons for various professional endeavors. "We were sitting in my living room," Linet relates, "and they told me that they were changing their names. Stan looked at me and said that he wanted to be called Paul Stanley, and Gene wanted to be Gene Simmons. They said that they'd been thinking about it for

some time."

Using their new names, Gene and Paul began working as background singers on several projects for Ron Johnsen, including an unreleased concept album (written by a young writer and a defrocked priest) called *Mr. Gee-Whiz,* and folk singer Lyn Christopher's debut album.

Lew Linet recalls, "At that time [early autumn 1972], we started to hold auditions for drummers. A million guys came through, a whole variety of people auditioning. Well, one day they tell me that they've got a drummer coming in from Brooklyn who had been playing in bar bands and his name is Peter Cris." ("Cris" was shortened from Peter's full surname "Criscuola." His last name eventually became "Criss" due to a typographical error on a set of business cards.)

A long-standing KISS myth regarding how Peter Criss came to be in Wicked Lester needs to be dispelled. Legend has it that Paul and Gene read an ad for a drummer "willing to do anything to make it," which appeared in an issue of *Rolling Stone*, and that the drummer was none other than Peter. That story is only partly true. Records kept by Lydia Criss (Peter's first wife) indicate that the ad did indeed appear in *Rolling Stone,* but that the text of the ad read as follows:

Experienced Rock and Roll Drummer
Looking for original group
doing soft and hard music
Peter XXX-7778, Brooklyn

Apparently, Paul and Gene read the ad, contacted Peter and arranged for a meeting at Electric Lady Studios where they were recording the background vocals on the Lyn Christopher album. Peter was accompanied by Lydia and his younger brother Joey. Ron Johnsen, who had engineered an album for Peter's old band Chelsea, recollects: "It was very casual. Paul and Gene were standing in the hallway when Peter came in, and I introduced them." Joey Criscuola continues, "I was with Georgie [Peter's given name is George], and we went down to meet Gene and Stan at Electric Lady. Ron Johnsen was there and he was doing some work on a song called 'Celebration' [actually a song divided into two parts titled 'Celebrate I' and 'Celebrate II']. He needed some guys to clap on the record, so after the meeting, my brother and I went into the booth, put on headphones, and clapped." As fate would have it, "Celebrate" was also the track for which Paul and Gene were recording background vocals that day. As amazing as it seems, on the very same day Peter first met Paul and Gene, the three future bandmates made their first appearance on an album together. No one has ever mentioned the recording in this context before, strongly indicating that Paul, Gene, and Peter remain wholly unaware that they appeared on an album together before becoming bandmates.

Unfortunately, Peter failed to impress Paul and Gene at his first audition; he had been forced to use Tony Zarrella's drums and claimed his poor performance was due to his unfamiliarity with Zarrella's kit. Gene and Paul granted him a second audition. Linet recalls: "He came in with a gorgeous set of drums which took up half the room; obviously he was a professional. I thought he was the one right away, but it was Paul and Gene's audition. I called them the next day and asked them what they thought of Peter. They thought he was great and said they were going to hire him."

Gene and Paul had continued to rehearse with the other members of Wicked Lester throughout this backroom audition process, but with the band's new direction eventually becoming apparent, Brooke Ostrander sought and obtained his release from the band. By early fall 1972, Tony Zarrella and Ron Leejack had followed Ostrander out the door, though Leejack did not procure his official, legal release from the band until January 1973.

Sticking with the Wicked Lester name for the moment, the new three-piece began a brutal regimen of rehearsals at 10 East Twenty-third Street, where they had moved from the fourth floor to a second-floor loft. Their recording contract had been terminated and no gigs were being booked, but the merciless rehearsal routine was engraining an unwavering work ethic in the band that would serve them well in the years to come. Linet relates: "When they started to rehearse, I began to see a pattern of this loud, theatrical, blast-off kind of band. I also began to see that this was not really my taste, but I figured I'd see where they went." Alice West, Linet's former assistant and later a co-executive producer for the television series *Ally McBeal*, remembers: "At one point they were rehearsing in a loft that belonged to a friend of mine. There was an antiques dealer underneath the loft, and their music was so loud and the vibrations were so intense that we were asked to leave the rehearsal space because we were damaging the antiques."

As winter 1972 approached, another opportunity to impress Don Ellis of Epic Records arose, and the trio set up showcases for November 20th and 28th, though it appears that they used only one of the two dates. "We bought the record," Werman recalls, "but Wicked Lester had broken up. The deal was dead, and everyone was a free agent by the time of this showcase. Gene or Paul called me and wanted to audition as a three-piece for my boss Don Ellis and me. We went up to this rehearsal loft on Twenty-third Street. It was early evening, and they played a great set with Peter; they blew me away—I really loved it. At the end of the set Paul threw a bucket of silver confetti at us. We all thought it was water. It was really cool. That was the first time I'd seen even a taste of theater in an audition.

"Unfortunately, when we got down to the sidewalk my boss, may he rest in peace, turned to me and said, 'What the fuck was that?' At that point, I thought hopes were dim for this band. I didn't argue with him. I wimped out. I didn't have the clout or the confidence at the time to say, 'No, they're great, they're really good, they're gonna be big.'"

Wicked Lester was a dead issue, yet as late as December 1972, Epic was still planning on releasing the album. In an interview with a local newspaper, Peter (who is listed as "Peter Cris of Wicked Lester") mentioned that the Wicked Lester album would be out on January 1, 1973.

Although the Wicked Lester album from Epic remains unreleased, the cover commissioned for it (shot in front of a house near Fifty-fifth Street and Tenth Avenue in Manhattan) was used on The Laughing Dogs's debut album for CBS Records in June 1979. KISS and the president of Casablanca Records, Neil Bogart, jointly bought back the rights to the Wicked Lester album from Epic in 1978 for $137,500; KISS eventually bought out Bogart's share, thus assuring they had full control of the album.

SPRING 1971 (TWO SETS)

Staten Island, New York
Richmond Community College
No Opening Act
Archived: Audio

■ This was Rainbow's lone gig. Surprisingly, an audio recording of the concert does exist. "Stan used to talk with a fake British accent during the shows," offers Brooke Ostrander, "partially to appear British and partially to torment Gene."

The set list opened with "Little Lady" (a song later retitled "Goin' Blind") and included, among others, "Suitor," "Eskimo Sun," "Keep Me Waiting," and "Love Her All I Can." Several songs that were never recorded for the album were included in the set lists at all three of the band's gigs.

APRIL 23, 1971 (TWO SETS)

South Fallsburg, New York
Rivoli Theatre
No Opening Act

■ This was the first of Wicked Lester's two concerts. Brooke Ostrander relates the details: "Gene got us the gig. We were looking for places to play, and the opportunity just presented itself. We got my brother's van and another friend's van and hauled all of our gear up there. We played, and the next day we went to Emerson, Lake & Palmer who were preparing to play the Fillmore the following week. They were playing in a hotel ballroom in the area. We were up there for a few days."

SUMMER 1971 (MULTIPLE SETS)

Atlantic City, New Jersey
No Opening Act

■ The final Wicked Lester gig was part of a B'nai B'rith Youth Organization event held at a major hotel in Atlantic City. They performed three sets on a Saturday night.

The Rivoli Theatre in South Fallsburg, New York, site of Wicked Lester's debut concert.

CHAPTER 2

THE CLUBS

Number of Shows: 24
Start Date: January 30, 1973 — Queens, New York
End Date: December 22, 1973 — New York, New York
Countries: U.S.A.
Headlining Acts: The Brats; Isis; Queen Elizabeth featuring Wayne County; Wild Honey
Opening Acts: Bloontz; City Slicker; The Detroit Dogs; Flaming Youth; Jackdaw; Luger; Planets; Rags; Rebillot Quartet; Street Punk

Unsuccessful, but not discouraged, the trio began to search for a lead guitarist. Paul placed an ad in *The Village Voice* on December 1, 1972 reading: "Lead Guitarist wanted with flash and ability." The ad ran in the December 7th and 14th issues of the paper.

To filter through the many candidates who responded to the ad, the band held two sets of auditions, both at the Twenty-third Street loft, through which a ragged menagerie of amateur and professional New York musicians paraded. Among them was Bob Kulick, who recalled: "The audition was fairly brief. We ran through maybe five songs, one Zeppelin tune and three or four of their originals."

One of the guitarists who auditioned was a strange man by the name of Paul Frehley. The various legends surrounding his audition have Frehley dressed in all manner of multicolored footwear, interrupting Kulick's audition several times, and otherwise nearly sabotaging his own cause. Regardless of what actually happened during the audition, if the press kit material is true, the four found kismet in the middle of "Deuce" and KISS had their man. Nearly.

Paul Stanley reflected on the audition in a 1977 TV interview with Alison Steele: "When Ace first played with us we were really pleased with the way it sounded, and yet we didn't ask him to join us immediately. I, for one, thought he was a little too weird. I said, 'Let's wait a week (and) try some more people.'"

Frehley was not officially hired until he auditioned a second time in mid-December. (The exact date when Ace joined the band cannot be substantiated, though Lydia Criss insists that he had joined the band before the holidays. None of the previously reported dates of hire can be verified.) To avoid having two Pauls in the band, Frehley chose to use his nickname, "Ace," a handle that had followed him around since his teenage days in the Bronx.

KISS in the stairwell outside their Jams Studios rehearsal loft on Twenty-third Street, January 1973.

While still a trio, the band had begun to discuss new names. If one is to believe the apocryphal stories, supposedly, while driving down Queens Boulevard, Peter mentioned in passing that a former band of his had been named Lips; Paul then quipped that these three should name themselves Kiss. The joke fell flat, but the suggestion held more and more appeal as they considered it.

Lew Linet, however, recalls a different version of the story, one in which Ace was already in the band. "We were in the loft on Twenty-third Street. We all sat around and decided that we needed a new name. I remember where I was sitting exactly. We were sitting around talking, and we came up with all kinds of names and one of them came up with the name Kisses or Kiss, and it went around the room and everyone said, 'Yeah, that's a great name.'"

KISS. The name stuck.

———————

KISS's look went through more alterations in 1973 than in any other year in their career. Originally, KISS looked like another transsexual cast-off from the line of established glitter bands like the Harlots of 42nd Street, the Fast, and the visionary New York Dolls. Lew Linet comments on the glam trappings: "KISS decided they wanted to do makeup. So, they started to do it, Alice Cooper style, with eye shadow, mascara, blush on the cheeks, white pancake, etc. It was girly, transgender stuff and they started wearing more dramatic clothing as well."

At the onset, KISS's look was definitely derivative. However, it progressed from thrift-shop attire and virtually no makeup at their debut gigs in January 1973, to fully articulated greasepaint, heavy leather, and thigh-high platform boots at the very same club (Coventry) by December.

Most of the venues that KISS played in 1973

were dives like The Daisy on Long Island and the considerably less-than-five-star Hotel Diplomat in Manhattan. "KISS couldn't even get a club gig in Manhattan," notes Brats singer Keith West, "the Mercer Arts Center, Club 82, and Max's Kansas City wouldn't have them." Soundman Eddie Solan who, with Bobby McAdams (both longtime friends of Frehley) and Joey Criscuola, comprised the KISS road crew for most of 1973, adds: "Paul Stanley and I would go around on nights when we weren't doing anything and try to get gigs. I brought him to Westchester one weekend, and we went to some clubs to book some shows, but nobody wanted them. That's why we did so many Daisy gigs."

"When they first started," Lew Linet recalls, "I worked them at Coventry and The Daisy. The reception was horrible. They were so loud and so unsubtle and so crude that they didn't do well at all. The audiences didn't like them, and the reviewers that I had come out just unanimously hated them."

Hated or not, KISS would usually bludgeon their way through their sets, which consisted of a mix of leftover Wicked Lester material like "Simple Type" or "Keep Me Waiting," and newer songs such as "100,000 Years" and "Baby, Let Me Go."

JANUARY 30, 1973 (TWO SETS)
Queens, New York
Coventry (Popcorn Pub)
No Opening Act
Capacity: 600
Promoter: In-house
■ SET LIST (FIRST SET)
Deuce
Watchin' You
Love Her All I Can
She
Simple Type
Keep Me Waiting
Life in the Woods
Baby, Let Me Go
Firehouse
Black Diamond
■ SET LIST (SECOND SET)
Deuce
Love Her All I Can
She
Life in the Woods
Simple Type
Keep Me Waiting
Baby, Let Me Go
Watchin' You

■ This was KISS's debut show. A poster-sized portrait of their first official photo session—taken in the stairwell outside their rehearsal loft—was displayed in the entryway of the venue. KISS's performance was the first at the newly named Coventry, which had previously been called the Popcorn Pub.

For a band that became renowned the world over for its garish, ridiculous appearance, KISS's attire for their first concert was, simply put, dull. Of the four, only Gene wore makeup that even hinted at what was to come, with white pancake covering his face and black greasepaint smudged formlessly around his eyes. Peter wore a small amount of rouge, and neither Paul nor Ace wore any makeup whatsoever. The band's clothing was very pedestrian as well. Gene wore bellbottoms and a sailor suit top. Ace wore jeans and a shirt, as did Paul,

who included a dark sports jacket in his ensemble.

A handful of Polaroids from one of the first Coventry shows exists and was sold at a June 2000 auction.

JANUARY 31, 1973 (TWO SETS)
Queens, New York
Coventry (Popcorn Pub)
No Opening Act
Capacity: 600
Promoter: In-house
■ Coventry was a small club in the Sunnyside neighborhood of Queens. Owner Paul Sub describes the club: "As you came in, there was a small stage on your right and a large one on your left. The P.A. equipment was the size that you'd put into Madison Square Garden, and we occasionally had problems with the neighbors. From floor to ceiling, the club was maybe 15' high. There was also a basement where people could go relax. It was a hang-out room that was sealed off to the public, but sometimes the bands would take their guests down there."

Cyndi Lauper, who also got her start at Coventry, recalls: "Coventry was a big glitter club. I was in a band called Doc West, and we would play at Coventry at the tail end of glitter. We played on dead nights sometimes for just five people."

FEBRUARY 1, 1973 (TWO SETS)
Queens, New York
Coventry (Popcorn Pub)
No Opening Act
Capacity: 600
Promoter: In-house
■ Paul Sub: "There was no real formal booking at Coventry. KISS came in like all the bands did and asked if they could play. Whoever came in . . . we just booked them. We never turned anyone down. On average, KISS drew about 60 or 70 people. They didn't draw at all."

MARCH 9, 1973 (TWO SETS)
Amityville, New York
The Daisy
No Opening Act
Promoter: In-house
■ Eddie Solan: "The first night we played at The Daisy, there was no one there. They even did a cover, 'Go Now' by the Moody Blues, which they used to do from the first rehearsals we ever did. I think they included it at the end of the set at some of the other club gigs."

"The first couple of gigs," continues Solan, "I set up the mixing board on the side of the stage because we didn't have a mike snake. Someone said, 'Oh, you're the keyboard player in KISS!' After that, I brought a mike snake so I could sit out in the room. I also brought a camera to one of those gigs and gave it to Bobby McAdams. He was going around the stage and taking pictures. Unfortunately, he never took the lens cap off the whole night."

MARCH 10, 1973 (TWO SETS)
Amityville, New York
The Daisy
No Opening Act
Promoter: In-house
■ The March 9 and 10 shows were the first gigs

at which KISS wore makeup that resembled their famous designs. There was no real costuming to speak of yet, but the androgynous rouge and mascara look had been replaced with greasepaint.

It's important to note that Peter actually con-

KISS's fifth concert, March 10, 1973 at The Daisy.

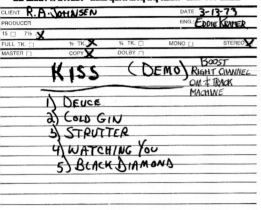

This is the tape box cover from the band's original five-song demo. Notice the date, which pre-dates the commonly accepted date for the demo tapes (June 1973) by three months.

tinued to gig with his former Lips bandmate Stan Penridge at clubs like the King's Lounge in Brooklyn through the spring of 1973. "At the time," mentions Solan, "Ace was delivering mail and Gene was typing, but Peter was still playing in the lounge bands, and we used to go out and see his lounge group. Gene and Paul would get up and play a song with the lounge band's equipment."

By March 13, KISS and producer Eddie Kramer had completed work on a five-song demo at Electric Lady Studios. Kramer remembers, "Ron Johnsen asked me to do the demos because it wasn't his cup of tea. It was done very quickly, within a 24-hour period." During the recording of their demo, Peter began singing lead on "Black Diamond," a duty that had previously fallen to Paul.

The only still-existing handbill for KISS's second set of gigs at The Daisy, April 1973. The photo in the upper right corner was taken during the band's March 10, 1973 appearance at the club.

EDDIE SOLAN COLLECTION/COURTESY OF CURT GOOCH

APRIL 13, 1973 (TWO SETS)

Amityville, New York
The Daisy
No Opening Act
Promoter: In-house

■ Solan recollects: "We would go out to The Daisy on the Thursday night before the weekend gigs and we'd set up the gear. I used to have this Volkswagen Beetle, and Peter had a car, too, so we used to do most of the driving. I would come through the Bronx and pick up Ace and sometimes Paul in Queens, and we'd go out to the job.

"One night we were all set up, and they were in the dressing room doing their makeup. Gene asked for his bass because he wanted to tune it. We all looked at one another because we had no bass. It was Paul's fault; he had them in his apartment, and he brought his guitar and never thought of bringing the bass. They're sitting in there with the makeup on, and we're thinking 'Holy shit, what are we going to do?!'

"I went out into the audience and asked people if they played bass guitar. This one kid said yes, and I talked him into going home and bringing his bass back. He came back with this blue Hagström bass with nylon strings on it. This thing would not stay in tune for even one song, but Gene had to make do.

"After the first set, Gene said that he couldn't play the thing. So, we got yet another kid to go home, and he came back with a semi-acoustic bass, which Gene played for the second set.

APRIL 14, 1973 (TWO SETS)

Amityville, New York
The Daisy
No Opening Act
Promoter: In-house

■ At this juncture, KISS's viability as a live act was a good news/bad news story. The good news was that they were getting gigs. The bad news was that they were all at Coventry or The Daisy, and neither location had anything on Max's Kansas City. Linet explains: "We would have band meetings and I would ask them, 'Is this really what you want, because the reaction that we're getting is rough.'

"The funny thing was that all four of them, especially Gene and Paul, would say to me over and over and over again, 'Lew, don't worry about a thing. Doesn't matter what they say or what they write, we don't care because we are going to be the biggest band in the world.' Understand that this is coming from two guys who were recently playing songs on the corner in Greenwich Village with their guitar cases open collecting quarters, a guy who was a refugee from a bar band in Queens and was ready to give up music entirely, and this crazy Ace Frehley guy from Mars.

"'We will be the biggest rock and roll band in the world.' They used those exact words with me.

"I never saw such confidence in my life, neither before nor since."

MAY 4, 1973

New York, New York
Bleecker Street Loft, Eighth Floor
Headlining Acts: Queen Elizabeth, featuring Wayne County, The Brats
Promoter: The Brats

■ Keith West of The Brats: "I had a record store in Queens called The Music Box, which had become the center of the early glitter scene. One day Paul comes in and says, 'You guys are really big and we're just playing some dive out in Amityville. Can we play with you guys?'"

"We told him that we were having a loft party and that they were welcome to open the show," continues Brats guitarist Rick Rivets. "On the afternoon of the show, we went over and picked up their equipment and that was the first time I met Ace and Peter. Ace had just gotten these Keds sneakers, and he put silver glitter all over them so everywhere he walked he left a trail of glitter behind. They had two Marshall stacks, one each for Paul and Ace, and I think Gene had an SVT [a speaker cabinet made by Ampeg] and Peter had this giant drum kit. We were freaking out, because none of the bands had equipment like that.

"While they did their soundcheck, our drummer and I were standing by the door listening and as soon as they hit the first song, he and I looked at one another and said, 'We're dead.' It was like playing on a bill with a band like Zeppelin or Deep Purple; everything was so tight. They had the harmonies down, they had the leads down, and sheer volume was amazing, but you could hear everything clearly. And that was just the sound check!

"After that, they said they had to go get ready. We had no idea what they meant by 'get ready.' I told them they could use the bathrooms in the loft, but they said 'No, we've got a hotel room.'"

The Bleecker Street Loft was hardly the Taj Mahal; in fact, it didn't even register a blip on the New York glam scene radar. The venue was chosen for two simple reasons: it was The Brats's rehearsal loft and it was cheap. West continues, "The loft kind of had an interesting look

The Bleecker Street Loft circa May 2001.

when you walked in; there was equipment all over the place. The guy who owned the factory would always think that people were going to steal things, so he would pack up everything and just leave the machines out. You would set up between the rivet makers in this factory that took up the eighth floor. We would have the windows open because it was so hot, and people would be doing drugs and hanging out the windows; in those days you just made your parties anywhere."

Rivets: "There were a lot of Warhol people in the crowd: Jackie Curtis, Hollywood Lon, Taylor Mead, and Eric Emerson. All the Dolls were there and I'm pretty sure that Joe Perry and Steve Tyler were there as well.

"It was time for KISS to go on and we're wondering where they are. Then the elevator opened and they came walking out in full costume; everybody was just freaking out because no one had ever seen anything like that. 'What the fuck are they going to do?' They started their set and it was just flawless. People's mouths were hanging down. They didn't do any encores and that was it, they got up and walked out. Then, we had to follow them . . . "

West: "We were on the floor with the audience and they were right on top of you. We encircled the band with this rope to keep the

gear from getting ripped off, and that little rope is all that separated the audience from the band." The rope wasn't much of a security measure— Paul's LoBue guitar was stolen anyway. Eddie Solan recollects: "He and Gene had a matching LoBue guitar/bass set. I was doing the sound, and we weren't watching the equipment and someone walked off with Paul's guitar."

Headliner Wayne (now Jayne) County performed a theatrical transvestite act that was popular at the time. Part of the extreme act occasionally included blood-spitting, which may have inspired an attentive Gene Simmons to add the stunt to his repertoire. "It wasn't really part of my act but I had done it a couple of times," recalls Jayne County. "My act was also big on the tongue thing. They knew if KISS did a show with Wayne County it would be a big audience, so when they got the loft party together, we were booked. I have very fond memories of that evening. It was a great night. It was kind of a shock to see them for the first time."

A review in *The Village Voice* noted that a man in a cowboy hat was archiving Wayne County's set on videotape. While no one knows whether any of KISS's set was taped by this mystery archivist, if any of their set were archived, it would be the earliest known footage of the band.

Palisades, New York
Lamont Hall @ Lamont-Doherty Earth Observatory
Opening Acts: Bloontz, Jackdaw, Rebillot Quartet
Attendance: 200+
Promoter: R.A. Johnsen

■ This show was part of an event called the "1973 Library Party," which was a benefit for the Palisades Free Library. The live music at the event was a showcase for several artists associated with Ron Johnsen. Couples were charged a $25 admission fee for an evening of dining, dancing, and live music, and the $1,500 profit went to the Palisades Free Library Fund.

Virginia Barrett was in charge of booking the event. She relates: "Columbia University has a set of laboratories that are part of their geological center, and the party was held on the grounds of this campus in a house called Lamont Hall.

"I had a neighbor, Ron Johnsen, who was the manager for Electric Lady Studios, and we had almost booked Blood, Sweat and Tears, who were working with Ron. He couldn't get ahold of them at the last minute, but he said that he had this new group KISS who could do the show. So, they came out the night before and stayed at his house. I even remember that they came over and helped us set up.

"While we were setting up, I was talking to Gene about how messed up the school systems were, and I had no idea what their act was. I asked if it was going to take a long time to put on their outfits, and he said: 'Wait 'til you see them.' They had to go back to Ron's house to get dressed. I remember they came on some time around 11 or 12. It was a very warm night, so all the windows and doors were open, and people were dancing in the hall all around them and also on the lawn, all over the place. Some people even went home and woke up their kids and brought them back.

"There was a table of really old people, all in their eighties, real proper types. Suddenly, KISS came out and they were like: 'Ooh. Look at that! Oh my!' Paul grabbed the microphone and yelled 'OK babies, move your ass.' All of a sudden this wild music started, and these old people's mouths were hanging open: 'WOW!' They had never seen anything like that, but they were into it; they stayed for hours, clapping their hands and dancing, carrying on. We had a ball.

"The next day KISS showed up to help us clean, and they commented what a mellow place it was. We raised more money at that event than had ever been raised before."

New York, New York
Bleecker Street Loft, Eighth Floor
Headlining Act: The Brats
Promoter: The Brats

■ The KISS look was beginning to come together; Peter's mother had made up several T-shirts with the KISS logo in glitter, and Paul wore one at this gig along with jeans decorated in blue glitter. Ace wore what has become known in fan circles as his "eagle shirt," presumably for the first time, in addition to a silver belt and matching pants. Gene donned his black skull and crossbones T-shirt, and wore studded, black jeans. Not to

The east wing of Lamont Hall in Palisades, New York, site of KISS's May 26, 1973 performance for the Palisades Free Library charity event. KISS performed in the room adjacent to the glass atrium in what is now a classroom.

A custom-made handbill designed by The Brats for their June 1 performance with KISS. According to Rick Rivets, only 25 of these were printed.

be outdone, Peter showed up in gold pants, a silver-studded belt, a yellow shirt (with a drawing of a drum on it), and a Mylar jacket. The band's makeup was coming along as well, although Ace still hadn't applied whiteface, and Paul had yet to flesh out his star with red lipstick or mascara around his left eye, which left him looking like a depressed clown.

Rick Rivets: "There were more people at this show. Naturally, they blew us away again, though I remember we had a bigger P.A. system than before."

Two nights later, KISS attended Alice Cooper's Billion Dollar Babies concert at Madison Square Garden. According to Eddie Solan, the band was inspired enough by the theatrics to begin incorporating flashing red lights into their own shows by July.

JUNE 8, 1973 (TWO SETS)

Amityville, New York
The Daisy
No Opening Act
Promoter: In-house

JUNE 9, 1973 (TWO SETS)

Amityville, New York
The Daisy
No Opening Act
Promoter: In-house

■ Solan: "We'd come back to Manhattan on the last night of every gig to bring the equipment back, and we used to buy a bottle for this old guy who would run the elevator in the loft. If he didn't show up, then we'd have to carry the equipment all the way up the stairs or bring it to Gene's apartment out in Brooklyn."

JUNE 15, 1973 (TWO SETS)

Amityville, New York
The Daisy
No Opening Act
Promoter: In-house

JUNE 16, 1973 (TWO SETS)

Amityville, New York
The Daisy
No Opening Act
Promoter: In-house
Archived: Audio

■ SET LIST (FIRST SET)

Nothin' to Lose
Firehouse
Life in the Woods
Simple Type
Acrobat
Deuce
100,000 Years
Black Diamond

■ PARTIAL SET LIST (SECOND SET)

Strutter
Watchin' You
Let Me Know

■ A California collector granted coauthor Jeff Suhs access to a 65-minute digital audiotape (DAT) recorded at The Daisy. Jeff explains, "The collector mistakenly thought the tape was from KISS's final show at The Daisy in August, but Paul provides a clue to the date of the recording when, out of the blue, he makes a very unusual comment to the small crowd: 'Don't forget about

The Brats, circa 1973, one of several bands comprising the New York glam scene who performed with KISS in 1973.

unwed Father's Day.' In 1973, Father's Day fell on June 17, indicating the tape was recorded the night before, at KISS's June 16 gig.

"The band sounds exactly like what they were: a brand new band playing a small dive. The songs are in dire need of tighter arrangements. In places, both 'Deuce' and 'Firehouse' barely resemble the songs KISS fans are familiar with, and both are considerably longer than normal. 'Nothin' to Lose' has slightly different lyrics than the recorded version, and 'Simple Type' is almost completely unrecognizable, with Gene and Paul switching vocal parts, compared to the Wicked Lester recordings.

"For all Gene's claims to the contrary, the band apparently had no reservations with regard to jamming and extending songs to lengthy running times. 'Life in the Woods' is a loose, 8-minute, riff-driven song with granola lyrics. In a breakdown during the song's middle section, the band even invited members of the crowd up on stage to sing with them.

"It is also surprising to note that KISS was performing the 'Do you feel all right?' live arrangement of '100,000 Years,' and a version of 'Black Diamond' that is similar to the one on the band's debut album, with the repetitive one-chord ending that goes on several minutes longer than it should.

"By far the most amusing aspect of the recording is the onstage banter.

"Peter Criss introduces 'Firehouse': 'This is our last show here in Amityville tonight, so we want all you people to get into it with us, 'cause you're a hell of a good crowd out here. We do have a mailing list, so you put your name on it, and we'll send you a postcard with our fuckin' faces on it. Especially you horny bitches who want to do yourselves in with it, right down

there, ladies. OK. We want to thank Sid for getting us down here. Especially our friends we made out here in Amityville and our old friends from the Bronx. All right, [Paul starts to rip into 'Firehouse'] let's take this place down!'

"Gene later gives the mailing list another sales pitch: 'Oh yeah. Here's something that's really important. Anybody that feels like using their right hand for something besides *this*. . . Go to the back of the room and pick up a pen, and you put down your name and where you live, and we'll come over to your house and give you head, if you're a guy. No, you just put your name down on the back, and we'll send you all the stuff that comes with KISS!'"

A brief explanation regarding "Acrobat" is important. The first portion is instrumental and appeared on KISS's debut album under the title "Love Theme from KISS." The second half is commonly (and mistakenly) referred to as "You're Much Too Young," despite the fact that it is not a separate song. KISS would sometimes perform both sections of the song, and sometimes just the "You're Much Too Young" portion of it. The entire song was performed at this gig.

JULY 13, 1973

New York, New York
The Crystal Room @ Hotel Diplomat
Headlining Act: The Brats
Opening Act: Planets
Attendance: 500
Promoter: KISS

■ For the first of what would be only two gigs at the Hotel Diplomat, KISS performed a 65-minute set.

Rick Rivets: "They told us they were going to rent the Diplomat because it was legal, and the cops wouldn't be coming like they did at the loft. Then both bands would just split the money, and if there were any losses, it wouldn't be that great.

"Ace had drawn up the ad for the show. He called me up and said that KISS would headline since we headlined last time. I said it was fine with me; I didn't really care because most of the people left after they had finished anyway. Unfortunately, our singer found out, and he went nuts. He called up Paul and was yelling at him over the phone, 'You guys are nothing without us!' I was thinking, 'What the hell are you doing? You know those guys are going to blow us off the stage. Let them go on after us.' But he insisted that we were the stars."

In an attempt to turn this gig into an unofficial showcase of sorts, the band sent out press kits to key industry contacts.

For this show, Paul and Gene rented a brown Mercedes limousine to bolster Peter's sagging spirits and his overall feeling that the band was going nowhere.

Longtime KISS fan Rik Fox (who dated Peter Criss's sister Joann Criscuola) remembers: "I used to sneak out of my house to go see them. For the first Diplomat Hotel gig, my friend and I bought a whole bag of balloons, blew each one of them up and drew the KISS logo and all of the band's faces on them. Then I deflated them, and carefully placed them back in the box. Right before the band came onstage, we blew the balloons back up, and when the lights came up we'd assault them with all the balloons. The band's reaction was: 'What the fuck? Where'd all the balloons come from?'

"The Diplomat had these huge mirrored columns at the corners of the stage, which had a lip to it that stuck out a few inches. During the show, Ace would walk out to the edge, then around the front of the column very slowly before finally walking around back, wrapping his cord around it."

Sylvain Sylvain of the New York Dolls: "When KISS did their first show at the Diplomat, I went to see them. It was so sold out and so hyped up. I remember Peter's mom was there selling T-shirts. Later Paul came up to me in the bathroom and asked me if we wanted to do shows with them, which we did do once they were signed."

Rick Rivets: "They must have had at least 100 people on the guest list; it was all record company people. When we got there, the place was packed. You couldn't even move, it was so jammed. But as soon as they finished, the place cleared out."

"I was with Rick Rivets, David Leeds [Brats bassist], and Ace after the gig," Keith West reflects, "and we headed over to Chinatown with the ten bucks we each made. By five in the morning we were really hammered, and Ace grabbed some old lady's bag and started throwing it around in the middle of the street. She has no idea who this guy is, and he's yelling 'Bonsai!' We crashed somewhere, and when we woke up in the morning David's pants were down. He had whipped cream all over him. That was Ace. "

AUGUST 10, 1973

New York, New York
The Crystal Room @ Hotel Diplomat
Opening Acts: Street Punk, Luger
Promoter: KISS

21

THIS PERMIT MUST BE PRODUCED ON DEMAND

THE CITY OF NEW YORK

$10.00

№ 61081

PUBLIC DANCE OR BALL

License No. 0275-8#

DEPARTMENT OF CONSUMER AFFAIRS

DATE OF ISSUANCE JULY 2/73
NEW YORK, 19

To whom it may Concern:

That in consideration of the sum of TEN DOLLARS, receipt of which is hereby acknowledged,

STANLEY EISEN

is permitted to hold a PUBLIC DANCE OR BALL

at the Public Dance Hall known as DIPLOMAT HOTEL Located at 108 W. 43rD. STREET

Borough of MANHATTAN on JULY 13/73 19

This Permit is issued subject to the strict observance of all laws, rules and regulations applicable thereto, and is to remain in force unless suspended or revoked and IS NOT TRANSFERABLE.

Commissioner.

An official permit from the City of New York issued to Stanley Eisen for a public dance or ball.

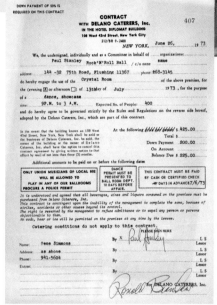

The contract for KISS's July 13, 1973 appearance at the Hotel Diplomat. This is the earliest known Paul Stanley signature in existence.

KISS onstage at the Hotel Diplomat in Manhattan. Show #14, July 13, 1973.

LYDIA CRIS

■ KISS could not have known it at the time, but this gig, perhaps more than any other in its career, was the linchpin upon which its story rests because future manager Bill Aucoin was in the audience.

Aucoin recollects in detail: "The reason I went to see this group was because Gene sent me these little notes every week inviting me to see his band and kept saying that he watched my television show *Flipside*. One night, I was out at dinner with a friend, and I said to the guy, 'C'mon, they're playing over at the Diplomat, let's go check them out.' Of course the Diplomat is this old, broken-down, rat trap of a hotel. Literally, there were holes in the floor. That's how bad the hotel was. The show itself was in the second floor ballroom. KISS had black jeans on, and they didn't have all the makeup or whiteface yet, but they were really different, and I love things that are different. The more extreme it is, the more I like it."

Nicky Martyn of opening act Street Punk: "Gene liked us, and Street Punk had a really good draw in New York; he knew that we'd get people down there. Gene was very smart about it; he made sure that Bill Aucoin came after we were well off the stage. He later tried to repay us by getting Street Punk signed with Aucoin. Bill thought he could do nothing for us. He told Gene, 'These guys aren't even a band.' KISS had a business sense about them, and we were a bunch of lunatics."

Producer Eddie Kramer: "It was an amazing show. I certainly saw the potential for the band to turn the world on its ear in terms of show. It was very raw, and they couldn't play very well, but I was impressed."

Joey Criscuola recalls, "The act was coming together. My sister Joann and her friend Annmarie Hughes [Pat Benatar's cousin] were wearing KISS T-shirts, screaming and going wild." The sight of the two girls in the audience screaming throughout the show made an important impression on Aucoin. After the show, Aucoin approached Eddie

Solan at the soundboard, told him he'd enjoyed KISS's show, and asked if Solan could arrange for him to speak with the band.

"I talked to Gene and Paul," Aucoin continues, "and said, 'Look, I'd like to have a meeting with you and see if we get along and if we'd like to work together.' About a week later they came by, and I met Peter and Ace and told them, 'Why don't you give me 30 days, and if I can get you a deal and if you want to work together, we'll go forward.'"

KISS may not have had a manager, a record contract, or a favorable relationship with the music press, but they were already converting the crowds into believers, no matter who they were. Ivan Kral, guitarist for opening act Luger, remembers the gig: "We played a very short set. It was maybe seven or eight songs. I remember my brother came in afterward and told me, 'You guys look pretty good, but *those* guys are outrageous!'"

The bigger-is-better approach was beginning

to become the band's mantra, as Eddie Solan relates: "We needed a bigger P.A. system for this gig, and we really didn't have any money. So we sold the speakers, and I built four Altec Lansing speakers myself. Paul drove this rented bread truck to Scarsdale, and we picked up the P.A., and that's what we used at the Hotel Diplomat."

AUGUST 17, 1973 (TWO SETS)

Amityville, New York
The Daisy
No Opening Act

AUGUST 18, 1973 (TWO SETS)

Amityville, New York
The Daisy
No Opening Act
Promoter: In-house

■ To promote the August 17 and 18 gigs, Long Island newspaper *The Express* featured the first-ever published photo of KISS in their "Do-Wah-Diddy" entertainment section.

Bill Aucoin's first look at KISS: the Hotel Diplomat, August 10, 1973.

LYDIA CRISS

AUGUST 24, 1973 (TWO SETS)

Amityville, New York
The Daisy
No Opening Act
Promoter: In-house

■ The sparse crowds at early Daisy gigs soon disappeared, as Solan relates: "Before long the place was packed to the rafters. I guess word got around about these nuts with the makeup. As The Daisy called them back three or four times, they got to be pretty popular."

AUGUST 25, 1973 (TWO SETS)

Amityville, New York
The Daisy
No Opening Act
Promoter: In-house

■ Unlike previous Daisy appearances, which had little promotion, KISS took out an ad in *The Village Voice* to promote the August 24 and 25 appearances.

AUGUST 31, 1973

Queens, New York
Coventry
Headline Act: Wild Honey
Opening Act: The Detroit Dogs
Capacity: 600
Promoter: In-house

■ Headline act Wild Honey were signed to Poly-dor at the time, and the obscure punk band The Detroit Dogs eventually renamed themselves the Dogs and released an album.

SEPTEMBER 1, 1973

Queens, New York
Coventry
Headline Act: Wild Honey
Opening Act: The Detroit Dogs
Capacity: 600
Promoter: In-house

■ Paul Sub: "KISS never really got paid. One day they came in and said that they insisted they could not play unless I gave them 50 bucks. So I asked what the $50 was for. They told me it was for a hotel they had to get so that they could put on their makeup."

Stanley Mieses reviewed one of the Coventry appearances for the *New York Daily News.* In his hilariously literal report, he writes, " . . . his [Stanley's] black-and-red striped platform shoes should win the Alan Ladd Footwear Award."

KISS performing at Coventry for the final time, December 1973.

They're so high that you can crawl through the gap between the heels and the layered soles. He also serves as the spokesman for the group. 'We didn't come here to talk no politics, we're goin' to rock and roll,' he shouts to the small audience at Coventry. He winks with the one eye that isn't painted black. 'I hope everyone here's been drinking . . . ' and the thought trails off, sentence incomplete, into a number called 'Sloe Gin Time.' [sic] 'We'd rather you dance than ponder the lurics [sic],' he advises. The bass player sneers and the lead guitarist strikes an I-dare-you-punk pose. 'We're not the smartest boys around, y'know,' the rhythm guitarist says, and the whole band laughs."

SEPTEMBER 2, 1973 CANCELED

Queens, New York
Coventry
Headline Act: Wild Honey
Opening Act: The Detroit Dogs
Capacity: 600
Promoter: In-house

■ This concert was only advertised on posters made by KISS. In all other advertisements, only the August 31 and September 1 dates were mentioned. A charity event related to Jerry Lewis's annual Labor Day telethon was scheduled at Coventry for this date.

––––––––

With the Aucoin agreement imminent, KISS ended their relationship with Lew Linet. "At this juncture," Linet recalls, "I had some talks with them, and I told them I knew what they needed, but I didn't think I could give it to them. They soon came to me and said they had met a television producer whose enthusiasm and contacts were just what they needed. I said, 'Sounds great to me. Let me give you a formal release, and I'll wish you the best.'"

Aucoin, in the meantime, had been moguling to keep his promise on delivering KISS a record deal in 30 days. Longtime Buddah Records executive Neil Bogart seemed to be Bill's man. Neil, who is often described as the P.T. Barnum of rock and roll, played a major part in KISS's success. The former Buddah Records executive had left his six-figure salaried position at the label earlier in the year only to find himself (under the alias Wayne Roberts) taking on a clothed role in a 1973 soft-core porn film called *Sin in the Suburbs.* However, the resourceful Bogart quickly reversed his fortunes when he scored a $3 million dollar distribution deal. Aucoin remembers: "Neil had just found out that the Warner Group was going to give him money to start up a label with Warner Bros." KISS's demo tape ended up on top of the slush pile in Bogart's office where record producer Kenny Kerner rescued it one Friday afternoon. Kerner liked it enough to play it for Bogart the following Monday. Aucoin picks up the story again: "Neil called me and told me, 'Everyone seems to want to do this band. Let's do a little showcase so that everyone in the future company knows what we're going to sign. And if everything's OK, then we'll sign them to the new label.'"

The showcase took place in Manhattan in late September. "Everyone was taken aback at the showcase," Aucoin comments, "which was done at about 5 or 6 o'clock at night in this little ballet studio called Le Tang's."

Prior to seeing KISS, Bill Aucoin had been partners with Joyce Biawitz in a company called Direction Plus, which shot promotional films for record companies. Aucoin had had some success in the television industry, working his way up from cameraman to director at Boston's WGBH before doing two TV pilots for Celebrity Productions. Aucoin sold one of the pilots, *Flipside,* to 143 markets around the country. Aucoin offers, "After the first 13-week run, I was getting bludgeoned and thought 'Screw this, I'm going to go into the music business.' So, I started Rock Steady Productions with Joyce."

Sean Delaney, a talented musician and song-writer, was brought in to help develop KISS. "I first started working with them during the Le Tang's period," Delaney explains. "When KISS were at Le Tang's, Neil, Joyce, and Bill were sitting in front of the guys, and I was sitting on the side, clinically depressed, wanting to hate them because all of a sudden I was no longer the center of attention. The band started playing, and they were loud. After the first song, Neil, Joyce, and Bill didn't react. They just sat there looking at them. That's when Gene walked over to Neil, grabbed his wrists and made him clap. That took me out of my depression right there. I said, 'Holy fuck, this guy is serious.' That's when I took on my role of making sure that nothing bad was going to happen to these four guys.

"Maybe two weeks after that they walked into my loft/basement to start rehearsing.

"The show that KISS does would not exist if it weren't for me. I did the original choreography, I blocked it, and I showed them how to do it. I showed Paul how to walk. Gene was not a demon; I turned Gene into a demon. I showed him how to walk like a monster and stay in character. The moment I started doing the demon with Gene, Paul wanted his fair share. That's how the whole he/she thing started.

"When I colored their hair black, the dye irritated Paul's scalp. Paul wanted to be Johnny Thunders, so he would stand there trying to strike these Johnny Thunders poses, and then he would reach up and scratch his head. I asked him, 'What was that man? You can't look like a rock star and then reach up and scratch your scalp.' 'Well, it itches; what am I supposed to do?'

"That's when I came up with his first move. He would throw the guitar behind him and take both hands and just rip them into his hair. Then throw his hands up in the air and walk forward like he's some kind of beauty model. Those were the first two things that I started doing with them. I carried a whistle, and I would use it the moment someone was out of character.

"KISS was a jam band. I had to tell them how to bring the music down into songs. I took all the bullshit out and tightened up the music. We were down there for several months."

KISS signed an artist's agreement with Bill Aucoin on October 15, 1973. Initially, KISS themselves were not signed directly to a recording contract. Instead, Aucoin's Rock Steady Productions inked a production agreement with Casablanca Records on November 1.

As the ink dried on that paperwork, KISS began recording their debut album. The eponymous album was recorded at Bell Sound Studios on Fifty-fourth Street in Manhattan from November 13 to November 30.

After the album was completed, Peter "Moose" Oreckinto was hired for his special effects expertise and wound up becoming one of the original traveling road crew. Peter relates: "I went down to the business district on Church Street, and they were rehearsing in some build-ing two floors below street level, and I met Bill Aucoin and the band. Sean had video equipment set up. It was the basic, black-and-white ½" video deck with a monitor, and he was just taping the band so they could go back and review their rehearsals. They didn't have the equipment set up that long, but they recorded rehearsals quite often."

DECEMBER 21, 1973

Queens, New York
Coventry
Headlining Act: Isis
Opening Acts: Rags, City Slicker, Flaming Youth
Capacity: 600
Promoter: In-house

■ This is the first show where all four members of KISS performed with full whiteface makeup.

A band called Actress was scheduled on the bill for both Coventry shows, but was replaced by Flaming Youth. (Actress is not to be confused with the early version of the New York Dolls that allegedly went by the same name.)

During the show, Paul announced to the crowd that KISS had signed a record contract. The announcement and portions of the show were archived on some form of video or Super 8mm. The film, which is the earliest confirmed live footage of KISS, has been lost. Paul Stanley in a March 2000 interview with the *Oklahoma Entertainer* recalled the final Coventry gigs: "I remember doing the shows with brand new amps and feeling very good about the prospects of the future."

Isis manager Ron Gitman: "Both Isis and KISS realized that it was just a big problem to play together, especially in these small clubs, because there was just too much equipment. But it was a great package. Years later, I bumped into Paul Stanley when I lived on the West Side. I told him who I was, and I said, 'Do you remember when you opened up for Isis?' He said 'We never opened up for Isis. They opened up for us.' OK, Paul, if you say so."

DECEMBER 22, 1973

Queens, New York
Coventry
Headlining Act: Isis
Opening Acts: Rags, City Slicker, Flaming Youth
Capacity: 600
Promoter: In-house

■ Opening act Flaming Youth who, according to Ron Blanchard of Rags, had "a beautiful French lead singer," ended up providing the title for a song on the *Destroyer* album.

This show was KISS's final appearance at Coventry and their last as a New York club band.

DECEMBER 23, 1973   CANCELED

Queens, New York
Coventry
Headlining Act: Isis
Opening Acts: Rags, City Slicker, Flaming Youth
Capacity: 600
Promoter: In-house

■ Three shows at Coventry were listed in the advertisement in *The Village Voice*. However, as Solan offers, "The final Coventry gig was canceled for some reason. I can't remember why. It might have been the weather."

CHAPTER 3

KISS TOUR

Number of Shows: 84
Start Date: December 31, 1973 - New York, New York
End Date: October 4, 1974 - Houston, Texas
Countries: Canada, U.S.A.
Headlining Acts: 10cc; Aerosmith; Argent; Billy Preston; Blue Öyster Cult; The "All New" Fleetwood Mac; Iggy & the Stooges; James Gang; Kathi McDonald; Manfred Mann's Earth Band; Nazareth; New York Dolls; Quicksilver Messenger Service; Redbone; Renaissance; Rory Gallagher; Rush; Savoy Brown; Silverhead; Suzi Quatro; Teenage Lust; Uriah Heep
Opening Acts: 13th Floor; Barbarossa; Chris Jagger; Conqueror Worm; Fat Chance; Flight; Fludd; Flying Saucer; Isis; Island; Les Variations; Max Onion; Michael Fennelly; Mike Quatro; Mojo Boogie Band; Mood Jga Jga; Outlaws; Redbone; Ritual; Ronny Legg; Ross; Rush; Silverhead; Smack Dab; Sweetwater; Thunderhead; Wizzard
Average Attendance: 2,645* (Does not include 3/31/74 or 4/29/74 appearances.)

After concluding their final stint at Coventry, KISS returned to Sean Delaney's loft on Church Street to rehearse for a New Year's Eve show at the Academy of Music in Manhattan.

While Sean Delaney was again running the band through rehearsals and designing and refining the stage show, the respective staffs of Casablanca Records and Rock Steady Productions were busy gearing up the promotions machine. Blurbs reporting on the band's progress were constantly fed to industry publications. The blurbs appeared almost weekly from January through June 1974 and were essential in creating the initial national buzz about the band. Both Neil Bogart and Bill Aucoin felt it was important to imprint the band's image and name into the consciousness of the American public, even if many of the blurbs were very mundane, such as the one that appeared in the March 9, 1974 issue of *Amusement Business*: "Joyce Biawitz reports that KISS employs a video system to review their rehearsals."

Meanwhile, Bogart was working his seemingly endless list of friends and key industry contacts to help the band get some high-profile gigs, such as ABC-TV's *In Concert* (courtesy of Dick Clark) and *The Mike Douglas Show* (through the efforts of talent coordinator Vince Calandra).

The most successful promotional idea, however, came in the spring of 1974. On April 20, Fort Lauderdale radio station WSHE staged a kissing contest to promote the band. The contest was a huge success, and Scott Shannon at WMAK in Nashville was inspired to suggest that KISS record a cover of Bobby Rydell's "Kissin' Time." The band was very reluctant to do so, but Neil Bogart was convinced that the idea would work and, on April 26, KISS entered Bell Sound Studios for a 12-hour session to record the song. "Kissin' Time" was released as a single and began appearing on pressings of the first album in June. Bogart parlayed the single and the kissing contest into a brilliant promotions coup, and arranged for 13 additional kissing contests to be held on or around May 10 under the title "The Great KISS-Off." Not coincidentally, many of the 13 markets chosen directly corresponded to the cities listed in the refurbished "Kissin' Time" lyrics. The contests were well covered by local press, though oddly enough, KISS, the intended beneficiary of all this promotional activity, was often not mentioned in connection with the events.

Regardless, the primary promotions tool was getting the band out on the road and keeping it there.

KISS onstage during the first gig of 1974

MARK RAVITZ

As a point of fact, from March 1974 until April 1978, KISS played an astonishing 504 concerts, going four years without a significant break from touring.

Determining the exact route that KISS took when they began to tour is exceptionally difficult because their schedule changed on a day-to-day basis. Moreover, the band's commitment to non-stop touring was so stringent that its early itineraries made almost no geographic sense whatsoever, especially considering that it traveled via station wagon between the gigs. The roadcrew dubbed the early dates "The Star of David Tour," jesting that if you were to draw lines on a map linking the sites of the concerts, the result would be a Star of David. Some of the billings were almost laughably mismatched, with KISS paired up with the likes of tranquil art-rockers Renaissance, folk singer Kathi McDonald, and Billy Preston. Equally impressive is the list of bands whom KISS was scheduled to, but for various reasons did not play with, among them Badfinger, Genesis, and Queen. All of this is testimony that KISS would play anywhere, at any time, with anyone who would have them.

At the heart of this meat-grinder of a tour was KISS's road crew, which started with only three people: Cris Griffin, Peter Oreckinto, and Sean Delaney, who served as interim road manager. The relentless crew that would see KISS through the chaos of the next two years took shape quickly when Mick Campise, Paul Chavarria, Mike McGurl, Rick Munroe, and longtime road manager JR Smalling, among others, all came on board by the end of May. This road crew had a profound impact in building KISS's concerts from slightly amateurish shows to performances of nearly mythical proportions. KISS unquestionably owes a large part of its success to its original road crew's creativity, loyalty, and perseverance. Oreckinto relates, "I remember having their truck parked out in my driveway for weeks at a time, with all the purple Anvil cases sitting in my garage. I built fog machines in the garage, T-shirts in the living room; we were doing everything we could to get this band out on the road, everything we could to make it happen for our boys."

Smalling recalls, "We were really like commandos, and that's the way we looked at it. When we rolled into town, we were the party; we were the reason why people got dressed up and came out. And it was a major rush, that's why we did it. In those days it was *the* scene."

What separated KISS from many other bands was the fact that its show started the instant they got into town. "The whole attitude was set long before the band hit the stage," Smalling continues. "It was almost a motorcycle gang mentality. I'm 6'3", Ace and Gene were 6'2" or 6'3", and Moose's name speaks for itself, and we were all walking around on 4- or 5-inch platform heels in head-to-toe leather. When we walked in the door, people were like, 'Who the fuck are these guys?!'"

Creating a lasting impression was the goal, and KISS was achieving it wherever it played. The fact that KISS was routinely burying the headlining act was both an accomplishment and a detriment, and the band quickly found that the

headliners did not appreciate their antics. "There were a lot of bands who hated us," relates production manager Mick Campise. Tension between KISS and the headlining acts and crews was frequently high; the Aerosmith/KISS pairing did not survive beyond two shows, and KISS was bounced from a tour with Argent just as quickly. "When we first went out there we ambushed, literally, a lot of bands," Smalling remembers, "the headliners rarely had much tolerance for being blown off the stage; their train of thought was: what fun is it to have the crowd chanting the name of the opening act all through your set? The number of shows that we did as openers began to become pretty few."

The set lists for the KISS tour were comprised almost exclusively of KISS material, with "She" the only remaining holdover from the Wicked Lester repertoire. The running order was also beginning to fall into place, with "Deuce" locked into the opening slot, "100,000 Years" home to Peter's drum solo, and "Black Diamond" typically closing out the set. "Baby, Let Me Go" (later recorded as "Let Me Go, Rock 'n Roll"), was the usual encore.

KISS began using its lighted logo at the New Year's Eve gig in 1973. A surprise gift from Aucoin, the sign was designed and built by Mark Ravitz of Jules Fischer Associates, a Broadway staging-design company. Ravitz relates, "Bill and Jules called me in to design the logo and get involved with their first flashpots. Their first logo was built by me and a couple of friends in what is now my living room." Aucoin was resolute that the sign be used at every gig, no matter how difficult the logistics proved. Rick Munroe recalls, "My job was to get the sign visible, it didn't have to be on stage. Sometimes I would put it on the speakers or in the balcony or on the side of the stage." Anything to imprint a flashing "KISS" in the audience's memory . . .

Ravitz was also responsible for designing KISS's stage, minimal as it was. Three stacks of amplifiers—Marshalls on stage left, Ampegs on stage right—flanked the drum riser, which typically sat only a foot off the floor and was fringed with white tassels. The riser levitated eight feet in the air via a very unreliable chain-link mechanism. "Peter hated that thing," states Smalling, "he was scared to death of it, and I don't blame him; half the time the chain would slip off the sprocket, and the entire riser would plummet until the chain-link caught again. But he did it every night; anything for the show."

Various gimmicks were already incorporated into the stage show by this time. Perhaps inspired by the Crazy World of Arthur Brown, or New York crazies The Magic Tramps, Gene had learned to breathe fire, and Peter was using drumsticks (white copper tubes, actually) that shot out sparks like a Roman candle. Gene's blood-spitting routine wouldn't appear until February 17 (its first confirmed appearance) at a show in Long Beach.

DECEMBER 31, 1973

New York, New York
Academy of Music
Headlining Acts: Blue Öyster Cult, Iggy & the Stooges,
   Teenage Lust

Capacity: 3,383
Promoter: Howard Stein Presents
Archived: Audio

■ SET LIST

Deuce
Cold Gin
Nothin' to Lose
Firehouse
Let Me Know
100,000 Years
Black Diamond

■ Eddie Solan remembers, "We went over all of these tricks at rehearsals with a magician. After Gene did the fire-breathing stunt he was supposed to lean over and stick the dagger-shaped torch into this foam block at center stage." Unfortunately, there was no foam block onstage that night. "Gene had done his fire-breathing stunt," Peter Oreckinto continues, "with this torch that had cloth attached to the end with picture-hanging wire. He went to the front of the stage and tried to jam it into the floor, which was solid hardwood, and as he was bending over, the torch caught the right side of his hair on fire."

As if immolating himself was not bad enough, Gene set a personal record—yet to be matched—by nearly setting a second person aflame during the show.

Solan: "I was sitting next to Bill Aucoin doing sound at the mixing board when Gene almost set some guy on fire. Gene had this trick where he would throw fire out of his hands by using flash-paper, which he lit with his candelabra." "He was so nervous that he threw it into the audience and burned a kid's face," Aucoin adds. "Fortunately, he just singed his eyebrows and forehead. Joyce and I set him up with KISS, and he was a terrific kid; we just wanted to make sure that he was OK. But, boy, that was a scary scene. That could have been the end of their career right there."

Preproduction was no cakewalk either, as Solan recalls: "I remember getting to the gig and there was no P.A. there. It was coming in from Colorado, and it got there at the last minute. In fact, we were still setting up microphones as people were filing in. From my standpoint, things were really screwed up. Gene's microphone wouldn't work so I had the stagehands take a drum mike off Peter's kit and set it up for Gene. We didn't even have a chance to do a sound check. But the gig was pretty exciting with the way they went over, considering they weren't even on the bill. The other bands were coming on, and people were still calling for KISS. It pissed off Blue Öyster Cult."

A planned encore of "Baby, Let Me Go" was scrapped, most likely due to time constraints. Nor did KISS perform at the evening's second show, which was scheduled for midnight.

American Talent International (ATI) was responsible for getting KISS booked for this gig and shortly thereafter became the band's booking agency, a position they held for the next ten years. ATI president Jeff Franklin was also instrumental in KISS's success and owned a portion of Casablanca.

This is the first known occasion when a KISS concert was privately recorded on audiotape.

Paul onstage at the Fillmore East, January 8, 1974.

Mark Ravitz's sketch of a spider-web prop, used at the band's January 8 gig at the Fillmore East.

JANUARY 8, 1974

New York, New York
Bill Graham's Fillmore East
No Opening Act
Promoters: Warner Bros. Records, Casablanca Records
■ KISS had moved to the Fillmore to rehearse for the week prior to the show.

Aucoin: "It wasn't a press party so much as it was a gathering to get people interested in promoting them. ATI was there just to kind of see what was going to happen. The idea of getting the Fillmore East was that their stage was big enough for us to do a big show, and if ATI wanted to bring people down to promote the band, then we could do that as well as get some of the rock and roll press in there."

"While we were rehearsing at the Fillmore," Aucoin continues, "Neil called me and told me to please ask the guys to take off the makeup. I told him that it was not going to happen. But he insisted, 'Please just ask them, Bill.' I called back and told him that there was no way. So he relented and agreed that we'd go with it."

Perhaps as a compromise with Bogart, who wasn't quite sold on the androgynous lover concept, Paul wore what would become known as the Bandit makeup at this show, one of only two occasions when he did so. Bogart introduced the band at this particular gig, though that duty would eventually fall to whomever the road manager for a particular tour was (Sean Delaney, JR Smalling, or Mike McGurl).

Rick Rivets: "One day in the Village I ran into Eddie Solan. He told me to come over to the Fillmore because KISS was doing a warm-up show, so the Dolls and I went over there. When we got there, the Fillmore was empty, and they were pulling people off the streets to fill the place. But it was the most unbelievable show. It dawned on me that they could be the new Beatles for the '70s."

After the Fillmore gig, KISS changed their rehearsal facilities to Carroll's Music on Forty-second Street.

JANUARY 26, 1974

New York, New York
Academy of Music
Headlining Acts: The "All New" Fleetwood Mac, Silverhead
Attendance: 3,383   Capacity: 3,383
Promoter: Howard Stein Presents
Archived: Super 8mm
■ The Fleetwood Mac appearing at this gig was Fleetwood Mac in name only. A contract dispute

had created a rift between the band members and management. Fleetwood's management decided to press forward with replacement players, whom they dubbed The "All New" Fleetwood Mac. Because their lead singer was too ill to perform, they offered refunds prior to their set, a 43-minute instrumental performance.

Paul wore the Bandit makeup at this gig, marking the second and final time he wore it for a live performance.

One minute and 53 seconds of silent, Super 8mm film from this concert was discovered in Eastern Europe in 2001, making this the earliest known color footage of KISS.

FEBRUARY 5, 1974

Edmonton, Alberta, Canada
Dinwoodie Lounge @ University of Alberta
Opening Act: Barbarossa
Attendance: 46   Capacity: 540
Promoter: Scenemaker Productions
■ Mike Quatro was originally penciled in to headline the February 5, 6, and 8 shows but wanted too much money ($5,000) for the gigs, and the promoters opted to go with KISS. They were paid $500 per show. Neil Bogart even called the promoter to thank him for booking the shows, and sent him an advance copy of the first album.

With relatively short notice, the band and four

crewmembers (Sean Delaney, JR Smalling, Peter Oreckinto, and Cris Griffin) flew from New York to Toronto and on to Calgary before driving the final stretch of the trip up to Edmonton in a station wagon and rental truck.

They were joined by soundman Bill Welch, who had flown up from California. Welch remembers: "The show was held in a big cafeteria with lots of glass. We had the levitating drum riser, two Marshall stacks per guitar player, four SVTs for Gene, then all the flashpots and lights. However, the sound company we were using was brand new, and they didn't have a snake for the soundboard, so I mixed sound right at the edge of the stage with headphones on the whole time. I was so close to the action that I had to learn the flashpot cues so I didn't get zapped. Fortunately, it was more of a rehearsal to get a feel of how the audience was going to respond to their extravagance in some place where they had never seen anything like that."

The ceiling in the lounge was so low that the KISS sign was flown only two feet off the floor.

FEBRUARY 6, 1974

Calgary, Alberta, Canada
Student Gymnasium @ Southern Alberta Institute of
    Technology
Opening Act: Barbarossa
Attendance: 161   Capacity: 800
Promoter: Scenemaker Productions
■ While in Calgary, KISS did what is probably their first radio interview, with station CHED's Jim McKeough. The promoter arranged for the interview but forgot to inform the front desk that KISS, whose first album wasn't even out, would be showing up in full costume and makeup. A female secretary screamed and ran into a back room when they entered the station.

FEBRUARY 8, 1974

Winnipeg, Manitoba, Canada
Tache Hall Auditorium @ University of Manitoba
Opening Act: Mood Jga Jga
Attendance: 750   Capacity: 750
Promoter: Frank Weipert
■ This gig was part of a yearly musical cultural program called "The 4th Annual Festival of Life and Learning" and was held in a ballroom inside of one of the university's residence halls.

During the show, a bottle containing the kerosene for Gene's fire-breathing act was accidentally kicked over and spilled across the stage. Paul slipped in the pool of kerosene but continued playing, pretending that it was all part of the show.

The scaffold that framed the KISS sign broke during load-out, sending the sign crashing to the floor. Fortunately, no one was injured.

Promotional black T-shirts with the KISS logo sewn on the front in rhinestones first appeared around this time.

While KISS was playing to small crowds in Canadian college dorms, Casablanca Records, according to copyright paperwork on file at the Library of Congress, released the album *KISS* on February 8. The more commonly reported release date, February 18, is inaccurate.

FEBRUARY 17, 1974

Long Beach, California
Long Beach Auditorium

Headlining Act: Rory Gallagher
Attendance: 4,000   Capacity: 4,000
Promoter: Pacific Presentations
Archived: Super 8mm
■ The "All New" Fleetwood Mac was scheduled for this show, but canceled.

In 2000, 27 minutes of silent, Super 8mm footage from an early KISS concert was put up for auction online. Judging by the costumes, set list, and what little can be seen of the venue, the footage was almost certainly shot at this gig. The set list contained, but was not necessarily limited to: "Deuce," "Strutter," "Firehouse," "She," "Nothin' to Lose," "Cold Gin," "100,000 Years," "Black Diamond," and "Acrobat."

KISS spent the week out in Los Angeles rehearsing (most likely at Studio Instrument Rentals) on February 14, 15, 16, and 20.

FEBRUARY 18, 1974

Los Angeles, California
Los Angeles Room @ Century Plaza Hotel
Promoters: Casablanca Records, Warner Bros. Records
■ The Los Angeles Room was a large ballroom that had been rented to celebrate the launch of Casablanca Records. Jules Fisher's organization decorated the ballroom to look like Rick's Café from *Casablanca*, and many guests dressed as characters from the famous 1942 film.

Bill Welch: "There were all the bigwigs from the record industry and people you didn't normally see at concerts sitting all dressed up at these fancy banquet tables; dinner and speeches came before the show. Then they introduced KISS, and they were just deafeningly loud. People were 10 to 15 feet away from the speaker cabinet . . . Well, I don't know what they were expecting with all that equipment on stage."

Legendary journalist Lisa Robinson wrote in the May 1974 issue of *Creem*: "When the drums levitated eight feet off the stage, Alice Cooper whispered to me, 'Some people will do anything to get attention.'"

KISS buttons featuring the debut album's cover were distributed to attendees.

FEBRUARY 21, 1974

Los Angeles, California
Aquarius Theater
Promoter: Dick Clark Productions
Archived: Video
■ **SET LIST**

Deuce
Nothin' to Lose
Firehouse
Black Diamond

■ This performance was staged specifically for an episode of *In Concert*. The taping was the band's first television appearance, and Paul gave a memorable introduction, shouting, "Hey, World; we're KISS! We want everybody here to come along with us; 'cause you've got nothin' to lose. Two, three, four . . ."

The show, episode 31 of the series, was first broadcast on ABC-TV, on March 29. The band taped performances of "Deuce," "Nothin' to Lose," "Firehouse," and "Black Diamond," though "Deuce" was never broadcast. The master tapes remain missing to this day.

"It was a disaster," as Bill Aucoin recalls. "They were so nervous and played so loud that you could

hardly decipher what was happening. I knew Josh White, the director that night, and when we looked at the footage it was really bad. We actually paid Josh and Dick Clark to go back and fix it to make it work. We couldn't have them look bad on their first network show. Josh went in and spent hours and hours covering the mistakes up and putting effects on it; anything to make it look more exciting."

Redbone, Foghat, Kool & the Gang, and Melissa Manchester also recorded appearances for the show on this date.

MARCH 1, 2, & 3, 1974   CANCELED

New York, New York
Felt Forum @ Madison Square Garden Center
Capacity: 4,300
Promoter: Richard Nader
■ It's a little known fact that during the relatively lengthy break that followed the taping of *In Concert*, KISS nearly did a show in Madison Square Garden. New York music promoter Richard Nader tells the story: "I was putting together a world music festival for Madison Square Garden. I proposed the event and blocked out days at the Garden, after which we did a press release and announced it. It was a three-night event where we were going to use the old Felt Forum, and the exhibit hall in the Garden, which was called The Rotunda. The new-era acts were going to perform in the Felt Forum and there would be this walk-through display on how records are made and the business end of the music industry in The Rotunda. KISS was scheduled to play one of the nights. The New York Dolls were scheduled, as was Alice Cooper.

"In the aftermath of the big petroleum crisis, the industry cut back their budgets and because of that squeeze, we didn't go through with the festival."

MARCH 22, 1974

Devon (Philadelphia), Pennsylvania
Valley Forge Music Fair
Headlining Act: Redbone
Capacity: 2,800
■ This gig appears on the earliest known KISS itinerary and members of the band's road crew have confirmed that it took place. It is possible that a third act (perhaps Argent) headlined over KISS and Redbone.

MARCH 23, 1974

New York, New York
Academy of Music
Headlining Acts: Argent, Redbone
Attendance: 3,383   Capacity: 3,383
Promoter: Howard Stein Presents
■ Nazareth and Graham Central Station were scheduled to appear on the bill over KISS, but were replaced by Argent and Redbone.

MARCH 24, 1974

Owings Mills (Baltimore), Maryland
Painter's Mill Music Fair
Headlining Act: Aerosmith
Opening Act: Redbone
Capacity: 2,450
Promoter: Entertainment Concept Corp.
■ This was the first of only two gigs KISS ever did with Aerosmith, and it featured an in-the-round stage setup. Sean Delaney recalls: "I got into

several shoving matches with Aerosmith's guys over being told that we couldn't use Peter's riser. They wanted him to set up on the floor, which we never did.

"We also had a fire start that night. The kids had all these banners along the front of the stage. When Gene spit fire, they set the signs on fire. The whole front of the stage was in flames; they even set the balcony on fire." Gene's bass head was also stolen at the show.

Aerosmith guitarist Joe Perry reminisced about this gig in Aerosmith's official autobiography *Walk This Way: The Autobiography of Aerosmith,* but he mistakenly claimed the gig had taken place in Marion, Ohio.

The original headliner, Badfinger, canceled on the day of the show. Aerosmith was moved up from their original opening-act slot, and KISS was added to open the gig. Sean Delaney also recalled that portions of the show were captured on video or film. The whereabouts of this footage are presently unknown.

MARCH 25, 1974 (TWO SHOWS: 8:00 P.M., 10:30 P.M.)

(Georgetown), Washington, D.C.
The Bayou
No Opening Act
Attendance: (1) 500; (2) 500   Capacity: 500
Promoter: Barry Richards
Archived: Audio (10:30 show)

■ SET LIST
Deuce
Strutter
She
Firehouse
Acrobat
Let Me Know
Black Diamond
Baby, Let Me Go

■ Peter Oreckinto: "There was no opening act because the stage was too small, one of the smallest stages we ever played on. It was maybe 15' x 15'. I actually used the flashpots that night even with the eight-foot ceilings; I just made little baby ones. We even got the levitation machine up there. We had the fog machines off in the dressing room with a stack of hoses (leading out to the stage); we had stuff all over the place."

At this gig, both sections of "Acrobat" were performed. This is the last known instance when the song was performed in its entirety.

After the show, KISS and their crew remained in D.C., where they caught the Badfinger gig the following night. Then, on March 27, the band taped a now-long-forgotten, lip-synched performance for a local *American Bandstand* clone called *Barry Richards' Rock 'n' Soul Show.* KISS most likely performed several songs at the 6 P.M. taping at WDCA-TV in Chevy Chase, Maryland, outside Washington, D.C. Production assistant for the show Lee Payton recalled, "I remember they didn't tell anyone they were going to be using pyro. For the big finale of one of their numbers, their drummer shot pyro out of his drumsticks. It scared the hell out of everyone on the show." There are no known tapes of this performance in existence, although a WDCA staff member remarked that Barry Richards may have retained a copy of the episode.

MARCH 29, 1974

Asbury Park, New Jersey
Sunshine In Concert Hall
Headlining Acts: Renaissance, 10cc
Promoter: Friendship Productions
■ After the gig, the band rushed to their hotel room to watch the broadcast of their first television appearance, on *In Concert,* only to find the reception was extremely poor due to inclement weather in the area.

MARCH 31, 1974

St. Louis, Missouri
Forest Park
Opening Act: 13th Floor
Attendance: 40,000–100,000
Promoter: KSHE
■ This daytime, outdoor concert was held in an area of Forest Park known as the aviator fields. It was part of an event called the "4th Annual KSHE Kite Fest" that was organized by the local rock radio station.

In a 1989 interview on KSHE, Gene remembered: "Someone said 'Hey, you're going to be playing a little park.' We figured it would be a nice little cozy [gig]. We figured a hundred to two hundred people." Paul continued, "They drove us up in a van that didn't have windows. Then they open the doors and it was like an ocean made out of people."

As the musical acts were only one of many attractions at the event, the attendance figure doesn't reflect how many people attended the concert itself. *Billboard* listed the attendance figure as "an estimated 100,000" while KSHE's own estimates put the figure at over 40,000. Ironically, if the attendance surpassed 43,000, then KISS played to the largest American crowd of its career just six weeks after the release of its debut album. One would think that in a crowd that size, someone would have a Super 8mm camera or tape recorder . . . Anyone?

APRIL 1, 1974

Cleveland, Ohio
The Agora
Headlining Act: Rory Gallagher
Attendance: 1,250   Capacity: 1,250
Promoter: Agora Presents
■ The show got off to a bad start when KISS was introduced as being from New York, and the crowd responded with a loud chorus of boos. The band won the crowd over and eventually came back for two encores, only to have Peter pass out from lack of oxygen and fall off the back of the drum riser near the end of "Black Diamond." He was caught by JR Smalling, who carried him back to the dressing room. The Rory Gallagher band refused to allow Smalling to bring Peter into the dressing room to recover. An ambulance was dispatched to the venue to transport Criss to nearby Charity Hospital.

Neil Bogart wrote a letter to a local Cleveland rag refuting a bad review of this show.

Although the Rory Gallagher performance was broadcast on radio station WMMS as part of their "Nights Out At The Agora" series, contrary to local legend, KISS's performance was not.

APRIL 2, 1974

Toledo, Ohio   **KISS CANCELED**
The Agora
Headlining Act: Rory Gallagher
Promoter: Agora Presents
■ In order to allow Peter Criss time to recover from the previous night, KISS was replaced by a local opening act.

APRIL 3, 1974

Columbus, Ohio
The Agora
Headlining Act: Rory Gallagher
Attendance: 2,000   Capacity: 2,000
Promoter: Agora Presents

Mark Ravitz's schematic for the original KISS sign.

MARK RAVITZ COLLECTION

■ This concert was the final attraction of a day-long event called the "WABX Kite-In and Balloon Fly" at the Scott Fountain area of Belle Island in Detroit. It was a benefit concert for the cleanup of Belle Isle. The concert was broadcast live on WABX radio.

APRIL 8, 1974

DeKalb, Illinois
University Center Ballroom @ Northern Illinois
　University
Opening Act: Conqueror Worm
Promoter: Northern Illinois University Student
　Association

■ The show was part of an event called the "Ed Paschke Memorial Glitter Ball." Some students made an entire day of it, getting dressed in costumes and handing out leaflets on the day of the show. A costume party was held between sets by Conqueror Worm and KISS, who took the stage at midnight.

APRIL 12, 1974

Detroit, Michigan
Michigan Palace
Headlining Acts: Suzi Quatro, Blue Öyster Cult
Attendance: 5,000　Capacity: 5,000
Promoter: Steve Glantz Productions

■ Nazareth was scheduled for both the April 12 and 13 shows, but they did not appear at either. The first advertisements for these shows in the *Ann Arbor Sun* listed the billing as Blue Öyster Cult and Captain Beyond.

APRIL 13, 1974

Detroit, Michigan
Michigan Palace
Headlining Acts: Suzi Quatro, Blue Öyster Cult
Attendance: 5,000　Capacity: 5,000
Promoter: Steve Glantz Productions

APRIL 14, 1974

Louisville, Kentucky
Beggar's Banquet
Opening Act: Thunderhead
Promoter: Jim Goodwin

■ According to Sean Delaney, Beggar's Banquet had once been a supermarket.

APRIL 15, 1974

Nashville, Tennessee
Muther's Music Emporium
Opening Act: Max Onion
Promoter: Sound 70 Concerts

■ This show was part of an event called the "Second Annual Coyote Concert" hosted by local DJ Coyote McCloud. The venue's ceiling was so low that Gene caught it on fire with his fire-breathing act.

APRIL 16, 1974

Nashville, Tennessee
Muther's Music Emporium
Opening Act: Max Onion
Promoter: Sound 70 Concerts

APRIL 17, 1974

Memphis, Tennessee
Lafayette's Music Room
Headlining Act: Kathi McDonald
Promoter: Overton Square, Inc.

■ According to Sean Delaney, Kathi McDonald jumped onstage during KISS's show and feigned performing fellatio on Gene.

APRIL 4, 1974　CANCELED

Warren, Ohio
W.D Packard Music Hall
Headlining Act: Badfinger
Capacity: 2,500
Promoter: Starshine Productions

APRIL 4, 1974

Hartland (Flint), Michigan
Nordic Arena
Opening Acts: Mike Quatro, Smack Dab
Promoter: Brass Ring Productions

APRIL 6, 1974　CANCELED

Fort Wayne, Indiana
Fort Wayne Armory
Opening Act: Babe Ruth
Promoter: Carousel Productions

■ This show was originally scheduled for the Embassy Theatre. The earliest KISS itinerary (dated March 21, 1974) lists the show as a KISS headline appearance at the Fort Wayne Armory with Babe Ruth as the opening act. That changed when KISS was apparently slotted as the opening act for Genesis. On April 4, a local newspaper mentioned that the announcement for the Genesis/KISS concert, initially made on March 27, was erroneous and that Genesis would play the April 6 gig at the Armory by themselves.

APRIL 7, 1974

Detroit, Michigan
Michigan Palace
Headlining Act: Aerosmith
Opening Acts: Mojo Boogie Band, Michael Fennelly
Attendance: 5,000　Capacity: 5,000
Promoter: Steve Glantz Productions
Archived: Audio

■ SET LIST

Deuce
Strutter
She
Firehouse
Nothin' to Lose
Cold Gin
100,000 Years
Black Diamond
Baby, Let Me Go

APRIL 18, 1974

Memphis, Tennessee
Lafayette's Music Room
Headlining Act: Kathi McDonald
Promoter: Overton Square, Inc.
Archived: Audio

■ **SET LIST**

Deuce
Strutter
Firehouse
She
Nothin' to Lose
Cold Gin
100,000 Years
Black Diamond
Acrobat

■ This show was broadcast on local radio station WMC FM-100.

APRIL 19, 1974

Chicago, Illinois
Aragon Ballroom
Headlining Act: Quicksilver Messenger Service
Opening Acts: Les Variations, Flying Saucer
Attendance: 2,000   Capacity: 5,000
Promoter: Wayne Mackie Productions

■ Aerosmith and Roxy Smith were listed on the bill on one early KISS itinerary, though neither act performed.

APRIL 20, 1974

Charleston, West Virginia **TEMP HOLD DATE**
Charleston Civic Center
Promoter: National Shows

■ A temporary hold date (commonly referred to as a "temp hold date") is when a concert is tentatively scheduled. A promoter will have been lined up for the gig, a date and (in most instances) a venue will have been reserved for the show, but advertising will not have taken place and tickets will not have been put on sale.

APRIL 21, 1974 (TWO SHOWS)

Charlotte, North Carolina
Flashes
Opening Act: Ritual
Promoter: Rod Guion

■ Flashes was a very small club on the outskirts of Charlotte. The venue was so cramped that when Gene pumped his fist into the air, he accidentally punched a hole in the ceiling panels above the stage.

Sean Delaney: "[Opening act] Ritual had all kinds of pyrotechnics, snakes, and effects set up on stage before we were set up. I walked in and told them they couldn't do that because that's what we do, and they got belligerent with me. Casablanca P.R. reps Bucky Reingold and Larry Harris came in and told me they wanted Ritual to do their entire show. So I proceeded to kick the band, Bucky Reingold, and Larry Harris out and told them to find their own venue. Ritual played, but they didn't use any of their stuff."

APRIL 27, 1974

Passiac, New Jersey
Capitol Theatre
Headlining Act: Blue Öyster Cult
Opening Act: Ross
Capacity: 3,256
Promoter: John Scher Presents

■ KISS was added to the bill on relatively short notice, just a few days prior to the show. It is

likely that the band debuted new costumes at this show, though the costumes' first confirmed appearance did not take place until the April 29 taping of *The Mike Douglas Show*. Gene's new costume featured large black horns on his shoulders and a skull and crossbones design on his chest. Paul wore a new jacket with silver lapels, and Ace began wearing what is commonly referred to as his Hotter Than Hell outfit.

APRIL 29, 1974

Philadelphia, Pennsylvania
KYW-TV Studios
Attendance: 100   Capacity: 100
Archived: Video

■ **SET LIST**

Firehouse

■ KISS taped their segment for an appearance on *The Mike Douglas Show*. The episode premiered in syndication on May 21. Dr. Joyce Brothers also appeared on the show and remarked, "Well, I think they're a little bit too subdued for my taste. I met the lead man [Gene] backstage, and as he walked by he said, 'Dr. Brothers, do I have a problem?'"

Eartha Kitt also performed on the episode.

MAY 2, 1974

Comstock Park (Grand Rapids), Michigan
Thunder Chicken
Headlining Act: Argent
Promoter: Dick Bickler

MAY 3, 1974

St. Louis, Missouri
Ambassador Theatre
Headlining Act: Argent
Capacity: 3,006
Promoter: Panther Productions

■ After Argent canceled several shows with KISS earlier in the year, the bands were finally set to do a tour. It did not last long for KISS, as they were thrown off the tour after only the second show. JR Smalling recalls: "They had this road manager, a British guy from Pakistan named Solomon, and

he was pretty much a pain in the ass." After refusing to give KISS a sound check, and then pulling the plug on them during an encore, Smalling sought out and found the pest and promptly locked him in an Anvil case to contemplate the error of his ways. KISS was immediately thrown off the tour.

MAY 4, 1974

Atlanta, Georgia **KISS CANCELED**
Alexander Memorial Coliseum
Headlining Acts: Blue Öyster Cult, Manfred Mann's Earth Band, Hydra
Promoter: Alex Cooley Presents

■ KISS and their crew drove straight through from St. Louis the night before but arrived too late to set up the equipment and play. The rest of the acts performed as scheduled.

MAY 7, 1974

Mt. Clemens, Michigan
The Penthouse @ Hillcrest Ballroom & Convention Center **TEMP HOLD DATE**
Promoter: Howard Tyner

MAY 9, 1974

Parsippany, New Jersey
The Joint in the Woods
Opening Act: Sweetwater
Promoter: In-house

■ Ace got food poisoning from his chicken dinner before the show, which was a tutorial gig for lighting director Rick Munroe: "I remember Gene coming to me at the first gig, and he said 'What's very important to us is our presentation on stage. We want people to be able to get a big bang for their entertainment dollar here, to not only hear the music but to watch something that you're not going to see just by playing the album. We need your lighting cues to be right where they need to be, when they need to be there.' We were an opening act so we didn't have a lot of lighting to work with.

"I used to make these 3 x 5 cards that had the name of the song on top, and I wrote whatever color palette I had come up with for that particular song on each one. I had about ten or twelve cards with all the songs that they could potentially do. Just before each show, I would have a meeting with the band and go over the setlist and would put the cards in the order we were going to do them."

Bill Aucoin's company Direction Plus may have filmed portions of this show for an unreleased eleven-minute promotional film. Footage from this promotional film was later used in the Hotter Than Hell television commercial.

Opening act Sweetwater was the first band to grace the stage at Woodstock and, many years later, was the subject of a VH1 movie.

MAY 10, 1974 ~~CANCELED~~

Warren, Ohio
W.D. Packard Music Hall
Capacity: 2,500
Promoter: Major Productions

MAY 12, 1974

Wyandotte (Detroit), Michigan
Benjamin F. Yack Arena
Headlining Act: Savoy Brown
Opening Act: Silverhead
Attendance: 2,400   Capacity: 3,300
Promoter: Brass Ring Productions

■ Rick Munroe: "After this long, drawn-out first day on the job in Wyandotte, I was walking down the hotel hallway, and I heard this screaming and saw one of the crew guys dragging this chick by the hair, and she's got no clothes on. He goes to our room and opens the door, throws her in there, and shuts the door. I asked him, 'Hey, what's going on?' 'Oh, man, she's just causing trouble,' and he threw a bunch of clothes in there with her and yelled at her to get dressed. So, I went down to the room that he had taken her out of. All of a sudden I hear all kinds of fire engines and red lights and then pounding on our door. Turned out the chick was trying to get out, and she ended up catching a T-shirt on fire and throwing it out the window and someone saw the burning T-shirt on the fire escape, and they pulled the fire alarm. I was thinking, 'Such long days, and then you don't even get to go to sleep. This is just not going to work out.'"

MAY 14, 1974

Fraser (Detroit), Michigan
Fraser Hockeyland Arena
Headlining Act: Savoy Brown
Opening Act: Silverhead
Attendance: 2,170   Capacity: 2,500
Promoter: Brass Ring Productions

■ On this evening, two Detroit-area youngsters, Bruce Redoute and Lee Neaves, snuck out of their houses to attend their first KISS show. The two would later be photographed at Cobo Arena in May 1975 for the back of the Alive! album jacket.

Opening act Silverhead was fronted by Michael Des Barres, who would figure frequently in the KISS equation throughout the 1970s by opening several concerts in 1977 with his band Detective and by appearing on Gene's solo album in 1978.

MAY 16, 1974

Winnipeg, Manitoba, Canada
Manitoba Centennial Concert Hall
Headlining Acts: Savoy Brown, Manfred Mann's Earth Band
Attendance: 1,500   Capacity: 2,663
Promoter: Frank Weipert

■ Peter Oreckinto: "Cris Griffin, Ace, and I were on our way to the Edmonton show when Cris tried to pull up to a gas station and went into a V-ditch because of all the snow. The rest of the band drove by and didn't see us. We stayed up with Ace playing cards at this gas station while drinking coffee and waiting for the tow trucks to show up the next morning. It took three tow trucks to pull the truck out of the ditch."

MAY 17, 1974

Edmonton, Alberta, Canada
Kinsmen Fieldhouse
Headlining Acts: Savoy Brown, Manfred Mann's Earth Band
Attendance: 6,000   Capacity: 7,000
Promoter: Accident Productions

■ KISS's P.A. system did not arrive until 6 P.M. Unfortunately, things only got worse from there as brown-outs occurred every time the air conditioning kicked in. By the end of the show, only a few of the P.A. amplifiers were still powered.

MAY 18, 1974

Saskatoon, Saskatchewan, Canada
Saskatoon Arena
Headlining Acts: Savoy Brown, Manfred Mann's Earth Band
Attendance: 1,950   Capacity: 5,000
Promoter: Lucifer Productions

MAY 19, 1974

Lethbridge, Alberta, Canada
Lethbridge Exhibition Pavilion
Headlining Acts: Savoy Brown, Manfred Mann's Earth Band
Attendance: 1,000   Capacity: 2,000
Promoter: Accident Productions

■ The Royal Canadian Mounted Police woke everyone up at the hotel after the show when Savoy Brown trashed their room at the Holiday Inn.

MAY 20, 1974

Calgary, Alberta, Canada
Foothills Arena @ University of Calgary
Headlining Acts: Savoy Brown, Manfred Mann's Earth Band
Attendance: 2,500   Capacity: 3,000
Promoter: Lucifer Productions

MAY 23, 1974 ~~CANCELED~~

Fresno, California
Warnors Theatre @ Warnors Center for the Performing Arts
Headlining Acts: Savoy Brown, Manfred Mann's Earth Band
Capacity: 2,165
Promoter: Get Down Productions

■ The show was canceled due to lack of ticket sales, according to the Fresno Bee.

MAY 24, 1974

Portland, Oregon
Paramount Northwest Theatre
Headlining Acts: Savoy Brown, Manfred Mann's Earth Band

Capacity: 3,040
Promoter: Get Down Productions

■ "Kissin' Time" made its first of only two known appearances in the setlist.

MAY 25, 1974

Seattle, Washington
Paramount Northwest Theatre
Headlining Acts: Savoy Brown, Manfred Mann's Earth Band
Capacity: 2,976
Promoter: Get Down Productions

■ Patrick MacDonald wrote a now-infamous comment in his May 27 Seattle Times review: "I hope the four guys who make up the group, whose names don't matter, are putting away money for the future. The near future, because Kiss won't be around long. Flash doesn't last." One wonders if Patrick was embarrassed 27 years later when his quote wound up on the back of a T-shirt for the band's Farewell Tour.

A young man by the name of Frank Ferrano (aka Nikki Sixx) attended this show. Nine years later, his band Mötley Crüe would open for KISS.

MAY 26, 1974

Spokane, Washington
John F. Kennedy Pavilion @ Gonzaga University
Headlining Acts: Savoy Brown, Manfred Mann's Earth Band
Attendance: Near Capacity   Capacity: 4,000
Promoter: Concerts West

■ The billing of Savoy Brown, Manfred Mann, and KISS was a strange, somewhat uncomfortable mix of musicians. Munroe remembers: "At Gonzaga University, all three bands were in the same, tiny dressing room. In one corner, we had Savoy Brown drinking it up and getting rowdy. In another were the Manfred Mann guys deep into the meditation they were fond of, and then in our corner was a bunch of clowns in makeup."

MAY 27, 1974

Lacey, Washington
Capitol Pavilion @ St. Martin's College
Headlining Acts: Savoy Brown, Manfred Mann's Earth Band
Capacity: 4,400   TEMP HOLD DATE
Promoter: L & M Productions

■ This was most likely just a temp hold date as neither the venue nor the school newspaper has any record of the performance.

MAY 28, 1974

Vancouver, British Columbia, Canada
The Gardens
Headlining Acts: Savoy Brown, Manfred Mann's Earth Band
Attendance: 1,824   Capacity: 4,800
Promoter: Accident Productions

■ Rick Munroe: "After a while, we all noticed that the Savoy Brown guys were pretty much a bunch of British drunks. It was nothing out of the ordinary if during the middle of their show one of them wandered to the backline area and just took a leak off the back of the stage."

According to a fan who attended the show, "Kissin' Time" was performed, marking its second and final known live performance. However, it is likely that the song was included in the set list for some of the shows between May 24 and June 4.

Live onstage at the Long Beach Auditorium, May 31, 1974. Why Gene had playing cards taped to his bass and mike stand is a mystery.

M. JULIAN BAUM

MAY 30, 1974

San Diego, California
San Diego Sports Arena
Headlining Acts: Savoy Brown, Manfred Mann's Earth
    Band
Capacity: 14,585
Promoter: Concert Associates

MAY 31, 1974

Long Beach, California
Long Beach Auditorium
Headlining Acts: Savoy Brown, Manfred Mann's Earth
    Band
Promoter: Pacific Presentations
Archived: Audio

■ SET LIST

Deuce
Nothin' to Lose
She
Firehouse
Strutter
Gene Simmons Bass Solo
100,000 Years
Peter Criss Drum Solo - reprise
Black Diamond
Baby, Let Me Go
■ The show was broadcast live on local radio station KNAC.

JUNE 1, 1974

San Francisco, California
Winterland
Headlining Acts: Savoy Brown, Manfred Mann's Earth
    Band
Attendance: 2,300   Capacity: 5,400
Promoter: Bill Graham Presents
■ Rick Munroe: "When we played Winterland, it was like nothing else we'd ever done. We had never played in a venue that was dedicated to concert music like that place was, everything else was a hockey rink or a theater or an outdoor stage of some sort. When you went to Winterland, you got a feeling of history and awe. Then security wouldn't let the band leave after sound check. It was a Winterland policy that the artist doesn't leave once they get there. After awhile it was worked out, and we could go back to the hotel."

As was the case with most shows at Winterland, the concert was archived on videotape by Bill Graham Presents. The master was destroyed in a fire in the early 1980s. The loss is especially harsh considering that it is likely that "Kissin' Time" was performed live.

JUNE 2, 1974

Anchorage, Alaska
Sundowner Drive-In Theatre
Headlining Act: Savoy Brown
Opening Acts: Flight, Island
Attendance: 2,000+
Promoter: Nebula Productions
■ This was a daytime, outdoor show. Rick Munroe: "We played this drive-in theatre, which was just useless in the summer up there because it never got dark. They put spotlights up for us to use, but that's all we had." JR Smalling continues, "I remember the Savoy Brown crew carrying singer Kim Simmonds from the limousine to the stage. He was blind drunk. The night before, one of their guys had slipped a microphone into Simmonds' hotel room where he and his wife, who had just flown in from England that day,

were staying. Needless to say, they recorded some interesting material. So, prior to the show, the crew played the tape back over the P.A., filling the entire venue with 'Oh! Kimmy! Ride me; ride me, Kimmy!'"

JUNE 4, 1974

Eielson Air Force Base (Fairbanks), Alaska
Baker Field House
Headlining Act: Savoy Brown
Promoter: Nebula Productions
■ Peter Oreckinto: "There were all these young lieutenants getting out there to dance with their dates and all dressed up really straight and nice, when here come these guys in leather and paint blowing their ears off. That may be the weirdest gig we ever did." Munroe continues, "No matter who you talked to, everyone knew how many days, how many minutes and seconds were left before they could leave. I remember loading out, and it was still light outside and felt like it was five o'clock in the afternoon."

JUNE 6, 1974

Salt Lake City, Utah TEMP HOLD DATE
Terrace Ballroom
Headlining Act: Queen
Opening Act: Dino Valente
Promoter: United Concerts

JUNE 7, 1974 TEMP HOLD DATE

Garden City (Boise), Idaho
Exhibition Building @ Western Idaho Fairgrounds
Headlining Act: Queen
Opening Act: Dino Valente
Promoter: United Concerts

JUNE 10, 1974 CANCELED

Rapid City, South Dakota
Central States Fairgrounds
Headlining Act: Styx
Capacity: 6,000
Promoter: Mike Chambers
■ A severe thunderstorm on the day of the show forced this outdoor gig to be canceled. One of two local bands, either White Wall or Free Fall, was scheduled to open the show, though the promoter could not recall which band had been booked. James Young of Styx recalls: "We were on the same airplane with them going up there, and they were supposed to open for us. They had just come on the scene at that time, and

'Lady' had actually been a hit for us in Rapid City in 1973, that's why they were opening for us. Unfortunately, the gig got washed away."

JUNE 12, 1974

Flint, Michigan
I.M.A. Sports Arena
Headlining Act: New York Dolls
Attendance: 2,112   Capacity: 5,300
Promoter: Brass Ring Productions
■ KISS was already creating a buzz in Michigan as Daniel E. Richards reported in the *Flint Journal:* "Stanley said the band has caused near-riots in Detroit, and pointed to a lot of jewelry around his neck and on his hands. All of it was thrown to him onstage by enthused fans.

"A young girl wandered up to Stanley and told him he looked 'really weird.' 'Why, thank you,' he replied with a pleased grin."

JUNE 13, 1974 TEMP HOLD DATE

Grand Rapids, Michigan
Grand Rapids Ice Arena
Promoter: Brass Ring Productions
■ The only known reference to this show is in a KISS itinerary dated June 3, 1974. The absence of any existing advertisements indicates that this was a temp hold date, though it is possible that the concert took place.

JUNE 14, 1974

Cleveland, Ohio
Allen Theatre
Headlining Act: New York Dolls
Promoter: Belkin Productions
■ The show, originally advertised for June 8, got underway in true Spinal Tap form when KISS got lost on their way to the stage, in Cleveland no less. Future KISS drummer Eric Singer was in the audience.

Arthur Kane of the New York Dolls: "We didn't really know KISS that well, but after the show we thought we'd hang out. We brought KISS over to someone's house that we knew, and her mom threw us out when we started raiding the refrigerator. That lady has got a story to tell: 'Yeah, I threw both the Dolls and KISS out of my house.'"

JUNE 15, 1974

Toronto, Ontario, Canada
Massey Hall

Headling Act: New York Dolls
Attendance: 2,800   Capacity: 2,800
■ WEA Canada (a division of Warner Bros.) promoted the show by having four girls in KISS makeup chauffeured around town to hand out red wax lips to radio stations and promoters.

JUNE 17, 1974
Asbury Park, New Jersey
Sunshine In Concert Hall
No Opening Act
Promoter: Bob Fisher
■ This show was originally scheduled for June 15, supporting the Eleventh House with Larry Coryell, and Truth. The subsequent ad read: "Buy a ticket for Larry Coryell and see KISS for free." The ad in *The Village Voice* promoted the rescheduled show as "an evening with KISS."

JUNE 19, 1974
Atlanta, Georgia
Alex Cooley's Electric Ballroom
Opening Acts: Outlaws, Fat Chance
Capacity: 1,100
Promoter: Alex Cooley Presents

JUNE 20, 1974
Atlanta, Georgia
Alex Cooley's Electric Ballroom
Opening Acts: Outlaws, Fat Chance
Capacity: 1,100
Promoter: Alex Cooley Presents
■ The audiotape rumored to be from this show is a fraud. At present, no recording of this show is known to exist.

JUNE 21, 1974
Atlanta, Georgia
Alex Cooley's Electric Ballroom
Opening Acts: Outlaws, Fat Chance
Capacity: 1,100
Promoter: Alex Cooley Presents

JUNE 22, 1974
Atlanta, Georgia
Alex Cooley's Electric Ballroom
Opening Acts: Outlaws, Fat Chance
Capacity: 1,100
Promoter: Alex Cooley Presents
■ During the final set of the four-night stand, Paul collapsed. Legend has it that he was suffering from exhaustion, but Mick Campise sets the record straight: "He didn't actually collapse. It was just that they didn't have any more songs to do. They did three encores, and the kids were just going absolutely crazy. So they did 'Deuce' again and right at the end of 'Deuce,' that was it, there Paul was lying on the stage. I remember JR picking Paul up by the arms, and I had him by the legs. We were walking up the stairs backstage when Paul opened his eye and winked at me. That's when I knew he didn't pass out. I got him upstairs and said 'What the hell are you doing?' He said, 'Man, we didn't have any more songs to do, I had to do something. We couldn't keep playing the songs over and over.'"

JUNE 23, 1974   KISS CANCELED
Jeffersonville, Indiana
Sportsdome Speedway
Headlining Acts: Canned Heat, Quicksilver Messenger Service, Nitty Gritty Dirt Band, Roger McGuin, Maggie Bell

Attendance: 10,000
Promoter: Starship Entertainment
■ After the June 22 appearance at the Electric Ballroom, Paul underwent minor surgery to remove polyps from his vocal chords. This resulted in KISS canceling all of the scheduled shows up to and including the July 8 gig in Memphis.
    The entire scenario was tidied up for press purposes by claiming Paul's June 22 collapse was the result of exhaustion, and that the subsequent downtime for the band was scheduled to give Paul some time to recover.

JUNE 25, 1974   KISS CANCELED
Greenville, South Carolina
Greenville Memorial Auditorium
Headlining Acts: Blue Öyster Cult, Lynyrd Skynyrd, Nazareth
Promoter: Beach Club Promotions

JUNE 26, 1974   KISS CANCELED
Hampton, Virginia
Hampton Coliseum
Headlining Acts: Blue Öyster Cult, Maggie Bell
Promoter: The Webb Organization

JUNE 27, 1974   KISS CANCELED
Salem, Virginia
Roanoke County Civic Center
Headlining Acts: Blue Öyster Cult, Lynyrd Skynyrd, Maggie Bell
Attendance: 2,295   Capacity: 7,500
Promoter: The Webb Organization
■ Lynyrd Skynyrd was listed on the bill in the June 3 KISS itinerary, but they did not perform. An article in *The Roanoke Times* indicated that Rock Steady Productions had telegrammed the venue informing them that KISS would not perform due to a band member's [Paul's] illness. Over 150 people received refunds when it was announced that KISS would not appear.

JUNE 28, 1974   KISS CANCELED
Charlotte, North Carolina
Charlotte Park Center Auditorium
Headlining Acts: Blue Öyster Cult, Nazareth, Brownsville Station
Promoter: Beach Club Promotions

JUNE 29, 1974   KISS CANCELED
Asheville, North Carolina
Asheville Civic Center Auditorium
Headlining Acts: Blue Öyster Cult, Nazareth, Brownsville Station
Promoter: Beach Club Promotions
■ This was the first rock concert at the venue.

JUNE 30, 1974   KISS CANCELED
Alexandria, Virginia
Alexandria Roller Rink
Headlining Acts: Blue Öyster Cult, Nazareth
Attendance: Sold Out
Promoter: Entertainment Concept Corp.

JULY 1, 1974   KISS CANCELED
Clarkston, Michigan
Pine Knob Music Theatre
Headlining Act: Blue Öyster Cult
Attendance: 13,700   Capacity: 13,700
Promoter: Nederlander Productions

JULY 3, 1974   KISS CANCELED
Indianapolis, Indiana
Indianapolis Convention Center

Headlining Acts: ZZ Top, Nazareth
Promoter: Sunshine Promotions
■ Blue Öyster Cult was the originally scheduled headliner, but they canceled, as did KISS. Both bands rescheduled and played the venue on August 3.

JULY 4, 1974   KISS CANCELED
Knoxville, Tennessee
Chillhowee Park Amphitheatre
Headlining Acts: Nazareth, New York Dolls
Attendance: 3,000   Capacity: 3,000
Promoter: Concerts South
■ This event was called "Summer Jam #2."

JULY 5, 1974   POSTPONED
Baton Rouge, Louisiana
Independence Hall
Headlining Acts: Blue Öyster Cult, Nazareth
Promoter: Beaver Productions
■ This show was rescheduled for July 16.

JULY 6, 1974   KISS CANCELED
Chattanooga, Tennessee
Engel Stadium
Headlining Acts: Blue Öyster Cult, Rare Earth, Nazareth
Promoter: Concerts South

JULY 8, 1974   KISS CANCELED
Memphis, Tennessee
Ellis Auditorium
Headlining Acts: Blue Öyster Cult, Nazareth
Capacity: 4,300
Promoter: Alex Cooley Presents
■ Several gas receipts retained by Peter Oreckinto show the road crew traveling from Elk Ridge, Maryland to Emporia, Virginia on July 9 and on to Fayetteville, North Carolina on July 10. This strongly indicates that KISS did not perform in Memphis on July 8.

JULY 11, 1974
West Palm Beach, Florida
West Palm Beach Auditorium
Headlining Acts: Blue Öyster Cult, Nazareth
Capacity: 5,895
Promoter: Performance Assoc.

JULY 12, 1974
Winter Park (Orlando), Florida
Orlando Jai-Alai Fronton
Headlining Acts: Blue Öyster Cult, Nazareth, Uriah Heep
Opening Act: Isis
Attendance: 3,500   Capacity: 3,500
Promoter: L & S Productions

JULY 13, 1974
Tampa, Florida
Curtis Hixon Convention Hall
Headlining Acts: Blue Öyster Cult, Nazareth
Attendance: 7,400   Capacity: 7,400
Promoters: L & S Productions, Gulf Artists
■ Gene caught his hair on fire during the show.
    Rick Munroe: "We were opening for BÖC, in Florida, and they were having a party in the hotel. We all ended up there, and after a while things started getting a little out of hand. Somebody put a lampshade on and cut eyeholes in it so he could see. Then Ace and some of the BÖC guys were doing something out on the balcony. They had taken a chair and thrown it into this river that was beneath the hotel, and they were listening for the splash. They got a kick out of

that. Next thing you know, the room is mostly empty of furniture. We snuck out after that. Word has it somebody downriver called back to the hotel and said, 'I got a chair and a dresser and some drawers clogging up our sawmill.'"

JULY 14, 1974

Birmingham, Alabama
Municipal Auditorium
Headlining Acts: Blue Öyster Cult, Nazareth
Capacity: 5,200
Promoter: Alex Cooley Presents

JULY 16, 1974

Baton Rouge, Louisiana
Independence Hall
Headlining Acts: Blue Öyster Cult, New York Dolls
Attendance: Near Capacity   Capacity: 4,000
Promoter: Beaver Productions
Archived: Audio
■ **SET LIST**
Deuce
Strutter
She
Firehouse
100,000 Years
Peter Criss Drum Solo - reprise
Black Diamond
■ Nazareth was originally on the bill, but the New York Dolls replaced them when the show was postponed from its original date.

JULY 17, 1974

New Orleans, Louisiana
A Warehouse   **TEMP HOLD DATE**
Headlining Acts: Lou Reed, New York Dolls
Promoter: Beaver Productions
■ This show was never advertised, but it did appear on several itineraries. Interestingly, A Warehouse was closed at the time due to permit problems with city hall, which calls the veracity of the itineraries into question.

JULY 17, 1974

Atlanta, Georgia
Alex Cooley's Electric Ballroom
Opening Act: Fat Chance
Capacity: 1,100
Promoter: Alex Cooley Presents

JULY 18, 1974

Atlanta, Georgia
Alex Cooley's Electric Ballroom
Opening Act: Fat Chance
Capacity: 1,100
Promoter: Alex Cooley Presents

JULY 19, 1974

Fayetteville, North Carolina
Cumberland County Memorial Arena
Headlining Acts: Blue Öyster Cult, New York Dolls
Opening Act: Nazareth
Capacity: 7,000
Promoter: Beach Club Promotions

JULY 21, 1974

Baltimore, Maryland / Washington, D.C.
Unconfirmed Appearance
■ A KISS travel itinerary prepared by the Majestic Travel Agency in mid-July 1974 indicates that the band was scheduled to drive from Fayetteville to Charlotte on July 20, and stay in a hotel in Charlotte that evening. This does mildly support a theory that a KISS concert occurred in Charlotte. However, it is doubtful such a show took

A never-before published outtake from a late August, 1974 publicity shoot. Note that Ace was only able to apply makeup to half his face due to injuries sustained in a recent car accident.

place as no proof of the concert could be located in any local publications and this would have been the fifth consecutive night KISS performed, an unusually lengthy run. Additionally, since there was no major airport in Fayetteville, it is likely that a day off would have been included in the schedule to allow the band and crew to drive to the nearest major airport in Charlotte where they were slated to depart for Washington National Airport in the early afternoon of July 21.

KISS was then scheduled to stay that evening in a Glen Burnie, Maryland (a suburb of Baltimore) Holiday Inn. While no itinerary lists a show in the Baltimore/Washington, D.C. area for the 21st, and no ads have surfaced in any local newspapers, two factors indicate that a show took place. First, there would have been no reason for KISS to stop in Baltimore for an evening on their way home to New York, unless they were playing a gig. Secondly, a bootleg tape of KISS's performance in Washington, D.C. (which is actually from March 25, 1974) has frequently been mislabeled with the date July 21, 1974, which is a coincidence too big to overlook. Hence, it is likely that a show took place somewhere in the Baltimore/D.C. area on that date.

JULY 25, 1974

London, Ontario, Canada
Centennial Hall
Opening Acts: Rush, Ronny Legg
Capacity: 1,500
Promoter: Mister Sound
■ This marked the first of 51 times that Rush and KISS would share a bill, but the only instance

when drummer John Rutsey was playing with Rush.

Mick Campise: "It was this one-off gig that had to be done for some reason. We blew out the P.A. during the first song. The whole show was a disaster." Peter Oreckinto continues: "They had these old A4 Altec-Lansing speakers that were designed to show movies. What a piece-of-shit sound system; you couldn't hear anything."

AUGUST 3, 1974

Indianapolis, Indiana
Indianapolis Convention Center
Headlining Acts: Blue Öyster Cult, James Gang
Opening Act: Chris Jagger
Attendance: 7,950
Promoter: Sunshine Promotions

AUGUST 4, 1974

South Bend, Indiana
Morris Civic Auditorium
Headlining Act: Blue Öyster Cult
Capacity: 2,468

AUGUST 31, 1974   CANCELED

Englishtown, New Jersey
Raceway Park
Headlining Acts: Faces, Black Oak Arkansas, Lou Reed, Blue Öyster Cult
Opening Acts: Graham Central Station, Flash Cadillac & the Continental Kids, New York Dolls, Mercury, Styx
Promoter: Mang Bros.
■ The festival was canceled when the Faces postponed their tour (which KISS had initially been scheduled to open), and construction of the venue's main stage fell too far behind schedule for the production work to be done in time for the show. Over 50,000 tickets had been sold at the time of cancellation.

SEPTEMBER 2, 1974   CANCELED

Detroit, Michigan
Olympia
Headlining Act: Faces
Opening Act: Haystacks
Promoter: Brass Ring Productions

SEPTEMBER 13, 1974

Kitchener, Ontario, Canada
Sir Wilfred Laurier Theatre
Opening Act: Fludd
Attendance: 1,178   Capacity: 1,500
Promoter: SRO Productions

SEPTEMBER 14, 1974
(TWO SHOWS: 8:00 P.M., 11:00 P.M.)

Toronto, Ontario, Canada
Victory Theatre
Opening Act: Fludd
Attendance: 1,035   Capacity: 1,200
Promoter: SRO Productions

SEPTEMBER 15, 1974

Lock Haven, Pennsylvania
Thomas Field House
Headlining Act: Blue Öyster Cult
Opening Act: Rush
Attendance: 2,000
Promoter: Fang Productions

■ Neil Peart had joined Rush by this time, as Mick Campise relates: "Neil was incredible. I remember that when Neil joined the band and started writing the songs with them, Paul Stanley told me, 'I love Neil to death, but he ruined that band. They will never be anything.'"

SEPTEMBER 16, 1974

Wilkes-Barre, Pennsylvania
Paramount Theatre
Headlining Act: Blue Öyster Cult
Opening Act: Rush
Attendance: 2,000   Capacity: 2,000
Promoter: Fang Productions

SEPTEMBER 18, 1974

Atlanta, Georgia
Alex Cooley's Electric Ballroom
Headlining Act: Rush
Opening Act: Fat Chance
Capacity: 1,100
Promoter: Alex Cooley Presents

SEPTEMBER 19, 1974

Atlanta, Georgia
Alex Cooley's Electric Ballroom
Opening Acts: Rush, Fat Chance
Capacity: 1,100
Promoter: Alex Cooley Presents

SEPTEMBER 20, 1974

Atlanta, Georgia
Alex Cooley's Electric Ballroom
Opening Acts: Rush, Fat Chance
Capacity: 1,100
Promoter: Alex Cooley Presents

SEPTEMBER 21, 1974

Atlanta, Georgia
Alex Cooley's Electric Ballroom
Opening Acts: Outlaws, Fat Chance
Capacity: 1,100
Promoter: Alex Cooley Presents

■ On September 14, a fourth KISS show was added to the run at the Electric Ballroom when British art-rock band Nektar postponed their scheduled September 21 appearance until October 3.

Backstage at Alex Cooley's Electric Ballroom, September 1974.

SEPTEMBER 27, 1974   TEMP HOLD DATE

Louisville, Kentucky
Commonwealth Convention Center
Opening Act: Rush

■ This show was listed in *Performance* magazine, though there was never any advertising for the show.

SEPTEMBER 27, 1974
(TWO SHOWS)   KISS CANCELED

St. Louis, Missouri
Ambassador Theatre
Headlining Act: Steppenwolf
Opening Act: Pavlov's Dog
Attendance: 4,000 (combined)   Capacity: 3,006
Promoter: Panther Productions

■ KISS was originally scheduled to open both shows for Steppenwolf. However, Steppenwolf refused to allow KISS to do their full stage show, and rather than compromise their production, KISS canceled on the day of the show. Local art-rock band Pavlov's Dog was brought in at the last minute to open the two shows.

SEPTEMBER 28, 1974

Detroit, Michigan
Michigan Palace
Opening Act: Wizzard
Attendance: 5,000+   Capacity: 5,000
Promoter: Steve Glantz Productions

■ Paul had been a longtime fan of Roy Wood, the frontman for Wizzard. When the crowd gave Wizzard an icy reception, Stanley took exception and wanted to chastise the crowd. His point was that if Roy Wood hadn't existed, KISS would not be around either. Sean Delaney talked him out of it.

SEPTEMBER 29, 1974

Evansville, Indiana
Roberts Municipal Stadium
Headlining Act: Billy Preston
Opening Act: Rush
Promoter: Rogers Attractions

OCTOBER 1, 1974

Jacksonville, Alabama
Leone Cole Auditorium @Jacksonville State University
Opening Act: Rush
Attendance: 1,000   Capacity: 5,000
Promoter: S.G.A. Productions

OCTOBER 4, 1974

Houston, Texas
Music Hall
Opening Act: Rush
Promoter: Bruce Dyson

■ This was the final show of the tour, after which KISS flew back to New York for a short break.

Mick Campise: "The thing that used to kill me about KISS was that they couldn't play anyone else's music. Ace could do his Page-Yardbirds thing, and Peter could play a bit. But Paul and Gene really couldn't do much; they couldn't jam.

"When we first played in Houston, they came and jammed with my younger brother's band in this old furniture warehouse. These kids were 15 or 16 years old, and they were floored; they could not believe it. Peter, Ace and Paul, and Alex and Geddy all got together and were going to jam with them. But Paul couldn't play much of anything; he played 'All Right Now' and that was about it. I will never forget that my little brother's guitar player was playing and Paul was wearing his guitar and leaning against the amps because he couldn't play."

CANCELED SAVOY BROWN / ARGENT TOUR

■ Beginning on March 26, KISS was scheduled to open a series of shows for Savoy Brown and Argent. Argent experienced some difficulty obtaining the proper work visas and, as a result, ten shows were canceled.

MARCH 26, 1974

Winnipeg, Manitoba, Canada
Winnipeg Arena
Headlining Acts: Savoy Brown, Argent
Promoter: Frank Weipert

■ Although neither KISS nor Argent appeared at the gig as scheduled, Savoy Brown did perform with Blue Öyster Cult and Flash Cadillac & the Continental Kids opening.

MARCH 27, 1974

Duluth, Minnesota
Duluth Arena Auditorium
Headlining Acts: Savoy Brown, Argent
Promoter: Yan Qui Productions

MARCH 29 & 30, 1974

San Francisco, California
Winterland
Headlining Acts: Savoy Brown, Argent
Promoter: Bill Graham Presents

APRIL 1, 1974

Spokane, Washington
John F. Kennedy Pavilion @ Gonzaga University
Headlining Acts: Savoy Brown, Argent

APRIL 4, 1974

Fresno, California
Fox Theatre
Headlining Acts: Savoy Brown, Argent
Promoter: Fun Productions

APRIL 5, 1974

Portland, Oregon
Paramount Northwest Theatre
Headlining Acts: Savoy Brown, Argent

APRIL 6, 1974

Seattle, Washington
Paramount Northwest Theatre
Headlining Acts: Savoy Brown, Argent

Memphis, Tennessee
Ellis Auditorium
Headlining Acts: Savoy Brown, Argent
Promoter: Mid-South Concerts
■ Both KISS and Argent canceled, but Savoy Brown did perform at a different venue (Auditorium North Hall) with opening act Fanny.

APRIL 13, 1974

Little Rock, Arkansas
T.H. Barton Coliseum
Headlining Acts: Savoy Brown, Argent
Promoter: Mid-South Concerts

CANCELED ARGENT TOUR

■ KISS had lined up another short tour with Argent scheduled to begin in late April. The initial gigs were canceled for reasons unknown. When the tour finally started on May 2, KISS was given the boot the following night. Listed below are the canceled shows from the beginning of the tour, plus the post-May 3 shows, none of which KISS played.

APRIL 26, 1974
(TWO SHOWS: 7:30 P.M., 11:00 P.M.)

Toronto, Ontario, Canada
Victory Theatre
Headlining Act: Argent
Capacity: 1,100
Promoter: SRO Productions
■ The show was canceled by April 19. Vinnie Toro and Louise Heath were scheduled to attend this show as their prize for winning the first kissing contest, an event that had been sponsored by WSHE in Fort Lauderdale on April 20. To make up for the cancellation, Toro and Heath were invited to appear on *The Mike Douglas Show* along with KISS. During the taping of the show, Gene made reference to the cancellation of the April 26 show and commented on

the world finals that were planned for May 25. Ultimately, Toro and Heath went on to win the world finals of "The Great KISS-Off," which were delayed until June 8 and were held at Woodfield Mall in Schaumburg, Illinois, just outside of Chicago. Neil Bogart attended the Saturday morning event, which was held under the guise of a benefit for the St. Jude's Children's Hospital and was backed by the likes of *Playboy Magazine*, radio station WCFL, and World Football League franchise Chicago Fire. Local DJ Larry Lujack and comedian Jan Murray were also in attendance.

APRIL 27, 1974

Millersville, Pennsylvania
Pucillo Gym @ Millersville State College
Headlining Act: Argent
Promoter: Entertainment Concepts Corp.
■ Argent's appearance is listed as postponed until May 5 in the Millersville State College newspaper. This newspaper also mentioned that this was to be the first date of Argent's tour. There is no evidence in the university's paperwork that KISS played the May 5th gig.

APRIL 28, 1974

Cambridge, Massachusetts
The Performance Center
Headlining Act: Argent
Promoter: Roger Abramson

APRIL 29, 1974

Reading, Pennsylvania
The Watch Tower
Headlining Act: Argent
Promoter: Terry Snyder

MAY 1, 1974

Mansfield, Pennsylvania
Decker Gymnasium @ Mansfield State College
Headlining Act: Argent
Capacity: 3,000
Promoter: Concerts East

■ This gig was supposed to have been part of a two-day festival held at the school, though ultimately neither KISS nor Argent appeared.

MAY 7, 1974

Upper Darby (Philadelphia), Pennsylvania
Tower Theatre
Headlining Act: Argent
Capacity: 3,000
Promoter: Midnight Sun Concerts

MAY 10, 1974

Asbury Park, New Jersey
Sunshine In Concert Hall
Headlining Act: Argent
■ Brian Auger's Oblivion Express was originally listed on the bill.

MAY 11, 1974

Blue Bell (Philadelphia), Pennsylvania
Montgomery County Community College Gym
Headlining Act: Argent
Promoter: Paul Berrel
■ Canceled by April 26. *The Montgomery Gazette* reported that the school did not have adequate funds or time to meet the necessary production requirements, one of which was a request for a forklift.

MAY 12, 1974

Columbus, Ohio
The Agora
Headlining Act: Argent
Capacity: 2,000
Promoter: Agora Presents
■ The show was postponed until May 13 and then canceled.

MAY 14, 1974

Toledo, Ohio
Renaissance Valentine Theatre
Headlining Act: Argent
Promoter: Lynn Martin
■ The original date for the show was May 13.

Taken during the final week of the KISS Tour, September 28, 1974 at the Michigan Palace.

CHARLIE AURINGER

CHAPTER 4

HOTTER THAN HELL TOUR

Number of Shows: 53
Start Date: October 17, 1974 - Comstock Park, Michigan
End Date: February 22, 1975 - Schererville, Indiana
Countries: Canada, U.S.A.
Headlining Acts: Black Oak Arkansas; Dr. John; Foghat; Golden Earring; Jo Jo Gunne; Quicksilver Messenger Service; REO Speedwagon; Rush; Wishbone Ash; ZZ Top
Opening Acts: Arosa; Ballin' Jack; Camel; Cannonball; Clowns; Cockney Rebel; Easy Stream; Eddie Boy Band; Eli; Fancy; Fantasy; Heartsfield; Hickock; Hydra; If; James Gang; James Montgomery Band; Joe; John Hammond; Kenny Kramer; Man; Mercury; Mike Quatro; Neil Merryweather & Space Rangers; Pezband; Point Blank; Raspberries; The Road Crew; Rockets; Rush; The Sam Hurrie Band; Scream; Skyhook; Smokehouse; Stampeders; Stone Wall; T. Rex; Third Rail; Tongue; Trapeze; UFO; Yesterday & Today
Average Attendance: 3,936

Initially titled *The Harder They Come,* the *Hotter Than Hell* album was recorded at The Village Recorder in West Los Angeles between August 16 and September 4, 1974 for a mere $15,511.92.

The recording sessions, which came during a break from the KISS Tour, were marred by misfortune and a feeling of discomfort for the band. KISS lighting director Rick Munroe notes: "This was the first time the band was alone on the road. They were away from New York and the road crew. I remember them calling and not being too happy there." An excerpt from an August 17 letter Ace wrote underscores this: "The second day of recording Paul got his Flying V stolen! The owner of the studio felt very bad and told Paul to order another guitar, and he would pay for it." He goes on to note, "I haven't

had a drink in two weeks, and it's very hard to adjust to, but I feel healthy." Ironically, Ace was involved in a car accident on August 23, forcing him to cancel a planned visit to Disneyland.

Frehley's letter also mentions, "Yesterday, we all went to get props and costumes for the pictures on the back of the album cover. The photographer [Norman Seeff] is the guy who did the Rolling Stones's postcards." The now legendary photo session, which reportedly dissolved into an orgy—partly planned by Seeff and designer John Van Hamersveld in an attempt to bring out the visceral vibe they got from the band—was shot on August 18 at The Stage in Hollywood.

During this short recording break from the KISS Tour, a bombshell landed in Neil Bogart's lap: an in-house memo had been issued at Warner

Bros. instructing the promotions staff to downplay the band. The label had reportedly soured on KISS due to the apparent lack of interest from radio stations, and at Bogart's request, Warner Bros. terminated the business relationship in early September. Never one to be easily discouraged, Bogart quickly lined up a distribution network comprised of new distributors and independents from his days at Buddah. Casablanca was ready to roll again by October, with Neil vowing to concentrate on TV advertising. Toward that end, he commissioned Direction Plus to produce a 60-second commercial for the *Hotter Than Hell* album which, in some markets, aired on all three network affiliates simultaneously.

KISS maintained a high profile during the break between tours by appearing alongside

Lydia and Peter Criss, circa 1974.

Wayne County on a panel discussing glitter rock. *Rock Scene* editor Richard Robinson hosted the event, which was part of a radio convention held in Manhattan on October 14.

The KISS and Hotter Than Hell Tours were, in a sense, essentially the same tour—the costuming and staging were virtually identical. The only real delineations between the two are a 12-day break from touring in early October and the release of the album *Hotter Than Hell* on October 22.

Despite the overall visual similarities, some other important differences did exist. The most impactful change was the presence of a dedicated sound crew and system. Enter Fanfare Sound, who had previously been contracted by KISS for their upper-Midwest gigs. Fanfare employee and longtime KISS soundman Jay 'Hot Sam' Barth notes, "We prided ourselves on being big and loud and KISS had taken a liking to us and these huge W-bins [bass cabinets] we had."

Despite what may have seemed like a fairly static state of production, the band and crew were continuing to refine and expand the show, and new effects were consistently developed and integrated into the act. Rick Munroe explains one such effect: "We were sitting around up at the Rock Steady office and reading mail, and this one piece came addressed to 'lighting person.' So they gave it to me, and this guy had sent me some gels that he had developed, which he called holography-gels. The gels were designed to break white light down into prisms. He had sent us some square samples of this gel and some cardboard 3-D glasses with the holograph gel in the frames. The idea was to hand these glasses out to everyone in the audience and for them to watch the show that way. I didn't think that was going to fly.

"I took one of the squares that he had sent, and I got an overhead projector from the office and shut the lights off and put the gel in front of the lamp. And this very strange explosion of purples, yellows, golds, and reds filled the room. Armed with only two pieces of gel, we went to the Capitol Theatre out in Passaic and took them

to the spot operators. I said, 'Look, at a certain time in the show, I want you to take this gel and stick it in front of your lamp.' At the beginning of 'Black Diamond,' I put a very tight spot on Paul from his waist up with the gel on it. When I put the gel in front of the spotlight, I kept rotating it, and it looked like Paul was in the middle of this prism. It was a very stunning effect for the time."

Ace had also begun using an effect in which he would shoot a bottle-rocket-type device from the back of his guitar neck.

When headlining at the beginning of the tour, KISS was contracted to play 55 minutes, a figure that extended to 70 minutes by tour's end. Determining how KISS filled those minutes is difficult, as there is a severe lack of set list information available for the tour, with only three set lists known to exist. Surprisingly, the band initially included just two new songs from *Hotter Than Hell* in the set: "Got to Choose" and "Parasite," though several others were eventually added and the newly renamed "Let Me Go, Rock 'n Roll" (originally known as "Baby, Let Me Go") was still typically used for an encore.

OCTOBER 17, 1974
Comstock Park (Grand Rapids), Michigan
Thunder Chicken
Opening Act: Rush
Promoter: Dick Bickler

OCTOBER 18, 1974
Hammond, Indiana
The Parthenon Theatre
Opening Act: Rush
Capacity: 2,000
Promoter: S & J Productions
Archived: Audio

■ SET LIST
[Deuce]
[Strutter]
Got to Choose
Firehouse
She
Ace Frehley Guitar Solo
Nothin' to Lose
Parasite
100,000 Years
Peter Criss Drum Solo - reprise
Black Diamond
Let Me Go, Rock 'n Roll
Cold Gin

OCTOBER 19, 1974
Toledo, Ohio
Renaissance Valentine Theatre
Opening Act: Rockets
Promoter: Brass Ring Productions

OCTOBER 21, 1974
East Lansing, Michigan
The Brewery
Opening Act: Rush
Attendance: 750   Capacity: 750
Promoter: Bill Smith
Archived: Audio

■ SET LIST
Deuce
Strutter
Got to Choose
Firehouse
She
Ace Frehley Guitar Solo
Nothin' to Lose

Parasite
100,000 Years
Peter Criss Drum Solo - reprise
Black Diamond
Let Me Go, Rock 'n Roll
Cold Gin

OCTOBER 22, 1974
East Lansing, Michigan
The Brewery
Opening Act: Rush
Attendance: 750   Capacity: 750
Promoter: Bill Smith

OCTOBER 25, 1974
Passaic, New Jersey
Capitol Theatre
Headlining Act: Golden Earring
Opening Act: John Hammond
Promoter: John Scher Presents

■ Due to immigration problems, original headliners Climax Blues Band canceled three days prior to the show. Blues guitarist John Hammond and KISS were then added to the bill, and Golden Earring was moved up from their opening slot to that of headliner.

OCTOBER 27, 1974
Youngstown, Ohio
Tomorrow
Opening Act: Cannonball
Attendance: 2,000   Capacity: 2,000
Promoter: Agora Presents

■ Agora promoter Henry LaConti had originally intended to book the New York Dolls for this show and the subsequent show in Columbus and to promote the shows as Halloween parties. Unfortunately, the Dolls's booking agent took the idea and booked two gigs for the band in New York instead. LaConti booked KISS as a back-up and never regretted the decision, remarking that the Columbus show in particular was "a madhouse."

OCTOBER 30, 1974
Columbus, Ohio
The Agora
Opening Act: If
Attendance: 2,000   Capacity: 2,000
Promoter: Agora Presents

OCTOBER 31, 1974
Peru, Indiana
Circus Center Building
Opening Act: Stone Wall
Attendance: 1,000   Capacity: 1,000
Promoter: B&E Productions

■ This venue is on the campus of a genuine circus school. The Circus Center Building itself was a large tent, complete with support poles and bleachers. Inexplicably, KISS was allowed to use their full complement of pyrotechnics, despite the fact that the entire floor of the venue was covered with sawdust. This is especially ironic considering that sawdust (saturated with a flammable solution and densely packed into short cylinders) was the primary ingredient used in most flamethrowers of that era.

NOVEMBER 2, 1974
Des Plaines (Chicago), Illinois
Herman L. Rider Memorial Gymnasium @ Maine
    Township High School West
Opening Act: Smokehouse
Capacity: 3,600

NOVEMBER 3, 1974

Duluth, Minnesota
Duluth Arena Auditorium
Headlining Act: Dr. John
Opening Act: Easy Stream
Attendance: 2,193   Capacity: 8,000
Promoter: Yan Qui Productions
■ Raspberries are listed in the advertisements for the show, but they did not perform.

NOVEMBER 7, 1974

St. Louis, Missouri
Kiel Auditorium
Opening Acts: Heartsfield, T. Rex, Neil Merryweather & Space Rangers
Attendance: 10,154   Capacity: 10,154
Promoter: KSHE
■ This was KISS's first sold-out headlining performance at a full-sized arena. Promoted as the "KSHE 7th Anniversary Party," tickets for the event were only $1.95. The line-up was rather unusual in that KISS was advertised as the headliner, and the majority of the crowd was clearly there to see KISS. However, for some reason, Heartsfield was the last band to take the stage.

NOVEMBER 8, 1974

Chicago, Illinois
Aragon Ballroom
Opening Acts: UFO, Hydra
Attendance: 4,000   Capacity: 4,000
Promoter: JAM Productions
■ T. Rex was the scheduled headliner, but KISS was added as the last-minute replacement when T. Rex canceled.

NOVEMBER 10, 1974

University City (Saginaw), Michigan
Delta College Gymnasium
Opening Act: Skyhook
Attendance: Sold Out
Promoter: WTAC
■ Opening act Skyhook was a local band and should not be confused with the Australian band Skyhooks.

NOVEMBER 12, 1974

Minot, North Dakota
Minot Municipal Auditorium
Opening Act: Clowns
Attendance: 1,085   Capacity: 5,056
Promoter: Galaxy Productions

NOVEMBER 16, 1974

Asbury Park, New Jersey
Sunshine In Concert Hall
Opening Acts: Fantasy, Mercury
Promoter: Bob Fisher
■ It's possible that this concert was initially scheduled for October 24. This date cannot be confirmed with any existing paperwork, though several road crew members recall playing the venue a third time.

NOVEMBER 21, 1974

Evansville, Indiana **KISS CANCELED**
Roberts Municipal Stadium
Headlining Act: Black Oak Arkansas
Opening Acts: Montrose, James Montgomery Band
Promoter: Rogers Attractions
■ KISS backed out of this gig and opted to appear in Des Moines as the opener for Foghat.

NOVEMBER 21, 1974

Cedar Rapids, Iowa
Veterans Memorial Coliseum
Headlining Act: Foghat
Attendance: 4,000+   Capacity: 4,000
Promoter: Celebration Concerts
■ A KISS itinerary lists Black Oak Arkansas as the opener, but BOA was never scheduled to do the show. The attendance exceeded the venue's capacity, and the fire marshal issued a hazard warning to the venue.

NOVEMBER 23, 1974

Atlanta, Georgia
Alexander Memorial Coliseum
Headlining Act: Black Oak Arkansas
Opening Acts: Trapeze, the Stampeders
Promoter: Alex Cooley Presents

NOVEMBER 24, 1974   CANCELED

Columbia, South Carolina
Carolina Coliseum
Headlining Act: Black Oak Arkansas
Promoter: Entertainment Concepts

NOVEMBER 27, 1974

Greenville, South Carolina
Greenville Memorial Auditorium
Headlining Act: Black Oak Arkansas
Opening Act: James Montgomery Band
Attendance: 3,800
Promoter: Beach Club Promotions

NOVEMBER 28, 1974

Charlotte, North Carolina
Charlotte Coliseum
Headlining Act: Black Oak Arkansas
Opening Act: James Montgomery Band
Attendance: 11,500   Capacity: 13,000
Promoter: Kaleidoscope Productions
■ "Mainline" was included in the set, according to a fan in attendance.

NOVEMBER 29, 1974

Charleston, South Carolina
Charleston Municipal Auditorium
Headlining Act: Black Oak Arkansas
Opening Acts: the Stampeders, James Montgomery Band
Capacity: 2,732
Promoter: Kaleidoscope Productions
■ A KISS itinerary incorrectly lists Camden, South Carolina as the site of the show.

NOVEMBER 30, 1974

Fayetteville, North Carolina
Cumberland County Memorial Arena
Headlining Act: Black Oak Arkansas
Opening Act: the Stampeders
Capacity: 7,000
Promoter: Beach Club Promotions
■ Mick Campise: "One day we were in Fayetteville when Ace had an emergency and had to go to the dentist to get his wisdom teeth out. They gave him some Percodan, and when he came back from the dentist he was just unconscious. Word from above was, 'Do whatever you have to do to get him on stage, we are not canceling the show.' And that was the first time that Ace did cocaine. He never smoked, never did anything. He just drank beer; that was it. When cocaine was exploding and everyone was doing it, Gene and Paul never did it, Ace never did it, and the only thing Pete did at the time was take prescrip-

tion drugs to get to sleep."

DECEMBER 1, 1974

Asheville, North Carolina
Asheville Civic Center
Headlining Act: Black Oak Arkansas
Opening Acts: the Stampeders, James Montgomery Band
Attendance: 7,654   Capacity: 7,654
Promoter: Beach Club Promotions
■ Mick Campise: "Black Oak used to have a trestle on their front lights, and they had a little black curtain over it. When Peter shot his exploding drumsticks off at the show in Asheville, he hit the curtain, and it caught on fire. Black Oak went crazy over it, but they should have been paying more attention to the kids walking out during their set than worrying about KISS catching their curtain on fire."

DECEMBER 6, 1974

Bowling Green, Kentucky
Van Meter Auditorium @ Western Kentucky University
No Opening Act
Attendance: 1,100   Capacity: 1,100
Promoter: Ron Beck
■ KISS's set-up time was pushed back as William F. Buckley, Jr. had delivered a lecture in the auditorium earlier in the afternoon.
    Jay Wethington, in his *College Herald Heights* review, listed "Watchin' You," "100,000 Years," and "Firehouse" as part of the set.

DECEMBER 8, 1974

Evansville, Indiana
Roberts Municipal Stadium
Headlining Act: ZZ Top
Opening Act: Point Blank
Promoter: Sunshine Promotions
■ KISS performed last despite the fact that ZZ Top was the headliner. Future KISS Army Commander-in-Chief, Bill Starkey, attended this show. It was Starkey's first time seeing the band in concert.

DECEMBER 10, 1974

Davenport, Iowa
Palmer Alumni Auditorium @ Palmer College of Chiropractic
Headlining Act: ZZ Top
Opening Act: Point Blank
Promoter: Celebration Concerts

DECEMBER 11, 1974

Cedar Grove, New Jersey **TEMP HOLD DATE**
The Meadowbrook Theatre Restaurant
Promoter: Meadowbrook Concerts

DECEMBER 12, 1974

Flint, Michigan
I.M.A. Sports Arena
Headlining Act: ZZ Top
Attendance: 4,100   Capacity 5,200
Promoter: Brass Ring Productions

DECEMBER 13, 1974

La Crosse, Wisconsin
Mary E. Sawyer Auditorium
Opening Acts: Tongue, Eddie Boy Band
Promoter: Hole in the Wall Productions
■ KISS's official itineraries list Savoy Brown as the headliner for this show and the December 18 show in La Porte, Indiana, though they did not appear at either concert.

DECEMBER 18, 1974

La Porte, Indiana
National Guard Armory
Opening Act: Scream
Capacity: 350
Promoter: Schzoid Productions

■ JR Smalling: "I was standing on the stage during load-in when I looked up at the ceiling and realized that the entire thing was made of sheet metal. It was a fairly low ceiling, so I took a coin and flipped it up in the air and it made this nice 'ping' sound, which confirmed my suspicions.

"At that time, we did not have a dedicated pyro man, and each of us would take turns setting the effects up. It was my turn to load the flame-throwers, and I really juiced them up, figuring I had nothing to lose with the ceiling being metal. So, it gets to the point in the show where the flamethrower cues are, I flipped the switch and up go these beautiful, enormous columns of flame. They shoot upwards, hit the ceiling, and then I watched in pure terror as they spread and spread and spread across the ceiling towards the walls, which were definitely *not* metal. I looked out over the audience and the entire crowd was staring like zombies at these flames; the whole venue had turned bright orange. What must have taken three seconds drew out to what felt like five minutes. Fortunately, the flames stopped just short of the walls; otherwise, none of us would have gotten out of there alive."

DECEMBER 20, 1974

Detroit, Michigan
Michigan Palace
Headlining Act: Rush (co-headliners)
Opening Act: Fancy
Attendance: 5,000+   Capacity: 5,000
Promoter: Steve Glantz Productions

■ Both Michigan Palace shows were oversold.

Rick Munroe: "After the first show in Detroit, we held a party for Peter's birthday up in the balcony of the Michigan Palace. Somebody came around with some brownies, and as soon as I bit into one I knew what was going on. I ate a bunch of them. Of course, we all got the munchies and had to get something to eat. Gene was there and asked if he could go with us. On our way out, I said, 'So what did you do at the party, Gene?' 'Oh, nothing. I ate some food that was there. It was pretty good.' 'Gene . . . you didn't have the brownies, did you?' 'Yeah! Very chocolatey, very fudgey. They were really good.' Remember that Gene is as straight as can be. He doesn't drink; he doesn't smoke; he doesn't do anything. 'Gene, didn't you know those brownies were spiked?' 'What do you mean by spiked?' 'There was marijuana in those brownies, Gene.' 'No! Is that why I'm so hungry?'

"By this time, the only place still open is this White Castle with the bright, white fluorescent lights; it was hard to walk into that; it was so bright for us. We were all just hammered. I remember Gene stood out—with his platform shoes and a tarantula for a belt-buckle, and skulls on his rings—and there is no one in there but a bunch of rednecks. They all turn around and look at us. We're just standing there, and he says to me: 'Um, why is everybody staring at me?'

Note the KISS sign on the side of the stage.

'Gene, take a look at yourself.' 'And why do I feel so stupid?' 'Because, Gene, you're high as a kite, and you don't know it.'"

Paul Stanley, in a March 2000 interview with the *Oklahoma Entertainer*, recalled: "Someone decided a nice touch would be hash brownies and, of course, didn't tell anybody. Gene, being the sweet freak that he is, scarfed down a few brownies and later on couldn't quite figure out why his head was shrinking, and his arms were getting so long."

Peter Criss, in an October 1994 interview with coauthor Curt Gooch, remembered: "I got a call at about three in the morning. It was Gene. He's giving me all these scenarios about his brain shrinking, his hands looked tiny, and his face didn't fit in the mirror. I told him, 'Gene, it's no big deal. Order up some brownies—without hash—and some milk and go make passionate love to some babe and you'll come down in a few hours. You'll thank me.' And he did. That was the only time he ever got high."

DECEMBER 21, 1974

Detroit, Michigan
Michigan Palace
Headlining Act: Rush (co-headliners)
Opening Act: Fancy
Attendance: 5,000+   Capacity: 5,000
Promoter: Steve Glantz Productions

DECEMBER 22, 1974

London, Ontario, Canada
London Arena
Opening Act: Joe
Capacity: 2,000
Promoter: CJOM

■ The show was scheduled to start at 8 P.M. but did not begin until 10:45, due to "nothing more than poor management" according to the review in the *London Free Press.*

DECEMBER 23, 1974

Wilkes-Barre, Pennsylvania
Paramount Theatre
Opening Act: Kenny Kramer
Attendance: 2,000   Capacity: 2,000
Promoter: Fang Productions

■ Moose: "We were on our way to the Wilkes-Barre gig and had just crossed the Peace Bridge coming down from Kitchener through Buffalo when the state troopers pulled us over. We were driving a station wagon, and we had these big plastic containers of vitamin C with us, which the troopers dumped out all over the back of the car. They searched us and found no drugs, which really pissed them off." Rick Munroe continues: "They found some flashpaper on Moose and arrested him for suspicion of gambling. Bookies would write their deals on flash-paper because if the cops busted into a room, you just had to set a match to the paper and it would evaporate in an instant. So, they strip-searched us right on the side of the highway in the middle of winter. They ended up taking us all to the police station, but Moose was the only one they retained."

With their gear arriving late, KISS did not go onstage until nearly midnight. During the delay between acts, the manager of the venue asked people in the audience to come up onstage and perform to keep the crowd entertained. The official opening act, comedian Kenny Kramer, was later the inspiration for the character Kramer on *Seinfeld.*

Hudson-Ford, consisting of former members of British folk band The Strawbs was listed as the headliner on one KISS itinerary but did not perform.

RICK MUNROE

JR Smalling backstage with Paul, an hour before showtime at the La Porte Armory.

Grand Rapids, Michigan
Civic Center **KISS CANCELED**
Headlining Act: REO Speedwagon
Promoter: Celebration Concerts
■ A snowstorm prevented KISS from making it to the gig.

DECEMBER 27, 1974
Des Moines, Iowa **KISS CANCELED**
Veterans Memorial Auditorium
Headlining Act: Wishbone Ash
Promoter: Celebration Concerts

DECEMBER 27, 1974
Fort Wayne, Indiana
Allen Co. War Memorial Coliseum
Headlining Acts: REO Speedwagon, Quicksilver
 Messenger Service
Promoter: Sunshine Promotions
■ The show was billed as the "First Annual Holiday Festival."

DECEMBER 28, 1974
Indianapolis, Indiana
Indianapolis Convention Center
Headlining Acts: REO Speedwagon, Quicksilver
 Messenger Service
Opening Act: Hydra
Capacity: 13,500
Promoter: Sunshine Promotions
■ The event was billed as the "Third Annual Holiday Festival." KISS, despite being advertised for the middle of the bill, performed last. Bill Starkey recalled Paul greeting the crowd by saying: "Hey Indianapolis! Better late than never!"

**DECEMBER 29, 1974
(TWO SHOWS)**
Milwaukee, Wisconsin **KISS CANCELED**
Performing Arts Center
Headlining Act: REO Speedwagon

DECEMBER 29, 1974
South Bend, Indiana
Morris Civic Auditorium

Headlining Act: Quicksilver Messenger Service
 (co-headliner)
Opening Act: Hydra
Attendance: 2,483   Capacity: 2,483
Promoter: Sunshine Promotions

DECEMBER 30, 1974
Springfield, Illinois
National Guard Armory
Opening Act: Mike Quatro
Promoter: Lenny Trumper
■ Despite the inherent danger of having so many pyrotechnic effects in their show, KISS had not had any major accidents until this night.

JR Smalling: "Peter had these white copper tubes, about 18" long and 1" in diameter. They were packed with flashpaper that was ignited by a connector and two AA batteries. When these things ignited, they looked like flaming drumsticks. Since he was Peter's roadie, the task of setting this effect up every night fell to Moose. Over the course of time, the unused flash powder had accumulated around the electrical connectors of one device, and it wasn't working. As I understand it, Moose had taken a screwdriver to scrape away the powder from one of the connectors. In scraping the stuff off he more than likely caused a spark, and it blew up in his hand."

Moose: "It was really weird that night: there was a man dressed all in black, with a cape and a handlebar moustache. He looked like he was out for a walk in the English fog; he was very surreal. He stood right in front of the box where I kept all my powder for the effects, and he asked me what I was doing. I told him that I was setting up my effects and then, after we talked for about a minute, he disappeared. Right after that, as I was setting up the toy, it blew up on me. I specifically recall that when the thing blew up, the audience started applauding because they thought it was something Mike Quatro had done."

JR Smalling: "I was hanging out by the soundboard when I heard the explosion. We had had a big discussion with Mike Quatro telling him in no uncertain terms that he could not use pyro because that was our gig. When I first heard the explosion, I thought 'Mike Quatro, you are a dead man,' and I took off backstage. When I got there, Moose was standing against a wall and holding on to his hand and screaming, and there was blood all over the place."

Peter Criss: "I never saw so much blood in my life. We kept wrapping his hand over and over, and there was all this white, brainy, ugly stuff coming out."

Moose continues: "I had the presence of mind to look down and see if I still had my hand, and it was a freaking mess. I was bleeding from underneath my chin, I got eight stitches there, and my hand had two inches of scar tissue on it and there was a hole in my stomach. My right finger got a little bit trashed, but my left hand was the one that almost got whacked.

"When I got to the hospital, there were two Illinois state troopers standing by as I signed the document authorizing the surgeon to remove my hand if he had to. I remember the troopers asking me if anyone had put me up to this. That was some question to ask. As I went into surgery, I

told the doctor, whose name I remember vividly, Dr. Hayes of Springfield Memorial: 'Whatever you do, sew it back on; I don't want it off.' He looked at it and told me: 'I just came back from 'Nam, so I've seen worse.'

"JR told me that when the surgeon came down he said that if my name wasn't Moose, I wouldn't have a hand."

DECEMBER 31, 1974
Evansville, Indiana
Evansville Coliseum
Opening Act: Raspberries
Promoter: Duncan Productions
■ Rush was listed as the opening act in some ads. This New Year's Eve gig was billed as a "70-minute headline performance" and was promoted as the "early show" since Black Oak Arkansas was also appearing in town later that night.

JANUARY 7, 1975
Lethbridge, Alberta, Canada
Lethbridge Exhibition Pavilion
Opening Act: Hickock
Attendance: 1,500   Capacity: 1,500
Promoter: Gold & Gold Productions
■ The New York Dolls were the original headliners for the show, but they were forced to cancel when they ran into trouble with the border patrol authorities in Montana while attempting to drive into Canada.

Mick Campise: "We tried playing 'Strange Ways' in Canada a couple of times in early 1975, but it had too much of a plodding, start-and-stop feel, and it never really went over live. The crew was always pulling for more material from Ace and Peter, but not much made it into the sets."

**JANUARY 9, 1975
(TWO SHOWS: 9:00 P.M., 11:00 P.M.)**
Vancouver, British Columbia, Canada
Commodore Ballroom
Opening Act: The Sam Hurrie Band
Attendance: Sold Out
Promoter: Accident Productions
■ The opening act was actually called Sam Hurrie's Diamond Reo Band, but they changed their name to avoid confusion with the New York band Diamond Reo.

The first known mention of the SS/Nazi controversy appeared in the Vancouver, Canada magazine *Georgia Straight*. An uncredited writer observed in their January 16 issue: "Embarrassed as I am to admit it, my colleague from this same periodical ventured the almost ludicrous proposition that the final two letters of the band's KISS logo held some innate, but dark significance, in that the final two "S's" resembled uncannily the double "S" of the Schutz-Staffel of Hitler's Germany. Needless to say, this was greeted by eight pointed fingers of derisive scorn and embarrassingly frank ridicule." Various religious zealots and other extreme conservatives brought up the issue over the years to come.

JANUARY 10, 1975
Portland, Oregon
Paramount Northwest Theatre
Opening Act: Ballin' Jack
Attendance: 2,300   Capacity: 3,040
Promoter: Get Down Productions

CHARLIE AURINGER

▲ **KISS in the men's room at Creem magazine, preparing for a photo session.**

▶ **Gene with Creem staffer Leslie Brown.**

CHARLIE AURINGER

JANUARY 14, 1975
Eugene, Oregon   TEMP HOLD DATE

JANUARY 11, 1975

Medford, Oregon
National Guard Armory
Opening Act: Arosa
Promoter: Rock 'n Roll Productions

JANUARY 12, 1975

Seattle, Washington
Paramount Northwest Theatre
Opening Act: Ballin' Jack
Attendance: 2,700   Capacity: 2,700
■ Mick Campise: "On the way down from Seattle, we got stuck at the Travelodge in San Francisco because we couldn't pay the hotel bill. The rest of the road crew had left and started driving back to New York, but JR and I stayed there with the band. We were stuck there for what seemed like two weeks. During the last few days, we

pitched in and bought some bread and peanut butter and that's what we lived on."

JANUARY 14, 1975

Eugene, Oregon   TEMP HOLD DATE
Lane County Fairgrounds Expo Hall

JANUARY 17, 1975

Long Beach, California
Long Beach Arena
Headlining Act: Wishbone Ash
Opening Act: Camel
Attendance: 9,500   Capacity: 9,500
Promoter: Pacific Presentations
■ Local radio station KNAC aired a "live concert preview" of the show.

JANUARY 18, 1975

San Bernardino, California

Swing Auditorium
Headlining Act: ZZ Top
Attendance: 7,400   Capacity: 7,400
Promoter: Pacific Presentations
■ Mick Campise: "ZZ Top and KISS just never got along. ZZ thought KISS was a joke and KISS didn't like one thing about ZZ. I'm from Texas, and ZZ and their crew used to get on my ass: 'Man, I don't know if I should even talk to you, working with those damn Yankees and living in New York. By the way, is that drummer still wearing those hot pants?' Peter used to wear silver-leather hot pants and they just thought it was the funniest thing ever. Of course, at the same time these guys were dressing like cowboys and brought a bunch of cattle onstage during their show."

JANUARY 19, 1975

San Diego, California
Golden Hall @ Convention & Performing Arts Center
Headlining Act: Wishbone Ash
Opening Act: Camel
Attendance: 3,000   Capacity: 3,000
Promoter: Jim Pagni
■ The local fire marshal prohibited Gene's fire-breathing act.

JANUARY 21, 1975

KISS CANCELED

Denver, Colorado
Regis College Fieldhouse
Headlining Act: Wishbone Ash
Opening Act: Camel
Promoter: Feyline Presents
■ KISS canceled due to Paul's strep throat.

JANUARY 23, 1975

KISS CANCELED

Salt Lake City, Utah
Terrace Ballroom
Headlining Act: Wishbone Ash
Opening Act: Camel
Attendance: Sold Out
■ KISS canceled due to Paul's strep throat.

JANUARY 24, 1975

TEMP HOLD DATE

Tucson, Arizona

JANUARY 26, 1975

Fresno, California
Selland Arena @ Fresno Convention Center
Headlining Acts: ZZ Top, Wishbone Ash
Opening Act: Camel
Capacity: 7,410
Promoter: Papa Productions

JANUARY 31, 1975

San Francisco, California
Winterland
Opening Acts: Third Rail, Eli
Attendance: 5,400   Capacity: 5,400
Promoters: Bill Graham Presents, FM Productions
Archived: Video
■ **SET LIST**
Deuce
Strutter
Got to Choose
Hotter Than Hell
Firehouse
Watchin' You
Ace Frehley Guitar Solo
Nothin' to Lose
Parasite
Gene Simmons Bass Solo
100,000 Years
Peter Criss Drum Solo - reprise
Black Diamond
Cold Gin
Let Me Go, Rock 'n Roll
■ This show was videotaped by Bill Graham Presents using the in-house system at Winterland. Bill Graham had to be talked into booking the show by ATI rep Sol Saffian. KISS pocketed over $12,000 on a $1,000 guarantee.

FEBRUARY 1, 1975

Santa Monica, California
Santa Monica Civic Auditorium
Headlining Act: Jo Jo Gunne
Opening Act: Yesterday & Today
Attendance: 3,000   Capacity: 3,000
Promoter: Fun Productions
■ This show was originally slated for January 31. The tour itself was scheduled to continue through February as evidenced by three temp. hold dates on February 10, 11, and 12 in Lafayette, Louisiana; Little Rock, Arkansas; and at Cain's Ballroom in Tulsa, Oklahoma, respectively. ATI was having some difficulty finding a promoter to purchase the Little Rock and Tulsa gigs, so the band cut their losses and took the opportunity to record their next album, *Dressed to Kill.*

FEBRUARY 20, 1975

St. Louis, Missouri
Kiel Auditorium
Opening Acts: Cockney Rebel, The Road Crew
Attendance: 5,600   Capacity: 5,700
Promoter: Panther Productions

FEBRUARY 21, 1975

Chicago, Illinois
Aragon Ballroom
Opening Acts: James Gang, Man
Attendance: 4,276   Capacity: 5,000
Promoter: JAM Productions
■ After the show, Lawrence Keenan of the *Prairie Sun* conducted an interview with the band, which may rank as the most hysterically funny interview that the band has ever conducted. It ran as part of a piece called "KISS: Subtle Truths and Harmless Lies," which was not printed until 1977. During the interview, Ace got in a fight with a lamp, and Gene offered interesting observations such as, "Mike Douglas sucks cock 13 to the dozen, but don't print that."

FEBRUARY 22, 1975

Schererville, Indiana
Omni 41
Opening Acts: James Gang, Pezband
Attendance: 4,321   Capacity: 5,000
Promoters: Celebration Concerts, JAM Productions

Ace in a hotel room somewhere on the Hotter Than Hell Tour.

KISS posing with Boy Howdy! beer for Creem magazine.

CHAPTER 5

DRESSED TO KILL TOUR

Number of Shows: 72

Start Date: March 19, 1975 - Northampton, Pennsylvania

End Date: August 28, 1975 - Indianapolis, Indiana

Countries: Canada, U.S.A.

Headlining Acts: Black Sabbath; Golden Earring; Hunter-Ronson; Johnny Winter; Marshall Tucker Band; Ozark Mountain Daredevils; Rare Earth; Uriah Heep; War; ZZ Top

Opening Acts: ASTIGAFA; Atlanta Rhythm Section; Brian Auger's Oblivion Express; Diamond Reo; The Flock; Heavy Metal Kids; Hydra; James Gang; Jo Jo Gunne; Journey; M-S Funk; Montrose; Mushroom; Nazareth; Passport; Point Blank; Pure Prairie League; REO Speedwagon; Rush; Salem Witchcraft; Skyscraper; Smokehouse; Status Quo; Stu Daye; Ted Nugent; Ted Nugent & the Amboy Dukes; Thin Lizzy; The Tubes; Vitale's Madman

Average Attendance: 5,973

The Hotter Than Hell Tour essentially came to an end on February 1, 1975, though three dates clustered in mid-February provided a coda to the tour. Several factors had brought about the somewhat sudden ending, the most significant of which were the sessions to record KISS's third album, *Dressed to Kill.*

The initial sessions for the album, which had originally been titled *KISS at Midnight,* were held at Larrabee Sound in Los Angeles on January 24 and 25, where tracks for both "Anything for My Baby" and "Rock and Roll All Nite" were laid down. Following a February 1 gig in Santa Monica, KISS departed for New York, where recording was quickly finished at Electric Lady Studios between February 6 and 25.

Despite the relative success KISS had enjoyed thus far, some issues had begun to fester between the group and its record label. Through early 1975, Casablanca had yet to pay the band any substantial royalties, although their November 1973 agreement clearly obligated them to do so. KISS was also displeased that Neil Bogart had yet to break them on a large-scale basis. To add to the tension, producers Kenny Kerner and Richie Wise were receiving offers for the band from other major labels.

To sort matters out, the band, Kerner and Wise, Bill Aucoin, and Joyce Biawitz held a meeting. The result was a decision to field the offers from other record companies. Biawitz was Aucoin's partner and had become Bogart's

girlfriend, thus her involvement in the meeting created a conflict of interest. When Bogart was informed of the meeting, he immediately fired Kerner and Wise and began to consider ways of removing Aucoin from the equation. One way was to cease all funding of KISS's tours, which he did at some point in early 1975. This left Aucoin and his accountant, Alan Cohen, with the unenviable task of covering KISS's touring expenses with their American Express cards.

When the dust finally settled, Aucoin had solidified his position by agreeing to buy out Joyce's share of their Rock Steady partnership for $50,000, and Neil Bogart had appointed himself as KISS's producer *du jour.* The band would eventually sign its first record contract with Casablanca on May 1.

KISS live in Boston at the Orpheum, May 11, 1975.

RON POWNALL/ WWW.ROCKROLLPHOTO.COM

Bogart's production ideas were decidedly different than his predecessors', as his comments in the February 15 issue of *Billboard* delineate: "What the market obviously needs now is upbeat, happy records that can make people forget their troubles." In fact, Bogart's insistence that the band needed an anthem brought about the writing of "Rock and Roll All Nite," which was penned at the Continental Hyatt House in Los Angeles. As Rick Munroe recalls, "I remember Neil finishing 'Rock and Roll All Nite' at Electric Lady. He kept trying to pile track on top of track to make the vocals sound like a crowd, and it wasn't working using just the band. I recall Mick Campise, Mike McGurl [tour manager], JR, Moose, Lydia Criss, and myself were there. So, he had all of us go in and record both clapping and vocals. I remember Moose couldn't clap with his bad hand, so he zippered with the zipper on his jacket."

Once the recording sessions were complete, KISS relocated to SIR studios in Manhattan, where tour rehearsals began in early March.

Every attempt was being made to keep the spotlight on the band. On April 1, KISS recorded a memorable appearance on NBC-TV's *The Midnight Special.* There was also a scheduled taping on May 5 for a Mary Tyler Moore variety special, which unfortunately never came to fruition.

For his part, Aucoin hired his Direction Plus associates, John Kelly and Angela Kirby, to produce two promotional films for the band. The videos for "C'mon and Love Me" and "Rock and Roll All Nite" were shot at the Michigan Palace in Detroit on May 15. Insert-shots for the videos, including backstage footage and shots of the crowd, were done at Cobo Arena the following day.

An interesting dichotomy arose as the tour got underway. Money was almost nonexistent, yet KISS was apparently starting to demand the rock-star lifestyle. Not that the budget supported it, but KISS and road manager JR Smalling now flew on commercial airlines between shows. KISS also found a way to justify hiring a designated pyro man, and Mark "Zero" Stinner joined the entourage as such on March 19.

Initially, there were very few changes to the set list. Only two *Dressed to Kill* tracks were in the show, "C'mon and Love Me" and "She," and the latter had already been a concert staple for two years. However, with the imminent recording of a live album, many tracks briefly found their way into the set, including "Rock Bottom," "Room Service," and older tracks like "Let Me Know." Oddly enough, the band's most famous song, "Rock and Roll All Nite," was not added to the set list until some time in May.

MARCH 19, 1975
(TWO SHOWS: 6:30 P.M., 9:30 P.M.)

Northampton, Pennsylvania
Roxy Theatre
Opening Act: Passport
Attendance: (1) 561; (2) 561   Capacity: 561
Promoter: Sound 70 Concerts

■ These two shows were more-or-less warm-up gigs for the tour. Due to its relative proximity to New York, The Roxy was frequently used for just such a purpose.

The following night, KISS did a photo shoot in and around Max's Kansas City in New York. "There was a time there when they'd throw on whatever they had just to make a costume," Rick Munroe recalls. "They had some kind of promotional thing at Max's Kansas City, and there was no central meeting place to get ready, as everyone lived out in Queens or Brooklyn. I offered my apartment, which was on McDougal Street in the Village, across from Café Wha? They showed up in a limousine, came into my apartment, and put their makeup on. Because the costumes weren't with us, they ended up going through my closet to see if there was something they could wear, and they pulled out anything they could find. Paul used a velvet cape that some girl had left there, and Ace ended up using this purple velvet jumpsuit. They all looked pretty ridiculous."

MARCH 21, 1975
(TWO SHOWS: 7:30 P.M., 11:00 P.M.)

New York, New York
Beacon Theatre
Opening Act: Jo Jo Gunne
Attendance: Both shows sold out
Promoter: Ron Delsener Presents
Archived: Audio (7:30 show)
■ SET LIST
Deuce
Strutter
Got to Choose
Hotter Than Hell
Firehouse
She
Ace Frehley Guitar Solo
Nothin' to Lose
Parasite
Gene Simmons Bass Solo
100,000 Years
Peter Criss Drum Solo - reprise
Black Diamond
C'mon and Love Me
Let Me Go, Rock 'n Roll

■ When first approached, promoter Ron Delsener didn't think the show would sell, so the band negotiated a deal such that Delsener was guaranteed not to lose money even if the draw was

RICK MUNROE

Lighting director Rick Munroe getting ready for the shows at the Beacon Theatre. Notice the state-of-the-art light board and original rhinestone KISS T-shirt.

poor. The first show sold out so quickly that a second show was added, which also sold out.

One of the two gigs was archived on audiotape, most likely the 7:30 show.

MARCH 27, 1975

Kenosha, Wisconsin
Kenosha Ice Arena
Opening Acts: Rush, Thin Lizzy
Capacity: 4,500
Promoter: Twin Productions

MARCH 28, 1975

Toledo, Ohio
Sports Arena
Headlining Act: ZZ Top
Capacity: 7,500
Promoter: Bamboo Productions

MARCH 29, 1975

Cleveland, Ohio   TEMP HOLD DATE
Allen Theatre
Opening Acts: Rush, Vitale's Madman
Promoter: Belkin Productions

■ This show is occasionally cited as one of the sources for the *Alive!* album. This is incorrect, as this show was nothing more than an early temp hold date and never took place.

APRIL 1, 1975

Burbank, California
NBC Studios
Promoter: NBC Productions
Archived: Video
■ SET LIST
Deuce
C'mon and Love Me
She
Ace Frehley Guitar Solo
Black Diamond

■ This gig was the taping of KISS's appearance on NBC-TV's *The Midnight Special.* Although KISS recorded "C'mon and Love Me," it was never aired. KISS had to be toned down and was asked that they not stick their tongues out or touch each other's knees during any choreographed moves. "Deuce," "She," and Ace's solo premiered on July 11, while "Black Diamond" aired on September 12.

Rick Munroe: "I remember that Pearl gave Peter a drum kit to use that night. By the end of the set, it was in pieces. He just kicked the crap out of the kit. I think the band was pissed off at Peter over that."

APRIL 4, 1975   TEMP HOLD DATE

Hempstead, New York
Calderone Concert Hall
Promoter: Phil Basile of Concerts East

APRIL 4, 1975

Hartland (Flint), Michigan
Nordic Arena
Opening Act: Rush
Attendance: 3,542   Capacity: 3,542
Promoter: Brass Ring Productions

APRIL 5, 1975   CANCELED

Williamsport, Pennsylvania
Williamsport Community College
Opening Act: Heavy Metal Kids

■ KISS was forced to cancel when the crew could not load the equipment into the venue because the doors to the stage were too small.

APRIL 6, 1975

Washington, D.C.
G.W. Lisner Auditorium @ George Washington
    University
Opening Acts: Rush, Heavy Metal Kids
Attendance: 1,506   Capacity: 1,506
Promoter: Cellar Door Concerts
■ This was a benefit performance for the Hillcrest Children's Medical Center.

APRIL 8, 1975

Akron, Ohio
Akron Civic Theatre
Opening Acts: Rush, Heavy Metal Kids
Capacity: 2,918
Promoter: Belkin Productions

APRIL 9, 1975

Erie, Pennsylvania
Erie County Fieldhouse
Opening Acts: Rush, Vitale's Madman
Capacity: 6,000
Promoter: Belkin Productions

APRIL 11, 1975

Dayton, Ohio
The Palace Theatre
Opening Act: Heavy Metal Kids
Capacity: 2,064
Promoter: Belkin Productions
■ A day-of-show ad was placed by the promoter in the *Dayton Daily News* with Victoria Opera House incorrectly listed as the venue. Fortunately for any concertgoers who may have been confused by the ad, The Palace was right across the street from the Opera House.

APRIL 12, 1975

Normal, Illinois
ISU Union & Auditorium
Opening Act: Rush
Capacity: 3,457
Promoter: Lenny Trumper

APRIL 13, 1975

Kansas City, Kansas
Soldier's & Sailor's Memorial Hall
Headlining Act: Golden Earring
Opening Act: Vitale's Madman
Attendance: 3,531   Capacity: 3,531
Promoter: Cowtown Productions

APRIL 15, 1975

Pittsburgh, Pennsylvania
Stanley Theatre
Opening Acts: Rush, Heavy Metal Kids
Attendance: 3,700   Capacity: 3,700
Promoters: DiCesare-Engler Productions, WDVE

APRIL 17, 1975

Burlington, Iowa
Memorial Auditorium
Opening Act: Rush
Capacity: 2,062
Promoter: Road Fever Productions
■ Heavy Metal Kids and Smokehouse were scheduled to play, but both canceled.

APRIL 19, 1975

Palatine (Chicago), Illinois
Fremd High School Gymnasium
Opening Act: Rush
Promoter: Prophet Productions
Archived: Audio

RICK MUNROE

Gene at war with the road crew, at a mini-mall somewhere on the Dressed to Kill Tour.

■ PARTIAL SET LIST

Deuce
Strutter
Got to Choose
Hotter Than Hell
Firehouse
She
Ace Frehley Guitar Solo
Nothin' to Lose
■ Rockandy was advertised as the first opening act but did not appear at the show. "Room Service" was run through several times at sound check and, during a recorded backstage, preshow conversation, Paul indicated that it was to be included in the set.

APRIL 21, 1975

Louisville, Kentucky
Louisville Memorial Auditorium
Opening Act: Rush
Capacity: 2,000
Promoter: Sunshine Promotions

APRIL 22, 1975

Indianapolis, Indiana
Indianapolis Convention Center
Opening Acts: Rush, Status Quo
Attendance: SRO
Promoters: Treble Clef, Sunshine Promotions
■ The venue was set up in theater-seating configuration. An ad in *Primo Times* listed KISS and America as the two bands on the bill, but America did not perform at the show.

APRIL 24, 1975

Johnson City, Tennessee
Freedom Hall Civic Center @ Science Hill High School
Opening Acts: Rush, Heavy Metal Kids

Attendance: 4,300   Capacity: 8,000
Promoter: Lyn-Lee Productions

APRIL 25, 1975

Charlotte, North Carolina
Charlotte Park Center Auditorium
Opening Acts: Rush, Heavy Metal Kids
Attendance: Sold Out
Promoter: Kaleidoscope Productions
■ A fan on his way to see KISS in Charlotte was killed in a car accident. The event provided the back-story for the narrative in "Detroit Rock City," in which a young person is killed in a collision on the way to a rock concert.

APRIL 26, 1975

Fayetteville, North Carolina
Cumberland County Memorial Arena
Opening Acts: Atlanta Rhythm Section, Rush
Attendance: 3,564   Capacity: 7,000
Promoter: Kaleidoscope Productions

APRIL 27, 1975

Richmond, Virginia
Mosque Theatre
Opening Acts: Rush, Brian Auger's Oblivion Express,
    M-S Funk
Capacity: 3,732
Promoter: Century Productions
■ M-S Funk, a band from Muscle Shoals, Alabama (hence, the "M-S" in its name) once included Tommy Shaw (future guitarist for Styx), though he was not a member of the band at this time. The promoter, who had booked KISS without much clue about what their stage show entailed, later publicly apologized for "allowing such subversive behavior within city limits."

APRIL 29, 1975

Lansing, Michigan
Metro Ice Arena
Opening Act: Salem Witchcraft
Attendance: 4,300   Capacity: 4,300
Promoters: Paul Stanley Productions, Belkin Productions
■ This gig was originally scheduled to be held at the Lansing Civic Center.

APRIL 30, 1975

Columbus, Ohio
Veterans Memorial Auditorium
Opening Act: Status Quo
Capacity: 3,898
Promoter: Bamboo Productions

MAY 3, 1975

Upper Darby (Philadelphia), Pennsylvania
Tower Theater
Opening Act: Ted Nugent & the Amboy Dukes
Attendance: 1,899
Capacity: 3,064
Promoter: Midnight Sun Concerts
Archived: Audio

■ PARTIAL SET LIST

Deuce
Strutter
Got to Choose
Hotter Than Hell
Firehouse
She
Ace Frehley Guitar Solo
Nothin' to Lose
Room Service
Gene Simmons Bass Solo
100,000 Years
Peter Criss Drum Solo - reprise

A rare shot of Paul onstage in sunglasses, at the **G. W. Lisner Auditorium, April 6, 1975.** An eye infection had prevented him from applying his star makeup.

MAY 6, 1975

Milwaukee, Wisconsin
Riverside Theater
Opening Act: Rush
Promoter: Daydream Productions

■ Jay Lengnick, writing for *The Bugle-American*, mentioned several songs included in the set list: "Rock Bottom," "Hotter Than Hell," "Firehouse," "Nothin' To Lose," "Room Service," Peter's drum solo, and "Black Diamond." This marks the only known occasion where both "Rock Bottom" and "Room Service" were performed live during the same show.

In a scene lifted straight from Woodstock, between the acts an announcement was made regarding bad pills circulating in the theater.

MAY 8, 1975

Lockport (Chicago), Illinois
John F. Kennedy Gymnasium @ Lewis University
Opening Act: Rush
Attendance: 2,200   Capacity: 2,200
Promoter: Tom Seymour

■ This area of Lockport has since been rezoned and is now part of Romeoville, Illinois. The show was archived on audiotape, only to be accidentally erased years later, presumably without a copy ever having been made.

MAY 9, 1975

Ada, Ohio
King Horn Convocation Center @ Ohio Northern University
Opening Acts: James Gang, Rush
Capacity: 5,000
Promoter: Ohio Northern University

■ Initially, REO Speedwagon was hired to do the show with the following running order: Rush, KISS, REO Speedwagon. When REO Speedwagon canceled, James Gang was signed to replace them and KISS became the headline act.

Legend has it that on the afternoon of the show, a faculty member spotted the members of KISS (minus the makeup) walking across campus to the cafeteria. She mistakenly thought they were destitute students, so she gave them four passes for lunch.

MAY 10, 1975

Wilkes-Barre, Pennsylvania
King's College Hall
Capacity: 2,600

MAY 10, 1975

Landover (Washington, D.C.), Maryland
Capital Centre
Headlining Act: ZZ Top
Attendance: 13,399
Capacity: 18,000
Promoter: Cellar Door Concerts

■ Brian Auger's Oblivion Express was replaced on the bill by KISS. As an opening act, KISS was most likely not allowed to take advantage of the in-house video system.

Larry Rohter, in his review of the show for the *Washington Post*, observed: "KISS's most warmly received number was called 'Rock 'n' Roll All Night and Party Every Day [sic].'" Although it was possibly added several days prior, this is the first known performance of the song.

MAY 11, 1975

Boston, Massachusetts
Orpheum Theatre
Headlining Act: Hunter-Ronson
Opening Act: Journey   Capacity: 2,868
Promoter: Don Law Presents
Archived: Audio

■ **SET LIST**

Deuce
Strutter
Hotter Than Hell
Firehouse
She
Ace Frehley Guitar Solo
C'mon and Love Me
Gene Simmons Bass Solo
100,000 Years
Peter Criss Drum Solo - reprise
Black Diamond
Rock and Roll All Nite

■ This was the last live appearance of the KISS/Hotter Than Hell outfits.

Due to a strict city ordinance, KISS's pyro was scaled back drastically. Because of these regulations, KISS did not perform a full-scale concert within the Boston city limits again until 1996.

_____

In many ways, the Dressed to Kill Tour is two tours. The first half, which ended on May 11, was merely a continuation of the Hotter Than Hell Tour, with identical costumes and similar staging and production. The second half began on May 16 in Detroit and featured totally different costumes, a new lighting system, and a redesigned stage.

The days between May 11 and May 16 were used for fitting costumes, filming promotional footage of the band, doing a photo session, and rehearsing the new stage show.

New York designer Moonstone developed the new costumes and constructed them from design sketches for $1,000 a piece. KISS ordered three costumes for each band member.

Promotional films were done at the Michigan Palace (where the band was rehearsing) on the days preceding the Cobo Arena gig. On May 14, some of the visual highlights of KISS's performance, e.g., flamethrowers and the levitating drum riser, were shot. On the 15th, the band was filmed lip-synching "C'mon and Love Me" and "Rock and Roll All Nite" for each song's promotional film. Additional production highlights were filmed that day, with the band lip-synching to "Firehouse" and "Black Diamond" and doing a live performance of "100,000 Years." Some of the footage from these three songs was used for insert-shots in the promo films for "C'mon and Love Me" and "Rock and Roll All Nite."

During the filming of "Firehouse," Gene lit his hair on fire. "I always kept a towel around my neck while I was running the sirens during 'Firehouse', just in case anything happened," recalls pyrotechnician Mark Stinner. "While they were shooting the video, Gene caught his hair on fire. I ran out to extinguish him and stopped just before I got to him, but as I tried to stop, I hit

CHUCK DIOTTE

Bruce Redoute and Lee Neaves about 30 seconds after posing for their famous photo on the back cover of the Alive! album.

the puddle of kerosene next to him. I slid right underneath his legs, turned around, stood up, patted his hair out, and ran offstage."

Photographer Fin Costello showed up at the Michigan Palace and shot posed live photos of KISS. An airbrushed collage of his photos from the session would become the cover of *Alive!* The famous photo on the back of the album jacket featuring teenagers Bruce Redoute and Lee Neaves holding up their homemade KISS sign in front of the May 16 crowd at Cobo Arena was also shot by Costello.

MAY 16, 1975

Detroit, Michigan
Cobo Arena
Opening Act: Diamond Reo
Attendance: 12,039
Capacity: 12,039
Promoter: Steve Glantz Productions
Archived: Audio, Film

■ This was the first of five concerts recorded for the *Alive!* album. Live footage of the show was projected onto a screen above the stage.

Mick Campise: "It was the very first time that we had headlined Cobo Arena and everybody had their families up for the show. It was a very big deal. During the day, the band was filmed putting the makeup on in the dressing room and walking down the corridor to the stage. At the beginning of the show, this footage was shown on a screen above the stage while the taped intro to 'Rock Bottom' was playing over the P.A. Then everyone took their positions on stage and the show started. That's the only time I remember opening with 'Rock Bottom.'"

Production for the gig did not go particularly well. "Grand Stage Lighting out of Detroit did the lighting for that show," Rick Munroe remembers. "Gui [Bill Aucoin] told me that I had to use them, so I said OK. I tried to get things to look the way they needed to look, and they just didn't have the proper equipment for the job because they were not a touring company, they were a stage company. We did a show in Johnstown the next day, and they didn't show up until three or four in the afternoon, at which point I had already rounded up enough local lighting to do the show without them. I never used them again."

In addition, Peter's drum riser didn't go up as scheduled at the end of "Black Diamond." "We didn't have enough power outlets," Mick Campise explains, "which is what we needed for both the fog machines and for Peter's drum riser. Something happened after 'Firehouse,' and when Paul Chavarria unplugged the fog machines, he forgot to plug in Peter's riser. So, here it was time for Peter's drum riser to go up at our first big headlining show, and it didn't happen. Paul Stanley hit the roof and fired Paul on the spot. I got him his job back about nine months later, and he worked for Gene from there on out."

Promoter Steve Glantz held an after-show party at the Cobo Hall Ballroom beginning at 11:30 P.M. (To clarify: Cobo Hall is not the name of the arena, but, rather, was the name for the convention/ballroom area of the complex.)

MAY 17, 1975

Johnstown, Pennsylvania
Cambria County War Memorial Arena
Opening Act: Rush
Capacity: 6,747
Promoter: Music Artisans Productions

■ *Creem* writer Jaan Uhelszki, as part of a feature titled "I Dreamed I Was On Stage With KISS In My Maidenform Bra," got up onstage wearing a guitar (which was unplugged) and performed the majority of "Rock and Roll All Nite" with the band as the unofficial "Fifth member of KISS." Uhelszki wore the collage makeup design from the back cover of the *Hotter Than Hell* album.

MAY 19, 1975

St. Paul, Minnesota
St. Paul Civic Center Theater
Opening Act: Hydra
Capacity: 2,687
Promoter: Van Horn Productions

MAY 22, 1975

Yakima, Washington
Capitol Theater
Opening Act: Rush

TEMP HOLD DATE

MAY 23, 1975

Medford, Oregon
National Guard Armory
Opening Act: Rush
Promoter: Get Down Productions

MAY 24, 1975

Portland, Oregon
Paramount Northwest Theatre
Opening Act: Rush
Attendance: 3,040   Capacity: 3,040

MAY 25, 1975

Seattle, Washington
Paramount Northwest Theatre
Opening Act: Rush
Capacity: 2,976

MAY 26, 1975

Portland, Oregon
Paramount Northwest Theatre
Opening Act: Rush
Capacity: 3,040

MAY 27, 1975

Spokane, Washington
Spokane Coliseum
Opening Act: Rush
Attendance: 4,000   Capacity: 8,500
Promoters: Double Tee Center Stage, Get Down
    Productions

MAY 29, 1975
(TWO SHOWS: 8:00 P.M., 2:00 A.M.)

Las Vegas, Nevada
Space Center @ Sahara
Opening Act: Rush
Capacity: 4,200
Promoters: Pacific Presentations, Gary Naseef

■ Jefferson Starship was originally scheduled to be on the bill, which was officially dubbed "Glitter Night on the Strip." The band did not perform at either show.

Gene accidentally singed his hair during the 2 A.M. concert.

MAY 30, 1975
Sacramento, California
Memorial Auditorium
Opening Acts: Rush, The Tubes
Promoter: Bill Graham Presents

MAY 30, 1975
Los Angeles, California
Shrine Auditorium
Opening Acts: Nazareth, Rush
Capacity: 6,500
Promoter: Fun Productions

MAY 31, 1975
Long Beach, California
Long Beach Arena
Opening Act: James Gang
Attendance: 7,000
Promoter: Pacific Presentations
Archived: Audio

■ SET LIST

Deuce
Strutter
Got to Choose
Hotter Than Hell
Firehouse
She
Ace Frehley Guitar Solo
C'mon and Love Me
Rock Bottom
Nothin' to Lose
Gene Simmons Bass Solo
100,000 Years
Peter Criss Drum Solo - reprise
Black Diamond
Cold Gin
Rock and Roll All Nite
Let Me Go, Rock 'n Roll

■ Leo Sayer was scheduled to appear initially, but he did not perform. Attendance was near capacity, though seating in the arena was scaled back.

Ace wrote in a May 31 letter: "I'm staying on the Queen Mary, it's really nice, everything is done in art deco. When I look out of the porthole I can see the arena we're playing at tonight, here in Long Beach. The James Gang are opening up the show, it should be really hot!

"Last night, Neil had a big party for us at his house. Gui and Joyce were there. Neil showed the new Monty Python movie, I couldn't stop laughing. Tonight the guy from Gibson is coming and giving us more guitars. I own seven guitars now, not bad for a poor kid from the Bronx."

This gig marks the first known appearance of JR Smalling's legendary intro: "You wanted the best, you got the best, the hottest band in the land . . . KISS!" Prior to this, the band had used various introductions to open their gigs; the most consistently used was: "Are you ready to rock? Are you ready to roll? Then put your two lips together and KISS!"

JR Smalling explains the surprisingly simple origin of the famous intro: "That was mine and I'm proud to say so. At the time, I was changing up the intro a little bit each night trying to find the right one for the band. One day, I was sitting at a hotel somewhere watching TV and this famous commercial for Toyota came on: 'You ask for it, you got it, Toyota.' I thought that was catchy, so I modified it a little and used it. And that's where the intro came from."

JUNE 1, 1975
San Francisco, California
Winterland
Opening Acts: Rush, The Tubes
Attendance: 2,200   Capacity: 5,400
Promoter: Bill Graham Presents

■ Once again, KISS's performance was archived in-house by Bill Graham Presents. Sadly, the same fire that claimed the June 1, 1974 tape destroyed this master tape. The loss is especially painful because it's likely the set featured one or both of the infrequently performed "Rock Bottom" and "Room Service."

Rick Munroe: "When we got to Winterland, the opening act was already set up on stage and rehearsing. 'What the hell is this?' we thought, 'An opening act on stage before the headliner?' I remember us doing our New York thing, getting brash, vocal, and walking right out into the middle of the stage, and all of us going 'What the fuck is going on out here?' Just then, Bill Graham came out on stage and he let us have it: 'This is my house. This is my stage. This is my group. You are going to be doing what I tell you to do, when I tell you to do it. Now, get the hell off the stage!' We all looked at each other, 'Well that's never happened to us before.' The band was the Tubes. Bill Graham used the sold-out KISS concert to showcase the Tubes. So we were stuck with them on stage and we had to build around them, even though we were the headliner."

JUNE 4, 1975   CANCELED
Salt Lake City, Utah
Terrace Ballroom
Opening Act: Rush
Promoter: United Concerts

JUNE 6, 1975
Fresno, California
Warnors Theatre @ Warnors Center for the Performing Arts
Opening Act: Rush
Capacity: 2,100
Promoter: Get Down Productions

JUNE 7, 1975
San Diego, California
Civic Theatre
Opening Act: Rush
Attendance: 1,600   Capacity: 3,000

■ The final gig (until November) with longtime opener Rush was a memorable one.

JR Smalling: "We ambushed them with shaving cream pies. Back in those days, bands developed a vibe together a little bit more than they do now. You try that these days and you'll get shot. We always did something screwy on the last night of any tour. That night was our last gig with them, and during their last song we pied them. Of course, then we had to clean the shit up, but it was fun."

Rick Munroe: "It started with our crew wanting to get their crew. Then KISS found out about it and said: 'Hell, we'll go out and cream the band.' It was a pretty well-organized sneak-attack to the point where the front-of-house people only saw the pies a split second before it hit them. We had people come out behind them to get them there. Rush retaliated by dancing around on stage during KISS's set dressed up in Indian costumes and war paint."

JUNE 11, 1975   CANCELED
Denver, Colorado
Denver Coliseum
Opening Act: Rush
Promoter: Feyline Presents

JUNE 13, 1975
Tulsa, Oklahoma
Tulsa Fairgrounds Pavilion
Headlining Act: Rare Earth
Opening Act: Point Blank
Promoter: Stone City Attractions
Archived: Audio

■ SET LIST

Deuce
Strutter
Got to Choose
Hotter Than Hell
Firehouse
She
Ace Frehley Guitar Solo
C'mon and Love Me
Gene Simmons Bass Solo
100,000 Years
Peter Criss Drum Solo - reprise
Black Diamond
Cold Gin
Rock and Roll All Nite

■ KISS was paid a flat $3,500 for a 60-minute performance. This concert was initially going to be held in the Tulsa Assembly Center but wound up at the Tulsa Fairgrounds Pavilion.

JUNE 14, 1975
Austin, Texas
City Coliseum
Opening Act: REO Speedwagon

JUNE 15, 1975
Corpus Christi, Texas
Memorial Coliseum
Headlining Act: Rare Earth
Attendance: 4,500   Capacity: 5,990
Promoter: Stone City Attractions

■ Despite being billed second, KISS performed after Rare Earth.

JUNE 18, 1975
Jackson, Michigan
Sports Arena
Opening Acts: Salem Witchcraft, ASTIGAFA
Promoters: Steve Glantz Productions, Paul Stanley Productions

■ ASTIGAFA, an acronym for "A Splendid Time Is GuAranteed For All," featured singer/songwriter Marshall Crenshaw.

JUNE 20, 1975
Salem (Roanoke), Virginia
Salem-Roanoke County Civic Center
Opening Act: Montrose
Attendance: 1,801   Capacity: 7,500
Promoter: Entam Ltd.

JUNE 21, 1975
Cleveland, Ohio
Music Hall
Opening Act: Journey
Capacity: 3,631
Promoter: Belkin Productions
Archived: Audio

■ PARTIAL SET LIST

Hotter Than Hell
Firehouse
Black Diamond

An interesting shot of the band with Peter, Ace, and Gene in their Dressed to Kill Tour outfits, and Paul still in his Hotter Than Hell Tour costume.

Let Me Know
Rock and Roll All Nite
■ This show was recorded for the *Alive!* album. It was originally scheduled to be two shows at the Allen Theatre but was consolidated to a single concert at the Music Hall.

The partial set list comes from an abbreviated tape of this show. Two additional pieces of the set list, "C'mon And Love Me" and "She" are mentioned in *Scene* magazine's review of the concert.

Neil Schon of Journey: "It was interesting just watching them, that whole thing. They were really great guys. Gene Simmons really fucked my head up when I saw him blowing fire for the first time."

JUNE 22, 1975

Charleston, West Virginia
Charleston Civic Center
Opening Acts: Montrose, Journey
Capacity: 8,348
Promoter: Entam Ltd.
■ The review in *The Charleston Gazette* mentions that "Hotter Than Hell," "She," "Nothin' To Lose," and "C'mon And Love Me" were all included in the set list.

JUNE 23, 1975 · TEMP HOLD DATE

Winston-Salem, North Carolina
Memorial Coliseum

JUNE 25, 1975

Asbury Park, New Jersey
Convention Hall
Opening Act: Skyscraper
Capacity: 3,800
Promoter: John Scher Presents

JUNE 27, 1975

Asheville, North Carolina
Asheville Civic Center
Opening Act: Montrose
Attendance: 3,150   Capacity: 7,654
Promoter: Kaleidoscope Productions

JUNE 28, 1975

Greenville, South Carolina
Greenville Memorial Auditorium
Opening Act: Montrose
Attendance: 10,220   Capacity: 10,220
Promoters: Kaleidoscope Productions, Beach Club Promotions

JUNE 29, 1975

Atlanta, Georgia · TEMP HOLD DATE
Promoter: Alex Cooley Presents

JULY 1, 1975

Port Chester, New York
Capitol Theatre
Opening Act: Stu Daye
Promoter: In-house
■ According to JR Smalling's 1975 dayplanner, this show was scheduled to be taped. It cannot be confirmed whether the date was supposed to be recorded for the *Alive!* album, but the taping apparently did not take place.

JULY 5, 1975

Tampa, Florida
Florida State Fairgrounds
Headlining Acts: ZZ Top, Johnny Winter, Marshall Tucker Band, Ozark Mountain Daredevils, War
Opening Acts: Pure Prairie League, Atlanta Rhythm Section, + local acts
Attendance: 40,000+
Promoters: Sid Clark Promotions, Marquee Promotions
■ The event was billed as the "Florida Jam." the *Tampa Tribune* reported: "Local talent will perform until noon, and a special female security force will protect the stars." The show ran until midnight.

JR Smalling: "KISS had a tentative stage time of 1–2 P.M. Obviously, KISS stuck out like a sore thumb, as the other acts were more country or southern rock; Ozark Mountain Daredevils and Atlanta Rhythm Section, those names pretty much speak for themselves."

The band flew into Tampa from New York early on the morning of the gig, and returned to New York in the late afternoon that same day.

Mick Campise: "There was a time in the early days where we were off the road, and we came home for about a week. Paul's parents were out of town, so I stayed with him. It was just he and I staying there being two kids, listening to records. It was strange walking down the street with him and having kids in the neighborhood call him by his real name, 'Hey, Stanley, how's it going?' Never knowing that he was in KISS, never knowing what was going on.

"There was a drug store about a block from Paul's house that had a magazine rack. And we walked in, and there was an old Jewish guy behind the counter, who said, 'Oh, hi Stanley! Do you still have your combo?' As we're going by, there is a *Circus* magazine with KISS on the cover with a big spread, and there were little kids there about 12 years old just going crazy over KISS. Paul and I were standing right behind

them and I knew, I *knew* it was killing Paul not to say 'That's me!' It was like being friends with Clark Kent.

"We ended up going back to the house, boiled some lobsters, and just kicked back all night listening to music, just hanging out. I have fond memories of little things like that, when they were themselves, when they weren't KISS."

JULY 15, 1975 · TEMP HOLD DATE

Cleveland, Ohio
Music Hall
Opening Act: Journey
■ This date appeared on one KISS itinerary, though it was never advertised. It may have been placed on the schedule to record additional material for *Alive!*

JULY 20, 1975 (TWO SHOWS)

Davenport, Iowa
RKO Orpheum Theatre
Opening Act: Journey
Attendance: 4,673 (combined)   Capacity: 2,803
Promotions: Windy City Productions
Archived: Audio
■ Both shows were recorded for the *Alive!* album. During "Let Me Go, Rock 'n Roll" at one of the shows, Gene yelled "C'mon Quad City!" This ended up appearing on the record, and is the only direct reference to a city on the entire album.

JULY 23, 1975

Wildwood, New Jersey
Wildwoods Convention Center
Opening Act: Mushroom
Capacity: 2,200
Promoter: Phil Cohen & Earth Productions
Archived: Audio

■ SET LIST

Deuce
Strutter
Got to Choose
Hotter Than Hell
[Firehouse]
She
Ace Frehley Guitar Solo
Nothin' to Lose
C'mon and Love Me
Gene Simmons Bass Solo
100,000 Years
Peter Criss Drum Solo - reprise
Parasite
[Black Diamond]
Cold Gin
[Rock and Roll All Nite]
Let Me Go, Rock 'n Roll
■ This was the fifth and final show recorded for *Alive!*

AUGUST 2, 1975

Baltimore, Maryland
Baltimore Civic Center
Headlining Act: Black Sabbath
Promoter: JH Productions
■ KISS was added to the bill when the original opening act, Brian Auger's Oblivion Express, canceled.

AUGUST 8, 1975 · POSTPONED

Syracuse, New York
Onondaga County War Memorial
Steve Glantz Productions

■ An ad for this show listing KISS with "Special Guests" appeared in the *Syracuse Herald-Journal*. For reasons unknown, this gig was postponed until October 2.

AUGUST 8, 1975

Providence, Rhode Island
Providence Civic Center
Headlining Act: Black Sabbath
Attendance: 12,500   Capacity: 12,500
Promoter: Concerts East
Archived: Audio
■ **SET LIST**
Deuce
Strutter
Hotter Than Hell
Firehouse
She
Ace Frehley Guitar Solo
C'mon and Love Me
Gene Simmons Bass Solo
100,000 Years
Peter Criss Drum Solo - reprise
Black Diamond
Cold Gin
Rock and Roll All Nite

AUGUST 9, 1975

Albany, New York
Palace Theatre
Capacity: 2,807
Promoter: Steve Glantz Productions
■ The opening act for this show is unknown.

AUGUST 14, 1975

Boston, Massachusetts
Orpheum Theatre
Headlining Act: Black Sabbath
Capacity: 2,868
Promoter: Don Law Presents

AUGUST 15, 1975

Saginaw, Michigan
Wendler Arena @ Saginaw Civic Center

Opening Act: The Flock
Attendance: 7,200   Capacity: 7,200
Promoter: Steve Glantz Productions
■ This show marked the first advance sellout in the venue's history.

AUGUST 16, 1975

Muskegon, Michigan
L.C. Walker Arena
Opening Act: The Flock

AUGUST 17, 1975

Pekin, Illinois
Pekin Community High School (East Campus) Stadium
Opening Acts: REO Speedwagon, Ted Nugent,
   Smokehouse
Attendance: 10,000   Capacity: 10,000
Promoter: Lenny Trumper
■ The show, which started in the afternoon and was scheduled to end at dusk, ran late, and the only lights available for KISS were two follow-spots, which were opened-up to canvas as much of the stage as possible. After this show, residents voted to ban rock concerts.

AUGUST 23, 1975

Hempstead, New York
Calderone Concert Hall
Opening Act: The Flock
Attendance: 2,435   Capacity: 2,435
Promoter: Phil Basile of Concerts East
Archived: Audio
■ **SET LIST**
Deuce
Strutter
Got to Choose
Hotter Than Hell
Firehouse
She
Ace Frehley Guitar Solo
Nothin' to Lose
C'mon and Love Me
Gene Simmons Bass Solo
100,000 Years

Peter Criss Drum Solo - reprise
Black Diamond
Cold Gin
Rock and Roll All Nite
Let Me Go, Rock 'n Roll

AUGUST 24, 1975

Hazelton, Pennsylvania
Harmon Geist Stadium
Opening Act: REO Speedwagon
■ This was listed on several *Performance* itineraries, including one as late as August 23, but the gig never transpired.

AUGUST 25, 1975

Harrisburg, Pennsylvania
State Farm Arena
Opening Act: REO Speedwagon
Promoter: East Coast Concerts

AUGUST 27, 1975

Owensboro, Kentucky
Sportscenter
Opening Act: Hydra
Attendance: 2,744   Capacity: 5,648
Promoter: Steve Glantz Productions
■ The venue's ceiling was scorched by pyro; KISS was summarily banned from the venue.

AUGUST 28, 1975

Indianapolis, Indiana
Indianapolis Convention Center
Headlining Act: Uriah Heep
Opening Act: Atlanta Rhythm Section
Attendance: 13,000   Capacity: 13,000
Promoter: Windy City Productions

AUGUST 30, 1975

Laurel (Washington, D.C.), Maryland
■ The show was listed on several *Performance* itineraries, but it never took place.

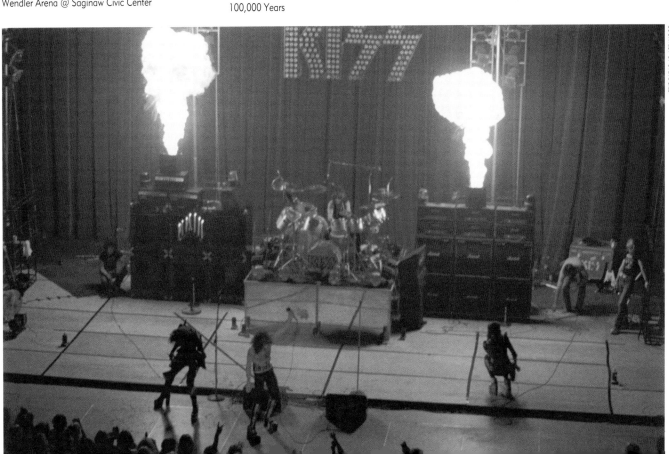

CHAPTER 6

ALIVE! TOUR

Number of Shows: 87
Start Date: September 10, 1975 - Chattanooga, Tennessee
End Date: March 28, 1976 - Springfield, Massachusetts
Countries: Canada, U.S.A.
Headlining Act: Black Sabbath
Opening Acts: .38 Special; Albatross; Artful Dodger; Atlanta Rhythm Section; Back Street Crawler; Black Sheep; Blue Öyster Cult; Bob Seger & the Silver Bullet Band; Booga Booga; Boz Scaggs; Brownsville Station; Diamond Reo; The Dixie Dregs; Double Yellow Line; Electromagnets; Fallen Angel; Gary Wright; Hammerhead; Harvest; Hot Lucy; Hydra; James Montgomery Band; (Lakeland String Quartet); The Leslie West Band; Little Feat; Montrose; Mott; Mountain Smoke; Point Blank; REO Speedwagon; Rockets; Rory Gallagher; Rush; Savoy Brown; Slade; Styx; Target; Thee Image

Average Attendance: 7,292

Originally planned as three sides of live material with new studio cuts on the fourth side, the *Alive!* album would take KISS to the next level of its career and turn a huge profit for Casablanca.

The initial producer targeted for the project, Ronnie Dean, declined the invitation that Eddie Kramer ultimately accepted. Kramer, in fact, passed up the opportunity to do Boston's debut album to work on *Alive!* Unfortunately, much of the live material recorded for the album was deemed useless, and the album had to be redone from top to bottom in the studio. Kramer himself admits, "The first live album was all overdubbed at Electric Lady. Only the drums were kept from the original live recordings; virtually everything else was replaced." JR Smalling continues, "I recall specifically that the explosion at the very top of the show did not record well live. I remember Eddie hunting for a sample of an explosion and dubbing it over the live explosion."

Using the ample time between the scattered gigs at the end of the Dressed to Kill Tour, KISS did the overdubs for *Alive!* at Electric Lady Studios. Most of the work was completed by August 7, 1975.

In the midst of this, the troubling royalty issue between Casablanca and Rock Steady Productions came to a head. Casablanca had consistently failed to pay KISS the royalties due them, which forced Bill Aucoin to notify Casablanca that Rock Steady wished to terminate the production agreement signed on November 1, 1973. "Eventually, when we didn't get any royalty payments, I had to stand up for the band," Aucoin recounts. "That turned into a major fight, and I could have easily left Casablanca. But, truth be known, I loved Neil and Casablanca, and Neil Bogart was the only person crazy enough to buy into all the nutty things we came up with; you really needed that kind of flamboyant person who shared your enthusiasm."

Despite dealing with the tension involving royalties, Aucoin's gift for shrewd marketing was not dulled. Two incidents in particular were opportunistic strokes of marketing genius. The first was the band's historic October 9 and 10 event in the tiny town of Cadillac, Michigan. The other was turning an overzealous group of Terre Haute KISS fans into the KISS ARMY.

Once again, the transition from shows of one tour into those of the next occurred with little fanfare. The costumes showed the least amount of change, though both Paul and Ace occasionally wore different boots, and Paul and Gene frequently mixed and matched various belts with their costumes.

For the first time in its career, KISS began to use the same set list night after night. The band went so far as to include the set list in their first tourbook, which debuted in January 1976. While KISS would continue to focus on promoting

KIT LUCE/THE TENNESSEAN

Alive!, two songs from the fourth studio album, *Destroyer*, were integrated into the show before the tour concluded, first "Shout it Out Loud" and then "Flaming Youth."

Alive! was certified Gold by the R.I.A.A. on December 4, 1975, and the album surpassed the 1-million-sold mark the following month. It was a first for KISS: an album was impacting their concerts, and not vice versa. The crowds on the Alive! Tour grew rapidly, and the band frequently established house records for their appearances. KISS's success was ballooning so quickly that a European tour, at first scheduled for fall 1975, was pushed back to spring 1976 so that the band could capitalize on *Alive!*'s success in the U.S. In fact, since Casablanca did not have distribution set up in all European territories, in most countries *Alive!* was not released until after *Destroyer*.

No matter, in the U.S., KISS's drawing power was growing exponentially; in November the band played before what is one of the largest crowds to ever see a rock concert in an arena when it drew nearly 22,000 to the Capital Centre outside of Washington, D.C. Aucoin's insistence that KISS take every opportunity to capture the public's eye was succeeding; the band had seeped into the public's consciousness, and they would soon become a part of American pop culture.

SEPTEMBER 10, 1975

Chattanooga, Tennessee
Soldiers and Sailors Memorial Auditorium
Opening Act: Slade
Attendance: 1,818   Capacity: 5,000
Promoters: Sound 70 Concerts, Entam Ltd.

SEPTEMBER 11, 1975

Knoxville, Tennessee
Knoxville Civic Coliseum
Opening Acts: Slade, Gary Wright
Attendance: 4,540   Capacity: 6,500
Promoters: Belkin Productions, Entam Ltd.

SEPTEMBER 12, 1975

Greensboro, North Carolina
Greensboro Coliseum
Opening Acts: Slade, Gary Wright
Attendance: 3,813   Capacity: 5,000
Promoters: Belkin Productions, Entam Ltd.

SEPTEMBER 13, 1975

Norfolk, Virginia
The Scope
Opening Acts: Slade, Gary Wright
Attendance: 2,727   Capacity: 5,000
Promoters: Belkin Productions, Entam Ltd.

SEPTEMBER 14, 1975

Wilkes-Barre, Pennsylvania
King's College Gymnasium
Opening Act: Diamond Reo
Attendance: 2,300   Capacity 3,000
Promoter: Fang Productions

SEPTEMBER 21, 1975   CANCELED

Mt. Vernon, New York
Memorial Field
Opening Acts: Fallen Angel, Frank Morgan, Brian
   Auger's Oblivion Express
Promoter: Concert Promotions Int'l
■ Advertisements for the show's cancellation appeared in several industry publications during the week prior to the gig. No reason for the cancellation was given.

OCTOBER 2, 1975

Syracuse, New York
Onondaga County War Memorial
Opening Act: James Montgomery Band
Capacity: 8,300
Promoter: Steve Glantz Productions
■ This concert was originally scheduled for August 8.

OCTOBER 3, 1975

Upper Darby (Philadelphia), Pennsylvania
Tower Theater
Opening Act: Fallen Angel
Attendance: 3,000   Capacity: 3,000
Promoter: Midnight Sun Concerts
■ The back of Paul's spandex jumpsuit was ripped open by a fan in the front row.

JR Smalling: "One time we were playing a gig in Pennsylvania, and we had a bit of a mishap with the confetti guns. The guns are designed to be loaded with confetti at one end of the barrel with lightweight tape masked over the opening. The tape allows the air pressure to build up enough to blast the confetti out of the barrel when you trigger the effect, but it isn't strong enough to totally contain it. Whoever set up one of the guns that night had overtaped it, and when we triggered the guns at the end of the show, the tape held. The guns were fastened to the top of the P.A. horns, which were sitting on the front of the stage. When the tape held, the air pressure had nowhere to go, and the entire gun and horn flew off the P.A. stack and into the front row of the audience. It hit some poor girl right in the head. I jumped into the audience, picked her up and took her backstage to get some medical attention. I don't know what ended up happening to her, but since we never heard anything about a lawsuit, I guess she was OK."

Opening act Fallen Angel was an early version of Starz.

OCTOBER 4, 1975
(TWO SHOWS: 8:00 P.M., 11:30 P.M.)

Passaic, New Jersey
Capitol Theatre
Opening Act: Savoy Brown
Attendance: (1) 3,397; (2) 3,397   Capacity: 3,397
Promoter: John Scher Presents

OCTOBER 5, 1975

Henrietta (Rochester), New York
The Dome Center
Opening Act: Black Sheep
Attendance: 5,600   Capacity: 5,600
Promoters: Concerts East, Steve Glantz Productions
■ Black Sheep was vocalist Lou Gramm's band prior to Foreigner.

OCTOBER 6, 1975

Allentown, Pennsylvania
Memorial Hall
Opening Act: REO Speedwagon
Attendance: 4,400   Capacity: 4,510
Promoter: DiCesare-Engler Productions

OCTOBER 7, 1975

Kalamazoo, Michigan
Herbert Reed Field House
Opening Acts: Styx, Hammerhead
Capacity: 10,900

OCTOBER 9, 1975

Cadillac, Michigan
Cadillac High School Auditorium
Opening Act: Double Yellow Line
Attendance: 2,000   Capacity: 2,000
Promoter: Steve Glantz Productions
■ This event may have been the shining example of expert marketing and PR by Bill Aucoin. KISS's appearance at Cadillac was anything but an impromptu decision. The groundwork had been laid in early summer 1974 when Aucoin and KISS began looking for suitable opportunities to stage an event. High schools were targeted in particular for the natural audience the student body would provide.

Then, in September 1974, Aucoin received a letter from Jim Neff, the assistant coach of the Cadillac High School football team. The team had become very successful as a result, he felt, of their interest in KISS's music, which he used to motivate the team at practices, even going so far as to incorporate KISS song titles into the names of various plays. Neff himself had seen firsthand what KISS could do to a crowd when he attended their June 1974 concert in Flint, so he contacted Aucoin in the hopes of scheduling a concert at Cadillac High. Nothing was arranged that autumn, but over the course of the next year the idea was developed greatly via correspondence between Neff and Alan Miller, director of promotion for Rock Steady. Alan was responsible for turning KISS's Cadillac appearance into a very memorable event by convincing several press members and photographers to travel (on KISS's dime) to the small Michigan town. This ultimately gave the public the impression that KISS's popularity was greater than it actually was. After all, you didn't see The Who or Led Zeppelin being invited to a breakfast with town officials or having Main Street renamed after them. And so, in the fall of 1975, KISS appeared at the Cadillac High homecoming.

Rick Munroe: "The Cadillac show was nothing like we'd ever done before. We couldn't fit everything in there that we needed for our show; we couldn't even put our sign in there. Someone from the school told us that the kids were making signs, so we said we'd take the best one and put it behind the drum kit. We covered the back wall with the banners that the kids had made.

"All these little kids showed up for sound check because any kid in KISS makeup could come see the sound check for free. The whole time the band was there was like one long public appearance, so they were in costume the whole time."

Mick Campise: "I remember Peter and Gene were at it that day, and it was always fun when those two would go head-to-head. During the show, Peter got behind the drums, decided he was going to mess with Gene a little, and started playing everything double-time. I thought Gene was going to kill him. Gene turned around and yelled at me: 'Tell him to get on the count.' Peter said: 'Well . . . I'll show that motherfucker!' and he sped up the count even more. The kids loved it, but afterwards JR had to pull them apart backstage."

The concert turned into a two-day event, complete with a parade, the presentation of the key to the city, the concert itself, and a large breakfast banquet on October 10 featuring mem-

bers of Cadillac's political establishment in full KISS makeup.

Filmmaker Lamarr Scott documented the second day of the event. He recalls, "At the behest of a couple of friends who knew I worked at a TV station and had access to a camera, we drove up to Cadillac. When we got there that Friday night, it was like we had landed on another planet. Everybody we saw on the street was dressed up in KISS makeup. The people in McDonalds and the people behind the counter had KISS makeup on. We could've shot the concert, but we got a late start and didn't get into town until the concert was over. We got live sound of the press conference, and we shot footage of the parade as well as the band leaving.

"The whole program, once we put it together, was about a half-hour. It actually aired on WUCF-TV, Channel 19. It aired within a week or two after the shoot to an audience that was unaware who they [the band] were and what was going on. It wasn't until years later that those people actually realized, even me, what we had done."

OCTOBER 11, 1975

Columbus, Ohio
Veterans Memorial Auditorium
Opening Act: Black Sheep
Capacity: 3,898
Promoter: Steve Glantz Productions
■ This concert was originally scheduled for October 12.

OCTOBER 19, 1975

Orlando, Florida
Orlando Sports Stadium
Opening Acts: Bob Seger & the Silver Bullet Band,
    Atlanta Rhythm Section
Capacity: 7,000
Promoter: Steve Glantz Productions

OCTOBER 20, 1975

St. Petersburg, Florida
Bayfront Center Arena
Opening Acts: Bob Seger & the Silver Bullet Band,
    Atlanta Rhythm Section
Capacity: 8,355
Promoter: Steve Glantz Productions
■ Rick Munroe: "I remember playing Tampa with Bob Seger. After Seger's set, Campise

looked at me and said: 'This guy just blew us off the stage.' And this was when absolutely no one could touch us."

OCTOBER 21, 1975

Mobile, Alabama   TEMP HOLD DATE
Expo Hall @ Mobile Municipal Auditorium
Opening Act: Bob Seger & the Silver Bullet Band

OCTOBER 22, 1975

Birmingham, Alabama
Municipal Auditorium
Opening Acts: Bob Seger & the Silver Bullet Band,
    Atlanta Rhythm Section
Promoter: Steve Glantz Productions

OCTOBER 26, 1975

Montgomery, Alabama
Garrett Coliseum
Opening Act: Harvest
Attendance: 1,857   Capacity: 6,000
Promoter: Good Times Productions
■ This show, which started at 2 P.M., is incorrectly listed as October 25 on KISS's itineraries. Opening act Harvest featured future Styx guitarist Tommy Shaw.

Tommy Shaw: "It was a huge gig for us, and Gene Simmons could not have been nicer to me. We were singing during our sound check and I didn't understand the hierarchy of all these things; a lot of times it is just not physically possible with all the load-in and set-up challenges to give a little no-name opening act a sound check. I didn't know any better, and I asked Gene about it. He walked me around the venue, and we were talking about all sorts of stuff; he was a total gentleman, and I still give him shit about it today: tough old Gene Simmons being a nice guy to a little nobody from Montgomery."

OCTOBER 30, 1975

Nashville, Tennessee
Nashville Municipal Auditorium
Opening Acts: Bob Seger & the Silver Bullet Band,
    Montrose
Attendance: 5,100   Capacity: 8,000
Promoter: Sound 70 Concerts

NOVEMBER 1, 1975

St. Louis, Missouri
Kiel Auditorium
Opening Act: Atlanta Rhythm Section
Attendance: 10,154   Capacity: 10,154
Promoter: Panther Productions

NOVEMBER 3, 1975

La Crosse, Wisconsin
Mary E. Sawyer Auditorium
Opening Act: Brownsville Station
Attendance: 3,187   Capacity: 4,100
Promoter: Daydream Productions

NOVEMBER 6, 1975

San Antonio, Texas
Municipal Auditorium
Opening Act: Mott
■ Rick Munroe: "In San Antonio, they had this venue that was famous for its terrible power supply. We called it Brown Out Arena. Sure enough, during the opening act the place browned out and fried the power supply. Hot Sam [Jay Barth] said, 'We don't have a show here, fellas.' I think all the amps had enough protection on them where it didn't affect them, but the board did not. We

thought, 'Where are we going to get the power to do this?'"

Jay Barth: "I had to steal the batteries out of the limousines to make the mixing console work. The power supply had gone out and I needed plus or minus 12 volts. If you take two car batteries and tie the minuses together, you've got your plus or minus 12 volts. So we hooked them up with C-clamps and vice-grips and, with just those two batteries, we actually made it through the show. The band was pissed when they couldn't leave right away because I had to get the batteries back to the limos, so they had to wait a few minutes. That was an adventure."

NOVEMBER 7, 1975

Beaumont, Texas
McDonald Gym @ Lamar University
Opening Act: Mott
Attendance: 3,000
Promoter: Redman Productions

■ This had all the earmarks of another thankless gig: a small school gymnasium in the B-market backwater of East Texas. Then, just prior to the show, word that *Alive!* had gone Gold reached the band: KISS had finally broken through and Casablanca had its ticket out of bankruptcy. The album would be officially certified Gold by the Recording Industry Association of America (R.I.A.A.) in December.

NOVEMBER 8, 1975

Arlington (Dallas), Texas
Texas Hall @ University of Texas-Arlington
Opening Act: Mott
Capacity: 2,800
Promoter: Concerts West

■ *Performance* magazine observed in its review of the November 8 show, "It is obvious now that they are no longer merely a regionally successful band but are in actuality a national phenomena."

NOVEMBER 9, 1975

Houston, Texas
Sam Houston Coliseum
Opening Act: Mott
Promoter: Concerts West

NOVEMBER 12, 1975

Toledo, Ohio
Sports Arena
Opening Act: Styx
Attendance: 7,500   Capacity: 7,500
Promoter: Steve Glantz Productions

■ *The Toledo Blade* reported that 13 people were arrested among the 200–300 persons who could not get inside.

NOVEMBER 15, 1975

Rockford, Illinois
National Guard Armory-Rockford
Opening Act: Rush
Attendance: 3,610   Capacity: 3,610
Promoter: Windy City Productions
Archived: Audio

■ SET LIST
Deuce
Strutter
Got to Choose
Hotter Than Hell
Firehouse
She
Ace Frehley Guitar Solo
Ladies in Waiting

Nothin' to Lose
Gene Simmons Bass Solo
100,000 Years
Peter Criss Drum Solo - reprise
Black Diamond
Cold Gin
Rock and Roll All Nite

■ The local fire marshal prohibited the use of all pyro at the show, including Gene's fire-breathing. For unknown reasons, KISS did not perform the usual final encore, "Let Me Go, Rock 'n Roll," at this show.

NOVEMBER 16, 1975

Flint, Michigan
I.M.A. Sports Arena
Opening Act: Mott
Attendance: 5,300   Capacity: 5,300
Promoter: Midwest Productions

NOVEMBER 17, 1975

Flint, Michigan
I.M.A. Sports Arena
Opening Act: Rush
Attendance: 5,300   Capacity: 5,300
Promoter: Midwest Productions

NOVEMBER 18, 1975

Port Huron, Michigan
McMorran Place
Opening Act: Rush
Attendance: 3,788   Capacity: 3,788
Promoter: Chris Cole

NOVEMBER 19, 1975

Traverse City, Michigan
Glacier Arena   **KISS CANCELED**
Opening Act: Styx
Attendance: 5,800   Capacity: 5,800
Promoter: Steve Glantz Productions

■ Around 9:15, after Styx's set, a shortage in the transformer forced KISS to cancel its performance. *The Record-Eagle* reported the band sat in the dressing room waiting for two hours and was willing to play without lighting effects if the sound equipment could be put back together. Eventually the show was canceled and tickets were refunded. The 5,800 tickets sold were a house record.

NOVEMBER 21, 1975

Terre Haute, Indiana
Hulman Civic University Center
Opening Act: Rush
Attendance: 10,000   Capacity: 10,000
Promoters: Entam Ltd., Belkin Productions, Sycamore
    Showcase Committee Presentation

■ Although its origins were nearly a year old, the KISS Army was more or less born in November 1975. In January of that year, two Terre Haute teenagers, Jay Evans and Bill Starkey, began to pester their local radio station (WVTS) to play KISS. After being tersely dismissed by the radio station's program director, Rich Dickerson, the two started a campaign. According to Starkey, Evans joked, "We would keep calling them and calling them, saying that we were the army. Yeah, the KISS Army." The two soon began signing their letters to the station, "Bill Starkey— President of the KISS Army," and "Jay Evans— Field Marshall."

By July 1975, there was evidence that the campaign was working as WTVS had begun to

KISS arrives at the airport in Terre Haute, ground zero for the KISS Army.

play KISS and often included a humorous reference to the KISS Army. The publicity resulted in people calling the radio station asking how they could enlist. When the November 21 gig in Terre Haute approached, Starkey and Evans had succeeded in creating such tremendous public interest that KISS's show sold out almost instantly. Starkey received word through WVTS that KISS's management was so impressed that they wanted to use the idea of the KISS Army for the band's national fan club. On November 10, Alan Miller contacted Starkey to discuss the KISS Army. Miller asked Starkey to go on the air to try to recruit as many new members as he could and Starkey and Evans obliged, taking phone calls at WVTS all night long.

Miller even arranged for members from the local U.S. Army base to provide a jeep escort for KISS from the airport to downtown Terre Haute; a "KISS Army meets the U.S. Army" stunt. KISS arrived in a private jet for a parade downtown that ended with the band's appearance as disc jockeys at the same radio station that only a year before had refused to play them.

During the concert, Starkey was brought out on stage before the encores and presented with a plaque from the band.

NOVEMBER 22, 1975

Chicago, Illinois
International Amphitheatre
Opening Acts: The Leslie West Band, Mott, Little Feat
Attendance: 10,140   Capacity: 10,140
Promoter: Windy City Productions

■ Rick Munroe: "Bill Aucoin had called me up to his seat when we were flying somewhere, and he told me that we were going to play Chicago as a headliner. It was going to be our first headlining gig in Chicago other than at a high school, and he wanted to make an impact, but we weren't allowed to use pyro. He wanted me to come up with some lighting effects that could replace pyro.

"That's when I came up with the flashballs effect for '100,000 Years.' I took a four-foot mirror ball, drilled holes in it, installed light sockets in it, and then put flashbulbs in the sockets. I had a company called Triad build the prototype for me. They built two mirror balls with something like 70 or 80 lights. Then, we needed to connect the mirror balls to the stage somehow. We ended up taking five strings of Christmas lights and wrapping them in a clear tube to create one long rope of lights. Paul would grab the end of the rope onstage, and the lights would chase up the lighting rig to the mirror balls.

"In the demonstration, I had the lights chase up to these two balls, and then the balls appeared to explode. Gui saw that and said: 'Build six of them.' So we put two in the front of the house, two in the middle, and two in the back of the house. I had this Frankenstein-type dimmer on my desk, and I would swing the handle from one end to the other to chase the lights up to the ceiling. When it would get to the top, I'd hit the button, and the first two balls would go off.

"It was funny to watch the whole audience follow the lights from Paul on stage up to the ceiling. Then, the flashbulbs would go off, burning everybody's retinas out. The second and third pairs would follow in sequential order.

"I had it built specifically for Chicago, but they liked it so much that we kept it. The Chicago show was also the first time that I used a front [lighting] truss with them. I'd never had a front truss with them. I always had the back and the side. Even when we were headlining, we didn't have any rigging. We had the pneumatic air-trees that went on either side of the stage, and then four of them along the back. I would use spotlights to highlight the guys because I didn't have any front lighting."

NOVEMBER 23, 1975
Evansville, Indiana
Roberts Municipal Stadium
Opening Acts: Rush, Mott
Attendance: 11,200   Capacity: 11,000
Promoter: Tom Duncan
■ KISS broke the Doobie Bros.'s record for attendance at the venue. The show was oversold by 200 tickets.

NOVEMBER 26, 1975
Huntington, West Virginia
Veterans Memorial Field House
Opening Acts: Rush, Mott
Attendance: 9,000   Capacity: 9,000
Promoters: Entam Ltd., Belkin Productions
■ For the second consecutive night, KISS broke the Doobie Bros.'s house attendance record.

NOVEMBER 27, 1975
Fayetteville, North Carolina
Cumberland County Memorial Arena
Opening Acts: Mott, Styx
Attendance: 7,000   Capacity: 7,000
Promoter: Kaleidoscope Productions

NOVEMBER 28, 1975
Asheville, North Carolina
Asheville Civic Center
Opening Acts: Mott, Styx
Attendance: 3,488   Capacity: 7,654
Promoter: Kaleidoscope Productions

NOVEMBER 29, 1975
Charlotte, North Carolina
Charlotte Park Center Auditorium
Opening Acts: Mott, Styx
Attendance: 3,000   Capacity: 3,000
Promoter: Kaleidoscope Productions

NOVEMBER 30, 1975
Greenville, South Carolina   TEMP HOLD DATE
Greenville Memorial Auditorium
Opening Acts: Mott, Styx
Promoter: Kaleidoscope Productions

NOVEMBER 30, 1975
Landover (Washington, D.C.), Maryland
Capital Centre
Opening Acts: Mott, Styx
Attendance: 21,897   Capacity: 21,897
Promoter: Cellar Door Concerts
Archived: Partial Video
■ **PARTIAL SET LIST**
Cold Gin
Rock and Roll All Nite
Let Me Go, Rock 'n Roll
■ KISS set the house record for attendance, breaking the mark set by the Rolling Stones. The record stands to this day.

DECEMBER 2, 1975
Columbus, Georgia
Columbus Municipal Auditorium
Opening Act: Styx
Promoter: Entam Ltd.

DECEMBER 3, 1975
Dothan, Alabama
Dothan Civic Center
Opening Act: Styx
Capacity: 3,100
Promoter: Belkin Productions

DECEMBER 5, 1975
Atlanta, Georgia
The Omni
Opening Acts: Styx, The Leslie West Band
Promoter: Alex Cooley Presents
■ The show was originally advertised for the Fox Theatre.

DECEMBER 6, 1975
Jacksonville, Florida
Jacksonville Veterans Memorial Coliseum
Opening Acts: Styx, The Dixie Dregs
Capacity: 10,228
Promoter: Jet Set Enterprises

DECEMBER 12, 1975
Syracuse, New York
Onondaga County War Memorial
Headlining Act: Black Sabbath
Attendance: 7,000   Capacity: 8,300
Promoter: Concerts East
■ This gig marked the last time KISS would open a show for anyone until August 20, 1988.

DECEMBER 14, 1975
Boston, Massachusetts
Orpheum Theatre
Opening Act: Black Sheep
Attendance: 1,700   Capacity: 2,868
Promoter Don Law Presents
■ Then-monitor-mixer, Fritz Postlethwaite: "When I first started, they didn't know me very well and I didn't know them very well, but I worked very hard for them and I think they appreciated and understood that. The previous monitor mixer had warned me that Gene would spit at you when he couldn't hear his monitors. He'll tell you the story of how it's part of the show, and he's all wrapped up in his persona, and he doesn't know what he's doing, etc. Gene was an amazing spitter; he could spit 30 or 40

feet and hit a three-inch target. Just incredible. One night, somewhere up in New England, it happened; he got some feedback on his mike, and he was upset about it. The lights had gone to dark, when I heard this sound near me and I looked down and there was this big hocker on the ground. I got through the rest of the show, but after the show was over I was backstage when Paul came up to me as he was taking his makeup off and said, 'How ya doing?'

"And I said: 'Not too good.' Paul asked, 'Why, what's the matter.' I told him: 'Well, Gene has just done some things that I can't live with.' 'Well, why don't you talk to him about it. Let him know how you feel.' 'OK. If you think that will do any good, I will.'

"So he called Gene out, and Gene and I went into a separate dressing room. Gene was in his nine-inch platforms and he's at least 6'3" to begin with, and I'm 5'7" so he was towering over me in this makeup. He asked, 'What's wrong?' I told him, 'You spit at me during the performance, and I wouldn't do that to a dog. I wouldn't treat anyone like that. It's rude, and more importantly, it's absolutely unacceptable.'

"He went into this spiel that I have heard 100 times of how in the throes of a show when you're all worked up, and you don't know what you're doing, and you've got the costume on you become another person, you become a demon and sometimes do things you wouldn't ordinarily do. So, I listened and I listened. When he got done I said, 'Bullshit. For the rest of your life, don't ever spit at me again. If you do, two things are going to happen: 1. I'm going to leave, and that will be the end of it. 2. Just before I leave, I'm going to throw you off the stage, and I will do it.'

"He paused for a second and thought about that, and he looked at me. I continued: 'Gene, understand this very carefully. I don't care how tall you are, I don't care how big you are. I am tenacious, I will find a way to throw you off the stage. If there's six feet to the pit, you're going to get hurt. If there's 30 feet to the pit, you're really going to get hurt. Either way, you're going off the front of the stage. So don't ever spit at me again.'

"And he said, 'OK.' And that was the end of that. He never spit on me or anyone else as far as I know."

DECEMBER 18, 1975
Waterbury, Connecticut
Palace Theatre
Opening Act: Black Sheep
Attendance: 3,100   Capacity: 3,100
Promoter: Cornucopia Productions
Archived: Audio, Super 8mm
■ **SET LIST**
Deuce
Strutter
C'mon and Love Me
Hotter Than Hell
Firehouse
She
Ace Frehley Guitar Solo
Ladies in Waiting
Nothin' to Lose
Gene Simmons Bass Solo
100,000 Years
Peter Criss Drum Solo - reprise

Black Diamond
Cold Gin
■ Gene's hair caught fire again.

Twice during the show, JR Smalling got on the P.A. to tell the crowd to settle down or the gig would be stopped. The show was ended following "Cold Gin" for reasons unknown. While there was a report that a break in a water main nearby forced the evacuation of the crowd, it is more likely that the fire marshal simply pulled the plug because of the unruly audience.

DECEMBER 19, 1975 ~~CANCELED~~
Cherry Hill, New Jersey
The Centrum
Capacity: 8,000
Promoter: Willow Productions
■ Willow Productions fraudulently advertised this show, which was never scheduled to happen as far as KISS was concerned. The promoter did succeed in selling over 6,000 tickets to the show.

DECEMBER 19, 1975
Binghamton, New York
Broome Co. Veterans Memorial Arena
Opening Act: Mott
Capacity: 6,855

DECEMBER 20, 1975
Pittsburgh, Pennsylvania
Civic Arena
Opening Acts: Rush, Mott
Attendance: 15,432   Capacity: 17,000
Promoter: DiCesare-Engler Productions
■ KISS set the house attendance record, breaking the mark held by Elton John.

DECEMBER 21, 1975
Richmond, Virginia
Richmond Coliseum
Opening Acts: Rush, Mott
Capacity: 12,300
Promoter: Belkin Productions
■ Fire extinguishers were accidentally set off immediately prior to KISS taking the stage.

This was the final gig at which Rush and KISS appeared together. "Rush was the perfect opening act for KISS," relates Mick Campise. "The bands and crews had a great rapport, and we had all become very good friends. But Bill Aucoin got rid of them because it got to the point where Rush was just nicking stuff left and right off of KISS. Neil had copped the phaser, and Alex started running around on stage trying to do Paul's moves, just so he wasn't standing still, though it doesn't quite go over the same without the makeup and everything."

DECEMBER 26, 1975 ~~KISS CANCELED~~
Fort Wayne, Indiana
Allen Co. War Memorial Coliseum
Opening Acts: Ted Nugent, Mott
Attendance: 7,000   Capacity: 7,000
Promoter: Sunshine Promotions
■ The show sold out in advance, but was canceled due to a severe snowstorm.

DECEMBER 27, 1975
Louisville, Kentucky
Louisville Gardens
Opening Acts: Styx, Black Sheep
Attendance: 7,200   Capacity: 7,200
Promoter: Sunshine Promotions

■ "Santa Claus" was also listed on the bill. The concert was billed as "The First Annual Holiday Festival."

DECEMBER 28, 1975
South Bend, Indiana
Morris Civic Auditorium
Opening Act: Styx
Attendance: 2,468   Capacity: 2,468
Promoter: JAM Productions

DECEMBER 29, 1975
Providence, Rhode Island
Providence Civic Center
Opening Act: The Leslie West Band
Attendance: 13,200   Capacity: 13,200
Promoter: Frank J. Russo
■ During his performance, Leslie West was hit with an M-80 thrown from the audience.

DECEMBER 31, 1975
Uniondale, New York
Nassau Veterans Memorial Coliseum
Opening Acts: Blue Öyster Cult, The Leslie West Band
Attendance: 13,000   Capacity: 16,688
Promoter: Ron Delsener Presents
■ This was a huge event for KISS, and the first time the band sold out an arena in its home-town. Casablanca had given the band money to improve the production for the show, which KISS spent touching-up the speaker cabinets on the stage backline and on hundreds of balloons for the show's finale.

The guest list for the show was a mile long and included Detroit promoter Steve Glantz, rock journalist Lester Bangs, Steve Coronel, Billy Squier, and others. The band spared no expense and even made arrangements for Bill Starkey and Cadillac High coach Jim Neff to be flown in for the event.

A claim is occasionally made that precisely a year before this show, KISS had been fourth on a bill with BÖC headlining at the Academy of Music. In fact, that concert had taken place two years prior. KISS had risen to astonishing popularity quickly, but not *that* quickly. Another erroneous claim is that an audiotape of this show exists, when in fact the audiotape in question was recorded at KISS's August 23 concert in Hempstead, New York.

Beginning at 2 A.M., an after-show pool party was held at the Excelsior Club on Fifty-seventh Street in Manhattan.

JANUARY 23, 1976
Erie, Pennsylvania
Erie County Fieldhouse
Capacity: 6,000
Promoters: Belkin Productions, Steve Glantz Productions
■ The opening act for this show is unknown.

There were no tech or dress rehearsals done during the three-week break prior to this gig, but the band did gather at Carroll's Music in Manhattan for a three-hour rehearsal on January 22.

JANUARY 25, 1976
Detroit, Michigan
Cobo Arena
Opening Act: Back Street Crawler
Attendance: 12,001   Capacity: 12,001
Promoters: Steve Glantz Productions, Mike Keener Productions
Archived: Video

■ SET LIST
Deuce
Strutter
C'mon and Love Me
Hotter Than Hell
Firehouse
She
Ace Frehley Guitar Solo
Ladies in Waiting
Nothin' to Lose
Gene Simmons Bass Solo
100,000 Years
Peter Criss Drum Solo - reprise
Black Diamond
[Cold Gin]
[Rock and Roll All Nite]
[Let Me Go, Rock 'n Roll]
■ This is the last known performance of "Ladies in Waiting."

Rather than deal with the glut of interview requests, on January 24 the band did a press conference at the Airport Hilton for key members of the Detroit media. No other interviews were granted during the band's three-day stay.

Upon arriving in Detroit on the 25th, Bill Aucoin went straight from the venue to a video suite where he spent the afternoon editing video together for the intro to the evening's show. The video was projected on a screen above the stage prior to the beginning of the concert. All three of KISS's January 1976 performances at Cobo Arena were archived on videotape by the Kelly-Kirby production team.

The band's first tourbook, *In Concert 1976*, debuted at this show. It was one of three initial pieces of merchandise sold by Boutwell Enterprises, who were brought on board in January to handle merchandising. Boutwell was also in charge of handling the band's fan club, the KISS Army.

JANUARY 26, 1976
Detroit, Michigan
Cobo Arena
Opening Act: Rory Gallagher
Attendance: 12,001   Capacity: 12,001
Promoters: Steve Glantz Productions, Mike Keener Productions
Archived: Video

■ SET LIST
Deuce
Strutter
C'mon and Love Me
Hotter Than Hell
Firehouse
She
Ace Frehley Guitar Solo
Parasite
Nothin' to Lose
Gene Simmons Bass Solo
100,000 Years
Peter Criss Drum Solo - reprise
Black Diamond
Cold Gin
Rock and Roll All Nite
Let Me Go, Rock 'n Roll
■ Photographer Fin Costello did a session with KISS from 8:30 to 9:15 featuring the band members on motorcycles in their new *Destroyer* costumes. (The costumes would appear on the album cover in March, but would not be worn in public until July 3.)

"Parasite" was added to the set, replacing "Ladies In Waiting."

JANUARY 27, 1976
Detroit, Michigan
Cobo Arena
Opening Act: Rory Gallagher
Attendance: 12,001   Capacity: 12,001
Promoters: Steve Glantz Productions, Mike Keener
    Productions
Archived: Video

■ SET LIST
Deuce
Strutter
C'mon and Love Me
Hotter Than Hell
Firehouse
She
Ace Frehley Guitar Solo
Parasite
Nothin' to Lose
Gene Simmons Bass Solo
100,000 Years
Peter Criss Drum Solo - reprise
Black Diamond
[Cold Gin]
[Rock and Roll All Nite]
[Let Me Go, Rock 'n Roll]

■ Promoter Steve Glantz held a private after-show party for the band at a restaurant called The Rooster Tail.

JANUARY 30, 1976
Mt. Pleasant, Michigan
Rose Arena
Opening Act: Hot Lucy
Attendance: 5,785   Capacity: 5,785
Promoter: Steve Glantz Productions

JANUARY 31, 1976
Dayton, Ohio
Hara Arena & Exhibition Center
Opening Act: The Leslie West Band
Attendance: 8,000   Capacity: 8,000
Promoters: Belkin Productions, Windy City Productions

■ Tom Scheidt, writing for *The Journal Herald*, observed in his February 2 review, "Last year it was the old Palace Theater downtown. Saturday night it was Hara Arena filled to the rafters. And by this summer, only football stadiums will be large enough for the crowds . . ." Scheidt's observation was correct: KISS had gone from 3,000-seaters to arenas and would play several stadium shows later that summer, all within an 18-month timespan.

FEBRUARY 1, 1976
Richfield (Cleveland), Ohio
The Coliseum
Opening Act: Hydra
Attendance: 13,000   Capacity: 20,000
Promoter: Belkin Productions

■ The show started a half-hour late due to traffic caused by severe weather.

FEBRUARY 4, 1976
Milwaukee, Wisconsin
Milwaukee Auditorium
Opening Act: Point Blank
Attendance: SRO   Capacity: 6,266
Promoters: Stardate Productions, Daydream
    Productions

FEBRUARY 5, 1976
Madison, Wisconsin
Dane County Expo Center Coliseum
Opening Act: Point Blank
Attendance: 8,755   Capacity: 10,100
Promoter: Stardate Productions

■ Cheap Trick was originally scheduled to open this concert.

FEBRUARY 6, 1976 (TWO SHOWS)
St. Paul, Minnesota
St. Paul Civic Center Theater
Opening Act: Point Blank
Attendance: (1) 2,687; (2) 2,687   Capacity: 2,687
Promoter: Schon Productions

■ *Alive!* reached its peak chart position at #9.

FEBRUARY 9, 1976
Salt Lake City, Utah
Terrace Ballroom
Opening Act: Point Blank
Promoter: United Concerts

FEBRUARY 11, 1976
Portland, Oregon
Memorial Coliseum
Opening Act: Point Blank
Attendance: 11,000
Promoter: Concerts West

FEBRUARY 12, 1976
Spokane, Washington
Spokane Coliseum
Opening Act: Point Blank
Attendance: 8,000   Capacity: 8,500
Promoter: Concerts West

FEBRUARY 13, 1976
Seattle, Washington
Paramount Northwest Theatre
Opening Act: Point Blank
Capacity: 2,976
Promoter: Concerts West

■ Patrick McDonald of *The Seattle Times* wrote, "There's no justice in the world when a group like KISS can sell out two shows at Paramount Northwest, and the Kinks couldn't even sell out the first floor last Friday night.

"The series of explosions that climaxed KISS's set shook the dust off the Paramount's chandeliers and were frightening enough to cause someone nearby to call the Fire Dept. The truck roared up, siren blaring, just about the time the crowd was streaming out of the exits. In fact, the act should be franchised now while it's having its run, like 'Hair' in its heyday. They could have several groups traveling the country doing the KISS routine, because it doesn't really matter who the guys are. And the music could be easily learned. They might as well cash in while they can."

His afterthought was eerily foretelling: " . . . But then maybe the microboppers will take them over and they'll have a KISS cartoon show on Saturday TV and special KISS issues of *Sixteen magazine*."

FEBRUARY 14, 1976
Seattle, Washington
Paramount Northwest Theatre
Opening Act: Point Blank
Capacity: 2,976
Promoter: Concerts West

FEBRUARY 16, 1976
Missoula, Montana
Harry Adams Fieldhouse
Opening Act: Point Blank
Attendance: 4,300   Capacity: 8,089
Promoter: Ken Kinnear

■ The venue's ceiling was scorched by pyro.

FEBRUARY 18, 1976   CANCELED
Eugene, Oregon
Lane County Fairgrounds Expo Hall
Opening Act: Point Blank
Promoter: Concerts West

■ This gig was canceled on the afternoon of the show when Paul was diagnosed with strep throat, forcing KISS to pay a $5,519 cancellation fee. Subsequent shows in San Jose, San Francisco, and Fresno were canceled as well.

FEBRUARY 20, 1976   CANCELED
San Jose, California
San Jose Civic Auditorium
Opening Act: Slade
Promoter: Bill Graham Presents

"Black Diamond" from backstage. Notice manager Bill Aucoin surveying the proceedings in the foreground.

COURTESY OF JACQUES VAN GOOL

KISS backstage with Elton John at The Forum outside of Los Angeles.

FEBRUARY 21, 1976   CANCELED

San Francisco, California
Winterland
Opening Acts: Slade, Point Blank
Promoter: Bill Graham Presents

FEBRUARY 22, 1976   POSTPONED

San Bernardino, California
Swing Auditorium
Opening Act: Montrose
Promoters: Fun Productions, Pacific Presentations
■ The show was rescheduled for February 26.

FEBRUARY 23, 1976

Inglewood (Los Angeles), California
The Forum
Opening Act: Montrose
Attendance: 16,283   Capacity: 18,679
Promoters: Fun Productions, Pacific Presentations
■ Despite the fact that KISS canceled shows immediately before and after their appearances in Los Angeles, due to the large number of tickets sold, KISS performed both shows at The Forum as scheduled. The show on the 23rd was added when tickets for the first show (on February 24) sold out in 36 hours.

FEBRUARY 24, 1976

Inglewood (Los Angeles), California
The Forum
Opening Act: Montrose
Attendance: 17,905   Capacity: 18,679
Promoters: Fun Productions, Pacific Presentations
■ Paul Stanley gave *Los Angeles Times* writer

Steve Ponds an amusing quote: "Rock has reached a point where most of your '60s bands are over the hill. You can't play good rock 'n' roll when you're 35 years old. Even Pete Townshend isn't playing the kind of rock he was playing five years ago. You get too tired, and when you're that tired it's easier to write lyrics, as opposed to rock 'n' roll. We're young and it's our time. We're gonna do it."

Gene's hair caught on fire once again during the show.

FEBRUARY 25, 1976   CANCELED

Fresno, California
Selland Arena @ Fresno Convention Center
Opening Act: Slade
Promoter: Fun Productions

FEBRUARY 26, 1976

San Bernardino, California
Swing Auditorium
Opening Act: Montrose
Attendance: 7,500   Capacity: 7,500
Promoters: Fun Productions, Pacific Presentations
■ This was the make-up date for the February 22 show.

FEBRUARY 27, 1976

San Diego, California
San Diego Sports Arena
Opening Act: Montrose
Attendance: 13,577   Capacity: 13,577
Promoter: Fun Productions
■ Slade was initially part of the bill, but canceled

during the week prior to the show.

FEBRUARY 29, 1976

Honolulu, Hawaii
Neal S. Blaisdell Memorial Center Arena
Opening Act: Booga Booga
Capacity: 8,500
Promoter: Third Eye Productions
■ This was KISS's first and only appearance in Hawaii.

Security chief Rick Stuart: "Paul, Zero [pyrotechnician Mark Stinner], and I had an interesting experience in Hawaii. The first time Paul introduced me to his parents, I was introduced as 'This is the guy who saved my life,' and it was a result of Honolulu. The day after the Honolulu gig, I was out on the beach and ran into Zero, and we decided to rent a catamaran. We went out, and the guide told us that as long as we stayed within the lagoon area that we'd be fine, but neither of us knew what we were doing. We took it out and were getting the hang of it when we noticed Paul standing out on the end of this pier waving to us, 'C'mon over!' We managed to make our way over and we picked him up.

"When we went back out, we saw some other guys from our crew, [roadies] Bob Davies and Tony Canal, on the other side of the reef, heading towards the break coming in. We're running parallel with them and thought we'd meet them at the opening. We shot out through the opening while they came in, and we got sucked right out to sea. We were less than two miles out, but we figured we had to do something about this.

"Suddenly, we got caught in these really big swells that were breaking in these giant Hawaiian waves. We're thinking, 'Do we dive off the boat, or what?' We decided to stay on, ride it out, and try to gain control. Paul panicked and dove off the catamaran, and he's in this turbulent water yelling 'Help!' We threw him a life preserver, which was gone in a second. I said to Zero, 'See ya later' and dove in.

"Paul and I managed to get to where the waves were breaking down over us. We were both a little numb and pretty scared. My foot hit the bottom, and it felt like I'd stepped on a razor, and I knew I was bleeding. We got through the waves into this dark murky water. I'm thinking my foot is bleeding really badly, and I'm waiting for the shark attack to happen. Paul was doing OK, but we were both pretty tired at this point. Turned out that Paul and I had both stepped on sea urchins. My foot was cut, but not as badly as I'd thought. What was really hurting were these sea urchins' spines.

"We got the catamaran guy to go out after Zero because Zero was floating further out to sea and he towed him in. Later on, Paul and I went to the hospital. They said there was really nothing that they can do about it. The only thing they could recommend for the pain was to pee in the sink and soak our feet in it. Paul and I looked at each other like: 'Yeah, OK . . . right.'

"We went back to the hotel and I unsuccessfully tried to remove the spines from my foot, when Paul calls and said, 'I tried peeing in the sink and soaking my foot in it and it works.' There we were in Hawaii, pissing in sinks."

MARCH 4, 1976

Oklahoma City, Oklahoma
Civic Center Music Hall
Opening Act: Mountain Smoke
Attendance: 3,200   Capacity: 3,200
Promoters: Concert Club, Cornucopia Productions
■ The local support act canceled literally minutes before the show. Country/bluegrass band Mountain Smoke, which featured future country star Vince Gill, was added as a last-second replacement. Hal Clifford, bassist for Mountain Smoke, recalls the details: "The promoter called me after 6 P.M. in the evening. He said that he had a problem and described the contract with KISS, which stated that they had to have an opening act or they wouldn't go on.

"The promoter said that if we could play he could get us $5,000. I called around and got some of the guys from Mountain Smoke, one of who was Vince Gill. Everybody raced down to the Civic Center and got there at about 8 P.M. As soon as they saw us walk out onstage the tone of the audience went from subdued amazement to a louder level of disapproval. They booed and booed and booed. We played several songs and made light of it and laughed. We said things like, 'Your enthusiasm is remarkable. You keep driving us on like this and we'll continue to play.'

"We thanked the audience again and I suggested that they be sure to get Mom and Dad's

car back in by 10. Then we left and Vince shot them the finger." Years later Vince Gill would talk about this concert on *The Tonight Show with Jay Leno.*

Steve Hoffman, writing for the *Oklahoma Journal,* mentions "Parasite" in his review. The inclusion of "Parasite" seems to indicate that KISS was still playing the exact set list that they used at the final two Cobo Arena shows in January.

MARCH 6, 1976

Lincoln, Nebraska
Pershing Auditorium
Opening Act: Boz Scaggs
Attendance: 8,056   Capacity: 8,056
Promoter: Contemporary Productions

MARCH 8, 1976

Tulsa, Oklahoma
Tulsa Assembly Center
Opening Act: Electromagnets
Promoter: Concerts West
■ Opening act Electromagnets featured guitarist Eric Johnson. The show was cut short when someone threw a beer bottle at Peter and knocked over several pieces of his drum kit.

MARCH 11, 1976

Huntsville, Alabama
Von Braun Civic Center
Opening Act: Albatross
Attendance: 9,559   Capacity: 9,559
Promoters: Concerts West, Sound 70 Concerts
■ "Shout It Out Loud" was performed, marking the first known appearance of *Destroyer* material in the set. The song had been released as a single on March 1.

MARCH 12, 1976

New Orleans, Louisiana
A Warehouse
Capacity: 3,500
Promoter: Beaver Productions
■ The opening act is unknown.
Rick Munroe: "We had a nice hepatitis scare in New Orleans. After the show, we were starting the load-out and they stopped us, literally told us to drop what we were doing because we were all going to the hospital. Barry Ackom, one of the guitar techs, had symptoms of hepatitis, and management didn't want to take any chances. So they lined us all up bent over on the gurneys and went down the line and injected us all, the band and everyone."

Following their brief trip to Charity Hospital, all four members of KISS ventured over to a nightclub in the French quarter called Ballinjax, where they attended a 2 A.M. performance by the New York Dolls. Surprisingly, Gene and Ace can be heard on a private recording of the concert playfully heckling the Dolls, who were performing that night minus Johnny Thunders and Jerry Nolan.

MARCH 13, 1976

Mobile, Alabama
Expo Hall @ Mobile Municipal Auditorium
Promoter: Beaver Productions
■ British rock band Dr. Feelgood was the original opening act, though which band ultimately opened the show cannot be confirmed. One attendee described the opening act as a small,

folk-rock outfit, a description implying that Albatross (openers for the March 11 show) may have opened the show.

MARCH 14, 1976

Memphis, Tennessee
Auditorium North Hall
Opening Act: Target
Attendance: 4,361   Capacity: 11,000
Promoter: Mid-South Concerts
■ The show was originally scheduled for Mid-South Coliseum with Dr. Feelgood opening. The lead singer for Target, Jimi Jamison, went on to front the mid-80's version of Survivor.

MARCH 18, 1976

Greenville, South Carolina   **CANCELED**
Greenville Memorial Auditorium
Promoter: Kaleidoscope Productions
■ Both this show and the subsequent gig in Macon appear on KISS's itineraries, but they are listed as canceled in official paperwork detailing the band's 1976 appearances.

MARCH 19, 1976

Macon, Georgia   **CANCELED**
Macon Coliseum
Promoter: Alex Cooley Presents

MARCH 20, 1976

Lakeland, Florida
Lakeland Civic Center
Opening Act: (Lakeland String Quartet)
Attendance: 10,000
Promoter: Cellar Door Concerts
■ Dr. Feelgood was the advertised opening act, but the band canceled on the day of the show.
Rick Munroe: "We were set to do a gig with Dr. Feelgood in Lakeland. And when we got to the show, they bitched so much about something—the dressing rooms, the food, the money—that Ted Wilson from Cellar Door told them to get the hell out of there and threw them off the tour. We never saw them again.

"I was thinking, 'OK, smarty-pants, what are you going to do for an opening act?' You know what they came up with? A string quartet. They told us that they'd just need five mikes and they wouldn't need an LD [lighting director]. Just put the spots on them and leave it on, don't worry about it. They came out in their black dresses and tuxedos, four of them, and started playing Beethoven or Bach and the shit started flying onstage like it was raining. I don't think they got through one whole number."

The official name of the string quartet is not known.

MARCH 21, 1976

Miami, Florida
Miami Jai-Alai Fronton
Opening Act: .38 Special
Attendance: 5,000   Capacity: 6,000
Promoter: Cellar Door Concerts
Archived: Audio
■ SET LIST
Deuce
Strutter
C'mon and Love Me
Hotter Than Hell
Firehouse
She
Ace Frehley Guitar Solo
Parasite
Nothin' to Lose
Shout It Out Loud
Gene Simmons Bass Solo
100,000 Years
Peter Criss Drum Solo - reprise
Black Diamond
Cold Gin
Rock and Roll All Nite
Let Me Go, Rock 'n Roll
■ There were no flashpots allowed at this show due to the low ceiling in the venue.

The night prior, WSHE DJ Cory James (from Miami) ran a radio promotion giving hourly reports on the Lakeland show. KISS did a photo session on top of the radio station and received a commemorative plaque from WSHE.

While in town, KISS attended a Sammy Davis, Jr. performance at the Diplomat Hotel in Hollywood, Florida.

MARCH 24, 1976

Philadelphia, Pennsylvania
Philadelphia Civic Center
Opening Act: Rockets
Attendance: 9,871   Capacity: 11,500
Promoters: Jennifer Productions, Dick Clark Concerts
■ This show was promoted with a disclaimer informing concertgoers that only tickets printed specifically for this show would be honored. Months earlier, a fraudulently advertised KISS show for December 19, 1975 had been put on sale by Willow Productions. Promoters were worried that ticketholders would think those tickets would be valid at this show.

MARCH 25, 1976

Johnstown, Pennsylvania
Cambria County War Memorial Arena
Opening Act: Thee Image
Promoter: Silver Bullet Productions

MARCH 26, 1976

Harrisburg, Pennsylvania
Farm Show Arena
Opening Act: Artful Dodger
Attendance: 13,000   Capacity: 13,000
Promoter: Jennifer Productions
■ According to one attendee, "Flaming Youth" was included in the set, marking the first known performance of the song.

MARCH 27, 1976   POSTPONED

Utica, New York
Memorial Auditorium
Opening Act: Ethos
Promoter: Cross Country Concerts
■ For reasons unknown, the show was postponed until April 13.

MARCH 28, 1976

Springfield, Massachusetts
Springfield Civic Center
Opening Act: Artful Dodger
Attendance: 10,000   Capacity: 10,000
Promoter: Concert Club
Archived: Super 8mm
■ SET LIST
Deuce
Strutter
C'mon and Love Me
Hotter Than Hell
Firehouse
She
Ace Frehley Guitar Solo
Nothin' to Lose
Flaming Youth
Shout It Out Loud
Gene Simmons Bass Solo
100,000 Years
Peter Criss Drum Solo - reprise
Black Diamond
Cold Gin
Rock and Roll All Nite
Let Me Go, Rock 'n Roll
■ An audience member who provided the above set list recorded this show. The authors lost contact with the attendee before the audiotape could be located. However, the set list information was provided to the authors before information on the Miami set list from March 21, 1976, which it closely parallels, was publicly available. Hence, it is reasonable to assume that the information is not fraudulent.

The concert was promoted as the final show of the Alive! Tour.

TEMP HOLD SHOWS

■ In the autumn of 1975, an entire run of tour dates appeared in *Performance*. Very little information was given regarding the shows beyond the date, city, and, occasionally, the venue. None of these gigs made it off the drawing board, but they are included here as an interesting point of reference.

October 29, 1975
Minneapolis, Minnesota
Promoter: Twin Productions

October 30, 1975
Madison, Wisconsin
Dane County Expo Center Coliseum
Promoter: Daydream Productions

November 2, 1975
Oklahoma City, Oklahoma
Civic Center Music Hall

November 3, 1975
Lubbock, Texas
■ Itineraries listed the city as Levitte, Texas.

November 4, 1975
Galveston, Texas

November 8 & 9, 1975
New York, New York
Beacon Theatre

November 14, 1975
Chalmette (New Orleans), Louisiana
St. Bernard Civic Center

November 15, 1975
Kansas City, Kansas
Soldier's & Sailor's Memorial Hall

December 7, 1975
Mobile, Alabama
Expo Hall @ Mobile Municipal Auditorium

December 13, 1975
Buffalo, New York
Veterans Memorial Auditorium

December 28, 1975
Springfield, Illinois
Nelson Center

January 1, 1976
Baltimore, Maryland
Baltimore Arena

CHAPTER 7

DESTROYER TOUR

Number of Shows: 67
Start Date: April 11, 1976 - Fort Wayne, Indiana
End Date: October 1, 1976 - New York, New York
Countries: Belgium, Canada, Denmark, England, France, The Netherlands, Sweden, Switzerland, U.S.A., West Germany
Opening Acts: .38 Special; Artful Dodger; Blue Öyster Cult; Bob Seger & the Silver Bullet Band; Brownsville Station; Earth Quake; Ethos; Finch; Hammersmith; Hoa Bihn; J. Geils Band; Johnny & Edgar Winter; Kansas; Montrose; Moon Pie; Point Blank; Scorpions; Starz; Stray; Ted Nugent; UFO
Average Attendance: 11,073* (Does not include 5/4/76 gig or European Tour.)

When the Alive! Tour concluded on March 28, 1976, KISS was still just a rock and roll band. However, changes made during the *Destroyer* era would alter that forever.

The recording of *Destroyer*, KISS's fourth studio album, was divided into two sections separated by five months of touring. Most of the album's basic tracks were laid down at Electric Lady between September 3 and 6, 1975, a full six months prior to its release on March 15, 1976; the recording was completed in January of that year. Although it's not often discussed, the mixing sessions for *Alive!* and the first *Destroyer* sessions were only separated by a matter of days.

Unfortunately, outside distractions prevented the band from being a focused unit during the recording sessions. Rick Munroe relates: "While we were recording *Destroyer*, Ace was supposed to do some guitar solo, and he couldn't get in the right mood for it. He said 'Ah, Curly, I need a blow job for this.' We all looked at each other thinking 'Ace, you're going to lose on this one. Nobody here wants to give you one!' Well, hey,

we're in New York City, why not go out and get a hooker off the streets? So Gene volunteered. He came back with the ugliest woman I have ever seen, so ugly that nobody wanted a part of her except Gene. Ace took one look at her and said, 'Are you kidding me? It's worse now than it was before.'"

The finished product was so dynamic and so foreign to previous KISS records that KISS's public initially revolted. The band's raw guitar solos, four-on-the-floor drums, and raspy rock vocals had been replaced by harmonized guitar melodies, asymmetric time signatures, and multi-layered vocal counterpoint. This was not a KISS that the fan base recognized, and while the album sold briskly on the strength of the single "Shout It Out Loud," *Destroyer* fell off the charts on August 13, well before it attained Platinum status. In the months following its release, both the band and management were disappointed with the album; as a follow-up to *Alive!*, it initially failed.

Nonetheless, KISS's touring revenue was bet-

ter than ever. The band was headlining and consistently selling out 10,000+ seat arenas, but the incessant touring was taking its toll: "No one took the success for granted," recalls Rick Munroe, "but we had been on the road constantly and we were getting very fed-up with the schedule. Things kept getting bigger and better as far as the audiences went, but the schedule was still the same shitty process of 'Do it, do it, and do it again, as many times as you can in a week.' Everyone was very worn out and was not really celebrating the fact that it was becoming as big as it was. *It* was taking us, rather than *us* taking it."

The band saw no need to rehearse during the down time between tours as the initial Destroyer Tour shows (April 11–June 6) used staging, costumes, and production identical to those on the Alive! Tour, though Paul did add a blonde streak to his hair sometime after May 1.

There are no full set lists available for the first month of the tour, but it is likely that they were very similar to those used at the end of the previous tour. Material from *Destroyer* began to appear

The opening night of Summer Tour '76 in Norfolk, Virginia, July 3, 1976.

MARK RAVITZ

when "Shout It Out Loud" and "Flaming Youth" were added to the set in March, and "God of Thunder" was worked into the show in April. (Initially, both Gene's solo/blood-spitting routine and Peter's drum solo were still part of "100,000 Years," though both would be integrated into "God of Thunder" some time in August. Additionally, for a brief period, Criss's solo was attached to the end of "Watchin' You.") It would seem natural for "Detroit Rock City" to have made it into the set, but its earliest confirmed inclusion is the beginning of the European tour in mid-May.

The prospect of KISS's debut engagements in Europe was the highlight of the first half of the Destroyer Tour. "I remember arriving in Europe," states Mick Campise, "and the band went to put their makeup on to make a grand first appearance. Unfortunately, we still had to go through customs. With the makeup on, the customs officials couldn't identify the band members by their passports, so they had to go remove the makeup, go through customs, and then put it right back on."

The 17-date tour was only marginally successful. The European crowds were considerably smaller than those in North America, and reports were that the attendees were generally unimpressed by KISS's garish theatrics. JR Smalling recalls: "The tour of Europe was a step backwards for us in some ways. The crowds and venues made it more like our first tour of the States than some big extravaganza."

APRIL 11, 1976

Fort Wayne, Indiana
Allen Co. War Memorial Coliseum
Opening Act: Artful Dodger
Attendance: 9,663   Capacity: 9,663
Promoter: Sunshine Promotions

APRIL 13, 1976

Utica, New York
Memorial Auditorium
Opening Act: Ethos
Attendance: almost 4,500
Promoter: Cross Country Concerts
■ This concert was originally scheduled for March 27.

APRIL 14, 1976

Niagara Falls, New York
Niagara Falls Convention & Civic Center Arena
Opening Act: Brownsville Station
Attendance: 9,500   Capacity: 9,500
Promoter: Ruffino & Vaughn

APRIL 16, 1976

Bangor, Maine
Municipal Auditorium
Opening Act: Ethos
Attendance: 6,932   Capacity: 6,932
Promoter: Cedric Kushner
■ Nearly 500 people were turned away at the door.

APRIL 18, 1976

Moncton, New Brunswick, Canada
Moncton Coliseum
Opening Act: Hammersmith
Attendance: 6,000   Capacity: 9,000
Promoter: Donald K. Donald

Just one of many occasions where Gene set himself aflame, in this instance, on April 22, 1976 in Ottawa, Ontario.

APRIL 19, 1976

Halifax, Nova Scotia, Canada
Halifax Forum Complex
Opening Act: Hammersmith
Attendance: 7,000   Capacity: 7,200
Promoter: Donald K. Donald

APRIL 21, 1976

Montréal, Quebec, Canada
Forum de Montréal
Opening Act: Hammersmith
Attendance: 6,000
Promoter: Donald K. Donald

APRIL 22, 1976

Ottawa, Ontario, Canada
Ottawa Civic Centre
Opening Act: Hammersmith
Attendance: 6,000
Promoter: Donald K. Donald
■ Gene's hair caught on fire during his fire-breathing stunt. Apparently, the advertised opening act, BIM, did not perform as only Hammersmith is mentioned in the review.

APRIL 23, 1976

Kitchener, Ontario, Canada
Memorial Auditorium
Opening Act: Hammersmith
Attendance: Nearly 6,000   Capacity: 7,600
Promoter: Donald K. Donald

APRIL 24, 1976

London, Ontario, Canada
London Gardens
Opening Act: Hammersmith
Attendance: 5,000   Capacity: 5,000
Promoter: Donald K. Donald
■ A review of the show indicates that 14 songs were performed and that "God of Thunder" was included in the set. This is the first known perfor-

mance of the song, though it is likely that it was added to the set at the beginning of the tour.

APRIL 26, 1976

Toronto, Ontario, Canada
Maple Leaf Gardens
Opening Act: Hammersmith
Attendance: 11,800   Capacity: 12,000
Promoter: Donald K. Donald
■ Security chief Rick Stuart: "Paul and I were in the Toronto airport, and we went to get something to eat. We were sitting next to a big window in this airport restaurant, and these two kids came over and saw Paul and started going nuts on the other side of the glass. Paul waved them in to say hi, and they asked for his autograph. Paul signed a napkin or something, and the kid just looked at it and said: 'I thought you were Freddie McMurray from Queen.' It just completely floored Paul that the kid thought he was Freddie Mercury, and then to top it off the kid said 'Freddie McMurray.' We had a good laugh about it."

After the concert, Quality Records threw a party for KISS at Sam The Chinese Food Man. Bob Ezrin and Alice Cooper were among the attendees.

Rick Munroe's flashballs effect was used for the final time at this concert.

APRIL 28, 1976

Winnipeg, Manitoba, Canada
Winnipeg Arena
Opening Act: Hammersmith
Promoter: Donald K. Donald
■ Security guard Eddie Balandas: "Ace was getting married on May 1, and the whole crew really wanted to be there. They told us it was too expensive to get the whole crew back to New York in time, so most of us drove back from Win-

nipeg with the equipment. We were in the crew bus, and Hot Sam and I wrote a song as we were thinking about Ace's wedding; we all had drinks on the bus and toasted them with a little blues song, 'We won't hear Curly say "I do," it's the road for me and you . . . '"

MAY 1, 1976

New York, New York
The Americana
Wedding Band: St. James Infirmary

■ At Ace and Jeanette's wedding reception, the band grabbed the opportunity to take the stage. Obviously, the band's impromptu appearance immediately took the focus off of the wedding festivities, and after playing only one song, Ace's new father in-law asked the band to stop.

Eddie Solan: "I hired this band called St. James Infirmary to do music for the reception. KISS ended up playing a song and used their instruments. "

MAY 4, 1976

Mount Prospect (Chicago), Illinois
River Trails Middle School Gymnasium
No Opening Act
Attendance: 350
Promoter: Mars Candy Corporation

■ In the spring of 1976, Mars Candy held a contest to promote their new Marathon Bar. The contestants were individual schools in the Midwest. The goal of the contest was to collect the most Mars Candy wrappers, and whichever school had the most would win its own personal KISS concert. Surprisingly, the contest was won by a small junior high school in a northwest suburb of Chicago. So, KISS performed a very scaled-back show in front of approximately 350 twelve- and thirteen-year-olds. The event was obviously a huge coup for the school, and one faculty member reported that every member of the student body attended except two individuals who had called in sick.

On May 10, the band departed for Europe. Tour rehearsals for Europe were held on May 11 and 12 at Shepperton Studios in Middlesex, England, where a relatively low-budget sci-fi film titled *Star Wars* had recently wrapped shooting.

MAY 13, 1976

Manchester, England
Free Trade Hall
Opening Act: Stray
Attendance: 2,529   Capacity: 2,529
Promoter: Straight Music
Archived: Audio

■ **SET LIST**
Deuce
Strutter
Flaming Youth
Hotter Than Hell
Firehouse
She
Ace Frehley Guitar Solo
Nothin' to Lose
Shout It Out Loud
Gene Simmons Bass Solo
100,000 Years
Peter Criss Drum Solo - reprise
Black Diamond
Detroit Rock City
Rock and Roll All Nite
Let Me Go, Rock 'n Roll

■ Some outstanding footage from this show was aired in an episode of the British series *So It Goes!* on August 2. During the pre-show interview, Ace remarked, "No one knows what I look like with my makeup off. So I sneak home, call some old friends, and we go into a pub and play."

Casablanca's British distributor, EMI International, spent a reported $60,000 on promotion for the U.K. leg of the KISS tour.

MAY 14, 1976

Birmingham, England
The Odeon Theatre
Opening Act: Stray
Attendance: 3,983   Capacity: 3,983
Promoter: Straight Music

MAY 15, 1976

London, England
Hammersmith Odeon Theatre
Opening Act: Stray
Attendance: 3,983   Capacity: 3,983
Promoter: Straight Music

■ A review in the *New Musical Express* notes: "At the top of the stairs belligerent and tanked-up youths ripped off large promo cardboard cut outs and posters." The review also mentions that KISS masks were handed out at the door.

MAY 16, 1976

London, England
Hammersmith Odeon Theatre
Opening Act: Stray
Capacity: 3,983
Promoter: Straight Music
Archived: Audio

■ **SET LIST**
[Deuce]
Strutter
Flaming Youth
Hotter Than Hell
Firehouse
She
Ace Frehley Guitar Solo
Nothin' to Lose
Shout It Out Loud
[Gene Simmons Bass Solo]
[100,000 Years]
[Peter Criss Drum Solo - reprise]
Black Diamond
Detroit Rock City
[Rock and Roll All Nite]
[Let Me Go, Rock 'n Roll]

MAY 18, 1976

Mannheim, West Germany
Saalbau Rosengarten
Promoter: MCP (Mama Concert Productions)

■ JR Smalling: "We were at a fancy restaurant somewhere in West Germany hoping to enjoy some of the famous local cuisine. The waiter, who was an older, very conservative-looking guy, was going around the table taking everyone's orders. He finally gets to Gene who orders a steak. The waiter asked him how he would like it cooked. Now Gene, despite the stage theatrics, practically faints at the sight of blood, so he tells the waiter to 'burn it to a crisp.' And in this venomous voice, the waiter hissed, 'Sir, ve vill *incinerate* it for you.' I was blown away that the outward contempt for Jews was still that strong."

MAY 19, 1976

Düsseldorf, West Germany
Philipshalle
Opening Act: Scorpions
Promoter: MCP

■ KISS remained in Düsseldorf on May 20 for a press conference.

MAY 22, 1976

Paris, France
Olympia Theatre
No Opening Act
Attendance: 1,900
Promoter: Koski Cauchoix Productions
Archived: Audio

■ **SET LIST**
See May 13, 1976.

■ This show was a 3 P.M. matinee.

Mick Campise: "KISS did the show in the afternoon so they could get off the stage in time for Jerry Lewis; he was still huge there. While we were in Paris, we stayed at the Grand Hotel right across the street from the Paris Opera House, and we walked to the gig."

MAY 23, 1976

Amsterdam, The Netherlands
RAI Congrescentrum-Amsterdam
Opening Act: Finch
Promoters: Mojo Concerts, Leon Ramakers
Archived: Audio

■ **SET LIST**
See May 13, 1976.

■ This show was recorded by a local radio station, most likely VARA, but it was deemed unusable, and it was never aired.

MAY 24, 1976

Offenbach (Frankfurt a.M.), West Germany
Stadthalle
Opening Act: Scorpions
Promoter: MCP

■ JR Smalling: "We were at a hotel in West Germany watching Muhammad Ali's comeback fight. As it would happen, he was fighting this big German guy (Richard Dunn) and while we were watching we had been, 'celebrating,' shall we say." Mick Campise continues, "Peter started to pull some shit, and he threatened to jump off the window ledge of the hotel. So, JR, Hot Sam, and I looked at each other and thought, 'Well, we have a choice. Either let him rip up the room and hope he passes out or he's going to jump.' We decided to let him rip up the room, including this antique armoire, to the tune of about $6,000. JR, Sam, and I woke up the next morning and went and had breakfast, and there's Bill Aucoin sitting across from us. We're thinking, 'How in the fuck did he already get word of what happened and is over here that fast?' We couldn't believe it."

MAY 26, 1976

Göteborg, Sweden
Scandinavium
No Opening Act
Attendance: 3,198   Capacity: 3,198
Promoter: EMA Telstar
Archived: Audio

■ **SET LIST**
Deuce
Strutter

Flaming Youth
Hotter Than Hell
Firehouse
She
Ace Frehley Guitar Solo
Nothin' to Lose
Shout It Out Loud
Gene Simmons Bass Solo
100,000 Years
Peter Criss Drum Solo - reprise
[Black Diamond]
[Detroit Rock City]
[Rock and Roll All Nite]
[Let Me Go, Rock 'n Roll]

■ Rick Munroe: "At the hotel in Gothenburg, we were all assembled at some wee hour of the morning. It was leaked to us that somebody had some super telephoto lenses and caught the band without makeup getting off the airplane. We were all handed a pile of money to go out and buy every newspaper we could buy and get it off the streets. The point was to try to make the newspaper unavailable; hit every newsstand that you can, and put the newspapers in the car. It only happened once, and I seem to recall it was on a day off. We quickly realized that it was a futile attempt, and the photos weren't that good, so we let it go."

MAY 28, 1976

Stockholm, Sweden
Stora Scenen @ Gröna Lund in Tivoli Gardens
No Opening Act
Attendance: 15,600   Capacity: 15,600
Promoter: EMA Telstar
Archived: Audio, Super 8mm

■ SET LIST

Deuce
Strutter
Flaming Youth
Hotter Than Hell
Firehouse
She
Ace Frehley Guitar Solo
Nothin' to Lose
Shout It Out Loud
Gene Simmons Bass Solo
100,000 Years
Peter Criss Drum Solo - reprise
Black Diamond
Detroit Rock City
Rock and Roll All Nite
[Let Me Go, Rock 'n Roll]

■ Jay Barth: "In Stockholm, we went to this restaurant where you order your food, and they send it around this water-filled channel on these little boats. We were all drunk as a skunk and Ace ended up wading in the water. We all were thrown out immediately."

MAY 29, 1976

København, Denmark
Falkoner Teatret
No Opening Act
Attendance: 1,300
Promoter: EMA Telstar

■ SET LIST

See May 13, 1976.

MAY 30, 1976

Lund, Sweden
Olympen
No Opening Act
Promoter: EMA Telstar
Archived: Audio

■ SET LIST

See May 13, 1976.

■ Ace may have intended to make his lead vocal debut at this gig. Just prior to "Let Me Go, Rock 'n Roll," Paul announced "All right. Ace is going to sing a song for you." Whether or not Paul was kidding, Ace didn't sing the song and his live lead vocal debut had to wait until July 1977.

JUNE 2, 1976

Zürich, Switzerland
Volkshaus
No Opening Act
Attendance: 1,497   Capacity: 1,497
Promoter: Good News Agency

■ Rick Munroe: "Casablanca had decided to go ahead and have a dinner for us at the hotel in Zürich. When they said we could have anything we wanted, Peter just went to the extreme immediately and started ordering very expensive bottles of wine. Then everybody started doing it. After a while, Paul Chavarria and I went back up to our room to get something or other. We came back down to the restaurant and no sooner had we stepped off the elevator when this guy goes flying by us, literally in midair. This huge brawl had broken out: a furniture-throwing, lip-cracking, nose-breaking, knock-out, drag-down fight. Upon getting out of the elevator, Paul is pushed back into my lap, and he's got blood coming out of his nose. I said, 'What the hell happened?' He said, 'Some guy just hit me!' We got up and just got into it."

JUNE 3, 1976

München, West Germany
Circus Krone
Opening Act: Scorpions
Promoter: MCP

■ A local TV show Szene 76 was on hand to film a KISS segment, which included "Detroit Rock City" from the concert.

JUNE 4, 1976

Fürth (Nürnberg), West Germany
M.T.V. Gründighalle
Opening Act: Scorpions
Promoter: MCP

JUNE 6, 1976

Harelbeke (Kortrijk), Belgium
Ontmoetingscentrum
Opening Act: Hoa Bihn
Attendance: 600   Capacity: 1,500
Promoters: VANSO (Etienne Vanneste, Soubry Louis)

■ The final show of the European tour was a mess from beginning to end. To start with, the local promoters purchased the gig at a moment's notice from an English booking agent, which left very little time for promotion. Then, on the morning of the gig, KISS awoke at the Hilton in Bruxelles to find that the bus driver they hired had quit during the night.

Rick Munroe: "We had been having bus problems the whole time we were in Europe. They kept giving us these touring buses for the blue-haired crowd with big windows and everything. And we'd get these drivers in jackets and suits, and they just didn't like the way we behaved after a show because we'd get on and drink beer. A lot of these buses didn't have bathrooms on them either.

"On the way into Belgium, I told the driver, 'Hey, you've got to pull over, we need to use the bathroom.' A long time went by and he didn't pull over. Finally, Paul Chavarria went up to him: 'Hey, buddy, you have GOT to pull over. We have got to take a leak here.' The guy said: 'You piss in bottles. You drink beer, you empty the bottles, now you piss in the bottles.' Paul shot back, 'Look, if I piss in this bottle, I'm going to smash you over the head with it, so you just better pull over.' He was very upset, and just pulled over to the side of the road. He then dropped us off at the hotel.

"We got up the next morning to find all of our bags in the lobby. The gear was at the gig, but we weren't, and we had no idea how to make it. Mike and JR scrambled and went to the train station to buy tickets for everybody. We got on a train full of peasants and chickens, it was right out of a Fellini movie to me. We did have a bus to take us back."

Jay Barth: "At least there was some reward for finally getting to the show. They had this keg of beer backstage with its own beer tapper. We tried our best to empty it."

Lastly, the venue's ceiling was so low that Gene scorched it during his fire-breathing act.

───────

With the group's first European tour behind them, KISS returned to the U.S. on June 7, 1976. A typically short break followed, and by June 21 the band had begun to rehearse in earnest for the American leg of the tour. Production and dress rehearsals were staged at Hangar E at Stewart International Airport in Newburgh, New York. The hangar was the home of Theatre Techniques, the stage construction company that had built the set.

The tour to support Destroyer technically began with the April 11 appearance in Fort Wayne, yet many fans of the band typically mention the Destroyer Tour in relation to the 10-week American leg, which began in July and was officially named Summer Tour '76.

May and June 1976 were watershed months in every sense of the word for KISS, as many changes in management and production took place. Quantum leaps were made on just about every front. Manager Bill Aucoin separated his operations into two separate enterprises: Rock Steady Productions, Inc. and Aucoin Management, Inc. (AMI). Operations were relocated from his single room office to a palatial location at 645 Madison Avenue, a move that was proudly announced by Aucoin with full-page ads in both Billboard and Performance.

The most significant change, however, was the hiring of the Glickman/Marks Management Corporation, who were brought on board to act as business managers for KISS. The hiring of Glickman/Marks was the primary landmark dividing the energetic, mad improvisation of '74 and '75 and the calculated extravaganza that was to follow. Gone were the days when a wide-eyed band and a small, loyal road crew criss-crossed the country on nothing but naïveté, ambition, and attitude: there was no mistaking that KISS was now a business, if not quite its own industry.

Even the KISS Army was making money, as Ron Boutwell (of Boutwell Enterprises) notes in a wickedly sarcastic letter to Aucoin: "I approach this subject with great trepidation, for I find myself in a rather embarrassing position. If you will recall our meeting in September of 1975, wherein you forced me to organize and manage a fan club, i.e., the KISS Army, my promise to you at that time was that we would do it and probably end up losing money, or at best, break even. However, the bottom line is that in spite of all my efforts, the fucking fan club has made money, too much goddamn money!"

In terms of the Summer Tour '76, one of the first noticeable differences was the departure of longtime road manager JR Smalling, and production manager Mick Campise. By tour's end, lighting director Rick Munroe, tour manager Mike McGurl, and Mark Stinner had left, as would Fanfare Sound and house engineer Jay Barth. Of the original crew, only Paul Chavarria would remain employed by KISS beyond the Destroyer Tour.

JR Smalling observes: "They basically outgrew the people they had been working with. I worked with them from the beginning when there were only a few of us—the band, the crew and Sean—in 1974, until June of 1976 when the crew was over 40, and we had eight tractor trailers' worth of equipment. Then Glickman/Marks came in with their people and filled all our positions without telling us."

Mick Campise continues: "By the time *Destroyer* had come around, the original road crew was very disenchanted because the fun had been taken out of it. There was no spontaneity any more; it wasn't rock and roll, it was big business. It was so completely foreign to what the original concept was that you could hardly recognize it. When Glickman/Marks came on board they wanted to bring their own people; Bill fired most of the original crew, saying that we couldn't handle the band, which was bullshit, because JR would tell them something and they would do it. But Bill had a goal: to keep KISS separated from everybody, keep the mystique up. It got to the point that Bill thought that we were too close to them. That's another reason why Bill Aucoin threw Rush off the KISS tours—they were getting too close to the band. Anybody that gave the band any kind of safety net was just yanked away from them."

Another significant difference between this tour and previous excursions was the amount of money available to invest in the show. The royalty dispute between Casablanca and KISS had been resolved when AMI received a check for $2 million. The influx of cash played out into an opportunity to bring some outlandish production ideas to fruition for the tour.

A change of attire was the first order of the day—all four band members wore completely new costumes during a live performance for the first time since May 16, 1975. The costumes were designed and constructed by L. LeGaspi.

In addition, to this point, KISS had certainly employed some unique production ideas, but nothing that compared with the outlandish props brought to bear on the Summer '76 outing. Sev-

Mark Ravitz's detailed scale model of the Destroyer stage. Note the multi-colored crystals and the center stage incline. The crystals were removed from the stage during rehearsals and the incline soon followed.

eral concepts never quite made it beyond the development phase, the most extreme of these being an onstage recreation of the "Detroit Rock City" narrative in which a car was to be hoisted high above the floor and would crash down upon the stage to begin the show.

The staging and production design was a joint effort between the band, Sean Delaney, and Mark Ravitz and Mark Krueger, who were representatives of the Jules Fischer Organization. A multi-level design was eventually decided upon, with the idea being that different portions of the stage would thematically correspond to a different band member's stage persona. For instance, two emerald-eyed cats flanked Peter's drum platform. The area where Frehley did portions of his solo was distinctly lunar in theme, and Simmons, in turn, would ascend to a crumbling gothic castle for his solo.

The Destroyer Tour marked the most radical staging change in KISS's touring history. The staging was so different that the band reacted quite harshly when they first saw it in Newburgh. "The designer had tried to literally represent the vision of the *Destroyer* cover," eventual tour manager Fritz Postlethwaite notes. "It was Broadway meets rock and roll and the first joint venture didn't work out too well. I remember Ace looking at the set pieces and saying, 'This fucking set looks like a fruit salad.'"

Mark Ravitz had designed a host of colorfully named stage props for the tour: the God of Thunder machine, The Tentacle Tree, and an enormous bloody stake.

The God of Thunder Machine had been originally designed by Ken Strickfaden; it had been used some 45 years earlier in the 1931 film *Frankenstein*. Despite the legendry and hype surrounding it, the device was nothing more than a gargantuan Tesla coil. AMI production manager Ken Anderson explains, "While the machine looked very impressive sitting in a 12' x 20'

room, the effect was totally lost when performing in a huge arena." Its unreliability, coupled with its meager production value, spelled a quick demise for the machine; Fritz Postlethwaite relates: "It was huge and we couldn't begin to lift it with eight stagehands. There was this enormous ring that had to be constructed each night and once it was ready, it worked about half the time."

The Tentacle Tree resembled a twisted parody of a tree. Placed upon a rotating platform on stage right, supposedly the tree was designed to spin around at a great velocity, the whip-like branches whirring into a blur. What photos/video exist of the Tentacle Tree show it as a stationary prop, and there remains no direct proof that the spinning effect was ever used during a concert.

Another prop of Ravitz's design was a giant, red stake that resembled a blood-soaked Washington Monument. The stake, which was originally designed as a belfry, would rise up behind Gene's gothic tower just prior to his bass solo. One undeveloped concept had Simmons standing atop his platform surrounded by a circular wall of flame.

Mark Stinner describes another of the tour's short-lived effects, "They had these foam rubber pieces that looked like buildings attached to the front of the amps. It was a major pain, and it took hours to set up. Late in the show, right before the encores, the buildings would crumble. Then the foam rubber pieces had to be cleared off the stage before the band could return.

"There was so much clean-up involved I think the buildings were cut pretty quickly. We eliminated some of the foam rubber pieces while we were still in Newburgh."

The remainder of the staging and variations on these elements, such as the staircases bordering Criss's drum platform, were included in many of the band's later stages.

The lighting trees were designed to mimic

high-tension steel utility towers. This was embellished by a cloud with red, white, and blue lightning bolts, which were mounted above the front of the stage. "We did the lightning bolts with that particular color scheme because of the Bicentennial," Mark Ravitz elaborates. "We started trying video projection then, too. We had built big cloud shapes to go along with the lightning bolts. The lightning bolts were part of one cloud, and adjacent to that was a bigger cloud, which was the rear-projection screen. I'm not sure if the projection screen was ever used."

Fleshing out the display even further were lengthy strands of chaser lights (essentially heavy-duty Christmas lights),-which were attached to the top of the vertical lighting columns and were then strung out into the auditorium. Ravitz explains: "The lighting towers were shaped like power towers out in the fields, so I added a little more truss-work up above to give it some shape, and then they were all linked by chase lights. Big strands of them went right into the balcony of the arena and would 'link' the arena electrically."

The lighting proved to be a big problem. Rick Munroe: "We were in Denmark when Aucoin showed me the new staging plans. I was stunned and asked him, 'Bill, where are all the lights?' 'Well, the lights are on these towers.' 'No, Bill, the towers are behind the band, where are the *front* lights?' 'Well, there are no front lights.' 'You're kidding me! You're building this band on how they look and on their faces and makeup and you use no light on them?' I was embarrassed to be behind the board running it, after all I had done to make them look good under much worse circumstances." When the stage was refurbished for the subsequent tour that winter, a front lighting truss was one of the first additions.

As a final touch, two, sometimes three large banners emblazoned with the newly-created KISS Army coat of arms were suspended from the steel towers and were typically unfurled during "Let Me Go, Rock 'n Roll" or "Shout It Out Loud."

The finale of this tour's performances involved an important addition to Peter's drum riser—the visage of a black cat (looking uncannily like the logo used on Black Cat fireworks) on an ebony curtain that unfurled beneath the rising drum platform. A similar effect was used for nearly all subsequent tours in which Peter Criss took part.

The set list for the Summer Tour '76 was a significant departure from the typical Dressed to Kill/Alive! Tour set list that had remained essentially the same since spring 1975. Both "Deuce" and "Strutter" had been removed from the opening slots that each had occupied for virtually every show dating to early 1974. Other standards such as "100,000 Years" and "She" were retired to make room for the inclusion of over half of the *Destroyer* album.

Bob Seger & the Silver Bullet Band, who had opened a handful of shows for KISS in December 1975, were tapped as the opening band for the tour. Although there were a few instances when Seger was not on the bill, this was the first time that KISS booked a particular opening band for the entire duration of a tour. The two acts turned out to be a great pairing, each pushing the other to their limits on a nightly basis.

JULY 1, 1976   POSTPONED
Richmond, Virginia
Richmond Coliseum
Opening Act: Bob Seger & the Silver Bullet Band
Promoters: Entam Ltd., Belkin Productions
■ Scheduled for the opening night of the tour, the show was postponed at the eleventh hour when it took longer than expected to complete portions of the staging. Fortunately, the Richmond Coliseum had a date available only a week later, and the show was rescheduled for July 8.

JULY 3, 1976
Norfolk, Virginia
The Scope
Opening Act: Bob Seger & the Silver Bullet Band
Attendance: 8,539   Capacity: 11,584
Promoters: Entam Ltd., Belkin Productions
■ SET LIST
Detroit Rock City
King of the Night Time World
Let Me Go, Rock 'n Roll
Gene Simmons Bass Solo
God of Thunder
Sweet Pain
Ace Frehley Guitar Solo
Shout It Out Loud
Strutter
Nothin' to Lose
Watchin' You
Peter Criss Drum Solo
Do You Love Me
Flaming Youth
Deuce
Firehouse
Black Diamond
Rock and Roll All Nite
■ This was the official concert debut of what are generally known as the Destroyer stage and the Destroyer costumes.

The above set list was typed out on a sheet of paper with the title "Rundown on new KISS concert," and it was given to stage designer Mark Ravitz, who attended the show. This is the only known performance of "Sweet Pain," which was quickly replaced by "Cold Gin."

JULY 6, 1976
Columbia, South Carolina
Carolina Coliseum
Opening Act: Bob Seger & the Silver Bullet Band
Attendance: 6,157   Capacity: 12,328
Promoter: Beach Club Promotions

JULY 8, 1976   CANCELED
Clemson, South Carolina
Littlejohn Coliseum
Opening Act: Bob Seger & the Silver Bullet Band
Promoter: Beach Club Promotions
■ Listed on the original itinerary and a pre-tour ad, this show was ousted from the schedule when it became apparent that the original July 1 date for Richmond was not feasible. Ticket sales for the Clemson show had been sluggish, and with the opportunity to play the rescheduled Richmond show to a larger audience, the decision to cancel was an easy one.

JULY 8, 1976
Richmond, Virginia
Richmond Coliseum
Opening Act: Bob Seger & the Silver Bullet Band
Attendance: 6,430   Capacity: 12,600
Promoters: Entam Ltd., Belkin Productions

■ This was the make-up date for the postponed show on July 1.
During the show, a fan threw a live M-80 onstage that landed on the drum riser near Peter and detonated. The impact of the blast nearly blew Peter off his drum stool and left him with only partial hearing for the rest of the show. Peter later mentioned this incident on *The Tomorrow Show*, though he incorrectly cited Memphis as the city in which the incident occurred.

JULY 10, 1976
Jersey City, New Jersey
Roosevelt Stadium
Opening Acts: Bob Seger & the Silver Bullet Band, J. Geils Band, Point Blank
Attendance: 13,867   Capacity: 30,000
Promoter: John Scher Presents
Archived: Video
■ SET LIST
[Detroit Rock City]
[King of the Night Time World]
[Let Me Go, Rock 'n Roll]
[Hotter Than Hell]
Cold Gin
Ace Frehley Guitar Solo
Shout It Out Loud
Strutter
Nothin' to Lose
Do You Love Me
Watchin' You
Peter Criss Drum Solo
Gene Simmons Bass Solo
God of Thunder
Flaming Youth
Deuce
Firehouse
Black Diamond
Rock and Roll All Nite
■ This was KISS's first headlining show at a stadium and one of six stadium shows on the tour. Unfortunately, ticket sales fell short of expectations despite the hometown crowd and a huge, albeit late, advertising push by promoter John Scher and AMI. Walk-up ticket sales were diminished considerably by news of a stabbing that had occurred at Roosevelt Stadium during a Yes concert on June 17.

The venue was a perplexing choice in that the park was in an advanced state of ruin and seemed more of a fire hazard than a stadium. Roosevelt Stadium was a bit of a story in and of itself: a wooden edifice built in 1937 during Franklin Roosevelt's Works Progress Administration, the stadium sat upon a landfill that stored dirt excavated from the Holland Tunnel.

The general admission crowd, already agitated by the long admission lines and oppressive heat and humidity (it was 95 degrees at show time), was surly and impatient. In an effort to help alleviate the discomfort of the crowd, stadium officials sent employees throughout the park to distribute free bottles of chilled orange juice. A preemptive strike against the rising tension in the crowd, the effort backfired as several fights erupted when angry concertgoers began throwing the glass bottles at one another.

The show was professionally videotaped in black-and-white, and a live feed was sent to monitors backstage.

The post-concert party was nothing short of

spectacular with a huge tent erected to house the throngs of partygoers that included the band, members of AMI and the newly partnered Glickman/Marks firm, industry members, and various celebrities such as Linda Lovelace.

A show at Roosevelt Stadium on July 12 does appear on some itineraries; however, this was reserved on the schedule as a potential makeup date if the July 10 show was rained out.

JULY 11, 1976
South Yarmouth, Massachusetts
Cape Cod Coliseum
Opening Act: Bob Seger & the Silver Bullet Band
Attendance: 7,200   Capacity: 7,200
Promoters: New England Productions, Don Law Presents

■ From a room at the Riviera Hotel in Cape Cod, Paul and Gene taped a post-concert interview for a radio show called *BackStage*. During the interview, Paul joked that "Gene liked the album *(Destroyer)*" even though none of the other band members cared for it, and mentioned that "Eddie Kramer will return to produce the next album."

JULY 13, 1976
Baltimore, Maryland
Baltimore Civic Center
Opening Act: Bob Seger & the Silver Bullet Band
Attendance: 6,940 Capacity 12,500
Promoter: L & S Productions

■ According to a fan attending the show, production was significantly scaled back compared to most shows, as neither Gene's castle nor Ace's moon garden were used.

The print ad for the show indicated that models from the Patricia Stevens Agency gave away free kisses in the venue's lobby. We presume they meant Hershey's kisses.

JULY 15, 1976
Knoxville, Tennessee
Knoxville Civic Coliseum
Opening Act: Bob Seger & the Silver Bullet Band
Attendance: 8,970   Capacity: 10,000
Promoters: Entam Ltd., Belkin Productions

JULY 17 & 18, 1976
Homewood (Chicago), Illinois
Washington Park **TEMP HOLD DATES**
Promoter: Windy City Productions

■ The July 17 and 18 shows at Washington Park, the Roosevelt Stadium show on July 10, and the gig at Anaheim Stadium in August were the earliest shows of this tour to be planned, appearing in long-range plans as early as April. The two concerts in Chicago never made it far beyond the planning stage.

Tickets for the shows were never put on sale and no advertising was done. Somewhere along the line, most likely in May, AMI and promoter Windy City Productions decided to consolidate the shows, and a single Chicago date was scheduled for July 31 at Comiskey Park.

JULY 17, 1976
Charleston, West Virginia
Charleston Civic Center
Opening Act: Bob Seger & the Silver Bullet Band
Attendance: 9,500   Capacity: 9,500
Promoters: Entam Ltd., Belkin Productions

■ In their July 18 edition, *The Charleston Gazette* reported:"Throughout a long set and four encores—FOUR—the band didn't let up." This indicates it's highly likely that "Flaming Youth" was still in the set at this point, although the song was dropped sometime between this show and the first St. Louis concert on July 28.

Peter performed the show with his hand wrapped in tape due to a fractured thumb.

JULY 19, 1976
Johnson City, Tennessee
Freedom Hall Civic Center @ Science Hill High School
Opening Act: Bob Seger & the Silver Bullet Band
Attendance: 8,000   Capacity: 8,000
Promoters: Entam Ltd., Belkin Productions

JULY 21, 1976
Nashville, Tennessee
Nashville Municipal Auditorium
Opening Acts: Bob Seger & the Silver Bullet Band, UFO
Attendance: 8,233   Capacity: 11,000
Promoter: Sound 70 Concerts

■ Felix Pappalardi & Creation were originally slated to be the third act on the bill, but they canceled a few days prior to the show.

JULY 23, 1976
Birmingham, Alabama
Rickwood Field
Opening Acts: Kansas, Bob Seger & the Silver Bullet Band
Attendance: 12,664   Capacity: 20,000
Promotes: Ruffino & Vaughn

■ For the second time in two weeks, KISS performed in an ancient minor league baseball park. Rickwood Stadium, the longtime home of the Birmingham Barons, was built in 1910 and was the oldest baseball park still in use in the world.

JULY 26, 1976
Kansas City, Missouri
Municipal Auditorium
Opening Act: Artful Dodger
Attendance: 8,234   Capacity: 11,000
Promoters: Cowtown Productions, Contemporary Productions

■ A date for a second Kansas City show was held open for July 25, but was never used.

JULY 28, 1976
St. Louis, Missouri
Kiel Auditorium
Opening Act: Bob Seger & the Silver Bullet Band
Attendance: 6,896   Capacity: 10,584
Promoters: Ron Delsener Presents, Panther Productions
Archived: Video

■ SET LIST
Detroit Rock City
King of the Night Time World
Let Me Go, Rock 'n Roll
Cold Gin
Ace Frehley Guitar Solo
Shout It Out Loud
Strutter
Nothin' to Lose
Do You Love Me
Watchin' You
Peter Criss Drum Solo
Gene Simmons Bass Solo
God of Thunder
Rock and Roll All Nite
Deuce

Firehouse
Black Diamond

■ Peter's drum solo here marks the last known occasion where it appeared after "Watchin' You," rather than its soon-to-become-standard position in "God of Thunder."

AMI archived the show on black-and-white videotape with a single camera stationed at the soundboard.

JULY 29, 1976
St. Louis, Missouri
Kiel Auditorium
Opening Act: Bob Seger & the Silver Bullet Band
Attendance: 8,969   Capacity: 10,584
Promoters: Ron Delsener Presents, Panther Productions

JULY 31, 1976   CANCELED
Chicago, Illinois
Comiskey Park
Opening Acts: Ted Nugent, Uriah Heep, Bob Seger & the Silver Bullet Band
Promoter: Windy City Productions

■ Bad luck continued for KISS and Chicago—this became the third show to be canceled in the Windy City in less than a month. While the removal of the two shows from the itinerary at Washington Park was relatively painless, canceling the Comiskey Park show was a blow to KISS. On July 22, AMI was notified that a city ordinance prohibited non-sporting events at Comiskey from running past 8 P.M. This meant that to complete the concert before the curfew, KISS would have to be on stage by 6 P.M. This was unacceptable to the band and AMI because the impact of their stage show would be dramatically reduced by the sunlight that would still be present throughout the show. AMI made the decision to cancel the show and nearly 20,000 tickets were refunded.

The concert was to have been "Game Two" of a running series of concerts called "The World Series of Rock." Aerosmith had headlined "Game One" on July 10.

JULY 31, 1976
Toledo, Ohio
Sports Arena
Opening Act: Starz
Attendance: 7,485   Capacity: 7,485
Promoter: Belkin Productions

■ Given the incredibly short amount of lead time that Belkin Productions had after the cancellation of the Chicago concert, the attendance figure of nearly 7,500 is quite remarkable. The opening act, Starz, which featured guitarist Richie Ranno, was another Bill Aucoin discovery recently signed to AMI.

An AMI business report indicates that the promoter's check KISS received for their share of this show's revenues bounced.

AUGUST 2, 1976
Indianapolis, Indiana
Market Square Arena
Opening Acts: Bob Seger & Silver Bullet Band, Artful Dodger
Attendance: 19,000   Capacity: 19,000
Promoter: Sunshine Promotions

■ That same night across town, 1970s sensations The Carpenters performed a concert of their own. Reportedly, Gene spent several hours conversing with Karen Carpenter after the shows ended.

AUGUST 4, 1976

Little Rock, Arkansas
T.H. Barton Coliseum
Opening Act: Bob Seger & Silver Bullet Band
Attendance: 14,000   Capacity: 14,000
Promoter: Mid-South Concerts

AUGUST 6, 1976

Evansville, Indiana
Roberts Municipal Stadium
Opening Acts: Bob Seger & Silver Bullet Band, Artful
    Dodger
Attendance: 11,480   Capacity: 11,480
Promoter: Sunshine Promotions

■ At Bill Starkey's request, Gene did a post-concert interview to help squelch rising controversy that KISS was skipping Terre Haute because it was too small for such a huge band. Simmons assured them that this was not the case, and KISS did play Terre Haute's Hulman Center the following January.

During the interview, Simmons also stated that KISS would never play "Beth" in concert, a claim that held true for all of three months.

A review mentions that the God of Thunder machine was used during the show. This marks the last known appearance of the device.

AUGUST 8, 1976   CANCELED

Tampa, Florida
Tampa Stadium
Opening Act: Bob Seger & Silver Bullet Band

■ Management's difficulties with stadium shows continued as a combination of factors caused the cancellation of a fourth big-venue concert. Lack of ticket sales played a part in the scenario, but at the heart of the matter were the concerns of stadium officials. NFL expansion team the Tampa Bay Buccaneers were about to open their inaugural season in the newly renovated Tampa Stadium. Several recent concerts, particularly a July appearance by Jethro Tull, had done more damage to the stadium's new sod than was expected. This left officials believing that the notoriously rowdy KISS crowd would wreak such havoc with the delicate turf that repairing the damage in time for the Buccaneers' home opener in September would prove impossible.

AUGUST 8, 1976

Dayton, Ohio
Hara Arena & Exhibition Center
Opening Acts: Bob Seger & Silver Bullet Band, Artful
    Dodger
Attendance: 8,300   Capacity: 8,300
Promoter: Belkin Productions

AUGUST 10, 1976

Shreveport, Louisiana
Hirsch Memorial Coliseum
Opening Act: Bob Seger & Silver Bullet Band
Attendance: 8,033   Capacity: 10,200
Promoter: Concerts West

■ Rick Munroe: "One of the girls that was with us said something to one of the African-American janitors at the venue, and he looked at her like he was looking at a ghost and ran away without saying a word to her. He came back later with this white guy. The white guy started yelling at

the girl, 'Listen, you don't talk to the niggers. OK?! You leave them alone.' We were just flabbergasted by that!

"We're thinking that first of all, they're not niggers. Secondly, we had one with us, and he was our best buddy. Where in the world do you live where you can't talk to somebody? We were very taken aback by this.

"Later, Sean showed up at that gig, I think, in purple hair. The state police showed up and came into the dressing room and took all the booze and said, 'Try to stop us.' The state trooper made him get on his knees and put a gun in his mouth and called him a faggot.

"We were glad to get out of town."

AUGUST 11, 1976

Fort Worth, Texas
Tarrant County Convention Center
Opening Acts: Bob Seger & Silver Bullet Band, Artful
    Dodger
Attendance: 13,956   Capacity: 13,956
Promoter: Concerts West

■ KISS was charged $543 for damages to the venue.

At the last minute, Artful Dodger was added to the bill for this show and the subsequent concert in Houston.

AUGUST 13, 1976

Houston, Texas
The Summit
Opening Acts: Bob Seger & Silver Bullet Band, Artful
    Dodger
Attendance: 15,196   Capacity: 15,196
Promoters: Concerts West, Pace Concerts
Archived: Video

■ SET LIST

Detroit Rock City
King of the Night Time World
Let Me Go, Rock 'n Roll
Strutter
Hotter Than Hell

Shout It Out Loud
Cold Gin
Ace Frehley Guitar Solo
Nothin' to Lose
[Do You Love Me]
Gene Simmons Bass Solo
God of Thunder
Peter Criss Drum Solo - reprise
Rock and Roll All Nite
Deuce
Firehouse
Black Diamond

■ This concert was videotaped by John Crow TV Productions, the in-house video team that typically ran a live feed of Summit concerts onto a large screen above the stage.

Despite the tight scheduling, KISS flew from Houston to Atlanta on Friday night to make a Saturday appearance at the Peaches Records store on Peachtree Boulevard. The band staged a costume contest, and girls could pay 93 cents for the opportunity to kiss the bandmember of their choice. All the proceeds from the event, which was heavily covered by the local media, went to the muscular dystrophy campaign. *The Atlanta Journal and Constitution* reported, "The occasion was honored with a proclamation of Kiss Day by Mayor Maynard Jackson." His representative later added that the city was "proud to welcome groups as popular and notorious as KISS."

AUGUST 15, 1976

El Paso, Texas
El Paso County Coliseum
Opening Act: Moon Pie
Attendance: 11,000   Capacity: 11,000
Promoters: Concerts West, Pace Concerts

■ Bob Seger opted to play a long-scheduled concert in Jackson, Michigan on July 14 and could not make the return trip to El Paso in time for the gig. Local musicians Moon Pie were brought in as last-minute replacements.

KATHERINE KONONCHEK /COURTESY OF RANDI MARX /WWW.ARCANEHARVEST.COM

Gene and Ace arrive at KISS's August 14, 1976 Peaches in-store appearance in Atlanta. Notice Alan Miller on Ace's left, the man responsible for bringing producer Bob Ezrin into the KISS camp.

AUGUST 17, 1976

Tempe, Arizona
Tempe Stadium
Opening Acts: Ted Nugent, Bob Seger & the Silver
   Bullet Band
Attendance: 15,915   Capacity: 25,000
Promoter: Fun Productions

AUGUST 20, 1976

Anaheim, California
Anaheim Stadium
Opening Acts: Ted Nugent, Montrose, Bob Seger & the
   Silver Bullet Band
Attendance: 42,987   Capacity: 53,970
Promoter: Fun Productions
Archived: Video

■ SET LIST

Detroit Rock City
King of the Night Time World
Let Me Go, Rock 'n Roll
Strutter
Hotter Than Hell
Nothin' to Lose
Cold Gin
Ace Frehley Guitar Solo
Shout It Out Loud
Do You Love Me
Gene Simmons Bass Solo
God of Thunder
Peter Criss Drum Solo - reprise
Rock and Roll All Nite
Deuce
Firehouse
Black Diamond

■ In what was certainly the highlight of the tour, KISS played to what was probably the largest American crowd of their concert history. The undertaking was a huge coup for both the band and the aggressive promoter David Forest of Fun Productions. KISS's already-monstrous stage production was even more exaggerated for this show; a lighting effect modeling the New York skyline was added above the main lighting rig, and a lengthy firework display followed the show's final encore, "Black Diamond."

The entire event resembled a giant carnival, with tightrope walker Unique McPeak giving a circus-like performance between sets by Montrose and Ted Nugent, and hot-air balloonist Captain Schossberg piloting his craft into the stadium between Nugent and KISS.

The concert was projected onto two large video screens and the live feed was captured on videotape. Additionally, AMI set up a single color video camera at the soundboard to capture wide shots of the production.

Following their performance, a fully made-up KISS attended a party at the Anaheim Club on the stadium's premises. At the party, Peter was photographed wearing green makeup on the area immediately surrounding his eyes, a makeup variation he had not been known to use since 1973. The variation had become standard by the time KISS taped their appearance on *The Paul Lynde Halloween Special* in October 1976.

August 21 was held open on the schedule for a possible second Anaheim show. Lastly, Ted Nugent was added to the bill when Uriah Heap backed out of the engagement.

AUGUST 22, 1976

Oakland, California
Oakland-Alameda County Coliseum Arena
Opening Acts: Bob Seger & the Silver Bullet Band, Earth
   Quake
Attendance: 9,897   Capacity: 9,897
Promoter: Bill Graham Presents
■ Uriah Heep was scheduled to perform, but they canceled several days prior to the show.

AUGUST 27, 1976

Greensboro, North Carolina
Greensboro Coliseum
Opening Acts: Point Blank, Artful Dodger
Attendance: 11,068   Capacity: 11,068
Promoter: Fun Productions

AUGUST 29, 1976

Atlanta, Georgia
Atlanta/Fulton County Stadium
Opening Acts: Johnny & Edgar Winter, Blue Öyster Cult,
   Bob Seger & the Silver Bullet Band, .38 Special
Attendance: 34,489   Capacity: 50,000
Promoter: Alex Cooley Presents
■ Artful Dodger is listed on the bill in some ads, but they did not appear.

Because of a preseason football game between the Atlanta Falcons and Baltimore Colts on Saturday afternoon, the staging was set up in an all-night session ending late Sunday morning.

The papier maché cats from Peter's drum riser were stolen during load-out. A replacement pair was made quickly and appeared shortly thereafter.

SEPTEMBER 1, 1976

South Bend, Indiana
Joyce Athletic & Convocation Center Arena
Opening Act: Bob Seger & the Silver Bullet Band
Attendance: 7,677   Capacity: 7,677
Promoter: Sunshine Promotions

SEPTEMBER 3, 1976

Richfield (Cleveland), Ohio
The Coliseum
Opening Act: Artful Dodger
Attendance: 15,769   Capacity: 15,769
Promoter: Belkin Productions
Archived: Audio

■ SET LIST

See August 20, 1976.

SEPTEMBER 4, 1976

Pittsburgh, Pennsylvania
Civic Arena
Opening Acts: Bob Seger & the Silver Bullet Band,
   Artful Dodger
Attendance: 11,615   Capacity: 12,000
Promoter: DiCesare-Engler Productions

SEPTEMBER 6, 1976

Toronto, Ontario, Canada
Varsity Stadium
Opening Acts: Blue Öyster Cult, Artful Dodger
Attendance: 13,650   Capacity: 35,000
Promoter: Concert Promotions Int'l
Archived: Audio

■ SET LIST

See August 20, 1976.
Artful Dodger replaced Bob Seger, who was the originally scheduled opening act.

SEPTEMBER 8, 1976

Louisville, Kentucky
Freedom Hall
Opening Acts: Bob Seger & the Silver Bullet Band,
   Artful Dodger
Attendance: 17,051   Capacity: 19,000
Promoter: Sunshine Promotions

SEPTEMBER 10, 1976

Cincinnati, Ohio
Riverfront Coliseum
Opening Acts: Bob Seger & the Silver Bullet Band,
   Artful Dodger
Attendance: 13,381   Capacity: 18,500
Promoter: Electric Factory Concerts

SEPTEMBER 11, 1976   CANCELED

Hartford, Connecticut
Colt Park
Opening Act: Blue Öyster Cult
Promoter: Cross Country Concerts
■ This concert was canceled during the first week of August when the Hartford City Council banned rock concerts from Colt Park. Nearby residents had issued a steady stream of complaints regarding the noise, loitering, assaults, and vandalism associated with concerts at the venue, and an August 2 bottle fight between concertgoers and local police proved to be the final straw. This was the second such ban imposed by the city

council in 1976 as they had outlawed concerts at Dillon Stadium earlier in the year. KISS never performed at the venue. Ironically, fraudulent concert posters of fictional KISS shows at Dillion Stadium would later surface.

Despite the early cancellation, an ad for the show (incorrectly listing September 10) appears in the weekly publication *The Aquarian* as late as September 7.

SEPTEMBER 12, 1976 ~~CANCELED~~
Allentown, Pennsylvania
Allentown Fairgrounds Grandstand
Opening Act: Bob Seger & the Silver Bullet Band
Promoter: Jennifer Productions
■ This show was listed on the early itineraries for the tour, but disappeared soon thereafter. The promoter has no record of the event, and the reason for the cancellation is unknown.

SEPTEMBER 12, 1976
Springfield, Massachusetts
Springfield Civic Center
Opening Act: Artful Dodger
Attendance: 8,409   Capacity: 10,000
Promoter: Cross Country Concerts
Archived: Audio
■ **SET LIST**
See August 20, 1976
■ This marked the second tour in a row to end in Springfield.

——————-——————

During the summer, Scott Shannon, vice president of promotion for Casablanca, had coerced Neil Bogart into putting "Beth" as the B-side to the "Detroit Rock City" single, which was released by the label on August 5 and promptly flopped.

It is very ironic, then, that "Beth" eventually became the most important single in the band's career, thanks largely to Shannon, who soon convinced a radio station in Columbus, Georgia to add it into rotation. Within days it was the station's most-requested song. Using Columbus as an example, Shannon and the other 24 Casablanca promotion men convinced a long list of stations nationwide to add the single to their playlists. Most were similarly bombarded by calls requesting "Beth," and the song was quickly issued as an A-side and landed on the *Billboard* charts, where it eventually peaked at #7.

It is clear that the overwhelming success of *Alive!* had broken KISS as a major act, but it is quite likely that without "Beth," KISS would have sunk into one-album-wonder oblivion as quickly as they had risen. Over the coming months, "Beth" would become a demographic-shattering phenomenon for KISS, infusing *Destroyer* with new energy on the charts, expanding the band's fanbase into the far reaches of adult contemporary music, and all the while being the antithesis of what the band was about.

OCTOBER 1, 1976
New York, New York
Puglia
■ While obviously not part of the tour, this occasion at a popular restaurant in Little Italy marked Howard Marks's birthday party, and the event would become an annual ritual. KISS took the opportunity to perform a short set of cover material, including Led Zeppelin and Beatles tunes.

Sometimes friends of the band and road crew would get bored while on the road and try to capture shots of the band members sans makeup. These pictures are Eddie Solan's attempt to do so while on a flight to Oakland in August 1976.

EDDIE SOLAN/COURTESY OF CURT GOOCH

CHAPTER 8

ROCK AND ROLL OVER TOUR

Number of Shows: 70
Start Date: November 24, 1976 - Savannah, Georgia
End Date: April 3, 1977 - Tokyo, Japan
Countries: Japan, U.S.A.
Opening Acts: Blackfoot; Bob Seger & the Silver Bullet Band; Bow Wow; Climax Blues Band; Dictators; Dr. Hook & the Medicine Show; Graham Parker & the Rumour; Head East; Jesse Bolt; Legs Diamond; Natural Gas; The Raisin Band; Sammy Hagar; Tom Petty and the Heartbreakers; Uriah Heep

Average Attendance: 10,868

The two-and-a-half months between the Destroyer and Rock and Roll Over Tours were the longest break KISS had taken from touring since 1973. "Beth" was still riding high on the charts, and though both Peter and Paul found time for short vacations in Hawaii, the band was not idle.

Immediately after the Destroyer Tour, KISS began work on its next album. Budgeted at $76,400, *Rock and Roll Over* was recorded at the Star Theatre in Nanuet, New York between September 13 and October 4. Eddie Kramer returned to produce the album, which abandoned Bob Ezrin's lush *Destroyer* approach in favor of the raw, live sound the band had used before. In an effort to capture the band's live sound, Kramer had chosen an actual concert

venue rather than a studio as the site for the recordings. He spent time experimenting with the sound, having the band members set up all over the theater, even placing the drums in one of the venue's bathrooms. At times, the band was so scattered throughout the venue that they communicated via video monitors. The album was released on November 1, 1976.

On October 19 and 20, KISS was in Hollywood taping lip-synched performances of "Detroit Rock City," "Beth," and "King of the Night Time World," for their appearance on *The Paul Lynde Halloween Special.* Drum tech Chuck Elias remembers, "Tim Conway was on the show and we pretty much laughed the whole time we were there. I remember talking to John Travolta about KISS as he was doing *Welcome Back, Kotter*

across the lot."

It wasn't quite *The Ed Sullivan Show,* but a rock band appearing on prime time television in 1976 in the United States was still a major event, to say the least. Its impact for KISS would be almost immediate. In fact, many of the fans who would go on to comprise the KISS fan base first became aware of the band on October 29, when ABC-TV broadcast the special. The band recognized the show's impact very quickly. Paul Stanley, in particular, first began to notice KISS's audience widening on December 2 in Memphis, Tennessee. He told a reporter the following night, "I saw parents there with four-year-old kids. I think the thing that sets KISS apart from so many other groups is that we appeal to such a wide audience." Paul was correct. KISS's audi-

CHUCK ELIAS

A mixing board and other studio components on location at Nanuet, New York's Star Theatre for the Rock and Roll Over sessions. Note the video monitor above the mixing board.

ence was expanding in two directions: towards a younger demographic, thanks to the exposure from the Paul Lynde show, and for a brief period, towards an older demographic too, due to the immense crossover success of "Beth."

The appeal to a wider audience made the Rock and Roll Over Tour KISS's most successful tour ever in terms of the percentage of tickets sold; 98.1 percent of the tickets available for the tour were purchased. This was a mark KISS would never eclipse, though several tours would average higher attendance figures per show.

Rehearsals for the Winter '76 –77 Tour, as it was officially dubbed, began at SIR studios in Manhattan on November 8 where the band rehearsed through November 12. Production and dress rehearsals were held on a military facility in Reading, Massachusetts and ran from November 15–21. During the rehearsals in Reading, promotional films for "I Want You," "Hard Luck Woman," and "Love 'em and Leave 'em" were videotaped specifically for Don Kirshner's Rock Concert. The three videos, which were broadcast on May 28, 1977, were eventually transferred to film and sent overseas for promotional use there.

KISS's business managers, Glickman/Marks, who had been officially on board since May 5, were beginning to assert their presence. Rick Munroe offers, "Up to this point, management listened to the band and what they wanted, then tried to realize those goals. For the longest time, the crew was making more money a week than anybody in the band was. Every dime the band made went back into the organization—to costumes, to makeup, to getting the marketing thing together. It seemed like it had all taken hold, and things were working, things were happening. Then, total strangers who had no idea what we were doing were brought in to run the operations. They were in a position where they had more say into what was going on than we did, and we'd been with the band for years.

"I was invited in to discuss my lighting schemes with Ken Anderson, the production manager. I came in and showed them what I planned on doing, and what I felt would really make it work. At that point it dawned on me that I was competing with other lighting companies. Ken called me shortly after my meeting with

him and said, 'Sorry, but we won't be using your design and we won't be needing you.' It was that quick, and that sudden."

Although the pairing would be brief, the band hired publicist Danny Goldberg prior to the release of Rock and Roll Over. Goldberg, a legend in his own right, had previously worked for Led Zeppelin, first as their publicist and ultimately as CEO of their imprint label, Swan Song. Part of Goldberg's task was to help KISS reconnect with the segment of their audience that had been alienated by Destroyer. Danny was able to use several of his press contacts to help get maximum coverage for the new album and tour, including a feature article in Rolling Stone. Years later, Goldberg would again prove to be an invaluable resource for KISS when he became CEO of the Mercury Records Group.

The Rock and Roll Over Tour used a refined version of the Destroyer Tour stage. Fritz Postlethwaite remarks: "The set pieces would start to disappear after a while until we got closer to what the band wanted, which was huge, black, chrome, and loud." The apocalyptic landscape and crystal frontispieces were significantly scaled back, the lighting towers were replaced with a more traditional lighting grid, and Peter was using a new drum riser that was bordered in chrome.

Not surprisingly, KISS retained the costumes from the Destroyer Tour with only slight modifications. Paul lost the blonde streak in his hair and in January began to wear a belt over his outfit. Also, at their Madison Square Garden appearance on February 18, Paul debuted a new costume which closely resembled a sleeveless version of his Destroyer garb, but with feathered armbands.

The concerts on the tour were scheduled to be 75 minutes long, and the set list was heavily weighted in favor of the Rock and Roll Over album, with "I Want You," "Take Me," "Ladies Room," and "Makin' Love" part of the standard set throughout the tour. "Hard Luck Woman" was included and appeared in concert as late as the December 4 show in New Orleans, but it was dropped some time during the following week. A sixth track from the album, "Love 'em and Leave 'em," appears on a rehearsal tape, and was most likely performed early on the tour, which Gene asserted in a 1998 interview with journalist Ken Sharp. Additionally, "Nothin' to Lose" was slightly rearranged, with Peter and Paul in a prominent call-and-response with Gene during the song's verses.

"Beth" was also added to the set list. The single had not attained hit status during the Destroyer Tour, but by November 1976 it was a national success, and the Rock and Roll Over Tour reaped the benefits. Aucoin made certain that many industry publications noted that KISS sold out the first 22 appearances of the tour in advance. While exact figures are not available for every show, the first attendance figure that did not reflect a sellout didn't appear until February 21, 1977, some 53 shows into the tour.

NOVEMBER 24, 1976 POSTPONED

Fayetteville, North Carolina
Cumberland County Memorial Arena
Promoter: Beach Club Promotions
■ The show was postponed for unknown reasons

and was rescheduled for December 27.

NOVEMBER 24, 1976

Savannah, Georgia
Civic Center
Opening Act: Graham Parker & the Rumour
Attendance: 8,000+   Capacity: 8,000
Promoter: Alex Cooley Presents
■ "Beth" was presumably performed live for the first time at this show. Despite the attempts made during sound checks and rehearsals to arrange the piece so the band could play it as a group, only the vocals were performed live; Ezrin's 70-piece orchestral arrangements from Destroyer were piped in over the P.A.

NOVEMBER 25, 1976

Charlotte, North Carolina
Charlotte Coliseum
Opening Act: Jesse Bolt
Attendance: 13,300   Capacity: 13,300
Promoter: Kaleidoscope Productions

NOVEMBER 27, 1976

Raleigh, North Carolina
J.S. Dorton Arena @ North Carolina State Fairgrounds
Opening Act: The Raisin Band
Attendance: 4,000   Capacity: 4,000
Promoter: Kaleidoscope Productions
■ In the weeks prior to the concert, both Bob Seger and the Climax Blues Band were listed in the opening act slot in local ads, before The Raisin Band ultimately got the gig.

NOVEMBER 28, 1976

Greenville, South Carolina
Greenville Municipal Auditorium
Opening Act: Climax Blues Band
Attendance: 6,153   Capacity: 6,153
Promoter: Kaleidoscope Productions

NOVEMBER 30, 1976

Columbus, Georgia
Columbus Municipal Auditorium
Opening Act: Tom Petty and the Heartbreakers
Attendance: Sold Out
Promoter: Bash Productions
■ This was Tom Petty's first performance in an arena.

DECEMBER 2, 1976

Memphis, Tennessee
Mid-South Coliseum
Opening Act: Dr. Hook & the Medicine Show
Attendance: 12,000   Capacity: 12,000
Promoters: Mid-South Concerts, Beaver Productions
■ The originally scheduled opening act, Tommy Bolin, canceled. In Miami, only two days later, Bolin was found dead of a drug overdose.

Pushing and shoving outside the gates for this general admission show caused glass in some of the venue's doors to break. According to the Commercial Appeal review by Walter Dawson, "An announcement (was made) by a tour person: 'The fire marshal asks that the aisles be cleared, please' . . . Three songs later, the man is back: 'The fire marshal has threatened to pull the plug and stop the show. Please move back' . . . Then, the fire marshal himself comes out on stage. Hundreds of youngsters give him an obscene gesture. After a few minutes the show is back on."

DECEMBER 3, 1976

Jackson, Mississippi

Mississippi Coliseum
Opening Act: Dr. Hook & the Medicine Show
Attendance: 12,000   Capacity: 12,000
Promoter: Beaver Productions
Archived: Super 8mm
■ **PARTIAL SET LIST**
Detroit Rock City
Take Me
Let Me Go, Rock 'n Roll
Strutter
Firehouse
I Want You
Hard Luck Woman
God of Thunder
Shout It Out Loud
Rock and Roll All Nite
Beth
Black Diamond

■ The set list is derived from the 8mm film footage and from Joe Leydon's review in *The Clarion-Ledger,* which mentions "Hard Luck Woman," "Firehouse," "Strutter," "Beth," and "Rock and Roll All Nite" were performed. This is the last known performance of "Strutter" until July 1980.

Leydon goes on to note, "Sprinkled among the thousands of teenagers at Mississippi Coliseum Friday night were a surprising number of middle-aged types, including quite a few parents with their children. Even without makeup Stanley enjoys the adulation of KISS freaks. While wandering about recently in a North Carolina shopping center, Stanley found himself followed by scores of fans."

DECEMBER 4, 1976

New Orleans, Louisiana
Municipal Auditorium
Opening Act: Blackfoot
Attendance: Sold Out
Promoter: Beaver Productions
Archived: Audio
■ **PARTIAL SET LIST**
Detroit Rock City
Take Me
Let Me Go, Rock 'n Roll
Firehouse
Do You Love Me
Ladies Room
Hard Luck Woman
I Want You
Gene Simmons Bass Solo
God of Thunder
Peter Criss Drum Solo - reprise
Cold Gin

DECEMBER 5, 1976

Mobile, Alabama
Mobile Municipal Auditorium
Opening Act: Blackfoot
Attendance: Sold Out
Promoter: Beaver Productions
■ Gene caught his hair on fire and was injured badly enough to cut the show short.

DECEMBER 7, 1976

Huntsville, Alabama
Von Braun Civic Center
Opening Act: Dr. Hook & the Medicine Show
Attendance: 11,521   Capacity: 10,500
Promoter: Sound 70 Concerts
■ The show was oversold by more than 1,000 tickets. Uriah Heep was the originally scheduled opening act, but the group did not perform.

DECEMBER 8, 1976

Macon, Georgia
Macon Auditorium
Opening Act: Uriah Heep
Attendance: 8,000   Capacity: 8,000
Promoter: Alex Cooley Presents

DECEMBER 10, 1976

Jacksonville, Florida
Jacksonville Veterans Memorial Coliseum
Opening Act: Uriah Heep
Attendance: 10,228   Capacity: 10,228
Promoter: Kaleidoscope Productions

DECEMBER 11, 1976

Pembroke Pines (Hollywood), Florida
The Sportatorium
Opening Act: Uriah Heep
Attendance: 12,943   Capacity: 12,943
Promoter: Kaleidoscope Productions

DECEMBER 12, 1976

Lakeland, Florida
Lakeland Civic Center
Opening Act: Uriah Heep
Attendance: 8,136   Capacity: 8,136
Promoter: Kaleidoscope Productions
■ During the opening number "Detroit Rock City," Ace touched the metal railing on the stage-left staircase, which was ungrounded, and he was nearly electrocuted. Longtime Peter Criss drum tech Chuck Elias recalls the details: "It happened very fast, right at the beginning of the show and basically right above my head. Ace was standing on top of the stairs. I saw him grabbing the rail and not being able to move, and then eventually hitting the ground. We were up there instantly, but he was stunned more than anything else, which was lucky because it could have been life-threatening." After a 30-minute delay, KISS restarted the show from the top, only to have Gene set his hair on fire later in the set.

To alleviate the threat of electrocution, production manager Ken Anderson began looking into using wireless guitars. Anderson recalls: "I was involved with a company called Vega who had developed some wireless mikes and I explained our problem to them. They understood the situation and had some of their engineers get to work on it. Through a lot of trial and error, we eventually got a wireless system working and the band was quite happy with it."

The band flew from Tampa to Buffalo immediately after the show.

DECEMBER 15, 1976

Buffalo, New York
Veterans Memorial Auditorium
Opening Act: Uriah Heep
Attendance: 12,182   Capacity: 17,500
Promoter: Festival East, Inc.

DECEMBER 16, 1976

Syracuse, New York
Onondaga County War Memorial
Opening Act: Uriah Heep
Attendance: 8,300   Capacity: 8,300
Promoter: Concerts East

DECEMBER 18, 1976

New Haven, Connecticut
New Haven Veterans Memorial Coliseum
Opening Act: Uriah Heep

Attendance: 9,300   Capacity: 9,300
Promoter: Cross Country Concerts

DECEMBER 19, 1976

Landover (Washington, D.C.), Maryland
Capital Centre
Opening Act: Bob Seger & the Silver Bullet Band
Attendance: 19,000+   Capacity: 19,000+
Promoter: Cellar Door Concerts
■ The show was broadcast on a video screen over the stage, although AMI apparently did not purchase a copy from the venue.

DECEMBER 21, 1976

Philadelphia, Pennsylvania
The Spectrum
Opening Act: Bob Seger & the Silver Bullet Band
Attendance: 19,500   Capacity: 19,500
Promoter: Electric Factory Concerts
■ All proceeds from the show went to charity. Fans were asked to bring toys and Christmas gifts to the show for distribution to the Children's Hospital of Philadelphia.

DECEMBER 27, 1976

Fayetteville, North Carolina
Cumberland County Memorial Arena
Opening Act: Blackfoot
Attendance: 7,000   Capacity: 7,000
Promoter: Beach Club Promotions
■ This was the make-up date for the November 24 concert.

DECEMBER 28, 1976

Roanoke, Virginia
Roanoke Civic Center
Opening Act: Uriah Heep
Attendance: 11,000   Capacity: 11,000
Promoter: Belkin Productions

DECEMBER 30, 1976

Augusta, Maine
Augusta Civic Center
Opening Act: Natural Gas
Attendance: 7,249   Capacity: 7,249
Promoters: Ruffino & Vaughn, Northeast Concerts

JANUARY 1, 1977

Providence, Rhode Island
Providence Civic Center
Opening Act: Uriah Heep
Attendance: 13,200   Capacity: 13,200
Promoter: Mark Puma
Archived: Audio
■ **SET LIST**
Detroit Rock City
Take Me
Let Me Go, Rock 'n Roll
Ladies Room
Firehouse
Makin' Love
I Want You
Cold Gin
Ace Frehley Guitar Solo
Do You Love Me
Nothin' to Lose
Gene Simmons Bass Solo
God of Thunder
Peter Criss Drum Solo - reprise
Rock and Roll All Nite
Shout It Out Loud
Beth
Black Diamond

JANUARY 5, 1977

Abllene, Texas

Peter performing "Beth" at the band's December 27, 1976 concert in Fayetteville. Notice the Anvil case serving as a stool, rather than the drum trap case he would come to favor.

Taylor County Coliseum
Opening Act: Uriah Heep
Attendance: 8,956   Capacity: 8,956
Promoter: Stone City Attractions
■ KISS broke the house record for attendance, previously held by Lawrence Welk. 600 people were turned away at the door.

JANUARY 6, 1977
Tulsa, Oklahoma
Tulsa Assembly Center
Opening Act: Uriah Heep
Promoter: Concerts West
■ Setup time for the show was greatly reduced when a severe snowstorm delayed the arrival of the crew and gear.

JANUARY 7, 1977
Norman, Oklahoma
Lloyd Noble Center
Opening Act: Uriah Heep
Attendance: Sold Out
Promoter: Concerts West

JANUARY 9, 1977
Wichita, Kansas
Henry J. Levitt Arena
Opening Act: Uriah Heep
Attendance: 10,886   Capacity: 10,886
Promoter: Feyline Presents

JANUARY 10, 1977
Amarillo, Texas

The Amarillo Civic Center
Opening Act: Uriah Heep
Attendance: 7,875   Capacity: 7,875
Promoter: Feyline Presents

JANUARY 11, 1977
Albuquerque, New Mexico
Tingley Coliseum
Opening Act: Uriah Heep
Attendance: 9,671
Promoter: Feyline Presents

JANUARY 13, 1977
Salt Lake City, Utah
O. Thayne Accord Arena @ Salt Palace Center
Opening Act: Uriah Heep
Promoter: United Concerts

JANUARY 15, 1977
Denver, Colorado
McNichols Sports Arena
Opening Act: Uriah Heep
Attendance: 16,137
Promoter: Feyline Presents
Archived: Audio
■ SET LIST
See January 1, 1977.

JANUARY 17, 1977
Grand Forks, North Dakota
University of North Dakota Fieldhouse
Opening Act: Uriah Heep
Capacity: 7,500
Promoter: Ken Brandt

JANUARY 18, 1977
Duluth, Minnesota
Duluth Arena Auditorium
Opening Act: Uriah Heep
Attendance: 8,114   Capacity: 8,000
Promoter: Yan Qui Productions
■ The arena's box office was robbed on the day of the show. Oddly enough, the perpetrators took no cash, only some tickets for the night's sold-out performance.

JANUARY 19, 1977
TEMP HOLD DATE
Springfield, Missouri
John Q. Hammons Student Center @ Southwest
    Missouri State University

JANUARY 20, 1977
Lincoln, Nebraska
Pershing Auditorium
Opening Act: Uriah Heep
Attendance: 8,387   Capacity: 8,387
Promoter: Feyline Presents
Archived: Audio
■ SET LIST
Detroit Rock City
Take Me
Let Me Go, Rock 'n Roll
Ladies Room
Firehouse
Makin' Love
I Want You
Cold Gin
Ace Frehley Guitar Solo
Do You Love Me
Nothin' to Lose
Gene Simmons Bass Solo
God of Thunder
Peter Criss Drum Solo - reprise
Rock and Roll All Nite
[Shout It Out Loud]
[Beth]
[Black Diamond]
■ Ace announced Paul's birthday to the crowd following "Rock and Roll All Nite."
    Eddie Balandas: "We all got dressed up in drag for Paul's birthday party. We joked that since we couldn't get any women to show up, we'd have to wear the dresses ourselves. Strange thing was that we couldn't figure out how this one dress went on, but when Paul got it and took it out he said, 'It goes on this way.' It was one of these wrap-around things. We thought it was weird that he knew how to put it on."

JANUARY 21, 1977
Des Moines, Iowa
Veterans Memorial Auditorium
Opening Act: Uriah Heep
Attendance: 14,234   Capacity: 14,234
Promoter: Celebration Concerts
■ KISS surpassed The Who's attendance record (set in 1975) by nearly 1,000 people.

JANUARY 22, 1977
Chicago, Illinois
Chicago Stadium
Opening Act: Uriah Heep
Promoter: Concerts West

JANUARY 24, 1977
Fort Wayne, Indiana
Allen Co. War Memorial Coliseum
Opening Act: Uriah Heep
Promoter: Sunshine Promotions

JANUARY 25, 1977
Terre Haute, Indiana
Hulman Civic University Center
Opening Act: Uriah Heep
Attendance: 11,027   Capacity: 11,000
Promoter: Entam Ltd.

JANUARY 27, 1977
Detroit, Michigan
Cobo Arena
Opening Act: Uriah Heep
Attendance: 11,041   Capacity: 11,041
Promoter: Belkin Productions

■ While in Detroit, KISS was interviewed on TV by local anchor Max Kinkel; the band appeared without makeup but with their backs to the camera, the first known time that they did so.

JANUARY 28, 1977
Detroit, Michigan
Cobo Arena
Opening Act: Uriah Heep
Attendance: 11,041   Capacity: 11,041
Promoter: Belkin Productions

■ During the afternoon of the 28th, the band was notified that "Beth" had won a *People's Choice Award*. The concert was videotaped, and the taped portions of "Beth" were then shown on February 10 when the actual show, the *3rd Annual People's Choice Awards*, aired, albeit with canned audio. Goldie Hawn presented the award, which Lydia Criss accepted on the band's behalf.

All three Cobo Arena gigs were broadcast live on an overhead video screen in the arena and may have been archived on videotape, most likely by the Kelly-Kirby production team. However, other than the aforementioned clips of "Beth," none of the footage has appeared either among collectors or from the band's archives.

JANUARY 29, 1977
Detroit, Michigan
Cobo Arena
Opening Act: Uriah Heep
Attendance: 11,041   Capacity: 11,041
Promoter: Belkin Productions

FEBRUARY 1, 1977
Milwaukee, Wisconsin
Milwaukee Auditorium
Opening Act: Uriah Heep
Attendance: 6,155   Capacity: 6,155
Promoter: Daydream Productions

FEBRUARY 2, 1977
Milwaukee, Wisconsin
Milwaukee Auditorium
Opening Act: Uriah Heep
Attendance: 6,155   Capacity: 6,155
Promoter: Daydream Productions

FEBRUARY 3, 1977
Green Bay, Wisconsin
Brown County Veterans Memorial Arena
Opening Act: Uriah Heep
Attendance: 7,008   Capacity 7,008
Promoter: Daydream Productions

FEBRUARY 4, 1977
Madison, Wisconsin
Dane County Expo Center Coliseum
Opening Act: Uriah Heep
Attendance: 10,050   Capacity: 10,050
Promoter: Daydream Productions

FEBRUARY 6, 1977
Bloomington (Minneapolis), Minnesota
Metropolitan Sports Center
Opening Act: Uriah Heep
Attendance: 16,800   Capacity: 16,800
Promoter: Schon Productions

■ Paul wore his Alive! Tour costume at this show. He also wore the outfit at the subsequent shows in Waterloo (February 10) and Hartford (February 16), and presumably at all the shows between February 6 and 16. Most likely, something happened to Paul's Destroyer outfit(s) around this time that forced him to wear his Alive! costume.

FEBRUARY 8, 1977
Omaha, Nebraska
Omaha Civic Auditorium
Opening Act: Uriah Heep
Attendance: 12,000   Capacity: 12,000
Promoter: Schon Productions

FEBRUARY 9, 1977
Kansas City, Missouri
Kemper Arena
Opening Act: Head East
Attendance: 14,931   Capacity: 14,931
Promoter: Cowtown Productions

FEBRUARY 10, 1977
Waterloo, Iowa
McElroy Auditorium
Opening Act: Dictators
Attendance: 7,800   Capacity: 7,800
Promoter: Fox Productions

FEBRUARY 12, 1977
Bismarck, North Dakota
Bismarck Civic Center
Opening Act: Dictators
Attendance: 8,000   Capacity: 8,000
Promoter: Amusement Conspiracy

FEBRUARY 13, 1977
Fargo, North Dakota **TEMP HOLD DATE**
Fieldhouse @ North Dakota State University
Promoter: Amusement Conspiracy

FEBRUARY 16, 1977
Hartford, Connecticut
Hartford Civic Center
Opening Act: Sammy Hagar
Attendance: 9,150
Promoter: Cross Country Concerts

■ **SET LIST**
Detroit Rock City
Take Me
Let Me Go, Rock 'n Roll
Ladies Room
[Firehouse]
Makin' Love
Cold Gin
Ace Frehley Guitar Solo
I Want You
[Do You Love Me]
[Nothin' to Lose]
Gene Simmons Bass Solo
God of Thunder
Peter Criss Drum Solo - reprise
Rock and Roll All Nite
[Shout It Out Loud]
[Beth]
Black Diamond

FEBRUARY 18, 1977
New York, New York
Madison Square Garden
Opening Act: Sammy Hagar
Attendance: 19,626   Capacity: 19,626
Promoter: Ron Delsener Presents
Archived: Video
■ **SET LIST**
Detroit Rock City
Take Me
Let Me Go, Rock 'n Roll
Ladies Room
Firehouse
Makin' Love
Cold Gin
Ace Frehley Guitar Solo
I Want You
Do You Love Me
Nothin' to Lose
Gene Simmons Bass Solo
God of Thunder
Peter Criss Drum Solo - reprise
Rock and Roll All Nite
Shout It Out Loud
Beth
Black Diamond

■ After three years of constant touring, KISS realized a dream when they headlined before a sold-out hometown crowd at Madison Square Garden. KISS could have very easily done this in late 1975, but Aucoin wisely held off until the show could rightly be billed as a "triumphant return of the conquering heroes."

Chuck Elias: "Ace was too drunk to do the sound check, so his buddy Bobby McAdams filled in, which did happen occasionally with all of them. The whole day was a big nightmare, from a crew standpoint more than anything else because we had to contend with the local union and they were brutal to deal with." The band tested Vega's wireless guitar system during sound check.

While the band appeared overexcited and the performance was rushed and sloppy, as an event it was an enormous success. It's ironic to note that given the overflowing attendance, the promoter, Ron Delsener, was hesitant to book more than one show at the Garden. Hence, the Nassau Coliseum was booked for a gig three days later. AMI put a more positive spin on the story, claiming that the Garden's tight schedule accounted for the lack of a second show there.

Aucoin used the "conquering heroes" tagline on the dinner menu for the massive after-show party held at the Parc Swim and Health Club on Fifty-sixth Street. The band showed up without makeup and proceeded to throw more than one of their guests into the pool, including Ace, who by some accounts lost his shoes in the pool.

FEBRUARY 21, 1977
Uniondale, New York
Nassau Veterans Memorial Coliseum
Opening Act: Sammy Hagar
Attendance: 13,759   Capacity: 16,688
Promoter: Phil Basile of Concerts East

FEBRUARY 23, 1977   **POSTPONED**
Hampton, Virginia
Hampton Coliseum
Promoter: Entam Ltd.

■ Peter was involved in a car accident with Paul Chavarria and had sustained injuries that left him unable to apply his makeup for a few days. The show was postponed until March 7.

FEBRUARY 26, 1977

Johnson City, Tennessee
Freedom Hall Civic Center @ Science Hill High School
Opening Act: Dictators
Attendance: 8,500   Capacity: 8,500
Promoter: Entam Ltd.
Archived: Audio
■ SET LIST
Detroit Rock City
Take Me
Let Me Go, Rock 'n Roll
Ladies Room
Firehouse
Makin' Love
I Want You
Cold Gin
Ace Frehley Guitar Solo
Do You Love Me
Nothin' to Lose
Gene Simmons Bass Solo
God of Thunder
Peter Criss Drum Solo - reprise
Rock and Roll All Nite
Shout It Out Loud
Black Diamond
■ Peter was apparently still suffering from the effects of his car accident as evidenced by the fact that "Beth" was not performed at the show, and Paul sang all of Peter's lines in "Black Diamond."

FEBRUARY 27, 1977

Columbia, South Carolina
Carolina Coliseum
Opening Act: Dictators
Attendance: 12,832   Capacity: 12,832
Promoter: Beach Club Promotions

MARCH 1, 1977

Asheville, North Carolina
Asheville Civic Center
Opening Act: Dictators
Attendance: 7,654   Capacity: 7,654
Promoter: Kaleidoscope Productions

MARCH 3, 1977

Birmingham, Alabama
Birmingham-Jefferson Civic Center
Opening Act: Dictators
Promoter: Ruffino & Vaughn

MARCH 5, 1977

Lexington, Kentucky
Rupp Arena
Opening Act: Legs Diamond
Attendance: 16,558   Capacity: 20,416
Promoter: Sunshine Promotions
Archived: Audio
■ SET LIST
See January 1, 1977.

MARCH 6, 1977

Columbus, Ohio
St. John Arena
Opening Act: Legs Diamond
Attendance: Sold Out
Promoter: Your Friends Productions

MARCH 7, 1977

Hampton, Virginia
Hampton Coliseum
Opening Act: Legs Diamond

Attendance: 9,949   Capacity: 12,075
Promoter: Entam Ltd.
■ This was the make-up date for the postponed February 23rd show.

————————

Though KISS and the Japanese culture seemed a perfect match in many respects, various issues had made a tour of Japan impractical thus far. Cost had been a considerable factor and since the North American market had been so robust for KISS, the band had been content to focus on domestic tours. Initially, the Japanese tour was also supposed to include stops in Australia and New Zealand, though those dates never came to fruition.

Getting KISS to Japan was an enormous task that involved the efforts of countless people over a period of several months. As far back as January 22, Al Ross, (who was Aucoin's silent partner in AMI), was busy coordinating the trip, ordering bilingual business cards for the band and management, and 1,000 lip-shaped stick-pins which were given out as gifts to various Japanese VIPs. "It was probably one of the most successful P.R. campaigns done," offers Ross. "I made a deal with Pan-Am to have them fly over some domestic press people and Pan-Am picked up ten first-class tickets. In exchange for that I guaranteed

them that in every story there would be a mention of Pan-Am. As it turned out, from that little junket we ended up with over 300 different publications. I then turned around and made a deal with Pan-Am that I would give them the right to carry all our cargo on the tour; in exchange for that, they painted the nose of a 747 with 'The KISS Clipper.' That plane, with that logo, flew an additional two years. I was getting pictures of it from all over the world.

"I also made a deal with Pan-Am to use the upper level of the 747 to allow the band to get into costume, so that when they got off the plane, they would be in costume and makeup."

The press junket was done in part to maintain a constant presence for KISS in the U.S. press during the downtime prior to the next album and tour. Aucoin was rightfully concerned that any inconsistencies in press coverage would diminish the incredible wave of popularity that KISS was riding. Bill had purposefully held KISS back from touring Japan, which had been feasible as early as late 1975, in order to build the anticipation for the tour to its highest level.

KISS arrived in Japan on March 19 at 3:40 P.M. on Pan-Am flight 801. Mr. Udo, the promoter for the tour, met the band with $5,000 in hand. The scene at the airport was nearly beyond

KISS posing for legendary photographer Bob Gruen in Japan.

Manager Bill Aucoin photographed on the band's 1977 tour of Japan.

description, as Eddie Balandas explains: "That was completely out of control; so much more than I expected. The building literally moved with the people. My fist was flying around into the chests of people just to keep them back; it was like an army coming in for an invasion, they just kept coming and coming."

On March 21, KISS held a press conference at Osaka Bampaku Hall in Suita City where rehearsals would be held from the 21st to the 23rd. "We did three days of rehearsals in Osaka," Chuck Elias recalls, "one tech rehearsal for the crew and then two with the band. The venue itself was right across the parking lot from the site of the 1970 World's Fair."

The Japanese officials were exceptionally strict with KISS, requiring the band to keep the concert volume at every show under 110 decibels (db), a level that the officials closely monitored. KISS was also forced to significantly reduce their use of pyro in some cities.

The band did not change costumes or set lists for the shows in Japan, but KISS did debut a completely new stage. The stage would be used for the succeeding two tours, though not all production aspects of the stage were in use for its debut.

Chuck Elias: "The new stage was a colossal clusterfuck when we first unloaded it in the rehearsal facility parking lot. A lot of it was new to everybody, and the Japanese officials had really screwed things up because they had gone through all of the gear at customs."

MARCH 24, 1977

Osaka, Japan
Osaka Kosei Nenkin Hall
Opening Act: Bow Wow
Capacity: 2,400
Promoter: Udo Artists

MARCH 25, 1977

Osaka, Japan
Osaka Kosei Nenkin Hall
Opening Act: Bow Wow
Capacity: 2,400
Promoter: Udo Artists

MARCH 26, 1977

Kyoto, Japan
Kyoto Kaikan
Opening Act: Bow Wow

Capacity: 2,000
Promoter: Udo Artists

MARCH 28, 1977

Nagoya, Japan
Aichi-Ken Taiiku-Kan
Opening Act: Bow Wow
Capacity: 6,000
Promoter: Udo Artists

MARCH 29, 1977

Osaka, Japan
Royal Festival Hall
Opening Act: Bow Wow
Capacity: 2,800
Promoter: Udo Artists
Archived: Audio
■ SET LIST
See January 1, 1977.

MARCH 30, 1977

Fukuoka, Japan
Kyuden Taiiku-Kan
Opening Act: Bow Wow
Capacity: 4,000
Promoter: Udo Artists

■ After the concert, Gene, Paul, Fritz Postlethwaite, and guitar tech Barry Ackom performed at a Tokyo club called Honey Pot #2.

Fritz Postlethwaite: "Honey Pot #2 was a dank, dark basement. The promoter had set aside this great party when we came in to Tokyo, but we didn't care. There was some stuff set up there and I think it was Gene who said, 'Let's get up and play,' and so we decided to jam through a couple of songs. I think we played 'Jumpin' Jack Flash' and a couple of tunes, but we left pretty soon because everyone was either drunk or dead tired."

APRIL 1, 1977

Tokyo, Japan
Nippon Budokan Hall
Opening Act: Bow Wow
Attendance: 11,000   Capacity: 11,000
Promoter: Udo Artists
Archived: Audio

■ SET LIST
See January 1, 1977.
■ Chuck Elias: "I remember us going to the toy store in the Ginza and Ace just went crazy in there. We all did to a certain extent, seven stories of just toys. We were somewhat awed by it all, plus the dollar to the yen was so good in those days that we spent thousands of dollars on little shit to bring home."

Eddie Kramer recorded at least one of the four Tokyo concerts for use on a Japanese-only live album that was planned at the time.

APRIL 2, 1977 (TWO SHOWS: 3:00 P.M., 7:00 P.M.)

Tokyo, Japan
Nippon Budokan Hall
Opening Act: Bow Wow
Attendance: (1) 11,000; (2) 11,000   Capacity: 11,000
Promoter: Udo Artists
Archived: Video (both shows)
■ SET LIST
See January 1, 1977.
■ Both shows were videotaped by the Japanese TV network NHK. A 50-minute, edited version of the performances aired during an episode of *Young Music Show* in Japan and on July 28, 1979, a slightly reedited version premiered on HBO.

Al Ross: "In exchange for shooting the two shows in Tokyo, NHK had the right to do a KISS documentary," which they eventually produced in 1997.

APRIL 4, 1977

Tokyo, Japan
Nippon Budokan Hall
Opening Act: Bow Wow
Attendance: 11,000   Capacity: 11,000
Promoter: Udo Artists
Archived: Audio
■ SET LIST
Detroit Rock City
Take Me

Lydia Criss filming home movies of the KISS entourage on the bullet train, Japan 1977.

Let Me Go, Rock 'n Roll
Ladies Room
Firehouse
Makin' Love
I Want You
Cold Gin
Ace Frehley Guitar Solo
Do You Love Me
Nothin' to Lose
Gene Simmons Bass Solo
God of Thunder
[Peter Criss Drum Solo - reprise]
Rock and Roll All Nite
Shout It Out Loud
Beth
Black Diamond

■ Chuck Elias: "We had to set the stage up, tear it down and then set it back up again because of a Japanese high school exam held at Budokan between shows. But the local crews there were just phenomenal."

Gene stayed behind to record material at Victor Recording Studios, presumably for his 1978 solo album.

CHAPTER 9

LOVE GUN TOUR

Number of Shows: 32
Start Date: July 8, 1977 - Halifax, Nova Scotia
End Date: September 5, 1977 - Fort Worth, Texas
Countries: Canada, U.S.A.
Opening Acts: Cheap Trick, Styx
Average Attendance: 9,476

By April 1977, a little over three years had passed since Casablanca Records was launched, yet it was already a 30 million-dollar-a-year operation. The label had merged with a film production company in November 1976, and was officially rechristened Casablanca Record and FilmWorks in January 1977. The company boasted a roster of 14 artists and 88 employees, most of them promotional and publicity personnel. KISS, along with the label's other frontline jewel Donna Summer, had turned Bogart's small, independent company into an industry benchmark with revenues of over $11 million for the first fiscal quarter of 1977 alone.

With Casablanca now a very successful endeavor, Bogart decided to sell 50% of the company to PolyGram. In order to finance even grander ideas, he was going to need deeper pockets and PolyGram would be the ideal financier. As opportunistic and profitable as the deal seemed to PolyGram's nine-member board of directors, the purchase proved to be a huge mistake because virtually every artist signed to Casa-

blanca was yesterday's news by 1981.

Aucoin Management was also growing by leaps and bounds, opening up two new divisions: The Press Office in December 1976, and Aucoin Productions in August. Bill Aucoin explains: "Once we started The Press Office, the idea was to really develop KISS in-house, almost like a studio structure, so that we wouldn't have to depend upon anyone outside for assistance." The Press Office also handled publicity for Paul McCartney in addition to other AMI clients, such as Toby Beau, Starz, and Piper.

The second new AMI division, Aucoin Productions, was designed to be the film/television production arm of AMI and eventually several projects were green-lighted, including: *Meatballs;* a disaster film; the *Rock and Roll Sports Classic;* and a Mick Jagger script. Aucoin Productions even began to develop career plans for actors, among the most notable of whom were Beverly D'Angelo and Danielle Brisebois *(Archie Bunker's Place).*

From most vantage points, this expansion

seems indicative of how financially healthy AMI was, though some involved were skeptical. "I think a problem arose when they were spending money and really couldn't afford it," offers AMI accountant Alan Cohen. "Bill was a spender and always believed that Starz was going to break, as well as Billy Squier (Piper) and Toby Beau. He figured KISS made it, so everyone else would, too. You could see it happening to Bill because he wouldn't listen. Bill didn't like to be told that you can't spend money."

KISS's initial efforts for Casablanca had been completed with frugal budgets in the $15,000–20,000 range. When KISS entered Electric Lady Studios to record *Love Gun* from May 2–22, 1977, their budget had swelled to a then-astronomical sum of $94,000. Eddie Kramer again returned to produce the album, which, despite the huge sum fronted by Bogart, went over budget by $19,968. Kramer was contractually obligated to cover any budget overruns, but KISS agreed to split the overage with him, stating in a June 21 meeting that it wasn't entirely his fault.

The album, which shipped Platinum, was released to great fanfare on June 17, 1977.

KISS was now a full-blown, worldwide success. Their presence was inescapable. In April, the *New York Post* proclaimed, "KISS is Rock's Rocky" and referred to the band as a "light industry." Following suit, the *New York Times Magazine* ran a lengthy piece on the band titled "An Outrage Called KISS" in their June 19 edition and rock journalist Alison Steele did a lengthy interview with the band for a syndicated TV special *Night Bird*. KISS even garnered mention in the normally conservative Gallup Poll who, on June 22, proclaimed KISS as the most popular "musical group or personality" among the 1,069 teenagers polled.

Expanding their presence even further, the band partnered with Marvel Comics to release an oversized KISS comic book officially known as *Marvel Super Special #1* on June 30. A door had been opened for a younger audience with KISS's appearance on *The Paul Lynde Halloween Special,* and the comic book effectively invited them through that door. The comic book, which went on to be the biggest seller in Marvel's history, was created by Steve Gerber of *Howard the Duck* fame, who collaborated with Sean Delaney to bring the new superhero KISS to fruition.

To hype the comic book, on May 25, KISS traveled to the Borden Chemical Co. plant in the Buffalo suburb of Depew, New York where the ink was being prepared. Buffalo television stations and local radio stations WKBW and WGRQ covered the high-profile event where KISS dumped vials of their own blood (drawn just before their February 21 gig on Long Island), into the mixing vats. This promotional event marked the last time KISS would appear in their Destroyer/Rock and Roll Over outfits.

On June 29, KISS returned to the Theatre Techniques facility in Newburgh, New York where rehearsals for the tour were held through July 3. During their stay, KISS filmed an interview with noted newsman Edwin Newman for an NBC-TV special *Land of Hype and Glory,* and did individual photo sessions with celebrated photographer Lynn Goldsmith. Additional dress rehearsals were done on July 7 at the Halifax Forum, site of the tour's debut concert. During rehearsals, KISS began using the wireless guitar system that Vega had developed. The system worked well enough to be implemented for the tour, making KISS the first band in history to use what would become a standard in the industry.

Officially dubbed the Can-Am Tour, KISS was at its visual peak with new costumes, new instruments, a revamped production, and a fully functional version of their new stage. Two stages were constructed, so that while KISS was performing on one stage, the second stage was being set up in the next city.

Many of the features that made the Love Gun stage so memorable debuted at the first show of the Can-Am Tour, as they had not been ready to go for Japan. The most prevalent features were the extensively used hydraulics. Above each section of amp stacks were balconies that lowered Gene, Paul and Ace to the stage at the beginning of the show, obviously inspired by a similar effect used on *The Paul Lynde Halloween Special.* At various points during the concert, portions of the stage floor would elevate Gene, Paul, or Ace up at a 60° angle over the crowd. An additional function, which had debuted in Japan, was added to Peter's drum riser so that it not only elevated up to 20 feet above the stage, but also slid forward towards the crowd during his drum solo. Lastly, Sam the Serpent, as the road crew dubbed Gene's stage prop, sat coiled around a large torch on stage right.

KISS's new costumes were constructed by Maria Contessa and Laurie Greenan, and the band traveled with three of each of the outfits while on tour. Gene and Ace used slightly altered versions of the original designs for touring purposes. The total cost for the new production, including the new stage, costumes, and instruments, was $194,910, although the show was hyped as a million-dollar production in most markets.

McManus Enterprises was hired to handle lighting responsibilities for the tour, and Newburgh-based Tasco was brought on board to handle sound reinforcement. House sound engineer, Don Ketteler, recalls: "Gene took me aside when I first began working for them and said, 'Here's what we want as far as the sound goes. We want no one to be able to speak with anyone sitting next to them. And when any of us takes a solo, it should be as loud as if we were all playing.' It was all about the power, and not about the subtleties of mixing. I had to mix as far back as we could go in the house because of the tremendous levels they had on stage, which made it difficult because I tended to mix it even louder so I could hear it in the back; meanwhile, the poor people in the tenth row were getting their ears melted.

"Ironically, despite the fact that Ace had 20-some-odd amps on stage, the only one that I miked was the little Fender Champ tuning amp sitting behind the stacks."

As stipulated by the tour's contract, the length of the concerts had been expanded to 90 minutes. Not surprisingly, the set list was skewed heavily towards promoting the *Love Gun* album with five songs from the record included in the show: "I Stole Your Love," "Love Gun," "Hooligan," "Christine Sixteen," and "Shock Me." "Calling Dr. Love," from *Rock and Roll Over,* was also added to the set.

KISS was such a part of the public's consciousness and was so successful on several different levels that promoters scaled back advertising quite significantly; word of mouth alone was nearly enough to sustain the tour. Despite claims that every show was sold out, there were several nights when attendance bubbled just under capacity. Since it was assumed that KISS sold out every concert, in most cases the promoters didn't bother to report the shows to the trade publications.

It is astonishing to realize that despite KISS's pervasive, overwhelming success, initial forecasts had the Canadian leg of the Love Gun Tour running at an $80,000 deficit, though the band's leasing of a private plane, used to jet between gigs on this leg of the tour, seems never to have been in jeopardy. Portions of the tour were eventually revamped, and it became a break-even proposal.

Gene onstage in Montréal, early in the Love Gun Tour. Note Gene's use of his boots from the original design of his Love Gun costume.

JULY 7, 1977
Halifax, Nova Scotia, Canada
Halifax Forum
Opening Act: Cheap Trick
Promoters: Concert Promotions Int'l, Donald K. Donald

TEMP HOLD DATE

JULY 8, 1977
Halifax, Nova Scotia, Canada
Halifax Forum
Opening Act: Cheap Trick
Attendance: 6,000   Capacity: 6,200
Promoters: Concert Promotions Int'l, Donald K. Donald
■ This date was originally slated for July 10, but was then changed to two shows on July 7 and 8. The gig on the 7th was eventually cleared from the schedule for budgetary reasons, leaving the gig on July 8 as the opening night of the tour.

Presumably, Ace sang "Shock Me" at this show, thus making his lead vocal debut.

Don Ketteler: "The first show we did was just jammed with kids. Of course, you had to play 'Stairway to Heaven' as the last song before the show starts, and the kids start screaming when they hear it begin. Then the lights went out, and the spotlights hit the mirrorball. Mind you, I'd been at rehearsal, so I knew that this was a loud fucking band. I put all the faders up to where they were supposed to be, KISS started playing, and all my needles start jumping all over the place, but I could not hear a single thing they were playing. I remember my hair standing on end with the excitement of the moment; I'd never really had that kind of experience, before or since. I had a state-of-the-art P.A., and I could not hear a thing, the crowd was so loud."

JULY 9, 1977
Moncton, New Brunswick, Canada
Moncton Coliseum
Opening Act: Cheap Trick

Capacity: 9,000
Promoters: Concert Promotions Int'l, Donald K. Donald
■ This was originally going to be the start date of the tour but became the second show when, on April 22, the decision was made to move the Halifax concert to July 8.

JULY 12, 1977

Montréal, Quebec, Canada
Forum de Montréal
Opening Act: Cheap Trick
Attendance: 12,000   Capacity: 13,000
Promoters: Concert Promotions Int'l, Donald K. Donald
Archived: Audio

■ **SET LIST**

Detroit Rock City
Take Me
Calling Dr. Love
Hooligan
Love Gun
Firehouse
Christine Sixteen
I Stole Your Love
Shock Me
Ace Frehley Guitar Solo
I Want You
Makin' Love
Gene Simmons Bass Solo
God of Thunder
Peter Criss Drum Solo - reprise
Rock and Roll All Nite
Shout It Out Loud
Beth
Black Diamond

JULY 14, 1977

Ottawa, Ontario, Canada
Ottawa Civic Centre
Opening Act: Cheap Trick
Attendance: 6,660   Capacity: 10,000
Promoters: Concert Promotions Int'l, Donald K. Donald

JULY 15, 1977

Toronto, Ontario, Canada
Maple Leaf Gardens TEMP HOLD DATE
Opening Act: Cheap Trick
Capacity: 18,400
Promoters: Concert Promotions Int'l, Donald K. Donald
■ As a result of difficulties with the crowds at recent rock concerts, including KISS's performance at Maple Leaf Gardens in April 1976, a bylaw had been passed which essentially banned all such events in Toronto. The bylaw was eventually repealed, as KISS performed at the venue in August 1979.

JULY 15, 1977 TEMP HOLD DATE

Kitchener, Ontario, Canada
Memorial Auditorium
Opening Act: Cheap Trick
Capacity: 7,600
Promoters: Concert Promotions Int'l, Donald K. Donald

JULY 16, 1977

Kitchener, Ontario, Canada
Memorial Auditorium
Opening Act: Cheap Trick
Attendance: 5,800   Capacity: 7,600
Promoters: Concert Promotions Int'l, Donald K. Donald

JULY 18, 1977

London, Ontario, Canada
London Gardens
Opening Act: Cheap Trick
Attendance: 4,400   Capacity: 5,740
Promoters: Concert Promotions Int'l, Donald K. Donald

In what is a very atypical move, Ace is pictured here in Montréal performing his guitar solo from one of the *Love Gun* stage's hydraulic lifts.

■ London was the last known show at which Gene wore the same boots that appear on the *Love Gun* album cover.

JULY 19, 1977

Sudbury, Ontario, Canada
Sudbury Arena
Opening Act: Cheap Trick
Capacity: 7,000
Promoters: Concert Promotions Int'l, Donald K. Donald

JULY 21, 1977

Winnipeg, Manitoba, Canada
Winnipeg Arena
Opening Act: Cheap Trick
Attendance: 8,000+   Capacity: 11,405
Promoters: Concert Promotions Int'l, Donald K. Donald

JULY 24, 1977

Vancouver, British Columbia, Canada
Pacific Coliseum
Opening Act: Cheap Trick
Attendance: 12,000   Capacity: 17,613
Promoters: Concert Promotions Int'l, Donald K. Donald
■ While in Vancouver, Gene spent time at Pinewood Studios continuing work on his solo album. Drummer Duris Maxwell of the band Doucette provided percussion for the session.

JULY 25, 1977 CANCELED

Victoria, Alberta, Canada
Victoria Memorial Arena
Opening Act: Cheap Trick
Capacity: 6,021
Promoters: Concert Promotions Int'l, Donald K. Donald
■ The venue was too small to accommodate production, which forced the cancellation of the show.

JULY 27, 1977

Edmonton, Alberta, Canada
Edmonton Coliseum
Opening Act: Cheap Trick
Attendance: 11,494
Promoters: Concert Promotions Int'l, Donald K. Donald
■ The show was listed for July 26 on an early itinerary.

JULY 28, 1977

Lethbridge, Alberta, Canada
Canada Games Sportsplex
Opening Act: Cheap Trick
Attendance: Almost 7,000   Capacity: 6,180
Promoters: Concert Promotions Int'l, Donald K. Donald

JULY 29, 1977

Edmonton, Alberta, Canada
Edmonton Coliseum
Opening Act: Cheap Trick
Promoters: Concert Promotions Int'l, Donald K. Donald

JULY 31, 1977

Calgary, Alberta, Canada
Corral Arena
Opening Act: Cheap Trick
Attendance: 7,500   Capacity: 7,500
Promoter: Brimstone Productions
■ Eddie Balandas: "We were in Calgary, we had a couple of days off, and Ace wanted to go to Vegas. He said, 'Why don't we get dressed up like rich cowboys, fly into Vegas, go do the town and laugh it up?' So, we went out and bought cowboy boots, and a shirt and hat. We flew into Vegas on Hughes Airlines, went to Caesar's and the room service came in on about 15 carts. We were hitting it big, rolling three-thousand-dollar hands."

AUGUST 1, 1977

Calgary, Alberta, Canada
Corral Arena **TEMP HOLD DATE**
Opening Act: Cheap Trick
Capacity: 7,500
Promoter: Brimstone Productions

AUGUST 2, 1977

Saskatoon, Saskatchewan, Canada
Saskatoon Arena **TEMP HOLD DATE**
Opening Act: Cheap Trick
Capacity: 5,000
Promoters: Concert Promotions Int'l, Donald K. Donald

AUGUST 2, 1977

Regina, Saskatchewan, Canada
Regina Agridome @ Regina Exhibition Park
Opening Act: Cheap Trick
Attendance: 6,900   Capacity: 6,900
Promoters: Concert Promotions Int'l, Donald K. Donald
■ The show, which was part of Regina's annual "Buffalo Days" exhibition, was originally scheduled for August 3. CPI, the promoter, took out an ad in the local newspaper thanking KISS for the sold-out performance.

AUGUST 4, 1977

Winnipeg, Manitoba, Canada
Winnipeg Arena **TEMP HOLD DATE**
Opening Act: Cheap Trick
Capacity: 11,405
Promoters: Concert Promotions Int'l, Donald K.
    Donald Some early Love Gun Tour itineraries included this date, but it was quickly stricken from the schedule and was never advertised or put on sale.

AUGUST 4, 1977

Salt Lake City, Utah
O. Thayne Accord Arena @ Salt Palace Center
Opening Act: Cheap Trick
Capacity: 13,075
Promoter: United Concerts

AUGUST 6, 1977

Missoula, Montana **CANCELED**
Harry Adams Fieldhouse
Opening Act: Cheap Trick
Promoter: Amusement Conspiracy
■ This show was advertised but never put on sale.

AUGUST 7, 1977

Billings, Montana
Metra
Opening Act: Cheap Trick
Attendance: 9,971   Capacity: 10,500
Promoter: Amusement Conspiracy
■ In Billings, the band was first made aware that KISS was supposedly an acronym for Knights In Satan's Service. Imagine their surprise; the laughable rumor was spread across the country over the next several months, usually by religious conservatives trying to get their names mentioned in the press.

AUGUST 8, 1977

Rapid City, South Dakota
Rushmore Plaza Civic Center
Opening Act: Cheap Trick
Capacity: 10,500
Promoter: Amusement Conspiracy

AUGUST 11, 1977

Spokane, Washington
Spokane Coliseum
Opening Act: Cheap Trick
Attendance: 8,500   Capacity: 8,500
Promoter: Concerts West

AUGUST 12, 1977

Seattle, Washington
Seattle Center Coliseum
Opening Act: Cheap Trick
Capacity: 15,000
Promoter: Concerts West
■ According to *The Seattle Times* review, "Beth" was not performed.

Eddie Balandas: "When we were in Seattle, Ace and I would always go fishing on our day off, so we rented a boat out on Lake Washington. We weren't supposed to go out through the locks and into the ocean, but I did it because Ace wanted to. The hotel we were staying at, the Edgewater Inn, sat on pilings directly above the water, and you could literally fish right out of your hotel window. So we took the boat underneath the hotel and tied up the fishing lines hanging from all the rooms. Then we pulled on them so everyone thought they had a fish. As we pulled away from the hotel, Ace mooned everybody from the boat.

"Then Ace and I went back to the boat rental facility. On our way, all of these huge, expensive yachts were going through the locks with us and guys were shouting to us, 'Hey. Watch your port bow!' We didn't know what the hell a bow was. Meanwhile, Ace is just sitting there kicking back a few beers and people are watching us from up above in their yachts. Ace said, 'I think the people are recognizing us.' I said, 'They're not recognizing you, they're watching your fucking balls that are sticking out of your shorts.'"

AUGUST 13, 1977

Portland, Oregon
Memorial Coliseum
Opening Act: Cheap Trick
Capacity: 12,600
Promoter: Concerts West
■ "Before the show one night, I had set up the cassette for 'Beth,'" recalls Don Ketteler. "At some point, one of the other guys on the sound crew decided that the music we should play as the crowd was leaving should be the Beatles' 'Magical Mystery Tour.' But he spaced out and put the tape in before they had done 'Beth.' The

MICHAEL MONFORT/SHOOTING STAR

spotlight comes on the stool in the middle of the stage, Peter comes out selling it, looking all serious and solemn, the crowd is completely hushed, I hit the tape and 'Magical Mystery Tour' starts playing. It was embarrassing and hilarious at the same time. It was so bad that the band didn't even say anything after the show."

AUGUST 14, 1977

Portland, Oregon
Memorial Coliseum **TEMP HOLD DATE**
Opening Act: Cheap Trick
Capacity: 12,600
Promoter: Concerts West

AUGUST 16, 1977

Daly City (San Francisco), California
Cow Palace
Opening Act: Cheap Trick
Attendance: 14,500   Capacity: 14,500
Promoter: Bill Graham Presents
Archived: Audio

■ SET LIST
I Stole Your Love
Take Me
Ladies Room
Firehouse
Love Gun
Hooligan
Christine Sixteen
Makin' Love
Shock Me
Ace Frehley Guitar Solo
I Want You
Calling Dr. Love
Shout It Out Loud
Gene Simmons Bass Solo
God of Thunder
Peter Criss Drum Solo - reprise
Rock and Roll All Nite
Detroit Rock City
[Beth]
Black Diamond

■ Despite the sellout crowd, the day was tinged with a somber tone as Elvis Presley's death was announced. In various ways, both direct and indirect, Presley had been an influence on KISS and an obvious inspiration for the band. Paul informed the crowd, "We're gonna dedicate the last song . . . to the King of Rock 'n' Roll: Elvis Presley! Rock and roll all nite, party every day!"

On the previous day, Alison Steele interviewed KISS over a picnic luncheon at San Francisco's scenic Victoria Park. KISS one-upped her by showing up in a streetcar sans makeup. Alison was taping a television version of her radio program *Night Bird.* The special aired in national syndication in January 1978.

Shortly after JR Smalling had departed in June 1976, security man Eddie Balandas had been given the honor of introducing the band. "I started doing that on the Destroyer Tour," relates Balandas. "Gene loved it right away because it scared the shit out of him. I think I had the ballsiest intro of anyone." Naturally, when it came time to record the intro for the beginning of *Alive II,* Balandas was tabbed for the job. "We were in San Francisco at the Cow Palace setting up for a gig, and Eddie Kramer came up to me with a recorder and said, 'Do it.' So, we went down to the bathroom, and I recorded it about five or six times. Afterwards, Kramer said: 'Did Eddie say

'KISS' or "piss"?' He didn't think I enunciated 'KISS' very well, so Gene ended up dubbing in the word 'KISS' on the *Alive II* album."

AUGUST 17, 1977

Fresno, California
Selland Arena @ Fresno Convention Center
Opening Act: Cheap Trick
Attendance: 7,410   Capacity: 7,410
Promoter: Avalon Attractions
Archived: Audio

■ SET LIST
I Stole Your Love
Take Me
Ladies Room
Firehouse
Love Gun
Hooligan
Christine Sixteen
Makin' Love
Shock Me
Ace Frehley Guitar Solo
[I Want You]
[Calling Dr. Love]
[Shout It Out Loud]
[Gene Simmons Bass Solo]
[God of Thunder]
[Peter Criss Drum Solo - reprise]
[Rock and Roll All Nite]
Detroit Rock City
Beth
Black Diamond

AUGUST 19, 1977

San Diego, California
San Diego Sports Arena
Opening Act: Cheap Trick
Attendance: 11,925   Capacity: 11,925
Promoter: Fun Productions

AUGUST 21, 1977

Tucson, Arizona
Tucson Community Center
Opening Act: Cheap Trick
Attendance: 6,591   Capacity: 9,400
Promoter: Avalon Attractions

■ Monitor engineer, Arnie Toshner: "There was an interesting incident between Peter Criss and his drum monitor mixer, Chris 'The Smoother'

Smythe. One night during Gene's bass solo, Peter came off his drum riser and went to get some refreshments. There was always a lot of dry-ice fog around the stage during the solo. There was a wall behind the riser with all the dry ice billowing up, and as Peter came off his drum riser he ran right into Smoother, who was wearing a Darth Vader helmet and black cloak and was holding a makeshift lightsaber. Peter completely freaked out."

AUGUST 22, 1977

Phoenix, Arizona
Arizona Veterans Memorial Coliseum
Opening Act: Cheap Trick
Capacity: 13,868
Promoter: Fun Productions

AUGUST 25, 1977

Inglewood (Los Angeles), California
The Forum
Opening Act: Cheap Trick **TEMP HOLD DATE**
Capacity: 16,026
Promoter: Fun Productions

AUGUST 26, 1977

Inglewood (Los Angeles), California
The Forum
Opening Act: Cheap Trick
Capacity: 16,026
Promoter: Fun Productions
Archived: Audio, Video

■ SET LIST
I Stole Your Love
Take Me
Ladies Room
Firehouse
Love Gun
Hooligan
Makin' Love
Christine Sixteen
Shock Me
Ace Frehley Guitar Solo
I Want You
Calling Dr. Love
Shout It Out Loud
Gene Simmons Bass Solo
God of Thunder
Peter Criss Drum Solo - reprise

Rock and Roll All Nite
Detroit Rock City
Beth
Black Diamond

■ Eddie Kramer recorded all three Forum shows for *Alive II.* Several thousand specialty KISS T-shirts reading "I Was There" were sold to commemorate the recording; the T-shirts were obviously done in quite a rush as Los Angels [sic] Forum was misprinted on the back of the shirts. The Love Gun tourbooks were first sold at this gig and complimentary "I Was There" buttons were handed out at the door.

Southern California KISS Army members received postcards in the mail notifying them of the concerts and the live album that was being recorded. To promote the concerts, KISS dropped by Ten-Q radio to chat with DJ "The Real" Don Steele. NBC News shot footage of KISS's appearance at Ten-Q and the first Forum show for inclusion in the *Land of Hype and Glory* piece. Steele later made a cameo appearance in *KISS Meets the Phantom of the Park* in which he played himself announcing the contestants at a KISS look-a-like contest.

For the first two Los Angeles appearances, Gene's costume was slightly modified to include two black horns on the shoulders of his collar. Oddly enough, they closely resemble the horns he wore during the latter shows on the KISS Tour.

AUGUST 27, 1977

Inglewood (Los Angeles), California
The Forum
Opening Act: Cheap Trick
Capacity: 16,026
Promoter: Fun Productions
Archived: Audio

■ Backstage, before the show, Peter was despondent and was acting very erratic. "I went into the dressing room to talk to Peter," explains Fritz Postlethwaite. "I asked him what was the matter, and he told me that he just wasn't feeling good, though it was obvious that there was something else that was going on; everyone could tell. And the longer I talked to him, the worse it got. It went from 'I don't feel good' to his speech slurring and eyes starting to close. We were in a very difficult position: there were 20,000 people there, what were we going to do with them? On the other hand, we had to look out for Peter's safety. As it got worse, they took me outside and asked what we could do about it. They may have talked to [Cheap Trick drummer] Bun E., too, it wouldn't surprise me, as he's a great drummer. But somehow, somebody figured out a solution, be it chemical or psychological or whatever it was. Peter did do the show."

Arnie Toshner: "During the second show in Los Angeles, there were two teenagers down in the front, and they were giving Gene shit all night long, spitting at him, etc. Gene asked the security people to get them out, but they didn't do anything about it. So we went to this roadie we called The Beast, Andy Barker, who was about 6'3" and weighed about 240 pounds. He went down front where the barrier was and, in coordination with the lighting director, the lights were blacked out, he grabbed the two guys, smacked each of them

once and carried both of them out of the building." Gene caught his hair on fire during the show.

AUGUST 28, 1977

Inglewood (Los Angeles), California
The Forum
Opening Act: Cheap Trick
Capacity: 16,026
Promoter: Fun Productions
Archived: Audio

■ SET LIST

I Stole Your Love
[Take Me]
[Ladies Room]
[Firehouse]
Love Gun
Hooligan
[Makin' Love]
Christine Sixteen
Shock Me
[Ace Frehley Guitar Solo]
[I Want You]
Calling Dr. Love
[Shout It Out Loud]
[Gene Simmons Bass Solo]
[God of Thunder]
[Peter Criss Drum Solo - reprise]
[Rock and Roll All Nite]
[Detroit Rock City]
[Beth]
[Black Diamond]

■ Prior to this show, Gene had the black horns from the shoulders of his costume removed, most likely due to the difficulty he had had with his fire-breathing act the previous night.

SEPTEMBER 1, 1977

Houston, Texas
The Summit
Opening Act: Styx
Attendance: 14,352
Promoters: Pace Concerts, Concerts West
Archived: Video

■ SET LIST

See August 26, 1977.

■ Pyro usage was drastically reduced for both Houston shows, which were professionally archived by John Crow TV Productions.

SEPTEMBER 2, 1977

Houston, Texas
The Summit
Opening Act: Styx
Attendance: 14,832
Promoters: Pace Concerts, Concerts West
Archived: Video

■ SET LIST

See August 26, 1977.

SEPTEMBER 4, 1977

Fort Worth, Texas
Tarrant County Convention Center
Opening Act: Styx
Attendance: 13,690   Capacity: 13,690
Promoter: Concerts West

■ Pete Oppel, in his review for the *Dallas Morning News,* wrote: "A kid in back of me had a portable tape recorder, destroying the illusion that no one comes to see Kiss for the 'music.'" To whomever that mystery kid is: contact the authors of this book!

At the Green Oaks Hotel, the party celebrating the end of the tour deteriorated into an enormous food fight involving the band, crew and management. Chuck Elias recalls: "I seem to remember Paul starting that one by pieing Bill right in the face. We were throwing just about everything that we could grab. I had to go up and shower afterwards because I was sticky as hell."

SEPTEMBER 5, 1977

Fort Worth, Texas
Tarrant County Convention Center
Opening Act: Styx
Capacity: 13,690
Promoter: Concerts West

■ This was the final performance of "Hooligan." "Take Me" was also dropped from the set.

MICHAEL MONFORT/SHOOTING STAR

CHAPTER 10

ALIVE II TOUR

Number of Shows: 52
Start Date: November 15, 1977 - Oklahoma City, Oklahoma
End Date: May 19, 1978 - Valencia, California
Countries: Japan, U.S.A.
Opening Acts: AC/DC; Bow Wow; Detective; Nantucket; Piper; Rockets
Average Attendance: 13,550* (Does not include the 5/19/78 performance.)

For well over two decades now, the legend of what KISS was in the 1970s has been passed from one generation of fans to the next, the story quite literally taking on mythic proportions. With each successive generation, another layer of hype has been added to the tale. The result is a wonderful, idealistic, and exaggerated version of the American Dream: KISS was nearly as big as the Beatles; their albums were certified Quadruple-Platinum in a matter or weeks; "Beth" was one of the biggest #1 singles of the decade; KISS was the top touring act in the world, their mind-melting concerts played before enormous stadium crowds.

The truth of course is that KISS was never that band. But if there were a time when they were even close, the Alive II Tour was it.

Having risen to fame in the post-Vietnam, pre-AIDS American culture, KISS really was the perfect band for the perfect time. And in 1977, times were good.

KISS was succeeding on just about every level possible: their albums were shipping Platinum, their singles were charting, and attendance at their concerts was better than ever. They were constantly in the public eye and, most importantly, they had placed an indelible mark on American pop culture. For once, KISS was—as they so-often liked to claim—larger than life.

Promotion did not cease; KISS merchandise was flooding the market: posters, jigsaw puzzles, belt buckles, notebooks, mirrors, and a whole host of other licensed products would flourish in the coming months. Documents dated November 14, 1977 indicate that no fewer than 20 companies had negotiated licensing agreements with AMI for the rights to manufacture and distribute KISS merchandise.

KISS obviously was becoming an inflated image of itself, though the negative consequences of that fact had yet to impact the band. *Alive II* itself, much in keeping with this direction, was an overblown studio recreation of a live concert. While source material for the three live sides of the album was recorded at live shows in Japan and in California, it was heavily overdubbed in the studio. The overdubs were done at the Capitol Theatre in Passaic, New Jersey. "We were in Passaic for at least a week," recalls Chuck Elias, "and we pretty much re-recorded the entire show. It was very difficult for them to play well live, considering all the running around they did, and the production details they had to pay attention to. With that kind of show you just never could get it musically perfect." KISS's second live album, *Alive II* was released on October 24.

Considering that promoters were more eager than ever to purchase KISS concerts, it's interesting to note that the Alive II Tour ran for only 11 weeks. And while not all figures are available, the tour likely had the highest average attendance per show of any KISS tour in history. Yet, despite the amazing heights of popularity to which the band had ascended, they weren't anywhere close to being the top touring act around. They were far, far outpaced (by thirty, forty, even fifty thousand people per show) by the Grateful Dead, Led Zeppelin, and especially Pink Floyd. In fact, in 1977, KISS placed only one concert on *Billboard's* Top 100 Concerts of the Year—which ranked the shows according to gross revenue—that being their February 18 appearance at Madison Square Garden.

Nonetheless, the tour was an unqualified success. Ric Aliberte had come on board to do promotion for the band in May 1977 and contributed heavily to the drawing power of the Love Gun and Alive II tours. "My mission was to get them on mainstream rock radio," explains Aliberte. "That was pretty hard to do because radio looked at KISS like a circus, and they didn't take it as seriously as if Queen was coming through. A lot of them, believe it or not, had not been to KISS concerts.

"I had a lot of friends in radio, and if they hadn't seen a KISS show I would set them up. There was always this space between the stage and the barrier, and I would take the radio people in attendance, give them earplugs, and tell them if they wanted to see what rock and roll was all about . . . well, come with me. At the beginning of the show, the stage would explode and the guys would come out rocking, and suddenly they got it: 'Wow! That's fucking rock and roll.'

"The kids got it, but the media, I guess, just didn't realize how much fun KISS was to see. What these radio people eventually found was that it wasn't just a bunch of tricks. The band had the capability of making you feel that any explosion or any of the effects was emanating from them, as if they were in control of it, because they had such command of the stage.

"Promotions for KISS was a machine. Every night before a show we would have a meet-and-greet, and, without fail, the band would turn up and do whatever was asked of them."

The tour was not without its eccentricities, which were starting to become more prevalent as KISS's fame grew. Fritz Postlethwaite was an interesting character who had ingratiated himself to the band, all of whom liked him a great

deal, as a jack-of-all-trades and had moved up the crew ranks from his original monitor engineer job to the tour manager position. One of the things Postlethwaite did was to take the unusual step of printing out biorhythm charts for each of the crewmembers in the hopes of gauging their moods.

The Alive II Tour was, in almost every way, the second half of the Love Gun Tour. No two tours in the band's history have been more alike: the staging, production, and costumes were nearly identical. The only noteworthy difference was a very slight change in the set list as "King of the Night Time World" replaced "Take Me," and "Hooligan" was abandoned in favor of "Let Me Go, Rock 'n Roll." Never has a KISS set list been more static; in only one known instance did KISS stray from the standard set, and even that was due to a unique mitigating circumstance.

The tour concluded with a short return trip to Japan, almost one year to the day since the band's 1977 Japanese tour. KISS did not tour the country on this venture, but instead did five shows at Nippon Budokan Hall in Tokyo. It's remarkable that another run of gigs in Japan was booked at all considering the previous tour there; though successful in terms of hype and attendance, had resulted in $150,000 in losses for the band.

NOVEMBER 15, 1977

Oklahoma City, Oklahoma
Myriad Convention Center
Opening Act: Detective
Attendance: near capacity
Promoter: Concerts West
Archived: Audio

■ SET LIST

I Stole Your Love
King of the Night Time World
Ladies Room
Firehouse
Love Gun
Let Me Go, Rock 'n Roll
Makin' Love
Christine Sixteen
Shock Me
Ace Frehley Guitar Solo
I Want You
Calling Dr. Love
Shout It Out Loud
Gene Simmons Bass Solo
God of Thunder
Peter Criss Drum Solo - reprise
Rock and Roll All Nite
Detroit Rock City
Beth
Black Diamond

NOVEMBER 17, 1977

Denver, Colorado
McNichols Sports Arena
Opening Act: Detective
Attendance: 10,586
Promoter: Feyline Presents

NOVEMBER 19, 1977

Abilene, Texas
Taylor County Coliseum
Opening Act: Detective
Attendance: 9,082   Capacity: 9,082
Promoter: Stone City Attractions
■ KISS broke their own venue attendance record, set in January, and 600 people were turned away at the door.

NOVEMBER 20, 1977

Lubbock, Texas
Lubbock Municipal Coliseum
Opening Act: Detective
Attendance: 10,250   Capacity: 10,250
Promoter: Stone City Attractions
■ KISS established the house attendance record.

NOVEMBER 22, 1977

San Antonio, Texas
Joe & Harry Freeman Coliseum
Opening Act: Detective
Promoter: Stone City Attractions
■ On November 22, at the behest of Carl Glickman, KISS signed paperwork investing several hundred thousand dollars in a coal mining company to provide the band with substantial tax shelters. Aucoin, Glickman, and Marks made similar investments in the company. The move later backfired when a change in the tax laws made KISS and the other members involved liable for the payment of millions of dollars in back taxes.

NOVEMBER 23, 1977

San Antonio, Texas
Joe & Harry Freeman Coliseum
Opening Act: Detective
Promoter: Stone City Attractions

NOVEMBER 26, 1977

Tulsa, Oklahoma
Tulsa Assembly Center
Opening Act: Detective
Attendance: 8,300
Promoter: Stone City Attractions

NOVEMBER 27, 1977

Kansas City, Missouri
Kemper Arena
Opening Act: Detective
Attendance: 13,369
Promoter: Contemporary Productions

NOVEMBER 29,1977

Des Moines, Iowa
Veterans Memorial Auditorium
Opening Act: Detective
Attendance: 13,000
Promoter: Celebration Concerts
Archived: Audio
■ SET LIST
I Stole Your Love
King of the Night Time World
Ladies Room
Firehouse
Love Gun

Let Me Go, Rock 'n Roll
Makin' Love
Christine Sixteen
Shock Me
Ace Frehley Guitar Solo
I Want You
Calling Dr. Love
Shout It Out Loud
Gene Simmons Bass Solo
God of Thunder
Peter Criss Drum Solo - [reprise]
[Rock and Roll All Nite]
[Detroit Rock City]
[Beth]
[Black Diamond]
■ The hydraulic balconies used to lower Gene, Paul, and Ace to the stage at the beginning of the concert were not used at this show.

According to a fan in attendance, Ace did not join Paul on the hydraulic platform during "Black Diamond," though Paul had motioned him over. During the same song, one of the cat faces on the black curtain beneath Peter's drum riser became unattached and was dangling from the curtain.

NOVEMBER 30, 1977

Omaha, Nebraska
Omaha Civic Auditorium
Opening Act: Detective
Attendance: 11,800   Capacity: 11,800
Promoter: Schon Productions

DECEMBER 2, 1977

St. Paul, Minnesota
St. Paul Civic Center
Opening Act: Detective
Attendance: 16,000   Capacity: 17,822
Promoter: Schon Productions

DECEMBER 3, 1977

Madison, Wisconsin
Dane County Expo Center Coliseum
Opening Act: Detective
Attendance: 10,100   Capacity: 10,100
Promoter: Stardate Productions
■ The show was stopped briefly when Paul was hit in the head with beer bottle thrown from the audience.

Gene remained in Madison the day after the show to record material at Full Compass Studios.

DECEMBER 6, 1977

Wichita, Kansas
Henry J. Levitt Arena
Opening Act: Detective
Attendance: 10,724
Promoter: Cowtown Productions
Archived: Audio
■ SET LIST
I Stole Your Love
[King of the Night Time World]
Ladies Room
Firehouse
[Love Gun]
Let Me Go, Rock 'n Roll
Makin' Love
Christine Sixteen
Shock Me
Ace Frehley Guitar Solo
I Want You
Calling Dr. Love
[Shout It Out Loud]
Gene Simmons Bass Solo
God of Thunder

Peter Criss Drum Solo - reprise
[Rock and Roll All Nite]
Detroit Rock City
Beth
[Black Diamond]

DECEMBER 7, 1977

St. Louis, Missouri
The Checkerdome
Opening Act: Detective
Attendance: 13,478
Promoter: Contemporary Productions
■ Eddie Balandas: "We were in St. Louis, and we decided to go over the state line to East St. Louis to go to a bar. We took a couple of local police guys with us and pulled up in a limo to this real hick bar. Rosie Licata (another KISS security guard) was with me at that time; he was with Peter, and I was with Ace. Somehow, those two got into a rumble in the bar, and the police guys got their guns taken away by some of the patrons at the bar. Baseball bats started coming out, and it got ugly in a hurry. I quickly pulled Peter out, and Rosie got the cops out.

"Then we looked around and realized Ace was still in there. I went back in to get Ace and as I covered Ace, I got hit over the head with a chair. And I got a gun pointed in my face, by a guy who took it from one of the cops. The guy was saying 'Hey, get your ass out of here!' I told him that I wanted to get my guy and that was it, and we rushed out of there.

"Then, Ace realizes that he left his jacket in the bar. There we are with a cop bleeding from his head, and Peter was yelling that we'd almost lost our lives. And Ace calmly says, 'I lost my jacket in the club. Eddie, go back in there and get my jacket.' He said, 'Bobby [McAdams] gave me that jacket.' So, I had to go back into the club to get the jacket. When I went back in, I almost got mobbed and, of course, somebody had taken the jacket. Management ended up posting a $500 reward the next day, and the jacket turned up again.'

DECEMBER 9, 1977

Memphis, Tennessee
Mid-South Coliseum
Opening Act: AC/DC
Attendance: 11,493   Capacity: 11,493
Promoters: Mid-South Concerts, Beaver Productions
■ Detective was listed as the opening act in several ads, but they did not appear.

DECEMBER 11, 1977

Indianapolis, Indiana
Market Square Arena
Opening Act: AC/DC
Attendance: 19,000   Capacity: 19,000
Promoter: Sunshine Promotions
■ In Miami, Minneapolis, Cleveland, and Houston, *Playboy Magazine* hosted a contest where four winners and a guest could spend a week on the road with KISS. The contest winners were treated to five KISS concerts (including three shows at Madison Square Garden), the first of which took place in Indianapolis. After the show the band, sans makeup, hosted a party for the winners that lasted until the wee hours of the morning.

DECEMBER 12, 1977

Louisville, Kentucky
Freedom Hall
Opening Act: AC/DC
Attendance: Near sellout   Capacity: 19,400
Promoter: Sunshine Promotions

DECEMBER 14, 1977

New York, New York
Madison Square Garden
Opening Act: Detective
Capacity: 19,626
Promoter: Ron Delsener Presents
Archived: Audio
■ **SET LIST**
See November 15, 1977.
■ Future KISS guitarist Bruce Kulick attended this show, along with his brother, guitarist Bob Kulick.

DECEMBER 15, 1977

New York, New York
Madison Square Garden
Opening Act: Piper
Capacity: 19,626
Promoter: Ron Delsener Presents

DECEMBER 16, 1977

New York, New York
Madison Square Garden
Opening Act: Piper
Capacity: 19,626
Promoter: Ron Delsener Presents
Archived: Audio
■ **SET LIST**
See November 15, 1977.
■ Following the concert, KISS held a private party at The Harkness Ballet School in Manhattan.

DECEMBER 19, 1977

Landover (Washington, D.C.), Maryland
Capital Centre
Opening Act: AC/DC
Attendance: 18,000   Capacity: 18,000
Promoter: Cellar Door Concerts

DECEMBER 20, 1977

Landover (Washington, D.C.), Maryland
Capital Centre
Opening Act: Piper
Attendance: 18,000   Capacity: 18,000
Promoter: Cellar Door Concerts
Archived: Video
■ **SET LIST**
See November 15, 1977.
■ The in-house staff professionally videotaped the show. Since they knew some footage would be used for *The American Music Awards*, special emphasis was placed upon the production value of the video. The result far surpasses the Houston shows from September, with generous amounts of wide-angle shots showcasing the entire stage, and an eye for production detail that is missing from those tapes. Thus far, no footage from the first show has ever surfaced, indicating that it was most likely not purchased by the band.
Portions of "Shout It Out Loud" and "Rock and Roll All Nite" aired January 16, 1978 on *The American Music Awards.*

DECEMBER 22, 1977

Philadelphia, Pennsylvania
The Spectrum
Opening Act: Piper

Capacity: 19,500
Promoter: Electric Factory Concerts
Archived: Audio
■ **SET LIST**
See November 15, 1977.
■ AC/DC was advertised as the opening act, but they did not perform.

DECEMBER 27, 1977

Baton Rouge, Louisiana
Riverside Centroplex
Opening Act: Piper
Promoter: Beaver Productions
Archived: Audio
■ **SET LIST**
I Stole Your Love
King of the Night Time World
Ladies Room
Firehouse
Love Gun
Let Me Go, Rock 'n Roll
Makin' Love
Christine Sixteen
Shock Me
Ace Frehley Guitar Solo
I Want You
Calling Dr. Love
Shout It Out Loud
Gene Simmons Bass Solo
God of Thunder
Peter Criss Drum Solo - [reprise]
[Rock and Roll All Nite]
[Detroit Rock City]
[Beth]
[Black Diamond]

DECEMBER 29, 1977

Birmingham, Alabama
Birmingham-Jefferson Civic Center
Opening Act: Piper
Attendance: 17,000   Capacity: 17,000
Promoter: Ruffino & Vaughn

DECEMBER 30, 1977

Atlanta, Georgia
The Omni
Opening Act: Piper
Attendance: 14,417   Capacity: 16,607
Promoter: Alex Cooley Presents
■ Billy Squier, formerly of Piper: "I thought their show was phenomenal. They were doing something on a scale that no one had done before. They really were very creative in terms of reshaping arena-rock entertainment. Gene, in particular, is a very smart guy and a very astute businessman, so I had a lot of respect for him in that way. They are very serious musicians, not really like they appear."

DECEMBER 31, 1977

Greensboro, North Carolina
Greensboro Coliseum
Opening Act: Piper
Attendance: 13,185   Capacity: 15,000
Promoters: Entam Ltd., Beach Club Promotions

JANUARY 3, 1978

Pembroke Pines (Hollywood), Florida
The Sportatorium
Opening Act: Detective
Attendance: 16,509   Capacity: 16,509
Promoter: Beach Club Promotions
Archived: Audio
■ **SET LIST**
See November 15, 1977.

JANUARY 4, 1978   TEMP HOLD DATE

Tampa, Florida
Egypt Shrine Auditorium
Promoter: Beach Club Promotions
■ This show was listed on the tour schedules distributed to members of the KISS Army circa November 1977. How or why KISS would have even placed a hold on a date in the venue's schedule is unclear as the venue has a capacity of only 1,500.
Additionally, there is an audiotape circulating that was allegedly recorded at a 1978 gig in Tampa. This information is fraudulent and the tape is actually from the September 24, 1979 show in Milwaukee.

JANUARY 5, 1978

Charlotte, North Carolina
Charlotte Coliseum
Opening Act: Nantucket
Attendance: 12,900   Capacity: 12,900
Promoter: Kaleidoscope Productions
■ Stan Orlen, who despite his enormous frame was nicknamed "Mr. Tiny," had been hired as tour manager at the beginning of the year. "I had worked for other bands like The Who and the Rolling Stones. But KISS was strange . . . I think the best way to put it is to say that KISS thrived on chaos. If things ran smoothly, I really believe that they weren't happy."

JANUARY 6, 1978

Columbia, South Carolina
Carolina Coliseum
Opening Act: Nantucket
Capacity: 12,800
Promoter: Beach Club Promotions
Archived: Audio
■ **SET LIST:**
[I Stole Your Love]
King of the Night Time World
Ladies Room
Firehouse
Love Gun
Let Me Go, Rock 'n Roll
[Makin' Love]
[Christine Sixteen]
[Shock Me]
[Ace Frehley Guitar Solo]
[I Want You]
Calling Dr. Love
[Shout It Out Loud]
Gene Simmons Bass Solo
God of Thunder
Peter Criss Drum Solo - reprise
Rock and Roll All Nite
[Detroit Rock City]
Beth
[Black Diamond]

JANUARY 8, 1978

Richfield (Cleveland), Ohio
The Coliseum
Opening Act: Rockets
Attendance: 17,500   Capacity: 17,500
Promoter: Belkin Productions
Archived: Audio
■ **SET LIST**
See November 15, 1977.
■ A severe snowstorm ravaged Cleveland throughout the day and evening, delaying KISS's arrival and departure from the venue. "It wasn't just a snowstorm in Cleveland," Stan Orlen remembers.

"For this tour, we had the KISS snowstorm. This snowstorm followed us through the whole Midwest. Wherever we went, it snowed. It was unbelievable. The arena in Cleveland was 20 miles from the city down this two-lane highway. We were going to the show, and we get caught in the traffic. We're stuck. I got out to talk to the drivers, and they got on the radio and got us a police escort. We finally got to the show." 250 audience members spent the night in the venue's marketing offices and dressing rooms. KISS did not depart from Cleveland until January 10.

Fortunately for the band, the protracted stay in Cleveland took place at the famous Swingos Celebrity Hotel. Something of a 1970s landmark, Swingos was renowned for catering to a rock star's every need. It was a place of garish excess, with uniquely themed rooms, e.g., the Blue Room or the Purple Room, etc. The hotel was immortalized in the 2000 Academy Award™ nominated movie, *Almost Famous*.

Ric Aliberte: "We were snowed in after the show. We couldn't leave the next day, and by that time the hotel was running out of food. You could walk around the place and still see a bunch of girls hanging around, but you could tell the party was over; we had had it. Then I heard Ace say: 'That's it, they're outta champagne. We gotta leave. Stan, do something!' So Stan went out and rented a bus, the biggest vehicle he could find to fit us all in. He ran around to stores and got potato chips and blankets and all this stuff, playing cards; it was hilarious all the stuff that he collected. I asked, 'What, are we going on a bus with a bunch of children? He said: 'Yep!' So we all climbed on this bus, which proceeded out of town at about 5 mph. It was the longest bus ride in the world.

"I stayed up the whole time and played cards with Ace and lost $2,000 to him in the process. He is the luckiest person in the world. You'd be sitting there with three-of-a-kind and he'd pull an inside straight. You'd have a flush, he'd have one higher. He'd say, 'Yeah, if you play with the Ace, you gotta take this kind of shit.' Here we were on this bus, and the only wine or booze was Night Train, which is basically fuel oil. But at least we were finally out of town."

On January 10, NBC News's *Land of Hype and Glory* special aired. In reference to KISS's finances, the broadcast included the line, ". . . and they are all millionaires." If the members of KISS were millionaires, nobody had told them; in fact, that specific question had been asked of Carl Glickman at a financial meeting the previous August. Glickman responded that the four KISS partners would probably each be worth over $1 million by the time they received their next royalty payments.

JANUARY 11, 1978

Huntington, West Virginia
Huntington Civic Center
Opening Act: Rockets
Attendance: 11,934   Capacity: 11,934
Promoter: Entertainment Amusement Company
Archived: Super 8mm

JANUARY 12, 1978

Cincinnati, Ohio

Riverfront Coliseum
Opening Act: Rockets
Attendance: 18,239   Capacity: 18,239
Promoter: Electric Factory Concerts

The snowstorm in Cleveland on the night of January 8 caused the Cincinnati show to be rescheduled from January 9.

JANUARY 13, 1978

Pittsburgh, Pennsylvania
Civic Arena
Opening Act: Rockets
Attendance: 17,053   Capacity: 18,000
Promoter: DiCesare-Engler Productions

■ Stan Orlen: "In Pittsburgh, someone threw a lighter out of the audience, and it hit Peter under the eye. He was a hypochondriac, and I don't think anyone in the history of music had his blood pressure taken more on one tour than this guy. If you told him that it was normal, he'd be really unhappy. I knew how to take blood pressure, so I always told him it was a little high or a little low. He made this big deal about being hit in the face, and we had to stop the show and tell him that his blood pressure was low."

JANUARY 15, 1978

Chicago, Illinois
Chicago Stadium
Opening Act: Rockets
Attendance: 16,700   Capacity: 16,700
Promoter: Concerts West
Archived: Audio

■ SET LIST
I Stole Your Love
King of the Night Time World
Ladies Room
Firehouse
Love Gun
Let Me Go, Rock 'n Roll
Makin' Love
Christine Sixteen
Shock Me
Ace Frehley Guitar Solo
I Want You
Calling Dr. Love
[Shout It Out loud]
[Gene Simmons Bass Solo]
God of Thunder
Peter Criss Drum Solo - reprise
[Rock and Roll All Nite]
[Detroit Rock City]
[Beth]
Black Diamond

JANUARY 16, 1978

Chicago, Illinois
Chicago Stadium
Opening Act: Rockets
Attendance: 16,700   Capacity: 16,700
Promoter: Concerts West
Archived: Audio

■ SET LIST
See November 15, 1977.

JANUARY 18, 1978

Lexington, Kentucky
Rupp Arena
Opening Act: Rockets
Attendance: 10,828   Capacity: 23,458
Promoter: Sunshine Promotions

JANUARY 20, 1978

Detroit, Michigan
Olympia

Opening Act: Rockets
Capacity: 16,400
Promoters: Belkin Productions, Brass Ring Productions

JANUARY 21, 1978

Detroit, Michigan
Olympia
Opening Act: Rockets
Capacity: 16,400
Promoters: Belkin Productions, Brass Ring Productions

JANUARY 23, 1978

Evansville, Indiana
Roberts Municipal Stadium
Opening Act: Rockets
Attendance: 14,144   Capacity: 14,144
Promoter: Sunshine Promotions
Archived: Audio

■ PARTIAL SET LIST
I Stole Your Love
King of the Night Time World
Ladies Room
Firehouse
Love Gun
Let Me Go, Rock 'n Roll
Makin' Love
Christine Sixteen
Shock Me
Ace Frehley Guitar Solo
I Want You
Calling Dr. Love
Deuce
Rock and Roll All Nite
Detroit Rock City

■ In the middle of the concert, the front stage-right lighting rig support collapsed, and the show was interrupted for approximately 30 minutes. Spotlight operator Thomas Mills, 26, fell from the rig to the floor, but did not sustain serious injuries. Eddie Balandas relates: "The Genie-lift simply bent over and snapped, which I've never seen happen in all the years I've worked with that equipment. It was a shock. It wasn't weighted down at all, it was just one guy on there with the spotlight. Fortunately, he lived to tell about it."

When KISS reappeared after the delay, they jump-started the show with "Deuce." Paul remarked, "'Since you people've been so patient, we got something we haven't done in a long time. You wanna hear it?" This marked the song's first appearance on tour since 1976, and its final performance in concert until April 1988.

JANUARY 25, 1978

Buffalo, New York
Veterans Memorial Auditorium
Opening Act: Rockets
Attendance: 17,500   Capacity: 17,500
Promoter: Festival East, Inc.

JANUARY 27, 1978

Springfield, Massachusetts
Springfield Civic Center
Opening Act: Rockets
Attendance: 10,395   Capacity: 10,395
Promoter: Cross Country Concerts
Archived: Audio

■ SET LIST
See November 15, 1977.

■ The hydraulic balconies were not used at this show.

JANUARY 28, 1978

New Haven, Connecticut
New Haven Veterans Memorial Coliseum
Opening Act: Rockets
Attendance: 10,407   Capacity: 10,407
Promoter: Cross Country Concerts
■ Paul and Ace briefly segued into the *Green Acres* theme during the show.

JANUARY 29 & 30, 1978

Uniondale, New York
Nassau Veterans Memorial Coliseum

JANUARY 30, 1978

Philadelphia, Pennsylvania
The Spectrum
Opening Act: Rockets
Attendance: 19,567   Capacity: 19,567
Promoter: Electric Factory Concerts

FEBRUARY 2, 1978

Providence, Rhode Island
Providence Civic Center
Opening Act: Rockets
Attendance: 12,307   Capacity: 13,200
Promoter: Frank J. Russo
Archived: Audio
■ **SET LIST**
See November 15, 1977.

FEBRUARY 3, 1978

Providence, Rhode Island
Providence Civic Center
Opening Act: Rockets
Attendance: 12,980   Capacity: 13,200
Promoter: Frank J. Russo
Archived: Audio
■ **SET LIST**
See November 15, 1977.
■ Just prior to "Detroit Rock City," Ace and Paul again went into the *Green Acres* theme.

Tour manager Fritz Postlethwaite: "Peter asked me if I would play this trick on Gene, and I said sure. So Richard Monier, KISS's wardrobe

man, put me into one of Gene's old costumes and makeup, which was kind of a stretch since I'm 5'7". At the end of the last song, Peter stepped down, and I jumped up there, and the riser started to go up. Gene looked up at me to get his cue, and he sort of stopped and turned back to the audience and kept playing. A second later, he stopped playing and put his hands by his sides and stared at me. Meanwhile, bombs are going off, I'm 25 feet in the air and Gene is just standing there staring at me. Somehow, we got the song ended and Gene unhooked the strap of his bass and it just dropped on the stage. He started walking around the end of the amp rail and one of the security guards had to grab him because he was about to walk right off the stage which was about six feet high. They pushed him back and threw him into the limousine and got him out of the building. The other three guys were going to fly home, and we had a Lear Jet to take us out of there. Gene didn't like to fly, so he was going to go back to Manhattan via limousine with Bill Aucoin.

"Bill relayed this story to me later. Gene got in the car and just sort of sat there and stared, and he wouldn't talk. And Bill said, 'What's the matter?' He said, 'Well, I looked back there, and I thought I saw myself playing drums.' And Gene, who is a very straight guy, said 'I think I'm losing my mind, Bill.' Bill said: 'That wasn't you, that was Fritz.' Gene was so angry that he wouldn't speak to me for a week. Not because I had played a trick on him, but because Gene was a purist about the show. The show was paramount; everything had to be professional. I had messed up Gene's show and he almost never forgave me for that. We laughed about it two weeks later, but he was very angry with me at first, and Peter, of course, just got a lot of delight out of that."

MARCH 28, 1978

Tokyo, Japan
Nippon Budokan Hall
Opening Act: Bow Wow
Attendance: 11,000   Capacity: 11,000
Promoter: Udo Artists
■ Chuck Elias: "I remember the second time we went to Japan we were much smarter about it and went over very early so we wouldn't have to deal with the jet lag. It was a crazy trip, although the crew was thrilled that this was all in one venue."

KISS stickers with all five of the Tokyo dates listed were given away in Japan, presumably at the venue.

MARCH 29, 1978

Tokyo, Japan
Nippon Budokan Hall
Opening Act: Bow Wow
Attendance: 11,000   Capacity: 11,000
Promoter: Udo Artists
■ Stan Orlen: "While we were in Japan, the guy who played Godzilla came by and brought the actual outfit with him. He suited up, and the band did a photo session with him. I was busy doing something, and I never got my picture with Godzilla. That's the single biggest regret of my life."

MARCH 31, 1978

Tokyo, Japan
Nippon Budokan Hall
Opening Act: Bow Wow
Attendance: 11,000   Capacity: 11,000
Promoter: Udo Artists
Archived: Audio
■ **SET LIST**
See November 15, 1977.
■ One of the five Budakon shows was archived on audio, although there is no way to determine which one. March 31, however, is most commonly listed as the source of the audiotape.

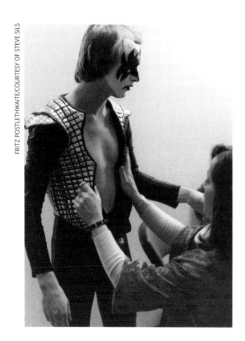

Fritz Postlethwaite in Providence, February 3, 1978, suiting up to play a joke on an unsuspecting Gene Simmons.

Paul and Peter heading for the limos at the conclusion of the Alive II Tour in North America.

APRIL 1, 1978

Tokyo, Japan
Nippon Budokan Hall
Opening Act: Bow Wow
Attendance: 11,000   Capacity: 11,000
Promoter: Udo Artists

APRIL 2, 1978

Tokyo, Japan
Nippon Budokan Hall
Opening Act: Bow Wow
Attendance: 11,000   Capacity: 11,000
Promoter: Udo Artists

■ An early estimate indicated that the Japanese tour grossed $272,000.

MAY 19, 1978

Valencia, California
Magic Mountain Amusement Park
Attendance: 8,000
Promoters: Belkin Productions, Brass Ring Productions
Archived: Audio, Film

■ **PARTIAL SET LIST**

I Stole Your Love
King of the Night Time World
Ladies Room
Firehouse
Love Gun
Let Me Go, Rock 'n Roll
Makin' Love
Christine Sixteen
Shock Me
Ace Frehley Guitar Solo
I Want You
Love Gun
Love Gun (lip-synched)
Love Gun (lip-synched)
Shock Me (lip-synched)

■ In order to have live footage for inclusion in *KISS Meets the Phantom of the Park,* this concert was staged and filmed in a parking lot at the Magic Mountain Amusement Park. Tickets, which could not be purchased, were distributed by KMET. The radio station made a single announcement that listeners could submit a SASE and would receive a pair of tickets and a parking pass to the event. Curiously, the station chose to make the announcement during the middle of the afternoon, a time when many members of the KISS fanbase would have been in school and unable to hear the announcement.

The attendees, at least those who stayed for the entire event, were treated to several hours of KISS. First, KISS performed their standard Alive II Tour show. After the concert concluded, KISS was filmed lip-synching to several songs and some production highlights were captured on tape. The shoot went long into the night, and as the filming process drew out, the band interacted with the crowd quite a bit. During an especially lengthy set of takes featuring Paul Stanley elevating on one of the stage's hydraulic platforms, Paul quipped, "If this takes much longer, I'm going to have to start offering rides to everyone in the front row."

Songwriter/producer Bill Bartell was in attendance and noticed "All American Man" listed on the set list that was visible on stage left. "My friend and I were so excited that we were going to be hearing one of the studio tracks from *Alive II* live. Before they came on, a roadie went over

to the set list and scratched it out. My heart sank.

"When I watched the movie I noticed that one scene was left on the cutting-room floor. They passed out fake red roses to us and told us to throw them at the camera. It was supposed to be a Paul point-of-view shot.

"I was also surprised to see 'Rip and Destroy' in the movie as that was definitely not done on the night of the concert. Although they did come out during the day and tell us to boo."

Chuck Elias: "That shoot was just brutally long. It was really the opposite of what we were used to doing, which was to get there and get out. That gig was: get there and sit around and wait; I know the band felt that way, too. I remember them building the roller coaster while we were filming. During the concert that they filmed, I remember the wind was so strong it almost picked up the stage and lifted it right off the ground."

Peter Criss and Fritz Postlethwaite were in a car accident on Sepulveda Boulevard on May 27, 1978, the last day of filming for the movie.

Stan Orlen: "We were playing Acey-Deucy. There was a $4,000 pot and Peter Criss won. There was so much money that he had to put it in a pillowcase. After that big pot, the game broke up, and Peter wanted to go for a ride. We always used to rent these cars from Economy Rental, which ironically had these Ferraris. I said no because I was pissed at the fact that I'd lost. The next thing I hear is that Fritz is burnt up, and Peter, of course, isn't injured. If there had been a third person in that car, they wouldn't have gotten out alive."

CHAPTER 11

1978–79

April 4, 1978 not only marked the end of the Alive II Tour, but also marked the end of what was essentially an exhausting, epic four-year tour. Even though KISS would not perform another concert—the Magic Mountain filming notwithstanding—until June 1979, the intervening 14 months were far from quiet; the band would release five more albums, make numerous public appearances, and continue to grow their rapidly expanding merchandising niche.

On April 24, the band's first greatest-hits package, *Double Platinum,* was released, albeit with very little involvement from the band. Sean Delaney was responsible for producing and remixing the album, which featured 21 songs from the band's first six albums, many of them considerably different from their original versions. Delaney recalls remixing the songs with Mike Stone: "Mike and I had just finished doing Toby Beau's album when Bill called up and said, 'You've got to do this.' We were already insane by that point from having been cooped up for so long. One of the girls from Bill's office literally hand-delivered the master tapes [for KISS's studio albums] to us in England, and then she flew right back. We had to remix 21 titles in 11 days."

Perhaps the most significant event during the downtime from touring was the recording and release of the band's four solo albums. The genesis of the solo albums is a very interesting story, with KISS perpetuating one version, and many other sources telling another. As KISS typically spins the tale, the band had been in a very fractured state during the filming of *KISS Meets the Phantom of the Park,* with Peter and Ace threatening to quit the band. The alleged resolution to appease them was for each band member

to release a solo album of their own material. In short, the time span from the formation of the idea to do the albums (roughly May 1978) to the release of the albums (September 18) was only three months.

Why the band claims this to be the case is unclear, as numerous sources provide irrefutable evidence to the contrary. Band members were advised in a June 21, 1977 business meeting to consider whom they would like to produce their solo albums. Additionally, Gene mentions working on a solo album in a July 1977 interview for Japanese radio; a review of the Vancouver Love Gun show cites Gene as recording solo album material in a local studio; and Ace talks about the solo albums in a Madison, Wisconsin interview from December 1977.

No matter how the idea came about, the solo albums were designed to be big from the earliest stages. The budgets for the albums were huge, Gene's especially, with a then almost absurd production cost of $300,000.

Sean Delaney was asked to produce Gene's album, which was primarily recorded in Oxford, England at a castle called The Manor. Delaney recalls: "Gene's solo album wasn't something that he went in and did by himself. The album began with Gene sitting there playing an acoustic guitar and singing songs. There was hardly any music for the album. You have five musicians that can verify and testify that I made up just about every single note on that album. Gene barely even played on it. This was also at the point where his ego was getting out of hand; Gene was a great asshole in England to the point where they blew up on him."

Drummer Allan Schwartzberg: "We'd be sitting in the dining room having breakfast and

Gene would say, 'Hey Drums,' or 'Hey Guitar.' He was all ego. After a bit, we called him on it: 'Look, Gene, we have names. Either use them or find somebody else.' He was cool about it after that.

"Cher was going out with Gene at the time and came over with her kids, Chastity and Elijah, and lived in the studio while we recorded the album. We recorded all over the castle: in a stone bathroom, and a hallway and so forth, but it ended up being a great album. Sean did an outstanding job of producing it."

Paul's album was much more aligned with his contributions to the six KISS albums. While all four solo albums were rather disingenuously "dedicated" to one another, Paul's had a special dedication to JB Fields and Victoria Medlin. JB Fields was one of the early KISS road crew members and had been KISS's truck and bus driver since 1974. Sadly, Fields, affectionately known as Captain 66, had died in an auto accident outside of Columbus, Georgia on April 12, 1978 while driving for Blue Öyster Cult. Fields had swerved to miss an oncoming car on a bridge and his truck went through the guardrail and into the river below; he was killed instantly.

Medlin, who had dated Paul, was an obscure actress whose lone role of note was in the 1971 cult classic *Vanishing Point.* She committed suicide on February 22, 1978.

Ace chose Eddie Kramer as producer for his album, though Frehley himself had been trying his hand at producing, too, apparently with less-than-desirable results. His clients, the New York proto-punk band The Brats, were calling in a favor. Brats singer Keith West recalls, "The Brats had this unwritten thing with KISS that

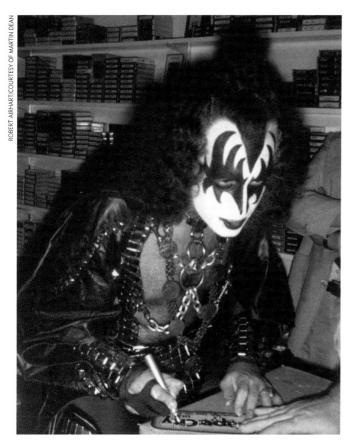

▲ November 18, 1978: Gene during an "in-store" at Tape City in Metairie, Louisiana, a New Orleans suburb.

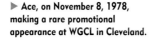

▶ Ace, on November 8, 1978, making a rare promotional appearance at WGCL in Cleveland.

whoever made it first would help the other band get a record deal. Eventually, Ace took us into the Record Plant while he was recording his solo album. Unfortunately, Ace was really fucked up most of the time and was heavily into cocaine. He'd even bring his golden retriever, and it would drink beers with him. He had control over the sessions, and the resulting mix was horrible." Ace may have had an unsteady hand when it came to producing, but his album was the only one of the KISS solo albums to spawn a legitimate hit single, "New York Groove."

Peter initially wanted to use Rod Stewart's producer, Tom Dowd, for his album before ending up with former Ringo Starr bandmate and producer Vini Poncia. "I was asked to do drums for both Gene and Peter's albums," recalls Allan Schwartzberg. "It was weird being asked to play for Peter because he's a good drummer himself; in fact, he still can do this live trick that I've never been able to figure out. But I relaxed pretty quickly because he was very nice about it. He even sat on the floor next to me when I was recording the drum parts."

A total of four or five million copies (depending upon which source you believe) of the solo albums were released simultaneously by Casablanca on September 18. Neil Bogart claimed it to be the largest shipment of product in industry history. While the albums immediately charted and sold well—they were certified Gold and Plat-

inum on October 2—none of them broke into the Top 10 and eventually the enormous number of albums in circulation collapsed back upon Casablanca. After the initial sell-through, the albums' omnipresence ceased to have a positive promotional impact and instead made it appear as if the albums were not selling. Casablanca ended up discounting hundreds of thousands of copies in cut-out bins. Unfortunately for the label, they either forgot or ignored one of the clauses in their contract with KISS, which stated they had to have the band's permission to do so first.

To help promote the solo albums, Gene, Paul, and, to a lesser degree, Ace, did promotional tours around the country consisting of radio-station interviews and a string of very successful in-store appearances. The lack of a concert tour had done nothing to dull fan enthusiasm as Ric Aliberte relates: "The in-stores were just insane. In New Orleans [November 18], we did an in-store with Gene at a place called Tape City, and there were at least 4,000 kids in line. Gene was amazing: he signed every last autograph, and when he was through, he took pictures with the fans." A brief press conference was held in conjunction with the in-store appearance, and Gene announced that KISS would serve as Grand Marshal at the annual Endymion Parade during Mardi Gras on February 24, 1979.

Unfortunately, KISS never made it to the

event. Ric Aliberte explains: "We were concerned about security for the band because the local police were on strike at the time. The people organizing the parade told us not to worry, that they would arrange for security. I told them that if they could give us enough security, we'd do the parade despite the strike. I got a call in my office in New York saying, 'Hi, my name is Joe. I am a member of the New Orleans Police, and we know who you are. We are on strike down here trying to make a living. If you break our strike, you're going to be sorry.' I blew it off and went down to New Orleans anyway. As I was walking into The Royal Orleans hotel to check into my room, a bullet smashed into the pillar above my head. I hit the floor immediately. Eventually, I got up, checked in and went to my room. After I'd been there for a few minutes, the phone rang and the voice on the other end said, 'I thought I told you that we didn't want you down here.' I called back and told the band that we were canceling the appearance and they should stay at home. Gene asked, 'Why? They were shooting at you, not us.'"

It wasn't just political confrontations in the Bible Belt that caused the band problems, as Aliberte continues: "In late 1978, I took Paul Stanley out to do a bunch of in-stores in San Francisco and several other locations in the Pacific Northwest. A particularly memorable one took place [at Peaches Records on December 6, the last

95

known in-store in this run of appearances] in Seattle where the line out front was something like 1,500 kids. The first person in line had waited a full 24 hours to see Paul. I was standing next to him when a woman came up and said: 'Never come to Everett, Washington or we will blow you away.' And then she left. She waited 24 hours in the rain just to tell him that. We couldn't believe it."

Aside from the frequent in-stores, KISS made many notable television appearances during this time. First and foremost, *KISS Meets the Phantom of the Park* aired on NBC-TV on October 28, 1978. It was panned by those critics who even bothered to watch it, though the ratings for the broadcast were among the best of the year for the network. The band also made several local and national television appearances on *PM Magazine.* Two other contracted projects never came to fruition: a KISS feature film deal with Universal Pictures and a prime-time animated Halloween special.

Just prior to KISS's 1978 tour of Japan, Gene had started dating Cher. Not surprisingly, from the onset the relationship had been a fairly public one and became especially high profile in early 1979. During Cher's March 2, 1979 appearance on *The Mike Douglas Show,* a skit was contrived where a camera crew was placed in a local Philadelphia Jack in the Box with Cher and Mike Douglas working undercover behind the walk-up counter. The producers decided to surprise Cher by having Gene appear in full costume and makeup and order "French-fried lizard tongues." Cher's son Elijah was also seen on the same episode carrying his KISS toy guitar, which was a present from Gene.

Gene, again in full makeup and costume, and Cher also cohosted the NARM Awards banquet, which took place at the Diplomat Hotel in Hollywood, Florida over the weekend of March 23–26, 1979.

Lastly, Gene and Ace (still using their Love Gun outfits) made an appearance on *The Robert Klein Hour* (a radio show taped in front of a live audience) in April 1979 with Robin Williams.

The long break between the Alive II and Dynasty Tours was a successful one for KISS. Despite the lack of concerts, they had managed to maintain their popularity through shrewd marketing, promotional appearances, and very extensive merchandising. But KISS had set themselves up for a fall. Simply put, KISS had become too visible. It is almost poetic that the same brilliant marketing and merchandising that had propelled KISS into a pop-culture phenomenon eventually crippled them.

Much like the dollar devalues when too much money is in circulation, too much KISS was eroding the band's popularity.

Paul making an in-store appearance at Peaches Records in Seattle, December 6, 1978. AMI promotions director Ric Aliberte is on his right.

CHAPTER 12
DYNASTY TOUR

Number of Shows: 79
Start Date: June 15, 1979 - Lakeland, Florida
End Date: December 16, 1979 - Toledo, Ohio
Countries: Canada, U.S.A.
Opening Acts: Breathless; Cheap Trick; Eli; John Cougar & the Zone; Jon Butcher Axis; Judas Priest; Loverboy; Michael Stanley Band; Nantucket; New England; Rockets; Sweet; Whiteface
Average Attendance: 10,523

OBJECTIVES:

• Make money.

• Most spectacular show ever to go on the road.

Those were the first words the members of KISS saw when they entered the Aucoin Management offices on December 21, 1978 to discuss plans for the upcoming 1979 tour. Production Manager Ken Anderson had been fielding bids from companies offering their special effects/production services to KISS and had compiled his findings and suggestions into a 38-page document, which he presented at the meeting.

The means of achieving the first objective were simple enough: generate revenue while keeping the overhead as low as possible. Sensible options such as efficient tour routing and consolidating the responsibilities for light, sound,

and production to one company were offered. Additionally, the production would be designed to allow all seats in each venue to be sold, even those behind the stage. The KISS partners voted and McManus Enterprises was awarded the responsibility for most of the tour's production.

Unfortunately, spectacular shows cost money, so the two objectives of the tour worked at cross-purposes. As logical as the above suggestions were, the list of production effects KISS wanted to include was prohibitively expensive and the Dynasty Tour quickly became impractical.

KISS was out of control on many levels—the four members assumed they could maintain professional and personal lifestyles that they could not realistically support. The tour not only generated significantly less profit than expected, it hemorrhaged money.

Making matters worse, throughout the tour, the band members became increasingly dysfunctional. Ace was drinking and partying fairly heavily, and Paul and Gene were distracted by their untethered egos, high-profile relationships with women, and the celebrity lifestyle that success provides. Peter was the worst of the group, with a hard-drug habit and a looming divorce from his wife Lydia making him a big liability. His drumming skills had deteriorated rapidly, and there were several instances, especially during the last weeks of the tour, where his bandmates and management questioned whether or not he was going to perform at a show. Fritz Postlethwaite recalls: "Peter's substance abuse got to the point where he couldn't make good decisions anymore, and he couldn't make it through a show. Paul and Gene both talked to me about it and said

RON POWNALL/WWW.ROCKROLLPHOTO.COM

97

they were not going to tour with him again if he was like that; it wasn't worth it. Paul had talked to other drummers, which wasn't unknown, and after the solo albums they'd worked with other people anyway. They had all of those other people in line." In at least two instances, Peter purposefully did his best to sabotage a concert.

Many people quickly dismiss the Dynasty Tour as a flop, but its success or failure should be judged in context. KISS's grandiose plans for the tour weren't entirely irrational, as huge budgets and free-spending were typical of the music industry, which enjoyed its biggest year to date in 1978, finally surpassing $1 billion in gross revenues. But an unforeseen combination of economic and political factors made the U.S. economy very unstable in 1979. The Consumer Price Index for 1979 was up 11.3% (the largest gain since World War I), and the growth rate for the Gross Domestic Product was down 42%. In essence, this meant there was less disposable income to spend on entertainment. Not surprisingly, the music industry suffered dramatically.

The tour averaged a little over 10,500 attendees per show, a disappointing figure in that it was 22% less than the Alive II Tour. But, considering the severe economic indicators, the Dynasty Tour can be looked at as a qualified success.

Ultimately, KISS was still inclined to view the tour as a bust because it failed to meet their expectations and Aucoin's as well, though Glickman/Marks had been more cautious, and repeatedly urged a more economic approach. Since the expectations were ridiculous to begin with, the Dynasty Tour's failure in that regard was predestined.

Outside factors were only part of the Dynasty Tour's problems. KISS created many problems of their own, mostly due to their stubborn adherence to a very expensive "bigger is better" approach, which is perfectly demonstrated in a concept called KISS World.

The plans for the tour were to have KISS perform multiple shows in at least one city each week, preferably more, with single shows in two other cities rounding out the weekly schedule. Outside the venue, a traveling KISS-themed amusement park called KISS World would set up shop and operate throughout the band's stay in the city. Multiple-show stays would reduce operating expenses significantly as they eliminated travel and much of the load-in and load-out process, and that, coupled with the money generated by the amusement park, would make the tour a revenue machine. In one of a small list of smart moves, KISS World was scrapped when the idea was recognized as impractical.

As far back as 1975, KISS had shown interest in incorporating a laser show into their concerts. For the Dynasty Tour, a group of laser effects was designed and an attempt was made to integrate them into the production. Bill McManus explains the difficulties that arose: "They never worked. I came in and listened to the laser show proposal in Aucoin's office and felt that they had no real concept of the physics involved. I figured it would require a 200-watt laser, and there wasn't such a thing that you could use in public. In fact,

a 65-watt laser will slice baloney at 50 paces and is powerful enough to do damage to the roof structures of buildings. I don't think the Bureau of Radiological Health would ever allow you to do what they wanted in public. I told them I would cooperate in every way with the laser company, Science Faction, but I insisted that I would not be the middleman for that, because I knew it would be dissatisfactory and they would be angry about the amount of money that they wasted on it.

"There were three items they used in rehearsals: they had the fiber-optic piece that was supposed to appear to be coming out of Paul's eye. The device had micro-switches and mercury switches in it (as a safety guard) so that it would never fire when he was looking at an audience, only when he was looking upwards. That didn't work well, but when it did work, I think it scared the shit out of Paul and, frankly, it should have: it was way too powerful. It was way too close to his eye. It was an ill-conceived thing.

"They also had one in Ace's guitar. We had this little flash-paper cannon on the back of his guitar that he would shoot up in the air and it would blow up what we called a mine-bag up in the truss. For this tour, they went one further and put a fiber-optic laser guide in the guitar. Again, it had safety switches built in."

Anderson's memo details the final laser effect: "Laser Curtain Light: This effect consists of vertical beams of light running between the stage and the truss, around the entire perimeter of the stage, approximately one foot apart. They will be red, green, and blue lines, which can appear alone or in combination. They will be able to chase in any direction and appear at any given portion of the stage . . . The system will come with two (2) operators and will cost approximately $10,000 per week." The initial design and construction fee was $148,000.

McManus continues: "The literal concept was to have a water-cooled laser under the stage, the lasers would then shoot out straight up through the stage, hit the mirror that was rotating at a high speed and bounce out to maybe 150 other mirrors that were around the truss that would reflect it down as though to create a curtain. Then, there was a triangular-shaped interrupter that was supposed to be pulled down in front of that rotating mirror to create the illusion that a curtain was being drawn open. Well, it sounds great, looks good on paper, even on a model. But it never did work, ever."

There were many ill-conceived effects proposed for each individual band member as well. A $6,000 pair of illuminated, strobing drumsticks was suggested for Peter. An animatronic lion was recommended for Peter's drum riser and even the laughable illusion of changing Peter into a lion and back again was offered.

An effect was proposed for Ace that would allow him to shoot sparks out of his hands.

Aside from his laser eye-trick, yet another effect was conceived for Paul that involved a laser beam that would shine down from the lighting truss, striking his newly-designed, fractured-mirror Ibanez Iceman, and then reflect off of it as if bolts of lightning were shooting from the guitar.

Gene had several rather dangerous effects proposed for the production. One involved Gene engulfed in flames after doing his fire-breathing act, only to magically appear at another part of the stage. The feasibility of allowing Gene to breathe fire more than once without any visible means of ignition was also explored; a device fitting inside of his mouth would produce the flame and was to be triggered by the action of his jaws: a nice idea, providing he never coughed or sneezed.

The suggestions got more and more ridiculous. One company offered an idea where strange little creatures would emerge from a flying saucer only to be destroyed by Gene's fire-breathing. Then, Dr. Doom would step out from the saucer, instruct the creatures to capture Paul and imprison him. Dr. Doom would then blow up the box in which Paul was imprisoned.

Costuming, too, was expensive, with proposals ranging from $5,000 to $25,000 for a set of four costumes. Even the band's now classic logo was ear-marked for an upgrade, though the proposed Spectracolor KISS logo edged in neon never survived the planning stages.

Eventually the pre-production phase wrapped, and initial rehearsals began in Nassau Community College on Long Island in early June. Renowned choreographer Ken Ortega of Dirty Dancing fame was present at the rehearsals to help KISS choreograph their moves. After concluding rehearsals at Nassau, the staging, crew, and band departed for Lakeland, Florida where rehearsals would continue from June 11–14. Bill McManus: "I was the one who chose Lakeland and the Lakeland Civic Center. They had a full-sized facility, and the public officials that managed the building would just about give you the building for free if you'd do a show there. Essentially, we could get a week's free setup and shakedown of all the hardware."

Another of the long list of changes was the addition of color to the band's costumes. KISS had been very much a monochromatic band to this point, but now each member had a color associated with him: Gene, red; Paul, purple; Ace, blue; and Peter, green. These colors had first appeared as backlighting on the front of each of the four solo albums, and elements of the colors were now incorporated into the costumes. Ace also added blue eye shadow to his makeup, while Peter continued to use green makeup around his eyes.

The stage was designed by Paul Stanley, Lenny Cowles, and Mark Duffy, and constructed by Theatre Techniques. It had a very low design to it to allow seating behind the stage, with short, curved ramps rather than staircases flanking Peter's drum riser. The riser itself was circular and could rotate 360 degrees.

Several new effects actually did make it to the show: for "God of Thunder," Gene flew up to the lighting truss via wires and a motorized winch; Ace's guitar flew up to the truss via a similar method during his solo in "2,000 Man;" and at the end of the show, KISS Army sponges spilled out of the large disco ball suspended high above the venue floor.

Because six KISS albums had been released since the band last toured, it's not surprising that the standard set list was dramatically different from the Alive II Tour. "I Was Made for Lovin' You" and "2,000 Man" from *Dynasty* were performed, and one song from each of the solo albums was added to the set as well: "Radioactive" from Gene's album, "Move On" from Paul's, "New York Groove" from Ace's album, with Peter offering a cover of "Tossin' and Turnin'" from his record. Both Gene and Peter's contributions were replaced early in the tour by more familiar fare, "Let Me Go, Rock 'n Roll" and "Christine Sixteen," respectively. Another song from *Dynasty*, Peter's "Dirty Livin'" was reportedly rehearsed for the tour, but was never performed live.

Several then-up-and-coming bands were offered the opening slot for KISS on the Dynasty Tour. Most passed on the offer, thinking that the KISS crowd would not be very appreciative. Gene wanted either The Cars or Van Halen, while Bill Aucoin was considering the laughable choice of Devo. Eventually most of the opening slots on the tour went to several long-forgotten acts like New England, Nantucket, and the Rockets, or complete unknowns like Eli and Breathless, though two of the tour's opening acts, Judas Priest and John Cougar, did go on to find great success.

The tour, which was advertised as "The Return of KISS," received heavy coverage in the local press, some of it quite negative. As the band became more popular, naturally the lunatic fringe began to target them more often and the idea that KISS was an acronym for Knights in Satan's Service was brought up several times on the tour, usually in the south.

———— · ————

Although it is not specifically cited in the set lists, throughout the tour Ace included brief excerpts of John Williams's score for *Close Encounters of the Third Kind* in his featured solo.

JUNE 8, 1979   TEMP HOLD DATE
New Orleans, Louisiana
Louisiana Superdome
Promoter: Beaver Productions

JUNE 14, 1979   CANCELED
Lakeland, Florida
Lakeland Civic Center
Opening Act: Nantucket
Promoter: Beach Club Promotions

■ The show was canceled due to poor ticket sales, though AMI fed the press a fabricated official story that Peter was recovering from a hand injury. Six other shows on the itinerary were either canceled or never put on sale. Tickets for this show were honored at the June 15th appearance.

The day prior to the canceled show, Paul, Gene, and Ace dropped by radio station WRBQ to promote the Lakeland show.

KISS ran through a full-scale dress rehearsal on June 14, which members of the local and national press attended.

JUNE 15, 1979
Lakeland, Florida
Lakeland Civic Center
Opening Act: Nantucket
Attendance: 8,136   Capacity: 8,136

■ Wardrobe manager Pixie Esmonde: "Lakeland was horrible: it was a million degrees, the air-conditioning just sucked, and the entire place smelled like a swamp. All of my stuff hadn't arrived, the road cases I'd ordered were too big and unwieldy; it was a nightmare.

"The repair-work I had to do to Gene's boots was done by mixing two plastics together. I would use the glue/plastic mixture to create the knobs/veins on the boots, and then finish it with silver paint. It really stunk, and it would knock you out if you inhaled too much of it, so I had to repair them outside in 95° heat. When I was repairing them I had to fend off these giant Palmetto bugs, and you'd occasionally even see an alligator.

"After the first show was over, we were in the dressing room and Gene was in his makeup with his jumpsuit down to his waist. Suddenly, I hear this scream like a girl: 'Pixie! Pixie! Pixie! Come in here.' So I run in and ask, 'What's the matter? You OK?' And I'm expecting him to be covered in blood, fallen down, an alligator, you name it. 'No, there's a Palmetto bug on the floor, and I need you to kill it.' I said, 'What? You big pussy!' So, I killed a big Palmetto bug. Unbeknownst to Gene, the next day, while I was outside polishing the boots, a couple of Palmetto bugs crawled up on them and got stuck in some glue. Because he behaved so badly the day before, I just let them lay there and die and then polished them silver."

Production manager Ken Anderson: "At the first show, the drum riser rolled downstage just fine. Then it came time for it to roll back upstage, and it wasn't going to move. I think it moved three feet and died. And, in full view of the audience, Gene and Paul and Ace got in front of it and pushed it back upstage. In the meantime, I was looking for an oven to stick my head in."

For this show and the subsequent performance on June 17, Gene wore an outfit that differs from his typical Dynasty costume.

JUNE 17, 1979
Pembroke Pines (Hollywood), Florida
The Sportatorium
Opening Act: Nantucket
Attendance: 7,300   Capacity: 7,300
Promoter: Beach Club Promotions

■ At this show, Gene did not fly up to the lighting truss.

JUNE 19, 1979
Savannah, Georgia
Civic Center
Opening Act: Sweet
Attendance: SRO
Promoter: Beach Club Promotions

■ While in Savannah, Ace was arrested for allegedly walking away from a charter fishing boat cruise without paying the tab.

Gene debuted his regular Dynasty outfit at this show.

JUNE 20, 1979   CANCELED
Savannah, Georgia
Civic Center
Promoter: Beach Club Promotions

■ This gig was canceled due to lack of ticket sales. Only 700 tickets had been sold at the time of cancellation.

A rare shot of Gene performing in his original Dynasty outfit.

The promotional films for "I Was Made for Lovin' You" and "Sure Know Something" were shot at the venue on June 20. John Goodhue produced and directed the films.

JUNE 22, 1979
Columbia, South Carolina
Carolina Coliseum
Opening Act: Whiteface
Capacity: 12,800
Promoter: Beach Club Promotions

JUNE 24, 1979
Charlotte, North Carolina
Charlotte Coliseum
Opening Act: Nantucket
Attendance: 10,000
Promoters: Kaleidoscope Productions, Beach Club Promotions

JUNE 26, 1979
Greenville, South Carolina
Greenville Memorial Auditorium
Opening Act: Nantucket
Capacity: 10,200
Promoters: Kaleidoscope Productions, Beach Club Promotions

JUNE 28, 1979
Asheville, North Carolina
Asheville Civic Center
Opening Act: Nantucket
Attendance: 4,500–5,000   Capacity: 7,654
Promoter: Kaleidoscope Productions

JUNE 30, 1979

Atlanta, Georgia
The Omni
Opening Act: New England
Promoter: Full House Productions

■ Reportedly, an early version of the Dynasty tourbook was accidentally shipped to the venue and sold during this show only.

JULY 1, 1979

Atlanta, Georgia
The Omni
Promoter: Full House Productions

JULY 3, 1979

Greensboro, North Carolina
Greensboro Coliseum
Opening Act: Nantucket
Attendance: 10,336   Capacity: 12,000
Promoters: Entam Ltd., Belkin Productions

■ Bill McManus: "I think one of the most important things to be said about KISS during that time period was their commitment to delivering the biggest and best show they possibly could. At one point, Wally Meyrowitz was trying to book us into some tight squeezes in some small halls, and it was my job to go out in advance to look at the halls and decide if the hall could handle the production and do what we called a "B" show. We did it once down in Greensboro, North Carolina. Afterwards, Gene said, 'If we can't fly and do our full pyro because of the size of the room or limitations of public officials, then we just won't do it. These people expect KISS, and they should get the whole wet sloppy KISS or they shouldn't get

anything.' And the battle cry from then on was that 'there are no B shows.'"

JULY 5, 1979

Hampton, Virginia
Hampton Coliseum
Opening Act: New England
Attendance: 8,682   Capacity: 10,000
Promoters: Entam Ltd., Belkin Productions

JULY 7, 1979

Landover (Washington, D.C.), Maryland
Capital Centre
Opening Act: New England
Attendance: 12,000
Promoter: Cellar Door Concerts
Archived: Video
■ SET LIST
King of the Night Time World
Radioactive
Move On
Calling Dr. Love
Firehouse
New York Groove
I Was Made for Lovin' You
Love Gun
2,000 Man
Ace Frehley Guitar Solo
Tossin' and Turnin'
Gene Simmons Bass Solo
God of Thunder
Peter Criss Drum Solo - reprise
Shout It Out Loud
Black Diamond
Detroit Rock City
Beth
Rock and Roll All Nite

■ Both shows were archived by the in-house video crew for the band. The first night, the band was so loud that it caused a fluctuation in the video signal and the tape was deemed useless. The second night is not much better, but it is in the band's library.

JULY 8, 1979

Landover (Washington, D.C.), Maryland
Capital Centre
Opening Act: New England
Promoter: Cellar Door Concerts
Archived: Video
■ SET LIST
See July 7, 1979.

■ As he would several times throughout the tour, Peter deliberately botched "Beth."

JULY 10, 1979

Roanoke, Virginia
Roanoke Civic Center
Opening Act: New England
Attendance: 11,000   Capacity: 11,000
Promoter: Entam Ltd.
Archived: Audio
■ SET LIST
See July 7, 1979.

JULY 13, 1979

Pontiac (Detroit), Michigan
Pontiac Mini-Dome
Opening Acts: Cheap Trick, New England
Attendance: 35,000+   Capacity: 35,000
Promoter: Belkin Productions
Archived: Audio

KISS rises to the stage at the Capital Centre in Landover, Maryland.

MARK OUELLETTE

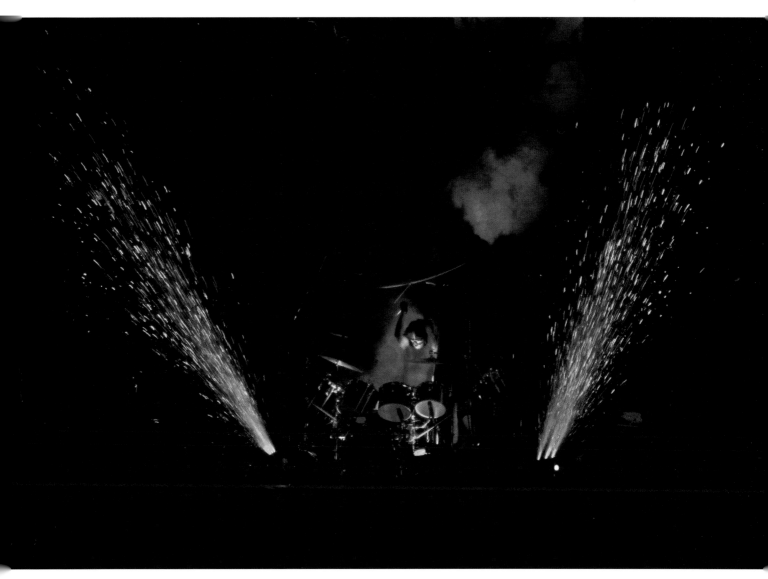

■ **SET LIST**
See July 7, 1979.

■ Pixie Esmonde: "At the show in Detroit, we were in the under-stage dressing room, Gene was really angry at somebody else for something that happened onstage and, in the heat of the moment, he grabbed me and drop-lifted me, which ended up leaving some bruises. So, the next day I glued fishing weights to his boots and to his codpiece. Gene said to me, 'Pixie, these boots are really heavy.' 'Oh, Gene, you're probably just tired, your legs get tired, you've been working too hard.' 'Are you sure?' 'Well, sometimes the costume doesn't have time to dry out and it gets heavier. That's probably it.' The moral of the story is: never piss off your wardrobe woman."

JULY 14, 1979   CANCELED

Pontiac (Detroit), Michigan
Pontiac Mini-Dome
Opening Acts: Cheap Trick, New England
Promoter: Belkin Productions

■ A TV commercial advertising this show was aired, but tickets were never put on sale.

JULY 16, 1979

Lexington, Kentucky
Rupp Arena
Opening Act: New England
Attendance: 9,480   Capacity: 23,000
Promoters: Entam Ltd., Sunshine Promotions

JULY 18, 1979

Richfield (Cleveland), Ohio
The Coliseum
Opening Act: New England
Capacity: 20,000
Promoter: Belkin Productions
Archived: Audio

■ **SET LIST**
King of the Night Time World
Let Me Go, Rock 'n Roll
Makin' Love
Calling Dr. Love
Firehouse
New York Groove
I Was Made for Lovin' You
Love Gun
2,000 Man
Ace Frehley Guitar Solo
Tossin' and Turnin'
Gene Simmons Bass Solo
God of Thunder
Peter Criss Drum Solo - reprise
Shout It Out Loud
Black Diamond
Detroit Rock City
Beth
Rock and Roll All Nite

■ This was the final known performance of "Tossin' and Turnin'." It was also the only known performance of "Makin' Love" on the tour.

ABC-TV's *20/20* taped parts of the show for a feature on KISS that aired on August 16, 1979.

JULY 19, 1979

Richfield (Cleveland), Ohio
The Coliseum
Opening Act: New England
Capacity: 20,000
Promoter: Belkin Productions

JULY 21, 1979

Pittsburgh, Pennsylvania
Civic Arena
Opening Act: New England
Attendance: 13,873   Capacity: 18,000
Promoter: DiCesare-Engler Productions

■ **SET LIST**
King of the Night Time World
Let Me Go, Rock 'n Roll
Move On

Calling Dr. Love
Firehouse
New York Groove
I Was Made for Lovin' You
Christine Sixteen
2,000 Man
Ace Frehley Guitar Solo
Love Gun
Gene Simmons Bass Solo
God of Thunder
Peter Criss Drum Solo - reprise
Shout It Out Loud
Black Diamond
Detroit Rock City
Beth
Rock and Roll All Nite

■ These are the first known performances of "Let Me Go, Rock 'n Roll" and "Christine Sixteen" on the Dynasty Tour.

JULY 24, 1979

New York, New York
Madison Square Garden
Opening Act: New England
Capacity: 19,626
Promoter: Ron Delsener Presents
Archived: Audio
■ **SET LIST**
See July 21, 1979

■ In a somewhat unusual approach to promoting rock concerts, Ron Delsener took out print ads in all of the major New York newspapers enticing readers to "Call KISS." When the toll-free call was made, callers were treated to a fifty-eight second message from the band. The promotion began in May and lasted for about a month.

Adding to the unusual marketing approach, KISS banners were flown at area beaches for the Memorial Day and July 4th weekends, and space was reserved on the back of 250 buses for a KISS sign to promote the Madison Square Garden appearances.

JULY 25, 1979

New York, New York
Madison Square Garden
Opening Act: New England
Capacity: 19,626
Promoter: Ron Delsener Presents
Archived: Audio
■ **PARTIAL SET LIST**
Move On
Calling Dr. Love
Firehouse
New York Groove
I Was Made for Lovin' You
Christine Sixteen
2,000 Man
Ace Frehley Guitar Solo
Love Gun
God of Thunder
Peter Criss Drum Solo - reprise

JULY 26, 1979

New York, New York
Madison Square Garden
Capacity: 19,626 TEMP HOLD DATE
Promoter: Ron Delsener Presents

JULY 27, 1979

New York, New York
Madison Square Garden
Capacity: 19,626 TEMP HOLD DATE
Promoter: Ron Delsener Presents

JULY 28, 1979

New York, New York TEMP HOLD DATE
Madison Square Garden
Capacity: 19,626
Promoter: Ron Delsener Presents

JULY 28, 1979

Portland, Maine
Cumberland County Civic Center
Opening Act: New England
Promoter: Frank J. Russo

JULY 29, 1979

New York, New York
Madison Square Garden
Capacity: 19,626 TEMP HOLD DATE
Promoter: Ron Delsener Presents

JULY 31, 1979

Providence, Rhode Island
Providence Civic Center
Opening Act: New England
Attendance: 7,052   Capacity: 13,200
Promoter: Frank J. Russo
Archived: Audio
■ **SET LIST**
See July 21, 1979.

AUGUST 1, 1979

Providence, Rhode Island
Providence Civic Center
Opening Act: New England
Attendance: 11,314 Capacity: 13,200
Promoter: Frank J. Russo
Archived: Audio
■ **SET LIST**
[King of the Night Time World]
Let Me Go, Rock 'n Roll
Move On
Calling Dr. Love
Firehouse
New York Groove
I Was Made for Lovin' You
Christine Sixteen
2,000 Man
Ace Frehley Guitar Solo
[Love Gun]
[Gene Simmons Bass Solo]
God of Thunder
Peter Criss Drum Solo - reprise
Shout it Out Loud
[Black Diamond]
Detroit Rock City
Beth
Rock and Roll All Nite

AUGUST 2, 1979

Providence, Rhode Island TEMP HOLD DATE
Providence Civic Center
Promoter: Frank J. Russo

AUGUST 4, 1979

Toronto, Ontario, Canada
Maple Leaf Gardens
Opening Act: New England
Attendance: 14,000   Capacity: 17,000
Promoter: Concert Productions Int'l
Archived: Audio
■ **SET LIST**
[King of the Night Time World]
[Let Me Go, Rock 'n Roll]
[Move On]
[Calling Dr. Love]
[Firehouse]
[New York Groove]
[I Was Made for Lovin' You]

[Christine Sixteen]
2,000 Man
Ace Frehley Guitar Solo
Love Gun
Gene Simmons Bass Solo
God of Thunder
Peter Criss Drum Solo - reprise
Shout It Out Loud
Black Diamond
Detroit Rock City
Beth
[Rock and Roll All Nite]

AUGUST 6, 1979

Montréal, Quebec, Canada
Forum de Montréal
Opening Act: New England
Promoter: Donald K. Donald
Archived: Audio
■ **SET LIST**
See July 21, 1979.
■ Gene did not breathe fire at this show.

AUGUST 8, 1979

Buffalo, New York
Veterans Memorial Auditorium
Opening Act: New England
Attendance: 8,900   Capacity: 17,500
Promoter: Festival East, Inc.
Archived: Audio
■ **SET LIST**
See July 21, 1979.
■ Gene's flying rig malfunctioned, causing a few moments of panic during "God of Thunder." The production was designed so that Gene would be lowered to the floor from the lighting rig while Peter did his drum solo. Gene did reach the floor safely, however, two of the wires attached to him were not unfastened quickly enough by Gene's roadie and as the winch began to retract the cables, Gene was again lifted off the floor. He dangled about five feet off the floor for several moments before the road crew successfully disconnected the wires.

AUGUST 10, 1979

Indianapolis, Indiana
Market Square Arena
Opening Act: Michael Stanley Band
Attendance: 13,283
Promoter: Sunshine Promotions
Archived: Audio
■ **SET LIST**
See July 21, 1979.

AUGUST 12, 1979

Memphis, Tennessee
Mid-South Coliseum
Opening Act: New England
Attendance: 11,999   Capacity: 11,999
Promoter: Beaver Productions
■ While in Memphis on August 13, Gene wrote a five-page treatment for *KISSTORY*, which was to be a documentary film on KISS.

AUGUST 14, 1979

Nashville, Tennessee
Nashville Municipal Auditorium
Opening Act: New England
Attendance: 9,900   Capacity: 9,900
Promoter: Sound 70 Concerts
■ A brief article in the *The Tennesseean* warned would-be attendees that counterfeit tickets were being sold to the show.

AUGUST 16, 1979

Birmingham, Alabama
Birmingham-Jefferson Civic Center
Opening Act: New England
Attendance: 12,213   Capacity: 19,100
Promoter: Ruffino & Vaughn
■ Ian Hunter was originally scheduled to open the show.

AUGUST 18, 1979

Baton Rouge, Louisiana
Riverside Centroplex
Opening Act: New England
Promoter: Beaver Productions
■ Local show *The Journal* videotaped highlights of the entire concert, which later aired in a lengthy segment about the band.

AUGUST 20, 1979

Mobile, Alabama
Mobile Municipal Auditorium
Opening Act: Eli
Attendance: 13,000
Promoter: Beaver Productions
■ Nantucket was listed as the opening act in some early advertisements, and New England was listed as the opening act in a day-of-show ad. Neither band appeared.
Hot Hero Sandwich was filmed for NBC-TV.

SEPTEMBER 1, 1979

Uniondale, New York
Nassau Veterans Memorial Coliseum
Opening Act: Judas Priest
Capacity: 16,500
Promoter: Ruffino & Vaughn
Archived: Audio
■ SET LIST
See July 21, 1979.
■ Backstage, KISS presented Jack Tessler, director of international operations for Aucoin Management, with a cake for his part in making "I Was Made for Lovin' You" an international hit.

SEPTEMBER 3, 1979

New Haven, Connecticut
New Haven Veterans Memorial Coliseum
Opening Act: Judas Priest
Attendance: 8,008   Capacity: 9,350
Promoter: Cross Country Concerts

SEPTEMBER 5, 1979

Springfield, Massachusetts
Springfield Civic Center
Opening Act: Judas Priest
Attendance: 7,650   Capacity: 10,000
Promoter: Cross Country Concerts

SEPTEMBER 7, 1979

Philadelphia, Pennsylvania
The Spectrum
Opening Act: Judas Priest
Attendance: 13,524   Capacity: 19,500
Promoter: Electric Factory Concerts
Archived: Audio
■ SET LIST
See July 21, 1979.
■ Paul sang all of "Black Diamond."
Pyrotechnician Hank Schmel and security man Eddie Balandas were both fired after the show. Balandas: "I think I must hold some sort of record for being fired by KISS. I got fired 13 times by Paul Stanley, three times by Ace, twice by Peter, and once by Gene. It was always a three-to-one vote to keep me. In this last case, Gene fired me. He was going out with Cher at the time, and the incident was more or less an ego trip. Gene started wanting me to pack up his suitcases for him. I said, 'No, why can't you fucking do it?' He responded, 'Because Cher had someone doing hers.' I wasn't going to stoop that low, so he fired me. We eventually made up, and I got to work with him when he went out with Diana Ross."

SEPTEMBER 10, 1979

Huntington, West Virginia
Huntington Civic Center
Opening Act: Judas Priest
Attendance: 9,798   Capacity: 11,934
Promoter: Entam Ltd.
■ KISS did not stay at a hotel in town as the local Holiday Inn required a $5,000 damage bond before they would make a reservation for the band.
On just 24-hours notice, Tom DeWilly of Pyro Tech, Inc. took over Hank Schmel's pyrotechnic responsibilities.
Dave Peyton, writing for *The Herald-Dispatch*, noted in his review of the concert: "Among those backstage was Bill Aucoin, the millionaire manager who has had much to do with putting KISS on top. He doesn't attend many concerts, but when he does it's a special event." Aucoin had garnered the nickname Good Gig Gui for his habit of only attending especially important shows.

SEPTEMBER 12, 1979

Knoxville, Tennessee
Knoxville Civic Coliseum
Opening Act: Judas Priest
Attendance: 9,442   Capacity: 9,442
Promoter: Entam Ltd.

SEPTEMBER 14, 1979

Cincinnati, Ohio
Riverfront Coliseum
Opening Act: Judas Priest
Capacity: 18,000
Promoter: Electric Factory Concerts

SEPTEMBER 16, 1979

Louisville, Kentucky
Freedom Hall
Opening Act: Judas Priest
Attendance: 7,000   Capacity: 19,400
Promoter: Sunshine Promotions

SEPTEMBER 18, 1979

Fort Wayne, Indiana
Allen Co. War Memorial Coliseum
Opening Act: Judas Priest
Attendance: 7,669   Capacity: 10,000
Promoter: Sunshine Promotions
Archived: Audio

Ace in Cincinnati with a tobacco sunburst Les Paul.

A mob of fans welcomes their heroes to Great American Music in Bloomington, Minnesota on September 27, 1979.

TOMMY SOMMERS

■ **SET LIST**
King of the Night Time World
Let Me Go, Rock 'n Roll
Move On
Calling Dr. Love
[Firehouse]
New York Groove
I Was Made for Lovin' You
Christine Sixteen
2,000 Man
Ace Frehley Guitar Solo
Love Gun
Gene Simmons Bass Solo
God of Thunder
Peter Criss Drum Solo - reprise
Shout It Out Loud
Black Diamond
Detroit Rock City
Beth
Rock and Roll All Nite

SEPTEMBER 20, 1979
Evansville, Indiana
Roberts Municipal Stadium
Opening Act: Judas Priest
Attendance: 8,220   Capacity: 13,600
Promoter: Sunshine Promotions

SEPTEMBER 22, 1979
Chicago, Illinois
International Amphitheatre
Opening Act: Judas Priest
Capacity: 11,000
Promoter: Celebration Concerts
Archived: Audio
■ **SET LIST**
See July 21, 1979.

SEPTEMBER 24, 1979
Milwaukee, Wisconsin

Milwaukee Arena
Opening Act: Judas Priest
Capacity: 12,000
Promoter: Stardate Productions
Archived: Audio
■ **SET LIST**
King of the Night Time World
Let Me Go, Rock 'n Roll
Move On
Calling Dr. Love
Firehouse
New York Groove
I Was Made for Lovin' You
Christine Sixteen
2,000 Man
Ace Frehley Guitar Solo
Love Gun
Gene Simmons Bass Solo
God of Thunder
Peter Criss Drum Solo - reprise
Shout It Out Loud
Black Diamond
Detroit Rock City
Beth
[Rock and Roll All Nite]

SEPTEMBER 26, 1979
Madison, Wisconsin
Dane County Expo Center Coliseum
Opening Act: Judas Priest
Attendance: 5,026   Capacity: 10,500
Promoter: Stardate Productions
■ Controversy over the fire code delayed the sale of tickets by three weeks, which drastically reduced attendance.

SEPTEMBER 28, 1979
Bloomington (Minneapolis), Minnesota
Metropolitan Sports Center
Opening Act: Judas Priest

Capacity: 16,800
Promoter: Schon Productions
■ On September 27, KISS made a rare in-store appearance at a Bloomington record store called Great American Music. Several thousand fans mobbed the record store for hours.

SEPTEMBER 30, 1979
Kansas City, Missouri
Municipal Auditorium
Opening Act: Judas Priest
Attendance: 10,000   Capacity: 10,429
Promoter: Contemporary Productions

OCTOBER 2, 1979
St. Louis, Missouri
The Checkerdome
Opening Act: John Cougar & the Zone
Attendance: 12,333   Capacity: 18,170
Promoter: Contemporary Productions
■ **SET LIST**
See July 21, 1979.
■ Gene and Paul were interviewed sans makeup with their backs to the camera from a dressing room in the venue for the local television show *Newsbeat* with KSDK anchors Dick Ford and John Auble.

OCTOBER 4, 1979
Des Moines, Iowa
Veterans Memorial Auditorium
Opening Act: John Cougar & the Zone
Attendance: 8,000   Capacity: 12,216
Promoter: Celebration Concerts
■ Walk-up ticket sales for the show were poor due to the Pope visiting Des Moines on the same day.

OCTOBER 6, 1979
Duluth, Minnesota
Duluth Arena Auditorium
Opening Act: John Cougar & the Zone
Attendance: 6,874   Capacity: 7,765
Promoter: Schon Productions

OCTOBER 8, 1979
Omaha, Nebraska
Omaha Civic Auditorium
Opening Act: John Cougar & the Zone
Capacity: 11,300
Promoter: Schon Productions

■ Pixie Esmonde: "Paul was a lot of things, but even-tempered was not one of them. He was always good to his audience, always good to the press, all that, but he was a bit of a bitch. He was obsessed about his weight, and understandably so. One day, he was breaking my chops about something and going on and on and on about it. So I took his jumpsuit in. He said to me, 'Pixie, did you shrink this?' 'No, why? I always wash it in cold water. Every night.' 'Are you sure?' 'Mmm, hmm. Maybe you're gaining weight.' He was horrified: 'I can't be!'"

OCTOBER 10, 1979
Cedar Rapids, Iowa
Five Seasons Center
Opening Act: John Cougar & the Zone
Attendance: 9,000
Promoter: Amusement Conspiracy

OCTOBER 12, 1979
Valley Center (Wichita), Kansas
Britt Brown Arena @ Kansas Coliseum
Opening Act: John Cougar & the Zone
Capacity: 12,000
Promoter: Contemporary Productions

OCTOBER 14, 1979
Pine Bluff, Arkansas
Pine Bluff Convention Center
Opening Act: John Cougar & the Zone
Attendance: 8,257   Capacity: 10,000
Promoter: Pace Concerts

OCTOBER 17, 1979
Norman, Oklahoma
Lloyd Noble Center
Opening Act: Breathless
Attendance: 10,500   Capacity: 10,500
Promoter: Little Wing Promotions

■ KISS's disco ball was damaged in transit and was not used in the show.

Breathless drummer Kevin Valentine would later appear on KISS's *Psycho Circus* album. John Cougar & the Zone were scheduled to appear at all of the shows up to and including the gig on November 7th at the Forum, but they did not appear at any of the concerts.

Ace did an interview with Gene Triplett of *The Oklahoma Journal* and observed, "Ticket sales are good but not as good as the last tour, but no one is doing as good as their last tour. It's the economy. A lot of places we used to do two nights in, we're only doing one now. Initially, when we started the tour, we thought it was us. We thought, wow, we've been away from the concert circuit too long."

OCTOBER 19, 1979
San Antonio, Texas

HemisFair Arena @ Henry B. Gonzalez Convention Center
Opening Act: Breathless
Attendance: 14,000   Capacity: 16,000
Promoter: Stone City Attractions
Archived: Audio

■ SET LIST
King of the Night Time World
Let Me Go, Rock 'n Roll
Move On
Calling Dr. Love
Firehouse
New York Groove
I Was Made for Lovin' You
Christine Sixteen
2,000 Man
Ace Frehley Guitar Solo
Love Gun
Gene Simmons Bass Solo
God of Thunder
Peter Criss Drum Solo - reprise
Shout It Out Loud
Black Diamond
Detroit Rock City
[Beth]
Rock and Roll All Nite

■ Jayne Grodd, assistant to the tour and road managers: "One night in October I got a call at 3:30 in the morning. It was Gene. He was sitting in a hotel room in Texas, he was bored and thought, 'Hey, good time to get my Christmas cards done! So, that's when he decided it was important to wake up the office staff in New York and get that taken care of."

OCTOBER 21, 1979
Houston, Texas
The Summit
Opening Act: Breathless
Attendance: 17,572   Capacity: 17,572
Promoter: Pace Concerts
Archived: Audio

■ SET LIST
King of the Night Time World
Let Me Go, Rock 'n Roll
[Move On]
Calling Dr. Love
Firehouse
New York Groove
I Was Made for Lovin' You
Christine Sixteen
2,000 Man
Ace Frehley Guitar Solo
Love Gun
Gene Simmons Bass Solo
God of Thunder
Peter Criss Drum Solo - reprise
[Shout It Out Loud]
Black Diamond
[Detroit Rock City]
[Beth]
[Rock and Roll All Nite]

■ Ace briefly jumped behind Peter's kit during the show.

OCTOBER 23, 1979
Fort Worth, Texas
Tarrant County Convention Center
Opening Act: Jon Butcher Axis
Attendance: 13,000   Capacity: 14,000
Promoter: Concerts West

■ Breathless was mistakenly reviewed in a local paper as the opening act for the show, but Jon Butcher Axis actually opened.

Peter Oppel of the *Fort Worth Star-Telegram*

was granted a rare preshow phone interview with Peter Criss, who mentioned that he had plans to begin acting school in early 1980, and also admitted, "This has been a hard tour for us."

OCTOBER 27, 1979
Abilene, Texas
Taylor County Coliseum
Opening Act: Breathless
Capacity: 9,082
Promoter: Stone City Attractions
Promoter: Pace Concerts
Archived: Partial Film

■ Segments of the concert were filmed for the PBS show *321 Contact*.

OCTOBER 29, 1979
Tulsa, Oklahoma
Tulsa Assembly Center
Opening Act: Breathless
Attendance: 7,500
Promoter: Stone City Attractions

■ KISS flew to New York the following day to tape an interview with Tom Snyder for *The Tomorrow Show*.

OCTOBER 31, 1979
Lubbock, Texas
Lubbock Municipal Coliseum
Opening Act: Breathless
Attendance: 6,700   Capacity: 10,000
Promoter: Stone City Attractions

■ Someone claiming to be a former missionary got himself a lot of press riding on KISS's coattails, claiming that he wanted to expose the evil influences that KISS seemed to produce. He even claimed that he could produce a witness who saw the band perform a blood sacrifice to the devil at their previous Lubbock concert, a statement that made for great copy in the local press. The band even held a makeshift press conference backstage to address the situation.

NOVEMBER 2, 1979
Midland, Texas
Al G. Langford Chaparral Center
Opening Act: Breathless
Promoter: Stone City Attractions

NOVEMBER 4, 1979
Denver, Colorado
McNichols Sports Arena
Opening Act: Breathless
Attendance: 10,543
Promoter: Schon Productions

NOVEMBER 6, 1979
Inglewood (Los Angeles), California
The Forum   **TEMP HOLD DATE**
Opening Act: Breathless
Capacity: 15,822
Promoter: Avalon Attractions

■ This date was originally held on the schedule for a second show at The Forum, but when that proved unnecessary, a concert in Anaheim was added in its place.

NOVEMBER 6, 1979
Anaheim, California
Anaheim Convention Center
Opening Act: Breathless
Attendance: 10,000   Capacity: 10,000
Promoter: Avalon Attractions

NOVEMBER 7, 1979

Inglewood (Los Angeles), California
The Forum
Opening Act: Breathless
Attendance: 15,822   Capacity: 15,822
Promoter: Avalon Attractions
Archived: Audio
■ SET LIST
See July 21, 1979.

■ Billy Crystal interviewed KISS backstage for *Dinah! and Friends.*

Jayne Grodd: "KISS was really living the celebrity lifestyle at this time. I was holed up in an L.A. hotel room with 80 million backstage passes and all these celebrities were calling me up. For some reason, Paul got friendly with Ron Howard, John Ritter, and Henry Winkler. It turns out that Paul and Henry Winkler grew up in the same neighborhood, and they got to talking about some famous local bakery. We received a call that Paul wanted us to buy five pounds of rugelach from this bakery and send it out to him in L.A. One of the girls from the New York office, Stephanie Tudor, had to go get the rugelach, take it by limo to the airport where she was met by the girlfriend of Arnie Silver, a road manager for another group that was touring with KISS. She was a stewardess for American Airlines and had agreed to take the pastries out to L.A. All of this just so Paul could impress Henry Winkler."

Following the performance, Casablanca threw a party for KISS in The Forum Club.

NOVEMBER 10, 1979

Phoenix, Arizona
Arizona Veterans Memorial Coliseum
Opening Act: Breathless
Attendance: 13,000
Promoter: Beaver Productions
■ At some point during this time frame, Paul stopped breaking guitars at the end of KISS's shows, possibly for legal reasons, though the gimmick returned for the Unmasked Tour. Phoenix is most likely the last concert where Paul broke a guitar on the Dynasty Tour.

NOVEMBER 19, 1979

Vancouver, British Columbia, Canada
Pacific Coliseum
Opening Act: Loverboy
Attendance: 14,271   Capacity: 17,613
Promoter: Perryscope Concert Productions
Archived: Audio
■ SET LIST
King of the Night Time World
Let Me Go, Rock 'n Roll
Move On
Calling Dr. Love
Firehouse
New York Groove
I Was Made for Lovin' You
Christine Sixteen
2,000 Man
Ace Frehley Guitar Solo
[Love Gun]
[Gene Simmons Bass Solo]
[God of Thunder]
[Peter Criss Drum Solo - reprise]
[Shout It Out Loud]
[Black Diamond]
Detroit Rock City
Beth
Rock and Roll All Nite

■ Loverboy was booed off the stage during their third song. During KISS's show, Peter fell off his drum stool between songs. Paul briefly went up and played drums while the band was throwing out towels prior to the encore.

According to the review in *The Vancouver Sun*, Gene did not fly at this performance.

NOVEMBER 21, 1979

Seattle, Washington
Seattle Center Coliseum
Opening Act: Rockets
Attendance: 14,000   Capacity: 14,000
Promoter: Concerts West
Archived: Audio
■ SET LIST
See July 21, 1979.

NOVEMBER 23, 1979   CANCELED

Portland, Oregon
Memorial Coliseum
Opening Act: Rockets
Promoter: Concerts West
■ This show was canceled when the Portland Fire Marshal refused to issue a permit for the pyrotechnics.

NOVEMBER 25, 1979

Daly City (San Francisco), California
Cow Palace
Opening Act: Rockets
Attendance: 14,500   Capacity: 14,500

Promoter: Bill Graham Presents

NOVEMBER 27, 1979

Fresno, California
Selland Arena @ Fresno Convention Center
Opening Act: Rockets
Attendance: 7,410   Capacity: 7,410
Promoter: Avalon Attractions
Archived: Audio
■ SET LIST
See July 21, 1979.

NOVEMBER 29, 1979

San Diego, California
San Diego Sports Arena
Opening Act: Rockets
Attendance: 7,180   Capacity: 14,585
Promoter: Avalon Attractions
Archived: Audio
■ SET LIST
See July 21, 1979.

DECEMBER 1, 1979

Albuquerque, New Mexico
Tingley Coliseum
Opening Act: Rockets
Attendance: 10,656   Capacity: 10,656
Promoter: Feyline Presents

DECEMBER 3, 1979

Amarillo, Texas
The Amarillo Civic Center
Opening Act: Rockets

Attendance: 6,000
Promoter: Stone City Attractions

DECEMBER 6, 1979

Lake Charles, Louisiana
Benton Memorial Coliseum
Opening Act: Rockets
Promoter: Beaver Productions

DECEMBER 8, 1979

Shreveport, Louisiana
Hirsch Memorial Coliseum
Opening Act: Rockets
Attendance: Sold Out
Promoter: Beaver Productions

■ The show was cut short when Peter purposefully dragged the tempo to a standstill at the end of his drum solo in "God of Thunder." KISS returned to the stage to play "Shout It Out Loud" and "Black Diamond," but there were no encores at all.

John-Andrew Prime, writing for *The Times*, noted, "Peter Criss has deteriorated. The band saved Criss by going into 'Shout It Out Loud' and the closing tune, 'Black Diamond.' The relative shortness of the set—just over an hour—and the exclusion of popular numbers like 'Beth' and 'Rock and Roll All Nite' was keenly felt."

DECEMBER 10, 1979

Jackson, Mississippi
Mississippi Coliseum
Opening Act: Rockets
Promoter: Beaver Productions

■ Peter stopped playing during "Move On" and walked off the stage. Paul, Ace, and Gene finished the song without him before leaving the stage themselves. All four band members returned after 15 minutes and explained that Peter had been hit in the eye with a fragment from a broken drumstick. Later, after finishing the vocals to "Beth," Peter threw the micro-

phone to the floor and stormed offstage again.

DECEMBER 12, 1979

Biloxi, Mississippi
Mississippi Coast Coliseum
Opening Act: Rockets
Promoter: Beaver Productions

■ In a 1994 interview with coauthor Curt Gooch, Peter Criss recalled an event that most likely happened during the final week of the tour: "I threw a drumstick at Gene, but I didn't mean it. I was always just throwing sticks out. It bounced off of Gene's head really cool; it really bounced. He turned around, and he was at one of his demonic stages where he didn't know where he was and he went crazy. When I got downstairs, he came around and walked up to me and kicked me in the ankle, and it really hurt. I said, 'You son of a bitch, what was that about?' He said, 'Don't you ever throw a drumstick at me.' I said, 'Gene, I was only doing it for a joke, man. I didn't mean it, but no one fuckin' hits me,' and I went crazy. The audience is screaming for us, and our road manager is going nuts. He rushes us up to the encore, and I was thinking all through the song, 'How do I get him in the next encore? Do I hit him immediately or do I whack him one in the back?' Sure enough, the minute the song ended, I quickly got off the drums, because I wanted to be the first one back there waiting for him to come through the curtain, so I could hit him in the face. He came walking back, and I grabbed a champagne bottle. I broke it, and I went at him with it, and everybody jumped in and broke it up. Later, in the dressing room, Paul said, 'Great. Gene Simmons kicks drummer of KISS; KISS drummer kills Gene Simmons, band's over with.'"

DECEMBER 14, 1979

Huntsville, Alabama

Von Braun Civic Center
Opening Act: Rockets
Attendance: 9,113   Capacity: 9,113
Promoter: Sound 70 Concerts

■ One attendee reported that Peter was screaming at someone backstage when he walked out to do "Beth."

DECEMBER 16, 1979

Toledo, Ohio
Sports Arena
Opening Act: Rockets
Attendance: 6,700   Capacity: 6,700
Promoter: Belkin Productions

■ This was Peter Criss's final show during his original tenure with KISS and was also the final live performance of "Move On." There was unusually high media coverage due to the tragedy at The Who's performance in Cincinnati just 13 days prior.

Several things happened during the show that were part of the typical end-of-tour hijinks. During Ace's solo, he was supposed to shoot a rocket from his guitar to a small pyro pack suspended in the lighting rig. At this show, the crew placed the pyro inside of a rubber chicken, which was left dangling from the lighting rig.

When the band came out for their curtain call, Ace sat down at Peter's drum kit and began playing. And during the final song, a crew member dressed as Santa Claus came out on stage with a sack over his shoulder. The sack was filled with guitar picks and KISS sponges (which usually fell into the audience via the mirror ball hung from the ceiling), which the crew member threw out to the crowd. Members of the road crew filtered out onstage and sang the final choruses of "Rock and Roll All Nite" with the band.

The band took a private jet home immediately after the show.

CHAPTER 13

UNMASKED TOUR

Number of Shows: 41
Start Date: July 25, 1980 - New York, New York
End Date: December 3, 1980 - Auckland, New Zealand
Countries: Australia, Belgium, Denmark, England, France, Italy, The Netherlands, New Zealand, Norway, Sweden, Switzerland, U.S.A., West Germany
Opening Acts: Eyes; Girl; Iron Maiden; The Rockats; Techtones
Average Attendance: 16,442* (Based upon a very limited number of available attendance figures.)

"And rock and roll shall stand on a wind-swept plateau at the edge of the 70's, readying a descent into the virgin valley of the new decade. Yet, who shall lead? Who shall carry on and march in the vanguard? It is written that the demon, the catman, the starman and the spaceman shall marshal the forces of rock and roll, and shall spearhead the crusades to conquer the 80's, while all the armies of rock shall joyously shout the words of victory: 'LONG LIVE THE DYNASTY'"

—From the Dynasty press kit.

Yeah, right.

The "dynasty" had all but crumbled before the 1980s even began, and the new decade would look far more skeptically upon the over-the-top hype that defined KISS. To be fair, some words in this overblown fantasy were very accurate, especially "plateau," in describing the state of KISS's popularity in 1978, and "descent," in describing what happened to KISS's popularity by 1980. Still others, like "catman," would play almost no part in the story at all.

Peter Criss's departure from KISS had been years in coming, with his drug habits, personal problems, and growing disinterest in the band accruing to the point where it was mutually agreed that he would leave the band while still retaining his 25% share of KISS.

Fritz Postlethwaite recalls: "My experience is that relationships usually end with a whimper and not with a bang, and this one seemed like that. In some cases, like this one, it's bittersweet because they've been together for such a long time, and they so closely and intensely played a part in each other's lives—being on tour is a very intense, 24-hour-a-day experience—that nobody wanted to see it end. Even though people said that they were going to throw him out, or that they didn't want him around anymore, there were plans to work things out. They proposed several solutions to him, both psychological and chemical, that could be taken to avert leaving the band. He even went and took drum lessons and complied with their requests. But the relationship was too far gone."

Another relationship that fell by the wayside was that with Neil Bogart. PolyGram, which owned 50% of Casablanca, bought out the remaining shares of the company, and Bogart officially resigned on February 8, 1980, ending a tumultuous but very successful seven-year relationship with KISS. Although PolyGram now owned the label, KISS's domestic releases would still bear the Casablanca imprint through 1982. Since KISS had a key-man clause as part of their deal with Casablanca, PolyGram was obligated to renegotiate KISS's contract. Fortunately for KISS, "I Was Made for Lovin' You" had been a huge

Eric Carr's first show, at the Palladium, July 25, 1980.

LYDIA CRISS

international hit and PolyGram felt compelled to keep the band on its roster of artists. Howard Marks handled the contract renegotiations for KISS; the results were more than the band could have hoped for, with PolyGram agreeing to advance KISS $2 million for each album it delivered. It was also a coup for Marks; he had succeeded in negotiating a major contract for KISS without much involvement from Bill Aucoin. This marked a significant turning point: in the band's eyes, the balance of power between Glickman/Marks and Bill Aucoin had clearly shifted in Glickman/Marks's direction.

Peter's relationship with KISS had not been completely severed, but he played no part in the recording of *Unmasked,* which was released on May 29, 1980, within days of the official announcement that Peter had left the band. Session drummer Anton Fig, who had worked on Ace's solo album and provided most of the percussion work on *Dynasty,* filled in for Peter on *Unmasked.*

Criss's last official appearance with KISS came in late spring, during the shooting of the "Shandi" promotional film in Studio B at Unitel Video in New York. "The 'Shandi' video was done all in one day," Pixie Esmonde recalls, "because the vibe was so horrible between the guys that if they didn't get it right then, they weren't ever going to get it."

Aucoin and the band immediately began the search for Peter's replacement. Not surprisingly, hundreds of applications poured into AMI's offices on Madison Avenue.

Jayne Grodd: "Ric Aliberte and Bill Aucoin ended up walking into my office and told me that I was going to be interviewing people. I couldn't believe it; what the heck did I know about interviewing a drummer? We made up a checklist of what they were going to need, and the main thing that the guys in the band required was they wanted the candidates to be able to sing. And they had to play double-kick. They had a list of questions for the candidates, including one which asked if they were married, because after the fiasco with Peter, they wanted someone with no obligations.

"They put the word out for a drummer and I took a week's vacation. When I returned, the piles of folders and résumés was so I high I literally could not see my desk, and there were at least 150–200 phone messages as well. I told Bill that I was going to start interviewing but that there was no way I was going to get all the way through the list of people that had accumulated. Bill told me to go ahead and choose some people to interview and that whomever made it past the initial screening with me would then go through another interview with him. And from that, we'd decide who would get an audition. We set up auditions at a place called Starr Sound, which was a rehearsal place on Lafayette opposite a restaurant called Lady Astor's.

"I went to sort through this huge stack of folders and résumés, and I saw an orange folder. I pulled out the folder and read about this guy named Paul Caravello. It was the first thing I picked up, and I only picked it up because it was orange. The picture of him looked good. I listened to the tape he provided and he could sing great. He could play double-kick, and everything else looked good, so I set up and did an interview with him. Then I had him go interview with Bill [June 19], and Bill liked him.

"There were a lot more interviews I had to do, a lot of big-name drummers with inside recommendations; I remember Carmine Appice was a choice. But I kept thinking that here was a guy working for $75 a week; what a great story that would be for him to get the job."

The auditions began on June 23 with Caravello scheduled for 1:30 P.M. "We only did about four days' worth of auditions," continues Grodd, "because that's all the guys could take; Gene and Paul were just completely unnerved. After that, we got down to the second set of auditions, and Paul Caravello [whose callback audition took place on June 27] and another guy [rumored to be Bobby Rondinelli, who went on to work with Rainbow] were running neck and neck, but KISS was leaning towards the other guy. Paul Caravello kept calling me and asking how it was going, how it was looking.

"At one point towards the end of the process, George Sewitt [tour manager from 1979–80], Paul Stanley, Gene, and I went across the street to Lady Astor's, where I was witness to one of the funniest conversations I have ever heard. Gene and Paul were discussing what the new character was going to be. Paul was having fun with it, and Gene was showing absolutely no sense of humor. Paul was saying things like, 'OK. We'll make him . . . a tailor! And he'll sew things on stage.' George and I were rolling on the floor, but Gene was deadly serious. Happily, Paul Caravello ended up getting the job."

Paul Caravello was officially named KISS's new drummer during the third week of July 1980. To avoid having another Paul in the band, Caravello changed his name to Eric, and shortened his last name to Carr. Eric had been a member of several different nondescript bands prior to KISS, one of which, Lightning, had released an album through Casablanca on August 13, 1979.

Carr made his official concert debut with KISS on July 25, 1980 at the Palladium in Manhattan where the band had been rehearsing for several days. Eric's costume and persona were in doubt less than 24 hours before the gig, as Pixie Esmonde explains, "Eric's outfit started out as a hawk, which they quickly decided looked too much like a canary. So we removed the feathers and switched it to a Fox persona with a leather jacket, little metal studs and silver fox fur that had been dyed orange. Eric and I and Bill Aucoin worked on the makeup the whole night before the first show; it was Bill who came up with the concept of the Fox. The makeup we designed was changed very quickly, however. We did the Palladium, and by the next gig, Eric's makeup was different, the jumpsuit's shape was altered, and we had redone the color of the boots."

Bill Aucoin: "That night [before the Palladium gig] was the only time I ever recall Gene and Paul turning to me and telling me, 'You're the manager. You fix it.' They were very frustrated over Eric's makeup and costume, and they were very nervous the night before his first show."

Ignoring the one-off show in Manhattan, the Unmasked Tour was and still is KISS's only full-length tour played exclusively outside the U.S. KISS's popularity in America had begun to wane significantly over the course of 1979 and 1980, to the point where a major tour of the U.S. was not a realistic possibility. *Unmasked* only inched its way to Gold certification in late July, stalling well short of Platinum status. The single show at the Palladium, notably a hometown venue, sold out, but ticket sales were slow enough that no additional shows were added, despite the venue's capacity of less than 4,000.

During this time, Gene, who was sporting a temporary set of clear braces, had moved from one highly visible relationship with Cher to another, and was now dating Diana Ross. The pair garnered considerable attention from the press.

Additional time in the spotlight was earned when Carol Kaye of The Press Office scored a prodigious marketing coup by landing KISS the cover story for *People* magazine's August 18th issue. On July 27, KISS taped their appearance on *Kids Are People Too,* a Sunday morning children's program. ABC-TV premiered the show on September 21, marking Eric's introduction to a nationwide audience.

The earliest plans for the Unmasked Tour were for a tour of Europe to commence in March as the second leg of the Dynasty Tour, which is why laminates from Dynasty read: "1979–1980 World Tour." The European tour was then rescheduled to begin in May, and even though advertising included Peter Criss's likeness, it was clear to both the band and management that Peter would not be touring with KISS. Announcements for several shows on the tour had been made, and tickets were put up for sale in several markets before KISS's booking agent Wally Meyrowitz canceled the tour on April 14, to allow the band time to find a new drummer. ATI had also talked about booking KISS shows in the Far East as part of the spring tour.

These were not the only cancellations to occur during this time period. In mid-summer, a Mexican promoter (Promociones Artistieasy Espectaculous Internacionales) had attempted to schedule a brief tour of Central America. This tour was announced at a press conference in July, though many details, such as the venues for the concerts, had not been determined. Three concerts were scheduled for Mexico City for August 9–11, as well as shows in Guadalajara on the 12th and Monterrey on 14th. The shows were canceled when the promoter failed to obtain the required permits.

The tour of Europe was finally rescheduled to begin late in August and was now intended to support *Unmasked* rather than *Dynasty.* Unfortunately, the initial financial projections were not encouraging and showed a running deficit similar to the Dynasty Tour. The cost of keeping this huge KISS show on the road overwhelmed the revenues, and the first budget showed a net loss of $675,000. A revised projection, which included the cancellation of two shows in Portugal leading off the tour, as well as scaled-back production costs, reduced that figure to $474,000. It is not very apparent, but a new condensed version of the Dynasty stage set was constructed for the 1980 European Tour, while the 1979 North American set was used for the larger outdoor shows in Italy and was then shipped to Australia. Additionally, a new flying rig was purchased for Gene.

For costumes on the Unmasked Tour, Ace used the same outfit he had on the previous excursion, while Gene's costume was very similar in design to his Dynasty Tour outfit, but with several slight modifications, including a somewhat smaller, darker breastplate. Paul wore an entirely new costume, however. The construction of Gene and Paul's costumes was costly, running $10,000 and $16,000, respectively.

The set list for the tour featured several songs from *Unmasked*, namely, "Is That You?," "Talk to Me," and "You're All That I Want," the last of which was dropped from the set two weeks into the European tour. A fourth track from the album, "Shandi," was added to the set list for the concerts in Australia and New Zealand. Additionally, "Strutter" and "Cold Gin" returned after being absent, respectively, since 1976 and 1977.

The addition of Eric Carr, who was a more technically accomplished drummer than Peter, revitalized the band, and they paid more attention to musical detail than they had in several years. The vocals were especially improved, with harmonized background vocals more apparent and stronger. Ace and Gene (joined occasionally by Paul and Eric) now shared lead vocal duties on "Cold Gin," a responsibility that had previously fallen to Gene, and while "Beth" had been dropped with Peter's departure, Eric took over lead vocals on "Black Diamond" and contributed background vocals on almost every song. Throughout the tour, Paul would often rearrange the vocal lines in "Detroit Rock City," adding a heightened sense of melody to the verses.

On the Unmasked Tour, Paul's intro to "Black Diamond" had become long enough to merit consideration as a solo. While the song's introduction was performed by Paul alone and typically was several minutes in length, we feel it did not deviate enough from the song's original chord structure to label it as a solo.

JULY 25, 1980

New York, New York
Palladium
Opening Act: The Rockats
Attendance: 3,383   Capacity: 3,383
Promoter: Mateus Presents
■ SET LIST
Detroit Rock City
Cold Gin
Strutter
Calling Dr. Love
Is That You?
Firehouse
Talk to Me
You're All That I Want
2,000 Man
Ace Frehley Guitar Solo
I Was Made for Lovin' You
Love Gun
Shout It Out Loud
Gene Simmons Bass Solo
God of Thunder
Eric Carr Drum Solo - reprise

Rock and Roll All Nite
New York Groove
King of the Night Time World
Black Diamond
■ This show marked Eric Carr's first performance with KISS.

The opening act, the Rockats, was a rockabilly band based in the New York area and is not to be confused with the Rockets, who opened several shows for KISS throughout the 1970s.

During the afternoon, footage of Eric performing behind his kit was shot for inclusion in a KISS promo film. According to Bill Aucoin and Chris Lendt, the rumor that this show was professionally videotaped is false.

A specialty T-shirt was sold at the venue.

AUGUST 24 & 25, 1980   CANCELED

Cascais (Lisboa), Portugal
Cascais Hall
Opening Act: Iron Maiden
■ Both shows appeared on early tour itineraries, but were canceled due to budgeting constraints.

AUGUST 29, 1980

Roma, Italy
Castel Sant'Angelo
Opening Act: Iron Maiden
Attendance: 15,500
Promoters: Francesco Sanavo, David Zard
Archived: Audio
■ SET LIST
Detroit Rock City
Cold Gin
Strutter
Calling Dr. Love
Is That You?
Firehouse
Talk to Me
You're All That I Want
2,000 Man
Ace Frehley Guitar Solo
I Was Made for Lovin' You
New York Groove
Love Gun
Gene Simmons Bass Solo
God of Thunder
Eric Carr Drum Solo - reprise
Rock and Roll All Nite
Shout It Out Loud
King of the Night Time World
Black Diamond
■ Bill McManus: "When we did the outdoor show at Castel Sant'Angelo, we were testing the sound system and the pyro during "God of Thunder." I remember a figure in white robes coming out on a third floor balcony about 150 yards away and looking at us and listening, seeing the columns of flames and shaking his head before finally going inside. Later that night, I mentioned this to one of the local interpreters, and he said that it was the Pope's residence and that it was probably the Pope looking at our rehearsal. I thought that was pretty heavy."

Pixie Esmonde: "There is an escape route from the Vatican to Castel Sant'Angelo so if the Vatican was ever stormed, the Pope could escape through an underground route. There is a giant stone wall behind the stage, and the way the lights were set up, it projected KISS's figures in giant shadow on the wall. The shadow effect was dramatic because it was dark, it was outdoors, and it was stark with the only lights

being whatever little lights the audience might have had. When Gene went up to do his blood routine, his figure was cast upon the wall, and it looked like the devil was reflected on the walls of Castel Sant'Angelo and the surrounding rock. In the background, you could see the Vatican and it was as if 'the devil takes the Vatican.' You can't buy that kind of effect; it was the coolest thing I've ever seen. The show was just electric."

The beginning of "New York Groove" was extended much longer than usual, due to difficulties with Ace's guitar.

AUGUST 30, 1980   TEMP HOLD DATE

Perugia, Italy
Stadion Communale
Opening Act: Iron Maiden
Capacity: 30,000

AUGUST 31, 1980   TEMP HOLD DATE

Bologna, Italy
Stadion Communale
Opening Act: Iron Maiden

AUGUST 31, 1980

Genova, Italy
Palasport
Opening Act: Iron Maiden
Promoters: Francesco Sanavo, David Zard
Archived: Audio
■ SET LIST
See August 29, 1980.
■ For the second time in as many shows, the opening bars of "New York Groove" were extended due to a guitar malfunction. Ace was forced to restart the song four times.

KISS flew to München on September 1 to lip-synch "She's So European" and "Talk To Me" for the TV show *RockPop*. AMI paperwork dated August 21 indicated that the above two songs would air in September, and that two additional songs, "Is That You?" and "Tomorrow," would be recorded for a back-up promotion to air later.

SEPTEMBER 2, 1980

Milano, Italy
Motovelodromo Vigorelli
Opening Act: Iron Maiden
Attendance: 30,000   Capacity: 30,000
Promoters: Francesco Sanavo, David Zard
Archived: Audio
■ SET LIST
See August 29, 1980.
■ The show was stopped for 30 minutes when a left-wing political group took control of the stage.

Bill McManus: "In Milano, we had a Molotov cocktail thrown at the stage and one thrown at the generator, too. We found out that in Italy, the political parties are basically older teenagers that we'd call gangs here in the U.S. The promoters, when they announce that they're going to do a concert, align themselves with one of these political parties as a cosponsor or beneficiary of the concert, and they do that in order to be politically correct and acceptable. The promoters try to pick the political party that they think will be in power by the time the concert happens. And the promoter that did this tour picked the wrong party. The one that was in power took it as an affront that they weren't the one chosen and they felt very passionate about that and decided to attack the concert.

KISS on tour in Europe, 1980.

"I had my hand on the dry-ice machine about to do a cue that would suddenly blanket the stage in CO_2 gas, and when I looked up I saw this flame twirling towards the stage. When I realized what it was, it was probably 35 feet out from the stage on its way in on a big arc. I dropped the basket right then and there, which released all the dry ice, and by the time the Molotov cocktail hit the deck, the dry ice fog was two to three feet deep. The CO_2 helped extinguish the flame before it turned into a bigger problem. The bottle actually never broke because our deck had a soft, grippy surface so the boys would be able to move around in their platform shoes without slipping. When the bottle hit, it bounced and the flame was extinguished so that most people never realized what it was.

Pixie Esmonde continues: "George Sewitt and several bodyguards rushed the band off the stage. They were terrified as they ran into the dressing rooms, which were literally in catacombs with electrical wire strung around them and bare lightbulbs hanging from the wire. The bathrooms were holes in the floor with little handles. Mirrors were broken shards from larger mirrors. As they ran into the dressing room, someone gave me a stick and said, 'Here, Pixie!' and I got pushed out into the hallway, and they shut the door on me! They were terrified they were going to be killed. When they were running down the hallway, you have never seen anything as funny in your life: these big guys in these huge boots, running and ducking, hitting their heads on the lights because the catacombs were low."

SEPTEMBER 5, 1980
Stafford, England
Bingley Hall
Opening Act: Girl
Promoter: Kennedy Street Entertainment
Archived: Audio
■ SET LIST
See August 29, 1980.
■ The band had flown into London on September 3, where a "reception by fans in makeup" (according to AMI paperwork) awaited them. The memo instructed band members as to what the appropriate protocol for the occasion would be: "You will have to duck cameras and jump into limousines and genuinely cause some excitement." KISS held a press conference in London on September 4 where press kits containing KISS stick pins and 30-minute, "open-ended" interview cassettes were passed out.

SEPTEMBER 6, 1980
Chester, England
Deeside Leisure Centre
Opening Act: Girl
Promoters: Kennedy Street Entertainment, MCP
Archived: Audio

■ SET LIST
See August 29, 1980.

SEPTEMBER 8, 1980
London, England
Wembley Arena
Opening Act: Girl
Promoter: Kennedy Street Entertainment
Archived: Audio
■ SET LIST
See August 29, 1980.

SEPTEMBER 9, 1980
London, England
Wembley Arena
Opening Act: No Opening Act
Promoter: Kennedy Street Entertainment
Archived: Audio
■ SET LIST
See August 29, 1980.
■ Opening act Iron Maiden had recently done a tour of England, so they opted not to perform at any of KISS's U.K. concerts. The British band Girl, featuring future Def Leppard guitarist Phil Collen and L.A. Guns vocalist Phil Lewis, was named to fill in for Maiden. Girl, who was booed off the stage at the first Wembley Arena gig, reportedly was thrown off the bill for performing their cover of KISS's "Do You Love Me." No replacement was named for the second Wembley show.

SEPTEMBER 11, 1980

Nürnberg, West Germany
Hessehalle
Opening Act: Iron Maiden
Promoter: MCP

■ **SET LIST**

See August 29, 1980.

■ This is the last known live performance of "You're All That I Want."

SEPTEMBER 12, 1980

Düsseldorf, West Germany
Philipshalle
Opening Act: Iron Maiden
Promoter: MCP

SEPTEMBER 13, 1980

Frankfurt a.M., West Germany
Rebstokgelände
Opening Act: Iron Maiden
Promoter: MCP
Archived: Audio

■ **SET LIST**

Detroit Rock City
Cold Gin
Strutter
Calling Dr. Love
Firehouse
Talk to Me
Is That You?
2,000 Man
Ace Frehley Guitar Solo
I Was Made for Lovin' You
New York Groove
Love Gun
Gene Simmons Bass Solo
God of Thunder
Eric Carr Drum Solo - reprise
Rock and Roll All Nite
Shout It Out Loud
King of the Night Time World
Black Diamond

■ This was an outdoor show. Child actor Ricky Schroeder was in attendance, and watched the concert from the soundboard.

While introducing "Shout It Out Loud," Paul mentioned that KISS would be making a September 16 in-store appearance at a Frankfurt record store called Main Radio.

SEPTEMBER 15, 1980

Dortmund, West Germany
Westfalenhalle
Opening Act: Iron Maiden
Promoter: MCP

SEPTEMBER 17, 1980

Sindelfingen (Stuttgart), West Germany
Sindelfingen Messehalle
Opening Act: Iron Maiden
Promoter: MCP

SEPTEMBER 18, 1980

München, West Germany
Olympiahalle @ Olympiapark München
Opening Act: Iron Maiden
Promoter: MCP
Archived: Partial Film

■ Pixie Esmonde: "Over in Europe is where I learned to rinse out their outfits in the bidet. After one concert, I had taken their jumpsuits in my luggage because I wanted to get them dried out and ready for the next show. But there was only one sink in my room so I used the bidet: suds 'em up, rinse 'em off, and you're done. I

kept thinking that if they knew what I was doing with their jumpsuits, they would have a heart-attack."

During the München concert, "Talk to Me," "I Was Made for Lovin' You," Gene's solo, Eric's solo, and "Black Diamond" were filmed for the West German TV show *Okay*. A crew from Phonogram Austria was reportedly also on hand to film the first three songs and to do a short pre-show interview with the band.

SEPTEMBER 20, 1980

Kassel, West Germany
Eissporthalle
Opening Act: Iron Maiden
Promoter: MCP

SEPTEMBER 21, 1980

Bruxelles, Belgium
Vorst Nationaal
Opening Act: Iron Maiden
Capacity: 9,000
Promoter: Make It Happen
Archived: Audio

■ **SET LIST**

See September 13, 1980.

SEPTEMBER 23, 1980

Avignon, France
Parc des Expositions
Opening Act: Iron Maiden
Promoter: KCP
Archived: Audio

■ **SET LIST**

See September 13, 1980.

SEPTEMBER 24, 1980

Lyon, France
Palais des Sports
Opening Act: Iron Maiden
Promoter: KCP

SEPTEMBER 26, 1980 ~~CANCELED~~

Lille, France
Parc des Expositions
Opening Act: Iron Maiden
Promoter: KCP

■ This show was canceled not too long before the show date, reportedly due to a lack of ticket sales.

SEPTEMBER 27, 1980

Paris, France
Le Bourget Exhibition Centre
Opening Act: Iron Maiden
Promoter: KCP
Archived: Audio

■ **SET LIST**

See September 13, 1980.

■ An edited version of this show was later broadcast on the radio.

The show at Le Bourget Exhibition Centre had one particularly memorable aspect: it actually rained indoors. The venue was a large tent-like structure, and it was so intensely hot indoors and unseasonably cold outdoors that the condensation collected on the ceiling of the venue and rained down on the crowd.

SEPTEMBER 28, 1980

Bâle, Switzerland
Sporthalle St. Jakob
Opening Act: Iron Maiden
Attendance: 6,000
Promoter: Good News Agency

SEPTEMBER 30, 1980

Köln, West Germany
Sporthalle
Opening Act: Iron Maiden
Promoter: MCP
Archived: Partial Film

■ Portions of this concert and the September 16 in-store appearance in Frankfurt were filmed for inclusion in a special, KISS-themed episode of *Schüler-Express*, a program which could best be described as a West German version of an *ABC After-School Special*. The story line revolved around a young teenage girl who is so absorbed by her devotion to KISS that she begins to let her entire life go. When her boyfriend gives her an ultimatum, "KISS or me," she initially chooses KISS. One dream-sequence features the girl fantasizing about riding on the back of a moped with Paul Stanley (portrayed by an actor) to the tune of "I Want You." Surprisingly, KISS even allowed themselves to be interviewed for the special.

OCTOBER 1, 1980

Bremen, West Germany
Stadthalle
Opening Act: Iron Maiden
Promoter: MCP
Archived: Audio

■ **SET LIST**

See September 13, 1980.

OCTOBER 2, 1980

Hannover, West Germany
Neidersachsenhalle
Opening Act: Iron Maiden
Promoter: MCP

OCTOBER 4, 1980

Hamburg, West Germany
Ernst-Merck Halle
Opening Act: Iron Maiden
Promoter: MCP

OCTOBER 5, 1980

Leiden, The Netherlands
Groenoordhal
Opening Act: Iron Maiden
Promoter: Wim Bosman
Archived: Audio

■ **SET LIST**

See September 13, 1980.

OCTOBER 6, 1980

Karlsruhe, West Germany
Schwarzwaldhalle   **TEMP HOLD DATE**
Opening Act: Iron Maiden

OCTOBER 9, 1980

Stockholm, Sweden
Eriksdalshalle
Opening Act: Iron Maiden
Attendance: 3,300   Capacity: 3,300
Promoter: Tomas Johanssen
Archived: Audio

■ **SET LIST**

See September 13, 1980.

OCTOBER 10, 1980

Göteborg, Sweden
Scandinavium
Opening Act: Iron Maiden
Attendance: 5,443   Capacity: 9,000
Promoter: Tomas Johanssen
Archived: Audio

OCTOBER 11, 1980

København, Denmark
Brøndby Hallen
Opening Act: Iron Maiden
Promoters: Gunnar Eide, Internasjonal Konsertdireksjon
Archived: Audio
■ SET LIST
See September 13, 1980.

OCTOBER 12, 1980

Drammen, Norway, **TEMP HOLD DATE**
Drammenshallen
Opening Act: Iron Maiden
Promoters: Gunnar Eide, Internasjonal Konsertdireksjon

OCTOBER 13, 1980

Drammen, Norway
Drammenshallen
Opening Act: Iron Maiden
Attendance: 6,000
Promoters: Gunnar Eide, Internasjonal Konsertdireksjon
Archived: Audio
■ SET LIST
See September 13, 1980.
■ This was the last show with Iron Maiden, and KISS bombarded them with cake during their set. It was also the last show for Iron Maiden guitarist Dennis Stratton, who was soon replaced by Adrian Smith.

This concert was originally slated to be the last stop on the European tour.

OCTOBER 16, 1980

Paris, France
Le Hippodrome de Pantin
Promoter: KCP
■ This show was added when the promoter for the concert (Albert Koski of KCP) requested that the band do a second gig in Paris due to the large number of people turned away at KISS's concert in Paris on September 27. It may also have been added as a favor to Koski when the September 24 show in Lille was canceled. Due to the last-minute scheduling, it is unlikely that there was an opening act.

———————

The success and popularity that KISS had achieved in the U.S. in 1977 and '78 was, without a doubt, staggering. But it was nothing compared to the sheer pandemonium of their 1980 tour of Australia and New Zealand. They were the primary news story in every city for weeks, and the hysteria they inspired surpassed even that created by The Beatles.

Remembering difficulties from similar scenes in Japan, KISS anticipated the hysteria surrounding their arrival and leaked information to the press that they would be arriving on November 2. The band quietly entered the country, landing to little fanfare on November 1. The following afternoon, KISS made a brief, three-minute appearance alongside Lord Mayor Doug Sutherland on the balcony of the Town Hall in downtown Sydney. During the brief event, Ace threw his armbands into the crowd of 3,000–4,000 fans waiting below.

Even before KISS arrived in Australia, and all throughout the tour, the press coverage and fan reaction was nearly unfathomable. In Melbourne,

fans mobbed the Southern Cross Hotel for days trying to get a glimpse of the band, causing the hotel to strictly enforce a "no children" rule. Photographers, who were set up in the adjacent buildings, were reportedly offered $1,000 for a shot of any band member sans makeup.

In Sydney and New Zealand, promoters ran daily newspaper ads counting down the number of days until KISS performed. The KISS tour was such an event that one of the Australian promoters, Kevin Jacobsen, frequently appeared on national talk shows.

Television coverage was inescapable. KISS was featured on numerous local news broadcasts as well as national television shows like *Countdown,* and *The Don Lane Show,* the latter of which was actually syndicated in America at the time.

After their appearance with the Lord Mayor, KISS held a press conference at the Sebel Town Hall in Sydney. The band was upstaged by an Australian comedian named Norman Gunston, who asked them, "Which one of you is the construction worker?" Later that night, KISS took a lengthy luxury cruise around Sydney Harbor where *Penthouse* "Pet of the Year" Tracy Wallace was seen hanging on Paul's arm.

Merchandising was just as extreme, perhaps even surpassing their 1978–79 merchandising zenith in the U.S. The Australian merchandising blitz was done through 20th Century Fox, who had been brought to the band's attention by Chris Lendt. There were 43 different licensed KISS products on the market in Australia in November 1980, including KISS ice cream. In the years following, KISS and its associated merchandise was looked upon as nothing more than a fad by many Australians, and as a result, most of the merchandise is exceptionally hard to come by, as many collections were thrown in the garbage by the mid-80s.

Success soon gave way to overkill as KISS merchandise quickly saturated the Australian market. Toward that end, a front-page article in the *Sydney Morning Herald,* on November 21, claimed that a decline in KISS fever had already begun, a conclusion they reached by noting the vast amount of "unsold trinkets and tickets." Supporting their assertion, 200,000 KISS cosmetic bags were manufactured by Plough Australia, of which only a little more than half were sold. There were additional reports of the slowdown and in some cases halting of sales of KISS merchandise in Australia. In one instance, a company called Aredol manufactured 20,000 KISS coins, of which only 419 sold. KISS may have finally begun to realize the negative impacts of over-merchandising, as Gene commented to Melbourne journalist Susan Maxwell, "We're now taking a couple steps back from the merchandising. We've been neglecting touring by spending so much time with business people."

Bill Aucoin: "The Australia tour really came off great. That was the first time that they were ever really treated like rock and roll stars." While KISS may have been living large, the Unmasked Tour was the first where Aucoin himself did not collect any money from gross tour income, an agreement that had been reached during a

September 1979 meeting with the band and Glickman/Marks while on the Dynasty Tour in Fort Wayne, Indiana. Up until 1980, Aucoin had taken a commission from KISS's gross touring revenue, but was now relegated to earning money from KISS's tours only if they turned a profit.

NOVEMBER 8, 1980

Perth, Australia
Entertainment Centre
Opening Act: Eyes
Attendance: 8,000   Capacity: 8,000
Promoters: Kevin Jacobsen Concert Promotions,
    Michael Edgely Int'l
■ Former member of The Zoot (which also featured Rick Springfield) Darryl Cotton was scheduled to open the entire Australian leg of the tour, per an article in *Juke* magazine. He did not appear at any shows, however.

At least one of the four Perth performances is believed to have been professionally archived on videotape.

NOVEMBER 9, 1980

Perth, Australia
Entertainment Centre
Opening Act: Eyes
Capacity: 8,000
Promoters: Kevin Jacobsen Concert Promotions,
    Michael Edgely Int'l
■ The Australian TV show *Countdown* was broadcast with KISS lip-synching "Is That You?" and "Talk to Me" presumably recorded during sound check at the Entertainment Centre on November 8.

NOVEMBER 10, 1980

Perth, Australia
Entertainment Centre
Opening Act: Eyes
Capacity: 8,000
Promoters: Kevin Jacobsen Concert Promotions,
    Michael Edgely Int'l
■ During one of the shows in Perth, a teenage boy risked death by allowing himself to drop from the balcony onto a narrow stage catwalk during the concert. Gene witnessed the incident and commented, "If he had missed he would have been killed."

NOVEMBER 11, 1980

Perth, Australia
Entertainment Centre
Opening Act: Eyes
Capacity: 8,000
Promoters: Kevin Jacobsen Concert Promotions,
    Michael Edgely Int'l

NOVEMBER 15, 1980

Waverley (Melbourne), Australia
Victorian Football League Park
Opening Act: Eyes
Attendance: 45,000   Capacity: 45,000
Promoters: Kevin Jacobsen Concert Promotions,
    Michael Edgely Int'l
■ Several fans who were lined up in the queue waiting for the gates to open at 3:00 P.M. began brawling, and the police riot squad had to be called in. Fourteen people were arrested, 239 people injured.

In Melbourne, Gene, his date, and a bodyguard were swarmed by fans while attending

KISS takes a bow at the end of a gig on the 1980 tour of Europe. Notice the use of the altered S's in the KISS sign.

Monty Python's *Life of Brian*. Additionally, National Nine News cameraman Bernie Bickerton captured Gene on video without makeup eating in a restaurant inside the Southern Cross Hotel.

NOVEMBER 18, 1980

Adelaide, Australia
Adelaide Oval
Opening Act: Eyes
Attendance: 20,000+
Promoters: Kevin Jacobsen Concert Promotions, Michael Edgely Int'l
Archived: Audio

■ SET LIST

Detroit Rock City
Cold Gin
Strutter
Shandi
Calling Dr. Love
Firehouse
Talk to Me
Is That You?
2,000 Man
Ace Frehley Guitar Solo

I Was Made for Lovin' You
New York Groove
Love Gun
Gene Simmons Bass Solo
God of Thunder
Eric Carr Drum Solo - reprise
Rock and Roll All Nite
Shout It Out Loud
King of the Night Time World
Black Diamond

■ The show was nearly canceled due to very high winds in the area, hence the pyro was drastically reduced for the performance. Opening band Eyes went over so poorly that the P.A. announcer apologized to the crowd for their performance, or lack thereof.

Production manager Ken Anderson: "Gene would fly from stage-right to stage-left and then back again. There was a small black curtain that hung in front of the truss and the flying system. It was a windy night, and Gene flew from stage-right to stage-left just fine, and flew back and got stuck right in the middle. The wind blew the cloth into the flying rigs motor or pulleys. It was pretty

funny seeing the God of Thunder hanging there like a sack of potatoes. He was up there for quite a while."

To hype the concert, a local TV station aired a half-hour special entitled *KISS In Adelaide*. Although their limousine driver and caterer appeared in the special, KISS did not.

NOVEMBER 21, 1980

Paddington (Sydney), Australia
Sydney Showground
Opening Act: Eyes
Attendance: 20,000   Capacity: 20,000
Promoters: Kevin Jacobsen Concert Promotions, Michael Edgely Int'l

■ As early as November 1, the hype surrounding KISS had reached such a fever pitch among the youth of Australia that the *Sydney Morning Herald* ran an article entitled "Parents: What to do about KISS." The author, a medical reporter, suggested the parents join the KISS Army, figuring that the drastic measure would get kids to lose interest in the band.

NOVEMBER 22, 1980

Paddington (Sydney), Australia
Sydney Showground
Opening Act: Eyes
Attendance: 20,000   Capacity: 20,000
Promoters: Kevin Jacobsen Concert Promotions,
    Michael Edgely Int'l
Archived: Video

■ SET LIST
See November 18, 1980.

■ In a November 20 article, a Sydney newspaper reported that 8,000 tickets remained for the second Sydney Showground concert. Promoter Kevin Jacobsen blamed the sluggish sales on media overkill.

At this show, KISS extended "Rock and Roll All Nite" by several minutes to include Paul's "Do you feel alright?" stage rap and its accompanying flamethrower effect that had long been part of "100,000 Years."

This concert was professionally videotaped for KISS. It was later edited to include several insert shots from what is believed to be one of the Perth performances.

A heavily edited and overdubbed version of the concert was broadcast on February 14, 1981, as *The Inner Sanctum*, on Channel 10.

NOVEMBER 25, 1980

Brisbane, Australia
Lang Park
Opening Act: Eyes
Attendance: 19,000   Capacity: 40,000
Promoters: Kevin Jacobsen Concert Promotions,
    Michael Edgely Int'l

NOVEMBER 30, 1980

Wellington, New Zealand
Athletic Park
Opening Act: Techtones
Attendance: 20,000   Capacity: 20,000
Promoters: Kevin Jacobsen Concert Promotions,
    Michael Edgely Int'l

■ A light rain fell throughout this outdoor show.

DECEMBER 3, 1980

Auckland, New Zealand
Western Springs Stadium
Opening Act: Techtones
Attendance: 25,000   Capacity: 25,000
Promoters: Kevin Jacobsen Concert Promotions,
    Michael Edgely Int'l
Archived: Audio

■ SET LIST
See November 18, 1980.

■ This was Ace Frehley's final concert during his original tenure with KISS. The show marked the final performance of "Is That You?"

To this day, while KISS's apex is usually considered to be 1977–78, both *Dynasty* and *Unmasked* mark the height of KISS's popularity in the minds of most of the Australian/New Zealand fanbase.

CANCELED DYNASTY/UNMASKED EUROPEAN TOUR

MAY 1980

Stockholm, Sweden
Eriksdalshalle
Promoter: Tomas Johansson

Göteborg, Sweden
Scandinavium
Promoter: Tomas Johansson

København, Denmark
Brøndby Hallen
Promoter: Int'l Concert Organization

Leiden, The Netherlands
Groenoordhal
Promoter: Wim Bosman

Bruxelles, Belgium
Vorst Nationaal
Promoter: Make It Happen

Paris, France
Promoter: KCP

Italy
Promoter: David Zard

West Berlin, West Germany
Promoter: MCP

MAY 19, 1980

Drammen, Norway
Drammenshalle
Promoter: Int'l Concert Organization

MAY 27, 1980

München, West Germany
Olympiahalle @ Olympiapark München
Promoter: MCP

JUNE 1980

London, England
Wembley Arena
Promoter: Kennedy Street Entertainment

Edinburgh, Scotland
Promoter: Kennedy Street Entertainment

JUNE 3, 1980

Saarbrucken, West Germany
Saarlandhalle
Promoter: MCP

JUNE 14, 1980

Zürich, Switzerland
Hallenstadion

JUNE 15, 1980

Stuttgart, West Germany
Messehalle

JUNE 16, 1980

Frankfurt a.M., West Germany
Festehalle

JUNE 18, 1980

Heidelberg, West Germany
Rhein-Neckar-Halle

JUNE 20, 1980

Köln, West Germany
Sporthalle

JUNE 21, 1980

Dortmund, West Germany
Westfalenhalle

JUNE 22, 1980

Bremen, West Germany
Stadthalle

JUNE 23, 1980

Hamburg, West Germany
Ernst-Merc Halle

CANCELED CENTRAL AMERICAN TOUR

(promoted by Promociones Artistieasy Espectaculous Internacionales)

AUGUST 9, 10 & 11, 1980

Ciudad de México, Mexico

AUGUST 12, 1980

Guadalajara, Mexico

AUGUST 14, 1980

Monterrey, Mexico

CHAPTER 14

MUSIC FROM THE ELDER

What are we going to do now?

That was the question KISS faced in 1981 with the Australian hysteria behind them and the prospect of a lifeless U.S. fanbase in front of them.

"The band and Bill were having a meeting figuring out what to do," remembers Ric Aliberte. "Someone said: 'I know, let's get Bob Ezrin back to do *Destroyer II*.' So, they contacted Bob Ezrin, and he came in, and they had another meeting. Everyone emerged saying they're going to have this album with a fat backbeat, and it's going to be a real rock record, etc. Ace had recently built this studio in his house up in Connecticut and everyone was excited: 'Yeah, we'll do it at Ace's!' And off they went.

"Weeks go by and no one in Aucoin's office is hearing from them, yet the bills are coming in, and I'm calling them and calling them and calling them: 'What's going on? Can we hear something?' A total of two months went by, and finally I told them I was coming up to Connecticut, and that I had to hear something. I drove up to Ace's and surprisingly found only Ace and Bob present. Bob proceeds to play me the album. I'm expecting to hear 'One! Two! Three! Four!. . .' and instead I hear Paul warbling in falsetto over an orchestra.

"I looked at Ezrin and said, "Bob: two months in the studio. $300,000. Backbeat. Rock and Roll. *Destroyer.* What is *this?*'

"He looked at me and shrugged: 'Who knew?'"

The answer was: no one. For the first seven years of their existence, the core of KISS's formula was simple: tour and record. And for seven years, the plan had worked almost flawlessly. However, by 1981, many factors had conspired to change the landscape of the music industry and KISS's formula had not changed with it. The result was that domestic album sales had dropped off a staggering 65% between *Dynasty* and *Unmasked;* the prospects for touring looked equally dismal, with the Dynasty Tour running at a huge deficit, and the Unmasked Tour—the self-contained success in Australia notwithstanding—posting similar losses. Merchandise was no longer a savior either; KISS had saturated that market as far back as 1978. With their main weapons more or less impotent, KISS was directionless.

In the meantime, KISS did manage to find some pleasant distractions, as tour assistant Jayne Grodd explains, "We had a big softball game in Central Park one day in May 1981. It was Aucoin vs. Glickman/Marks. Bill Aucoin was out there playing and co-captaining with me, and I remember us being really pissed because Glickman/Marks, the shysters, bought all four guys from the band for their team for a buck!

"A lot of people took part in the game: the entire band, a lot of crew members, and a bunch of people from Glickman/Marks. Bill's team had all the members from Spyder, including Anton Fig, and a couple of guys from the band New England, too. Believe it or not, Gene and Paul actually do have some athletic ability for a couple of Jewish guys from Queens and Israel. Ace was a big baseball fan, so he wasn't bad either. Paul hit a few out of the park; I was really bummed because we ended up losing. But it was a lot of fun."

Another of the summertime distractions was Ric Aliberte's wedding on July 19. Ace, Gene, and Paul performed briefly at the reception, which was held at The Covent Garden in New York.

KISS was going through a process of self-examination, trying to find a direction. "They were very intense about getting feedback from everyone in the office," Ida Langsam, the band's publicist, recollects, "and they spent a lot of time asking everybody, from Bill Aucoin down to the receptionist, what they thought. Did they have a song title? Did they have a song lyric phrase, or an anthem phrase that they could use to write a song? Should they leave the makeup on? Should they take it off?"

In a postcard to Langsam, Gene notes, "Understand that this is a time of readjustment for us, and we're not sure yet how we'll do or even how we'll look. Bear with us until we figure it out."

What Simmons, Aucoin, and producer Bob Ezrin figured out was that the new album, *Music From The Elder,* should be an elaborate concept piece. The album's narrative was a loose take on the heroic-quest archetype, with a naïve and bewildered young boy selected by a council of

GLENN A. BAKER/SHOOTING STAR

elders to champion the cause of good. Ezrin, whose previous effort with KISS, *Destroyer,* was easily their most-produced album, had recently completed the even-more-complex, overproduced, and successful concept piece *The Wall* with Pink Floyd.

As summer passed into fall, a promotional trip to Mexico was arranged on which the band would premiere their new short-haired look for the 1980s. *Dynasty* had been very successful in Mexico, and the band was scheduled to make several appearances, including one at an orphanage and one on Mexican television station Azteca 13, where they would lip-synch to "I Was Made for Lovin' You" and "Charisma." The September 25 taping of the show went smoothly, but the band's arrival in Mexico did not. Ric Aliberte elaborates: "I flew in early and squared it with the airport authorities to get the band in and out in a very different route than would be normal, by walking through steam-pipe hallways and the like. We came in through some basement antechamber and then through Customs. When we emerged from the Customs area, right in front of us were about 40 kids, and just beyond them were the doors to where the limousines were. To our left, because some idiot let the word out, were about 4,000 fans.

"We came out of the doorway and I heard 'Keeeessss! Keeessss!' And literally thousands of kids were coming at us in a dead run. I remember thinking, 'This is exactly what we wanted to avoid. Someone is going to get hurt.' I yelled to the band 'This way!' and took off running. I plowed through the small group of 40 kids, threw the guys into the car and off they went. As soon as the large group of kids saw that KISS was gone, they stopped running and started milling about.

"Then, this Mexican police sergeant came up to me and said, 'You gringo bastard! You knocked down our little Mexican kids!' I was looking at the guy and thinking how great it was that we had averted a major catastrophe when he took out his gun and pistol-whipped me. Then, his captain, who was the guy I'd squared things with—and bribed—in the first place, came up to me. I told him what happened, as did his own men and the kids that were there. They then took this guy into a room and beat him within an inch of his life for pistol-whipping me."

Music From The Elder was released on November 16, 1981. In a complete reversal from most of KISS's previous records, the album was greeted with substantial critical acclaim, but sales figures were deplorable. Though sales of the album have probably crept past the 500,000 figure, it has never been certified Gold by the R.I.A.A., thus becoming the first KISS album that failed to earn that distinction.

Though it never came to fruition, a full-blown tour for *Music From The Elder* was discussed in detail. In keeping with the spirit of trying to recreate *Destroyer,* set designer Mark Ravitz was again contacted to develop a theatrical production for KISS. Ravitz developed several ideas in a 21-page document that included such strange concepts as a simulated swarm of bees, a KISS temple, the "Well of the Unknown," and a stage designed to look like a spaceship. Perhaps the most noteworthy of the undeveloped concepts was a drum riser designed to look like a tank turret, an idea which KISS used on their two subsequent tours.

Two different budgets for the tour were put together (dated October 7, 1981 and February 10, 1982, respectively) and KISS commissioned an artist's rendering of the stage from Ravitz before projected cost overruns ultimately scrapped the idea.

Despite the lack of a tour to support the album, KISS made several television appearances, including spots on *Solid Gold* and *Fridays*. Ida Langsam recalls the *Solid Gold* taping where KISS lip-synched "I." "It was done at the Solid Gold studio in Los Angeles during the holiday season. KISS thought it was just ludicrous that there were these reindeer drawing a sled with Santa in it hanging from the palm trees."

---·---

Los Angeles, California
ABC Studios
■ **SET LIST**
The Oath
A World Without Heroes
I

Song writer/producer Bill Bartell attended the taping: "They did a complete dress rehearsal of the entire show. I was sitting in the bleachers with Blackie Lawless (W.A.S.P.) after the audience had left and Ace came over to talk to him. When Ace went backstage to get his makeup touched up, I went up to the sound booth just to see if the set list was going to be the same. There was an older woman in her fifties who was the sound tech. As I was asking her some questions, she asked me if I wanted something from the show. I was thinking maybe a set list when she reached into a tape deck and handed me a cassette of the dress rehearsal. The cool thing about the rehearsal is when they performed 'I,' they sang the original lyrics with the word 'balls' in it, but for the broadcast they changed 'balls' to 'guts.' I've still got that tape."

---·---

Later that month, on January 28, KISS again lip-synched "I," this time from Studio 54 in New York, a performance which was broadcast live in Italy for the *San Remo Festival.* "It was done pretty early in the day," Langsam remembers, "so it would synch with whatever time it was being shown overseas. They got some kids in to create an audience and, as if everyone wasn't nervous enough, Ace didn't show up, so they did it without him. The word was that he had woken up late, and then his limo got caught in traffic. I honestly don't even know if he got out of bed. It was bizarre and everyone was at the edge of his or her nerves. It was very tense."

Videos were produced for "A World Without Heroes" and "I." "Both videos were done at the same time [Halloween weekend, 1981]," relates Langsam. "I remember them putting the glycerin drop in Gene's eye so it would look like he was crying at the end." A second version of the "I" video was eventually done as well. The first version was shot on a soundstage in Manhattan which, as Glickman/Marks representative Chris Lendt recalls, "looked liked the landscape of another planet." The shoot featured a live audience (made up of fans and some AMI employees) cheering on the band. This version was ultimately scrapped as "the end result did not look KISS enough," according to Bill Aucoin. The second version, which did get released, was a compilation of various archival shots of the band with some performance footage from *Solid Gold* tacked on at the end.

The perfect vehicle for the videos had been born the previous summer when a new cable TV station, MTV, went on the air on August 1, 1981, and the music industry was never the same. Unfortunately, KISS's label PolyGram was one of two major record companies that refused to give any videos to MTV for free. Recalls Langsam, "The label's P.R. guy said that Europe had paid for them, and he saw no reason to just give the videos to MTV." Thus, no PolyGram artists were initially played on the cable network.

PolyGram eventually changed their minds once MTV proved they significantly impacted album sales, and in April 1982, "World Without Heroes" (MTV did not include the "A" from the title) became the first KISS video to be played on MTV.

While the relationship between MTV and KISS would eventually blossom, the band's relationship with manager Bill Aucoin drew to a close in late April 1982. "In 1981," Aucoin explains, "they were very nervous about *The Elder* and Gene and I had disagreed quite a few times. They also wanted to try a lot of new things, like taking off the makeup. They also didn't want to do merchandising anymore because they thought it was too kiddie-like. Since I had spent years developing that, it was real slap in the face to me, as was the idea of taking off their makeup. I had spent four years trying to get their faces copyrighted in the Library of Congress, a goal that we finally achieved, and then they wanted to take it off. You can imagine it was a real horror story for me.

"That wasn't enough for me to leave, but the relationship had gotten almost untenable, probably on both sides. I wouldn't have left, but they came into my office one day and said that it was probably coming to an end and I agreed. At that point there was no reason to go on."

Days later, on May 8, Casablanca Records founder Neil Bogart died at Cedars-Sinai Medical Center where he had resided for a month prior to his death. A victim of cancer, Bogart was only 39 years old. The memorial service, held on May 11 at the Hillside Memorial Park in Culver City, California, was filled with industry luminaries paying their final respects. Gene and Paul along with Burt Bacharach, Marvin Hamlisch, Bill Withers, the Isley Brothers, Neil Diamond, Gladys Knight and the Pips, Curtis Mayfield, Donna Summer, Brooklyn Dreams, Richard Fields, and Jill Bogart performed "Gonna Keep An Eye On Us" from *The First* at the funeral service.

A failed record, no tour, the dissolution of their relationship with Bill Aucoin, the death of Neil Bogart—things seemingly couldn't get worse...

CHAPTER 15

CREATURES OF THE NIGHT TOUR

Number of Shows: 56
Start Date: December 29, 1982 - Bismarck, North Dakota
End Date: June 25, 1983 - São Paulo, Brazil
Countries: Brazil, Canada, U.S.A.
Opening Acts: Dare Force; Defectors; Headpins; Herva Doce; Hotz; Molly Hatchet; Mötley Crüe; Night Ranger; Plasmatics; The Shoes; Why On Earth; Zebra
Average Attendance: 5,313* (Does not include Brazilian shows.)

Between 1979 and 1982, KISS's album sales dropped 75 percent. They had gone from averaging 10,500+ per concert in 1979, to *Music From The Elder* in 1981 where prospects were so poor that a tour never came into existence. The millions KISS had made in the 1970s had nearly evaporated; they needed a scapegoat and a solution.

The remedy they hit upon to help solve their financial problems was to sue Phonogram, PolyGram's Dutch parent company, for Casablanca's failure to obtain KISS's permission to discount the solo albums; Chris Lendt explains: "Paul Marshall had come to a business meeting with the KISS members at our (Glickman/Marks) offices on December 16, 1981, laid out the facts of the case, and asked for their consent to go ahead with the lawsuit against Phonogram . . . He reviewed the pertinent clauses of KISS's 1977 recording agreement with Casablanca that would affect the case . . . Paul emphasized the amount of money at stake. KISS's audit claimed $1.7 million was owed them. Potential compensatory and punitive damages would also be sought. KISS had an excellent case. . . ."[1]

Suit was filed in the U.S. Federal Court, and the trial was slated for early December 1982. It's interesting to note that Phonogram's list of witnesses included KISS Army founder Bill Starkey, though ultimately he was not called upon to testify. The verdict was rendered on December 13, with KISS as the victor. Unfortunately, KISS's hopes of a big payday were dashed when the jury awarded them only $520,000, far short of the nearly $7 million KISS had sought.

In the midst of this legal mess, Ace Frehley decided he wanted out, and with good reason. When Peter Criss departed in 1980, with him went the group dynamic within KISS. While Paul and Gene had helmed the band from the beginning, without Peter, even the appearance of democracy within the group had vanished. When deciding the course KISS would take, Paul and Gene often functioned as a single unit, and with Eric not involved in the KISS partnership, Ace was the lone member who could cast a dissenting vote against them. KISS's future was bleak, and for all intents and purposes, Ace was powerless to change it.

In June 1982, he called a meeting with Howard Marks, Gene, Paul, and his lawyer.[1] Ace announced that he wanted to leave the band, though unlike Peter Criss, the deal struck

between the two parties meant he would no longer be a partner in KISS.

Ace's departure was not immediate, as he would do promotional appearances with KISS through November and was not irretrievably out of the picture until June 1983, with Gene going so far as to phone Frehley at the end of the Creatures Tour to invite him back. Initially, KISS offered many excuses for Ace's absence: he had been in a bad auto accident in April 1982 (which was true), or, he developed an ear condition that prevented him from flying, so he couldn't tour. The excuses were given to the press in part to quell fans' concerns regarding Ace's status, though KISS had another vested interest in mind.

KISS's contract with PolyGram clearly stipulated that for the agreement to remain valid, at least three original members of KISS had to be in the band at all times. By claiming Ace's absence was temporary, the band could defend itself should PolyGram bring the contract into question, when in fact KISS was clearly in breach of contract. When it became apparent that Ace was not going to return, KISS was forced to address the issue.

"Now that it had been officially acknowledged by KISS that Ace wasn't in KISS any longer, KISS was in breach of the agreement. Phonogram felt it was high time for the group to get their comeuppance . . . They demanded that the contract be renegotiated. . .

"The framework of the new deal emerged. KISS would be Gene and Paul only. The royalty rates and most of the technical provisions remained . . . The biggest modification concerned the advances. They would be substantially reduced. Ace's departure from KISS would be very costly to Gene and Paul, shrinking their guaranteed income from delivering albums . . . Phonogram had exacted their pound of flesh."

Ironically, if KISS had refrained from suing Phonogram in the first place, they would have been in a much more advantageous position at the bargaining table when Phonogram addressed KISS's breach of contract. It is foreseeable that KISS could have leveraged Phonogram's failure to pay royalties against the company, which may have resulted in KISS being able to retain the points of the original contract.

Despite the chaos of litigation and departing band members, KISS did manage to release two albums in 1982: *Killers* and *Creatures of the Night.*

Killers, a compilation album, which included four new tracks, was recorded by Paul, Gene,

Eric, and Bob Kulick at the Record Plant in Los Angeles in spring 1982. The album never saw official release stateside, but debuted in Australia, Europe, and Japan around June 25. "*Killers* was put together in a very short period of time," relates Chris Lendt. "The foreign record companies wanted a KISS compilation album on the market with a lot of traditional songs on it because *The Elder* had done so poorly. They wanted to go right back into the marketplace to show the public that KISS was really a heavy metal group. They paid a sum of money to have KISS record some new songs that were in a heavy metal groove." Surprisingly, future KISS member Bruce Kulick actually made an uncredited appearance for his brother (who was ghosting for Ace) on at least one of the four new tracks.

Creatures of the Night, with Michael James Jackson producing, was recorded at the Record Plant from July through September and was released on October 25. *Creatures* was a purposeful, exacting change of direction for KISS, focusing on a darker, heavier sound and image than anything the band had attempted before. Song titles like "Killer" and "War Machine" sustained the atmosphere established by the eerie, cobalt-blue cover. The album was filled with the products of some of Paul and Gene's new writing

Ace's contributions to Creatures of the Night were mostly limited to a handful of promotional appearances. He is pictured here during an in-store in London, England.

COURTESY OF JACQUES VAN GOOL

---

[1] *Kiss and Sell* (CK Lendt. p. 254. Billboard Books 1996.)

partnerships, most notably with Bryan Adams and Vincent Cusano.

While Paul, Gene, and Eric certainly appear on *Creatures,* the issue of which guitarists appeared on the album has never been resolved satisfactorily. Although his image adorns the original cover of the album, it is clear that Ace did not appear on the album. Vincent Cusano, the songwriter/guitarist who would eventually replace Ace appears on two tracks that he cowrote, namely "I Still Love You," and "Killer," as well as contributing guitar work to "Danger" and "War Machine."

As part of the effort to keep PolyGram from realizing that Ace was leaving the band, Ace agreed to appear at KISS's promotional appearances in the fall, the first of which was an in-store/album release party at Much More in Richmond, Virginia on October 22.

Six days later, KISS held a press conference on Stage 5 at Francis Ford Coppola's Zoetrope Studios in Hollywood to announce the *Creatures of the Night* album and tour. The band would use the same facility to shoot the video for "I Love it Loud," an edited version of which MTV eventually put into medium rotation.

A promotional tour of Europe followed in November. "We visited England, Holland, Italy, and Germany," recalls Chris Lendt. "It was mostly TV appearances. We played in a TV studio in Germany with several other acts. We also did a TV show in Italy where we had skinheads as bodyguards."

The promo tour marked Ace's final appearances with KISS during his original tenure with the band; he had no intentions of being a part of the upcoming concert tour. KISS's official attempts at hiring another lead guitarist did not yield any exciting or at least viable options, and in the end, the job fell to Vincent Cusano. "When Vinnie came into the group," Chris Lendt explains, "he was nobody's choice, but there was no one that they thought would work out better. So he won by default, which is not necessarily the best way to bring in a musical partner."

During a 1990 interview with Bruce Kulick biographer Ken Gullic, Eric Carr recalled: "Vinnie was there through the whole audition process, not involved in it, but he was around the studio all the time. It just never occurred to anybody that he might be the guy that could work for the band. The album was almost done and we said, 'Look, we have to start thinking about touring, and we can't really find anybody that's standing out. Maybe since Vinnie's playing so great, he's got a great voice, he's writing great songs for the band, maybe we should just go with Vinnie.' So, we did some massive reconstruction on him and made him into a KISS person."

Cusano had enjoyed modest success as a songwriter, working with several artists, including Carmine Appice in 1981. Cusano met Gene

Vinnie Vincent portraying the shortest-lived of the six KISS personas: the Egyptian Warrior.

The band is pictured here taping an interview for the short-lived TV series TMT in Toledo.

through fellow songwriter Adam Mitchell when he happened to show up one day while Adam and Gene were writing together at Mitchell's home. Unbeknownst to Adam, Vinnie passed his phone number onto Gene. As a direct result, Vinnie wound up as a key session musician on the *Creatures* album and cowrote three songs that appeared on the album.

Eventually the job as lead guitarist for KISS fell to Cusano. Paul created an Egyptian warrior persona with a gold ankh makeup design for Cusano, whose name was changed to Vinnie Vincent. "Vinnie seemed to be at loggerheads with Gene and Paul all the time," remembers Lendt, "and you could sense that he really didn't fit in. His competence as a musician was undisputed, he was an excellent guitar player, and he was very important to the band in helping them write songs during that period, but in terms of personal relationships he wasn't terribly popular."

At the start, Vinnie was portrayed as a temporary member, a distinction that was purposefully made in case PolyGram objected to having only two original band members in KISS. Many people attending concerts on the tour had no clue Ace had left until they saw Vinnie's image on the merchandise sold at the shows. Some even wondered if Ace had simply changed his makeup.

The tour, which was advertised as the 10th Anniversary Tour, was the first over which Glickman/Marks had control without Bill Aucoin in the picture. The initial plans had the band playing over 100 shows, but that total never came close to being met. Attendance at KISS's concerts in the U.S. had been in steady decline since 1978, dropping a staggering 61 percent from the Alive II Tour to the time the Creatures of the Night Tour ended. Chris Lendt relates, "The tour was a constant struggle. The shows for the most part didn't come close to selling out. We were playing

a lot of smaller markets and there was a certain amount of resistance from some of the promoters taking shows." The average attendance of 5,313 was the smallest figure for a headlining tour in the band's history to that point and reflected nearly a 50 percent drop from the previous U.S. tour.

Merchandise for the tour was handled by the Michigan-based company Rock Tours, and showed similarly disappointing numbers. In an effort to recoup their losses, Rock Tours eventually sold the remaining stock of KISS merchandise to flea market merchants.

Despite the very disappointing turnout, the tour garnered a great deal of local and national press coverage, though not necessarily for reasons the band was proud of. The rumor that KISS was a malicious acronym was again in full swing. A short-lived fixation on rock bands backmasking subliminal messages in their music, coupled with the nationwide conservatism brought about by the Reagan administration, placed KISS on the agendas of many reactionary groups. Consequently, over the course of the tour, several of KISS's concerts were met with organized protests, and the band's appearances and effect on younger members of the audience was a frequent topic of discussion in the media and newspaper op-ed pages.

Rehearsals for the Creatures Tour took place at The Studios at Las Colinas, which is part of the Dallas Communications Complex in Irving, Texas. The rehearsals began immediately following the rendering of the verdict in the Phonogram lawsuit on December 13, and concluded just before Christmas.

Designed by M2 Research, the Creatures Tour stage was intended to look like an enormous tank, with lighted treads flanking the stage, and the drum riser serving as the gun turret complete with a functioning cannon and exhaust pipes.

The set list, not surprisingly, was a vast departure from the Unmasked Tour. All of the *Dynasty* and *Unmasked* material had been cut, and six of the nine tracks from *Creatures of the Night* had been added to the set: "Creatures of the Night," "I Still Love You," "I Love It Loud," "War Machine," "Keep Me Comin'," and "Rock and Roll Hell" were performed, though the last two were quickly dropped. "I Want You," which had not been performed live since the Alive II Tour, reappeared in the set, and a lengthy melodic coda had been added to "Black Diamond."

One of the band's timeworn production tricks, namely Gene's blood-spitting routine, was refurbished for the tour. During his solo, Gene would cower from an overhead spotlight, cringing Quasimodo-like as if stung by the light, with a tape of an iron bell tolling ominously in the background. All in all, it may have been the most melodramatic rendition of the blood-spitting routine that Gene has ever done.

There were several other new effects included in the production. During Eric's solo, the cannon on his gun-turret drum riser would fire and appear to destroy a dummy speaker cabinet above stage left. At the end of "Black Diamond," the band would join Eric on the riser, as the turret would rotate, spew exhaust, and fire its cannon over the audience. Lastly, during the early stages of the tour, Vinnie used a violin bow during his solo, but this was quickly dropped.

DECEMBER 27, 1982   CANCELED

Rapid City, South Dakota
Rushmore Plaza Civic Center
Promoter: Concert Presentation Company
■ The concert was canceled at 5:30 P.M. on the day of the show.

Some of the band's equipment, including their costumes, was scheduled to be routed from the rehearsal facility in Dallas through Denver and then to the venue in Rapid City. Unfortunately, Denver had been buried by 23 inches of snow on December 26, and Stapleton Airport was shut down. With their gear stuck in Denver, KISS was forced to cancel the Rapid City show.

DECEMBER 29, 1982

Bismarck, North Dakota
Bismarck Civic Center
Opening Act: Hotz
Attendance: 3,230   Capacity: 8,000
Promoter: Concert Presentation
■ When flights out of Denver were grounded prior to the Rapid City show, most of the equipment was placed on trucks that drove ahead to Bismarck, North Dakota. The band's wardrobe, however, was considered too valuable and fragile to be stowed on the cargo trucks, so it remained in Denver along with Wardrobe Manager Laurie Greenan until the airport reopened. The contingency plan was to have Pixie Esmonde, the band's wardrobe manager during 1979–80, fly into Bismarck with costumes from previous tours.

Pixie Esmonde: "I was working at *CBS News Nightwatch* at the time, and I got an emergency phone call from [Production Manager] Tom Marzullo. He explained that the band was in one city, and all the costumes were someplace else.

He asked if I would go to their warehouse and pick up clothes for all of them, jump on a plane, and fly out to meet them. They arranged for that, but I got as far as St. Louis and was snowed in. Then they rented a Lear jet: it was just me, the costumes, the pilot, and copilot, and we flew into Bismarck."

There are no photographs available to verify her assertion, but according to Esmonde, the band performed the gig in their Love Gun Tour costumes.

This was Vinnie Vincent's first performance with KISS.

Gene related an interesting story to journalist Mark Peel about the band's stay in Bismarck: "This girl comes up and hands Eric a bible. He sort of hesitated about taking it, thinking she was trying to convert him, but then he opened it, and found she had left her name and telephone number in it with a note that said, 'Call me.'"

DECEMBER 30, 1982

Sioux City, Iowa
Sioux City Municipal Auditorium
Opening Act: Dare Force
Attendance: 4,934   Capacity: 5,200
Promoter: Terry Drea Presents
Archived: Audio
■ SET LIST
Creatures of the Night
Strutter
Calling Dr. Love
Firehouse
I Love It Loud
Cold Gin
Keep Me Comin'
War Machine
I Want You
Vinnie Vincent Guitar Solo - reprise
Rock and Roll Hell
I Still Love You
Shout It Out Loud
Gene Simmons Bass Solo
God of Thunder
Eric Carr Drum Solo - reprise
Love Gun
Paul Stanley Guitar Solo
Black Diamond
Rock and Roll All Nite
Detroit Rock City

■ This was the second and final performance of "Keep Me Comin'." Interestingly the song had been recorded at the last minute in New York when another song was pulled from the album for legal reasons.

Glickman/Marks asserted that promoter Terry Drea claimed insolvency and stiffed the band. According to the promoter, KISS asked Drea for a percentage of the gate when news of brisk ticket sales came to their attention. Drea refused the request, which seems to have led to both sides feeling disgruntled.

Several citizens protested the booking of the show, as evidenced by the verbal war in the op-ed pages of the *Sioux City Journal*. Venue manager John Graham had to appear before the venue Board of Directors who wanted him to address if KISS was aligned with the devil. He had been quoted in the *Sioux City Journal* as saying they were, but he argued that the concert should go on as scheduled.

The rear stage curtain caught on fire during the show.

The all-girl rock band Vixen was scheduled to open the show, but they did not perform. They were replaced by Dare Force, which included the younger brother of Tommy Bolan.

DECEMBER 31, 1982

Rockford, Illinois
MetroCentre
Opening Act: The Shoes
Attendance: 3,500   Capacity: 9,213
Promoter: JAM Productions
Archived: Audio
■ SET LIST
Creatures of the Night
Strutter
Calling Dr. Love
Firehouse
I Love It Loud
Cold Gin
War Machine
I Want You
Vinnie Vincent Guitar Solo - reprise
Rock and Roll Hell
Shout It Out Loud
I Still Love You
Gene Simmons Bass Solo
God of Thunder
Eric Carr Drum Solo - reprise
Love Gun
Paul Stanley Guitar Solo
Black Diamond
Rock and Roll All Nite
Detroit Rock City

■ "Rock and Roll Hell" was performed for the third and final time at this show.

JANUARY 1, 1983

Terre Haute, Indiana
Hulman Center
Opening Act: Why On Earth
Attendance: 4,027   Capacity: 10,000
Promoter: Sunshine Promotions
Archived: Audio
■ SET LIST
Creatures of the Night
Detroit Rock City
Calling Dr. Love
Firehouse
I Want You
Vinnie Vincent Guitar Solo - reprise
I Love It Loud
Cold Gin
Gene Simmons Bass Solo
God of Thunder
Paul Stanley Guitar Solo
Love Gun
Eric Carr Drum Solo - reprise
War Machine
I Still Love You
Shout It Out Loud
Black Diamond
Strutter
Rock and Roll All Nite

JANUARY 4, 1983

Charleston, West Virginia
Charleston Civic Center
Opening Act: Defectors
Attendance: 4,717   Capacity: 8,032
Promoters: Belkin Productions, Future Entertainment
Archived: Audio, Super 8mm
■ SET LIST
See January 1, 1983.
■ It was at this point that the fourth verse in "I

Love It Loud" was dropped for live performances. The alleged reason for editing the song was that it was not a particular favorite of Paul's; he thought the song dragged and suggested that it would be improved if the verse were shortened. The unedited version reappeared in some performances during the band's 1995 conventions.

Paul's solo included part of the intro to "Black Diamond."

JANUARY 6, 1983

Lexington, Kentucky
Rupp Arena
Opening Act: Night Ranger
Attendance: 3,445   Capacity: 6,066
Promoter: Belkin Productions

JANUARY 7, 1983

Saginaw, Michigan
Wendler Arena @ Saginaw Civic Center
Opening Act: Night Ranger
Attendance: 5,409   Capacity: 7,169
Promoter: Belkin Productions

JANUARY 8, 1983

Toledo, Ohio
Sports Arena
Opening Act: Night Ranger
Attendance: 4,739   Capacity: 7,500
Promoter: Belkin Productions
■ SET LIST
Creatures of the Night
Detroit Rock City
Calling Dr. Love
Firehouse
I Want You
Vinnie Vincent Guitar Solo - reprise
I Love It Loud
Cold Gin
Gene Simmons Bass Solo
God of Thunder
Paul Stanley Guitar Solo
Love Gun
Eric Carr Drum Solo
War Machine
I Still Love You
Shout It Out Loud
Black Diamond
Strutter
Rock and Roll All Nite

■ Paul's solo included part of the intro to "Black Diamond" and what would become part of the live rendition of "Lick It Up." Paul continued using the song passages in his solo through the Rochester gig on January 20.

Before the show, KISS was interviewed for a nationally syndicated entertainment series called *TMT*.

JANUARY 9, 1983

Dayton, Ohio
University of Dayton Arena
Opening Act: Night Ranger
Attendance: 4,430   Capacity: 13,278
Promoter: Belkin Productions
Archived: Audio
■ SET LIST
Creatures of the Night
Detroit Rock City
Calling Dr. Love
Firehouse
I Want You
I Love It Loud
Cold Gin
Gene Simmons Bass Solo

God of Thunder
Paul Stanley Guitar Solo
Love Gun
Eric Carr Drum Solo
War Machine
I Still Love You
Shout It Out Loud
Black Diamond
Strutter
[Rock and Roll All Nite]

■ Vinnie's guitar solo was cut from the set at this gig and the following night in Quebec.

JANUARY 12, 1983

Quebec, Quebec, Canada
Colisée de Quebec
Opening Act: Headpins
Attendance: 8,893   Capacity: 11,285
Promoter: Donald K. Donald
Archived: Audio
■ SET LIST
Creatures of the Night
Detroit Rock City
Calling Dr. Love
Firehouse
I Want You
I Love It Loud
Cold Gin
Gene Simmons Bass Solo
God of Thunder
Paul Stanley Guitar Solo
Love Gun
Eric Carr Drum Solo
War Machine
I Still Love You
Shout It Out Loud
Black Diamond
Strutter
Rock and Roll All Nite

JANUARY 13, 1983

Montréal, Quebec, Canada
Forum de Montréal
Opening Act: Headpins
Attendance: 8,217   Capacity: 12,500
Promoter: Donald K. Donald
Archived: Partial Video, Audio
■ SET LIST
Creatures of the Night
Detroit Rock City
Calling Dr. Love
Firehouse
Paul Stanley Guitar Solo
I Want You
Vinnie Vincent Guitar Solo - reprise
I Love It Loud
Cold Gin
Gene Simmons Bass Solo
God of Thunder
Love Gun
Eric Carr Drum Solo
War Machine
I Still Love You
Shout It Out Loud
Black Diamond
Rock and Roll All Nite

■ Vinnie's solo contained the "Looney Tunes" melody and a brief excerpt of Beethoven's Fifth Symphony. Vinnie continued using the "Looney Tunes" theme at the next two shows in Toronto and Ottawa before dropping it. Most likely due to time constraints, "Strutter" was cut from the set list.

JANUARY 14, 1983

Toronto, Ontario, Canada
Maple Leaf Gardens
Opening Act: Headpins
Attendance: 9,565   Capacity: 12,541
Promoter: Concert Productions Int'l
Archived: Audio
■ SET LIST
Creatures of the Night
Detroit Rock City
Calling Dr. Love
Cold Gin
Paul Stanley Guitar Solo
I Want You
Vinnie Vincent Guitar Solo - reprise
I Love It Loud
Firehouse
Eric Carr Drum Solo
War Machine
Love Gun
Gene Simmons Bass Solo
God of Thunder
I Still Love You
Strutter
Black Diamond
Shout It Out Loud
Rock and Roll All Nite

JANUARY 15, 1983

Ottawa, Ontario, Canada
Ottawa Civic Centre
Opening Act: Headpins
Attendance: 4,919   Capacity: 10,000
Promoter: Concert Productions Int'l
Archived: Audio
■ SET LIST
Creatures of the Night
Detroit Rock City
Cold Gin
Calling Dr. Love
Paul Stanley Guitar Solo
I Want You
Vinnie Vincent Guitar Solo - reprise
I Love It Loud
Firehouse
Eric Carr Drum Solo
War Machine
Love Gun
Gene Simmons Bass Solo
God of Thunder
I Still Love You
Shout It Out Loud
Black Diamond
Rock and Roll All Nite

■ This gig marked the last known time that Vinnie used a bow in his featured solo. "Strutter" was again cut from the set list.

JANUARY 16, 1983

Glens Falls, New York
Glens Falls Civic Center
Opening Act: Night Ranger
Attendance: 4,637   Capacity: 7,713
Promoter: Festival East, Inc.
Archived: Audio
■ SET LIST
Creatures of the Night
Detroit Rock City
Cold Gin
Calling Dr. Love
Paul Stanley Guitar Solo
I Want You
Vinnie Vincent Guitar Solo - reprise
I Love It Loud

Firehouse
Eric Carr Drum Solo
War Machine
Love Gun
Gene Simmons Bass Solo
God of Thunder
I Still Love You
Shout It Out Loud
Black Diamond
[Strutter]
[Rock and Roll All Nite]

JANUARY 18, 1983

Syracuse, New York
Onondaga County War Memorial
Opening Act: Night Ranger
Attendance: 4,902   Capacity: 7,903
Promoter: Festival East, Inc.
■ KISS flew into Syracuse from New York City, where the band had taped an interview for ATI Video that became the basis for the USA Special KISS Yesterday and Today. The special premiered on August 8 on the USA Cable Network.

JANUARY 20, 1983

Rochester, New York
Rochester Community War Memorial
Opening Act: Night Ranger
Attendance: 4,267   Capacity: 10,200
Promoter: Festival East, Inc.
Archived: Audio
■ SET LIST
[Creatures of the Night]
[Detroit Rock City]
[Cold Gin]
Calling Dr. Love
Paul Stanley Guitar Solo
I Want You
[Vinnie Vincent Guitar Solo - reprise]
[I Love It Loud]
Firehouse
Eric Carr Drum Solo
War Machine
Love Gun
Gene Simmons Bass Solo
God of Thunder
I Still Love You
Shout It Out Loud
Black Diamond
Strutter
Rock and Roll All Nite

■ In the middle of Paul's guitar solo, the band and crowd sang "Happy Birthday" to him.

JANUARY 21, 1983

Portland, Maine
Cumberland County Civic Center
Opening Act: Night Ranger
Attendance: 4,608   Capacity: 10,000
Promoter: Ruffino & Vaughn

JANUARY 22, 1983

Worcester, Massachusetts
The Centrum
Opening Act: Night Ranger
Attendance: 9,952   Capacity: 13,014
Promoter: Frank J. Russo
Archived: Audio
■ SET LIST
Creatures of the Night
Detroit Rock City
Cold Gin
Calling Dr. Love
Paul Stanley Guitar Solo

I Want You
Vinnie Vincent Guitar Solo - reprise
I Love It Loud
Firehouse
Eric Carr Drum Solo
War Machine
Love Gun
Gene Simmons Bass Solo
God of Thunder
I Still Love You
Shout It Out Loud
Black Diamond
Strutter
Rock and Roll All Nite

■ There was no pyro used at this show.

A show scheduled for the following night in Providence, Rhode Island was canceled. Frank Russo, the promoter for both shows, made arrangements for tickets to the Providence concert to be honored at the show in Worcester. Additionally, ticket holders interested in attending the Worcester gig were bussed from Providence to the concert.

The band did an in-store appearance at a Strawberries record store on the day of the show.

JANUARY 23, 1983   CANCELED
Providence, Rhode Island
Providence Civic Center
Opening Act: Night Ranger
Promoter: Frank J. Russo

JANUARY 25, 1983
Norfolk, Virginia
The Scope
Opening Act: Night Ranger
Attendance: 5,191   Capacity: 13,800
Promoter: Whisper Concerts

JANUARY 27, 1983
Huntsville, Alabama
Von Braun Civic Center
Opening Act: Night Ranger
Attendance: 5,025   Capacity: 10,106
Promoter: Castleberry Creative Services

JANUARY 28, 1983
Birmingham, Alabama
Boutwell Auditorium
Opening Act: Night Ranger
Attendance: 4,635   Capacity: 5,778
Promoter: Ruffino & Vaughn
■ Paul dedicated "I Still Love You" to Paul "Bear" Bryant, legendary University of Alabama football coach who died on January 26.

JANUARY 29, 1983
Chattanooga, Tennessee
UTC Arena
Opening Act: Night Ranger
Attendance: 4,451   Capacity: 11,000
Promoter: Castleberry Creative Services
■ Vinnie split his pants during the show.

JANUARY 30, 1983
Nashville, Tennessee
Nashville Municipal Auditorium
Opening Act: Night Ranger
Attendance: 8,938   Capacity: 9,900
Promoter: Cumberland Concerts
Archived: Audio
■ **SET LIST**
See January 22, 1983.

FEBRUARY 1, 1983
Knoxville, Tennessee
Knoxville Civic Coliseum
Opening Act: Plasmatics
Attendance: 4,391   Capacity: 10,000
Promoter: Sunshine Promotions
Archived: Audio
■ **SET LIST**
See January 22, 1983.
■ This is the last confirmed performance of "Shout It Out Loud" on the Creatures Tour.

FEBRUARY 3, 1983
West Palm Beach, Florida
West Palm Beach Auditorium
Opening Act: Plasmatics
Attendance: 5,202   Capacity: 6,200

Promoter: Fantasma Productions
Archived: Audio
■ **SET LIST**
Creatures of the Night
Detroit Rock City
Cold Gin
Calling Dr. Love
Paul Stanley Guitar Solo
I Want You
Vinnie Vincent Guitar Solo - reprise
I Love It Loud
Firehouse
Eric Carr Drum Solo
War Machine
Love Gun
Gene Simmons Bass Solo
God of Thunder
[I Still Love You]
[Shout It Out Loud]
[Black Diamond]
[Strutter]
[Rock and Roll All Nite]
■ On February 2, KISS did an in-store appearance at the Specs Music store in Palm Beach Lakes Mall.

FEBRUARY 4, 1983
Lakeland, Florida
Lakeland Civic Center
Opening Act: Plasmatics
Attendance: 5,287   Capacity: 10,000
Promoter: Cellar Door Concerts
■ The rear stage curtain caught on fire during the show.

FEBRUARY 6, 1983
Charleston, South Carolina   TEMP HOLD DATE
Civic Center
Opening Act: Plasmatics
Promoter: Beach Club Promotions

FEBRUARY 8, 1983   TEMP HOLD DATE
Asheville, North Carolina
Asheville Civic Center Auditorium
Opening Act: Plasmatics
Promoter: Beach Club Promotions

MICHAEL MONFORT/SHOOTING STAR

FEBRUARY 9, 1983
Bristol, Tennessee **TEMP HOLD DATE**
Viking Hall Civic Center @ Tennessee High School
Opening Act: Plasmatics
Promoter: Beach Club Promotions

FEBRUARY 11, 1983
Pine Bluff, Arkansas
Pine Bluff Convention Center
Opening Act: Plasmatics
Attendance: 3,039   Capacity: 10,000
Promoter: Mid-South Concerts

FEBRUARY 14, 1983
New Orleans, Louisiana
Louisiana Superdome
Opening Act: Zebra
Attendance: 10,430   Capacity: 23,000
Promoter: Barry Mendelson Presents
■ The show was advertised as the "Mardi Gras
Eve Spectacular." Although KISS did not participate in the renowned Mardi Gras parade, silver
doubloons were distributed to commemorate the
concert. KISS had flown in several weeks prior
to hold a press conference and do an in-store
appearance. *Entertainment Tonight* covered the
performance.
   This concert was broadcast on a video screen,
rigged high above the stage, indicating that it
may have been archived.

FEBRUARY 16, 1983
Dubuque, Iowa
Dubuque Five Flags Center
Opening Act: Plasmatics
Attendance: 3,381   Capacity: 5,200
Promoter: Contemporary Productions

FEBRUARY 17, 1983
Duluth, Minnesota **CANCELED**
Duluth Arena Auditorium
Opening Act: Plasmatics

FEBRUARY 18, 1983
Bloomington (Minneapolis), Minnesota
Metropolitan Sports Center
Opening Act: Plasmatics
Attendance: 5,370   Capacity: 12,731
Promoter: Rose Productions
■ KISS's concert in Minneapolis prompted a
huge religious controversy involving two sib-
lings claiming to represent the local Christian
contingent. Gene made an on-air call to a local
TV station to talk live with one of the brothers,
both of whom were eventually allowed to meet
with the band backstage, an event which was
covered heavily by the local media. Ironically,
the brothers produced and sold cassette copies
of a one-hour program about KISS entitled "The
Truth About Rock," which included two songs
bootlegged from KISS's Met Center performance.

FEBRUARY 19, 1983
Sioux Falls, South Dakota
Sioux Falls Arena
Opening Act: Plasmatics
Attendance: 2,020   Capacity: 8,000
Promoter: R&R Productions

FEBRUARY 20, 1983
La Crosse, Wisconsin
Mary E. Sawyer Auditorium @ La Crosse Center
Opening Act: Plasmatics
Attendance: 3,613   Capacity: 8,000
Promoter: Belkin Productions

FEBRUARY 22, 1983
Richfield (Cleveland), Ohio
The Coliseum Theatre
Opening Act: Plasmatics
Attendance: 9,525   Capacity: 12,221
Promoter: Belkin Productions
Archived: Audio
■ **SET LIST**
Creatures of the Night
Detroit Rock City
Cold Gin
Calling Dr. Love
Paul Stanley Guitar Solo
I Want You
Vinnie Vincent Guitar Solo - reprise
I Love It Loud
Firehouse
Eric Carr Drum Solo
War Machine
Love Gun
Gene Simmons Bass Solo
God of Thunder
I Still Love You
[Black Diamond]
[Strutter]
[Rock and Roll All Nite]

■ Vinnie's solo contained the melody from the
"Star Spangled Banner."
   Gene was interviewed via satelite on the local
TV show *Live On Five*.

FEBRUARY 23, 1983
Detroit, Michigan
Cobo Arena
Opening Act: Plasmatics
Attendance: 7,620   Capacity: 12,191
Promoter: Belkin Productions
Archived: Audio
■ **SET LIST**
Creatures of the Night
Detroit Rock City
Cold Gin
Calling Dr. Love
Paul Stanley Guitar Solo
I Want You
Vinnie Vincent Guitar Solo - reprise
I Love It Loud
Firehouse
Eric Carr Drum Solo
War Machine
Love Gun
Gene Simmons Bass Solo

God of Thunder
I Still Love You
Black Diamond
Strutter
Rock and Roll All Nite.
■ Local TV show *Good Afternoon Detroit* interviewed the band and shot footage of the show.

FEBRUARY 24, 1983

Indianapolis, Indiana
Market Square Arena
Opening Act: Plasmatics
Attendance: 5,426   Capacity: 11,000
Promoter: Sunshine Promotions
■ This show was originally scheduled for January 2 at the Indianapolis Convention Center.

FEBRUARY 25, 1983

Springfield, Illinois
Prairie Capitol Convention Center
Opening Act: Plasmatics
Attendance: 3,384   Capacity: 6,888

FEBRUARY 27, 1983

St. Louis, Missouri
Kiel Auditorium

Opening Act: Plasmatics
Attendance: 2,802   Capacity: 5,646
Promoter: Contemporary Productions
■ All proceeds from this concert went to the Amy Hardin Relief Fund, which was established to help facilitate a liver transplant for a young St. Louis girl.

MARCH 1, 1983

Kansas City, Missouri
Municipal Auditorium
Opening Act: Molly Hatchet
Attendance: 3,929   Capacity: 10,372
Promoter: Chris Fritz Inc.

MARCH 9, 1983

Dallas, Texas
Dallas County Convention Center Arena
Opening Act: Plasmatics
Attendance: 5,408   Capacity: 7,474
Promoter: 462, Inc.

MARCH 10, 1983

Houston, Texas
Sam Houston Coliseum
Opening Act: Plasmatics

Attendance: 5,975   Capacity: 6,868
Promoter: Pace Concerts
■ SET LIST
Creatures of the Night
Detroit Rock City
Cold Gin
Calling Dr. Love
Firehouse
Paul Stanley Guitar Solo
I Want You
Vinnie Vincent Guitar Solo - reprise
I Love it Loud
Eric Carr Drum Solo
War Machine
Love Gun
Gene Simmons Bass Solo
God of Thunder
I Still Love You
Black Diamond
Strutter
Rock and Roll All Nite
■ On March 11, the decision was made not to book additional dates after April 3.
A local TV show, *Music News,* briefly caught Paul on videotape without makeup backstage.

MARCH 11, 1983

San Antonio, Texas
HemisFair Arena @ Henry B. Gonzalez Convention Center
Opening Act: Plasmatics
Attendance: 8,474   Capacity: 8,694
Promoter: Stone City Attractions

MARCH 13, 1983

Beaumont, Texas
Beaumont Civic Center
Opening Act: Plasmatics
Attendance: 2,663   Capacity: 6,300
Promoter: Three Phase Productions

MARCH 14, 1983

Corpus Christi, Texas
Memorial Coliseum
Opening Act: Plasmatics
Attendance: 6,000   Capacity: 6,000

MARCH 18, 1983

Biloxi, Mississippi
Mississippi Coast Coliseum
Opening Act: Plasmatics
Attendance: 4,645   Capacity: 7,000
Promoter: Barry Mendelson Presents

MARCH 19, 1983

Shreveport, Louisiana
Hirsch Memorial Coliseum
Opening Act: Plasmatics
Attendance: 4,059   Capacity: 10,200
Promoter: Drew Armstrong

MARCH 21, 1983

Norman, Oklahoma
Lloyd Noble Center
Opening Act: Plasmatics
Attendance: 3,699   Capacity: 12,260
Promoter: Little Wing Productions
■ SET LIST
Creatures of the Night
Detroit Rock City
Cold Gin
Calling Dr. Love
Firehouse
Paul Stanley Guitar Solo
I Want You
Vinnie Vincent Guitar Solo - reprise
I Love It Loud

Eric Carr Drum Solo
War Machine
Love Gun
Gene Simmons Bass Solo
God of Thunder
I Still Love You
Black Diamond
[Strutter]
[Rock and Roll All Nite]

MARCH 22, 1983
Amarillo, Texas
The Amarillo Civic Center
Opening Act: Plasmatics
Attendance: 3,419   Capacity: 7,850

MARCH 23, 1983
El Paso, Texas
El Paso County Coliseum
Opening Act: Plasmatics
Attendance: 5,171   Capacity: 8,000
Archived: Audio
■ SET LIST
See March 10, 1983.

MARCH 26, 1983
Laguna Hills, California
Irvine Meadows Amphitheatre
Opening Act: Mötley Crüe
Attendance: 5,786   Capacity: 5,969
Promoter: Avalon Attractions
Archived: Audio
■ SET LIST
Creatures of the Night
Detroit Rock City
Cold Gin
Calling Dr. Love
Firehouse
Paul Stanley Guitar Solo
I Want You
Vinnie Vincent Guitar Solo - reprise
I Love It Loud
Eric Carr Drum Solo
War Machine
Love Gun
Gene Simmons Bass Solo
God of Thunder
I Still Love You
Black Diamond
Strutter
Rock and Roll all Nite

MARCH 27, 1983
Universal City, California
Universal Amphitheatre
Opening Act: Mötley Crüe
Attendance: 6,251   Capacity: 6,251
Archived: Audio
■ SET LIST
See March 10, 1983.

MARCH 28, 1983
Phoenix, Arizona
Arizona Veterans Memorial Coliseum
Opening Act: Mötley Crüe
Attendance: 5,992   Capacity: 10,000
Promoter: Evening Star Productions
Archived: Audio
■ SET LIST
See March 10, 1983.

MARCH 31, 1983   CANCELED
San Diego, California
San Diego Sports Arena
Opening Act: Mötley Crüe
Promoter: Fahn & Silva Productions

APRIL 1, 1983

Las Vegas, Nevada
Aladdin Theatre for the Performing Arts
Opening Act: Mötley Crüe
Attendance: 4,702   Capacity: 7,548
Promoter: Evening Star Productions

APRIL 3, 1983

San Francisco, California
San Francisco Civic Auditorium
Opening Act: Mötley Crüe
Attendance: 7,299   Capacity: 8,500
Promoter: Bill Graham Presents
Archived: Audio

■ SET LIST

See March 10, 1983.

■ Prior to "Strutter," Paul told the audience: "This is the last night of the first part of the tour. We're going back to New York to do some recording before we hit the road."

JUNE 18, 1983

Rio de Janeiro, Brazil
Maracaña Stadium
Opening Act: Herva Doce
Attendance: 137,000   Capacity: 200,000
Promoter: Artteshow
Archived: Video

■ SET LIST

Creatures of the Night
Detroit Rock City
Cold Gin
Calling Dr. Love
Firehouse
Paul Stanley Guitar Solo
I Want You
Vinnie Vincent Guitar Solo - reprise
I Love It Loud
Eric Carr Drum Solo
War Machine
Love Gun
Gene Simmons Bass Solo
God of Thunder
I Still Love You
Black Diamond
[Strutter]
Rock and Roll All Nite

■ Initially, a show in Pôrto Alegre had been included on the itinerary for the Brazilian tour, but the show was never advertised and tickets did not go on sale.

Strangely, Paul had Vinnie introduce "Love Gun" to the crowd.

Edited versions of the show were later broadcast on radio and Central Globo TV.

JUNE 21, 1983

Belo Horizonte, Brazil
Estádio do Mineirão
No Opening Act
Attendance: 30,000   Capacity: 80,000
Promoter: Artteshow

■ This show was originally scheduled for June 20, but was postponed several hours in advance of show time due to difficulties with the power supply.

A ruling that no one under the age of 16 could attend the show without being accompanied by an adult guardian impacted the attendance.

JUNE 25, 1983

São Paulo, Brazil
Estádio do Morumbi
No Opening Act
Attendance: 65,000   Capacity: 100,000
Promoter: Artteshow
Archived: Video

■ SET LIST

Creatures of the Night
Detroit Rock City
Cold Gin
Calling Dr. Love
Firehouse
Paul Stanley Guitar Solo
I Want You
Vinnie Vincent Guitar Solo - reprise
I Love It Loud
Eric Carr Drum Solo
War Machine
Love Gun
Gene Simmons Bass Solo
God of Thunder
I Still Love You
Black Diamond
I Love It Loud
[Strutter]
Rock and Roll All Nite

■ June 24 was reserved on the schedule for a second São Paulo show.

Prior to the show date, KISS held a press conference from São Paulo wearing sunglasses and bandanas.

An hour's worth of highlights from the show was archived by a South American TV crew. As the band came out to do their encore, the audience began chanting the "I Love It Loud" intro. The band played along with the idea and proceeded to perform the song for a second time that evening. This was the final concert with makeup until June 15, 1996.

JULY 5, 6, 7, & 8, 1983   CANCELED

Ciudad de México, México
Palacio de los Deportes

AUGUST 19, 20, & 21, 1983

Buenos Aires, Argentina   CANCELED
Boca Juniors Stadium
Capacity: 50,000
Promoter: Demorcs Producciones

■ A combination of events factored into the cancellation, including troublesome production problems due to inadequate facilities at the venue, and the fact that local terrorists threatened to blow up the stadium if KISS performed there.

CHAPTER 16

LICK IT UP TOUR

Number of Shows: 93
Start Date: October 11, 1983 - Lisboa, Portugal
End Date: March 17, 1984 - Evansville, Indiana
Countries: Austria, Belgium, Canada, Denmark, England, Finland, France, Portugal, Scotland, Spain, Sweden, Switzerland, U.S.A., West Germany
Opening Acts: Accept; Axe; Great White; Heaven; Heavy Pettin'; Helix; Highfever; Pat Travers Band; Riot; Tigres de Oro; Vandenberg
Average Attendance: 5,052

Creatures of the Night successfully refocused KISS's musical direction, but it had done little else. Since firing Bill Aucoin in April 1982, KISS had been without a manager, subsisting on whatever opportunities their past glories afforded them. If they were to regain their footing, KISS clearly needed a transfusion of fresh blood, a necessity that led to the rekindling of their relationship with Danny Goldberg, who had enjoyed a short but successful run as their publicist in 1976.

"They didn't like the word 'manager' back then, because of what they'd been through with Aucoin," relates Goldberg, "but I played the role of the manager with the title of 'Creative Consultant.' The first big thing was to take the makeup off. I said, 'Guys, it's dead. You've got to do something to shake it up.' PolyGram really liked the idea, because it was a new story. Gerry Jaffe was the guy at Mercury then, and he was very pleased about it because it gave them a new look. That was my contribution, to get the makeup off of them. And then later [in 1996] getting it back on.

"They were pretty receptive to the idea. They knew that was always a card that they had in their pockets. They're smart guys: they went through the logic of being at the end of a cycle and that they needed to create a new one."

The new cycle began on MTV just after 11:30 P.M. on September 18, 1983, when the four members of KISS appeared for the first time in public without their makeup. The taped segment, which was hosted by VJ J.J. Jackson, was hyped for weeks on the fledgling cable channel and was later included on VH1's list of the *100 Greatest Rock & Roll Moments on TV.*

Initially, MTV was not very receptive to the idea, as Danny Goldberg explains: "They were pretty cold then. There was a little bit of groveling involved, but Les Garland and John Fleischer at MTV bought into it. Let's face it, the only way we were going to get them on to MTV was a gimmick like this because they had been played out as a commercial band at that time. Les and John understood that this was news at the moment, and that's what MTV was there for. The strategy was not only to get our value [in the press] of that particular moment, but it connected

KISS to the MTV era for the first time, because KISS had been a pre-MTV star and this made them part of MTV. It was a good soft-news piece, and it may have reached the national evening news.

"A big part of the unmasking was making the MTV executives feel invested in KISS. When we came out with the 'Lick It Up' video, MTV played it heavily because they were now in the KISS business."

Lick It Up was released on September 23 on PolyGram Records' Mercury imprint and sold briskly, producing considerably higher sales than KISS's last several efforts. Goldberg elaborates: "It brought them back to Gold and did about 800,000," a relatively mighty feat considering that no KISS album had been certified Gold by the R.I.A.A. since *Unmasked* in July 1980. Additionally, *Lick It Up* met with critical acclaim, and is very unusual among KISS albums in that the material was written entirely by KISS without influence of outside writers. But despite the reassuring success on some fronts, KISS remained fairly low profile in the context of the music world. In fact, several dates had been quietly put on sale for the band's autumn tour of Europe before KISS had abandoned their greasepaint.

The full Creatures of the Night Tour staging was retained throughout the Lick It Up Tour, though the makeup, exaggerated costumes, and personas were now mostly absent, and the band's use of pyro was exceptionally sparse. While pyro may not have been in great supply during the tour, KISS attempted to make up for it with newfound levels of energy. Naturally, the frontline members had been hindered to a great degree by the weight of their platform boots, but now that they had been mothballed, Gene, Vinnie, and Paul ran around with carefree abandon, often leaping onto the tank treads and sliding across them on their knees. KISS would maintain this high-energy level for the next two tours.

Not surprisingly, there was some initial concern as to how well the band members would adjust to performing without the safety net their personas and greasepaint had provided. After all, this would be the first time that Gene and Paul had been onstage as themselves in over 10 years. C.K. Lendt recollects: "We joked about what Gene would do without makeup and costume on stage. Wear a three-piece business suit?" There were some faltering steps and uncomfortable moments as the band made the adjustment to life without the clown white. Gene's solo, in particular, was difficult to watch because, for some reason, he was still using the same routine he had used on the Creatures of the Night Tour. But with no demonic greasepaint, no costuming, and most importantly, no blood, the overacted gesture of cowering from the spotlight and leering out at the audience as if he were some possessed demon came across as awkward, routine, or simply comical.

Following the conclusion of the European leg of the tour on November 25, Vinnie Vincent was fired from KISS. Several phone calls were placed in a hurried attempt to find a replacement for Vinnie, but, too pressed for time to do a thor-ough job, the quest proved futile and Vinnie was promptly rehired for the North American leg of the tour.

Merchandise duties fell to Bravado Merchandising Services on the European leg of the tour, while the San Francisco-based Winterland Productions stepped in for the North American leg. Winterland would continue to handle merchandise for KISS through the completion of the Revenge Tour in 1992.

The set list for the Lick It Up Tour was heavily slanted in favor of the band's two most recent albums, as two-thirds of the show were usually reserved for material from *Creatures of the Night* or *Lick It Up*. From the latter, the title track, "Fits Like a Glove," "Young and Wasted," and "Gimme More" were standards. "Exciter" was also played frequently on the first half of the tour with the album's second single, "All Hell's Breakin' Loose" typically part of the show throughout the last half. On several occasions, the band performed parts of cover songs, or briefly segued in and out of short portions of classic and/or obscure songs from their own back catalog, something that they had never done in the past.

Despite the success of the album and single, the Lick It Up Tour was the least-attended headlining tour the band had done to that point, averaging just 5,052 attendees per show. The musical material and individual performances were strong, but a combination of an uninspired concert production, a run of unsuccessful albums, and the cyclical nature of the music business relegated the Lick It Up Tour to relative obscurity. In several markets, including New York City—typically the strongest of KISS's A-market cities—the band was forced to perform in theater-sized venues for the first time since 1976. In an attempt to boost flagging ticket sales, KISS continued to make in-store appearances regularly .

Seemingly no amount of publicity could reverse the tour's fortunes, and the relationship between Vinnie and Paul and Gene grew from strained to unmanageable over the course of the tour's final weeks; if KISS's future remained uncertain as the tour concluded March 17, Vinnie's was all but decided.

OCTOBER 11, 1983

Lisboa, Portugal
Sports Palais
Opening Act: Helix
Capacity: 8,000
Promoter: Gay & Company
■ The band arrived in Portugal on October 8th and used the venue to rehearse the show on the 9th and 10th.

KISS was interviewed for a Portuguese music TV show, and the crew filmed and later broadcast "Creatures of the Night" and "Detroit Rock City." The footage was presumably from the Lisboa show, though there is some evidence that indicates the footage was shot in Spain, perhaps in Barcelona.

There is a persistent rumor that Gene spit blood at this show, which would have marked the only occasion he has ever done so without the makeup. However, there is no evidence to support this claim, and more than one KISS crew member interviewed for this book has emphatically denied that it took place.

Gene's bass tech, Dave "Romeo" Bonilla: "Gene used Lamplighter's Odorless Clear Lamp Oil to breathe fire. When I first started, no one would tell me what he would use to breathe fire. They claimed that they didn't know. So I went out and got him some white gasoline. The lamplighter's oil ignites and then extinguishes almost immediately. The white gasoline burned a lot longer. He used it at one gig and blew this fireball out that almost set the stage on fire. He melted the gels on the lighting rig. The gas got all over the mike stand, which was a problem because the guitar picks are flammable. And one by one the picks started igniting, the monitor was on fire, and I was running around trying to put out all these fires. Gene was pretty impressed."

OCTOBER 13, 1983

Madrid, Spain
Pabellon del Real Madrid
Opening Acts: Helix, Tigres de Oro
Capacity: 5,000
Promoter: Playsound Concerts
Archived: Audio
■ **SET LIST**
Creatures of the Night
Detroit Rock City
Cold Gin
Fits Like a Glove
Firehouse
Paul Stanley Guitar Solo
Exciter
War Machine
Gimme More
Vinnie Vincent Guitar Solo - reprise
Gene Simmons Bass Solo
I Love It Loud
I Still Love You
Eric Carr Drum Solo
Young and Wasted
Love Gun
Black Diamond
Lick It Up
Rock and Roll All Nite
■ Presumably at the first of the two shows in Madrid, a television crew from the U.S. Armed Forces videotaped the entire concert. "Detroit Rock City," "I Love It Loud," and "Lick It Up" were later broadcast during a KISS special.

OCTOBER 14, 1983

Madrid, Spain
Pabellon del Real Madrid
Opening Acts: Helix, Tigres de Oro
Capacity: 5,000
Promoter: Playsound Concerts
Archived: Audio
■ **SET LIST**
See October 13, 1983.

OCTOBER 15, 1983

San Sebastian, Spain
Velodromo de Anotea
Opening Acts: Helix, Tigres de Oro
Capacity: 8,000
Promoter: Playsound Concerts
Archived: Audio
■ **SET LIST**
Creatures of the Night
Detroit Rock City
Cold Gin

Fits Like a Glove
Firehouse
Paul Stanley Guitar Solo
Exciter
War Machine
Gimme More
Vinnie Vincent Guitar Solo - reprise
Gene Simmons Bass Solo
I Love It Loud
I Still Love You
Eric Carr Drum Solo
Young and Wasted
Love Gun
Black Diamond
Lick It Up
Whole Lotta Love
[Rock and Roll All Nite]

■ At both the San Sebastian and Barcelona gigs, Paul sang all of "Black Diamond."

OCTOBER 16, 1983

Barcelona, Spain
Estadio Deportes de Juventud
Opening Acts: Helix, Tigres de Oro
Capacity: 7,500
Promoter: Playsound Concerts
Archived: Audio

■ SET LIST

Creatures of the Night
Detroit Rock City
Cold Gin
Fits Like a Glove
Firehouse
Paul Stanley Guitar Solo
Exciter
War Machine
Gimme More
Vinnie Vincent Guitar Solo - reprise
Gene Simmons Bass Solo
I Love It Loud
I Still Love You
Eric Carr Drum Solo
Young and Wasted
Love Gun
Black Diamond
Lick It Up
Rock and Roll All Nite

OCTOBER 18, 1983

Toulouse, France
Palais des Sports
Opening Act: Helix
Capacity: 7,500
Promoter: KCP

OCTOBER 19, 1983

Clermont-Ferrand, France
Maison des Sports
Opening Act: Helix
Capacity: 6,000
Promoter: KCP
Archived: Audio

■ SET LIST

Creatures of the Night
Detroit Rock City
Cold Gin
Fits Like a Glove
Firehouse
Paul Stanley Guitar Solo
Exciter
War Machine
Gimme More
Vinnie Vincent Guitar Solo - reprise
Gene Simmons Bass Solo
I Love It Loud
I Still Love You

Eric Carr Drum Solo
Young and Wasted
Love Gun
Black Diamond
Lick It Up
Rock and Roll All Nite

OCTOBER 21, 1983

Leeds, England
Queens Hall
Opening Acts: Heavy Pettin', Helix
Capacity: 6,000
Promoters: Kennedy Street Entertainment, MCP
Archived: Audio

■ SET LIST

Creatures of the Night
Detroit Rock City
Fits Like a Glove
Cold Gin
Firehouse
Paul Stanley Guitar Solo
Exciter
War Machine
Gimme More
Vinnie Vincent Guitar Solo - reprise
Gene Simmons Bass Solo
I Love It Loud
I Still Love You
Eric Carr Drum Solo
Young and Wasted
Love Gun
Black Diamond
Lick It Up
Rock and Roll All Nite

■ Following the performance, a few fans ran into the band at the Leicester East Service Station on the M1. When their car wouldn't start, KISS reportedly helped push the vehicle around the parking lot to get it going.

OCTOBER 22, 1983

Stafford, England
New Bingley Hall
Opening Acts: Heavy Pettin', Helix
Capacity: 7,000
Promoters: Kennedy Street Entertainment, MCP
Archived: Audio

■ SET LIST

Creatures of the Night
Detroit Rock City
Cold Gin
Fits Like a Glove
Firehouse
Paul Stanley Guitar Solo
Exciter
War Machine
Gimme More
Vinnie Vincent Guitar Solo - reprise
Gene Simmons Bass Solo
I Love It Loud
I Still Love You
Eric Carr Drum Solo
Young and Wasted
Love Gun
Black Diamond
Lick It Up
Strutter
Rock and Roll All Nite

■ After "Strutter," Paul had the house lights brought up to quell fighting that had broken out in the audience.

OCTOBER 23, 1983

London, England
Wembley Arena
Opening Acts: Heavy Pettin', Helix

Capacity: 8,000
Promoters: Kennedy Street Entertainment, MCP
Archived: Audio

■ SET LIST

Creatures of the Night
Detroit Rock City
Cold Gin
Fits Like a Glove
Firehouse
Paul Stanley Guitar Solo
Exciter
War Machine
Gimme More
Vinnie Vincent Guitar Solo - reprise
Gene Simmons Bass Solo
I Love It Loud
I Still Love You
Eric Carr Drum Solo
Young and Wasted
Love Gun
Black Diamond
Lick It Up
Rock and Roll All Nite
Strutter

OCTOBER 24, 1983

Leicester, England
De Monfort Hall
Opening Acts: Heavy Pettin', Helix
Capacity: 2,300
Promoters: Kennedy Street Entertainment, MCP
Archived: Audio

■ SET LIST

Creatures of the Night
Detroit Rock City
Cold Gin
Fits Like a Glove
Firehouse
Paul Stanley Guitar Solo
Exciter
War Machine
Gimme More
Vinnie Vincent Guitar Solo - reprise
Gene Simmons Bass Solo
I Love It Loud
I Still Love You
Eric Carr Drum Solo
Young and Wasted
Love Gun
Black Diamond
Lick It Up
Rock and Roll All Nite

OCTOBER 25, 1983

Poole, England
Leisure Centre
Opening Acts: Heavy Pettin', Helix
Capacity: 2,500
Promoters: Kennedy Street Entertainment, MCP
Archived: Audio

■ SET LIST

Creatures of the Night
Detroit Rock City
Cold Gin
Fits Like a Glove
Firehouse
Paul Stanley Guitar Solo
Exciter
War Machine
Gimme More
Vinnie Vincent Guitar Solo - reprise
Gene Simmons Bass Solo
I Love It Loud
I Still Love You
Eric Carr Drum Solo
Young and Wasted

Love Gun
Black Diamond
Lick It Up
Rock and Roll All Nite
Strutter

OCTOBER 27, 1983

Glasgow, Scotland
Apollo Theatre
Opening Acts: Heavy Pettin', Helix
Capacity: 3,100
Promoters: Kennedy Street Entertainment, MCP
Archived: Audio
■ **SET LIST:**
Creatures of the Night
Detroit Rock City
Cold Gin
Fits Like a Glove
Firehouse
Paul Stanley Guitar Solo
Exciter
[War Machine]
Gimme More
Vinnie Vincent Guitar Solo - reprise
Gene Simmons Bass Solo
[I Love It Loud]
I Still Love You
[Eric Carr Drum Solo]
Young and Wasted
Love Gun
Black Diamond
Lick It Up
Strutter
Rock and Roll All Nite

OCTOBER 28, 1983

Edinburgh, Scotland
Playhouse Theatre
Opening Acts: Heavy Pettin', Helix
Capacity: 3,100
Promoters: Kennedy Street Entertainment, MCP
Archived: Audio
■ **SET LIST**
See October 24, 1983.

OCTOBER 29, 1983

Newcastle, England
City Hall
Opening Acts: Heavy Pettin', Helix
Capacity: 2,300
Promoters: Kennedy Street Entertainment, MCP
Archived: Audio
■ **SET LIST**
See October 24, 1983.

OCTOBER 31, 1983

Paris, France
Espace Ballard
Opening Act: Helix
Capacity: 6,000
Promoter: KCP
Archived: Audio
■ **SET LIST**
See October 24, 1983.

NOVEMBER 1, 1983

Offenbach (Frankfurt a.M.), West Germany
Stadthalle
Opening Act: Helix
Capacity: 3,000
Promoter: Top Concerts
Archived: Audio
■ **SET LIST**
Creatures of the Night
Detroit Rock City
Cold Gin
Fits Like a Glove

Firehouse
Paul Stanley Guitar Solo
Exciter
War Machine
Gimme More
Vinnie Vincent Guitar Solo - reprise
Gene Simmons Bass Solo
I Love It Loud
I Still Love You
Eric Carr Drum Solo
Young and Wasted
Love Gun
Black Diamond
Lick It Up
Rock and Roll All Nite
■ Paul and Gene played the main riff from "Almost Human," just prior to "Lick It Up."

NOVEMBER 2, 1983

München, West Germany
Löwenbraükeller
Opening Act: Helix

Capacity: 1,800
Promoter: Top Concerts
■ While in West Germany, KISS made a brief stop at a TV studio to lip-synch "All Hell's Breakin' Loose" for a show called *Bananas*.

NOVEMBER 3, 1983

Bâle, Switzerland
Sporthalle St. Jakob
Opening Act: Helix
Capacity: 8,000
Promoter: Top Concerts
Archived: Audio
■ **SET LIST**
See October 24, 1983.
■ Before "Lick It Up," Vinnie played an excerpt from "Oh Susannah."

NOVEMBER 4, 1983

Sindelfingen (Stuttgart), West Germany
Sindelfingen Messehalle
Opening Act: Helix

Capacity: 5,000
Promoter: Top Concerts
Archived: Audio
■ **SET LIST**
See November 1, 1983.

NOVEMBER 6, 1983

Nürnberg, West Germany
Hammerleinhalle
Opening Act: Helix
Capacity: 3,000
Promoter: Top Concerts
Archived: Audio
■ **SET LIST**
See October 24, 1983.
■ The band briefly segued into Led Zeppelin's "Whole Lotta Love" prior to "Rock and Roll All Nite." At various points throughout the concert, Paul sang some lead vocal melodies an octave lower than usual, apparently to ease the strain on his voice because he was suffering from a cold.

NOVEMBER 7, 1983

Linz, Austria
Stadthalle
Opening Act: Helix
Capacity: 3,800
Promoter: Stimmen De Weld Wien

NOVEMBER 8, 1983

Wien, Austria
Stadthalle
Opening Act: Helix
Attendance: 3,500   Capacity: 3,500
Promoter: Stimmen De Weld Wien
Archived: Audio
■ **SET LIST**
See November 1, 1983.
■ Tickets sold for a September 25 appearance in Wien were honored at the band's eventual November 8 appearance. The September concert was announced prior to the band removing their makeup, though no other tour dates for that time period are known to have been advertised.

NOVEMBER 9, 1983

Graz, Austria
Liedenan Stadthalle
Opening Act: Helix
Capacity: 5,000
Promoter: Stimmen De Weld Wien

NOVEMBER 11, 1983

Essen, West Germany
Grughalle
Opening Act: Helix
Capacity: 3,000
Promoter: Top Concerts
Archived: Video
■ **SET LIST**
Creatures of the Night
Detroit Rock City
Cold Gin
Firehouse
Fits Like a Glove
Paul Stanley Guitar Solo
Exciter
War Machine
Gimme More
Vinnie Vincent Guitar Solo - reprise
Gene Simmons Bass Solo
I Love It Loud
I Still Love You
Eric Carr Drum Solo
Young and Wasted

Love Gun
Black Diamond
Lick It Up
Rock and Roll All Nite

NOVEMBER 12, 1983

Lille, France
Fuire Internationale
Opening Act: Helix
Capacity: 5,000
Promoter: KCP

NOVEMBER 13, 1983

Bruxelles, Belgium
Vorst Nationaal
Opening Act: Helix
Attendance: 3,998   Capacity: 6,000
Promoter: Make It Happen
Archived: Audio
■ **SET LIST**
See October 24, 1983.

NOVEMBER 15, 1983

Lausanne, Switzerland
Halle des Festes
Opening Act: Helix
Attendance: 4,900
Archived: Audio
Promoter: Good News Agency
■ **SET LIST**
Creatures of the Night
Detroit Rock City
Cold Gin
Fits Like a Glove
Firehouse
Paul Stanley Guitar Solo
Exciter
War Machine
Gimme More
Vinnie Vincent Guitar Solo - [reprise]
Gene Simmons Bass Solo
I Love It Loud
I Still Love You
Eric Carr Drum Solo
Young and Wasted
Love Gun
Black Diamond
Lick It Up
Rock and Roll All Nite

NOVEMBER 17, 1983

Århus, Denmark
Vejlby-Risskov Hallen
Opening Act: Helix
Capacity: 2,500
Promoter: International Concert Organization

NOVEMBER 18, 1983

Göteborg, Sweden
Scandinavium
No Opening Act
Attendance: 7,774   Capacity: 7,774
Promoter: EMA Telstar
Archived: Audio
■ **SET LIST**
See October 24, 1983.
■ Helix was scheduled to open the show but canceled.

NOVEMBER 19, 1983

Johanneshov (Stockholm), Sweden
Hovet
Opening Act: Helix
Attendance: 9,200   Capacity: 9,200
Promoter: EMA Telstar
Archived: Audio

■ **SET LIST**
Creatures of the Night
Detroit Rock City
Cold Gin
Fits Like a Glove
Firehouse
Paul Stanley Guitar Solo
Exciter
War Machine
Gimme More
Vinnie Vincent Guitar Solo - reprise
Gene Simmons Bass Solo
I Love It Loud
I Still Love You
Eric Carr Drum Solo
Young and Wasted
Love Gun
Black Diamond
[Lick It Up]
[Rock and Roll All Nite]

NOVEMBER 20, 1983

Malmö, Sweden
Ishallen
Opening Act: Helix
Attendance: 4,000   Capacity: 5,000
Promoter: EMA Telstar
Archived: Audio
■ **SET LIST**
Creatures of the Night
Detroit Rock City
Cold Gin
Fits Like a Glove
Firehouse
Paul Stanley Guitar Solo
Exciter
War Machine
Gimme More
Vinnie Vincent Guitar Solo - [reprise]
Gene Simmons Bass Solo
I Love It Loud
I Still Love You
Eric Carr Drum Solo
Young and Wasted
Love Gun
Black Diamond
Lick It Up
[Rock and Roll All Nite]
■ Prior to "Gimme More," the band played part of "Winchester Cathedral," a 1966 hit by the New Vaudeville Band. Also, Vinnie Vincent's solo included a short interlude from "Over The Rainbow."

NOVEMBER 21, 1983

Hillerød, Denmark
Frederiksborg Hallen
No Opening Act
Promoter: International Concert Organization
Archived: Audio
■ **SET LIST**
[Creatures of the Night]
[Detroit Rock City]
Cold Gin
Fits Like a Glove
Firehouse
Paul Stanley Guitar Solo
Exciter
War Machine
Gimme More
Vinnie Vincent Guitar Solo - reprise
Gene Simmons Bass Solo
I Love It Loud
I Still Love You
Eric Carr Drum Solo
Young and Wasted

Love Gun
Black Diamond
Lick It Up
[Rock and Roll All Nite]

■ There was no opening act as Helix opted to play Århus instead of Hillerød on this evening.

Helsingfors, Finland
Icehalle
Opening Act: Helix
Capacity: 5,200
Promoter: International Concert Organization

Uleåborg (Oulu), Finland
Icehalle
Opening Act: Helix
Capacity: 4,000
Promoter: International Concert Organization
Archived: Audio
■ **SET LIST**
Creatures of the Night
Detroit Rock City
Cold Gin
Fits Like a Glove
Firehouse
Paul Stanley Guitar Solo
Exciter
War Machine
Gimme More
Vinnie Vincent Guitar Solo - reprise
Gene Simmons Bass Solo
I Love It Loud
I Still Love You
Eric Carr Drum Solo
Young and Wasted
Love Gun
Black Diamond
Medley: Polka/Country Jam - La Bamba - Honky Tonk
    Woman - Dixie - Oh Susannah - Dixie - Johnny B.
    Goode - instrumental jam
Whole Lotta Love
Lick It Up
[Rock and Roll All Nite]

■ This was the final show of the European tour.

Dave "Romeo" Bonilla: "Paul always did the rap before 'Love Gun' about going to the doctor's office and the nurse says, blah, blah, blah. One night, I came out in drag as a nurse. I told everyone except for the band that I was going to do this. I told the crew when I hit the stage that I want a blackout; I want one spotlight on Paul and the other on me. So, Paul started doing the rap about the doctor's office and the nurse. All of a sudden there is the blackout and the spotlight is on me. Paul said, 'As a matter of fact, here she is now.' And I came across the stage in a nurse's dress and pantyhose, with my hair up in a hat and makeup on. When he was talking about his dick, I gave him a tape measure, he grabbed one end and I had the other."

Atlanta, Georgia
The Omni
Opening Acts: Pat Travers Band, Axe
Attendance: 6,512   Capacity: 9,650
Promoter: High Tide Management
■ While in town, Gene and Paul taped an interview for a local TV program called *The Dance Show*.

Shortly after this concert, TV commercials to promote the tour began airing with live footage of the band from an unknown concert on the Lick It Up Tour. Since this was the band's first U.S. show without makeup, and knowing that The Omni did have an in-house video system, it is likely that the footage came from this concert, which was presumably archived and purchased by the band.

Augusta, Georgia
Augusta/Richmond County Civic Center
Opening Act: Axe
Attendance: 4,515   Capacity: 9,000
Promoter: High Tide Management
Archived: Audio
■ **SET LIST**
See November 1, 1983.

Lakeland, Florida
Lakeland Civic Center
Opening Acts: Pat Travers Band, Axe
Attendance: 6,256   Capacity: 8,136
Promoter: Cellar Door Concerts

Pembroke Pines (Hollywood), Florida
The Sportatorium
Opening Acts: Pat Travers Band, Axe
Capacity: 17,300
Promoter: Cellar Door Concerts
Archived: Audio
■ **SET LIST**
See November 19, 1983.

Jacksonville, Florida
Jacksonville Veterans Memorial Coliseum
Opening Acts: Pat Travers Band, Axe
Attendance: less than 3,000   Capacity: 10,228
Promoter: Cellar Door Concerts

Tallahassee, Florida
Tallahassee-Leon Co. Civic Center
Opening Act: Axe
Attendance: 2,343   Capacity: 4,000
Promoter: Fantasma Productions

Birmingham, Alabama
Boutwell Auditorium
Opening Acts: Vandenberg, Riot
Promoter: Ruffino & Vaughn
Archived: Audio
■ **SET LIST**
See October 24, 1983.

Memphis, Tennessee
Mid-South Coliseum
Opening Acts: Vandenberg, Riot
Attendance: 5,188   Capacity: 9,961
Promoter: Mid-South Concerts

New Orleans, Louisiana
Kiefer UNO Lakefront Arena
Opening Acts: Vandenberg, Riot
Promoter: Barry Mendelson Presents
Archived: Audio
■ **SET LIST**
Creatures of the Night
Detroit Rock City
Cold Gin
Fits Like a Glove

Paul Stanley Guitar Solo
Exciter
War Machine
Gimme More
Vinnie Vincent Guitar Solo - reprise
Gene Simmons Bass Solo
I Love It Loud
I Still Love You
Eric Carr Drum Solo
Young and Wasted
Love Gun
All Hell's Breakin' Loose
Black Diamond
Lick It Up
Rock and Roll All Nite

■ This is the first known live performance of "All Hell's Breakin' Loose." Additionally, Paul performed a few bars of "Beth" prior to "Rock and Roll All Nite." "Firehouse" was apparently not performed in New Orleans.

Biloxi, Mississippi
Mississippi Coast Coliseum
Opening Acts: Vandenberg, Riot
Attendance: 1,507   Capacity: 5,000
Promoter: Barry Mendelson Presents
■ The crowd of 1,507 was the smallest KISS has drawn in a full-sized arena since they began headlining regularly in 1975. Attendance was reportedly affected by a tropical storm on the evening of the show, though weather records do not indicate the presence of any tropical storms in the region.

Knoxville, Tennessee
Knoxville Civic Coliseum
Opening Acts: Vandenberg, Riot
Promoter: Sunshine Promotions
Archived: Audio
■ **SET LIST**
Creatures of the Night
Detroit Rock City
Cold Gin
Fits Like a Glove
Firehouse
Paul Stanley Guitar Solo
Gimme More
Vinnie Vincent Guitar Solo - reprise
War Machine
Gene Simmons Bass Solo
I Love It Loud
I Still Love You
Eric Carr Drum Solo
Young and Wasted
Love Gun
All Hell's Breakin' Loose
Black Diamond
[Lick It Up]
[Rock and Roll All Nite]
■ Vinnie incorporated "Mary Had a Little Lamb" into his solo at this gig.

Nashville, Tennessee
Nashville Municipal Auditorium
Opening Acts: Vandenberg, Riot
Attendance: 5,852   Capacity: 9,900
Promoter: Sound 70 Concerts
Archived: Audio
■ **SET LIST**
Creatures of the Night
Detroit Rock City
Cold Gin

Fits Like a Glove
Firehouse
[Paul Stanley Guitar Solo]
Gimme More
Vinnie Vincent Guitar Solo - reprise
War Machine
Gene Simmons Bass Solo
I Love It Loud
I Still Love You
Eric Carr Drum Solo
Young and Wasted
Love Gun
All Hell's Breakin' Loose
Black Diamond
Lick It Up
Rock and Roll All Nite

■ An edited version of the concert was later broadcast on the syndicated radio show the *King Biscuit Flower Hour.*

JANUARY 13, 1984

Dallas, Texas
Dallas County Convention Center Arena
Opening Acts: Vandenberg, Riot
Capacity: 7,500
Promoter: 462, Inc.
Archived: Audio
■ **SET LIST**
Creatures of the Night
Detroit Rock City
Cold Gin
Fits Like a Glove
Paul Stanley Guitar Solo
Exciter
War Machine
Gimme More
Vinnie Vincent Guitar Solo - reprise
Gene Simmons Bass Solo
I Love It Loud
I Still Love You
Eric Carr Drum Solo
Young and Wasted
Love Gun
All Hell's Breakin' Loose
Black Diamond
Lick It Up
Rock and Roll All Nite

■ Prior to "Rock and Roll All Nite," Gene was grabbed by the leg and pulled off the stage by an overzealous fan. He then jokingly sang the first line from "Beth." "Firehouse" was not performed, as no pyro was allowed at this show.

Reportedly, a week's worth of Polaroids from Gene's collection was stolen at the venue.

JANUARY 14, 1984

San Antonio, Texas
HemisFair Arena @ Henry B. Gonzalez Convention
   Center
Opening Acts: Vandenberg, Riot
Attendance: 6,659   Capacity: 8,701
Promoter: Stone City Attractions

JANUARY 16, 1984

Austin, Texas
City Coliseum
Opening Acts: Vandenberg, Riot
Attendance: 2,877   Capacity: 2,877
Promoter: Jam Presents of Texas

JANUARY 17, 1984

San Angelo, Texas
San Angelo Coliseum
Opening Acts: Vandenberg, Riot
Attendance: 2,770   Capacity: 3,500
Promoter: Jam Presents of Texas

JANUARY 18, 1984

Houston, Texas
Sam Houston Coliseum
Opening Acts: Vandenberg, Riot
Attendance: 4,870   Capacity: 6,818
Promoter: Pace Concerts
Archived: Audio
■ **SET LIST**
Creatures of the Night
Detroit Rock City
Cold Gin
Fits Like a Glove
Firehouse
Paul Stanley Guitar Solo
Gimme More
Vinnie Vincent Guitar Solo - reprise
War Machine
Gene Simmons Bass Solo
I Love It Loud
I Still Love You
Eric Carr Drum Solo
Young and Wasted
Love Gun
All Hell's Breakin' Loose
Black Diamond
Lick It Up
Rock and Roll All Nite

JANUARY 19, 1984

Corpus Christi, Texas
Memorial Coliseum
Opening Acts: Vandenberg, Riot
Attendance: 3,919   Capacity: 3,919
Promoter: Jam Presents of Texas
Archived: Audio
■ **SET LIST**
Creatures of the Night
Detroit Rock City
Cold Gin
Fits Like a Glove
Firehouse
Paul Stanley Guitar Solo
Gimme More
Vinnie Vincent Guitar Solo - reprise
War Machine
Gene Simmons Bass Solo
I Love It Loud
I Still Love You
Eric Carr Drum Solo
Young and Wasted
Love Gun
All Hell's Breakin' Loose
Black Diamond
[Lick It Up]
[Rock and Roll All Nite]

JANUARY 21, 1984

El Paso, Texas
El Paso County Coliseum
Opening Acts: Vandenberg, Riot
Attendance: 4,102   Capacity: 8,000
Promoters: Pace Concerts, Magic Concerts
Archived: Audio
■ **SET LIST**
Creatures of the Night
Detroit Rock City
Cold Gin
Fits Like a Glove
Firehouse
Paul Stanley Guitar Solo
Gimme More
Vinnie Vincent Guitar Solo - reprise
War Machine
Gene Simmons Bass Solo
I Love It Loud
I Still Love You

Eric Carr Drum Solo
Young and Wasted
Love Gun
All Hell's Breakin' Loose
Black Diamond
Lick It Up
[Rock and Roll All Nite]

JANUARY 22, 1984

Albuquerque, New Mexico
Tingley Coliseum
Opening Acts: Vandenberg, Riot
Capacity: 10,500
Promoter: Feyline Presents
Archived: Audio
■ **SET LIST**
Creatures of the Night
Detroit Rock City
Cold Gin
Fits Like a Glove
Firehouse
Paul Stanley Guitar Solo
Gimme More
Vinnie Vincent Guitar Solo - reprise
War Machine
Gene Simmons Bass Solo
[I Love It Loud]
I Still Love You
Eric Carr Drum Solo
Young and Wasted
Love Gun
All Hell's Breakin' Loose
Black Diamond
Lick It Up
Rock and Roll All Nite

■ Prior to "Rock and Roll All Nite," the band made a brief attempt to perform "Do You Love Me," and again Gene jokingly sang a few lines from "Beth."

JANUARY 23, 1984

Odessa, Texas
Ector County Coliseum
Opening Acts: Vandenberg, Riot
Attendance: 5,632   Capacity: 8,500
Promoters: Stardate Productions, Pace Concerts

JANUARY 25, 1984

Denver, Colorado
University of Denver Ice Arena
Opening Acts: Vandenberg, Riot
Capacity: 6,000
Promoter: Feyline Presents
■ Gene set his hair on fire during the show.

JANUARY 27, 1984

Long Beach, California
Long Beach Arena
Opening Acts: Vandenberg, Riot
Attendance: 7,383   Capacity: 12,750
Promoter: Avalon Attractions
Archived: Audio
■ **SET LIST**
See January 18. 1984.
■ Paul sang lead vocals on "Black Diamond."

JANUARY 28, 1984

Las Vegas, Nevada
Thomas & Mack Center
Opening Acts: Vandenberg, Riot
Capacity: 10,000
Promoter: Avalon Attractions
Archived: Audio
■ **SET LIST**
See January 18, 1984

JANUARY 29, 1984

Fresno, California
Selland Arena @ Fresno Convention Center
Opening Acts: Vandenberg, Riot
Attendance: 3,993   Capacity: 7,000
Promoter: Avalon Attractions
Archived: Audio
■ **SET LIST**
See January 19, 1984.

JANUARY 31, 1984

Reno, Nevada
Lawlor Events Center
Opening Acts: Vandenberg, Riot
Promoter: Bill Graham Presents
Archived: Audio
■ **SET LIST**
See January 18, 1984.
■ In Reno, a local union took out a full-page ad in the local campus paper *Stagebrush* urging fans to boycott the concert due to the hiring of non-union students at the venue. As if tickets sales weren't already bad enough on this tour . . .

FEBRUARY 1, 1984

Berkeley, California
Berkeley Community Theatre
Opening Acts: Vandenberg, Riot
Attendance: 5,773   Capacity: 5,773
Promoter: Bill Graham Presents
Archived: Audio
■ **SET LIST**
Creatures of the Night
Detroit Rock City
Cold Gin
Fits Like a Glove
Firehouse
Paul Stanley Guitar Solo
Gimme More
Vinnie Vincent Guitar Solo - reprise
War Machine
Gene Simmons Bass Solo
I Love It Loud
I Still Love You
Eric Carr Drum Solo
Young and Wasted
Love Gun
All Hell's Breakin' Loose
Black Diamond
Lick It Up
Rock and Roll All Nite

■ The show was originally scheduled for the San Francisco Civic Auditorium but was moved to a smaller venue due to slow ticket sales.

FEBRUARY 2, 1984

Bakersfield, California
Bakersfield Civic Auditorium
Opening Acts: Vandenberg, Riot
Attendance: 6,000   Capacity: 6,000
Promoter: Rock 'n' Chair Productions

FEBRUARY 3, 1984

San Bernardino, California
Orange Show Pavilion
Opening Acts: Vandenberg, Riot
Attendance: 4,173   Capacity: 6,000
Promoter: Avalon Attractions
Archived: Audio
■ **SET LIST**
See January 18, 1984.

FEBRUARY 5, 1984

Salt Lake City, Utah
O. Thayne Accord Arena @ Salt Palace Center
Opening Acts: Vandenberg, Riot
Capacity: 10,000
Promoter: United Concerts

FEBRUARY 8, 1984

Sioux City, Iowa
Sioux City Municipal Auditorium
Opening Acts: Vandenberg, Highfever
Attendance: 3,051   Capacity: 5,000
Promoter: Terry Drea Presents
■ There was a long pause prior to "Lick It Up" when Vinnie accidentally ripped the crotch out of his pants. Vixen was advertised as a second opening act, but they did not perform.

FEBRUARY 9, 1984

Omaha, Nebraska
Omaha Civic Auditorium
Opening Acts: Vandenberg, Heaven
Attendance: 5,059   Capacity: 11,000
Promoter: Contemporary Productions

FEBRUARY 10, 1984

Milwaukee, Wisconsin
Milwaukee Auditorium
Opening Acts: Vandenberg, Heaven
Promoter: Stardate Productions

Archived: Audio
■ **SET LIST**
Creatures of the Night
Detroit Rock City
Cold Gin
Fits Like a Glove
Firehouse
Paul Stanley Guitar Solo
Gimme More
[Vinnie Vincent Guitar Solo] - reprise
War Machine
[Gene Simmons Bass Solo]
I Love It Loud
I Still Love You
Eric Carr Drum Solo
Young and Wasted
Love Gun
All Hell's Breakin' Loose
Black Diamond
Lick It Up
Rock and Roll All Nite

FEBRUARY 11, 1984

Dubuque, Iowa
Dubuque Five Flags Center
Opening Acts: Vandenberg, Heaven
Attendance: 3,783   Capacity: 5,200
Promoter: Grandview Entertainment
Archived: Audio
■ **SET LIST**
See January 18, 1984.
■ Before "Rock and Roll All Nite," Paul performed a part of "Down On Your Knees," and Paul, Gene, and Eric briefly attempted "I Was Made for Lovin' You."

FEBRUARY 12, 1984

Bloomington (Minneapolis), Minnesota
Metropolitan Sports Center
Opening Acts: Vandenberg, Heaven
Attendance: 4,784   Capacity: 7,500
Promoter: Schon Productions

FEBRUARY 14, 1984

Green Bay, Wisconsin
Brown County Veterans Memorial Arena
Opening Acts: Vandenberg, Heaven
Attendance: 3,871   Capacity: 7,044
Promoter: Stardate Productions

FEBRUARY 15, 1984

Chicago, Illinois
University of Illinois-Chicago Pavilion
Opening Acts: Vandenberg, Heaven
Attendance: 2,500
Promoter: JAM Productions
Archived: Audio
■ **SET LIST**
See January 21, 1984.

FEBRUARY 16, 1984

Indianapolis, Indiana
Market Square Arena
Opening Acts: Vandenberg, Heaven
Attendance: 8,400   Capacity: 8,400
Promoter: Sunshine Promotions
Archived: Audio
■ **SET LIST**
Creatures of the Night
Detroit Rock City
Cold Gin
Fits Like a Glove
Firehouse
Paul Stanley Guitar Solo
Gimme More

KISS receiving their first gold albums in four years backstage in Long Beach.

ANASTASIA PANTSIOS

Vinnie Vincent Guitar Solo - reprise
War Machine
Gene Simmons Bass Solo
I Love It Loud
Exciter
Eric Carr Drum Solo
Young and Wasted
Love Gun
All Hell's Breakin' Loose
Black Diamond
Lick It Up
Rock and Roll All Nite

■ In what may have been an impromptu set list change, after "I Love It Loud" Paul began the intro to "I Still Love You," suddenly stopped, and then went into "Exciter."

FEBRUARY 17, 1984

Saginaw, Michigan
Wendler Arena @ Saginaw Civic Center
Opening Acts: Vandenberg, Heaven
Attendance: 7,300   Capacity: 7,300

Promoter: Belkin Productions
Archived: Audio
■ **SET LIST**
Creatures of the Night
Detroit Rock City
Cold Gin
Fits Like a Glove
Firehouse
Paul Stanley Guitar Solo
Gimme More
Vinnie Vincent Guitar Solo - reprise
War Machine
Gene Simmons Bass Solo
I Love It Loud
Exciter
Eric Carr Drum Solo
Young and Wasted
Love Gun
All Hell's Breakin' Loose
Black Diamond
Lick It Up
Rock and Roll All Nite

FEBRUARY 18, 1984

Detroit, Michigan
Cobo Arena
Opening Acts: Vandenberg, Heaven
Capacity: 13,000
Promoter: Belkin Productions
Archived: Audio
■ **SET LIST**
See January 18, 1984.
■ Vinnie's solo included a brief portion of Beethoven's Fifth Symphony.

FEBRUARY 19, 1984

Columbus, Ohio
Battelle Hall @ Ohio Center
Opening Acts: Vandenberg, Heaven
Capacity: 7,500
Promoter: Belkin Productions
Archived: Audio
■ **SET LIST**
Creatures of the Night
Detroit Rock City
Cold Gin
Fits Like a Glove
Firehouse
Paul Stanley Guitar Solo
Gimme More
Vinnie Vincent Guitar Solo - reprise
War Machine
Gene Simmons Bass Solo
I Love It Loud
I Still Love You
Eric Carr Drum Solo
[Young and Wasted]
[Love Gun]
[All Hell's Breakin' Loose]
[Black Diamond]
[Lick It Up]
[Rock and Roll All Nite]

FEBRUARY 21, 1984

Dayton, Ohio
Hara Arena & Exhibition Center
Opening Acts: Vandenberg, Heaven
Capacity: 8,000
Promoter: Belkin Productions

FEBRUARY 22, 1984

Richfield (Cleveland), Ohio
The Coliseum Theatre
Opening Acts: Vandenberg, Heaven
Promoter: Belkin Productions
Capacity: 9,000
Archived: Audio
■ **SET LIST**
[Creatures of the Night]
[Detroit Rock City]
[Cold Gin]
[Fits Like a Glove]
[Firehouse]
Paul Stanley Guitar Solo
Gimme More
Vinnie Vincent Guitar Solo - reprise
War Machine
Gene Simmons Bass Solo
I Love It Loud
I Still Love You
Eric Carr Drum Solo
Young and Wasted
Love Gun
All Hell's Breakin' Loose
Black Diamond
Lick It Up
Rock and Roll All Nite
■ KISS did an in-store at the Record Den in Great Northern Mall. Following the appearance, Gene,

Eric, and Paul were interviewed from the Record Den on *Live On Five*. The band explained Vinnie's absence as being due to an illness.

FEBRUARY 24, 1984

Worcester, Massachusetts
The Centrum
Opening Act: Accept
Attendance: 5,132   Capacity: 12,761
Promoter: Frank J. Russo
Archived: Audio

■ SET LIST
Creatures of the Night
Detroit Rock City
Cold Gin
Fits Like a Glove
Firehouse
Gimme More
Vinnie Vincent Guitar Solo - reprise
Paul Stanley Vocal Solo
I Still Love You
Gene Simmons Bass Solo
I Love It Loud
War Machine
Eric Carr Drum Solo
Young and Wasted
Love Gun
All Hell's Breaking Loose
Paul Stanley Guitar Solo
Black Diamond
Lick It Up

■ "Lick It Up" was the only encore; "Rock and Roll All Nite" was cut due to time constraints.

FEBRUARY 26, 1984

Hampton, Virginia
Hampton Coliseum
Opening Acts: Accept, Great White
Capacity: 7,000
Promoter: Cellar Door Concerts

■ Gene lit his hair on fire severely enough to send his bass crashing to the stage floor.

FEBRUARY 28, 1984

Baltimore, Maryland
Baltimore Civic Center
Opening Act: Accept

Attendance: 4,402   Capacity: 12,200
Promoter: Cellar Door Concerts
Archived: Audio

■ SET LIST
Creatures of the Night
Detroit Rock City
Cold Gin
Fits Like a Glove
Firehouse
[Paul Stanley Guitar Solo]
Gimme More
Vinnie Vincent Guitar Solo - reprise
War Machine
[Gene Simmons Bass Solo]
I Love It Loud
I Still Love You
Eric Carr Drum Solo
Young and Wasted
Love Gun
All Hell's Breakin' Loose
Black Diamond
Lick It Up
Rock and Roll All Nite

MARCH 1, 1984

New Haven, Connecticut
New Haven Veterans Memorial Coliseum
Opening Act: Accept
Attendance: 5,527   Capacity: 9,900
Promoter: Cross Country Concerts
Archived: Audio

■ SET LIST
See January 22, 1984.

MARCH 3, 1984

Upper Darby (Philadelphia), Pennsylvania
Tower Theater
Opening Act: Accept
Attendance: 3,020   Capacity: 3,020
Promoters: East Coast Concerts, Concert Co.
    Presentations
Archived: Audio

■ SET LIST
See January 19, 1984.

MARCH 4, 1984

Pittsburgh, Pennsylvania

Stanley Theatre
Opening Act: Accept
Attendance: 3,270   Capacity: 3,500
Promoter: DiCesare-Engler Productions
Archived: Audio

■ SET LIST
See January 18, 1984.

■ Due to the small size of the venue, no pyro was used.

MARCH 5, 1984

Erie, Pennsylvania
Lewis J. Tullio Arena @ Erie Civic Center
Opening Act: Accept
Capacity: 3,500
Promoter: Belkin Productions

■ The day after the gig in Erie, KISS made an in-store appearance at a Sam Goody's in Manhattan.

MARCH 7, 1984

Binghamton, New York
Broome Co. Veterans Memorial Arena
Opening Act: Accept
Capacity: 7,200
Promoter: Magic City Productions
Archived: Audio

■ SET LIST
Creatures of the Night
Detroit Rock City
Cold Gin
Fits Like a Glove
Firehouse
Paul Stanley Guitar Solo
Gimme More
Vinnie Vincent Guitar Solo - reprise
War Machine
Gene Simmons Bass Solo
I Love It Loud
Exciter
Eric Carr Drum Solo
Young and Wasted
Love Gun
All Hell's Breakin' Loose
Black Diamond
Lick It Up
Rock and Roll All Nite

■ Just prior to "Exciter," a brief attempt at "I Still Love You" was made. This is the last known performance of "Exciter."

MARCH 8, 1984

Poughkeepsie, New York
Mid-Hudson Civic Center
Opening Act: Accept
Capacity: 3,000
Promoter: Harvey & Corky

MARCH 9, 1984

New York, New York
Radio City Music Hall
Opening Act: Accept
Attendance: 5,874   Capacity: 5,874
Promoter: RCMH Productions
Archived: Audio

■ SET LIST
See February 10, 1984.

■ New Jersey act Monroe was initially scheduled to open both Radio City Music Hall shows, but was replaced by Accept.

At the Friday night show, Gene once again set his hair on fire and Peter Criss was in attendance. Also, Paul and Vinnie reportedly got into some sort of physical confrontation that was off stage yet still in view of the audience. "I recall

NORMAN BOUTHILLIER

something like that being talked about," C.K. Lendt recalls, "but I didn't witness it. It doesn't surprise me. They really didn't get along that well."

MARCH 10, 1984
New York, New York
Radio City Music Hall
Opening Act: Accept
Attendance: 5,874   Capacity: 5,874
Promoter: RCMH Productions
Archived: Audio
■ SET LIST
See January 18, 1984.

MARCH 12, 1984
Quebec, Quebec, Canada
Colisée de Quebec
Opening Act: Accept
Capacity: 11,285
Promoter: Donald K. Donald
Archived: Video
■ SET LIST
See January 18, 1984.

MARCH 13, 1984
Montréal, Quebec, Canada
Forum de Montréal
Opening Act: Accept
Attendance: 4,371   Capacity: 10,000
Promoter: Donald K. Donald
Archived: Audio
■ SET LIST
Creatures of the Night

Detroit Rock City
Cold Gin
Fits Like a Glove
Firehouse
[Paul Stanley Guitar Solo]
Gimme More
Vinnie Vincent Guitar Solo - reprise
War Muchine
Gene Simmons Bass Solo
[I Love It Loud]
I Still Love You
Eric Carr Drum Solo
Young and Wasted
Love Gun
All Hell's Breakin' Loose
Black Diamond
Lick It Up
Rock and Roll All Nite
■ On the day of the show, KISS made an in-store appearance at a Rock en Stock record store.

MARCH 15, 1984
Toronto, Ontario, Canada
Maple Leaf Gardens
Opening Act: Accept
Attendance: 14,000   Capacity: 14,000
Promoter: Concert Productions Int'l
Archived: Audio
■ SET LIST
See January 18, 1984.
■ During the afternoon, Paul and Eric stopped by City TV to cohost *Toronto Rocks*, which was broadcast live.

MARCH 17, 1984
Evansville, Indiana
Roberts Municipal Stadium
Opening Act: Accept
Attendance: 5,369
Promoter: Sunshine Promotions
Archived: Audio
■ SET LIST
Creatures of the Night
Detroit Rock City
Cold Gin
Fits Like a Glove
Firehouse
[Paul Stanley Guitar Solo]
Gimme More
Vinnie Vincent Guitar Solo - reprise
War Machine
[Gene Simmons Bass Solo]
I Love It Loud
I Still Love You
Eric Carr Drum Solo
Young and Wasted
Love Gun
All Hell's Breakin' Loose
Black Diamond
Lick It Up
Rock and Roll All Nite
■ Paul played a bit of the Rolling Stones' "Angie," during his intro to "Black Diamond."

This was Vinnie Vincent's final appearance as a member of KISS. The concert also marked the final live performances of "Gimme More" and "All Hell's Breakin' Loose."

CHAPTER 17

ANIMALIZE TOUR

Number of Shows: 119
Start Date: September 30, 1984 - Brighton, England
End Date: March 29, 1985 - East Rutherford, New Jersey
Countries: Belgium, Canada, Denmark, England, France, The Netherlands, Norway, Scotland, Sweden, Switzerland, U.S.A., West Germany
Opening Acts: Bon Jovi; Dokken; Krokus; Queensrÿche; Sentinel; Steelover; W.A.S.P.
Average Attendance: 6,209

KISS's short-lived relationship with Vinnie Vincent effectively ended with the conclusion of the Lick It Up Tour in March 1984, which left KISS looking for a new band member for the third time in four years. While canvassing the industry for a new guitar player, Paul sought the advice of renowned guitar luthier Grover Jackson, who suggested a guitar teacher from Orange County, California as the ideal candidate for the job.

Mark St. John was hired as KISS's lead guitarist in May. Chris Lendt recalls St. John joining the band: "Mark didn't have a lot of professional playing experience and he had difficulty fitting in, which was understandable because Mark came out of a small-town environment in Southern California, and all of a sudden he's playing in the big leagues. At first, KISS felt Mark's looks and the way he appeared on stage would make him fit in with KISS, and that he would be accepted."

The band's new album, *Animalize,* was recorded at Right Track Recording Studios in New York City in June and July 1984. The primary producer for the album was Paul Stanley, with Michael James Jackson producing the drum tracks, and Gene Simmons listed as the associate producer. As was typical, the album had several notable (though uncredited) musicians providing session work: Jean Beauvoir of the Plasmatics provided bass-work on several tracks, and drummer Allan Schwartzberg added various fills throughout the record. Most importantly, Bruce Kulick, who would soon figure into the equation more than he realized, contributed to two tracks including the guitar solo on "Lonely is the Hunter," and the solo at the end of "Murder in High Heels."

Gene's production credit was essentially a ceremonial title, as he was on location in Vancouver filming his feature-film debut *Runaway* throughout many of the *Animalize* recording sessions. Yet, despite Gene's absence, *Animalize* was KISS's most successful album of the 1980s. Bolstered by strong initial support from MTV and radio, *Animalize* became KISS's first LP since *Dynasty* to reach the top 20 on the *Billboard* charts, and eventually enjoyed the longest run on the charts of any KISS album since *Rock and Roll Over.* It was certified Gold on December 3, and Platinum nine days later on December 12.

KISS held rehearsals for the Animalize Tour in September at SIR. studios in New York City. During the rehearsals, Mark St. John began to experience problems with his hand and wrist; he was diagnosed with an arthritic condition known as Reiter's Syndrome that left him unable to rehearse or start the tour with KISS. In the interim, Bruce Kulick was hired as a temporary replacement and served as KISS's lead guitarist for the European leg of the tour, though Kulick also missed ten days of rehearsal due to tendonitis. When KISS returned to tour North America in November, Kulick was still performing with the band, though Mark St. John began traveling with them in hopes that his medical condition would resolve itself, and he would be able to rejoin the band.

Chris Lendt recalls the primary factor behind St. John's eventual dismissal: "He was very capable, but he had a difficult time rhythmically keeping in time with others, and he would play all of the solos different. That's not what KISS wanted. KISS wanted a guitar player that would play the solos note-for-note the way they had always been played. Apparently, that was something that Mark wasn't used to and he was much more extemporaneous.

"It's very hard to bring people into a band that's existed for so many years where you have two dominating forces that have very specific ideas about what they believe works and doesn't work. Gene and Paul felt they had a certain formula to KISS and, naturally, they wanted the integrity of that formula to be maintained."

NORMAN BOUTHILLIER

A side view of the stage used for KISS's European tour in 1984. Notice the refurbished portions of the band's stage from their 1980 Unmasked Tour of Europe.

"When Mark developed the arthritic condition in his hand it was really the final blow, but they were planning on having him out of the band in any case."

St. John's condition improved enough for him to perform in parts of three concerts on the tour, but on December 7, in Fort Wayne, St. John was fired and sent home. Bruce Kulick was named as KISS's permanent lead guitarist the following day in Detroit.

Bruce Kulick had first been introduced to KISS back in 1977 when he met Paul through his older brother Bob Kulick. Unlike Mark St. John, Bruce had a considerable amount of experience under his belt. In 1976, a band called The Andrea True Connection, which featured vocalist and former adult cinema actress Andrea True, had scored a hit with the single "More, More, More." Kulick was brought on board when a band was assembled to do promotional appearances in support of the album. The Andrea True Connection appeared on several television shows including *The Midnight Special* and *Don Kirshner's Rock Concert.* Later, Bruce became a member of Meatloaf's *Bat out of Hell* touring band and made a notable TV appearance when the band was the musical guest on *Saturday Night Live,* making him the only member of KISS to ever appear on *SNL.* It is not commonly known, but Bruce had first auditioned for KISS when a replacement was sought for Ace in 1982.

Chris Lendt: "I think that Bruce fit into the band very well, and the fact that he lasted until 1996 proves that. Bruce was a much more agreeable personality than Vinnie Vincent, and he was more mature and more experienced than Mark St. John. Bruce had grown up and lived in Queens and he had certain values and ways of thinking that were much closer to what Paul and Gene were all about, culturally and socially."

Most fans in the U.S. found out that Bruce had become a permanent member via the heavy metal news on "Hit Parader's Heavy Metal Heroes," a half-hour segment on the USA network's *Night Flight* series.

"Heaven's On Fire," the first single released from *Animalize,* received strong initial support on AOR stations, even crossing over to the current hits radio (CHR) format in some markets as a direct result of MTV's impact on radio programming. The cable network purchased the exclusive U.S. rights to the "Heaven's On Fire" video for the first month, even going so far as to repeatedly air a commercial announcing the video's pending world premiere. "*Animalize* was a big radio record," states Danny Goldberg, "and clearly it was something that was going to be some kind of a hit. MTV has always been sensitive to radio, and they cherry pick what they think will be hot. Anything that smelled like a hit was something that they wanted some sort of exclusivity on. For us, it was a matter of building on the success of *Lick It Up,* which had doubled the sales of the previous record. KISS had done their first tour without makeup and were reenergized in the community, and then they made this fantastic record. Part of it was creating the cultural environment for them, but they came through and wrote a hit."

On January 27, 1985, MTV broadcast an hour of KISS's December 8 concert in Detroit on their popular *MTV's Saturday Night Concert* series, a move that would have been unthinkable just a year prior. A more complete version of the concert was released as a home video on April 12, under the title *Animalize Live Uncensored.*

Much like the album, the tour was considerably more successful than any of the band's recent outings. Owing a great debt to the frequent coverage by MTV, attendance for the Animalize Tour was up more than 22 percent per show over the Lick It Up Tour.

Winterland continued to handle the merchandising responsibilities for KISS. Although it was nothing in comparison to the band's merchandizing zenith in the late 1970s, the Animalize era was easily the most heavily merchandized period of the band's non-makeup years. Winterland expanded the retail merchandise assortment considerably, which now included such useful items as: bandanas, headbands, a pillow, a scarf, a tour jacket, tapestries, a seemingly endless supply of buttons, and even guitar picks fashioned into earrings, to name just a few. Winterland also redesigned the tourbook and artwork on the T-shirts to include Bruce once he became a permanent member.

KISS used two entirely different stages for the Animalize Tour, one in Europe, and another in North America. For Europe, KISS brought back the European version of the Unmasked Tour stage. The four-year-old stage was given a new look, with an animal-skin motif painted on the stage floor, ramps, and amp stacks. Tait Towers designed the stage for the North American tour. It featured heavy-duty steel grate ramps in front of and flanking Eric's drum riser, with a platform and two short staircases built above and behind the riser. Steel grates also ran along the front border of the stage.

The production also featured an elaborate lighting rig. During "Black Diamond," one end of a large support truss would descend toward the stage, creating a ramp up which Paul, Gene, and Bruce would ascend. They would make their way to a platform in the center of the truss, which would then descend to bring the three back to the main stage.

KISS's costumes continued to be fairly clichéd, rock-star garb with an animal-pelt look added to mimic the *Animalize* album cover, and Gene was now wearing a none-too-subtle wig to cover the short haircut he had cultivated for his role in *Runaway.*

KISS's fourth lead guitarist, Bruce Kulick, pictured here on the Animalize Tour.

More than half of the *Animalize* album was included in the show over the course of the tour, with "Heaven's On Fire," "Under the Gun," "I've Had Enough (Into the Fire)," "Get All You Can Take," "Burn Bitch Burn," and "Thrills in the Night" each performed live at various points.

Several other changes were also evident. Eric Carr was featured more on the Animalize Tour than any other in his 11-year tenure with KISS: in addition to his drum solo and handling the lead vocals on "Black Diamond," Eric was also singing lead on "Young and Wasted," a responsibility previously charged to Gene. Additionally, the tour was KISS's first that did not include "Firehouse," which forced Gene's fire-breathing act to find a new home at the end of "War Machine." And, most of the older, classic KISS songs, especially "Cold Gin," were played at an almost laughably fast pace, in an attempt to give them a more contemporary feel.

Lastly, for the first time in KISS's career, Gene's solo was actually structured and musical in nature, as opposed to the one-note collection of "buffalo farts" (as *Rolling Stone's* Charles M. Young had aptly termed it) that had been typical of the bass accompaniment in his blood-spitting routine. On several occasions, Gene included excerpts of Edvard Grieg's "In the Hall of the Mountain King" in his solo.

SEPTEMBER 30, 1984

Brighton, England
The Brighton Centre
Opening Act: Bon Jovi
Capacity: 5,000
Promoters: Kennedy Street Entertainment, MCP
Archived: Audio
■ **SET LIST**
I've Had Enough (Into the Fire)
Detroit Rock City
Burn Bitch Burn
Cold Gin
Strutter
Paul Stanley Guitar Solo
Under the Gun
Fits Like a Glove
Get All You Can Take
Eric Carr Drum Solo
Young and Wasted
Heaven's On Fire
War Machine
I Still Love You
I Love It Loud
Love Gun
Creatures of the Night
Rock and Roll All Nite
Lick It Up
■ These were the first and final performances of "Burn Bitch Burn" and "Get All You Can Take."

OCTOBER 1, 1984

Southampton, England
Gaumont Theatre
Opening Act: Bon Jovi
Capacity: 2,200
Promoters: Kennedy Street Entertainment, MCP
Archived: Audio
■ **SET LIST**
Detroit Rock City
Cold Gin
Strutter
Fits Like a Glove
Paul Stanley Guitar Solo

Under the Gun
Heaven's On Fire
War Machine
Eric Carr Drum Solo
Young and Wasted
I've Had Enough (Into The Fire)
I Still Love You
Lick It Up
Love Gun
Gene Simmons Bass Solo
I Love It Loud
Rock and Roll All Nite
Creatures of the Night
Oh Susannah
Black Diamond

OCTOBER 2, 1984

St. Austell, England
Cornwall Coliseum
Opening Act: Bon Jovi
Capacity: 3,000
Promoters: Kennedy Street Entertainment, MCP
Archived: Audio
■ **SET LIST**
Detroit Rock City
Cold Gin
Strutter
Fits Like a Glove
Paul Stanley Guitar Solo
Under the Gun
Heaven's On Fire
War Machine
Eric Carr Drum Solo
Young and Wasted
I've Had Enough (Into the Fire)
I Still Love You
Lick It Up
Gene Simmons Bass Solo
I Love It Loud
Love Gun
Rock and Roll All Nite
Creatures of the Night
[Black Diamond]

OCTOBER 4, 1984

Manchester, England
Apollo Theatre
Opening Act: Bon Jovi
Capacity: 2,600
Promoters: Kennedy Street Entertainment, MCP
Archived: Audio
■ **SET LIST**
Detroit Rock City
Cold Gin
Strutter
Fits Like a Glove
Paul Stanley Guitar Solo
Under the Gun
Heaven's On Fire
War Machine
Eric Carr Drum Solo
Young and Wasted
I've Had Enough (Into the Fire)
I Still Love You
Lick It Up
Gene Simmons Bass Solo
I Love It Loud
Love Gun
Rock and Roll All Nite
Creatures of the Night
Black Diamond

OCTOBER 5, 1984

Glasgow, Scotland
Apollo Theatre
Opening Act: Bon Jovi
Capacity: 3,100

Promoters: Kennedy Street Entertainment, MCP
Archived: Audio
■ **SET LIST**
Detroit Rock City
Cold Gin
Strutter
Fits Like a Glove
Paul Stanley Guitar Solo
Under the Gun
Heaven's On Fire
War Machine
I've Had Enough (Into the Fire)
Eric Carr Drum Solo
Young and Wasted
I Still Love You
Lick It Up
Gene Simmons Bass Solo
I Love It Loud
Love Gun
Rock and Roll All Nite
Creatures of the Night
Black Diamond
■ An edited version of this concert was later broadcast on the radio.

OCTOBER 6, 1984

Edinburgh, Scotland
Playhouse Theatre
Opening Act: Bon Jovi
Capacity: 3,100
Promoters: Kennedy Street Entertainment, MCP
Archived: Audio
■ **SET LIST**
See October 4, 1984.

OCTOBER 7, 1984

Newcastle, England
City Hall
Opening Act: Bon Jovi
Capacity: 2,200
Promoters: Kennedy Street Entertainment, MCP
Archived: Audio
■ **SET LIST**
See October 2, 1984.

OCTOBER 8, 1984

Newcastle, England
City Hall
Opening Act: Bon Jovi
Capacity: 2,200
Promoters: Kennedy Street Entertainment, MCP
Archived: Audio
■ **SET LIST**
Detroit Rock City
Cold Gin
Strutter
Fits Like a Glove
Paul Stanley Guitar Solo
Under the Gun
Heaven's On Fire
War Machine
Eric Carr Drum Solo
Young and Wasted
I've Had Enough (Into the Fire)
I Still Love You
Lick It Up
Gene Simmons Bass Solo
I Love It Loud
Love Gun
Rock and Roll All Nite
Creatures of the Night
Oh Susannah
Black Diamond
■ Following "Creatures of the Night," the band played a portion of "Winchester Cathedral."

OCTOBER 10, 1984

Leicester, England
De Montfort Hall
Opening Act: Bon Jovi
Capacity: 2,500
Promoters: Kennedy Street Entertainment, MCP
Archived: Audio

■ SET LIST

Detroit Rock City
Cold Gin
Strutter
Fits Like a Glove
Paul Stanley Guitar Solo
Under the Gun
Heaven's On Fire
War Machine
Eric Carr Drum Solo
Young and Wasted
I've Had Enough (Into the Fire)
I Still Love You
Lick It Up
Gene Simmons Bass Solo
I Love It Loud
Love Gun
Rock and Roll All Nite
[Creatures of the Night]
[Black Diamond]

OCTOBER 11, 1984

Ipswich, England
Gaumont Hall
Opening Act: Bon Jovi
Capacity: 1,666
Promoters: Kennedy Street Entertainment, MCP
Archived: Audio

■ PARTIAL SET LIST

Detroit Rock City
Cold Gin
Strutter
Fits Like a Glove
Heaven's On Fire
Under the Gun
I've Had Enough (Into the Fire)
I Still Love You
I Love It Loud
Creatures of the Night
Love Gun

■ The songs listed above were later broadcast on the radio.

OCTOBER 12, 1984

Stafford, England
New Bingley Hall
Opening Act: Bon Jovi
Capacity: 9,000
Promoters: Kennedy Street Entertainment, MCP
Archived: Audio

■ SET LIST

Detroit Rock City
Cold Gin
Strutter
Fits Like a Glove
Heaven's On Fire
Paul Stanley Guitar Solo
Under the Gun
War Machine
Eric Carr Drum Solo
Young and Wasted
I've Had Enough (Into the Fire)
I Still Love You
Gene Simmons Bass Solo
I Love It Loud
Love Gun
Creatures of the Night
Rock and Roll All Nite

Lick It Up
Black Diamond

■ KISS's pyro scorched the ceiling of the venue.

OCTOBER 13, 1984

Leeds, England
Queens Hall
Opening Act: Bon Jovi
Capacity: 6,500
Promoters: Kennedy Street Entertainment, MCP
Archived: Audio

■ SET LIST

Detroit Rock City
Cold Gin
Strutter
Fits Like a Glove
Heaven's On Fire
Paul Stanley Guitar Solo
Under the Gun
War Machine
Eric Carr Drum Solo
Young and Wasted
I've Had Enough (Into the Fire)
Gene Simmons Bass Solo
I Love It Loud
I Still Love You
[Love Gun]
Creatures of the Night
Rock and Roll All Nite
Lick It Up
Oh Susannah
Black Diamond

OCTOBER 14, 1984

London, England
Wembley Arena
Opening Act: Bon Jovi
Capacity: 8,000
Promoters: Kennedy Street Entertainment, MCP
Archived: Audio

■ SET LIST

Detroit Rock City
Cold Gin
Strutter
Fits Like a Glove
Heaven's On Fire
Paul Stanley Guitar Solo
Under the Gun
War Machine
Eric Carr Drum Solo
Young and Wasted
I've Had Enough (Into the Fire)
Gene Simmons Bass Solo
I Love It Loud
I Still Love You
Creatures of the Night
Love Gun
Rock and Roll All Nite
Oh Susannah
Lick It Up
Black Diamond

OCTOBER 15, 1984

London, England
Wembley Arena
Opening Act: Bon Jovi
Capacity: 8,000
Promoters: Kennedy Street Entertainment, MCP
Archived: Audio

■ SET LIST

Detroit Rock City
Cold Gin
Strutter
Fits Like a Glove
Heaven's On Fire

Paul Stanley Guitar Solo
Under the Gun
War Machine
Eric Carr Drum Solo
Young and Wasted
I've Had Enough (Into the Fire)
Gene Simmons Bass Solo
I Love It Loud
I Still Love You
Creatures of the Night
Love Gun
Rock and Roll All Nite
Lick It Up
[Black Diamond]

■ Paul introduced Eric as "The Little Man in the Tub," in reference to an incident where Eric had unwittingly allowed a girl to photograph him nude in a bathtub. Naturally, the picture was quickly distributed throughout the region.

OCTOBER 17, 1984

Offenbach (Frankfurt a.M.), West Germany
Stadthalle
Opening Act: Bon Jovi
Capacity: 3,500
Promoter: Top Concerts
Archived: Audio

■ SET LIST

Detroit Rock City
Cold Gin
Strutter
Fits Like a Glove
Heaven's On Fire
Paul Stanley Guitar Solo
Under the Gun
War Machine
Eric Carr Drum Solo
Young and Wasted
I've Had Enough (Into the Fire)
Gene Simmons Bass Solo
I Love It Loud
I Still Love You
Creatures of the Night
Love Gun
Rock and Roll All Nite
Lick It Up
Black Diamond

OCTOBER 18, 1984

München, West Germany
Circus Krone
Opening Act: Bon Jovi
Capacity: 2,500
Promoter: Top Concerts
Archived: Audio

■ SET LIST

Detroit Rock City
Cold Gin
Strutter
Fits Like a Glove
Heaven's on Fire
Paul Stanley Guitar Solo
Under the Gun
War Machine
Eric Carr Drum Solo
Young and Wasted
I've Had Enough (Into the Fire)
Gene Simmons Bass Solo
I Love It Loud
I Still Love You
Creatures of the Night
Love Gun
Rock and Roll All Nite
Lick It Up
Oh Susannah

Black Diamond

■ The following day, "Heaven's On Fire" live from Circus Krone aired on the long-running TV show *Bayernjournal*.

OCTOBER 19, 1984

Nürnberg, West Germany
Hammerleinhalle
Opening Act: Bon Jovi
Capacity: 3,000
Promoter: Top Concerts
Archived: Audio
■ **SET LIST**
See October 17, 1984.

OCTOBER 21, 1984

København, Denmark
Falkoner Centret
Opening Act: Bon Jovi
Attendance: 2,000   Capacity: 2,800
Promoter: EMA Telstar
Archived: Audio
■ **SET LIST**
See October 17, 1984.

■ During the afternoon KISS lip-synched "I Love It Loud," "Lick It Up," and "Heaven's On Fire" for *Veronica's Strandrace*. This daytime, beachfront performance was taped in the seaside resort of Schevningen, The Netherlands.

OCTOBER 22, 1984

Drammen, Norway
Drammenshallen
No Opening Act
Attendance: 3,500   Capacity: 6,000
Promoter: EMA Telstar
Archived: Audio
■ **SET LIST**
See October 18, 1984.

■ Bon Jovi canceled because they were arrested at a McDonald's restaurant in Oslo.

OCTOBER 24, 1984

Lund, Sweden
Olympen
No Opening Act

Capacity: 2,500
Promoter: EMA Telstar
Archived: Audio
■ **SET LIST**
Detroit Rock City
Cold Gin
Strutter
Fits Like a Glove
Heaven's On Fire
Paul Stanley Guitar Solo
Under the Gun
War Machine
Eric Carr Drum Solo
Young and Wasted
I've Had Enough (Into the Fire)
Gene Simmons Bass Solo
I Love It Loud
I Still Love You
Creatures of the Night
Love Gun
Rock and Roll All Nite
Lick It Up
Black Diamond
■ Bon Jovi did not perform as there was insufficient room on stage for their equipment.

Paul played the riff from "Lick It Up" as part of his solo.

OCTOBER 25, 1984

Lund, Sweden   **TEMP HOLD DATE**
Olympen
Capacity: 2,500
Promoter: EMA Telstar

OCTOBER 26, 1984

Johanneshov (Stockholm), Sweden
Hovet
Opening Act: Bon Jovi
Attendance: 7,000   Capacity: 9,500
Promoter: EMA Telstar
Archived: Audio
■ **SET LIST**
See October 18, 1984.
■ Paul fell twice at the beginning of the show, and Gene took over the lead vocals briefly. KISS performed part of "Winchester Cathedral" prior

to "Black Diamond."

While in Sweden, the band appeared on a local TV show called *Gladgehurs* to lip-synch "Heaven's On Fire."

OCTOBER 27, 1984

Göteborg, Sweden
Scandinavium
Opening Act: Bon Jovi
Attendance: 5,023   Capacity: 9,000
Promoter: EMA Telstar
Archived: Audio
■ **SET LIST**
Detroit Rock City
Cold Gin
Strutter
Fits Like a Glove
Heaven's On Fire
Paul Stanley Guitar Solo
Under the Gun
War Machine
Eric Carr Drum Solo
Young and Wasted
Creatures of the Night
Gene Simmons Bass Solo
I Love It Loud
I Still Love You
I've Had Enough (Into the Fire)
Love Gun
Rock and Roll All Nite
Lick It Up
Oh Susannah
Medley: Bang a Gong (Get It On) - Hey Joe - La Bamba
Black Diamond
■ Paul briefly played the riff from Zeppelin's "Immigrant Song," prior to "Black Diamond."

OCTOBER 29, 1984

Hannover, West Germany
Stadium Sporthalle
Opening Act: Bon Jovi
Capacity: 2,500
Promoter: Top Concerts

OCTOBER 30, 1984

Düsseldorf, West Germany
Philipshalle
Opening Act: Bon Jovi
Capacity: 8,000
Promoter: Top Concerts
Archived: Audio
■ **SET LIST**
Detroit Rock City
Cold Gin
Strutter
Fits Like a Glove
Heaven's On Fire
Paul Stanley Guitar Solo
Under the Gun
War Machine
Eric Carr Drum Solo
Young and Wasted
Creatures of the Night
Gene Simmons Bass Solo
I Love It Loud
I Still Love You
I've Had Enough (Into the Fire)
Love Gun
Rock and Roll All Nite
Lick It Up
Oh Susannah
Sunshine of Your Love
Medley: Hey Joe - La Bamba
Whole Lotta Love
Black Diamond
■ Gene sang "Sunshine of Your Love," while

The drum riser before a show on KISS's European tour, autumn 1984. Note the unusual panther face props on the bass drum heads.

Paul handled lead vocal duties on "Hey Joe" and "La Bamba" just as he had at the Göteborg gig on October 27.

OCTOBER 31, 1984

Ludwigshafen (Mannheim), West Germany
Friedrich-Ebert-Halle
Opening Act: Bon Jovi
Capacity: 5,000
Promoter: Top Concerts
Archived: Audio

■ SET LIST

Detroit Rock City
Cold Gin
Strutter
Fits Like a Glove
Heaven's On Fire
Paul Stanley Guitar Solo
Under the Gun
War Machine
Eric Carr Drum Solo
Young and Wasted
Creatures of the Night
Gene Simmons Bass Solo
I Love It Loud
I Still Love You
I've Had Enough (Into the Fire)
Love Gun
Rock and Roll All Nite
Lick It Up
Black Diamond

NOVEMBER 1, 1984

Lausanne, Switzerland
Palais De Beauleiu, Halle 18
Opening Act: Bon Jovi
Attendance: 6,800
Promoter: Good News Agency
Archived: Audio

■ SET LIST

Detroit Rock City
Cold Gin
Strutter
Fits Like a Glove
Heaven's On Fire
Paul Stanley Guitar Solo
Under the Gun
War Machine
Eric Carr Drum Solo
Young and Wasted
Creatures of the Night
Gene Simmons Bass Solo
I Love It Loud
I Still Love You
I've Had Enough (Into the Fire)
Love Gun
Rock and Roll All Nite
Lick It Up
Oh Susannah
Black Diamond

NOVEMBER 3, 1984

Bruxelles, Belgium
Vorst Nationaal
Opening Acts: Bon Jovi, Steelover
Attendance: 4,651   Capacity: 6,000
Promoter: Make It Happen
Archived: Audio

■ SET LIST

Detroit Rock City
Cold Gin
Strutter
Fits Like a Glove
Heaven's On Fire
Paul Stanley Guitar Solo

Under the Gun
War Machine
Eric Carr Drum Solo
Young and Wasted
Creatures of the Night
Gene Simmons Bass Solo
I Love It Loud
I Still Love You
[I've Had Enough (Into the Fire)]
Love Gun
Rock and Roll All Nite
Lick It Up
Oh Susannah
Black Diamond

NOVEMBER 4, 1984

Zwolle, The Netherlands
Ijsselhal
Opening Act: Bon Jovi
Attendance: 3,500   Capacity: 5,000
Promoter: Mojo Concerts
Archived: Audio

■ PARTIAL SET LIST

Detroit Rock City
Cold Gin
Strutter
Fits Like a Glove
Heaven's On Fire
Paul Stanley Guitar Solo
Under the Gun
War Machine
Eric Carr Drum Solo
Young and Wasted
La Bamba

■ Gene and Paul briefly played drums during the show. Paul also included a brief excerpt of "Deuce" during his solo.

KISS made their first appearance at a KISS convention, which was held by the Dutch KISS Army within the venue on the floor above the concert hall.

NOVEMBER 5, 1984

Paris, France
Le Zenith
Opening Act: Bon Jovi
Capacity: 6,000
Promoter: KCP
Archived: Audio

■ SET LIST

Detroit Rock City
Cold Gin
Strutter
Fits Like a Glove
Heaven's On Fire
Paul Stanley Guitar Solo
Under the Gun
War Machine
Eric Carr Drum Solo
Young and Wasted
Creatures of the Night
Gene Simmons Bass Solo
I Love It Loud
I Still Love You
[I've Had Enough (Into the Fire)]
Love Gun
Rock and Roll All Nite
Lick It Up
Black Diamond

■ This was the final performance of "Strutter" on the Animalize Tour.

Dave Bonilla: "On the last show of the tour, Bon Jovi dropped something like 2,000 ping pong balls on KISS. It was hilarious. At first there

were only one or two that you saw, then three, then four, and then the entire lot of them. And of course when they hit the stage floor, they'd bounce right up again, which made it look like this wall of white."

NOVEMBER 15, 1984

Bethlehem (Allentown), Pennsylvania
Stabler Arena
Opening Act: Queensrÿche
Attendance: 4,472   Capacity: 5,450
Promoter: Makoul Productions
Archived: Audio

■ SET LIST

Detroit Rock City
Cold Gin
Fits Like a Glove
Heaven's On Fire
Paul Stanley Guitar Solo
Under the Gun
War Machine
Eric Carr Drum Solo
Young and Wasted
Creatures of the Night
Gene Simmons Bass Solo
I Love It Loud
I Still Love You
I've Had Enough (Into the Fire)
Love Gun
Black Diamond
Lick It Up
Rock and Roll All Nite

NOVEMBER 16, 1984

Glens Falls, New York
Glens Falls Civic Center
Opening Act: Queensrÿche
Capacity: 8,100
Promoter: Magic City Productions
Archived: Audio

■ SET LIST

Detroit Rock City
Creatures of the Night
Cold Gin
Fits Like a Glove
Heaven's On Fire
Paul Stanley Guitar Solo
Under the Gun
War Machine
Eric Carr Drum Solo
Young and Wasted
Gene Simmons Bass Solo
I Love it Loud
I Still Love You
I've Had Enough (Into the Fire)
Love Gun
Black Diamond
Oh Susannah
Lick It Up
Rock and Roll All Nite

NOVEMBER 17, 1984

Rochester, New York
Rochester Community War Memorial
Opening Act: Queensrÿche
Attendance: 6,018   Capacity 9,300
Promoter: John Scher Presents
Archived: Audio

■ SET LIST

Detroit Rock City
Creatures of the Night
Cold Gin
Fits Like a Glove
Heaven's On Fire
Paul Stanley Guitar Solo

NORMAN BOUTHILLIER

Under the Gun
War Machine
Eric Carr Drum Solo
Young and Wasted
Gene Simmons Bass Solo
I Love It Loud
I've Had Enough (Into the Fire)
I Still Love You
Love Gun
Black Diamond
Oh Susannah
Lick It Up
Rock and Roll All Nite

NOVEMBER 18, 1984

Buffalo, New York
Veterans Memorial Auditorium
Opening Act: Queensrÿche
Capacity: 9,100
Promoter: Harvey & Corky
Archived: Audio
■ SET LIST
Detroit Rock City
Cold Gin
Creatures of the Night
Fits Like a Glove
Heaven's On Fire
Paul Stanley Guitar Solo
Under the Gun
War Machine
Eric Carr Drum Solo
Young and Wasted
Gene Simmons Bass Solo
I Love it Loud
I Still Love You
I've Had Enough (Into the Fire)
Love Gun
Black Diamond
Oh Susannah
Lick It Up
Rock and Roll All Nite
■ This is the final known performance of "I've Had Enough (Into the Fire)." The venue was set up in an intimate theater seating configuration.

NOVEMBER 20, 1984

Syracuse, New York
Onondaga County War Memorial
Opening Act: Queensrÿche
Capacity: 8,000
Promoter: Magic City Productions

NOVEMBER 21, 1984   POSTPONED

Uniondale, New York
Nassau Veterans Memorial Coliseum
Opening Act: Queensrÿche
Promoter: Ron Delsener
■ The show was postponed until November 26 because Paul was sick.

NOVEMBER 23, 1984

Worcester, Massachusetts
The Centrum
Opening Act: Queensrÿche
Attendance: 9,756   Capacity: 9,756
Promoter: Frank J. Russo
Archived: Audio
■ PARTIAL SET LIST
Detroit Rock City
Cold Gin
Creatures of the Night
Fits Like a Glove
Heaven's On Fire
Paul Stanley Guitar Solo
Under the Gun
War Machine
Eric Carr Drum Solo
Young and Wasted
Gene Simmons Bass Solo
Oh Susannah
Lick It Up
Rock and Roll All Nite
■ The band began to play "Firehouse" prior to "Rock and Roll All Nite," but the attempt was cut short before the first verse.

NOVEMBER 24, 1984

New Haven, Connecticut
New Haven Veterans Memorial Coliseum
Opening Act: Queensrÿche
Attendance: 9,315   Capacity: 9,315
Promoter: Cross Country Concerts
Archived: Audio
■ SET LIST
Detroit Rock City
Cold Gin
Creatures of the Night
Fits Like a Glove
Heaven's On Fire
[Paul Stanley Guitar Solo]
Under the Gun
War Machine
Eric Carr Drum Solo
Young and Wasted
Gene Simmons Bass Solo

I Love It Loud
I Still Love You
Love Gun
Black Diamond
Oh Susannah
Lick It Up
Rock and Roll All Nite

NOVEMBER 25, 1984

Philadelphia, Pennsylvania
The Spectrum
Opening Act: Queensrÿche
Attendance: 7,788   Capacity: 10,000
Promoter: Concert Co. Presentations
Archived: Audio
■ SET LIST
Detroit Rock City
Cold Gin
Creatures of the Night
Fits Like a Glove
Heaven's On Fire
Paul Stanley Guitar Solo
Under the Gun
War Machine
Eric Carr Drum Solo
Young and Wasted
Gene Simmons Bass Solo
I Love It Loud
I Still Love You
Love Gun
Black Diamond
Oh Susannah
Lick It Up
Rock and Roll All Nite

NOVEMBER 26, 1984

Uniondale, New York
Nassau Veterans Memorial Coliseum
Opening Act: Queensrÿche
Attendance: 10,000   Capacity: 10,000
Promoter: Ron Delsener Presents
Archived: Audio
■ SET LIST
Detroit Rock City
Cold Gin
Creatures of the Night
Fits Like a Glove
Heaven's On Fire
Paul Stanley Guitar Solo
Under the Gun
War Machine
Eric Carr Drum Solo
Young and Wasted
Gene Simmons Bass Solo
I Love It Loud
I Still Love You
Love Gun
Black Diamond
Oh Susannah
Lick It Up
[Rock and Roll All Nite]

NOVEMBER 27, 1984

Baltimore, Maryland
Baltimore Civic Center
Opening Act: Queensrÿche
Attendance: 5,759   Capacity: 6,200
Promoter: American Amusement Co.
Archived: Audio
■ SET LIST
See November 25, 1984.
■ This was Mark St. John's first performance with KISS. Bruce Kulick performed during the first third of the show before Mark joined the band onstage at the beginning of "Under the Gun." All five members bowed together.

NOVEMBER 28, 1984

Poughkeepsie, New York
Mid-Hudson Civic Center
Opening Act: Queensrÿche
Attendance: 3,020   Capacity: 3,020
Promoter: Harvey & Corky
■ Mark St. John played the entire show.

NOVEMBER 29, 1984

Binghamton, New York
Broome Co. Veterans Memorial Arena
Opening Act: Queensrÿche
Capacity: 7,200
Promoter: Magic City Productions
Archived: Audio
■ SET LIST
Detroit Rock City
Cold Gin
Creatures of the Night
Fits Like a Glove
Heaven's On Fire
Paul Stanley Guitar Solo
Under the Gun
War Machine
Eric Carr Drum Solo
Young and Wasted
Gene Simmons Bass Solo
I Love It Loud
I Still Love You
Love Gun
Black Diamond
Oh Susannah
[Lick It Up]
Rock and Roll All Nite
■ Mark St. John again played the entire show; it was his third and final performance with KISS.

DECEMBER 2, 1984

Indianapolis, Indiana
Market Square Arena
Opening Act: Queensrÿche
Attendance: 10,393   Capacity: 10,500
Promoter: Sunshine Promotions
Archived: Audio
■ SET LIST
Detroit Rock City
Cold Gin
Creatures of the Night
Fits Like a Glove
Heaven's On Fire
Paul Stanley Guitar Solo
Under the Gun
War Machine
Eric Carr Drum Solo
Young and Wasted
Gene Simmons Bass Solo
I Love It Loud
I Still Love You
Love Gun
Black Diamond
Lick It Up
Rock and Roll All Nite

DECEMBER 4, 1984

St. Louis, Missouri
Kiel Auditorium
Opening Act: Queensrÿche
Attendance: 4,380   Capacity: 5,700
Promoter: Contemporary Productions
■ SET LIST
Detroit Rock City
Cold Gin
Creatures of the Night
Fits Like a Glove
Heaven's On Fire
Thrills in the Night

Paul Stanley Guitar Solo
Under the Gun
War Machine
Eric Carr Drum Solo
Young and Wasted
Gene Simmons Bass Solo
I Love It Loud
I Still Love You
Love Gun
Black Diamond
Oh Susannah
Lick It Up
Rock and Roll All Nite
■ This was the first performance of "Thrills in the Night."

DECEMBER 5, 1984

Evansville, Indiana
Roberts Municipal Stadium
Opening Act: Queensrÿche
Attendance: 4,424   Capacity: 9,500
Promoter: Sunshine Promotions

DECEMBER 6, 1984

Terre Haute, Indiana
Hulman Center
Opening Act: Queensrÿche
Attendance: 3,792   Capacity: 8,500
Promoter: Sunshine Promotions
Archived: Audio
■ SET LIST
Detroit Rock City
Cold Gin
Creatures of the Night
Fits Like a Glove
Heaven's On Fire
Paul Stanley Guitar Solo
Under the Gun
War Machine
Eric Carr Drum Solo
Young and Wasted
Gene Simmons Bass Solo
I Love It Loud
I Still Love You
Love Gun
Black Diamond
Oh Susannah
Lick It Up
Rock and Roll All Nite

DECEMBER 7, 1984

Fort Wayne, Indiana
Allen Co. War Memorial Coliseum
Opening Act: Queensrÿche
Attendance: 6,577   Capacity: 9,800
Promoter: Sunshine Promotions
Archived: Audio
■ SET LIST
Detroit Rock City
Cold Gin
Creatures of the Night
Fits Like a Glove
Heaven's On Fire
Thrills in the Night
Paul Stanley Guitar Solo
Under the Gun
War Machine
Eric Carr Drum Solo
Young and Wasted
Gene Simmons Bass Solo
I Love It Loud
I Still Love You
Love Gun
Black Diamond
Lick It Up
Rock and Roll All Nite

■ After only six months and three performances with KISS, Mark St. John was fired as KISS's lead guitarist. St. John, who had been traveling with the band, was sent home during the day.

During the show, bottles were repeatedly thrown at the stage—perhaps the fans didn't like Gene's wig.

DECEMBER 8, 1984

Detroit, Michigan
Cobo Arena
Opening Act: Queensrÿche
Capacity: 8,500
Promoter: Belkin Productions
Archived: Video
■ SET LIST
Detroit Rock City
Cold Gin
Creatures of the Night
Fits Like a Glove
Heaven's On Fire
Thrills in the Night
Paul Stanley Guitar Solo
Under the Gun
War Machine
Eric Carr Drum Solo
Young and Wasted
Gene Simmons Bass Solo
I Love It Loud
I Still Love You
Love Gun
Black Diamond
Oh Susannah
Lick It Up
Rock and Roll All Nite
■ Bruce Kulick was made an official member of KISS, and the concert was broadcast live on radio station WLLZ.

As a publicity stunt, WLLZ arranged for Bruce Redoute and Lee Neaves—the two youths who had been featured prominently on the back of the *Alive!* album's jacket in 1975—to be reunited with KISS at the show. Gene and Paul went out to dinner with them after the concert.

DECEMBER 11, 1984

Saginaw, Michigan
Wendler Arena @ Saginaw Civic Center
Opening Act: Queensrÿche
Capacity: 7,500
Promoter: Belkin Productions
Archived: Audio
■ SET LIST
Detroit Rock City
Cold Gin
Creatures of the Night
Fits Like a Glove
Heaven's On Fire
Paul Stanley Guitar Solo
Under the Gun
War Machine
Eric Carr Drum Solo
Young and Wasted
Gene Simmons Bass Solo
I Love It Loud
I Still Love You
Love Gun
Black Diamond
Oh Susannah
Lick It Up
Rock and Roll All Nite

DECEMBER 12, 1984

Columbus, Ohio
Battelle Hall @ Ohio Center

Opening Act: Queensrÿche
Capacity: 7,000
Promoter: Belkin Productions
■ The lighting rig ramp and flamethrowers were not used at this concert.

DECEMBER 13, 1984
Dayton, Ohio
Hara Arena & Exhibition Center
Opening Act: Queensrÿche
Capacity: 8,000
Promoter: Belkin Productions

DECEMBER 14, 1984
Richfield (Cleveland), Ohio
The Coliseum Theatre
Opening Act: Queensrÿche
Capacity: 12,500
Promoter: Belkin Productions
Archived: Audio
■ PARTIAL SET LIST
Thrills in the Night
Paul Stanley Guitar Solo
Under the Gun
War Machine
Eric Carr Drum Solo
Gene Simmons Bass Solo
I Love It Loud
■ Audience shots for the "Thrills in the Night" video were filmed in Richfield. Some of the footage later wound up in Paul's "Rockers Against Drugs" public service announcement. This marks the final live performance of "Thrills in the Night."

Runaway, Gene's first theatrical film opened nationwide.

DECEMBER 15, 1984
Louisville, Kentucky
Commonwealth Convention Center
Opening Act: Queensrÿche
Attendance: 4,665   Capacity: 8,000
Promoter: Sunshine Promotions
Archived: Audio
■ SET LIST
Detroit Rock City
Cold Gin
Creatures of the Night
Fits Like a Glove
Heaven's On Fire
Paul Stanley Guitar Solo
Under the Gun

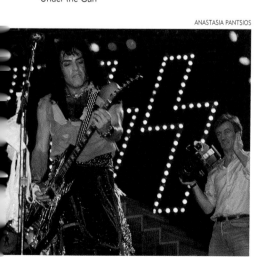

ANASTASIA PANTSIOS

Paul onstage in Richfield, Ohio, December 14, 1984 while filming the "Thrills in the Night" video.

War Machine
Eric Carr Drum Solo
Young and Wasted
Gene Simmons Bass Solo
I Love It Loud
I Still Love You
Love Gun
Black Diamond
Oh Susannah
Lick It Up
Rock and Roll All Nite
■ All close-up shots and conceptual footage for the "Thrills in the Night" video were filmed at the Commonwealth Convention Center on December 16. Originally, the director intended to include conceptual footage featuring band members in various roles, such as Eric portraying an office manager. Once shot, the footage was deemed too hokey and remains unreleased to this day. The video was re-edited to include licensed videotape excerpts from the *Animalize Live Uncensored* home video. Unfortunately, PolyGram (who does not own the footage) didn't option the home video rights, thus the absence of "Thrills in the Night" on KISS's 1987 home video *Exposed*.

DECEMBER 17, 1984
Peoria, Illinois
Carver Arena @ Peoria Civic Center
Opening Act: Queensrÿche
Attendance: 3,566   Capacity: 8,000
Promoter: Grandview Entertainment
Archived: Audio
■ SET LIST
See December 15, 1984.

DECEMBER 18, 1984
Cedar Rapids, Iowa
Five Seasons Center
Opening Act: Queensrÿche
Attendance: 6,800
Promoter: JAM Productions

DECEMBER 26, 1984
Kansas City, Missouri
Municipal Auditorium
Opening Act: Queensrÿche
Capacity: 9,200
Promoter: Schon Productions

DECEMBER 27, 1984
Lincoln, Nebraska
Pershing Auditorium
Opening Act: Queensrÿche
Attendance: 4,779   Capacity 6,000
Promoter: Contemporary Productions

DECEMBER 29, 1984
St. Paul, Minnesota
St. Paul Civic Center
Opening Act: Queensrÿche
Capacity: 12,500
Promoter: Schon Productions
Archived: Audio
■ SET LIST
Detroit Rock City
Cold Gin
Creatures of the Night
Fits Like a Glove
Heaven's On Fire
[Paul Stanley Guitar Solo]
Under the Gun
War Machine
[Eric Carr Drum Solo]

Young and Wasted
Gene Simmons Bass Solo
I Love It Loud
I Still Love You
Love Gun
Black Diamond
Oh Susannah
Lick It Up
Rock and Roll All Nite

DECEMBER 30, 1984
Milwaukee, Wisconsin
Mecca Auditorium
Opening Act: Queensrÿche
Attendance: 4,754   Capacity: 6,120
Promoter: Stardate Productions
Archived: Audio
■ SET LIST
Detroit Rock City
Cold Gin
Creatures of the Night
Fits Like a Glove
Heaven's On Fire
Paul Stanley Guitar Solo
Under the Gun
War Machine
[Eric Carr Drum Solo]
Young and Wasted
[Gene Simmons Bass Solo]
I Love It Loud
I Still Love You
Love Gun
Black Diamond
Oh Susannah
Lick It Up
Rock and Roll All Nite

DECEMBER 31, 1984   CANCELED
Chicago, Illinois
University of Illinois-Chicago Pavilion
Opening Act: Queensrÿche
Promoter: JAM Productions
■ The show was canceled due to production difficulties.

JANUARY 3, 1985
Greenville, South Carolina
Greenville Memorial Auditorium
Opening Act: Krokus
Attendance: 6,153   Capacity: 6,153
Promoter: Beach Club Promotions
■ Local lighting tech John Addington fell to his death from the lighting rig during the changeover between acts. Gene's bass tech, Dave "Romeo" Bonilla recalls: "We were standing looking at the band walking down to come onto the stage and next thing we knew there was a blur. This guy fell, hit the P.A., and then bounced into the barricade. He was one of the house riggers, I think. They took him to the hospital, and we went ahead with the show. During the concert, we were told that he died. The load-out was a real downer."

JANUARY 4, 1985
Johnson City, Tennessee
Freedom Hall Civic Center @ Science Hill High School
Opening Act: Krokus
Attendance: 8,575   Capacity: 9,000
Promoter: Sunshine Promotions

JANUARY 5, 1985
Fayetteville, North Carolina
Cumberland County Memorial Arena
Opening Act: Krokus

Attendance: 5,964   Capacity 6,500
Promoter: Beach Club Promotions

JANUARY 6, 1985

Charlotte, North Carolina
Charlotte Coliseum
Opening Act: Krokus
Attendance: 9,768   Capacity: 9,768
Promoter: Beach Club Promotions
Archived: Audio

■ SET LIST
See December 15, 1984.

JANUARY 8, 1985

Knoxville, Tennessee
Knoxville Civic Coliseum
Opening Act: Krokus
Attendance: 5,626   Capacity: 8,289
Promoter: Sunshine Promotions

JANUARY 9, 1985

Atlanta, Georgia
The Omni
Opening Act: Krokus
Attendance: 6,357   Capacity: 9,686
Promoter: Chesapeake Concerts
Archived: Audio

■ SET LIST
See December 15, 1984.

JANUARY 10, 1985

Orlando, Florida
Orlando Sports Stadium
Opening Act: Krokus

JANUARY 11, 1985

Fort Lauderdale, Florida
Sunrise Musical Theatre
Opening Act: Krokus
Attendance: 3,795   Capacity: 3,795
Promoter: Cellar Door Concerts
Archived: Audio

■ SET LIST
See December 15, 1984.

JANUARY 12, 1985

Fort Lauderdale, Florida
Sunrise Musical Theatre
Opening Act: Krokus
Attendance: 3,795   Capacity: 3,795
Promoter: Cellar Door Concerts
Archived: Audio

■ SET LIST
Detroit Rock City
Cold Gin
Creatures of the Night
Fits Like a Glove
Heaven's On Fire
Paul Stanley Guitar Solo
Under the Gun
[Eric Carr Drum Solo]
War Machine
[Young and Wasted]
Gene Simmons Bass Solo
I Love It Loud
I Still Love You
Love Gun
Black Diamond
Lick It Up
Rock and Roll All Nite

JANUARY 13, 1985

St. Petersburg, Florida
Bayfront Center Arena
Opening Act: Krokus
Capacity: 8,355
Promoter: Cellar Door Concerts

Archived: Audio

■ SET LIST
Detroit Rock City
Cold Gin
Creatures of the Night
Fits Like a Glove
Heaven's On Fire
Paul Stanley Guitar Solo
Under the Gun
Eric Carr Drum Solo
War Machine
[Young and Wasted]
Gene Simmons Bass Solo
I Love It Loud
I Still Love You
Love Gun
Black Diamond
Oh Susannah
Lick It Up
Rock and Roll All Nite

JANUARY 15, 1985

New Orleans, Louisiana
Kiefer UNO Lakefront Arena
Opening Act: Krokus
Promoters: Barry Mendelson Presents, Pace Concerts
Archived: Audio

■ SET LIST
See January 13, 1985.

JANUARY 16, 1985

Biloxi, Mississippi
Mississippi Coast Coliseum
Opening Act: Krokus

JANUARY 17, 1985

Huntsville, Alabama
Von Braun Civic Center
Opening Act: Krokus
Attendance: 6,458   Capacity: 10,106
Promoter: Sound 70 Concerts

JANUARY 18, 1985

Birmingham, Alabama
Boutwell Auditorium
Opening Act: Krokus
Attendance: 5,778   Capacity: 5,778
Promoter: High Tide Management
Archived: Audio

■ SET LIST
Detroit Rock City
Cold Gin
Creatures of the Night
Fits Like a Glove
Heaven's On Fire
Paul Stanley Guitar Solo
Under the Gun
War Machine
[Eric Carr Drum Solo]
[Young and Wasted]
[Gene Simmons Bass Solo]
I Love It Loud
[I Still Love You]
Love Gun
Black Diamond
[Oh Susannah]
Lick It Up
Rock and Roll All Nite

JANUARY 19, 1985

Nashville, Tennessee
Nashville Municipal Auditorium
Opening Act: Krokus
Attendance: 9,900   Capacity: 9,900
Promoter: Sound 70 Concerts

■ The "Thrills in the Night" video first aired on this date.

JANUARY 21, 1985

Chattanooga, Tennessee   **CANCELED**
UTC Arena

■ This concert was canceled sometime in January.

JANUARY 21, 1985

Pensacola, Florida
The Pensacola Civic Center
Opening Act: Krokus
Attendance: 4,713   Capacity: 10,318
Promoter: Barry Mendelson Presents

■ This was the very first event at The Pensacola Civic Center, and it was added to the itinerary when the Chattanooga concert was canceled.

JANUARY 22, 1985

Memphis, Tennessee
Mid-South Coliseum
Opening Act: Krokus
Attendance: 4,861
Promoter: Sunshine Promotions

JANUARY 24, 1985

Lubbock, Texas
Lubbock Municipal Coliseum
Opening Act: Queensrÿche
Promoters: Pace Concerts, Stardate Productions

JANUARY 25, 1985

Abilene, Texas
Taylor County Coliseum
Opening Act: Queensrÿche

JANUARY 26, 1985

Austin, Texas
Frank C. Erwin, Jr., Special Events Center
Opening Act: Queensrÿche
Attendance: 5,691   Capacity: 6,853
Promoter: Jam Presents of Texas
Archived: Audio

■ SET LIST
Detroit Rock City
Cold Gin
Creatures of the Night
Fits Like a Glove
Heaven's On Fire
Paul Stanley Guitar Solo
Under the Gun
War Machine
Eric Carr Drum Solo
Young and Wasted
Gene Simmons Bass Solo
I Love It Loud
I Still Love You
Love Gun
Black Diamond
Oh Susannah
[Lick It Up]
[Rock and Roll All Nite]

JANUARY 27, 1985

Corpus Christi, Texas
Memorial Coliseum
Opening Act: Queensrÿche
Promoter: Jam Presents of Texas
Archived: Audio

■ SET LIST
See December 15, 1984.

JANUARY 29, 1985

Dallas, Texas
Reunion Arena
Opening Act: Queensrÿche
Promoter: 462, Inc.
Archived: Audio

SET LIST
See December 15, 1984.

JANUARY 30, 1985
San Antonio, Texas
HemisFair Arena @ Henry B. Gonzalez Convention Center
Opening Act: Queensrÿche
Attendance: 7,221   Capacity: 7,748
Promoter: Stone City Attractions

JANUARY 31, 1985
Houston, Texas
Sam Houston Coliseum
Opening Act: Queensrÿche
Archived: Audio
■ SET LIST
Detroit Rock City
Cold Gin
Creatures of the Night
Fits Like a Glove
Heaven's On Fire
Paul Stanley Guitar Solo
Under the Gun
War Machine
Eric Carr Drum Solo
Young and Wasted
Gene Simmons Bass Solo
I Love It Loud
I Still Love You
Lick It Up
Love Gun
Black Diamond
Oh Susannah
[Rock and Roll All Nite]

FEBRUARY 1, 1985
Waco, Texas
Convention Center
Opening Act: Queensrÿche
Capacity: 4,500
Promoter: Jam Presents of Texas
Archived: Audio
■ SET LIST
Detroit Rock City
Cold Gin
Creatures of the Night
Fits Like a Glove
Heaven's On Fire
Paul Stanley Guitar Solo
Under the Gun
[War Machine]
[Eric Carr Drum Solo]
[Young and Wasted]
[Gene Simmons Bass Solo]
[I Love It Loud]
[I Still Love You]
[Love Gun]
[Black Diamond]
[Lick It Up]
[Rock and Roll All Nite]

FEBRUARY 3, 1985
Odessa, Texas
Ector County Coliseum
Opening Act: Queensrÿche
Promoter: Stardate Productions
Capacity: 8,500

FEBRUARY 4, 1985
Amarillo, Texas
The Amarillo Civic Center
Opening Act: Queensrÿche
Attendance: 6,000   Capacity: 8,500
Promoter: Stardate Productions

FEBRUARY 5, 1985
El Paso, Texas
Special Events Center
Opening Act: Queensrÿche
Capacity: 7,000
Promoter: Stardate Productions
Archived: Audio
■ SET LIST
Detroit Rock City
Cold Gin
Creatures of the Night
Fits Like a Glove
Heaven's On Fire
Paul Stanley Guitar Solo
Under the Gun
War Machine
Eric Carr Drum Solo
[Young and Wasted]
[Gene Simmons Bass Solo]
I Love It Loud
I Still Love You
Love Gun
Black Diamond
Lick It Up
Rock and Roll All Nite

FEBRUARY 6, 1985
Phoenix, Arizona
Arizona Veterans Memorial Coliseum
Opening Act: Queensrÿche
Attendance: 10,409   Capacity: 16,300
Promoter: Evening Star Productions

FEBRUARY 7, 1985
Las Vegas, Nevada
Aladdin Theatre for the Performing Arts
Opening Act: Queensrÿche
Attendance: 4,704   Capacity: 7,066
Promoter: Evening Star Productions
Archived: Audio
■ SET LIST
Detroit Rock City
Cold Gin
Creatures of the Night
Fits Like a Glove
Heaven's On Fire
Paul Stanley Guitar Solo
Under the Gun
War Machine
Eric Carr Drum Solo
Young and Wasted
Gene Simmons Bass Solo
I Love It Loud
I Still Love You
Love Gun
Black Diamond
Lick It Up
Rock and Roll All Nite

FEBRUARY 9, 1985
Oakland, California
Henry J. Kaiser Auditorium
Opening Act: Queensrÿche
Attendance: 7,182   Capacity: 7,182
Promoter: Bill Graham Presents
Archived: Audio
■ SET LIST
See December 15, 1984.

FEBRUARY 11, 1985
Salt Lake City, Utah
O. Thayne Accord Arena @ Salt Palace Center
Opening Act: Queensrÿche
Capacity: 11,500
Promoter: United Concerts

FEBRUARY 13, 1985
Seattle, Washington
Seattle Center Arena
Opening Act: Queensrÿche
Capacity: 6,000
Promoter: Albatross Productions

FEBRUARY 14, 1985
Portland, Oregon
Memorial Coliseum
Opening Act: Queensrÿche
Capacity: 9,040
Promoter: Albatross Productions

FEBRUARY 17, 1985
Long Beach, California
Long Beach Arena
Opening Act: Queensrÿche
Attendance: 9,084   Capacity: 9,084
Promoter: Avalon Attractions
Archived: Audio
■ SET LIST
See December 15, 1984.

FEBRUARY 18, 1985
Long Beach, California
Long Beach Arena
Opening Act: Queensrÿche
Attendance: 6,105   Capacity: 9,084
Promoter: Avalon Attractions
Archived: Audio
■ SET LIST
See December 15, 1984.

FEBRUARY 20, 1985
San Bernardino, California
Orange Show Pavilion
Opening Act: Queensrÿche
Capacity: 6,000
Promoter: Avalon Attractions
Archived: Audio
■ SET LIST
See February 7, 1985.

FEBRUARY 21, 1985
Bakersfield, California
Bakersfield Civic Auditorium
Opening Act: Queensrÿche
Attendance: 5,075   Capacity 6,000
Promoter: Rock 'n' Chair Productions

FEBRUARY 22, 1985
San Diego, California
San Diego Sports Arena
Opening Act: Queensrÿche
Attendance: 7,395   Capacity: 8,882
Promoter: Fahn & Silva Productions
Archived: Audio
■ SET LIST
See December 15, 1984.

FEBRUARY 24, 1985
Sacramento, California
Sacramento Memorial Auditorium
Opening Act: Queensrÿche
Attendance: 4,364   Capacity: 4,364
Promoter: Bill Graham Presents
Archived: Audio
■ SET LIST
See December 15, 1984

FEBRUARY 26, 1985
Spokane, Washington
Spokane Coliseum
Opening Act: Queensrÿche
Attendance: 6,800   Capacity: 8,500

FEBRUARY 27, 1985

Vancouver, British Columbia, Canada
Pacific Coliseum
Opening Act: Queensrÿche
Attendance: 4,000   Capacity: 17,613
Promoter: Albatross Productions

MARCH 1, 1985

Edmonton, Alberta, Canada
Kinsmen Fieldhouse
Opening Act: Sentinel
Attendance: 3,767   Capacity 5,000
Promoter: Perryscope Concert Productions

■ Local band Sentinel was named as the opening act on the day of the show. Queensrÿche canceled when several band members contracted the flu.

MARCH 2, 1985

Lethbridge, Alberta, Canada
Canada Games Sportsplex
Opening Act: Queensrÿche
Attendance: 5,144   Capacity: 6,000
Promoter: Perryscope Concert Productions

MARCH 3, 1985

Calgary, Alberta, Canada
Corral Arena
Opening Act: Queensrÿche
Attendance: 5,942   Capacity: 7,000
Promoter: Perryscope Concert Productions
Archived: Audio

■ PARTIAL SET LIST

Detroit Rock City
Cold Gin
Creatures of the Night
Fits Like a Glove
Heaven's On Fire
Paul Stanley Guitar Solo
Under the Gun
War Machine
Young and Wasted
Gene Simmons Bass Solo
I Love It Loud
I Still Love You

MARCH 7, 1985

Regina, Saskatchewan, Canada
Regina Agridome @ Regina Exhibition Park
Opening Act: Dokken
Attendance: 4,366   Capacity 6,500
Promoters: Concert Productions Int'l, Donald K. Donald

MARCH 9, 1985

Winnipeg, Manitoba, Canada
Winnipeg Arena
Opening Act: Dokken
Attendance: 5,877   Capacity 10,761
Promoters: Concert Productions Int'l, Donald K. Donald
Archived: Audio

■ SET LIST

Detroit Rock City
Cold Gin
Creatures of the Night
Fits Like a Glove
Heaven's On Fire
Paul Stanley Guitar Solo
Under the Gun
War Machine
Eric Carr Drum Solo
Young and Wasted
Gene Simmons Bass Solo
I Love It Loud
I Still Love You
Love Gun
Black Diamond

[Oh Susannah]
[Lick It Up]
[Rock and Roll All Nite]

MARCH 10, 1985

Grand Forks, North Dakota
University of North Dakota Fieldhouse
Opening Act: Dokken
Attendance: 6,330   Capacity: 6,330
Promoter: Stardate Productions
Archived: Audio

■ SET LIST

Detroit Rock City
Cold Gin
Creatures of the Night
Fits Like a Glove
Heaven's On Fire
Paul Stanley Guitar Solo
Under the Gun
War Machine
[Eric Carr Drum Solo]
Young and Wasted
Gene Simmons Bass Solo
I Love It Loud
I Still Love You
Love Gun
Black Diamond
Oh Susannah
Lick It Up
Rock and Roll All Nite

MARCH 11, 1985

Bismarck, North Dakota
Bismarck Civic Center
Opening Act: Dokken
Attendance: 4,973   Capacity: 6,000
Promoter: Stardate Productions

MARCH 13, 1985

Duluth, Minnesota
Duluth Arena Auditorium
Opening Act: Dokken
Attendance: 4,795   Capacity: 8,000
Promoter: Stardate Productions

MARCH 14, 1985   POSTPONED

Marquette, Michigan
Lakeview Arena
Opening Act: Dokken

■ On the day of the show, the concert was postponed until March 20, 1985.

MARCH 15, 1985

La Crosse, Wisconsin
Mary E. Sawyer Auditorium @ La Crosse Center
Opening Act: Dokken
Attendance: 8,000   Capacity: 8,000
Promoter: Stardate Productions

MARCH 17, 1985

Des Moines, Iowa
Veterans Memorial Auditorium
Opening Act: Dokken
Attendance: 9,910   Capacity: 9,910
Promoter: Contemporary Productions

■ No pyro was used at the show.

MARCH 19, 1985

Madison, Wisconsin
Dane County Expo Center Coliseum
Opening Act: W.A.S.P.
Attendance: 5,321   Capacity: 8,000
Promoter: Stardate Productions
Archived: Audio

■ SET LIST

See February 7, 1985

■ During the "Black Diamond" intro, Paul played

several bars of "Stairway to Heaven." He would continue to do this through the March 28 concert in Springfield, Massachusetts.

MARCH 20, 1985

Marquette, Michigan
Lakeview Arena
Opening Act: W.A.S.P.

MARCH 22, 1985

East Lansing, Michigan
Lansing Civic Center
Opening Act: W.A.S.P.
Capacity: 5,000
Promoter: Belkin Productions
Archived: Audio

■ SET LIST

[Detroit Rock City]
[Cold Gin]
[Creatures of the Night]
[Fits Like a Glove]
Heaven's On Fire
Paul Stanley Guitar Solo
Under the Gun
War Machine
Eric Carr Drum Solo
Young and Wasted
Gene Simmons Bass Solo
I Love It Loud
I Still Love You
Love Gun
Black Diamond
Oh Susannah
Lick It Up
Rock and Roll All Nite

MARCH 23, 1985

South Bend, Indiana
Joyce Athletic & Convocation Center Arena
Opening Act: W.A.S.P.
Attendance: 5,527   Capacity: 10,000
Promoter: Sunshine Promotions

MARCH 24, 1985

Cincinnati, Ohio
Cincinnati Gardens
Opening Act: W.A.S.P.
Capacity: 9,000
Promoter: Belkin Productions
Archived: Audio

■ SET LIST

Detroit Rock City
Cold Gin
Creatures of the Night
Fits Like a Glove
Heaven's On Fire
Paul Stanley Guitar Solo
Under the Gun
War Machine
Eric Carr Drum Solo
Young and Wasted
Gene Simmons Bass Solo
I Love It Loud
I Still Love You
Love Gun
Black Diamond
Oh Susannah
Whole Lotta Love
Lick It Up
Rock and Roll All Nite

■ Very brief portions of "Shout It Out Loud" and "Firehouse" preceded "Whole Lotta Love."

For what was presumably a practical joke, the band and audience sang "Happy Birthday" to Bruce, whose real birthday is December 12; however, the band did not mention his birthday to the crowd at their gig in Columbus on that date. Neither Bruce nor Chris Lendt recalled the event.

MARCH 25, 1985

Toledo, Ohio
Sports Arena
Opening Act: W.A.S.P.

MARCH 26, 1985

Pittsburgh, Pennsylvania
Civic Arena
Opening Act: W.A.S.P.
Attendance: 8,759   Capacity: 12,000
Promoter: DiCesare-Engler Productions
Archived: Audio
■ SET LIST
See December 15, 1984

MARCH 28, 1985

Springfield, Massachusetts
Springfield Civic Center
Opening Act: W.A.S.P.
Attendance: 6,623   Capacity: 7,000
Promoter: Cross Country Concerts
Archived: Audio
■ SET LIST
[Detroit Rock City]
[Cold Gin]
[Creatures of the Night]
[Fits Like a Glove]
[Heaven's On Fire]
[Paul Stanley Guitar Solo]
[Under the Gun]
[War Machine]
Eric Carr Drum Solo
Young and Wasted
Gene Simmons Bass Solo
I Love It Loud

I Still Love You
Love Gun
Black Diamond
Oh Susannah
Lick It Up
Rock and Roll All Nite
■ Following "Oh Susannah," KISS performed the first verse and chorus of "Strutter."

MARCH 29, 1985

East Rutherford, New Jersey
Brendan Byrne Arena
Opening Act: W.A.S.P.
Attendance: 15,928   Capacity: 15,928
Promoter: Monarch Entertainment
Archived: Audio
■ SET LIST
Detroit Rock City
Cold Gin
Creatures of the Night
Fits Like a Glove
Heaven's On Fire
Paul Stanley Guitar Solo
Under the Gun [edit]
War Machine
Eric Carr Drum Solo
Young and Wasted
Gene Simmons Bass Solo
I Love It Loud
I Still Love You
Love Gun
Black Diamond
[Oh Susannah]
[Lick It Up]
[Rock and Roll All Nite]
■ This was the last appearance of the classic KISS logo sign. This show was promoted on the weekend edition of *Entertainment Tonight.*

CHAPTER 18

ASYLUM TOUR

Number of Shows: 91
Start Date: November 29, 1985 - Little Rock, Arkansas
End Date: April 12, 1986 - Pittsburgh, Pennsylvania
Countries: Canada, U.S.A.
Opening Acts: Black 'N Blue; Blue Öyster Cult; King Kobra; Kix; W.A.S.P.
Average Attendance: 6,181

As the Animalize Tour drew to a close in March 1985, KISS had seen a top-20 album, a memorable single/video on AOR and MTV, a solidified lineup, and a tour that had witnessed the band's attendance rise over 20 percent. KISS had successfully reinvented themselves.

At first, the growth seemed to continue with KISS's next album, *Asylum.* MTV paid for the first-month rights to the "Tears Are Falling" video, and in the latter half of 1985 KISS had a higher media profile in the U.S. than at any other point during their non-makeup era. Unfortunately, the album would fail to duplicate the Platinum success of *Animalize,* and the band's attendance figures stalled and did not continue the pattern of growth established on the previous tour.

KISS began rehearsals for *Asylum* in mid-May and, during June and July, the band returned to the familiar confines of Electric Lady Studios to record the album. For the first time in their career, there was no outside producer presiding over the recording sessions, as Paul and Gene produced the album on their own. Additional work at Right Track Recording Studios was completed before the album was released on September 12, 1985. *Asylum* peaked at #20 on the *Billboard* charts and was certified Gold in November.

Two important administrative changes were made prior to the end of the year. First, The Press Office was rehired to do publicity for KISS, and a large number of television appearances ensued: Paul was seen on MTV with Martha Quinn (October 7); Eric cohosted *Radio 1990* (October 9); and Paul hosted MTV's *Heavy Metal Mania* (October 17). However, easily the most watched appearance made by any KISS member during this time was Gene's portrayal of drug runner Newton Blade on the second season premiere of *Miami Vice,* which aired on September 27.

Secondly, Danny Goldberg once again parted ways with the band: "They didn't replace me," remarks Goldberg, "I think it was: 'Let's save some money. We don't need this extra person here.' We had accomplished what we needed to do, they had been reinvented. Howard Marks just managed them himself for the next couple of years."

Three videos, each directed by David Mallet, were lensed to promote *Asylum.* "Tears Are Falling" was shot in August, while Gene and Paul were wrapping up a promotional tour of the U.K. The band returned to England in October to simultaneously film the other videos "Uh! All Night" and "Who Wants to Be Lonely."

The "Tears Are Falling" video, which had come and gone rather quietly after its September 27 world premiere, was resurrected when the popular request program, *Dial MTV,* first went on the air in January 1986. Through early May, the video typically landed in the top five on the show, a sustained presence which clearly bolstered sales for both the album and tour.

The Asylum Tour was KISS's first to remain exclusively within North America since 1979, and overall its attendance was nearly identical to the Animalize Tour. In many ways, the Asylum Tour was aptly named, as the band changed aspects of the show's production with almost schizophrenic confusion. The set lists were changed with great frequency and seemingly without a clear purpose, production effects were added and then quickly dropped, and three different stage sets were used before the tour concluded.

Tait Towers once again designed the new staging. Appearing rather deep and empty, Stage #1 was only used for the first eight shows. Its features included a rendering of the album cover artwork painted on the floor of the stage, a feature that was removed reportedly because the band kept slipping on it. "I think the stage floor was illuminated," remembers Tait Towers owner Mike Tait, "and that would have been made out of plastic, which is slippery. Normally, if something is too slippery, you just spill 7-Up on it, and that stops it from being slippery. In the end, I think they truthfully just didn't want their faces on there."

Additional features of the stage included a three-level drum riser painted black with yellow stripes; a huge, 40-foot-tall KISS logo, which required its own generator; and four steep, yellow lightning-bolt-shaped staircases placed on stage right and left. Depending on the size of the venue, sometimes only one set of staircases would be used on each side. Bruce Kulick recalls: "I hated those freaking stairs. I fell once on them and roughed up my knee. Thankfully, we lost them after awhile."

Stage #2 made its debut at the December 11 show in Richfield, Ohio. The second production filled out the stage rather nicely and no longer featured the album artwork on the floor of the stage, but retained the giant KISS logo and lightning stairs. Eric's black-and-yellow drum riser was replaced by a somewhat larger, silver, three-level riser, which now sat in the middle of the refurbished Animalize stage centerpiece.

The third and final stage debuted on February 2, 1986 in Tucson and was used for the remaining 51 shows of the Asylum tour. It featured a rounded backline of amplifiers set up on both sides of Eric's riser. Silver plating adorned the facing of the amplifiers, which were mostly empty cabinets, and gave the stage a look very

PAUL LEVASSEUR

The second of the three stages used on the Asylum Tour debuted just nine shows into the tour. Notice the recycled portions of the Animalize stage.

COURTESY OF STEVEN REEDER

The third and final stage used on the Asylum Tour. This stage made its debut in early 1986.

similar to Van Halen's 1984 Tour stage. Utilizing the new backline, band members would appear atop the amplifiers to start the show in a fashion similar to the Dynasty/Unmasked intro. Nonetheless, the third stage did appear less impressive than the refurbished Animalize stage. Since the apparent consensus was that not enough revenue was flowing to the bottom line, the band scaled back on the tour's production costs, and set pieces such as the lightning bolt stairs and the revamped Animalize staging were dropped. Removal of the excess staging would allow the band to use fewer trucks and require less local crew at each gig.

The garish costumes the band wore featured a blindingly bright palette of colors and an extremely heavy use of sequins. For the most part, Paul, Eric, and Bruce managed to pull it off, but Gene looked like a two-bit Madame impersonator. Years later, *Late Night With Conan O'Brien* cohost Andy Richter would compare Gene's look to that of Bea Arthur.

Several special effects were designed for the Asylum Tour.

- Paul performed a short-lived stunt where he would swing via trapeze from atop one of the lighting stairs diagonally down to the opposite side of the stage during "Lick It Up," before grabbing a guitar, which he would then break.

- A pyro effect at the conclusion of Eric's solo (which featured a newly added set of electronic drums) was designed to make his drums look as if they were engulfed in red flames, though local fire marshals often prohibited its use.

- Another idea, which was discussed but never implemented, was to open the show by having a guided missile fly from the back of the arena and detonate at center stage.

Two old effects that had fallen into disuse were brought back for the tour. A storm of confetti once again rained down on the audience at the conclusion of "Rock and Roll All Nite,"

though the gimmick was not nearly as impressive as it once had been. Additionally, Ace's rocket effect from the Dynasty/Unmasked era was taken up by Gene, who now used it in his solo.

For the first time, "Black Diamond" was no longer part of the show and the number of songs in the set from the band's 1970s repertoire (four, occasionally five) reached an all-time low. The number of actual songs in the set was also very low as most shows not only included a solo from all four band members, but also Paul's excruciatingly long (typically exceeding five minutes) scripted stage rap preceding "Love Gun." The rap often included poet laureate material like "I told her that we're doctors and we've come to [insert city name] to perform a *major operation*," "You have just entered the *danger zone*" and the modern day classic, "I'm not in *a* band, I'm in *the* band."

Only four songs from Asylum were performed on the tour: "Tears Are Falling," "Uh! All Night," "King of the Mountain," and "Any Way You Slice It" and of those, only the first two made the set on a nightly basis. Throughout the tour, KISS frequently covered The Who's "Won't Get Fooled Again" with Paul on lead vocals, and Gene and Eric each singing lead on a verse. Beginning in January and ending in late March, Paul's guitar solo occasionally included the famous "Streets of Cairo" melody and a short blues jam which some fans mistook for an ad hoc rendition of George Thorogood's "Bad to the Bone."

With the growing sales of portable video cameras in the US, in 1985 there was a natural increase in individuals privately videotaping concerts. By the time the tour was over, five concerts were widely available on videotape, far more than any other KISS tour up to that point.

NOVEMBER 29, 1985

Little Rock, Arkansas
T.H. Barton Coliseum
Opening Act: Black 'N Blue
Attendance: 7,559   Capacity: 10,000
Promoter: Mid-South Concerts
Archived: Audio

■ SET LIST
Detroit Rock City
Fits Like a Glove
King of the Mountain
Cold Gin
Paul Stanley Guitar Solo
Uh! All Night
Any Way You Slice It
Eric Carr Drum Solo
War Machine
I Still Love You
Under the Gun
Bruce Kulick Guitar Solo
Tears Are Falling
Gene Simmons Bass Solo
I Love It Loud
Love Gun
Rock and Roll All Nite
Heaven's On Fire
Lick It Up
■ The band rehearsed at the venue from November 26th through the 28th.

The first and final performance of "Any Way You Slice It."

NOVEMBER 30, 1985

Nashville, Tennessee
Nashville Municipal Auditorium
Opening Act: Black 'N Blue
Attendance: 9,379   Capacity: 9,900
Promoter: Sound 70 Concerts
■ *Entertainment Tonight* covered the show.

DECEMBER 1, 1985

Memphis, Tennessee
Mid-South Coliseum
Opening Act: Black 'N Blue
Capacity: 12,000
Promoter: Sunshine Promotions

DECEMBER 3, 1985

San Antonio, Texas
HemisFair Arena @ Henry B. Gonzalez Convention Center
Opening Act: Black 'N Blue
Attendance: 3,149   Capacity 4,109
Promoter: Stone City Attractions

ANASTASIA PANTSIOS

Coming this fall: Gene Simmons IS the Bea Arthur Experience.

■ A city ordinance prohibited anyone under the age of 14 from attending shows of this nature. The statute was not technically in effect for the KISS show, but the controversy surrounding the issue left many people with the impression that it would be enforced.

DECEMBER 4, 1985

Dallas, Texas
Reunion Arena
Opening Act: Black 'N Blue
Capacity: 17,000
Promoter: 462, Inc.
Archived: Audio, Partial Video

■ SET LIST

Detroit Rock City
Fits Like a Glove
Cold Gin
Paul Stanley Guitar Solo
Uh! All Night
Eric Carr Drum Solo
War Machine
I Still Love You
Under the Gun
Bruce Kulick Guitar Solo
Tears Are Falling
Gene Simmons Bass Solo
I Love It Loud
Love Gun
Rock and Roll All Nite
Heaven's On Fire
Oh Susannah
Lick It Up

■ Highlights from one of the first eight shows of the Asylum Tour were captured on film; the footage was most likely shot during this performance.

DECEMBER 6, 1985

Lafayette, Louisiana
Cajundome
Opening Act: Black 'N Blue
Capacity: 11,000
Promoter: Barry Mendelson Presents
Archived: Audio

■ SET LIST

Detroit Rock City
Fits Like a Glove
Cold Gin
Paul Stanley Guitar Solo
Uh! All Night
Eric Carr Drum Solo
War Machine
I Still Love You
Under the Gun
Bruce Kulick Guitar Solo
Tears Are Falling
Gene Simmons Bass Solo
I Love It Loud
Love Gun
Rock and Roll All Nite
Heaven's On Fire
Lick It Up

DECEMBER 7, 1985

Houston, Texas
Sam Houston Coliseum
Opening Act: Black 'N Blue
Capacity: 11,000
Promoter: Pace Concerts
Archived: Partial Video

■ SET LIST

[Detroit Rock City]
[Fits Like a Glove]
[Cold Gin]

[Paul Stanley Guitar Solo]
Uh! All Night
Eric Carr Drum Solo
War Machine
I Still Love You
Under the Gun
Bruce Kulick Guitar Solo
Tears Are Falling
Gene Simmons Bass Solo
[I Love It Loud]
[Love Gun]
[Rock and Roll All Nite]
[Heaven's On Fire]
[Won't Get Fooled Again]
[Lick It Up]

DECEMBER 8, 1985

Austin, Texas
Frank C. Erwin, Jr., Special Events Center
Opening Act: Black 'N Blue
Attendance: 4,324   Capacity: 6,455
Promoter: Texas Amusement Media
Archived: Audio, Partial Video

■ SET LIST

Detroit Rock City
Fits Like a Glove
Cold Gin
Paul Stanley Guitar Solo
Uh! All Night
Eric Carr Drum Solo
War Machine
I Still Love You
Under the Gun
[Bruce Kulick Guitar Solo]
Tears Are Falling
Gene Simmons Bass Solo
I Love It Loud
Love Gun
Rock and Roll All Nite
Heaven's On Fire
Won't Get Fooled Again
Lick It Up

■ Gene caught his hair on fire during the show.

DECEMBER 9, 1985

Springfield, Illinois **TEMP HOLD DATE**
Prairie Capital Convention Center
Opening Act: Black 'N Blue

DECEMBER 11, 1985

Richfield (Cleveland), Ohio
The Coliseum Theatre
Opening Act: Black 'N Blue
Promoter: Belkin Productions
Archived: Video

■ SET LIST

Detroit Rock City
Fits Like a Glove
Cold Gin
Paul Stanley Guitar Solo
Uh! All Night
Eric Carr Drum Solo
War Machine
I Still Love You
Under the Gun
Bruce Kulick Guitar Solo
Tears Are Falling
Gene Simmons Bass Solo
I Love It Loud
Love Gun
Rock and Roll All Nite
Heaven's On Fire
Won't Get Fooled Again
Lick It Up

■ The second Asylum Tour stage debuted at this show.

Much to the amusement of his bandmates, Eric tripped while running up one of lightning bolt staircases.

DECEMBER 12, 1985

Louisville, Kentucky
Freedom Hall
Opening Act: Black 'N Blue
Attendance: 5,000   Capacity: 19,000
Promoter: Sunshine Promotions
Archived: Audio

■ SET LIST

See December 11, 1985.

■ After the show, Paul and Bruce performed live at a club with a local band called Mannekin.

DECEMBER 13, 1985

Dayton, Ohio
Hara Arena & Exhibition Center
Opening Act: Black 'N Blue
Capacity: 8,000
Promoter: Belkin Productions

DECEMBER 14, 1985

Detroit, Michigan
Cobo Arena
Opening Act: Black 'N Blue
Capacity: 12,000
Promoter: Belkin Productions
Archived: Video

■ SET LIST

See December 11, 1985.

■ After "Heaven's On Fire," Eric again tripped while attempting to run up one of the lightning bolt staircases. The band and crowd egged him on to attempt the stage right staircase, which, after taking a running start, he did manage to negotiate. This is the first known appearance of Paul's trapeze stunt.

Paul's solo featured an excerpt of "Oh Susannah."

DECEMBER 16, 1985

New York, New York
Madison Square Garden
Opening Act: Black 'N Blue
Attendance: 13,500   Capacity: 13,500
Promoter: Ron Delsener Presents
Archived: Video

■ SET LIST

See December 11, 1985.

■ This was KISS's first appearance at Madison Square Garden since 1979. During the last two songs of the set, fans invaded the stage, as Dave Bonilla explains: "We were playing the Garden and as he normally would Paul yelled 'Hey! C'mon up! Let's get up here and have fun.' The lightning bolt stairs would extend close to the railings in the upper tiers of the arenas. And at this particular gig they were almost attached to the tier. When Paul yelled that, it looked like they had just opened the doors at Macy's during a big sales weekend; all of these kids came jumping over the railing and running down the steps. It looked like an escalator."

Paul's solo again featured an excerpt of "Oh Susannah."

KISS held a private party following their performance.

DECEMBER 17, 1985

Philadelphia, Pennsylvania
The Spectrum

Opening Act: Black 'N Blue
Attendance: 10,301   Capacity 14,972
Promoter: Concert Co. Presentations
Archived: Audio
■ **SET LIST**
See December 6, 1985.
■ A professionally-shot videotape of the show may exist as many concerts at The Spectrum were archived by their in-house video crew.

DECEMBER 19, 1985

Glens Falls, New York
Glens Falls Civic Center
Opening Act: Black 'N Blue
Capacity: 8,100
Promoter: Magic City Productions
Archived: Audio
■ **SET LIST**
Detroit Rock City
Fits Like a Glove
Cold Gin
Paul Stanley Guitar Solo
Uh! All Night
Eric Carr Drum Solo
War Machine
I Still Love You
Under the Gun
Bruce Kulick Guitar Solo
Tears Are Falling
Gene Simmons Bass Solo
I Love It Loud
Love Gun
Rock and Roll All Nite
Heaven's On Fire
[Lick It Up]
■ At the end of "Rock and Roll All Nite," Gene jumped into the audience and allegedly punched a concertgoer who was spitting on him.
  Earlier in the evening, "Uh! All Night" debuted on MTV.

DECEMBER 20, 1985

Worcester, Massachusetts
The Centrum
Opening Act: Black 'N Blue
Attendance: 9,132   Capacity: 10,200
Promoter: Frank J. Russo
Archived: Audio
■ **SET LIST**
Detroit Rock City
Fits Like a Glove
Cold Gin
Paul Stanley Guitar Solo
Uh! All Night
Eric Carr Drum Solo
War Machine
I Still Love You
Under the Gun
Bruce Kulick Guitar Solo
Tears Are Falling
Gene Simmons Bass Solo
I Love It Loud
Love Gun
[Rock and Roll All Nite]
[Heaven's On Fire]
[Lick It Up]

DECEMBER 21, 1985

New Haven, Connecticut
New Haven Veterans Memorial Coliseum
Opening Act: Black 'N Blue
Capacity: 11,000
Promoter: Cross Country Concerts
Archived: Audio

■ **SET LIST**
Detroit Rock City
Fits Like a Glove
King of the Mountain
Cold Gin
Uh! All Night
Eric Carr Drum Solo
War Machine
I Still Love You
Under the Gun
Bruce Kulick Guitar Solo
Tears Are Falling
Gene Simmons Bass Solo
I Love It Loud
Love Gun
Rock and Roll All Nite
Heaven's On Fire
Won't Get Fooled Again
Lick It Up

DECEMBER 22, 1985

Providence, Rhode Island
Providence Civic Center
Opening Act: Black 'N Blue
Attendance: 8,888   Capacity: 10,200
Promoter: Frank J. Russo
Archived: Audio
■ **SET LIST**
Detroit Rock City
Fits Like a Glove
Cold Gin
Uh! All Night
Eric Carr Drum Solo
War Machine
I Still Love You
Under the Gun
Bruce Kulick Guitar Solo
Tears Are Falling
Gene Simmons Bass Solo
I Love It Loud
Love Gun
Rock and Roll All Nite
Heaven's On Fire
Won't Get Fooled Again
Lick It Up
■ Paul split his pants during "Cold Gin" and changed them backstage during the song.

DECEMBER 27, 1985

Columbia, South Carolina
Carolina Coliseum
Opening Act: Black 'N Blue
Attendance: 5,341   Capacity: 9,500
Promoter: Beach Club Promotions

DECEMBER 28, 1985

Charlotte, North Carolina
Charlotte Coliseum
Opening Act: Black 'N Blue
Attendance: 9,458   Capacity 12,900
Promoter: Kaleidoscope Productions
Archived: Audio
■ **SET LIST**
Detroit Rock City
Fits Like a Glove
Uh! All Night
Cold Gin
Under the Gun
Bruce Kulick Guitar Solo
I Still Love You
Gene Simmons Bass Solo
I Love It Loud
Tears Are Falling
Eric Carr Drum Solo
War Machine
Love Gun

NORMAN BOUTHILLIER

Rock and Roll All Nite
Heaven's On Fire
[Lick It Up]

DECEMBER 29, 1985

Greensboro, North Carolina
Greensboro Coliseum
Opening Act: Black 'N Blue
Capacity: 13,500
Promoter: Beach Club Promotions

DECEMBER 30, 1985

Augusta, Georgia
Augusta/Richmond County Civic Center
Opening Act: Black 'N Blue
Attendance: 4,518   Capacity: 9,000
Promoter: Chesapeake Concerts

DECEMBER 31, 1985

Atlanta, Georgia
The Omni
Opening Act: Black 'N Blue
Attendance: 7,144   Capacity: 7,982
Promoter: Chesapeake Concerts
Archived: Audio
■ **SET LIST**
Detroit Rock City
Fits Like a Glove
Uh! All Night
Cold Gin
Under the Gun
Bruce Kulick Guitar Solo
I Still Love You
Gene Simmons Bass Solo
I Love It Loud
Tears Are Falling
Eric Carr Drum Solo
War Machine
Love Gun
Rock and Roll All Nite
La Bamba
Whole Lotta Love
Heaven's On Fire
Oh Susannah
Won't Get Fooled Again
Lick It Up

155

■ A professionally-shot video of the concert may exist, as The Omni possessed similar in-house video capabilities to The Spectrum in Philadelphia.

To celebrate the new year, "La Bamba" was played at the stroke of midnight. Paul also added vocals to this performance of "Oh Susannah."

JANUARY 3, 1986

Johnson City, Tennessee
Freedom Hall Civic Center @ Science Hill High School
Opening Act: W.A.S.P.
Attendance: 6,016   Capacity: 8,000
Promoter: Sunshine Promotions
Archived: Audio
■ SET LIST
Detroit Rock City
Fits Like a Glove
Uh! All Night
Cold Gin
Under the Gun
Bruce Kulick Guitar Solo
I Still Love You
Gene Simmons Bass Solo
I Love It Loud
Tears Are Falling
Eric Carr Drum Solo
War Machine
Love Gun
Rock and Roll All Nite
Heaven's On Fire
Oh Susannah
Lick It Up

JANUARY 4, 1986

Knoxville, Tennessee
Knoxville Civic Coliseum
Opening Act: W.A.S.P.
Attendance: 5,356
Promoter: Sunshine Promotions
Archived: Audio
■ SET LIST
Detroit Rock City
Fits Like a Glove
Uh! All Night
Cold Gin
Under the Gun
Bruce Kulick Guitar Solo
I Still Love You
Gene Simmons Bass Solo
I Love It Loud
Tears Are Falling
Eric Carr Drum Solo
War Machine
Love Gun
Rock and Roll All Nite
Heaven's On Fire
Won't Get Fooled Again
Whole Lotta Love
Lick It Up
■ The band played the *Green Acres* theme prior to "Won't Get Fooled Again."

JANUARY 5, 1986

Huntsville, Alabama
Von Braun Civic Center
Capacity: 10,100   TEMP HOLD DATE
Promoter: Sunshine Promotions

JANUARY 5, 1986

CANCELED
Chattanooga, Tennessee
UTC Arena
Opening Act: W.A.S.P.
Capacity: 12,200
Promoter: Sunshine Promotions

■ The concert was canceled at 7 P.M. on the night prior to the show due to the lack of tickets sold. This was the second cancellation in Chattanooga for KISS within a year.

NORMAN BOUTHILLIER

JANUARY 7, 1986

Tampa, Florida
USF Sundome
Opening Act: W.A.S.P.
Capacity: 10,400
Promoter: Cellar Door Concerts
Archived: Audio
■ SET LIST
Detroit Rock City
Fits Like a Glove
Uh! All Night
Cold Gin
Under the Gun
Bruce Kulick Guitar Solo
I Still Love You
Gene Simmons Bass Solo
I Love It Loud
Tears Are Falling
Eric Carr Drum Solo
War Machine
Love Gun
Rock and Roll All Nite
Heaven's On Fire
Oh Susannah
Won't Get Fooled Again
Lick It Up
■ Eric Carr was interviewed backstage for a regional cable music show called *V-32*.

JANUARY 8, 1986

West Palm Beach, Florida
West Palm Beach Auditorium
Opening Act: W.A.S.P.
Attendance: 5,063   Capacity: 6,400
Promoter: Cellar Door Concerts
Archived: Audio
■ SET LIST
Detroit Rock City
Fits Like a Glove
Cold Gin
Uh! All Night
Paul Stanley Guitar Solo
Under the Gun
Bruce Kulick Guitar Solo
I Still Love You

Gene Simmons Bass Solo
I Love It Loud
Tears Are Falling
Eric Carr Drum Solo
War Machine
Love Gun
Rock and Roll All Nite
Heaven's On Fire
Won't Get Fooled Again
Lick It Up

JANUARY 9, 1986

North Fort Myers, Florida
Lee County Arena
Opening Act: W.A.S.P.
Capacity: 7,100
Promoter: Cellar Door Concerts

JANUARY 10, 1986

Jacksonville, Florida
Jacksonville Veterans Memorial Coliseum
Opening Act: W.A.S.P.
Capacity: 10,228
Promoter: Cellar Door Concerts

JANUARY 12, 1986

San Juan, Puerto Rico
Coliseo Roberto Clemente
No Opening Act
Attendance: 5,000   Capacity: 10,000
Promoter: Sunshine Promotions
Archived: Audio
■ SET LIST
See January 8, 1986.
■ KISS's lighted logo was not used at the show.

While in San Juan, Paul went out to a nightclub called Shannon's Pub and performed "Strutter" with the house band. Someone who worked at the venue jokingly announced, "See you next week at Coventry," causing several fans to believe that the existing audiotape of this performance was in fact from 1973.

JANUARY 14, 1986

Norfolk, Virginia
The Scope
Opening Act: W.A.S.P.
Capacity: 11,300
Promoter: Beach Club Promotions
Archived: Audio
■ SET LIST
Detroit Rock City
Fits Like a Glove
Cold Gin
Uh! All Night
Paul Stanley Guitar Solo
Under the Gun
Bruce Kulick Guitar Solo
I Still Love You
Gene Simmons Bass Solo
I Love It Loud
Tears Are Falling
Eric Carr Drum Solo
War Machine
Love Gun
Rock and Roll All Nite
Heaven's On Fire
Lick It Up
■ The band made a very brief attempt to play "Oh Susannah" prior to "Lick It Up."

JANUARY 15, 1986

Charleston, West Virginia
Charleston Civic Center
Opening Act: W.A.S.P.

Attendance: 6,962   Capacity 10,195
Promoter: Belkin Productions
■ SET LIST
Detroit Rock City
Fits Like a Glove
Cold Gin
Uh! All Night
Under the Gun
Bruce Kulick Guitar/Bass Solo
I Still Love You
Gene Simmons Bass Solo
I Love It Loud
[Paul Stanley Guitar Solo]
Tears Are Falling
Eric Carr Drum Solo
War Machine
Love Gun
Rock and Roll All Nite
Heaven's On Fire
Lick It Up

■ The band jokingly refused to return to the stage on cue at the end of Bruce's solo, leaving him to his own devices to entertain the audience. Kulick extended his solo and eventually did a short bass solo to fill the time before his bandmates finally returned to the stage. Michael Lipton, writing for *The Charleston Gazette,* noted Bruce's "extended" solo and added "he tossed the guitar to the ground and left the stage."

The band played a portion of ZZ Top's "LaGrange" before segueing into "Heaven's On Fire." Then, Paul and Eric very briefly played the riff from "Firehouse" prior to "Lick It Up."

Joel Smith's review of the concert in *The Charleston Daily Mail* clearly references Paul's trapeze stunt. This is the last known appearance of the gimmick.

JANUARY 16, 1986
Indianapolis, Indiana
Market Square Arena
Opening Act: W.A.S.P.
Attendance: 13,538   Capacity: 16,000
Promoter: Sunshine Promotions
Archived: Audio
■ SET LIST
Detroit Rock City
Fits Like a Glove
Cold Gin
Uh! All Night
Bruce Kulick Guitar Solo
I Still Love You
Gene Simmons Bass Solo
I Love It Loud
[Paul Stanley Guitar Solo]
Tears Are Falling
Eric Carr Drum Solo
War Machine
Love Gun
Rock and Roll All Nite
Heaven's On Fire
Oh Susannah
Whole Lotta Love
Won't Get Fooled Again
Lick It Up

JANUARY 17, 1986
Chicago, Illinois
University of Illinois-Chicago Pavilion
Opening Act: W.A.S.P.
Capacity: 10,600
Promoter: JAM Productions
Archived: Audio
■ SET LIST
Detroit Rock City

Fits Like a Glove
Cold Gin
Uh! All Night
Under the Gun
Bruce Kulick Guitar Solo
I Still Love You
Gene Simmons Bass Solo
I Love It Loud
Paul Stanley Guitar Solo
Tears Are Falling
Eric Carr Drum Solo
War Machine
Love Gun
[Rock and Roll All Nite]
Heaven's On Fire
Won't Get Fooled Again
Lick It Up

JANUARY 20, 1986
Milwaukee, Wisconsin
Mecca Auditorium
Opening Act: W.A.S.P.
Attendance: 4,254   Capacity 6,100
Promoter: Stardate Productions
Archived: Audio
■ SET LIST
Detroit Rock City
Fits Like a Glove
Cold Gin
Uh! All Night
Under the Gun
Bruce Kulick Guitar Solo
I Still Love You
Gene Simmons Bass Solo
I Love It Loud
Paul Stanley Guitar Solo
Tears Are Falling
Eric Carr Drum Solo
War Machine
Love Gun
Rock and Roll All Nite
Heaven's On Fire
Lick It Up

■ The band and audience sang "Happy Birthday" to Paul prior to "Lick It Up."

JANUARY 21, 1986
St. Paul, Minnesota
St. Paul Civic Center
Opening Act: W.A.S.P.
Attendance: 8,770   Capacity: 11,000
Promoter: Schon Productions
Archived: Audio
■ SET LIST
Detroit Rock City
Fits Like a Glove
Uh! All Night
Cold Gin
Under the Gun
Bruce Kulick Guitar Solo
Gene Simmons Bass Solo
I Love It Loud
Heaven's On Fire
Eric Carr Drum Solo
War Machine
I Still Love You
Love Gun
Lick It Up
Tears Are Falling
Oh Susannah
Won't Get Fooled Again
Rock and Roll All Nite

■ Paul, who was hit by a bottle during the show, dedicated "Tears Are Falling" to Michael Streicher, a fan who died while hookie-bobbing (hanging onto the back of a car while skateboarding).

JANUARY 22, 1986
Rockford, Illinois
MetroCentre
Opening Act: W.A.S.P.
Attendance: 5,890   Capacity: 8,000
Promoter: JAM Productions

JANUARY 23, 1986
St. Louis, Missouri
Kiel Auditorium
Opening Act: W.A.S.P.
Attendance: 5,949   Capacity: 10,532
Promoter: Contemporary Productions
Archived: Audio
■ SET LIST
Detroit Rock City
Fits Like a Glove
Cold Gin
Uh! All Night
Under the Gun
Bruce Kulick Guitar Solo
I Still Love You
Gene Simmons Bass Solo
I Love It Loud
Paul Stanley Guitar Solo
Tears Are Falling
Eric Carr Drum Solo
War Machine
Love Gun
Rock and Roll All Nite
Heaven's On Fire
Won't Get Fooled Again
Lick It Up

JANUARY 24, 1986
Omaha, Nebraska
Omaha Civic Auditorium
Opening Act: W.A.S.P.
Attendance: 6,426   Capacity: 8,000
Promoter: Concert Presentation
Archived: Audio
■ SET LIST
Detroit Rock City
Fits Like a Glove
Cold Gin
Uh! All Night
Young and Wasted
Bruce Kulick Guitar solo
Heaven's On Fire
Gene Simmons Bass Solo
I Love It Loud
I Still Love You
Eric Carr Drum Solo
War Machine
Love Gun
Lick It Up
Tears Are Falling
Rock and Roll All Nite

■ Paul, Gene, and Eric played a 12-bar blues riff briefly before "Uh! All Night."

KISS's performance was delayed almost an hour from its scheduled time. The barricade that KISS used to separate the crowd from the front of the stage broke, and the venue's barricade had to be erected in its place. Road crew members asked the crowd to step back so that the barricade could be installed, but most of the audience refused to move.

JANUARY 25, 1986
Kansas City, Missouri
Municipal Auditorium
Opening Act: W.A.S.P.
Attendance: 6,922   Capacity: 9,000
Promoter: Schon Productions

■ On January 28, HBO premiered an episode of *The Hitchhiker* entitled "O.D. Feelin,'" starring Gene Simmons, who played a high-end drug dealer named Mr. Big.

JANUARY 28, 1986

Albuquerque, New Mexico
Tingley Coliseum   **TEMP HOLD DATE**
Capacity: 10,000
Promoter: Feyline Inc.

JANUARY 30, 1986

Inglewood (Los Angeles), California
The Forum   **POSTPONED**
Opening Act: W.A.S.P.
Promoter: Parc Presentations

■ The concert was postponed until February 11, 1986.

FEBRUARY 2, 1986

Reno, Nevada   **TEMP HOLD DATE**
Lawlor Events Center
Opening Act: W.A.S.P.
Promoter: Evening Star Productions

FEBRUARY 2, 1986

Tucson, Arizona
McKale Memorial Center
Opening Act: W.A.S.P.
Attendance: 4,493   Capacity: 8,352
Promoter: Evening Star Productions
Archived: Audio

■ **SET LIST**

Detroit Rock City
Fits Like a Glove
Uh! All Night
Cold Gin
Young and Wasted
Bruce Kulick Guitar Solo
Gene Simmons Bass Solo
I Love It Loud
Paul Stanley Guitar Solo
Heaven's On Fire
Eric Carr Drum Solo
War Machine
I Still Love You
Love Gun
Rock and Roll All Nite
Tears Are Falling
Won't Get Fooled Again
[Lick It Up]

■ This is the last known performance of "Young and Wasted."

FEBRUARY 4, 1986

Daly City (San Francisco), California
Cow Palace
Opening Act: W.A.S.P.
Attendance: 5,699   Capacity: 10,000
Promoter: Bill Graham Presents
Archived: Audio

■ **SET LIST**

Detroit Rock City
Fits Like a Glove
Uh! All Night
Cold Gin
Under the Gun
Bruce Kulick Guitar Solo
Gene Simmons Bass Solo
I Love It Loud
Paul Stanley Guitar Solo
Heaven's On Fire
Eric Carr Drum Solo
War Machine
I Still Love You

Love Gun
Rock and Roll All Nite
Tears Are Falling
Won't Get Fooled Again
Lick It Up

FEBRUARY 5, 1986

Sacramento, California
Sacramento Memorial Auditorium
Opening Act: W.A.S.P.
Attendance: 2,603   Capacity: 4,181
Promoter: Bill Graham Presents
Archived: Audio

■ **SET LIST**

Detroit Rock City
Fits Like a Glove
Uh! All Night
Cold Gin
Bruce Kulick Guitar Solo
Strutter
Gene Simmons Bass Solo
I Love It Loud
Paul Stanley Guitar Solo
Heaven's On Fire
Eric Carr Drum Solo
War Machine
I Still Love You
Love Gun
Rock and Roll All Nite
Tears Are Falling
Won't Get Fooled Again
[Lick It Up]

FEBRUARY 7, 1986

Las Vegas, Nevada
Thomas & Mack Center
Opening Act: Black 'N Blue
Attendance: 4,295   Capacity 6,751
Promoter: Evening Star Productions
Archived: Audio

■ **SET LIST**

Detroit Rock City
Fits Like a Glove
Uh! All Night
Cold Gin
Bruce Kulick Guitar Solo
Strutter
Gene Simmons Bass Solo
I Love It Loud
Paul Stanley Guitar Solo
Heaven's On Fire
Eric Carr Drum Solo
War Machine
I Still Love You
Love Gun
Rock and Roll All Nite
Tears Are Falling
Won't Get Fooled Again
Lick It Up

■ W.A.S.P. was unable to perform because they were banned from playing Las Vegas.

FEBRUARY 8, 1986

San Bernardino, California
Orange Show Pavilion
Opening Act: W.A.S.P.
Capacity: 6,000
Promoter: Parc Presentations
Archived: Audio

■ **SET LIST**

See February 7, 1986.

FEBRUARY 9, 1986

Fresno, California   **CANCELED**
Selland Arena
Opening Act: W.A.S.P.

Promoter: Avalon Attractions

■ This concert, originally scheduled for February 11, was moved to the 9th before being canceled.

FEBRUARY 9, 1986

Phoenix, Arizona
Arizona Veterans Memorial Coliseum
Opening Act: W.A.S.P.
Attendance: 8,996   Capacity: 16,000
Promoter: Evening Star Productions
Archived: Audio

■ **SET LIST**

Detroit Rock City
Fits Like a Glove
Uh! All Night
Cold Gin
Bruce Kulick Guitar Solo
Strutter
Gene Simmons Bass Solo
I Love It Loud
Eric Carr Drum Solo
War Machine
Heaven's On Fire
I Still Love You
Love Gun
Rock and Roll All Nite
Tears Are Falling
Won't Get Fooled Again
Lick It Up

FEBRUARY 10, 1986

San Diego, California
San Diego Sports Arena
Opening Act: W.A.S.P.
Attendance: 6,101   Capacity: 8,300
Promoter: Fahn & Silva Productions
Archived: Audio

■ **SET LIST**

Detroit Rock City
Fits Like a Glove
Uh! All Night
Cold Gin
Bruce Kulick Guitar Solo
Strutter
Gene Simmons Bass Solo
I Love It Loud
Eric Carr Drum Solo
War Machine
Paul Stanley Guitar Solo
Heaven's On Fire
I Still Love You
Love Gun
Rock and Roll All Nite
Tears Are Falling
Won't Get Fooled Again
Lick It Up

FEBRUARY 11, 1986

Bakersfield, California   **CANCELED**
Bakersfield Civic Auditorium
Opening Act: W.A.S.P.
Capacity: 6,000

FEBRUARY 11, 1986

Inglewood (Los Angeles), California
The Forum
Opening Act: W.A.S.P.
Attendance: 10,630   Capacity: 18,000
Promoter: Parc Presentations
Archived: Audio

■ **SET LIST**

Detroit Rock City
Fits Like a Glove
Uh! All Night
Strutter
Cold Gin

Bruce Kulick Guitar Solo
Gene Simmons Bass Solo
I Love It Loud
Eric Carr Drum Solo
War Machine
Paul Stanley Guitar Solo
Heaven's On Fire
I Still Love You
Love Gun
Rock and Roll All Nite
Tears Are Falling
Won't Get Fooled Again
Lick It Up

FEBRUARY 13, 1986
Portland, Oregon
Memorial Coliseum
Opening Act: W.A.S.P.
Capacity: 9,000
Promoter: Media One
Archived: Audio
■ SET LIST
Detroit Rock City
Fits Like a Glove
Uh! All Night
Cold Gin
Bruce Kulick Guitar Solo
Strutter
Gene Simmons Bass Solo
I Love It Loud
Eric Carr Drum Solo
War Machine
Paul Stanley Guitar Solo
Heaven's On Fire
I Still Love You
Love Gun
Rock and Roll All Nite
Oh Susannah
Tears Are Falling
[Lick It Up]

FEBRUARY 14, 1986
Seattle, Washington
Seattle Center Coliseum
Opening Act: W.A.S.P.
Attendance: 5,500   Capacity: 14,300
Promoter: Media One
Archived: Audio
■ SET LIST
Detroit Rock City
Fits Like a Glove
Uh! All Night
Cold Gin
Bruce Kulick Guitar Solo
Strutter
Gene Simmons Bass Solo
I Love It Loud
Eric Carr Drum Solo
War Machine
Paul Stanley Guitar Solo
Heaven's On Fire
I Still Love You
Love Gun
Rock and Roll All Nite
Tears Are Falling
Won't Get Fooled Again
Oh Susannah
Lick It Up
■ Prior to "Lick It Up," Gene briefly played "La Bamba."

FEBRUARY 15, 1986   CANCELED
Pullman, Washington
Beasley Performing Arts Center
Opening Act: W.A.S.P.
Capacity: 4,700

■ The concert was canceled on the day of show due to a massive snowstorm. It was originally scheduled for the Washington State University Arena.

FEBRUARY 16, 1986   TEMP HOLD DATE
Boise, Idaho
BSU Pavilion
Capacity: 13,000
Promoter: United Concerts

FEBRUARY 17, 1986
Salt Lake City, Utah
O. Thayne Accord Arena @ Salt Palace Center
Opening Act: W.A.S.P.
Capacity: 11,500
Promoter: United Concerts
■ Due to technical difficulties with the P.A., no encores were performed at this show.

FEBRUARY 19, 1986
Denver, Colorado
McNichols Sports Arena
Opening Act: W.A.S.P.
Capacity: 19,000
Promoter: Feyline, Inc.
Archived: Audio
■ SET LIST
Detroit Rock City
Fits Like a Glove
Uh! All Night
Cold Gin
Bruce Kulick Guitar Solo
Strutter
Gene Simmons Bass Solo
I Love It Loud
Eric Carr Drum Solo
War Machine
Paul Stanley Guitar Solo
Heaven's On Fire
I Still Love You
Love Gun
Rock and Roll All Nite
Oh Susannah
Tears Are Falling
Won't Get Fooled Again
[Lick It Up]

FEBRUARY 21, 1986
Norman, Oklahoma
Lloyd Noble Center
Opening Act: W.A.S.P.
Attendance: 6,116   Capacity: 6,116
Promoter: Contemporary Productions
Archived: Audio
■ SET LIST
Detroit Rock City
Fits Like a Glove
Uh! All Night
Cold Gin
Bruce Kulick Guitar Solo
Strutter
Gene Simmons Bass Solo
I Love It Loud
Eric Carr Drum Solo
War Machine
Paul Stanley Guitar Solo
Heaven's On Fire
I Still Love You
Love Gun
Rock and Roll All Nite
Oh Susannah
Tears Are Falling
Won't Get Fooled Again
Lick It Up

FEBRUARY 22, 1986
Tulsa, Oklahoma
Expo Square Pavilion
Opening Act: W.A.S.P.
Attendance: 6,600   Capacity: 8,100
Promoter: Little Wing Attractions

FEBRUARY 23, 1986
Waco, Texas
Convention Center
Opening Act: W.A.S.P.
Capacity: 4,500
Promoter: Jam Presents of Texas

FEBRUARY 24, 1986
Corpus Christi, Texas
Memorial Coliseum
Opening Act: W.A.S.P.
Attendance: 5,200   Capacity: 6,000
Promoter: Jam Presents of Texas
■ A heated controversy developed in the local press when the Corpus Christi City Council considered regulating rock concerts. Gene and Paul participated in a last-minute press conference to comment on the event. Some City Council members attended the concert to monitor the proceedings.

FEBRUARY 26, 1986
Beaumont, Texas
Beaumont Civic Center
Opening Act: W.A.S.P.
Capacity: 6,500
Promoter: 462, Inc.

FEBRUARY 27, 1986
Abilene, Texas
Taylor County Coliseum
Opening Act: W.A.S.P.
Attendance: 3,500   Capacity: 6,500
Promoter: Jam Presents of Texas
Archived: Partial Video
■ KISS met with 18-year old Brad Miller at the request of the Make a Wish Foundation of West Texas. Brad was suffering from Duchenne's muscular dystrophy.

A few minutes of this performance was privately videotaped. The privately recorded audiotape of this show is a fake, and is actually from the band's April 11 concert in East Rutherford, New Jersey.

FEBRUARY 28, 1986
Fort Worth, Texas
Tarrant County Convention Center
Opening Act: W.A.S.P.
Capacity: 8,600
Promoter: 462, Inc.
Archived: Video
■ SET LIST
Detroit Rock City
Fits Like a Glove
Creatures of the Night
Cold Gin
Bruce Kulick Guitar Solo
Uh! All Night
Eric Carr Drum Solo
War Machine
Love Gun
I Still Love You
Gene Simmons Bass Solo
I Love It Loud
Paul Stanley Guitar Solo
Heaven's On Fire

Rock and Roll All Nite
Tears Are Falling
Won't Get Fooled Again
[Lick It Up]
■ This was KISS's last known performance of "Won't Get Fooled Again."

MARCH 1, 1986

Shreveport, Louisiana
Hirsch Memorial Coliseum
Opening Act: W.A.S.P.
Attendance: 6,100   Capacity: 10,300
Promoter: Beaver Productions

MARCH 2, 1986

New Orleans, Louisiana
Kiefer UNO Lakefront Arena
Opening Act: W.A.S.P.
Capacity: 6,250
Promoter: Barry Mendelson Presents
Archived: Audio

■ SET LIST

Detroit Rock City
Fits Like a Glove
Creatures of the Night
Cold Gin
Bruce Kulick Guitar Solo
Uh! All Night
Eric Carr Drum Solo
War Machine
Love Gun
I Still Love You
Gene Simmons Bass Solo
I Love It Loud
Paul Stanley Guitar Solo
Heaven's On Fire
Rock and Roll All Nite
Oh Susannah
Tears Are Falling
Lick It Up

■ As an end-of-tour prank, members of W.A.S.P. entered the photo pit during "Lick It Up" and threw raw meat at KISS.

MARCH 5, 1986

Green Bay, Wisconsin
Brown County Veterans Memorial Arena
Opening Act: King Kobra
Attendance: 6,532   Capacity: 7,000
Promoter: Stardate Productions

■ The audience was cleared out of the facility during King Kobra's set due to a bomb threat. After a security sweep of the building, the audience was allowed back into the venue and the concert continued.

MARCH 6, 1986

Saginaw, Michigan
Wendler Arena @ Saginaw Civic Center
Opening Act: King Kobra
Attendance: 6,133   Capacity: 6,746
Promoter: Belkin Productions

MARCH 7, 1986

Port Huron, Michigan
McMorran Place
Opening Act: King Kobra
Attendance: 2,946   Capacity: 5,500
Promoter: Charlevoix Productions
Archived: Video

■ SET LIST

Detroit Rock City
Fits Like a Glove
Creatures of the Night
Cold Gin
Bruce Kulick Guitar Solo

Uh! All Night
Eric Carr Drum Solo
War Machine
Love Gun
I Still Love You
Gene Simmons Bass Solo
I Love It Loud
Paul Stanley Guitar Solo
Heaven's On Fire
Rock and Roll All Nite
Tears Are Falling
Medley: Deuce - Shout It Out Loud - Deuce - Firehouse
    - Calling Dr. Love - Beth - I Was Made for Lovin'
    You
[Lick It Up]

MARCH 8, 1986

Springfield, Illinois
Prairie Capital Convention Center
Opening Act: King Kobra
Attendance: 5,025   Capacity: 6,020
Promoter: JAM Productions
Archived: Audio

■ SET LIST

Detroit Rock City
Fits Like a Glove
Creatures of the Night
Cold Gin
Bruce Kulick Guitar Solo
Uh! All Night
Eric Carr Drum Solo
War Machine
Love Gun
[I Still Love You]
Gene Simmons Bass Solo
I Love It Loud
Paul Stanley Guitar Solo
Heaven's On Fire
Rock and Roll All Nite
Tears Are Falling
Medley: Firehouse - Beth - I Was Made for Lovin' You -
    Calling Dr. Love - Shout It Out Loud
Oh Susannah
Lick It Up

MARCH 9, 1986

Salina, Kansas
Bicentennial Center
Opening Act: King Kobra
Attendance: 4,633   Capacity: 6,000
Promoters: New West Presentations, Concert
    Presentation

MARCH 12, 1986

La Crosse, Wisconsin
Mary E. Sawyer Auditorium @ La Crosse Center
Opening Act: King Kobra
Attendance: 3,063   Capacity: 8,000
Promoter: Stardate Productions

MARCH 13, 1986

Duluth, Minnesota
Duluth Arena Auditorium
Opening Act: King Kobra
Attendance: 3,365   Capacity: 7,755
Promoter: Rose Productions

■ Dave Bonilla: "Steve Habl, the production manager, joked around quite a bit. He'd write messages on the exploding P.A. cabinets. When Gene would shoot them with the rockets, the front would hinge open, and there'd be a message, 'You stink,' and he'd shoot the other one down, and it'd say 'Fat Boy.' Another great joke Steve pulled involved a pair of underwear. He bought a pair of Fruit of the Looms, around size 68 or something like that, and smeared brown

shoe polish on the ass of the underwear. Then he chucked them onstage. The band was totally grossed out. Gene put it on Paul's mike when he wasn't looking, and then he'd put it on Gene's mike."

MARCH 14, 1986

Jamestown, North Dakota
Jamestown Civic Center
Opening Act: King Kobra
Attendance: 4,187   Capacity: 6,500
Promoter: X.F.R. Productions

MARCH 16, 1986

Des Moines, Iowa
Veterans Memorial Auditorium
Opening Act: King Kobra
Attendance: 7,169   Capacity: 7,500
Promoters: Contemporary Productions, Pace Concerts
Archived: Video

■ SET LIST

Detroit Rock City
Fits Like a Glove
Creatures of the Night
Cold Gin
Bruce Kulick Guitar Solo
Uh! All Night
Eric Carr Drum Solo
War Machine
Love Gun
I Still Love You
Gene Simmons Bass Solo
I Love It Loud
Paul Stanley Guitar Solo
Heaven's On Fire
Rock and Roll All Nite
Tears Are Falling
Lick It Up

■ The City Council forbade the use of pyro at the show.

MARCH 17, 1986

Sioux City, Iowa
Sioux City Municipal Auditorium
Opening Act: King Kobra
Attendance: 2,389   Capacity: 4,600
Promoter: Terry Drea Presents

MARCH 18, 1986

Cedar Rapids, Iowa
Five Seasons Center
Opening Act: King Kobra
Attendance: 6,000   Capacity: 10,000
Promoter: JAM Productions

MARCH 20, 1986

Fort Wayne, Indiana
Allen Co. War Memorial Coliseum
Opening Act: King Kobra
Attendance: 6,384   Capacity: 7,500
Promoter: Sunshine Promotions

MARCH 21, 1986

Cincinnati, Ohio
Cincinnati Gardens
Opening Act: King Kobra
Capacity: 9,000
Promoter: Belkin Productions
Archived: Audio

■ SET LIST

Detroit Rock City
Fits Like a Glove
Creatures of the Night
Cold Gin
Bruce Kulick Guitar Solo
Uh! All Night

Eric Carr Drum Solo
War Machine
Love Gun
I Still Love You
Gene Simmons Bass Solo
I Love It Loud
Paul Stanley Guitar Solo
Heaven's On Fire
Rock and Roll All Nite
Medley: Calling Dr. Love - Oh Susannah - I Was Made
   for Lovin' You - Beth
Tears Are Falling
Lick It Up
■ Prior to "Lick It Up," Gene played an excerpt of a Jeff Beck Group song.

MARCH 22, 1986
Carbondale, Illinois
SIU Arena
Opening Act: King Kobra
Attendance: 5,233   Capacity: 9,340
Promoter: JAM Productions

MARCH 23, 1986
Terre Haute, Indiana
Hulman Center
Opening Act: King Kobra
Attendance: 4,788   Capacity: 7,000
Promoter: Sunshine Promotions

MARCH 25, 1986
Evansville, Indiana
Roberts Municipal Stadium
Opening Act: King Kobra
Attendance: 6,220   Capacity: 8,000
Promoter: Sunshine Promotions
Archived: Audio
■ SET LIST
Detroit Rock City
Fits Like a Glove
Creatures of the Night
Cold Gin
Bruce Kulick Guitar Solo
Uh! All Night
Eric Carr Drum Solo
War Machine
Love Gun
I Still Love You
Gene Simmons Bass Solo
I Love It Loud
Paul Stanley Guitar Solo
Heaven's On Fire
Rock and Roll All Nite
Medley: Beth - I Was Made for Lovin' You - Shout It
   Out Loud
Tears Are Falling
[Lick It Up]

MARCH 26, 1986
Battle Creek, Michigan
Kellogg Center Arena
Opening Act: King Kobra
Attendance: 6,302   Capacity: 7,100
Promoter: Belkin Productions
Archived: Audio
■ SET LIST
Detroit Rock City
Fits Like a Glove
Creatures of the Night
Cold Gin
Bruce Kulick Guitar Solo
Uh! All Night
Eric Carr Drum Solo
[War Machine]
Love Gun
I Still Love You

Gene Simmons Bass Solo
I Love It Loud
Paul Stanley Guitar Solo
Heaven's On Fire
Rock and Roll All Nite
Medley: Calling Dr. Love - Beth
Tears Are Falling
[Lick It Up]

MARCH 27, 1986
Erie, Pennsylvania
Lewis J. Tullio Arena @ Erie Civic Center
Opening Act: King Kobra
Attendance: 4,600   Capacity: 7,500
Promoter: Belkin Productions
Archived: Audio
■ SET LIST
See March 16, 1986.

MARCH 28, 1986
Toledo, Ohio
Sports Arena
Opening Act: King Kobra
Capacity: 7,500
Promoter: Belkin Productions
Archived: Video
■ SET LIST
Detroit Rock City
Fits Like a Glove
Creatures of the Night
Cold Gin
Bruce Kulick Guitar Solo
Uh! All Night
Eric Carr Drum Solo
War Machine
Love Gun
Calling Dr. Love
Gene Simmons Bass Solo
I Love It Loud
Paul Stanley Guitar Solo
Heaven's On Fire
Rock and Roll All Nite
Medley: Deuce - Beth - I Was Made for Lovin' You
Oh Susannah
Tears Are Falling
Lick It Up

MARCH 29, 1986
Columbus, Ohio
Battelle Hall @ Ohio Center
Opening Act: King Kobra
Capacity: 7,100
Promoter: Belkin Productions
Archived: Audio
■ SET LIST
Detroit Rock City
Fits Like a Glove
Creatures of the Night
Cold Gin
Bruce Kulick Guitar Solo
Uh! All Night
Eric Carr Drum Solo
War Machine
Love Gun
Gene Simmons Bass Solo
I Love It Loud
Paul Stanley Guitar Solo
Heaven's On Fire
Rock and Roll All Nite
Whole Lotta Love
Tears Are Falling
Lick It Up
■ KISS played a brief part of Ratt's "Round and Round" prior to "Whole Lotta Love."

MARCH 30, 1986
Hammond, Indiana
Civic Center
Opening Act: King Kobra
Capacity: 4,100
Promoter: Holiday Star Theatre Productions
■ "King of the Mountain" was included in the set, and after "Rock and Roll All Nite," Paul performed part of "Beth."

APRIL 1, 1986
Bethlehem (Allentown), Pennsylvania
Stabler Arena
Opening Act: King Kobra
Attendance: 2,758   Capacity: 6,500
Promoter: Makoul Productions
Archived: Audio
■ SET LIST
Detroit Rock City
Fits Like a Glove
Creatures of the Night
Cold Gin
Bruce Kulick Guitar Solo
Uh! All Night
Calling Dr. Love
Eric Carr Drum Solo
War Machine
Love Gun
Gene Simmons Bass Solo
I Love It Loud
Paul Stanley Guitar Solo
Heaven's On Fire
Rock and Roll All Nite
Tears Are Falling
Lick It Up
■ Following a very brief attempt at "Oh Susannah," the intro to "Black Diamond" was performed, and then KISS launched into "Tears Are Falling." KISS also performed part of "Round and Round" prior to "Lick It Up."

APRIL 2, 1986
Utica, New York
Memorial Auditorium
Opening Act: King Kobra
Capacity: 6,500
Promoter: Magic City Productions
Archived: Audio
■ SET LIST
King of the Mountain
Fits Like a Glove
Creatures of the Night
Cold Gin
Bruce Kulick Guitar Solo
Calling Dr. Love
Uh! All Night
Eric Carr Drum Solo
War Machine
Love Gun
Gene Simmons Bass Solo
I Love It Loud
Lick It Up
Paul Stanley Guitar Solo
Heaven's On Fire
Rock and Roll All Nite
Tears Are Falling
Detroit Rock City
■ This is the last known live performance of "King of the Mountain."

APRIL 3, 1986
Pittsburgh, Pennsylvania   **POSTPONED**
Civic Arena
Opening Act: King Kobra
Promoter: DiCesare-Engler Productions

■ The gig was postponed until April 12th due to electrical difficulties at the venue.

APRIL 4, 1986

Poughkeepsie, New York
Mid-Hudson Civic Center
Opening Act: King Kobra
Attendance: 2,878   Capacity: 2,940
Promoter: Harvey, Corky & Tice Productions
Archived: Audio

■ SET LIST

Detroit Rock City
Fits Like a Glove
Creatures of the Night
Cold Gin
Bruce Kulick Guitar Solo
Calling Dr. Love
Uh! All Night
Eric Carr Drum Solo
War Machine
Love Gun
Gene Simmons Bass Solo
I Love It Loud
Paul Stanley Guitar Solo
Heaven's On Fire
Rock and Roll All Nite
Medley: Firehouse - Black Diamond - Shout It Out Loud
Tears Are Falling
Lick It Up

APRIL 6, 1986

Springfield, Massachusetts
Springfield Civic Center
Opening Act: King Kobra
Capacity: 10,000
Promoter: Cross Country Concerts
Archived: Audio

■ SET LIST

[Detroit Rock City]
[Fits Like a Glove]
[Creatures of the Night]
[Cold Gin]
Bruce Kulick Guitar Solo
Calling Dr. Love
Uh! All Night
Eric Carr Drum Solo
War Machine
Love Gun
Gene Simmons Bass Solo
I Love It Loud
Paul Stanley Guitar Solo
Heaven's On Fire
Rock and Roll All Nite
Tears Are Falling
[Lick It Up]

■ The power blew after two songs. A 45-minute break ensued, during which refunds were offered.

APRIL 7, 1986

Rochester, New York
Rochester Community War Memorial
Opening Act: King Kobra
Capacity: 10,200
Promoter: John Scher Presents

APRIL 8, 1986

Toronto, Ontario, Canada
Maple Leaf Gardens
Opening Act: King Kobra
Attendance: 6,991   Capacity: 8,500
Promoter: Concert Productions Int'l
Archived: Video

■ SET LIST

Detroit Rock City
Fits Like a Glove

ANDREW ALLIN

Creatures of the Night
Cold Gin
Bruce Kulick Guitar Solo
Calling Dr. Love
Uh! All Night
Eric Carr Drum Solo
War Machine
Love Gun
Gene Simmons Bass Solo
I Love It Loud
Paul Stanley Guitar Solo
Heaven's On Fire
Rock and Roll All Nite
Tears Are Falling
Lick It Up

■ King Kobra and some bikini-clad female friends joined KISS onstage for the first half of "Lick It Up." King Kobra vocalist Mark Free later had a sex change operation and became Marcie Free.

APRIL 10, 1986

Baltimore, Maryland
Baltimore Arena
Opening Act: Blue Öyster Cult
Attendance: 4,896   Capacity: 7,452
Promoter: Cellar Door Concerts
Archived: Audio

■ SET LIST

Detroit Rock City
Fits Like a Glove
Creatures of the Night
Cold Gin
Bruce Kulick Guitar Solo
Calling Dr. Love
Uh! All Night
Eric Carr Drum Solo
War Machine
Love Gun
Gene Simmons Bass Solo
I Love It Loud
Paul Stanley Guitar Solo
Heaven's On Fire
Rock and Roll All Nite

King of the Night Time World
Tears Are Falling
Lick It Up

APRIL 11, 1986

East Rutherford, New Jersey
Brendan Byrne Arena
Opening Act: Blue Öyster Cult
Attendance: 14,693   Capacity: 14,953
Promoter: John Scher Presents
Archived: Audio

■ SET LIST

Detroit Rock City
Fits Like a Glove
Creatures of the Night
Cold Gin
Bruce Kulick Guitar Solo
Calling Dr. Love
Uh! All Night
Eric Carr Drum Solo
War Machine
Love Gun
Gene Simmons Bass Solo
I Love It Loud
Paul Stanley Guitar Solo
Heaven's On Fire
Rock and Roll All Nite
Oh Susannah
Whole Lotta Love
Tears Are Falling
Lick It Up

APRIL 12, 1986

Pittsburgh, Pennsylvania
Civic Arena
Opening Act: Kix
Attendance: 6,192   Capacity: 12,500
Promoter: DiCesare-Engler Productions
Archived: Audio

■ SET LIST

Detroit Rock City
Fits Like a Glove
Creatures of the Night
Cold Gin
Bruce Kulick Guitar Solo
Calling Dr. Love
Uh! All Night
Eric Carr Drum Solo
War Machine
Love Gun
Gene Simmons Bass Solo
I Love It Loud
Paul Stanley Guitar Solo
Heaven's On Fire
Rock and Roll All Nite
Oh Susannah
Tears Are Falling
Medley: Strutter - Deuce - Round and Round
Lick It Up

■ This show was rescheduled from April 3rd. As part of the typical end-of-tour pranks, the road crew came on stage and did a chorus line during "Lick It Up."

C.K. Lendt: "We had a corporate jet to take us to and from the show that day."

This was the final live performance of "Uh! All Night."

Fairly soon after the Asylum Tour ended, it became clear that 1986 would be the first year in KISS's twelve-year history in which it would not release an album. Asylum continued to maintain some public presence for awhile, as the "Tears Are Falling" video still had some legs on Dial MTV, pushing the "Who Wants to Be Lonely" video back to a May 15 debut during *Heavy Metal Mania.*

At some point during this time, KISS received offers to tour in Europe and even perform at the Sun City resort in South Africa. As far as can be determined, the offers were never inked. But recently, a KISS "Live in Sun City" concert poster surfaced with April 4–15 advertised as the show dates, indicating that the concerts were, at the very least, seriously considered.

While the current members relaxed, all four ex-KISS members were busy during this time. In July 1986, Peter Criss, who had finally relinquished his share of the KISS partnership earlier in the summer, began gigging around Los Angeles with the short-lived band Balls Of Fire. Vinnie Vincent formed a band and released the much-hyped, self-titled Vinnie Vincent Invasion album on August 26 through Chrysalis Records, and Mark St. John formed White Tiger and released an independent album in October.

Ace Frehley, who had done some club gigs in 1985, made his first national public appearance without makeup in 1986 via a print ad for Laney Amplifiers. Ace had made numerous attempts to record and release an album, and he finally succeeded on May 5, 1987 with *Frehley's Comet.*

Gene filled the downtime by continuing to produce acts like Black 'N Blue and EZO in addition to acting in several movies. *Never Too Young To Die* (which was filmed prior to the release of *Asylum*) was released on June 13, 1986; the long-forgotten *Trick Or Treat,* which saw Gene playing an aging DJ, was released on October 24, and *Wanted Dead Or Alive,* after a delay of several months, was released on January 16, 1987. Gene also acted in an unaired pilot produced for ABC-TV called *Sable.* Outside of an onscreen kiss with co-star Rene Russo, Gene had little to show for his effort as his part was eventually recast.

Paul continued to make TV appearances, showing up when least expected on shows like *CBS News Nightwatch* on May 13, 1986 and later at MTV's premiere party for *American Anthem* where he hyped up "a band that he was going to possibly be producing an album for" that he "didn't want to mention." Although it never came to fruition, the unmentioned band was Guns N' Roses and the album was *Appetite For Destruction.* One can't help but wonder what might have transpired for KISS or Guns N' Roses had Paul been hired for the production job.

Perhaps the most interesting aspect of this time period was the effort of the fans themselves. Unofficial KISS conventions were beginning to take place in some parts of the country, and while most were short-lived, some continue annually to this day. By 1986–87, several memorabilia dealers dealing exclusively in KISS merchandise were starting to flourish, some producing monthly catalogs and selling everything from secondhand 1970s memorabilia to professionally-shot concerts of the original band, which had recently become available in fan circles.

KISS fanzines were also quite in vogue during this time and would often prove to be an invaluable source for information about the band. KISS even participated with most of the publications by doing interviews or faxing over answers to questionnaires. The fanzines helped KISS to establish an intimacy with their fans, the likes of which remain unprecedented. It was not at all uncommon for all four band members to know fanzine editors/staff on a first-name basis.

ANASTASIA PANTSIOS

CHAPTER 19

CRAZY NIGHTS TOUR

Number of Shows: 130
Start Date: November 13, 1987 - Jackson, Mississippi
End Date: October 3, 1988 - Belfast, Northern Ireland
Countries: Canada, Denmark, England, Finland, France, Hungary, Iceland, Italy, Japan, The Netherlands, Northern Ireland, Norway, Scotland, Sweden, U.S.A., West Germany
Headlining Acts: David Lee Roth; Iron Maiden
Opening Acts: Anthrax; Balaam & the Angel; Chastain; David Lee Roth; Dirty Looks; Edda; Foringjarnir; Great White; Guns N' Roses; Helix; Helloween; Kings of the Sun; Mantis; Megadeth; Royal Air Force; Ted Nugent; Testament; Treat; White Lion
Average Attendance: 5,691* (Does not include club gigs, Japanese, or Monsters of Rock dates.)

The two-year gap between *Asylum* and its follow-up, *Crazy Nights,* was the longest period between albums in KISS's career up to that point, and there was a corresponding gap between tours as well. *Asylum* had made a mediocre showing, and the break-even results of the tour had failed to generate much capital. And with their two primary sources of revenue—album and concert-ticket sales—both on hold, KISS was not in an enviable financial state.

To help bridge the gap, on May 18, 1987, PolyGram released their first KISS home video. Titled *Exposed,* the video contained new conceptual footage shot during August 1986 at Gray Hall in Beverly Hills intercut with vintage live clips and several of the band's 1980s videos. To promote *Exposed,* which quickly went Platinum, a compilation video for "Rock and Roll All Nite (Live)" was released and debuted on MTV's *Headbangers Ball* on May 23.

Paul and Gene were adamant that a huge album was needed to rekindle interest in the band.

The two were responsible for most of the production on both of the band's previous albums and, as they considered their options for the follow-up to *Asylum,* they reached the conclusion that a big-name, outside producer was the cure to KISS's ills. Gene and Paul wanted a producer who had worked career-reviving miracles for other artists. The producer they eventually targeted was Ron Nevison, who had been Paul's first choice to produce his 1978 solo album. There was one small problem: Nevison's schedule was booked through March 1987. Nonetheless, KISS decided to wait.

Crazy Nights was eventually recorded at several southern California studios. It was KISS's first foray into recording an all-digital album and the result was a very polished, but somewhat cold-sounding pop record. As summer 1987 drew to a close, *Crazy Nights* was released on September 21.

"Crazy Crazy Nights," the first single, did virtually nothing on U.S. radio and not much more on MTV. But, in mid-December, the video for *Crazy Night's* second single, "Reason to Live,"

was put into heavy rotation by MTV. The frequent airings lasted through the early part of February with the video usually in the #1 position on *Dial MTV,* and the song was on the verge of becoming a huge hit when it abruptly lost its momentum and seemed to vanish. The moderate success of "Reason to Live" was enough to push *Crazy Nights* to Platinum status on February 18, but it was not enough to keep the album afloat; when "Reason to Live" crashed, so did the band's hopes for a Multi-Platinum album.

After the long wait for Nevison, coupled with KISS's desperate need for a very successful album, the realization that *Crazy Nights* had fallen well short of expectations came as a grievous blow. A problem in the equation needed to be located, and in their desperation to find one, Glickman/Marks became a convenient target. On January 14, 1988, Paul and Gene met in Cleveland with Chris Lendt, Howard Marks, and financial advisor Dick Weidenbaum to discuss their finances. Chris Lendt explains: "KISS had

RIKARD GORANSSON

asked us to provide them with more details about their financial condition. . . Howard told Gene and Paul that their financial situation had deteriorated, something we'd been telling them for a long time. Years of excessive spending on all fronts were to blame. Their income had decreased sharply over the past few years, and their cash problems had been exacerbated by the two-year hiatus (between albums). . . Dick Weidenbaum handed out a chart that summarized the last twelve years of KISS's income and expenses. Seeing their financial history deduced to a chart was quite a jolt for Gene and Paul."[1]

To make matters far worse, the specter of the IRS and the huge sum KISS would owe on back taxes for its 1970s coal mine investment loomed large.

The meeting was the last between KISS and the Glickman/Marks firm. On March 3, 1988, prior to a concert in Peoria, Illinois, Paul and Gene notified Howard that Glickman/Marks had been fired as the band's business managers, ending an 11½-year relationship.

KISS then executed what may be the most inexplicable move of its entire career when it hired Dr. Jesse Hilsen (Paul's psychiatrist since the early 1970s) as the band's business manager. Larry Mazer, who would begin managing KISS in 1989, provides the consensus take on Hilsen: "I am still confused to this day as to what Jess Hilsen's role with KISS was. The first time I was introduced to Jess Hilsen he was positioned as their business manager, and I had to deal with him on budgets and anything having to do with business. But it was obvious to me that this guy didn't have a clue, and that he was there for other reasons. I never really had any respect for him in that sense whatsoever and tried to stay as far away from him as possible through the whole five years." Hilsen also seemed to play the role of a guru for Paul, much like Eugene Landy allegedly had for the Beach Boys's Brian Wilson. When asked about the analogy, Bruce Kulick replied: "I didn't really pry into it that much, but I don't think that description is incorrect."

Michael Levine of the Public Relations Co., who wound up scoring some impressive, or at least interesting, appearances for the band, handled publicity for the Crazy Nights Tour. In Los Angeles, KISS taped a segment for the British TV show *Top Of The Pops,* performing "Crazy Crazy Nights," with canned music but live vocals. (The single was in the top five in the U.K. that week.) The segment aired on October 23. Months later, on April 15, 1988, Gene and Paul made an appearance on *The Oprah Winfrey Show.* During the taping, Oprah innocently asked Gene how long his tongue was; Gene responded, "Long enough to make me your very closest friend." The exchange ended up on a "Best-of Oprah" episode several years later.

When the tour got under way in November 1987, some noteworthy changes to the crew were apparent. Chris Lendt, who had been on the road with KISS in one capacity or another since joining the Glickman/Marks firm in 1976, was now working out of the Glickman/Marks

[1] KISS and Sell. (C.K. Lendt. p 331–33. Billboard Books, 1996.)

offices, and Rich Nesin was handling tour manager duties. Additionally, John Harte, KISS's longtime security director, returned in that capacity for his first tour with KISS since Creatures of the Night.

Perhaps the most impactful change to the touring roster was the addition of Gary Corbett as the band's offstage keyboardist. "It really freed Paul up to entertain," remarks Bruce Kulick. "I didn't mind us without the keyboard, but it did help fill it in; Paul was sometimes barely in the mix he was entertaining so much. And that was an era where it didn't hurt to have the band sound more like the records. Since Ozzy and other people were using keyboard players, it wasn't so taboo."

Corbett explains further, "I was playing a lot on every song. I mostly played fat, nasty, timpani or guitarish pads, doubling guitar or bass parts. The only samples that we used were the siren for 'Firehouse' and some explosion samples. Some venues were too small for the fire marshals to allow explosives and percussion bombs. In those places, when Gene would do his rocket effect and blow up the guitar cabinets, I would hit the explosion samples to cover for the lack of pyro."

Initial rehearsals for the tour were held at the Orange County Pavilion in San Bernardino. Production rehearsals were done in Jackson, Mississippi on November 11 and 12.

As KISS attempted to keep overhead costs to a minimum, Corbett became a luxury the band felt they could afford only sporadically. He came and went several times over the course of the tour. "We started the tour, and after about three weeks they came to me and told me that they couldn't afford to keep me on the road. The original agreement was that I was to be traveling on the road as the fifth band member. When things weren't going as well as they needed to, that was the first place where they tried to reduce expenses."

Despite the grand hopes that the band harbored, the tour, much like the album, was a big disappointment. Often cited by fans as the worst KISS tour ever, the attendance for the North American leg of the tour (5,691) was down almost 500 people per show, an 8 percent falloff from the Asylum Tour. This may not seem like a particularly steep drop, but considering the expectations were for it to significantly improve upon the numbers from the previous tour, a drop of any type was considered a disaster. Gary Corbett relates, "The band's mood changed with the attendance. I remember Paul would always joke, 'Why don't we order two pizzas for the audience?'"

Perhaps part of the negative reaction to the North American leg of the tour stemmed from the use of "Love Gun" as the opening song (a tactic which worked better in theory) and the rather short set list, which was initially only 80–85 minutes. The show was not helped by the preponderance of *Crazy Nights* material included in the set, most of which did not come across well live. "Crazy Crazy Nights," "Reason to Live," "Bang Bang You," and "No, No, No" were staples on the tour and "Hell or High Water" and "When Your Walls Come Down" were also performed. The return of "Shout It Out Loud" to the set in early January, and the occasional inclusion of "Strutter," marked the start of a trend which

would see more and more of the band's 1970s repertoire performed live over the coming tours. Beginning with the first performance of the tour, the intro to "Lick It Up" had been dropped and the song now began with Paul singing the first line of the tune *a capella.*

Los Angeles, California
Grand Olympic Auditorium
No Opening Act
Archived: Audio

■ SET LIST
Cold Gin
Lick It Up
Detroit Rock City
Whole Lotta Love

■ The video shoot for "Crazy Crazy Nights" wound up becoming something of a mini-concert when the band decided to perform a few numbers for the crowd. Free tickets to the event were distributed by KNAC radio. The video world-premiered on September 12 during *Headbangers Ball.* Eventually appearing on *Dial MTV* several weeks later, on October 19, the "Crazy Crazy Nights" video had all but disappeared prior to the start of the tour in mid-November. The first single had failed, and ticket sales for the first few weeks of the tour reflect this.

Prior to "Cold Gin," the band jammed briefly, playing excerpts of Led Zeppelin's "Whole Lotta Love" and "Bring It On Home."

NOVEMBER 13, 1987
Jackson, Mississippi
Mississippi Coliseum
Opening Act: White Lion
Attendance: 5,577   Capacity: 10,000
Promoters: Be-Bop Productions, Mid-South Concerts

■ A meeting with the Mississippi Fair Commission was held when several religious extremists again thought KISS was aligned with the devil. Surprisingly, after the meeting adjourned, Paul showed up to defend KISS for the media who had gathered to cover the rather absurd event.

NOVEMBER 14, 1987
Pensacola, Florida
The Pensacola Civic Center
Opening Act: White Lion
Attendance: 3,196   Capacity: 9,748
Promoters: Cellar Door Concerts, Odgen-Allied Entertainment
Archived: Audio

■ PARTIAL SET LIST
Love Gun
Cold Gin
Hell or High Water
Bang Bang You
Fits Like a Glove
Crazy Crazy Nights
Eric Carr Drum Solo
No, No, No
Bruce Kulick Guitar Solo
When Your Walls Come Down

NOVEMBER 15, 1987
Memphis, Tennessee
Mid-South Coliseum
Opening Act: White Lion
Attendance: 7,189   Capacity: 9,931
Promoter: Mid-South Concerts

NOVEMBER 17, 1987

Lake Charles, Louisiana
Lake Charles Civic Center
Opening Act: White Lion
Capacity: 8,000
Promoter: Pace Concerts

NOVEMBER 18, 1987

Corpus Christi, Texas
Memorial Coliseum
Opening Act: White Lion
Capacity: 5,000
Promoter: Jam Presents of Texas

NOVEMBER 20, 1987

Belton, Texas
Bell County Expo Center
Opening Act: White Lion
Attendance: 2,717   Capacity: 9,000
Promoter: Jam Presents of Texas

NOVEMBER 21, 1987

Lubbock, Texas
Lubbock Municipal Coliseum
Opening Act: White Lion
Attendance: 3,924   Capacity: 5,000
Promoters: Pace Concerts, Stardate Productions
Archived: Video

■ SET LIST

Love Gun
Cold Gin
Bang Bang You
Fits Like a Glove
Crazy Crazy Nights
Eric Carr Drum Solo
No, No, No
Bruce Kulick Guitar Solo
When Your Walls Come Down
War Machine
Reason to Live
Heaven's On Fire
Gene Simmons Bass Solo
I Love It Loud
Lick It Up
Detroit Rock City
Tears Are Falling
Rock and Roll All Nite

■ The start of the show was delayed when the one of the band's trucks broke down on the way to the venue.

NOVEMBER 23, 1987

Valley Center (Wichita), Kansas
Britt Brown Arena @ Kansas Coliseum
Opening Act: White Lion
Attendance: 4,850   Capacity: 11,000
Promoter: Contemporary Productions
Archived: Audio

■ SET LIST

Love Gun
Cold Gin
When Your Walls Come Down
Fits Like a Glove
Bang Bang You
War Machine
Eric Carr Drum Solo
No, No, No
Crazy Crazy Nights
Heaven's On Fire
Bruce Kulick Guitar Solo
Reason to Live
Gene Simmons Bass Solo
I Love It Loud
Lick It Up
Rock and Roll All Nite
Tears Are Falling

■ Due to time constraints, KISS did not perform the final encore, "Detroit Rock City." This is the last known performance of "When Your Walls Come Down."

NOVEMBER 24, 1987

Tulsa, Oklahoma
Expo Square Pavilion
Opening Act: White Lion
Attendance: 3,193   Capacity: 5,000
Promoter: Little Wing Attractions

NOVEMBER 25, 1987

Norman, Oklahoma
Lloyd Noble Center
Opening Act: White Lion
Attendance: 3,788   Capacity: 4,000
Promoter: Contemporary Productions
Archived: Audio

■ SET LIST

Love Gun
Cold Gin
Bang Bang You
Fits Like a Glove
Crazy Crazy Nights
Eric Carr Drum Solo
Bruce Kulick Guitar Solo
No, No, No
War Machine
Reason to Live
Heaven's On Fire
Gene Simmons Bass Solo
I Love It Loud
Lick It Up
Rock and Roll All Nite
Tears Are Falling
Detroit Rock City

■ This show was originally advertised for November 13, though tickets were never put up for sale. Paul played part of "Stairway to Heaven" prior to "Tears Are Falling."

KATT radio held a contest where a grand prizewinner and a guest could eat a Thanksgiving Eve dinner backstage with the band.

NOVEMBER 26, 1987

Topeka, Kansas
Landon Arena @ Kansas ExpoCentre
Opening Act: White Lion
Attendance: 8,763   Capacity: 8,763
Promoter: Little Wing Attractions

NOVEMBER 27, 1987

Omaha, Nebraska
Omaha Civic Auditorium
Opening Act: White Lion
Capacity: 9,000
Promoter: Rose Productions
Archived: Audio

■ SET LIST

Love Gun
Cold Gin
Bang Bang You
Fits Like a Glove
Crazy Crazy Nights
Eric Carr Drum Solo
Bruce Kulick Guitar Solo
No, No, No
[War Machine]
[Reason to Live]
Heaven's On Fire
Gene Simmons Bass Solo
I Love It Loud
Lick It Up
Rock and Roll All Nite
Tears Are Falling

[Detroit Rock City]

NOVEMBER 28, 1987

Davenport, Iowa
Palmer Alumni Auditorium @ Palmer College of Chiropractic
Opening Act: White Lion
Capacity: 4,800
Promoter: JAM Productions
Archived: Video

■ SET LIST

Love Gun
Cold Gin
Bang Bang You
Fits Like a Glove
Crazy Crazy Nights
Eric Carr Drum Solo
Bruce Kulick Guitar Solo
No, No, No
War Machine
Reason to Live
Heaven's On Fire
Gene Simmons Bass Solo
I Love It Loud
Lick It Up
Rock and Roll All Nite
Oh Susannah
Tears Are Falling
Detroit Rock City

■ Brief clips of many songs were included in the set: Gene played part of Grieg's "Hall of the Mountain King" during his solo; part of "La Bamba" was done before "Oh Susannah"; the band played a bit of "Firehouse" and Gene played the riff from "Almost Human" just before the band went into "Tears Are Falling."

DECEMBER 1, 1987

St. Paul, Minnesota
St. Paul Civic Center
Opening Act: White Lion
Capacity: 15,406
Promoter: Rose Productions
Archived: Audio

■ SET LIST

Love Gun
Cold Gin
Bang Bang You
Fits Like a Glove
Crazy Crazy Nights
Eric Carr Drum Solo
Bruce Kulick Guitar Solo
No, No, No
Reason to Live
War Machine
Heaven's On Fire
Gene Simmons Bass Solo
I Love It Loud
Lick It Up
Rock and Roll All Nite
Whole Lotta Love
Tears Are Falling
Detroit Rock City

■ KISS briefly segued into Zeppelin's "You Shook Me" before going into "Whole Lotta Love."

DECEMBER 2, 1987

Rochester, Minnesota
Mayo Civic Center
Opening Act: White Lion
Capacity: 6,600
Promoter: Rose Productions

DECEMBER 4, 1987

Des Moines, Iowa
Veterans Memorial Auditorium

Opening Act: White Lion
Attendance: 5,795   Capacity: 8,000
Promoter: Contemporary Productions

■ Before the concert, MTV world-premiered the video for "Reason to Live" and, for the first time since the "Tears Are Falling" video, purchased the exclusive first-month rights to broadcast the video. The video was filmed during tour rehearsals at the Orange County Pavilion in San Bernardino, California.

DECEMBER 6, 1987

Springfield, Illinois
Prairie Capital Convention Center
Opening Act: White Lion
Capacity: 7,004
Promoter: JAM Productions

DECEMBER 7, 1987

Toledo, Ohio
Sports Arena
Opening Act: White Lion
Attendance: 3,000   Capacity: 7,500
Promoter: Belkin Productions
Archived: Video
■ SET LIST
Love Gun
Cold Gin
Bang Bang You
Fits Like a Glove
Crazy Crazy Nights
Eric Carr Drum Solo
Bruce Kulick Guitar Solo
No, No, No
Reason to Live
War Machine
Heaven's On Fire
Gene Simmons Bass Solo
I Love It Loud
Lick It Up
Rock and Roll All Nite
Tears Are Falling
Detroit Rock City
■ Prior to "Tears Are Falling," the band played an excerpt of Zeppelin's "How Many More Times," which was followed by a brief R & B jam.

DECEMBER 9, 1987

Erie, Pennsylvania
Lewis J. Tullio Arena @ Erie Civic Center
Opening Act: Ted Nugent
Capacity: 7,500
Promoter: Belkin Productions

DECEMBER 10, 1987

Toronto, Ontario, Canada
Maple Leaf Gardens
Opening Act: Ted Nugent
Attendance: 8,832   Capacity: 10,000
Promoter: Concert Promotions Int'l
Archived: Video
■ SET LIST
Love Gun
Cold Gin
Bang Bang You
Fits Like a Glove
Crazy Crazy Nights
Bruce Kulick Guitar Solo
No, No, No
Eric Carr Drum Solo - reprise
Reason to Live
War Machine
Heaven's On Fire
Gene Simmons Bass Solo
I Love It Loud
Lick It Up

STEVE SILS

Rock and Roll All Nite
Tears Are Falling
Detroit Rock City

DECEMBER 11, 1987

Glens Falls, New York
Glens Falls Civic Center
Opening Act: Ted Nugent
Promoter: Magic City Productions

DECEMBER 12, 1987

Providence, Rhode Island
Providence Civic Center
Opening Act: Ted Nugent
Attendance: 10,106   Capacity: 12,100
Promoter: Gemini Concerts
Archived: Audio
■ SET LIST
Love Gun
Cold Gin
Bang Bang You
Fits Like a Glove
No, No, No
Bruce Kulick Guitar Solo
Eric Carr Drum Solo
Crazy Crazy Nights
War Machine
Reason to Live
Heaven's On Fire
Gene Simmons Bass Solo
I Love It Loud
Lick It Up
Rock and Roll All Nite
Tears Are Falling
White Christmas
Detroit Rock City
■ Prior to "Detroit Rock City," the band and crowd sang "Happy Birthday" to Bruce, who turned 34.

DECEMBER 13, 1987

Portland, Maine
Cumberland County Civic Center
Opening Act: Ted Nugent
Attendance: 6,608   Capacity: 9,500
Promoter: Gemini Concerts
Archived: Audio
■ SET LIST
Love Gun

Cold Gin
Bang Bang You
Fits Like a Glove
No, No, No
Bruce Kulick Guitar Solo
[Eric Carr Drum Solo]
[Crazy Crazy Nights]
[War Machine]
Reason to Live
Heaven's On Fire
Gene Simmons Bass Solo
I Love It Loud
Lick It Up
Rock and Roll All Nite
[Tears Are Falling]
[White Christmas]
[Detroit Rock City]

DECEMBER 14, 1987   TEMP HOLD DATE

Goose Bay, Newfoundland, Canada
■ The audio tape listed for this date is actually from the band's December 20 show in East Rutherford.

DECEMBER 16, 1987   CANCELED

Syracuse, New York
Onondaga County War Memorial
Opening Act: Ted Nugent

DECEMBER 18, 1987

Philadelphia, Pennsylvania
The Spectrum
Opening Act: Ted Nugent
Attendance: 10,294   Capacity: 14,080
Promoter: Electric Factory Concerts
Archived: Video
■ SET LIST
Love Gun
Cold Gin
Bang Bang You
Fits Like a Glove
No, No, No
Bruce Kulick Guitar Solo
Eric Carr Drum Solo
Crazy Crazy Nights
War Machine
Reason to Live
Heaven's On Fire
Gene Simmons Bass Solo

I Love It Loud
Lick It Up
Rock and Roll All Nite
White Christmas
Detroit Rock City

■ "Tears Are Falling" was cut due to time constraints. The concert was professionally videotaped.

DECEMBER 19, 1987

New Haven, Connecticut
New Haven Veterans Memorial Coliseum
Opening Act: Ted Nugent
Capacity: 9,900
Promoter: Cross Country Concerts
Archived: Video

■ **SET LIST**

See December 12, 1987.

DECEMBER 20, 1987

East Rutherford, New Jersey
Brendan Byrne Arena
Opening Act: Ted Nugent
Attendance: 14,867   Capacity: 18,014
Promoter: John Scher Presents
Archived: Audio

■ **SET LIST**

See December 12, 1987.

■ Paul made an appearance on WNBC-TV's *Live At Five* to promote the concert.

This was Gary Corbett's last show with KISS until January 8, 1988. "I was in New York," recalls Corbett, "and stopped in to Electric Lady Studios; while I was there, I got a call from Paul who said 'I'm really sorry. We can't afford to have you on the road anymore.' They were scheduled to leave on December 26th to go back out on the road and because of how quickly it happened, all my gear went with them. Tony Byrd, who was my keyboard tech as well as Paul's guitar tech, went back out with them, and since he was a bit of a keyboard player, too, when he wasn't helping Paul out he was triggering whatever I had programmed into the keyboards.

"The day after the first show, Paul called me up and said, 'We need to get you back out here. This really sucks without the keyboards. We're going to work this out.' They were going to hire me back for three weeks because they were going to play a bunch of major markets again. And they told me that they wanted to do the whole tour like this: have me do the major markets, and when they weren't playing the major markets, we wouldn't do it. At the end of this first three weeks, at the Nassau Coliseum (January 29), I asked them what the next leg was going to be, and they told me they couldn't afford to have me around any more. It was just on-again, off-again depending upon how many tickets they were selling."

DECEMBER 26, 1987

Fort Wayne, Indiana
Allen Co. War Memorial Coliseum
Opening Act: Ted Nugent
Capacity: 10,000
Promoter: Sunshine Promotions

■ "White Christmas" was performed.

DECEMBER 27, 1987

Indianapolis, Indiana
Market Square Arena

Opening Act: Ted Nugent
Capacity: 17,500
Promoter: Sunshine Promotions

■ This concert, along with the December 30 show, was promoted as the "Holiday Festival Jam '87."

DECEMBER 29, 1987

Louisville, Kentucky
Freedom Hall
Opening Act: Ted Nugent
Capacity: 18,000
Promoter: Sunshine Promotions
Archived: Audio

■ **SET LIST**

Love Gun
Cold Gin
Bang Bang You
Fits Like a Glove
No, No, No
Bruce Kulick Guitar Solo
Eric Carr Drum Solo
Crazy Crazy Nights
War Machine
Reason to Live
Heaven's On Fire
Gene Simmons Bass Solo
I Love It Loud
Lick It Up
Rock and Roll All Nite
Tears Are Falling
Detroit Rock City

DECEMBER 30, 1987

Evansville, Indiana
Roberts Municipal Stadium
Opening Act: Ted Nugent
Capacity: 13,600
Promoter: Sunshine Promotions

DECEMBER 31, 1987

Dayton, Ohio
Hara Arena & Exhibition Center
Opening Act: Chastain

Attendance: 6,715   Capacity: 7,900
Promoter: Belkin Productions
Archived: Audio

■ **SET LIST**

Love Gun
Cold Gin
Bang Bang You
Fits Like a Glove
Hell or High Water
Bruce Kulick Guitar Solo
Eric Carr Drum Solo
Crazy Crazy Nights
War Machine
Reason to Live
Heaven's On Fire
Gene Simmons Bass Solo
I Love It Loud
Lick It Up
Rock and Roll All Nite
Strutter
Tears Are Falling
Detroit Rock City

■ White Lion was scheduled to open the show, but canceled. There was no pyro used at the concert.

JANUARY 1, 1988

Johnson City, Tennessee
Freedom Hall Civic Center @ Science Hill High School
Opening Act: Ted Nugent
Attendance: 9,058   Capacity: 9,200
Promoter: Sunshine Promotions

JANUARY 2, 1988

Knoxville, Tennessee
Knoxville Civic Coliseum
Opening Act: Ted Nugent
Attendance: 6,810   Capacity: 7,500
Promoter: Sunshine Promotions
Archived: Audio

■ **SET LIST**

Love Gun
Cold Gin
Bang Bang You

Fits Like a Glove
Hell or High Water
Bruce Kulick Guitar Solo
Eric Carr Drum Solo
Crazy Crazy Nights
War Machine
Reason to Live
Heaven's On Fire
Gene Simmons Bass Solo
I Love It Loud
Lick It Up
Rock and Roll All Nite
Tears Are Falling
Detroit Rock City

JANUARY 3, 1988
Toledo, Ohio
Sports Arena
Opening Act: Ted Nugent
Promoter: Belkin Productions

JANUARY 5, 1988
Marquette, Michigan
Lakeview Arena
Opening Act: Ted Nugent
Attendance: 2,977   Capacity: 6,500
Promoter: Stardate Productions

JANUARY 6, 1988
Green Bay, Wisconsin
Brown County Veterans Memorial Arena
Opening Act: Ted Nugent
Attendance: 5,005   Capacity: 7,044
Promoter: Stardate Productions

JANUARY 7, 1988
Milwaukee, Wisconsin
Mecca Arena
Opening Act: Ted Nugent
Attendance: 4,713   Capacity: 8,700
Promoter: Stardate Productions
Archived: Audio
■ SET LIST
Love Gun
Cold Gin
Bang Bang You
Fits Like a Glove
Crazy Crazy Nights
Bruce Kulick Guitar Solo
Eric Carr Drum Solo
Shout It Out Loud
War Machine
Reason to Live
Heaven's On Fire
Gene Simmons Bass Solo
I Love It Loud
Lick It Up
[Rock and Roll All Nite]
[Tears Are Falling]
[Detroit Rock City]
■ No pyro was used.

JANUARY 8, 1988
Chicago, Illinois
University of Illinois-Chicago Pavilion
Opening Act: Ted Nugent
Capacity: 10,595
Promoter: JAM Productions
Archived: Audio
■ SET LIST
Love Gun
Cold Gin
Bang Bang You
Fits Like a Glove
Shout It Out Loud
Crazy Crazy Nights
Bruce Kulick Guitar Solo

Eric Carr Drum Solo
War Machine
Reason to Live
Heaven's On Fire
Gene Simmons Bass Solo
I Love It Loud
Lick It Up
Rock and Roll All Nite
Tears Are Falling
Detroit Rock City
■ Gary Corbett rejoined KISS on tour.

JANUARY 9, 1988
St. Louis, Missouri
Kiel Auditorium
Opening Act: Ted Nugent
Attendance: 8,184   Capacity: 10,522
Promoter: Contemporary Productions
Archived: Video
■ SET LIST
See January 8, 1988.
■ KISS briefly segued into "Oh Susannah" prior to "Tears Are Falling."

JANUARY 11, 1988
Muskegon, Michigan
L.C. Walker Arena
Opening Act: Ted Nugent
Attendance: 6,706   Capacity: 7,501
Promoter: Belkin Productions

JANUARY 12, 1988
Saginaw, Michigan
Wendler Arena @ Saginaw Civic Center
Opening Act: Ted Nugent
Attendance: 6,141   Capacity: 6,586
Promoter: Belkin Productions
Archived: Video
■ SET LIST
Love Gun
Cold Gin
Bang Bang You
Fits Like a Glove
Shout It Out Loud
Crazy Crazy Nights
[Bruce Kulick Guitar Solo]
[Eric Carr Drum Solo]
War Machine
Reason to Live
Heaven's On Fire
Gene Simmons Bass Solo
I Love It Loud
Lick It Up
Rock and Roll All Nite
Tears Are Falling
Detroit Rock City

JANUARY 13, 1988
Columbus, Ohio
Battelle Hall @ Ohio Center
Opening Act: Ted Nugent
Attendance: 5,536   Capacity: 7,500
Promoter: Belkin Productions
Archived: Audio
■ SET LIST
See January 8, 1988.

JANUARY 15, 1988
Richfield (Cleveland), Ohio
The Coliseum
Opening Act: Ted Nugent
Attendance: 14,935   Capacity: 15,522
Promoter: Belkin Productions
Archived: Video
■ SET LIST
Love Gun

Cold Gin
Bang Bang You
Fits Like a Glove
Shout It Out Loud
Crazy Crazy Nights
Bruce Kulick Guitar Solo
Eric Carr Drum Solo
War Machine
Reason to Live
Heaven's On Fire
Gene Simmons Bass Solo
I Love It Loud
Lick It Up
Rock and Roll All Nite
La Bamba
Whole Lotta Love
Tears Are Falling
Detroit Rock City
■ Prior to going on, a very somber Paul Stanley taped an interview backstage for a local TV show called *The Cleveland Rock Beat*.

After "La Bamba," at Gene's insistence, the audience sang "Happy Birthday" to Paul despite the fact that Paul's birthday wasn't until January 20. Perhaps this was an attempt on Gene's part to bolster Paul's spirits after the unsettling financial meeting with Glickman/Marks the previous day.

JANUARY 16, 1988
Pittsburgh, Pennsylvania
Civic Arena
Opening Act: Ted Nugent
Attendance: 8,808   Capacity: 12,500
Promoter: DiCesare-Engler Productions
Archived: Audio
■ SET LIST
See January 8, 1988.
■ Gene's bass solo included a brief part of "Almost Human."

JANUARY 17, 1988
Detroit, Michigan
Cobo Arena
Opening Act: Helix
Capacity: 12,199
Promoter: Belkin Productions
Archived: Video
■ SET LIST
See January 8, 1988.
■ Originally scheduled opening act Megadeth canceled. The band played parts of "La Bamba" and "Stairway to Heaven" prior to "Tears Are Falling."

JANUARY 18, 1988
Charleston, West Virginia
Charleston Civic Center
Opening Act: Ted Nugent
Capacity: 11,000
Promoters: Concert/Southern Promotions
Archived: Audio
■ SET LIST
See January 8, 1988.
■ The concert was initially slated to take place in Huntington, West Virginia. However, Huntington town officials banned KISS from performing, and the show was moved to Charleston. Paul nonetheless referred to the audience as Huntington throughout the show.

Once again, part of "Stairway to Heaven" was performed prior to "Tears Are Falling."

JANUARY 20, 1988
Norfolk, Virginia
The Scope

Opening Act: Ted Nugent
Capacity: 13,800
Promoter: Cellar Door Concerts
Archived: Audio

■ SET LIST

Love Gun
Cold Gin
Bang Bang You
Shout It Out Loud
Fits Like a Glove
Crazy Crazy Nights
Bruce Kulick Guitar Solo
Eric Carr Drum Solo
War Machine
Reason to Live
Heaven's On Fire
Gene Simmons Bass Solo
I Love It Loud
Lick It Up
Rock and Roll All Nite
[Tears Are Falling]
Detroit Rock City

JANUARY 22, 1988

Utica, New York
Memorial Auditorium
Opening Act: Ted Nugent
Capacity: 6,000
Promoter: Magic City Productions
Archived: Audio

■ SET LIST

Love Gun
Cold Gin
Bang Bang You
Fits Like a Glove
Crazy Crazy Nights
Shout It Out Loud
Bruce Kulick Guitar Solo
Eric Carr Drum Solo
War Machine
Reason to Live
Heaven's On Fire
Gene Simmons Bass Solo
I Love It Loud
Lick It Up
Rock and Roll All Nite
Tears Are Falling
Detroit Rock City

JANUARY 23, 1988   CANCELED

Wilkes-Barre, Pennsylvania
Kingston Armory
Opening Act: Ted Nugent
Capacity: 6,000
Promoter: Magic City Productions

JANUARY 23, 1988

Johnstown, Pennsylvania
Cambria County War Memorial Arena
Opening Act: Ted Nugent
Attendance: 4,915   Capacity: 7,000
Promoter: Benmore Enterprises

JANUARY 24, 1988

Buffalo, New York
Veterans Memorial Auditorium
Opening Act: Ted Nugent
Capacity: 18,000
Promoter: Magic City Productions
Archived: Audio

■ SET LIST

Love Gun
Cold Gin
Bang Bang You
Fits Like a Glove
Crazy Crazy Nights
Shout It Out Loud
Bruce Kulick Guitar Solo

Eric Carr Drum Solo
War Machine
Reason to Live
Heaven's On Fire
Gene Simmons Bass Solo
I Love It Loud
Lick It Up
Rock and Roll All Nite
[Tears Are Falling]
Oh Susannah
La Bamba
Detroit Rock City

■ Prior to "Detroit Rock City," the band played part of Mountain's "Mississippi Queen."

JANUARY 26, 1988

Poughkeepsie, New York
Mid-Hudson Civic Center
Opening Act: Ted Nugent
Attendance: 3,000   Capacity: 3,000
Promoter: Magic City Productions
Archived: Audio, Partial Video

■ SET LIST

Love Gun
Cold Gin
Bang Bang You
Fits Like a Glove
Crazy Crazy Nights
Shout It Out Loud
Bruce Kulick Guitar Solo
Eric Carr Drum Solo
War Machine
Reason to Live
Heaven's On Fire
Gene Simmons Bass Solo
I Love It Loud
Lick It Up
Rock and Roll All Nite
Whole Lotta Love
Detroit Rock City

■ No staging or logo was used at the show. Gene played the riff from The Beatles's "Day Tripper" prior to "Whole Lotta Love."

JANUARY 27, 1988

Worcester, Massachusetts
The Centrum
Opening Act: Ted Nugent
Attendance: 7,877   Capacity: 10,200
Promoter: Frank J. Russo
Archived: Audio

■ SET LIST

Love Gun
Cold Gin
Turn On the Night (lip-synched)
Turn On the Night (lip-synched)
Bang Bang You
Fits Like a Glove
Crazy Crazy Nights
Shout It Out Loud
Bruce Kulick Guitar Solo
Eric Carr Drum Solo
War Machine
Reason to Live
Heaven's On Fire
Gene Simmons Bass Solo
I Love It Loud
Lick It Up
Rock and Roll All Nite
Turn On the Night (lip-synched)
Turn On the Night (lip-synched)
Tears Are Falling
Strutter
Detroit Rock City

■ The "Turn On the Night" video was filmed prior to and during the concert. The studio version of the song was played over the P.A. and

the band lip-synched to it; the song has never been performed live. The video world premiered during *Headbangers Ball* on April 9.

The band played part of "How Many More Times" prior to "Strutter."

JANUARY 28, 1988

Springfield, Massachusetts
Springfield Civic Center
Opening Act: Ted Nugent
Capacity: 10,000
Promoter: Cross Country Concerts
Archived: Audio

■ SET LIST

Love Gun
Cold Gin
Bang Bang You
Fits Like a Glove
Crazy Crazy Nights
Shout It Out Loud
Bruce Kulick Guitar Solo
Eric Carr Drum Solo
War Machine
Reason to Live
Heaven's On Fire
Gene Simmons Bass Solo
I Love It Loud
Lick It Up
Rock and Roll All Nite
[Tears Are Falling]
Detroit Rock City

JANUARY 29, 1988

Uniondale, New York
Nassau Veterans Memorial Coliseum
Opening Act: Ted Nugent
Capacity: 14,503
Promoter: Ron Delsener Presents
Archived: Audio, Partial Video

■ SET LIST

See January 22, 1988.

■ Gary Corbett: "At Nassau, I was going to show up, do the show, pack up my gear and leave. Some of the gear had been purchased by them for me to use, and that would remain with them out on the road. Tony Byrd asked me to set him up with the sounds, and I told him I'd come in early before sound check and show him how everything was done. I got there, and he had the equipment set up, and while he was doing something else, I set all the keyboards back to their factory settings. He didn't know I was doing that. He came to me afterwards and said, 'How come everything sounds different? Paul told me to get the sounds from you.' I told him 'If Paul has a problem: tell him to come see me.'

"Rich Nesin, the tour manager, comes looking for me demanding to know what's going on. 'I heard that you fucked up the keyboards or something?' I said, 'No, I have them for the show tonight, and I have them on cartridges, but I'm not putting them on the keyboards. It's my work; I spent years learning how to do it. I spent hours programming it and I'm not going to leave it set up so that any monkey can walk up to the keyboards and do what I do. I'll do the show tonight, and if they can afford to keep me out here, I will be here, and if they can't afford me, they're not getting my work.'

"I went and did the show, never looked at them once, and I split without even saying goodbye. I didn't talk to them again until that summer. We got off to a rocky start, but with those guys, if you stand up to them, they respect you more. In a strange way, I think it helped in the long run that I did that. But at the time, it was really ugly."

JANUARY 30, 1988

Rochester, New York
Rochester Community War Memorial
Opening Act: Ted Nugent
Attendance: 5,404   Capacity: 10,150
Promoters: John Scher Presents, Monarch Entertainment
Archived: Audio
■ SET LIST
Love Gun
Cold Gin
Bang Bang You
Fits Like a Glove
Crazy Crazy Nights
Shout It Out Loud
Bruce Kulick Guitar Solo
Eric Carr Drum Solo
War Machine
Reason to Live
Heaven's On Fire
Gene Simmons Bass Solo
I Love It Loud
Lick It Up
Rock and Roll All Nite
Blue Suede Shoes
Tears Are Falling
Detroit Rock City

FEBRUARY 1, 1988

Landover (Washington, D.C.), Maryland
Capital Centre
Opening Act: Ted Nugent
Promoter: Cellar Door Concerts
■ "Strutter" was performed.

FEBRUARY 3, 1988

Greenville, South Carolina
Greenville Memorial Auditorium
Opening Act: Ted Nugent
Promoter: Beach Club Promotions

FEBRUARY 5, 1988

Greensboro, North Carolina
Greensboro Coliseum
Opening Act: Ted Nugent
Attendance: 6,391   Capacity: 15,781
Promoter: Cellar Door Concerts
Archived: Audio
■ SET LIST
See January 22, 1988.

FEBRUARY 6, 1988

Fayetteville, North Carolina
Cumberland County Memorial Arena
Opening Act: Ted Nugent
Attendance: 6,076   Capacity: 6,076
Promoter: C & C Entertainment
■ "Strutter" was again performed.

FEBRUARY 7, 1988

Charlotte, North Carolina
Charlotte Coliseum
Opening Act: Ted Nugent
Attendance: 7,365   Capacity: 10,000
Promoter: C & C Entertainment
Archived: Audio
■ SET LIST
Love Gun
Cold Gin
Bang Bang You
Fits Like a Glove

Tears Are Falling
Shout It Out Loud
Bruce Kulick Guitar Solo
Eric Carr Drum Solo
War Machine
Reason to Live
Heaven's On Fire
Gene Simmons Bass Solo
I Love It Loud
Lick It Up
Rock and Roll All Nite
Crazy Crazy Nights
Detroit Rock City

NELSON MARÉ

FEBRUARY 9, 1988

Nashville, Tennessee
Nashville Municipal Auditorium
Opening Act: Ted Nugent
Attendance: 6,439   Capacity: 9,000
Promoter: Concert/Southern Promotions

FEBRUARY 10, 1988

Atlanta, Georgia
The Omni
Opening Act: Ted Nugent
Attendance: 7,526   Capacity: 17,000
Promoter: Concert/Southern Promotions
Archived: Audio
■ SET LIST
Love Gun
Cold Gin
Bang Bang You
Fits Like a Glove
Crazy Crazy Nights
Shout It Out Loud
Bruce Kulick Guitar Solo
Eric Carr Drum Solo
War Machine
Reason to Live
Heaven's On Fire
Gene Simmons Bass Solo
I Love It Loud
Lick It Up
Rock and Roll All Nite
[Tears Are Falling]

Detroit Rock City
■ The electronic drums in Eric's solo malfunctioned, prompting him to cut his solo short.

FEBRUARY 12, 1988

Pembroke Pines (Hollywood), Florida
The Sportatorium
Opening Act: Ted Nugent
Attendance: 6,366
Promoter: Cellar Door Concerts
Archived: Video
■ SET LIST
Love Gun
Cold Gin
Bang Bang You
Fits Like a Glove
Crazy Crazy Nights
Shout It Out Loud
Bruce Kulick Guitar Solo
Eric Carr Drum Solo
War Machine
Reason to Live
Heaven's On Fire
Gene Simmons Bass Solo
I Love It Loud
Lick It Up
Rock and Roll All Nite
Oh Susannah
Tears Are Falling
Detroit Rock City

FEBRUARY 13, 1988

St. Petersburg, Florida
Bayfront Center Arena
Opening Act: Ted Nugent
Attendance: 5,628
Promoter: Cellar Door Concerts
Archived: Audio
■ SET LIST
See January 22, 1988.
■ The band ran through parts of several songs after "Rock and Roll All Nite," including: "Cat Scratch Fever," "La Bamba," "Calling Dr. Love," "Wipeout," "Good Times Bad Times," and "Stairway to Heaven."

FEBRUARY 14, 1988

Jacksonville, Florida
Jacksonville Veterans Memorial Coliseum
Opening Act: Ted Nugent
Attendance: 3,653   Capacity: 10,228
Promoter: Cellar Door Concerts

FEBRUARY 15, 1988

Columbus, Georgia
Columbus Municipal Auditorium
Opening Act: Ted Nugent
Attendance: 5,263   Capacity: 5,500
Promoter: Colson Bros. Promotions
■ Gene was arrested after the show for indecent exposure. Vari-Lite Operator Warren Flynn captured the arrest on video. Gene's bass tech, Dave "Romeo" Bonilla, recalled: "Gene (while changing in a partially obscured area on the side of the stage) flashed the audience really quickly. The cops were waiting for him when he came off the stage, threw a robe on him, and hauled him off."

FEBRUARY 16, 1988

Columbia, South Carolina
Carolina Coliseum
Opening Act: Ted Nugent
Promoter: Beach Club Promotions

LORI BIRNBAUM

FEBRUARY 18, 1988
Terre Haute, Indiana
Hulman Center
Opening Act: Ted Nugent
Attendance: 4,444   Capacity: 10,464
Promoter: Sunshine Promotions

FEBRUARY 19, 1988
Dubuque, Iowa
Dubuque Five Flags Center
Opening Act: Ted Nugent
Attendance: 3,411   Capacity: 4,200
Promoter: Concert Presentation

FEBRUARY 20, 1988
Kansas City, Missouri
Municipal Auditorium
Opening Act: Ted Nugent
Attendance: 8,000

FEBRUARY 21, 1988
Little Rock, Arkansas
T.H. Barton Coliseum
Opening Act: Ted Nugent
Attendance: 7,365   Capacity: 10,000
Promoter: Mid-South Concerts

FEBRUARY 23, 1988
New Orleans, Louisiana
Kiefer UNO Lakefront Arena
Opening Act: Ted Nugent
Attendance: 2,388   Capacity: 8,000
Promoter: Concert/Southern Promotions
Archived: Audio
■ SET LIST
See January 22, 1988.

FEBRUARY 24, 1988
Houston, Texas
The Summit
Opening Act: Ted Nugent
Attendance: 6,188   Capacity: 9,600
Promoter: Pace Concerts
Archived: Audio
■ SET LIST
Love Gun
Cold Gin
Bang Bang You

Fits Like a Glove
Crazy Crazy Nights
Bruce Kulick Guitar Solo
Eric Carr Drum Solo
War Machine
Reason to Live
Heaven's On Fire
Gene Simmons Bass Solo
I Love It Loud
Lick It Up
Shout It Out Loud
Rock and Roll All Nite
Tears Are Falling
Detroit Rock City

FEBRUARY 25, 1988
San Antonio, Texas
HemisFair Arena @ Henry B. Gonzalez Convention
    Center
Opening Act: Ted Nugent
Attendance: 2,761   Capacity: 3,756
Promoter: Stone City Attractions

FEBRUARY 26, 1988
Austin, Texas
Frank C. Erwin, Jr. Special Events Center
Opening Act: Ted Nugent
Attendance: 3,972   Capacity: 6,757
Promoter: Stone City Attractions
Archived: Audio
■ SET LIST
See February 24, 1988.

FEBRUARY 27, 1988
Fort Worth, Texas
Tarrant County Convention Center
Opening Act: Ted Nugent
Promoter: 462, Inc.
Archived: Audio
■ SET LIST
See February 24, 1988.
■ KISS pennies were sold inside the venue at this show.

MARCH 1, 1988
Madison, Wisconsin
Dane County Expo Center Coliseum
Opening Act: Anthrax

Attendance: 3,553   Capacity: 8,000
Promoter: Stardate Productions

MARCH 2, 1988
Merrillville, Indiana
Star Plaza Theatre
Opening Act: Anthrax
Attendance: 3,288   Capacity: 3,288
Promoter: In-house
Archived: Audio
■ SET LIST
Love Gun
Cold Gin
Bang Bang You
Fits Like a Glove
Crazy Crazy Nights
Bruce Kulick Guitar Solo
Eric Carr Drum Solo
War Machine
Reason to Live
Heaven's On Fire
I Love It Loud
Lick It Up
Shout It Out Loud
Rock and Roll All Nite
Tears Are Falling
Detroit Rock City
■ While attempting to do his bass solo, Gene jumped into the audience to confront a fan who was bothering him.

MARCH 3, 1988
Peoria, Illinois
Carver Arena @ Peoria Civic Center
Opening Act: Anthrax
Attendance: 3,899   Capacity: 8,000
Promoters: Rose Productions, JAM Productions
Archived: Audio
■ SET LIST
Love Gun
Cold Gin
Bang Bang You
Fits Like a Glove
Crazy Crazy Nights
Bruce Kulick Guitar Solo
Eric Carr Drum Solo
War Machine
Reason to Live
Heaven's On Fire
Gene Simmons Bass Solo
I Love It Loud
Lick It Up
Shout It Out Loud
Rock and Roll All Nite
Strutter
Detroit Rock City
■ Gene sang part of "Tutti Frutti" before "Shout It Out Loud." Beginning with this show, "Tears Are Falling" was sporadically added to and dropped from the set list throughout the remainder of the U.S. leg of the tour.

MARCH 5, 1988
Winnipeg, Manitoba, Canada
Winnipeg Arena
Opening Act: Anthrax
Attendance: 4,611   Capacity: 10,000
Promoter: Perryscope Concert Productions
Archived: Audio
■ SET LIST
See February 24, 1988.
■ Paul played part of Led Zeppelin's "Heartbreaker" before "Fits Like a Glove." He continued doing this (presumably at every show) through the March 14 gig in Portland, Oregon and sporad-

ically throughout the spring and summer.

MARCH 8, 1988

Edmonton, Alberta, Canada
Edmonton Coliseum
Opening Act: Anthrax
Attendance: 5,057   Capacity: 7,500
Promoter: Perryscope Concert Productions
Archived: Audio
■ SET LIST
See March 2, 1988.

MARCH 9, 1988

Calgary, Alberta, Canada
Olympic Saddledome
Opening Act: Anthrax
Attendance: 5,641   Capacity: 7,500
Promoter: Perryscope Concert Productions

MARCH 11, 1988

Vancouver, British Columbia, Canada
Pacific Coliseum
Opening Act: Anthrax
Attendance: 4,814   Capacity: 7,500
Promoter: Perryscope Concert Productions
Archived: Audio
■ SET LIST
See February 24, 1988.

MARCH 13, 1988

Central Point (Medford), Oregon
Jackson County Expo Park
Opening Act: Anthrax
Attendance: 5,055   Capacity: 5,700
Promoter: Media One

MARCH 14, 1988

Portland, Oregon
Memorial Coliseum
Opening Act: Anthrax
Attendance: 4,235   Capacity: 9,000
Promoter: Media One
Archived: Audio
■ SET LIST
Love Gun
Cold Gin
Bang Bang You
Fits Like a Glove
Crazy Crazy Nights
Bruce Kulick Guitar Solo
Eric Carr Drum Solo
War Machine
Reason to Live
Heaven's On Fire
Gene Simmons Bass Solo
I Love It Loud
Lick It Up
Shout It Out Loud
Rock and Roll All Nite
Detroit Rock City

MARCH 15, 1988

Spokane, Washington
Spokane Coliseum
Opening Act: Anthrax
Attendance: 3,808   Capacity: 8,500
Promoter: Media One
Archived: Audio
■ SET LIST
See March 14, 1988.

MARCH 17, 1988

Seattle, Washington
Seattle Center Coliseum
Opening Act: Anthrax
Attendance: 5,945   Capacity: 14,327
Promoter: Media One

Archived: Audio
■ SET LIST
See March 14, 1988.

MARCH 19, 1988

Rapid City, South Dakota
Rushmore Plaza Civic Center
Opening Act: Anthrax
Attendance: 5,000

MARCH 20, 1988

Casper, Wyoming
Casper Events Center
Opening Act: Anthrax
Attendance: 3,869   Capacity: 10,424
Promoter: In-house

MARCH 21, 1988

Salt Lake City, Utah
O. Thayne Accord Arena @ Salt Palace Center
Opening Act: Anthrax
Attendance: 7,000   Capacity: 13,000
Promoter: United Concerts

MARCH 23, 1988

Denver, Colorado
McNichols Sports Arena
Opening Act: Anthrax
Attendance: 5,575   Capacity: 10,137
Promoter: Feyline Presents

MARCH 25, 1988

Chandler (Phoenix), Arizona
Compton Terrace
Opening Act: Anthrax
Attendance: 5,363   Capacity: 10,535

MARCH 26, 1988

Costa Mesa, California
Pacific Amphitheatre
Opening Act: Anthrax
Promoter: In-house
Archived: Audio
■ SET LIST
See March 14, 1988.

MARCH 28, 1988

Sacramento, California
ARCO Arena
Opening Act: Anthrax
Attendance: 3,579   Capacity: 4,500

Promoter: Bill Graham Presents
Archived: Audio
■ SET LIST
Love Gun
Cold Gin
Bang Bang You
Fits Like a Glove
Crazy Crazy Nights
Bruce Kulick Guitar Solo
Eric Carr Drum Solo
War Machine
Reason to Live
Heaven's On Fire
Tears Are Falling
I Love It Loud
Lick It Up
Shout It Out Loud
Rock and Roll All Nite
Detroit Rock City
■ "Tears Are Falling" returned to the set and Gene's solo during this show was reduced to a few notes prior to "I Love It Loud." He did not play a solo at either of the subsequent two shows.

MARCH 30, 1988

San Francisco, California
San Francisco Civic Auditorium
Opening Act: Anthrax
Attendance: 4,644   Capacity: 7,000
Promoter: Bill Graham Presents
Archived: Audio
■ SET LIST
Love Gun
Cold Gin
Bang Bang You
Fits Like a Glove
Crazy Crazy Nights
Bruce Kulick Guitar Solo
Eric Carr Drum Solo
War Machine
Heaven's On Fire
Tears Are Falling
I Love It Loud
Lick It Up
Shout It Out Loud
Whole Lotta Love
Rock and Roll All Nite
Detroit Rock City
■ "Reason to Live" was not performed at this show.

CHAD COPPESS

MARCH 31, 1988

Inglewood (Los Angeles), California
The Forum **CANCELED**
Opening Act: Anthrax
Promoter: Parc Presentations

APRIL 1, 1988

San Diego, California
San Diego Sports Arena
Opening Act: Anthrax
Attendance: 4,089   Capacity: 8,893
Promoter: Bill Silva Presentations
Archived: Audio

■ **SET LIST**

Love Gun
Cold Gin
Strutter
Bang Bang You
Fits Like a Glove
Crazy Crazy Nights
Bruce Kulick Guitar Solo
Eric Carr Drum Solo
War Machine
Reason to Live
Heaven's On Fire
Tears Are Falling
I Love It Loud
Lick It Up
Shout It Out Loud
Rock and Roll All Nite
Detroit Rock City

APRIL 2, 1988

Las Vegas, Nevada
Thomas & Mack Center
Opening Act: Anthrax
Attendance: 3,562   Capacity: 8,465
Promoter: Evening Star Productions
Archived: Audio

■ **SET LIST**

Love Gun
Cold Gin
Strutter
Bang Bang You
Fits Like a Glove
Crazy Crazy Nights
Bruce Kulick Guitar Solo
Eric Carr Drum Solo
War Machine
Reason to Live
Heaven's On Fire
Gene Simmons Bass Solo
I Love It Loud
Lick It Up
Shout It Out Loud
Rock and Roll All Nite
Tears Are Falling
Detroit Rock City

■ This was the final appearance of the 40-foot-tall KISS logo and the U.S. stage set.

APRIL 4, 1988 ~~TEMP HOLD DATE~~

Phoenix, Arizona
Arizona Veterans Memorial Coliseum
Opening Act: Anthrax
Promoter: Evening Star Productions

After a 10-year absence, KISS was brought back by the renowned promoter Mr. Udo for a well-received tour of Japan. The prestigious Japanese TV network NHK, which had broadcast the April 1977 KISS concert, was also back on board and purchased the rights to record and broadcast the April 22 Tokyo concert. KISS was even inter-viewed by a puppet on the Japanese TV show *Pure Rock*.

In Japan, KISS used a different stage than it had during its previous North American excursion. The stripped-down production was nothing more than rows of black amplifier cabinets stacked three high on either side of a black drum riser, which had three steps in front of it.

The set list was revised as the band increased the amount of 1970s material they performed, adding "Black Diamond," "I Was Made for Lovin' You," "Calling Dr. Love," and "Strutter" to the set list. Reportedly, the set lists for the shows in Japan were constructed from requests submitted by KISS's Japanese fan club.

An entirely different tourbook was sold during the concerts, and PolyStar released a new greatest hits KISS CD entitled *Chikara* on May 25.

APRIL 16, 1988

Nagoya, Japan
Civic Assembly Hall
No Opening Act
Promoter: Udo Artists
Archived: Audio

■ **SET LIST**

Love Gun
Cold Gin
Bang Bang You
Fits Like a Glove
Crazy Crazy Nights
Bruce Kulick Guitar Solo
Eric Carr Drum Solo
War Machine
Reason to Live
Heaven's On Fire
Tears Are Falling
Gene Simmons Bass Solo
I Love It Loud
Lick It Up
Black Diamond
Shout It Out Loud
Rock and Roll All Nite
Detroit Rock City

■ Paul mentioned that fans had been writing to the band requesting that Eric sing "Black Diamond," which had been included in the set for the first time since March 1985.

APRIL 18, 1988

Osaka, Japan
Royal Festival Hall
No Opening Act
Promoter: Udo Artists
Archived: Audio

■ **SET LIST**

Love Gun
Cold Gin
Bang Bang You
Calling Dr. Love
Fits Like a Glove
Crazy Crazy Nights
Bruce Kulick Guitar Solo
No, No, No
Reason to Live
Heaven's On Fire
Eric Carr Drum Solo
War Machine
Tears Are Falling
Gene Simmons Bass Solo
I Love It Loud
Lick It Up
Black Diamond
I Was Made for Lovin' You
Shout It Out Loud
Strutter
Rock and Roll All Nite
Detroit Rock City

■ "No, No, No" returned to the set for the first time since December 1987.

APRIL 20, 1988

Yokohama, Japan
Bunka Taiikukan
No Opening Act
Promoter: Udo Artists
Archived: Audio

■ **SET LIST**

See April 18, 1988.

APRIL 21, 1988

Tokyo, Japan
Nippon Budokan Hall
No Opening Act
Promoter: Udo Artists
Archived: Audio

■ **SET LIST**

Love Gun
Cold Gin
Bang Bang You
Calling Dr. Love
Fits Like a Glove
Crazy Crazy Nights
Bruce Kulick Guitar Solo
No, No, No
Reason to Live
Heaven's On Fire
Eric Carr Drum Solo
War Machine
Tears Are Falling
Gene Simmons Bass Solo
I Love It Loud
Lick It Up
Black Diamond
I Was Made for Lovin' You
Shout It Out Loud
[Strutter]
Rock and Roll All Nite
Detroit Rock City

APRIL 22, 1988

Tokyo, Japan
Nippon Budokan Hall
No Opening Act
Promoter: Udo Artists
Archived: Video

■ **SET LIST**

Love Gun
Cold Gin
Bang Bang You
Calling Dr. Love
Fits Like a Glove
Crazy Crazy Nights
Bruce Kulick Guitar Solo
No, No, No
Reason to Live
Heaven's On Fire
Eric Carr Drum Solo
War Machine
Gene Simmons Bass Solo
I Love It Loud
Lick It Up
Black Diamond
I Was Made for Lovin' You
Shout It Out Loud
Strutter
Rock and Roll All Nite
Detroit Rock City

■ This concert was professionally archived by NHK-TV and was broadcast in Japan.

APRIL 24, 1988

Tokyo, Japan
Yoyogi Olympic Pool
No Opening Act
Promoter: Udo Artists
Archived: Audio

■ **SET LIST**

Love Gun
Cold Gin
Bang Bang You
Calling Dr. Love
Fits Like a Glove
Crazy Crazy Nights
Bruce Kulick Guitar Solo
No, No, No
Reason to Live
Heaven's On Fire
Eric Carr Drum Solo
War Machine
Tears Are Falling
Gene Simmons Bass Solo
I Love It Loud
Lick It Up
Black Diamond
I Was Made for Lovin' You
Rock and Roll All Nite
Detroit Rock City

As the summer of 1988 began, PolyGram issued their second KISS home video, simply titled *Crazy Nights*. Released on June 6, the video consisted of nothing more than an introduction plus the three music videos produced to promote the album, but still managed to ship enough units to be certified Gold—KISS video cassettes were becoming a cash cow for PolyGram.

On June 26, Gene and Paul stopped by The Limelight Club in Manhattan to check out a show on Ace Frehley's Second Sighting Tour. They were watching the show from above the stage—in plain sight of the fans—when just prior to the first encore, Ace invited them to perform with his band. Stanley and Simmons obliged and got up on stage for an impromptu rendition of "Deuce" with Paul on guitar and Gene simply singing lead vocals. Rock journalist Adrianne Stone: "When they walked out on the stage the place just exploded. People were freaking out. Some of the guys from Kingdom Come and the Scorpions were sitting in the balconies wondering why the audience got so loud. It was really an incredible moment to witness."

Rehearsals for the upcoming Monsters of Rock/European tour had already started when KISS performed at a one-off concert in western New Hampshire. Offstage keyboardist Gary Corbett was brought back for the gig and would remain with KISS through June 1992.

The prospects for the European tour were exciting because "Crazy Crazy Nights" had been a hit single in the U.K. Additionally, on the brief, five-date Monsters of Rock (MOR) tour, KISS would find themselves performing in front of the largest audiences of their non-makeup period, as well as opening for other acts for the first time since December 1975. Both Iron Maiden, who had opened for KISS in 1980, and David Lee Roth, whose career in Van Halen had been jump-started through Gene's involvement with their

demo tapes, headlined over KISS: Iron Maiden at all five MOR shows, Roth at two.

The five daytime, outdoor MOR shows were already booked when KISS decided to do their own tour and 18 additional shows were added, including another "warm-up" gig, this time for the grand reopening of London's infamous Marquee club. KISS visited 13 countries on the tour including three countries they had never previously visited: Iceland, Hungary, and Northern Ireland.

For the European trek, KISS brought back the silver amplifier backline from the third version of the Asylum stage and added additional cabinets in front of Eric's new and rather tall drum riser. The set list closely resembled what it had in Japan, though the addition of 1970s material continued with "Deuce" and "Firehouse" both appearing in the set. Additionally, Paul played excerpts of "Heartbreaker" and/or "Whole Lotta Love" prior to "Fits Like a Glove" on most of the European tour dates.

JULY 4, 1988

North Swanzey, New Hampshire
Cheshire Fairgrounds
Opening Acts: Balaam & the Angel, Dirty Looks, Mantis
Attendance: 8,307   Capacity: 15,000
Promoter: Creative Productions Inc.
Archived: Audio

■ **SET LIST**

Love Gun
Cold Gin
Bang Bang You
Calling Dr. Love
Crazy Crazy Nights
Fits Like a Glove

MIKE NAIMOLI

Paul plays to the holiday crowd in New Hampshire, July 4, 1988.

Bruce Kulick Guitar Solo
No, No, No
Reason to Live
Heaven's On Fire
Eric Carr Drum Solo
War Machine
Tears Are Falling
I Love It Loud
Lick It Up
Black Diamond
Deuce
Shout It Out Loud
Strutter
Rock and Roll All Nite
Detroit Rock City

■ L.A. Guns were originally on the bill, but they canceled their appearance at this daytime, outdoor show. "Deuce" was performed in full for the first time since January 1978. KISS used the Asylum Tour amplifiers for this show before shipping the set off to England.

This was KISS's first and only concert performed in New Hampshire, leaving Delaware and Vermont as the remaining two states in which KISS has never performed.

JULY 8, 1988   CANCELED

Halifax, Nova Scotia, Canada
Halifax Forum
Promoter: Donald K. Donald

AUGUST 12, 1988

New York, New York
The Ritz
Opening Act: Dirty Looks
Attendance: 1,500   Capacity: 1,500
Promoter: John Scher Presents
Archived: Audio

■ **SET LIST**

Deuce
Love Gun
Fits Like a Glove
Heaven's On Fire
Cold Gin
Black Diamond
Bang Bang You
No, No, No
Firehouse
Crazy Crazy Nights
Calling Dr. Love
War Machine
Reason to Live
Tears Are Falling
I Love It Loud
Strutter
Shout It Out Loud
Lick It Up
Rock and Roll All Nite
Detroit Rock City

■ The first night was broadcast live on radio station WNEW.

At both Ritz shows Paul wore a fire hat at the beginning of "Firehouse." It was the first time he had done so since March 17, 1984. These shows mark the last known occasion that he threw a fire hat into the audience.

Reportedly, the band had a bet going with Gene that he couldn't get through the shows without extending his tongue.

AUGUST 13, 1988

New York, New York
The Ritz
Opening Act: Dirty Looks

Attendance: 1,500   Capacity: 1,500
Promoter: John Scher Presents
Archived: Video
■ **SET LIST**
See August 12, 1988.

AUGUST 16, 1988

London, England
Marquee
No Opening Act
Attendance: 500
Archived: Audio
■ **SET LIST**
See August 12, 1988.
■ Dave Bonilla remembers, "We were the first band to play there after it opened. They literally told us, 'Don't touch the wall, guys, the paint is still wet.'"

AUGUST 20, 1988

Leistershire, Donington, England
Donington Park
Headlining Act: Iron Maiden
Opening Acts: David Lee Roth, Megadeth, Guns N' Roses, Helloween
Attendance: 97,595   Capacity: 97,595
Promoter: MCP
Archived: Audio
■ **SET LIST**
Deuce
Love Gun
Fits Like a Glove
Heaven's On Fire
Cold Gin
Black Diamond
No, No, No
Firehouse
Crazy Crazy Nights
Calling Dr. Love
Tears Are Falling
I Love It Loud
Strutter
Shout It Out Loud
Lick It Up
Rock and Roll All Nite
Detroit Rock City
■ Monsters of Rock show #1. At this show, Iron Maiden became the first band to open for KISS and then headline over them.

British DJ Neil Kay was Master of Ceremonies for the show and a special tourbook was issued to commemorate the event.

Two people were crushed to death during the Guns N' Roses set.

AUGUST 27, 1988

Schweinfurt, West Germany
Mainwiesen
Headlining Acts: Iron Maiden, David Lee Roth
Opening Acts: Anthrax, Great White, Testament, Treat
Attendance: 60,000
Archived: Audio, Partial Video
■ **SET LIST**
Deuce
[Love Gun]
Fits Like a Glove
Heaven's On Fire
Cold Gin
Black Diamond
[Bruce Kulick Guitar Solo]
No, No, No
[Firehouse]
Crazy Crazy Nights
Tears Are Falling
I Love It Loud

Gene, Bruce, and Paul during the Monsters of Rock Tour in Europe, summer 1988.

[Strutter]
Shout It Out Loud
[Lick It Up]
Rock and Roll All Nite
Detroit Rock City
■ Monsters of Rock show #2. Megadeth was forced to cancel their scheduled appearance when their bassist sustained an injury to his arm; they were replaced by Testament. Warlock vocalist Doro Pesch introduced KISS.

The night before this concert Gene and Paul appeared on a live edition of the RTL-TV program, *Metal Hammer* in front of a group of fans. RTL broadcast two songs from the concert live and, later, an edited version of the concert aired on the network. Gary Corbett was purposefully kept hidden from the crowd at most shows, but one of the RTL cameramen unwittingly videotaped Corbett during the performance and the footage was included in the television broadcast.

AUGUST 28, 1988

Bochum, West Germany
Ruhr Stadion
Headlining Acts: Iron Maiden, David Lee Roth
Opening Acts: Anthrax, Great White, Testament
Attendance: 40,000+
Archived: Video
■ **SET LIST**
Deuce
Love Gun
Fits Like a Glove
Heaven's On Fire
Cold Gin
Black Diamond
Bruce Kulick Guitar Solo
No, No, No
Crazy Crazy Nights
Tears Are Falling
I Love It Loud

Shout It Out Loud
Lick It Up
Rock and Roll All Nite
Detroit Rock City
■ Monsters of Rock show #3. Testament again replaced Megadeth, and the first opening band, Treat, had their show canceled when a lighting truck's late arrival delayed setup of some of the staging.

AUGUST 30, 1988

Víðidalur, Árbær (Reykjavík), Iceland
Reiðhöllin
Opening Act: Foringjarnir
Attendance: 8,000
Promoters: Bobby Harrison & Tony Sandy
■ Víðidalur is a community in the Árbær suburb of Reykjavík. The area is world-renowned for its horse breeding, and the venue name, Reiðhöllin, translates: "horse stadium."

"It was a shitty facility, sweaty and hot, and a lot like a barn," remembers Bruce Kulick. "But I thought that Reykjavik was very alien and beautiful. I remember it had a great Hard Rock Café and a cool hotel."

Gary Corbett: "Reykjavík was really strange. The venue was a big metallic building and it was very damp inside. During the show, because of the metal building, the warm climate inside the place, and the very cool air outside, there was actually a cloud that had formed and was hanging above the audience. Driving from the airport to the hotel we were staying in, it was just like driving on the moon, nothing but rubble and rock without any buildings for miles."

This was KISS's first and only appearance in Iceland.

Budapest, Hungary
Kisstadion Lelàtò
Opening Act: Edda
Attendance: 8,000
Promoter: Multimedia Concerts
Archived: Audio, Video

■ SET LIST

Deuce
Love Gun
Fits Like a Glove
Heaven's On Fire
Cold Gin
Black Diamond
Bang Bang You
Bruce Kulick Guitar Solo
No, No, No
Crazy Crazy Nights
I Was Made for Lovin' You
War Machine
Reason to Live
Tears Are Falling
I Love It Loud
Strutter
Shout It Out Loud
Lick It Up
Rock and Roll All Nite
Detroit Rock City

■ The concert was originally scheduled for a venue called Népstadion. Advertisements for the show appeared to designate the concert as another in the "Monsters of Rock" series, however, it was clearly a KISS concert only.

Gary Corbett: "Budapest was really beautiful. I believe Gene's parents were from Budapest, so going to Hungary for him was a trip to his parent's birthplace. He perked up a bit. I have footage of Gene on the bus, and he's got the microphone tour guide thing going on up front, talking about the histories of the various buildings. He was all proud that he was doing this, but after five minutes we were all telling him to go sit down in the back of the bus. Later, we took him out to this bar out in the country. There was this Hungarian liqueur that was brought over special by the guy who owned the place. We were all doing shots and were trying to get him to do it, and we were giving him this Hungarian guilt-trip. At one point, he had one in his hand, and he just couldn't do it.

"The venue was gorgeous and was one of the most beautiful places we went. The show itself was hit by a torrential downpour about halfway through. It was heavier than anything I had ever seen. The stage was mostly covered except for the first eight feet or so, but I remember that Bruce was standing out on stage during his guitar solo, and he was totally, completely drenched. The crowd was wearing garbage bags, and it was just a mess."

Paul played parts of "Heartbreaker" and Aerosmith's "Walk This Way" prior to "Fits Like a Glove."

Tilburg, The Netherlands
Willem II Stadium
Headlining Act: Iron Maiden
Opening Acts: David Lee Roth, Anthrax, Helloween, Great White
Attendance: 35,000   Capacity: 35,000

Promoter: Mojo Concerts
Archived: Audio

■ SET LIST

Deuce
Love Gun
Fits Like a Glove
Heaven's On Fire
Cold Gin
Black Diamond
Bruce Kulick Guitar Solo
No, No, No
Crazy Crazy Nights
Tears Are Falling
I Love It Loud
Strutter
Shout It Out Loud
Rock and Roll All Nite
Detroit Rock City

■ Monsters of Rock show #4.

Gary Corbett relates the following story regarding Eric: "Eric was pissed because they weren't going to let him do his drum solo, and Paul and Gene justified it because it was a short set due to all the acts on the bill. But once we started to headline, there was time to do it. They told him in Amsterdam that he wasn't going to be able to do it on the European Tour either. So, he was really bummed and was not talking to them. He came to me and told me, 'I want to go to one of those cafés and get stoned.' He didn't want to smoke; he just wanted to eat the brownies. We went to the place and ate a bunch of stuff and nothing happened. He was really bummed about that, too.

"The next day, Bruce came up to me and told me that he'd found a little café that was off the beaten path, more of a local place, not a tourist place, and that the muffins there were supposedly amazing. I asked Eric if he wanted to try it again and that this time he'd really feel it. We get to this place, and he was chowing with the same enthusiasm that he was the day before. So, he and I and Bruce and 'Night' Bob are walking around, and Eric finally starts getting high, because it takes a while to kick in when you eat it. We sit down at another café and all of a sudden he started getting really paranoid. Then Gene and Paul showed up, and he didn't want to see them like that so he said, 'Let's get out of here.'

"We're walking back to my hotel room, and we put on a CD and are listening to Jeff Beck with like 20 different kinds of weed and hash. Every time I pan across the room with the camera, Eric is sitting in this armchair stiff as a board waving me to move the camera away from him. Finally, I told him, 'Eric, if you just sit down and eat something, you'll get down again.' We order room service and he takes one bite of it and he throws it down, saying, 'I can't eat this! If I eat it, I will choke on it and I'll die.' 'OK, why don't you just lie down for awhile and go to sleep?' 'No way! If I go to sleep, I'll never wake up and I'll die!' We babysat him the entire night.

"I met up with the band at the next stop in Italy, at which point I found out that Eric hadn't come out of his room for the last three days. Paul gave me shit later at this Italian restaurant; he kept saying, 'Hey look, it's the Pusher Man!' because Eric confessed everything to him."

Modena, Italy
Festa Della Unità
Headlining Act: Iron Maiden
Opening Acts: Anthrax, Helloween, Kings of the Sun, Royal Air Force
Attendance: 20,000   Capacity: 50,000
Promoter: Barley Arts Promotions
Archived: Audio, Video

■ SET LIST

Deuce
Love Gun
Fits Like a Glove
Heaven's On Fire
Cold Gin
Black Diamond
Bruce Kulick Guitar Solo
No, No, No
Firehouse
Crazy Crazy Nights
I Was Made for Lovin' You
War Machine
Tears Are Falling
I Love It Loud
Shout It Out Loud
Lick It Up
Rock and Roll All Nite
Detroit Rock City

■ This was the fifth and final Monsters of Rock show.

Yngwie J. Malmsteen's Rising Force was scheduled on the bill for this show, as well as the subsequent shows in Paris, Göteborg, and Johanneshov, but was forced to back out of all shows when Yngwie sustained serious injuries in an automobile accident. The concert was part of the annual festival held by Unità, the Italian Communist Party.

Paris, France
Le Zenith
Opening Act: Kings of the Sun
Attendance: 3,500   Capacity: 6,300
Archived: Audio, Video

■ SET LIST

Love Gun
Fits Like a Glove
Heaven's On Fire
Cold Gin
Black Diamond
Bang Bang You
No, No, No
Firehouse
Crazy Crazy Nights
I Was Made for Lovin' You
Deuce
Reason to Live
Tears Are Falling
I Love It Loud
Strutter
Shout It Out Loud
Lick It Up
Rock and Roll All Nite
Detroit Rock City

■ Gary Corbett: "We did two days' worth of rehearsals at Le Zenith before our tour started. The hotel we stayed in was beautiful and had been used as SS headquarters during WWII. While we where there, there were these French fans that had made this miniature replica of Eric's drum kit that was simply amazing. All the details were totally exact. Eric and I came down to the lobby, and they said, 'Oh please let us give you these things that we made for you.' They had the entire kit exact, along with the electronic pads. Eric was so taken by it, that he had it shipped home and put it in a glass viewing case."

SEPTEMBER 15, 1988

Frederiksberg (København), Denmark
K.B. Hallen
Opening Act: Kings of the Sun
Capacity: 3,000
Archived: Video
■ SET LIST
Love Gun
Fits Like a Glove
Heaven's On Fire
Cold Gin
Black Diamond
Bang Bang You
No, No, No
Firehouse
Crazy Crazy Nights
I Was Made for Lovin' You
Deuce
Reason to Live
Tears Are Falling
I Love It Loud
Strutter
Shout It Out Loud
Medley: La Bamba - Black Dog - How Many More
    Times
Lick It Up
Rock and Roll All Nite
Detroit Rock City

SEPTEMBER 16, 1988

Göteborg, Sweden
Frölundaborg
Opening Act: Kings of the Sun
Attendance: 4,000   Capacity: 4,500
Promoter: EMA Telstar
Archived: Video
■ SET LIST
Love Gun
Fits Like a Glove
Heaven's On Fire
Cold Gin
Black Diamond
Bang Bang You
No, No, No
Firehouse
Crazy Crazy Nights
I Was Made for Lovin' You
Deuce
Reason to Live
Tears Are Falling
I Love It Loud
Strutter
Shout It Out Loud
Lick It Up
Rock and Roll All Nite
Detroit Rock City

SEPTEMBER 17, 1988

Johanneshov (Stockholm), Sweden
Hovet
Opening Act: Kings of the Sun
Attendance: 7,500   Capacity: 9,500
Promoter: EMA Telstar
Archived: Audio
■ SET LIST
See September 16, 1988.
■ Prior to the show, Gene, Paul, Eric, and Bruce sat down backstage to film an interview for TV Scandinavia's *Nightflight*. The interview, during which the band constantly antagonize and belittle each other, can only be described as *The Tomorrow Show* of the 1980s.

Before playing "Reason to Live," Bruce performed a brief portion of "Turn On the Night" on keyboards.

SEPTEMBER 19, 1988

Helsingfors, Finland
Icehalle
Opening Act: Kings of the Sun
Attendance: 3,000   Capacity: 3,000
Archived: Audio
■ SET LIST
Love Gun
Fits Like a Glove
Heaven's On Fire
Cold Gin
Black Diamond
Bang Bang You
No, No, No
Firehouse
Crazy Crazy Nights
I Was Made for Lovin' You
Deuce
Reason to Live
Tears Are Falling
I Love It Loud
Strutter
Shout It Out Loud
Lick It Up
Rock and Roll All Nite
Detroit Rock City
■ Gary Corbett: "When we were in Helsinki, there were girls who attended the shows and had to sneak out of Russia to get there, which was not an easy or smart thing to do. That was the closest we got to the Russian border."

Bruce played an excerpt from Van Halen's "Jump" prior to "Reason to Live."

SEPTEMBER 21, 1988

Lilleström, Norway
Skedmohallen
Opening Act: Kings of the Sun
Attendance: 4,500
Promoters: Gunnar Eide, Internasjonal Konsertdireksjon
Archived: Audio
■ SET LIST
See September 13, 1988.

SEPTEMBER 24, 1988

London, England
Wembley Arena
Opening Act: Kings of the Sun
Capacity: 8,000
Promoters: MCP, Kennedy Street Entertainment
Archived: Audio
■ SET LIST
Love Gun
Fits Like a Glove
Heaven's On Fire
Cold Gin
Black Diamond
Bang Bang You
No, No, No
Firehouse
Crazy Crazy Nights
I Was Made for Lovin' You
Deuce
Reason to Live
Tears Are Falling
I Love It Loud
Strutter

Shout It Out Loud
Lick It Up
Rock and Roll All Nite
[Detroit Rock City]

SEPTEMBER 25, 1988

London, England
Wembley Arena
Opening Act: Kings of the Sun
Capacity: 8,000
Promoters: MCP, Kennedy Street Entertainment
Archived: Video
■ SET LIST
Love Gun
Fits Like a Glove
Heaven's On Fire
Cold Gin
Black Diamond
Bang Bang You
No, No, No
Firehouse
Crazy Crazy Nights
I Was Made for Lovin' You
Reason to Live
Tears Are Falling
I Love It Loud
Strutter
Shout It Out Loud
Lick It Up
Rock and Roll All Nite
Detroit Rock City

SEPTEMBER 26, 1988

Birmingham, England
National Exhibition Centre
Opening Act: Kings of the Sun
Capacity: 2,360
Promoters: MCP, Kennedy Street Entertainment
Archived: Audio
■ SET LIST
See September 25, 1988.

SEPTEMBER 27, 1988

Birmingham, England
National Exhibition Centre
Opening Act: Kings of the Sun
Capacity: 2,360
Promoters: MCP, Kennedy Street Entertainment
Archived: Video
■ SET LIST
Love Gun
Fits Like a Glove
Heaven's On Fire
Cold Gin
Black Diamond
Bang Bang You
Eric Carr Drum Solo
No, No, No
Firehouse
Crazy Crazy Nights
Deuce
I Was Made for Lovin' You
Reason to Live
Tears Are Falling
I Love It Loud
Strutter
Shout It Out Loud
La Bamba
Oh Susannah
Lick It Up
Rock and Roll All Nite
Detroit Rock City
■ KISS played part of "Whole Lotta Love" prior to "Lick It Up."

SEPTEMBER 28, 1988

Bradford, England
St. George's Hall
Opening Act: Kings of the Sun
Attendance: Sold Out
Promoters: MCP, Kennedy Street Entertainment
Archived: Video

■ SET LIST

Love Gun
Fits Like a Glove
Heaven's On Fire
Cold Gin
Black Diamond
Bang Bang You
Eric Carr Drum Solo
No, No, No
Firehouse
Crazy Crazy Nights
Deuce
I Was Made for Lovin' You
Oh Susannah
Medley: La Bamba - Wipeout - Jump - Runnin' With
     the Devil
Reason to Live
Tears Are Falling
I Love It Loud
Strutter
Shout It Out Loud
Medley: Badge - Winchester Cathedral - Faith - Black
     Sabbath - Sunshine of Your Love
Whole Lotta Love
Lick It Up
Rock and Roll All Nite
Detroit Rock City

SEPTEMBER 29, 1988

Newcastle, England
City Hall
Opening Act: Kings of the Sun
Attendance: Sold Out
Promoters: MCP, Kennedy Street Entertainment
Archived: Video

■ SET LIST

Love Gun
Fits Like a Glove
Heaven's On Fire
Cold Gin
Black Diamond
Bang Bang You
Eric Carr Drum Solo
No, No, No
Firehouse
Crazy Crazy Nights
I Was Made for Lovin' You
Deuce
Reason to Live
Tears Are Falling
I Love It Loud
Strutter
Shout It Out Loud
Lick It Up
Rock and Roll All Nite
Detroit Rock City

OCTOBER 1, 1988

Edinburgh, Scotland
Playhouse Theatre
Opening Act: Kings of the Sun
Attendance: 3,100   Capacity: 3,100
Promoters: MCP, Kennedy Street Entertainment
Archived: Audio

■ SET LIST

Love Gun
Fits Like a Glove
Heaven's On Fire
Cold Gin

Black Diamond
Bang Bang You
Eric Carr Drum Solo
No, No, No
Firehouse
Crazy Crazy Nights
Deuce
I Was Made for Lovin' You
Reason to Live
Tears Are Falling
I Love It Loud
Strutter
Shout It Out Loud
Oh Susannah
Medley: La Bamba - You Shook Me All Night Long -
     Good Times Bad Times
Lick It Up
Rock and Roll All Nite
Detroit Rock City

■ A power failure part of the way through "Love Gun" stopped the show dead in its tracks and the band restarted the show from the top.

OCTOBER 2, 1988

Edinburgh, Scotland
Playhouse Theatre
Opening Act: Kings of the Sun
Attendance: 3,100   Capacity: 3,100
Promoters: MCP, Kennedy Street Entertainment
Archived: Audio

■ SET LIST

Love Gun
Fits Like a Glove
Heaven's On Fire
Black Diamond
Bang Bang You
Cold Gin
Eric Carr Drum Solo
No, No, No
Firehouse
Crazy Crazy Nights
Deuce
I Was Made for Lovin' You
Reason to Live
Tears Are Falling
I Love It Loud
Strutter
Shout It Out Loud
Oh Susannah
Medley: Sunshine of Your Love - Communication
     Breakdown
Lick It Up
Rock and Roll All Nite
Detroit Rock City

■ Paul performed a bit of "Stairway to Heaven" during the introduction to "Black Diamond." Prior to "Reason to Live," Bruce again played a few bars of "Jump," prompting Paul to say "If we did something like that, we would have a big hit." A part of "Stairway to Heaven" was also played before "Oh Susannah."

OCTOBER 3, 1988

Belfast, Northern Ireland
King's Hall
Opening Act: Kings of the Sun
Attendance: 7,000
Promoter: Wonderland Promotions Ltd.
Archived: Video

■ SET LIST

Love Gun
Fits Like a Glove
Heaven's On Fire
Cold Gin
Black Diamond

Bang Bang You
Eric Carr Drum Solo
No, No, No
Firehouse
Crazy Crazy Nights
Deuce
I Was Made For Lovin' You
Reason to Live
Tears Are Falling
I Love It Loud
Strutter
Shout It Out Loud
Oh Susannah
Medley: La Bamba - Whole Lotta Love
Lick It Up
Rock and Roll All Nite
Detroit Rock City

■ This show marked the final performance for most of the *Crazy Nights* tracks, such as "Bang Bang You," "No, No, No," and "Reason to Live" and it was the last time that KISS used their "You wanted the best. . . " intro until 1996. Paul played the first part of "Stairway to Heaven" before "Whole Lotta Love."

Gary Corbett: "The funny thing about that part of the world, so they told us, is that if they approve of you, they spit at you and so when the show ended, Paul was basically covered in spit. But there was one guy in front who just kept getting them. He got shit all over the guitar neck and fingers and Paul finally just lost it. He walked up to the front of the stage and motioned to the people to part and move aside and single out the one guy who had been getting him and Paul spit right in the guy's face. When you look at the video footage, the spit is flying around so heavily that it just looks like the footage is really grainy. I was very happy to be offstage that night."

Bruce Kulick: "That was the most disgusting KISS gig ever. The promoters were saying "Oh, they love you!" Yeah, right. So there I am negotiating lead playing with strangers' phlegm dripping off my fingerboard and dripping off my hair. That truly defined rock and roll and punk all into one."

———————

Even before they departed for Europe to wind down the marathon Crazy Nights Tour, KISS was already promoting their next album, a greatest-hits package entitled *Smashes, Thrashes & Hits*.

The compilation album included remixed versions of some of the band's greatest hits as well as a new version of "Beth" with Eric Carr on lead vocals. Additionally, two new songs were recorded and produced by Paul for the album, "Let's Put the X in Sex" and "(You Make Me) Rock Hard." Both songs were a lot closer in sound to dance music than hard rock and on the heels of the pop sounds of *Crazy Nights* it was a bit much for some fans to take. Despite this, *Smashes . . .* wound up being a surprise hit for the band and was eventually certified Multi-Platinum.

Smashes . . . was released on November 14, 1988 and two days later, Paul made an appearance on the short-lived MTV show *Mouth To Mouth* to world-premiere the "Let's Put the X in Sex" video and to perform a one-man version of "Rock and Roll All Nite" for the studio audience. Paul also took up a week-long slot as a fill-in VJ on MTV starting on December 23.

A second video was also produced to promote the album. The quickly forgotten "(You Make Me) Rock Hard" video world-premiered on April 22, 1989 during an episode of *Headbangers Ball*.

Gene kept busy over the next several months as he launched the ill-fated Simmons Records, acted in the movie *Red Surf* with then-unknown actor George Clooney, and became a father when his son Nicholas was born to him and long-time paramour Shannon Tweed on January 22.

Eric continued to manage the all-girl group Hari Kari (as he had since 1986), as well as continuing to develop and shop his "Rockheads" cartoon concept with some assistance from Bruce, who helped Eric with the music for the potential series.

The initial plan for 1989 called for KISS to perform a short tour; a T-Shirt was even released with the slogan "Live Tour '89" on the back. When that tour failed to materialize, Paul opted to do his first series of concerts as a solo artist and performed 25 concerts in February, March, and April. Paul hired Gary Corbett, Dennis St. James, Bob Kulick, and Eric Singer to perform with him on the tour. The set list included a cross-section of KISS classics, three songs from Paul's 1978 solo album, and an unreleased song that had been recorded for the *Crazy Nights* album, "Hide Your Heart."

CHAPTER 20

HOT IN THE SHADE TOUR

Number of Shows: 124
Start Date: March 11, 1990 - Galveston, Texas
End Date: November 9, 1990 - New York, New York
Countries: Canada, U.S.A.
Headlining Act: Whitesnake
Opening Acts: Danger, Danger; Downtown Bruno; Faster Pussycat; The Good Rats; Joe Lynn Turner; Little Caesar; The Red & The Black; Saraya; Shake City; Slaughter; Vixen; Winger

Average Attendance: 6,589* (Does not include the Galveston show.)

With the release of *Smashes, Thrashes & Hits,* KISS had fulfilled its recording contract, and in 1989, Paul and Gene sought to re-sign with PolyGram. Two Platinum albums in the last fifteen months put KISS in a surprisingly advantageous position at the bargaining table and the result of the negotiations was a 10-year, seven-album contract. The timing of the deal was very fortunate for KISS as their next album would struggle to achieve Gold status and none of the band's subsequent albums have been officially certified Platinum.

With a new recording contract in place, KISS turned its collective attention to eliminating their debt to the IRS. Allegedly as a means of resolving that issue, Gene and Paul sold their publishing rights to KISS's back catalog, as well as licensed a percentage of their future publishing rights, to Hori Productions America.

Contractual matters behind them, KISS immersed themselves in the writing and recording of their next album. They decided that the new material should be less pop oriented, with a more stripped-down rock and roll feel. Ironically, Vini Poncia, who had produced two very pop-oriented records for the band, *Dynasty* and *Unmasked,* was brought in to write with both Gene and Paul. By April, Gene had begun recording 24-track demos with Eric Carr and former Black 'N Blue guitarist Tommy Thayer at a tiny Hollywood, California studio called The Fortress, while Paul worked on his demos with Bruce Kulick and the drummer from his solo tour, Eric Singer. The band decided that The Fortress would suit their needs, and recording of what was then tentatively titled *Crimes of Passion* began on June 15 and ran through late August.

Jesse Hilsen was still presiding over much of the band's business affairs at this time, yet KISS sought to bring a manager on board and they eventually hired Larry Mazer and his company Entertainment Services Unlimited. Mazer would handle the creative direction of the band, playing Bill Aucoin to Jesse Hilsen's Glickman/Marks. "I had been

working with Cinderella and then Nelson," recalls Mazer, "before getting a call from Gene and Paul asking me to come to work for KISS. Before I came on, they had sold their catalog to Hori, which I never would have done in a million years."

Retitled *Hot in the Shade,* the album was released on October 17, 1989 and became the last KISS album to be mass-produced on vinyl.

A lengthy five-month period separated the release of the album and the Hot in the Shade Tour, as initial tour projections were not encouraging. Gene and Paul decided to bide their time and went on two extensive promotional tours, the first to focus on promoting the album, and the second to hype the tour.

Three singles were released off *Hot in the Shade* and a video was produced for each one. The first single, "Hide Your Heart," had actually preceded the release of the album, and the accompanying video world-premiered during an episode of the MTV series *Hard 30* on October 23. With promoters not biting, the band took

a drastic step to generate interest in their next video "Rise to It," with Gene and Paul donning their KISS makeup for the first time in over six years during the taping on November 21. Larry Mazer comments: "I did come up with the makeup idea for 'Rise to It' but the video was one of their least popular. That sent the signal to me that the makeup generation had passed and the new kids didn't really care about it." The video nonetheless presented an obvious implication: that a reunion tour may have been in the works. Mazer continues, "[New York promoter] John Scher contacted us at one point to ask if KISS was interested in doing a makeup show for pay-per-view, but I told him no. The number one question for my entire tenure was, 'When are they putting the makeup back on?' Everyone saw that as the thing to do, whereas I saw it as the endgame." Ultimately, the "Rise to It" video was shelved for several months before finally being released in April 1990.

In early December 1989, "Forever," the ballad Paul Stanley had penned with Michael Bolton, was selected to be the second single/video from *Hot in the Shade*. The video was filmed on December 16 and world-premiered on January 20, 1990 during *Headbangers Ball*. The single and video would both prove to be exactly what KISS had hoped for, a bona fide smash hit. The video enjoyed a lengthy stay at number one on *Dial MTV* and was put into heavy rotation by the channel that more than a few fans became burned out on it. Radio also took rabidly to the song and it became KISS's second-highest charting single ever, peaking at number eight on *Billboard's* Top 10 Singles. PolyGram even printed new point-of-purchase posters touting the single as "The first *great* power ballad of the 90s," and recut the album's TV commercial to include excerpts from the "Forever" video.

Larry Mazer: "When I initially tried to set the tour up, there was no excitement among the promoters whatsoever. I went to Gene and Paul and told them that I didn't think we had enough going at that point do to a tour. So we waited. Then 'Forever' came out and was a hit. I booked the tour on the strength of the single, and the vibe among the promoters was like day and night compared to earlier."

"Larry was the nuts and bolts behind that tour," notes Bruce Kulick. "That guy does not get enough credit and he should. He did a lot to get KISS back on track."

Hot in the Shade had been certified Gold by the R.I.A.A. in December, three months after its release. But relative to the success of many bands within the same genre at this time—Skid Row, Guns N' Roses, and Great White among them—the reception to the album had been lukewarm.

Although the album was not hugely successful, the Hot in the Shade Tour was widely embraced by the band's fans. Like the Asylum Tour, it was exclusively a North American venture and, totaling 124 concerts, it was one of the longest tours in the band's career. And though the attendance was similar to the previous three tours, it did show an increase from the Crazy Nights Tour of more than 12%, rising to a nightly average of 6,589, a figure the band had not surpassed in the U.S. since 1979.

Larry Mazer: "I did try to talk to them about having Ace Frehley as the opening act, with the idea being that it would be cool to have him come out and do the encore. I was looking for a way to help sell tickets because at that time there weren't many acts who could help us do that. I had Gene and Paul convinced into doing it and then Ace turned it down."

One act that could help KISS sell tickets was Slaughter, who was booked as an opening act at 111 of the tour's shows. Slaughter not only provided a tenuous link to KISS's past (band members Dana Strum and Mark Slaughter had been members of the Vinnie Vincent Invasion), but also brought fresh interest to the tour on the strength of their Multi-Platinum debut album *Stick It to Ya*. Slaughter, along with two other rising bands who opened shows on the tour—Winger and Faster Pussycat—undoubtedly impacted ticket sales.

The tour not only featured new staging, lighting, and a heavily revamped set list, but an effort was made by Larry Mazer and the band to change the very thought process behind the design of the show. "The challenge for any tour is this," remarks Mazer, "normally you have a starting point, which can be a lighting configuration, a stage set, or even a set list. For KISS, everything started at the back center of the stage with the electric KISS logo; it had been that way for most of their career. My attitude was, 'How many times can you have a stage with a KISS logo in the middle?' It was boring at that point and, also, we had such a unique gift with the Sphinx on the album cover that the idea was obvious. Hey, take it right off the album cover and you have your center of the stage." The prop was eventually given the nickname "Leon Sphinx."

Part of the thorough reconstruction of KISS's live production was the elimination of several of their oldest effects, two of which dated back to 1973. Along with the lighted KISS logo, the "You wanted the best" intro, Paul's guitar-breaking routine, and Gene's fire-breathing stunt were all eliminated. For the first few shows, KISS experimented with a new intro where Paul would start the show by asking the audience: "What do you say we kick some ass?" The intro did not last long and was abandoned by mid-May.

The elaborate staging was designed by Robert Roth and Jim Chapman and was constructed by Tait Towers and there were many new props and effects added to the production.

Larry Mazer recalls, "We had come up with the way to include the KISS sign towards the end, by having the Sphinx disintegrate. We knew we had to include the sign, but we didn't want it there the entire time. We wanted Act Three drama, which came during the encore in 'I Want You' with the mirrorball, and then 'boom!' the sign would come up. The production manager, Charlie Hernandez, kept a box of sunglasses on the soundboard to give to all the working personnel because during that part of the show the lights were so bright."

Dallas-based Showlazers designed a laser show for KISS. During the show's dramatic intro, lasers would spread out around the band members in a fan of turquoise lines as they emerged from the mouth of the Sphinx. Lasers were also featured in several songs throughout the latter portion of the set and quite prominently in Eric's drum solo.

The stage also included a drainage pipe with running water. Robert Roth: "It was just a little prop that splurged water. The Hot in the Shade stage started out as 'M.C. Escher-meets-the-Sphinx' and a whole series of renderings was done and when we got into costing it, it was impractical to detail it to that level. We simplified it and that's one of the props that stayed."

The formula behind the Hot in the Shade Tour set list was a distinct departure from the past. Of the album's 15 tracks, only three were played regularly: "Hide Your Heart," "Forever," and "Rise to It" with two other *Hot in the Shade* songs, "Betrayed," and "Little Caesar," dropped from the set almost immediately. Gene, Paul, and Bruce all had their solos eliminated from the show and, with one exception, Eric's solo was not present until July 11.

In the absence of solos and *Hot in the Shade* material, KISS opted to give many fans what they had been clamoring to hear for years: classic 1970s KISS songs. Most of the set lists from the previous three tours had included only four or five classic era songs; the Hot in the Shade Tour set lists increased that count to as many as 13 in some instances. The show started off with "I Stole Your Love" and "Deuce," both of which had been used to open sets in the 1970s. And while the band had done "Deuce" at the end of the Crazy Nights Tour, "I Stole Your Love" had not been performed since May 1978, and the two songs back-to-back were akin to a religious epiphany for many fans. With an emphatic one-two punch that gave fans a feeling that their requests had been vindicated, KISS could not lose.

Keyboardist Gary Corbett was brought back to fill out KISS's live sound and though he contributed even more to the Hot in the Shade Tour than he had to the Crazy Nights Tour, he was still stationed offstage. "By the end of Hot in the Shade," Corbett recalls, "I was singing background vocals on at least half of the songs. At the beginning of the tour, they decided to succumb to the vocal samples and accept it as the way to do it. I would do the background vocals on about 12 songs as samples, in addition to everyone singing, including myself. We didn't actually pull the vocal samples off the record because the band played down a half-step live. We actually recorded the rehearsal live, and that's what I sampled, so it still had a very live sound to it. I had choruses for everything from 'Heaven's On Fire' to 'Shout It Out Loud.' I even did the talking Sphinx in 'God of Thunder.'"

Four noteworthy arrangements were made to the set:

- "Black Diamond" concluded abruptly at the end of the final chorus and immediately segued into "Shout It Out Loud."

- With one known exception, performances of the album's third single, "Rise to It," included a fairly lengthy blues-oriented intro that was not present on the album.

- Eric's solo contained a sample of the intro to The Who's "Who Are You."

- Paul frequently sang the second verse of "Cold Gin."

Despite the overall success of the tour, some misfortunes did transpire, especially for Paul, who suffered fairly serious injuries on two different occasions, first, in a limousine accident on July 4, and then again on October 10 when he ran into a guardrail onstage and cracked several ribs.

Additionally, Eric Carr and Paul Stanley were not on speaking terms at the start of the tour. Bruce Kulick notes: "I don't know the cause of it, but I do know that there was a period of time where they did not want to speak with one another. It lasted about a month." Gary Corbett offers: "I remember that it was really uncomfortable for the beginning of the tour. I remember it being more about something that Gene and Paul were imposing on Eric that he hated, like cutting out the drum solo altogether. He was so fed-up with them at that point, that for the entire first month or two he would get on the bus with his sunglasses and headphones, he would sit in the front lounge where everyone else was sitting, but he'd purposefully face away from everybody. He really wouldn't talk to anybody except me."

OCTOBER 21 & 22, 1989   CANCELED

Melbourne, Australia
Wallen
Co-Headliner: Joe Cocker
Promoter: Australian Rock Promotions Pty Ltd.
■ This two-day event was hyped as "World Rock 1989." It allegedly had been planned many months in advance, though KISS claimed to have no knowledge of the concert until September.

MARCH 11, 1990

Galveston, Texas
West Beach Pocket Park #1
Opening Act: Downtown Bruno
Attendance: 2,500
Promoter: KKBQ
Archived: Video
■ **SET LIST**
Detroit Rock City
Calling Dr. Love
Shout It Out Loud
Love Gun
Forever
Rock and Roll All Nite
Cold Gin
■ The show was a free, daytime, outdoor Spring Break mini-concert sponsored by KKBQ radio. The stage was located on the beach off the Gulf of Mexico. Set list requests had been fielded by the radio station during the days leading up to the show and KISS videotaped portions of this show (and the subsequent Reseda and Dallas shows) for the eventually scrapped home video *Exposed II*.

The unruly crowd threw debris at the stage throughout the show. Gary Corbett: "It was a very short show done in front of a couple thousand hot, sweaty drunks. I played the entire show out at the soundboard."

Tour Coordinator Steve Wood: "The Galveston show was the first public event I did with them. The night before the gig, we rented a studio so the band could rehearse. It wasn't a particularly great event; just a bunch of drunks on a beach. The promotion of it was certainly bigger than the actual event. The show was very short, but it was planned that way."

APRIL 14, 1990

Asbury Park, New Jersey
The Stone Pony
Opening Acts: Saraya, Joe Lynn Turner, The Good Rats, The Red & The Black
Archived: Video
■ **SET LIST**
I Stole Your Love
Deuce
Heaven's On Fire
Fits Like a Glove
Rise to It
Betrayed
C'mon and Love Me
Calling Dr. Love
Hide Your Heart
Love Gun
Detroit Rock City
I Love It Loud
Black Diamond
■ Despite the fact that KISS was the event's headliner, Saraya played after KISS. The concert was one of three benefit events for Tishna Rollo (the eight-year-old daughter of producer/engineer John Rollo) who was suffering from Wilms tumor disease.

The show was stopped briefly during the intro to "Fits Like a Glove," when Gene blew out his bass cabinet. He performed the remainder of the show running his bass through a Marshall stack. After the first few bars of "Fits Like a Glove," Paul segued into the intro to "Heartbreaker." He followed that with a brief attempt at "Oh Susannah," before eventually restarting and singing the first verse of "Fits Like a Glove." This was one of only three public performances of "C'mon and Love Me" by this lineup and was the song's first known performance since 1976.

Steve Wood: "We stayed down the street at the Berkeley Carteret Hotel. We did no rehearsals whatsoever for the gig, even the sound check was done by the crew. The band arrived in a van, walked through the front door, through the crowd—though the place was absolutely packed—got up on stage, played, and left."

Reseda, California
Chuck Landis' Country Club
Opening Act: Shake City
Attendance: Sold Out
Promoter: Avalon Attractions
Archived: Audio

■ SET LIST

I Stole Your Love
Deuce
Heaven's On Fire
Rise to It
Fits Like a Glove
Crazy Crazy Nights
Strutter
Calling Dr Love
Hide Your Heart
Betrayed
Black Diamond
Shout It Out Loud
Little Caesar
C'mon and Love Me
Cold Gin
Forever
God of Thunder
Under the Gun
[Lick It Up]
[Tears Are Falling]
[I Love It Loud]
[Love Gun]
[Detroit Rock City]
[I Want You]
[Rock and Roll All Nite]

■ Paul and Gene had appeared on Pirate Radio as far back as October 11, 1989 to announce that the first gig of the tour would be a special event for the station. The only way concertgoers could acquire tickets was to win them from the radio station.

This show marks the second and final performance of "Betrayed."

MAY 3, 1990

Lubbock, Texas
Lubbock Municipal Coliseum
Opening Acts: Faster Pussycat, Slaughter
Capacity: 10,500
Promoters: Stardate Productions, Pace Concerts

■ This full-dress rehearsal was attended by winners of a local radio promotion and various VIP guests. "Little Caesar" was performed live for the last time on this night, much to the dismay of Eric, who continued to believe that Gene and Paul were intentionally diminishing his presence in the band.

Earlier in the day, the band performed "Rise to It" live for a Japanese TV crew.

Steve Wood: "We were in Lubbock getting ready to do the dress rehearsals for the Hot in the Shade Tour. We had rented the arena for five days, and had the entire stage erected, with the full complement of crew, buses, trucks, etc. Charlie Hernandez, who was hired for production, came in and went to a windscreen shop and had a huge pair of Raybans made out of windscreen for Leon. "The pair of sunglasses never made it out on the tour," remembers Robert Roth. "They hung in my warehouse for years. Gene and Paul didn't like the way they turned out and decided to cut them."

Steve Wood continues, "At this point, KISS had never met the lighting designer, Dino DeRose.

Now, mind you, Gene Simmons is one of the only people I've ever worked with who can tell almost immediately whether or not the lights are good. Gene said to me, 'Steve, go and get Lights.' He often referred to people simply by whatever function they provided; the guitar tech was Guitar, the lighting guy was Lights, etc. I went and tracked down Dino, who is a fairly sheepish man, at best. Dino walked into the dressing room quite timidly and said, 'You called for me?' At which point, Gene simply waved his hand in front of Dino's face to see if he was paying attention, if there was any sign of life in there. He then walked over to the light switch and stood there, got into a position as if holding an imaginary bass, raised one arm and one leg and pretended to hit a enormous chord on the bass. As he did this, the lights went out; BANG! Then, he repeated the same procedure again and then said to Dino, 'Thank you. Bye!' It was so typical of Gene."

MAY 4, 1990

Lubbock, Texas
Lubbock Municipal Coliseum
Opening Acts: Faster Pussycat, Slaughter
Attendance: 9,641   Capacity: 10,500
Promoters: Stardate Productions, Pace Concerts
Archived: Video

■ SET LIST

I Stole Your Love
Deuce
Heaven's On Fire
Rise to It
Fits Like a Glove
Crazy Crazy Nights
Strutter
Calling Dr. Love
Hide Your Heart
Black Diamond
Shout It Out Loud
Lick It Up
C'mon and Love Me
Cold Gin
Forever
God of Thunder
Eric Carr Drum Solo
Under the Gun
Tears Are Falling
I Love It Loud
Love Gun
Detroit Rock City
I Want You
Rock and Roll All Nite

■ Gene sang the second verse of "Lick It Up" and Eric's solo was performed at the end of "God of Thunder," as opposed to its more typical spot in the middle of the song. Both "C'mon and Love Me" and Eric's drum solo were dropped from the set list after this show.

MTV talent Rikki Rachtman flew in to interview the band and shoot live footage for a special "On the Road" edition of *Headbangers Ball*, which aired on May 12. *Entertainment Tonight* also covered the show.

Stage designer Robert Roth: "Their understanding and our understanding of what a KISS sign was going to be was a little different, so we ended up making a second KISS sign. I remember sitting in Atlanta having dinner with my wife and my pager started melting down. It was Jim Chapman. He said, 'We got a problem, they

don't like the KISS sign.' So I went back to the office and started fooling with what needed to be done to get it right. Over the course of about twelve or eighteen hours, we got that done and went to a fabricator and in three days had a new one made and wired. It was big, something like 200 and some-odd bulbs. We airfreighted it to Lubbock. We bolted the logo on a frame, got it circuited and literally less than ten seconds later was the cue to fly it. I had shown up backstage dressed in loafers and slacks just to be account executive and to support the tour on opening night, when I suddenly found myself sitting there sweating with a screw driver in my hand yelling back and forth to one of the other techs. This was happening with all the pyro and the Sphinx coming down over us. It was a photo finish."

MAY 5, 1990

Dallas, Texas
Starplex Amphitheatre
Opening Acts: Faster Pussycat, Slaughter
Attendance: 6,367   Capacity: 10,000
Promoter: Pace Concerts

■ Larry Mazer: "The weakest relationship I probably had was with Eric Carr because the very first thing I said to him was, 'Eric, I gotta tell ya, honestly, don't take this the wrong way, but I hate drum solos. I prefer we didn't have a drum solo in the show.' And he completely lost his mind and hated me, but we became friendly during the tour."

The USA network series *Youthquake* taped an interview with the band and also recorded portions of the concert. The segment later aired on May 29.

MAY 6, 1990

Austin, Texas
Frank C. Erwin, Jr. Special Events Center
Opening Acts: Faster Pussycat, Slaughter
Attendance: 3,611   Capacity: 6,563
Archived: Video

■ SET LIST

I Stole Your Love
Deuce
Heaven's On Fire
Rise to It
Fits Like a Glove
Crazy Crazy Nights
Strutter
Calling Dr. Love
Hide Your Heart
Black Diamond
Shout It Out Loud
Lick It Up
Cold Gin
Forever
God of Thunder
Tears Are Falling
Under the Gun
I Love It Loud
Love Gun
Detroit Rock City
I Want You
Rock and Roll All Nite

■ Due to technical difficulties, the band did their encores without the P.A. system.

MAY 8, 1990

Tulsa, Oklahoma
Expo Square Pavilion
Opening Acts: Faster Pussycat, Slaughter

Attendance: 6,626   Capacity: 8,000
Promoter: Little Wing Attractions
Archived: Video
■ **SET LIST**
I Stole Your Love
Deuce
Heaven's On Fire
Rise to It
Fits Like a Glove
Crazy Crazy Nights
Strutter
Calling Dr. Love
Hide Your Heart
Black Diamond
Shout It Out Loud
Lick It Up
Cold Gin
Forever
God of Thunder
Under the Gun
Tears Are Falling
I Love It Loud
Love Gun
Detroit Rock City
I Want You
Rock and Roll All Nite

MAY 9, 1990

Valley Center (Wichita), Kansas
Britt Brown Arena @ Kansas Coliseum
Opening Acts: Faster Pussycat, Slaughter
Attendance: 4,968   Capacity: 6,000
Promoter: Contemporary Productions

MAY 10, 1990

Omaha, Nebraska
Omaha Civic Auditorium
Opening Acts: Faster Pussycat, Slaughter
Attendance: 7,420   Capacity: 12,000
Promoter: Contemporary Productions
Archived: Audio
■ **SET LIST**
I Stole Your Love
Deuce
Heaven's On Fire
Rise to It
Fits Like a Glove
Crazy Crazy Nights
Strutter
Calling Dr. Love
Hide Your Heart
Black Diamond
Shout It Out Loud
Lick It Up
Cold Gin
Forever
God of Thunder
Tears Are Falling
I Love It Loud
Under the Gun
Love Gun
[Detroit Rock City]
I Want You
[Rock and Roll All Nite]
■ This is the last known occasion where Paul used the "What do you say we kick some ass?" introduction to the show.

MAY 11, 1990

Sioux Falls, South Dakota
Sioux Falls Arena
Opening Acts: Faster Pussycat, Slaughter
Attendance: 8,000   Capacity: 8,000
Promoter: Steve Litman Productions

ANDREW ALLIN

MAY 12, 1990

Bonner Springs (Kansas City), Kansas
Sandstone Amphitheatre
Opening Acts: Faster Pussycat, Slaughter
Attendance: 9,333   Capacity: 18,000
Promoter: In-house
Archived: Video
■ **SET LIST**
I Stole Your Love
Deuce
Heaven's On Fire
Rise to It
Fits Like a Glove
Crazy Crazy Nights
Strutter
Calling Dr. Love
Hide Your Heart
Black Diamond
Shout It Out Loud
Lick It Up
Cold Gin
Forever
God of Thunder
Tears Are Falling
Under the Gun
I Love It Loud
Love Gun
Detroit Rock City
I Want You
Rock and Roll All Nite

MAY 15, 1990

Saginaw, Michigan
Wendler Arena @ Saginaw Civic Center
Opening Acts: Faster Pussycat, Slaughter
Attendance: 4,983   Capacity: 5,500
Promoter: Belkin Productions

MAY 17, 1990

Terre Haute, Indiana
Hulman Center
Opening Acts: Faster Pussycat, Slaughter
Attendance: 3,061   Capacity: 8,000
Promoter: Sunshine Promotions

MAY 18, 1990

Auburn Hills (Detroit), Michigan
The Palace of Auburn Hills
Opening Acts: Faster Pussycat, Slaughter
Attendance: 12,019   Capacity: 16,000
Promoter: Belkin Productions
Archived: Video
■ **SET LIST**
I Stole Your Love
Deuce
Heaven's On Fire
Rise to It
Fits Like a Glove
Crazy Crazy Nights
Strutter
Calling Dr. Love

Hide Your Heart
Black Diamond
Shout It Out Loud
Lick It Up
Cold Gin
Forever
God of Thunder
Under the Gun
I Love It Loud
Tears Are Falling
Love Gun
Detroit Rock City
I Want You
Rock and Roll All Nite
■ This show was professionally videotaped.

MAY 19, 1990

Toledo, Ohio
Sports Arena
Opening Acts: Faster Pussycat, Slaughter
Attendance: 7,266   Capacity: 7,266
Promoter: Belkin Productions
Archived: Audio
■ SET LIST
See May 18, 1990.

■ Prior to "I Want You," Gene introduced Eric as: "The man with the biggest dick in Ohio."

Steve Wood explains: "Eric used to have this habit where he would walk around the dressing room completely naked. He had this huge cock and Gene and Paul were really put off by it because they were so private. Everyone of course felt awkward about it, with him standing there like the John Holmes of rock. I'm sure he did it just to rile Gene and Paul."

MAY 20, 1990

Fort Wayne, Indiana
Fort Wayne Expo Center
Opening Acts: Faster Pussycat, Slaughter
Attendance: 7,019   Capacity: 10,000
Promoter: Sunshine Promotions
Archived: Audio
■ SET LIST
See May 18, 1990.

MAY 22, 1990

Cape Girardeau, Missouri
Show Me Center
Opening Acts: Faster Pussycat, Slaughter
Attendance: 5,240   Capacity: 6,500
Promoters: Joseph Entertainment Group, Stardate
    Productions

MAY 23, 1990

Cedar Rapids, Iowa
Five Seasons Center
Opening Acts: Faster Pussycat, Slaughter
Attendance: 9,493   Capacity: 10,000
Promoter: JAM Productions
Archived: Audio
■ SET LIST
See May 18, 1990.

MAY 25, 1990

Bloomington (Minneapolis), Minnesota
Metropolitan Sports Center
Opening Acts: Faster Pussycat, Slaughter
Attendance: 9,326   Capacity: 14,000
Promoter: Rose Productions
Archived: Audio
■ SET LIST
See May 18, 1990.

MAY 26, 1990

West Fargo, North Dakota

Red River Valley Speedway
Opening Acts: Faster Pussycat, Slaughter
Attendance: 9,200   Capacity: 9,200
Promoters: Joseph Entertainment Group, Stardate
    Productions
Archived: Audio
■ SET LIST
I Stole Your Love
Deuce
[Heaven's On Fire]
Rise to It
Fits Like a Glove
Crazy Crazy Nights
Strutter
Calling Dr. Love
Hide Your Heart
Black Diamond
Shout It Out Loud
Lick It Up
Cold Gin
Forever
God of Thunder
[Under the Gun]
I Love It Loud
Tears Are Falling
Love Gun
[Detroit Rock City]
I Want You
Rock and Roll All Nite

MAY 27, 1990

Duluth, Minnesota
DECC
Opening Acts: Faster Pussycat, Slaughter
Attendance: 4,450   Capacity: 6,400
Promoters: JAM Productions, Eclipse Productions
Archived: Audio
■ SET LIST
See May 18, 1990.

MAY 28, 1990

Green Bay, Wisconsin
Brown County Veterans Memorial Arena
Opening Acts: Faster Pussycat, Slaughter
Attendance: 6,744   Capacity: 7,044
Promoters: Joseph Entertainment Group, Stardate
    Productions
Archived: Audio
■ SET LIST
I Stole Your Love
Deuce
Heaven's On Fire
Crazy Crazy Nights
Black Diamond
Shout It Out Loud
Strutter
Calling Dr. Love
Rise to It
Fits Like a Glove
Lick It Up
God of Thunder
Under the Gun
Forever
Hide Your Heart
Cold Gin
Tears Are Falling
I Love It Loud
Love Gun
Detroit Rock City
I Want You
Rock and Roll All Nite

MAY 30, 1990

Peoria, Illinois
Carver Arena @ Peoria Civic Center
Opening Acts: Faster Pussycat, Slaughter

Attendance: 4,664   Capacity: 8,675
Promoter: JAM Productions

MAY 31, 1990

Evansville, Indiana
Mesker Music Theatre
Opening Acts: Faster Pussycat, Slaughter
Attendance: 5,576   Capacity: 8,703
Promoter: JAM Productions

JUNE 1, 1990

St. Louis, Missouri
Kiel Auditorium
Opening Acts: Faster Pussycat, Slaughter
Attendance: 6,427   Capacity: 10,275
Promoter: Contemporary Productions
Archived: Audio
■ SET LIST
See May 28, 1990.

JUNE 2, 1990

Des Moines, Iowa
Veterans Memorial Auditorium
Opening Acts: Faster Pussycat, Slaughter
Attendance: 9,757   Capacity: 9,757
Promoter: Contemporary Productions
Archived: Audio
■ SET LIST
See May 28, 1990.

■ A fanatical 27-year-old male fan offered his 21-year-old girlfriend to Gene at the pre-show meet-and-greet. Gene politely declined.

On this lone occasion, "Lick It Up" featured the blues intro that usually preceded "Rise to It."

JUNE 3, 1990

Tinley Park (Chicago), Illinois
New World Music Center
Opening Acts: Faster Pussycat, Slaughter
Attendance: 8,064   Capacity: 10,500
Promoter: JAM Productions
Archived: Audio
■ SET LIST
See May 28, 1990.

JUNE 6, 1990

Columbus, Ohio
Battelle Hall @ Ohio Center
Opening Acts: Slaughter, Little Caesar
Attendance: 5,764   Capacity: 5,764
Promoter: Belkin Productions
Archived: Audio
■ SET LIST
See May 28, 1990.
■ No pyro was used at this show.

JUNE 7, 1990

Dayton, Ohio
Hara Arena & Exhibition Center
Opening Acts: Slaughter, Little Caesar
Attendance: 7,058   Capacity: 7,058
Promoter: Belkin Productions
Archived: Audio
■ SET LIST
I Stole Your Love
Deuce
Heaven's On Fire
Crazy Crazy Nights
Black Diamond
Shout It Out Loud
Strutter
Calling Dr. Love
Rise to It
Fits Like a Glove
Lick It Up
God of Thunder

Under the Gun
Forever
Hide Your Heart
Cold Gin
Tears Are Falling
I Love It Loud
[Love Gun]
[Detroit Rock City]
[I Want You]
[Rock and Roll All Nite]

JUNE 8, 1990

Noblesville (Indianapolis), Indiana
Deer Creek Music Center
Opening Acts: Slaughter, Little Caesar
Attendance: 6,595   Capacity: 14,000
Promoter: Sunshine Promotions

■ Thunderstorms were prevalent throughout the latter part of the show. Faster Pussycat was originally advertised in place of Little Caesar.

JUNE 9, 1990

Richfield (Cleveland), Ohio
The Coliseum
Opening Acts: Slaughter, Little Caesar
Attendance: 13,048   Capacity: 14,000
Promoter: Belkin Productions
Archived: Video

■ SET LIST
See May 28, 1990.

■ This is the last known performance of "Under the Gun."

JUNE 12, 1990

Cincinnati, Ohio
Cincinnati Gardens
Opening Acts: Slaughter, Little Caesar
Attendance: 2,595   Capacity: 4,000
Promoter: Belkin Productions

JUNE 13, 1990

Muskegon, Michigan
L.C. Walker Arena
Opening Acts: Slaughter, Little Caesar
Attendance: 4,773   Capacity: 4,773
Promoter: Belkin Productions

JUNE 15, 1990

Toronto, Ontario, Canada
C.N.E. Stadium
Co-headlining Act: Whitesnake
Opening Acts: Faster Pussycat, Slaughter
Attendance: 13,262   Capacity: 15,000
Promoter: Concert Promotions Int'l
Archived: Audio

■ SET LIST
I Stole Your Love
Deuce
Heaven's On Fire
Crazy Crazy Nights
Black Diamond
Shout It Out Loud
Strutter
Calling Dr. Love
Rise to It
Fits Like a Glove
Lick It Up
Forever
Hide Your Heart
Cold Gin
Tears Are Falling
I Love It Loud
Detroit Rock City
I Want You
Rock and Roll All Nite

■ Whitesnake refused to allow KISS to use their full compliment of pyro and production effects

at this show, which created serious tension between the bands, especially between Paul Stanley and David Coverdale. Paul appeared on *MuchMusic* the day prior to the show and voiced his complaints on the issue.

Larry Mazer: "David Coverdale and I, up to that point, were really good friends. Paul insulted David Coverdale onstage to no end. And to this day, David Coverdale will not speak to me. What happened was that they opened for Whitesnake in a stadium and Whitesnake would not let them use their pyro. My attitude was, 'Who gives a fuck? Go play your show, you're a rock and roll band.' If Whitesnake want to follow KISS doing all these hits, God bless America. Paul, in his normal verbal diarrhea way went onstage and said, "People. The headliners won't let us use our pyro, but we're going to rock your ass anyway and fuck him." Coverdale got on stage and put down KISS. It was silly."

Due to KISS's co-headlining status, the set list was shorter than normal, as "God of Thunder," and "Love Gun" were not performed and the introduction to "I Want You" was shortened.

Bad English were originally scheduled as an opening act, but were replaced by Faster Pussycat.

JUNE 16, 1990

Weedsport (Syracuse), New York
Cayuga County Fairgrounds
Opening Acts: Slaughter, Little Caesar
Attendance: 3,157   Capacity: 7,200
Archived: Video

■ SET LIST
I Stole Your Love
Deuce
Heaven's On Fire
Crazy Crazy Nights
Black Diamond
Shout It Out Loud
Strutter
Calling Dr. Love
Rise to It
Fits Like a Glove
Lick It Up
God of Thunder
Forever
Hide Your Heart
Cold Gin
Tears Are Falling
I Love It Loud
Love Gun
Detroit Rock City
I Want You
Rock and Roll All Nite

■ Prior to "I Want You," Paul and Bruce briefly segued into Rodgers and Hammerstein's "Do-Re-Mi."

JUNE 17, 1990

Middletown, New York
Orange County Fair Speedway
Opening Acts: Slaughter, Little Caesar
Attendance: 4,090   Capacity: 9,600
Archived: Video

■ SET LIST
See June 16, 1990.

JUNE 20, 1990

Providence, Rhode Island
Providence Civic Center
Opening Acts: Slaughter, Little Caesar

Attendance: 6,943   Capacity: 10,000
Promoter: Frank J. Russo
Archived: Audio

■ SET LIST
I Stole Your Love
Deuce
Heaven's On Fire
Crazy Crazy Nights
Black Diamond
Shout It Out Loud
Strutter
Calling Dr. Love
I Was Made for Lovin' You
Rise to It
Fits Like a Glove
Lick It Up
God of Thunder
Forever
Hide Your Heart
Cold Gin
Tears Are Falling
I Love It Loud
Love Gun
Detroit Rock City
I Want You
Rock and Roll All Nite

■ Gene briefly played "Happy Trails" prior to "Strutter." "I Was Made for Lovin' You" was added to the set for the first time in the U.S. since 1979.

Larry Mazer: "I single-handedly resurrected 'I Was Made for Lovin' You.' They didn't want to do it at all, so I had to put a gun to their head to convince them that though it had been lame once that it was cool again. I told them 'Trust me on this. The place will go apeshit.' And sure enough it did; every night the place went nuts for 'I Was Made for Lovin' You.'"

JUNE 21, 1990

CANCELED

Rochester, New York
Rochester Community War Memorial
Opening Acts: Slaughter, Little Caesar

■ This concert was canceled on June 20.

JUNE 22, 1990

Binghamton, New York
Broome Co. Veterans Memorial Arena
Opening Acts: Slaughter, Little Caesar
Attendance: 4,758   Capacity: 5,760
Promoter: Magic City Productions
Archived: Video

■ SET LIST
See June 20, 1990.

■ A very brief portion of "Stairway to Heaven" was played by Paul during the intro to "I Want You."

JUNE 23, 1990

Burgettstown (Pittsburgh), Pennsylvania
Coca-Cola Star Lake Amphitheatre
Opening Acts: Slaughter, Little Caesar
Attendance: 7,936   Capacity: 14,000
Promoter: Concert Co. Presentations
Archived: Audio

■ SET LIST
[I Stole Your Love]
[Deuce]
[Heaven's On Fire]
[Crazy Crazy Nights]
[Black Diamond]
Shout It Out Loud
Strutter
Calling Dr. Love
I Was Made for Lovin' You

Rise to It
Fits Like a Glove
Lick It Up
God of Thunder
Forever
Hide Your Heart
Cold Gin
Tears Are Falling
I Love It Loud
Love Gun
Detroit Rock City
[I Want You]
[Rock and Roll All Nite]

■ Torrential rains and high winds were prevalent throughout the show.

JUNE 26, 1990

Philadelphia, Pennsylvania
The Spectrum
Opening Acts: Slaughter, Little Caesar
Attendance: 8,980   Capacity: 12,339
Promoter: Electric Factory Concerts
Archived: Video

■ SET LIST

I Stole Your Love
Deuce
Heaven's On Fire
Crazy Crazy Nights
Black Diamond
Shout It Out Loud
Strutter
Calling Dr. Love
I Was Made for Lovin' You
Rise to It
Fits Like a Glove
Lick It Up
God of Thunder
Forever
Hide Your Heart
Cold Gin
Tears Are Falling
I Love It Loud
Love Gun
Detroit Rock City
I Want You

NORMAN BOUTHILLIER

KISS magazine publisher Nico Ciccarone backstage with Paul in Albany, New York, on July 7. You'd be smiling this big too, if Paul Stanley just gave you money.

Rock and Roll All Nite

JUNE 27, 1990

Allentown, Pennsylvania
Allentown Fairgrounds Grandstand
Opening Acts: Slaughter, Little Caesar
Attendance: 6,190   Capacity: 10,000
Promoter: Electric Factory Concerts
Archived: Video

■ SET LIST

I Stole Your Love
Deuce
Heaven's On Fire
Crazy Crazy Nights
Black Diamond
Shout It Out Loud
Strutter
Calling Dr. Love
I Was Made for Lovin' You
Rise to It
Fits Like a Glove
Hide Your Heart
Lick It Up
God of Thunder
Forever
Cold Gin
Tears Are Falling
I Love It Loud
Love Gun
Detroit Rock City
I Want You
Rock and Roll All Nite

JUNE 28, 1990

Uniondale, New York
Nassau Veterans Memorial Coliseum
Opening Acts: Slaughter, Little Caesar
Attendance: 9,203   Capacity: 13,300
Promoter: Metropolitan Entertainment
Archived: Video

■ SET LIST

See June 27, 1990.

JUNE 29, 1990

Mansfield (Boston), Massachusetts
Great Woods Center for the Performing Arts Amphitheatre
Opening Acts: Slaughter, Little Caesar
Attendance: 8,441   Capacity: 12,000
Promoter: In-house
Archived: Audio

■ SET LIST

See June 27, 1990.

JUNE 30, 1990

East Rutherford, New Jersey
Brendan Byrne Arena
Opening Acts: Slaughter, Little Caesar
Attendance: 14,071   Capacity: 14,958
Promoter: Metropolitan Entertainment
Archived: Video

■ SET LIST

See June 27, 1990.

JULY 3, 1990

Springfield, Massachusetts
Springfield Civic Center
Opening Acts: Slaughter, Little Caesar
Attendance: 4,433   Capacity: 5,528
Promoter: Cross Country Concerts
Archived: Audio, Partial Video

■ SET LIST

See June 27, 1990.

■ Following the show, while en route to Manhattan, Paul was asleep in the back of the limo when it was struck by another vehicle in Pelham,

New York. Both Paul and his driver wound up under the dashboard following a 200-foot skid during which the limo knocked over a road light, crossed an embankment and finally crashed into an iron gate. Paul had to have fourteen X-rays and KISS wound up postponing the July 5 show in New Haven due to his injuries.

JULY 5, 1990   POSTPONED

New Haven, Connecticut
New Haven Veterans Memorial Coliseum
Opening Acts: Slaughter, Little Caesar

■ The show was postponed until October 27, due to the injuries Paul suffered in his July 4 auto accident.

JULY 6, 1990

Old Orchard Beach, Maine
Seashore Performing Arts Center
Opening Acts: Slaughter, Little Caesar
Attendance: 7,186   Capacity: 10,000
Promoter: Frank J. Russo
Archived: Audio

■ SET LIST

I Stole Your Love
Deuce
Heaven's On Fire
Crazy Crazy Nights
Black Diamond
Shout It Out Loud
Calling Dr. Love
I Was Made for Lovin' You
Rise to It
Fits Like a Glove
Hide Your Heart
Lick It Up
God of Thunder
Forever
Cold Gin
Tears Are Falling
I Love It Loud
Love Gun
Detroit Rock City
I Want You
Rock and Roll All Nite

■ Local authorities told the band that they were not allowed to curse on stage. "Strutter" was cut from the set due to time constraints.

JULY 7, 1990

Albany, New York
Knickerbocker Arena
Opening Acts: Slaughter, Little Caesar
Attendance: 4,814   Capacity: 10,000
Promoter: Magic City Productions
Archived: Audio, Partial Video

■ SET LIST

I Stole Your Love
Deuce
Heaven's On Fire
Crazy Crazy Nights
Black Diamond
Shout It Out Loud
Strutter
Calling Dr. Love
I Was Made for Lovin' You
Rise to It
Fits Like a Glove
Hide Your Heart
Lick It Up
God of Thunder
Forever
Cold Gin
Tears Are Falling

I Love It Loud
Love Gun
Detroit Rock City
I Want You
Rock and Roll All Nite

■ Longtime *KISS* magazine publisher Nico Cicca-rone: "A couple of days prior to the Albany show someone had broken into my hotel room in New York and stole my still camera, my video camera, and two hundred dollars cash. After the show in Albany, Paul came up to me and asked me about what had happened. He left for a few minutes and when he came back he put something in my hand. I didn't even look, but I figured out it was money. I told him that he didn't have to do that and not to worry about it but he insisted and said, 'The band wants you to have this.' He gave me the exact amount of money that I told him I lost. I was in shock. That's the nicest thing they ever did for me."

JULY 8, 1990

Harrisburg, Pennsylvania
City Island Sports Complex
Opening Acts: Slaughter; Little Caesar
Attendance: 8,199   Capacity: 9,600
Promoter: Makoul Productions

■ Eric Carr performed briefly with opening act Little Caesar, who were making their final appearance on the tour.

JULY 10, 1990

Fairfax, Virginia
The Patriot Center
Opening Acts: Slaughter; Danger, Danger
Attendance: 4,962   Capacity: 6,600
Promoter: Cellar Door Concerts
Archived: Video
■ SET LIST
See July 7, 1990.

JULY 11, 1990

Roanoke, Virginia
Roanoke Civic Center
Opening Acts: Slaughter; Danger, Danger
Attendance: 4,884   Capacity: 8,880
Promoter: Cellar Door Concerts
Archived: Audio
■ SET LIST
I Stole Your Love
Deuce
Heaven's On Fire
Crazy Crazy Nights
Black Diamond
Shout It Out Loud
Calling Dr. Love
Strutter
I Was Made for Lovin' You
Rise to It
Fits Like a Glove
Hide Your Heart
Lick It Up
God of Thunder
Forever
Eric Carr Drum Solo
Cold Gin
Tears Are Falling
I Love It Loud
Love Gun
Detroit Rock City
I Want You
Rock and Roll All Nite

■ Starting with this show, Eric Carr's drum solo returned to the set.

JULY 12, 1990

Richmond, Virginia
Richmond Coliseum
Opening Acts: Slaughter; Danger, Danger
Attendance: 4,012   Capacity: 10,000
Promoter: Cellar Door Concerts

JULY 13, 1990

Norfolk, Virginia
The Scope
Opening Acts: Slaughter; Danger, Danger
Attendance: 4,739   Capacity: 11,000
Promoter: Cellar Door Concerts
Archived: Audio
■ SET LIST
I Stole Your Love
Deuce
Heaven's On Fire
Crazy Crazy Nights
Black Diamond
Shout It Out Loud
I Was Made for Lovin' You
Strutter
Calling Dr. Love
Rise to It
Fits Like a Glove
Hide Your Heart
Lick It Up
God of Thunder
Eric Carr Drum Solo - reprise
Forever
Cold Gin
Tears Are Falling
I Love It Loud
Love Gun
Detroit Rock City
I Want You
Rock and Roll All Nite

JULY 14, 1990   POSTPONED

Charleston, West Virginia
Charleston Civic Center
Opening Acts: Slaughter; Danger, Danger
Promoter: Belkin Productions
■ The concert was postponed until November 1.

JULY 17, 1990   POSTPONED

Lexington, Kentucky
Rupp Arena
Opening Acts: Slaughter; Danger, Danger
Promoter: Sunshine Promotions
■ The concert was rescheduled for October 31.

JULY 18, 1990

Johnson City, Tennessee
Freedom Hall Civic Center @ Science Hill High School
Opening Acts: Slaughter; Danger, Danger
Attendance: 5,142   Capacity: 6,800
Promoter: Sunshine Promotions

JULY 19, 1990

Knoxville, Tennessee
Knoxville Civic Coliseum
Opening Acts: Slaughter; Danger, Danger
Attendance: 5,664   Capacity: 10,000
Promoter: Sunshine Promotions

JULY 20, 1990

Atlanta, Georgia
Lakewood Amphitheatre
Opening Acts: Slaughter; Danger, Danger
Attendance: 5,064   Capacity: 10,000
Promoters: MCA Concerts, Pace Concerts
Archived: Audio
■ SET LIST
I Stole Your Love

Deuce
Heaven's On Fire
Crazy Crazy Nights
Black Diamond
Shout It Out Loud
Strutter
Calling Dr. Love
I Was Made for Lovin' You
Rise to It
Fits Like a Glove
Hide Your Heart
Lick It Up
God of Thunder
Eric Carr Drum Solo - reprise
Forever
Cold Gin
Tears Are Falling
I Love It Loud
Love Gun
Detroit Rock City
I Want You
Rock and Roll All Nite

JULY 21, 1990

Antioch (Nashville), Tennessee
Coca-Cola Starwood Amphitheatre
Opening Acts: Slaughter; Danger, Danger
Attendance: 6,231   Capacity: 10,000
Promoter: Pace Concerts
Archived: Audio
■ SET LIST
I Stole Your Love
Deuce
Heaven's On Fire
Crazy Crazy Nights
Black Diamond
Shout It Out Loud
Strutter
Calling Dr. Love
I Was Made for Lovin' You
Oh Susannah
Rise to It
Fits Like a Glove
Hide Your Heart
Lick It Up
God of Thunder
Eric Carr Drum Solo - reprise
Forever
Cold Gin
Tears Are Falling
I Love It Loud
Love Gun
Detroit Rock City
Oh Susannah
I Want You
Rock and Roll All Nite

■ Paul played a very brief part of "Hard Luck Woman" prior to Rise to It."

JULY 24, 1990

Columbia, South Carolina
Carolina Coliseum
Opening Acts: Slaughter; Danger, Danger
Attendance: 3,761   Capacity: 3,761
Promoter: Cellar Door Concerts

JULY 25, 1990

Charlotte, North Carolina
Charlotte Coliseum
Opening Acts: Slaughter; Danger, Danger
Attendance: 6,455   Capacity: 9,646
Promoter: C & C Entertainment
Archived: Audio
■ SET LIST
I Stole Your Love
Deuce

Heaven's On Fire
Crazy Crazy Nights
Black Diamond
Shout It Out Loud
Strutter
Calling Dr. Love
I Was Made for Lovin' You
Rise to It
Fits I ike a Glove
Hide Your Heart
Lick It Up
God of Thunder
Eric Carr Drum Solo - reprise
Forever
Cold Gin
Tears Are Falling
I Love It Loud
Love Gun
Detroit Rock City
I Want You
[Rock and Roll All Nite]

■ Prior to "I Want You," Paul remarked, "This is a very special night for us. Eric Carr, our drummer, has been in the band 10 years today." After which, Paul and Gene began to chide one another, Gene: "I'd like you all to know that besides singing and really playing a fucking great guitar, Paul sucks a mean dick. You know what I mean." Paul: "Just for that, tomorrow, I'm gonna put starch in your bra."

JULY 26, 1990
Greenville, South Carolina
Greenville Memorial Auditorium
Opening Acts: Slaughter; Danger, Danger
Attendance: 4,824   Capacity: 4,824
Promoter: Cellar Door Concerts

JULY 27, 1990
Greensboro, North Carolina
Greensboro Coliseum
Opening Acts: Slaughter; Danger, Danger
Attendance: 5,427   Capacity: 7,877
Promoter: Cellar Door Concerts

JULY 28, 1990
Fayetteville, North Carolina
Cumberland County Memorial Arena
Opening Acts: Slaughter; Danger, Danger
Attendance: 4,345   Capacity: 5,886
Promoter: C & C Entertainment

JULY 31, 1990   CANCELED
Savannah, Georgia
Civic Center
Opening Acts: Slaughter; Danger, Danger
Capacity: 8,500
Promoter: Cellar Door Concerts

■ The concert was canceled during the week of the show.

AUGUST 1, 1990
Jacksonville, Florida
Jacksonville Veterans Memorial Coliseum
Opening Acts: Slaughter; Danger, Danger
Attendance: 3,779   Capacity: 9,340
Promoter: Cellar Door Concerts

AUGUST 2, 1990
Orlando, Florida
Orlando Centroplex Arena
Opening Acts: Slaughter; Danger, Danger
Attendance: 6,297   Capacity: 15,500
Promoter: Cellar Door Concerts
Archived: Video

■ SET LIST
See July 20, 1990.

■ Paul and Gene briefly segued into "Firehouse" prior to "I Want You."

AUGUST 3, 1990
Miami, Florida
Miami Arena
Opening Acts: Slaughter; Danger, Danger
Attendance: 7,194   Capacity: 13,000
Promoter: Cellar Door Concerts
Archived: Video

■ SET LIST
See July 20, 1990.

AUGUST 4, 1990
Tampa, Florida
USF Sundome
Opening Acts: Slaughter; Danger, Danger
Attendance: 6,596   Capacity: 8,850
Promoter: Cellar Door Concerts
Archived: Video

■ SET LIST
I Stole Your Love
Deuce
Heaven's On Fire
Crazy Crazy Nights
Black Diamond
Shout It Out Loud
Strutter
Calling Dr. Love
I Was Made for Lovin' You
Rise to It
Fits Like a Glove
Hide Your Heart
Lick It Up
God of Thunder
Eric Carr Drum Solo - reprise
Forever
Cold Gin
Tears Are Falling
I Love It Loud
Love Gun
Detroit Rock City
I Want You
Rock and Roll All Nite

■ Leon did not disintegrate during "Detroit Rock City." The logo, which was present and visible high above center stage throughout the show, was lowered down during "I Want You."

AUGUST 7, 1990
Pelham (Birmingham), Alabama
Oak Mountain Amphitheatre
Opening Acts: Slaughter; Danger, Danger
Attendance: 5,563   Capacity: 6,800
Promoter: New Era Promotions

■ Part of "Sweet Home Alabama" was performed.

AUGUST 8, 1990
Memphis, Tennessee
Mid-South Coliseum
Opening Acts: Slaughter; Danger, Danger
Attendance: 5,896   Capacity: 9,600
Promoter: Mid-South Concerts

AUGUST 16, 1990
Huntsville, Alabama
Von Braun Civic Center
Opening Acts: Winger, Slaughter
Attendance: 6,741   Capacity: 8,080
Promoter: New Era Promotions
Archived: Audio

■ SET LIST
See July 20, 1990.

AUGUST 17, 1990
Jackson, Mississippi
Mississippi Coliseum
Opening Acts. Winger, Slaughter
Attendance: 5,947   Capacity: 8,000
Promoter: Mid-South Concerts
Archived: Video

■ SET LIST
See July 20, 1990.

AUGUST 18, 1990
Shreveport, Louisiana
Hirsch Memorial Coliseum
Opening Acts: Winger, Slaughter
Attendance: 7,689   Capacity: 8,000
Promoter: Beaver Productions
Archived: Video

■ SET LIST
I Stole Your Love
Deuce
Heaven's On Fire
Crazy Crazy Nights
Black Diamond
Shout It Out Loud
Strutter
Calling Dr. Love
I Was Made for Lovin' You
Rise to It
Fits Like a Glove
Hide Your Heart
Lick It Up
God of Thunder
Eric Carr Drum Solo - reprise
Forever
Cold Gin
[Tears Are Falling]
[I Love It Loud]
[Love Gun]
[Detroit Rock City]
[I Want You]
[Rock and Roll All Nite]

AUGUST 19, 1990
Biloxi, Mississippi
Mississippi Coast Coliseum
Opening Acts: Winger, Slaughter
Attendance: 5,711   Capacity: 9,000
Promoter: Beaver Productions
Archived: Video

■ SET LIST
See July 20, 1990.

■ Gene was sick and sang many of his lead vocals in a lower register than normal. To help cover for him, Eric and Paul shared the lead vocal duties with Gene on "Rock and Roll All Nite."

AUGUST 21, 1990
Houston, Texas
The Summit
Opening Acts: Winger, Slaughter
Attendance: 6,757   Capacity: 9,576
Promoter: Pace Concerts
Archived: Video

■ SET LIST
See July 20, 1990.

AUGUST 22, 1990
San Antonio, Texas
Joe & Harry Freeman Coliseum
Opening Acts: Winger, Slaughter
Attendance: 3,198   Capacity: 10,000
Promoter: Pace Concerts
Archived: Video

■ SET LIST
See July 20, 1990.

AUGUST 24, 1990

Little Rock, Arkansas
T.H. Barton Coliseum
Opening Acts: Winger, Slaughter
Attendance: 9,721   Capacity: 10,000
Promoter: Mid-South Concerts
Archived: Video
■ SET LIST
See July 20, 1990.
■ No pyro was used at this concert.

AUGUST 25, 1990

Oklahoma City, Oklahoma
Myriad Convention Center
Opening Acts: Winger, Slaughter
Attendance: 5,560   Capacity: 9,600
Promoter: Contemporary Productions
Archived: Video
■ SET LIST
See July 20, 1990.
■ "I Love It Loud" began with its standard drum intro, then the audience and band sang "Happy Birthday" to Gene. A party for Gene was held in a hot tub backstage after the show.

AUGUST 26, 1990

Salina, Kansas
Bicentennial Center
Opening Acts: Winger, Slaughter
Attendance: 4,394   Capacity: 7,200
Promoter: Contemporary Productions

AUGUST 28, 1990

Rapid City, South Dakota
Rushmore Plaza Civic Center
Opening Acts: Winger, Slaughter
Attendance: 4,508   Capacity: 11,000
Promoters: JAM Productions, Feyline Presents

AUGUST 29, 1990

Billings, Montana
Metra Park
Opening Acts: Winger, Slaughter
Attendance: 5,269   Capacity: 12,700
Promoters: JAM Productions, Feyline Presents

AUGUST 30, 1990   CANCELED

Casper, Wyoming
Casper Events Center
Opening Acts: Winger, Slaughter
Promoter: United Concerts
■ The concert was canceled on the day of the show.

AUGUST 31, 1990

Morrison (Denver), Colorado
Red Rocks Amphitheatre
Opening Acts: Winger, Slaughter
Attendance: 9,000   Capacity: 9,000
Promoter: Feyline Presents

SEPTEMBER 1, 1990

Magna (Salt Lake City), Utah
SaltAir Resort Main Pavilion
Opening Acts: Slaughter; Danger, Danger
Attendance: 12,724   Capacity: 12,724
Promoter: United Concerts

SEPTEMBER 3, 1990

Boise, Idaho
BSU Pavilion
Opening Acts: Winger, Slaughter
Attendance: 5,943   Capacity: 8,500
Promoter: United Concerts

SEPTEMBER 6, 1990

Vancouver, British Columbia, Canada
Pacific Coliseum
Opening Act: Winger
Attendance: 5,299   Capacity: 10,000
Promoter: Perryscope Concert Productions
■ Slaughter skipped this show to appear on the *MTV Video Music Awards*.

SEPTEMBER 7, 1990

Seattle, Washington
Seattle Center Coliseum
Opening Acts: Winger, Slaughter
Attendance: 6,315   Capacity: 12,000
Promoter: Media One

SEPTEMBER 8, 1990

Spokane, Washington
Spokane Coliseum
Opening Acts: Winger, Slaughter
Attendance: 7,690   Capacity: 7,690
Promoter: Media One
■ On early itineraries, Raceway Park was listed as the venue for this show.

SEPTEMBER 9, 1990

Portland, Oregon
Memorial Coliseum
Opening Acts: Winger, Slaughter
Attendance: 6,340   Capacity: 9,600
Promoter: Media One

SEPTEMBER 12, 1990

Sacramento, California
California Expo Amphitheatre
Opening Acts: Winger, Slaughter
Attendance: 7,922   Capacity: 10,000
Promoter: Bill Graham Presents
Archived: Audio
■ SET LIST
I Stole Your Love
Deuce
Heaven's On Fire
Crazy Crazy Nights
Black Diamond
Shout It Out Loud
Strutter
Calling Dr. Love
I Was Made for Lovin' You
Rise to It
Fits Like a Glove
Hide Your Heart
[Lick It Up]
[God of Thunder]
Eric Carr Drum Solo - reprise
Forever
Cold Gin
Tears Are Falling
I Love It Loud
Love Gun
Detroit Rock City
I Want You
Rock and Roll All Nite

SEPTEMBER 13, 1990

Concord, California
Concord Pavilion
Opening Acts: Winger, Slaughter
Attendance: 6,197   Capacity: 8,725
Promoter: In-house
Archived: Audio
■ SET LIST
I Stole Your Love
Deuce
Heaven's On Fire
Crazy Crazy Nights
Black Diamond
Shout It Out Loud
Strutter
Calling Dr. Love
I Was Made for Lovin' You
Rise to It
Fits Like a Glove
Hide Your Heart
Lick It Up
[God of Thunder]
[Eric Carr Drum Solo - reprise]
Forever
Cold Gin
Tears Are Falling
I Love It Loud
Love Gun
Detroit Rock City
I Want You
Rock and Roll All Nite

SEPTEMBER 14, 1990

Long Beach, California
Long Beach Arena
Opening Acts: Winger, Slaughter
Attendance: 13,500   Capacity: 13,500
Promoter: Avalon Attractions
Archived: Audio
■ SET LIST
I Stole Your Love
Deuce
Heaven's On Fire
Crazy Crazy Nights
Black Diamond
Shout It Out Loud
Strutter
Calling Dr. Love
I Was Made for Lovin' You
Rise to It
Fits Like a Glove
Hide Your Heart
[Lick It Up]
God of Thunder
Eric Carr Drum Solo - reprise
Forever
Cold Gin
Tears Are Falling
I Love It Loud
Love Gun
Detroit Rock City
I Want You
Rock and Roll All Nite
■ Mark St. John was in attendance.

Vibrations from the pyro knocked tiles off the back wall during "Detroit Rock City."

Steve Wood: "I had hired a fellow by the name of Patrick Prendergast as the security man for the Hot in the Shade Tour. He was an Australian guy who had been Tina Turner's tour manager. We were well into the tour at Long Beach Arena, and Gene was wandering around backstage after the sound check. Gene asked, 'Patrick, how is the pass thing going to work tonight?' The answer was: 'Well, a triangular pass with the ibix of the square . . . ' and basically the history of the stick-on pass began to come out of Patrick's mouth. Gene is looking at him like: 'You complete, freaking idiot.' Patrick was shocked that Gene cut him off mid-sentence. Gene said, 'Patrick, allow me to explain. You know, there are two types of people that come to a KISS concert. There is scum. And then there's cool people. I don't care where the scum are going. Understand?'"

SEPTEMBER 15, 1990

San Diego, California
San Diego Sports Arena
Opening Acts: Winger, Slaughter
Attendance: 6,620   Capacity: 8,652
Promoter: Avalon Attractions
Archived: Audio
■ SET LIST
See July 20, 1990.

SEPTEMBER 16, 1990

Phoenix, Arizona
Arizona Veterans Memorial Coliseum
Opening Acts: Winger, Slaughter
Attendance: 8,892   Capacity: 14,042
Promoter: Evening Star Productions
Archived: Audio
■ SET LIST
See September 12, 1990.

SEPTEMBER 19, 1990

El Paso, Texas
Special Events Center
Opening Acts: Winger, Vixen
Attendance: 3,560   Capacity: 5,000
Promoters: Stardate Productions, Pace Concerts

SEPTEMBER 20, 1990

Odessa, Texas
Ector County Coliseum
Opening Acts: Winger, Vixen
Attendance: 4,863   Capacity: 8,500
Promoters: Stardate Productions, Pace Concerts

SEPTEMBER 21, 1990

Fort Worth, Texas
Tarrant County Convention Center
Opening Acts: Winger, Vixen
Attendance: 2,594   Capacity: 10,000
Promoter: 462, Inc.

SEPTEMBER 22, 1990

Amarillo, Texas
The Amarillo Civic Center
Opening Acts: Winger, Vixen
Attendance: 6,438   Capacity: 7,800
Promoters: Stardate Productions, Pace Concerts
Archived: Video
■ SET LIST
See July 20, 1990.

SEPTEMBER 24, 1990

Springfield, Missouri
John Q. Hammons Student Center @ Southwest
    Missouri State University
Opening Acts: Winger, Vixen
Attendance: 5,259   Capacity: 5,369
Promoter: Howard Cotner Productions

SEPTEMBER 25, 1990

Columbia, Missouri
The Hearns Center
Opening Acts: Winger, Vixen
Attendance: 3,351   Capacity: 10,000
Promoter: Contemporary Productions

SEPTEMBER 26, 1990

Lincoln, Nebraska
Pershing Auditorium
Opening Acts: Winger, Vixen
Attendance: 3,230   Capacity: 7,500
Promoter: Contemporary Productions
Archived: Audio
■ SET LIST
See July 20, 1990.

SEPTEMBER 28, 1990

Carbondale, Illinois
SIU Arena
Opening Acts: Winger, Vixen
Attendance: 3,592   Capacity: 8,800
Promoter: JAM Productions

SEPTEMBER 29, 1990

East Troy, Wisconsin
Alpine Valley Music Theatre
Opening Acts: Winger, Slaughter
Attendance: 18,862   Capacity: 20,000
Promoter: Joseph Entertainment Group
Archived: Audio
■ SET LIST
See July 20, 1990.

SEPTEMBER 30, 1990

Dubuque, Iowa
Dubuque Five Flags Center
Opening Acts: Winger, Slaughter
Attendance: 4,672   Capacity: 5,200
Promoter: JAM Productions

OCTOBER 2, 1990

Bismarck, North Dakota
Bismarck Civic Center
Opening Acts: Winger, Slaughter
Attendance: 6,454   Capacity: 8,000
Promoter: Joseph Entertainment Group

OCTOBER 4, 1990

Marquette, Michigan
Lakeview Arena
Opening Acts: Winger, Slaughter
Attendance: 5,731   Capacity: 6,000
Promoter: Joseph Entertainment Group

OCTOBER 5, 1990

Rochester, Minnesota
Mayo Civic Center
Opening Acts: Winger, Slaughter

Attendance: 5,732   Capacity: 7,100
Promoter: Joseph Entertainment Group

OCTOBER 6, 1990

Topeka, Kansas
Landon Arena @ Kansas ExpoCentre
Opening Acts: Winger, Slaughter
Attendance: 7,344   Capacity: 8,000
Promoter: Little Wing Attractions

OCTOBER 7, 1990

Sioux City, Iowa
Sioux City Municipal Auditorium
Opening Acts: Winger, Slaughter
Attendance: 6,000   Capacity: 6,000
Promoter: Contemporary Productions
Archived: Audio
■ SET LIST
I Stole Your Love
Deuce
Heaven's On Fire
Crazy Crazy Nights
Black Diamond
Shout It Out Loud
Strutter
Calling Dr. Love
I Was Made for Lovin' You
Rise to It
Fits Like a Glove
Hide Your Heart
Lick It Up
God of Thunder
Eric Carr Drum Solo - reprise
Forever
Cold Gin
Tears Are Falling
I Love It Loud
Love Gun
Detroit Rock City
Oh Susannah
I Want You
Rock and Roll All Nite

OCTOBER 10, 1990

Johnstown, Pennsylvania
Cambria County War Memorial Arena
Opening Act: Winger
Attendance: 4,031   Capacity: 5,145
Promoter: Magic City Productions
■ Slaughter canceled their appearance. Paul ran into the guardrail on stage and cracked his ribs, which would cause the cancellation of the Sydney, Halifax, and Moncton dates later in the month.

OCTOBER 12, 1990

Hamilton, Ontario, Canada
Copps Coliseum
Opening Acts: Winger, Slaughter
Attendance: 8,271   Capacity: 10,000
Promoter: Concert Promotions Int'l
Archived: Audio
■ SET LIST
See July 20, 1990.

OCTOBER 13, 1990

London, Ontario, Canada
London Gardens
Opening Acts: Winger, Slaughter
Attendance: 4,667   Capacity: 4,667
Promoter: Concert Promotions Int'l
Archived: Video
■ SET LIST
I Stole Your Love
Deuce

Paul playing through a rib injury in New Haven, Connecticut, on October 27, 1990.

Heaven's On Fire
Crazy Crazy Nights
Black Diamond
Shout It Out Loud
Strutter
Calling Dr. Love
Rise to It
Fits Like a Glove
I Was Made for Lovin' You
Hide Your Heart
Lick It Up
God of Thunder
Eric Carr Drum Solo - reprise

Forever
Cold Gin
Tears Are Falling
I Love It Loud
Love Gun
Detroit Rock City
I Want You
Rock and Roll All Nite

OCTOBER 14, 1990

Auburn Hills (Detroit), Michigan
The Palace of Auburn Hills
Opening Acts: Winger, Slaughter

Attendance: 12,448   Capacity: 15,000
Promoter: Belkin Productions
Archived: Video
■ **SET LIST**
See July 20, 1990.

■ This show was professionally archived by the in-house video crew.

OCTOBER 15, 1990

Kalamazoo, Michigan
Wings Stadium
Opening Acts: Winger, Slaughter
Attendance: 6,741   Capacity: 6,741
Promoter: Cellar Door Concerts

OCTOBER 16, 1990

Erie, Pennsylvania
Lewis J. Tullio Arena @ Erie Civic Center
Opening Acts: Winger, Slaughter
Attendance: 5,247   Capacity: 10,000
Promoter: Belkin Productions
Archived: Audio
■ **SET LIST**
See July 20, 1990.

OCTOBER 18, 1990

Ottawa, Ontario, Canada
Ottawa Civic Centre
Opening Acts: Winger, Slaughter

Attendance: 5,241   Capacity: 10,000
Promoter: Donald K. Donald
Archived: Audio
■ **SET LIST**
See July 20, 1990.

OCTOBER 19, 1990

Montréal, Quebec, Canada
Forum de Montréal
Opening Acts: Winger, Slaughter
Attendance: 6,956   Capacity: 10,000
Promoter: Donald K. Donald
Archived: Audio, Partial Video
■ **SET LIST**
I Stole Your Love
Deuce
Heaven's On Fire
Crazy Crazy Nights
Black Diamond
Shout It Out Loud
Strutter
Calling Dr. Love
I Was Made for Lovin' You
Rise to It
Fits Like a Glove
Hide Your Heart
Lick It Up
God of Thunder
Eric Carr Drum Solo - reprise

Forever
Cold Gin
[Tears Are Falling]
[I Love It Loud]
Love Gun
[Detroit Rock City]
[I Want You]
[Rock and Roll All Nite]

OCTOBER 21, 1990   CANCELED

Sydney, Nova Scotia, Canada
Centre 200
Opening Acts: Winger, Slaughter
Promoter: Donald K. Donald
■ This show and the subsequent shows in Halifax and Moncton were cancelled due to Paul suffering lingering effects of the rib injury he sustained onstage on October 10th.

OCTOBER 22, 1990   CANCELED

Halifax, Nova Scotia, Canada
Halifax Forum
Opening Acts: Winger, Slaughter
Promoter: Donald K. Donald

OCTOBER 23, 1990   CANCELED

Moncton, New Brunswick, Canada
Maritime Coliseum
Opening Acts: Winger, Slaughter

NORMAN BOUTHILLIER

194

Promoter: Donald K. Donald

OCTOBER 25, 1990

Portland, Maine
Cumberland County Civic Center
Opening Acts: Winger, Slaughter
Attendance: 6,120   Capacity: 9,150
Promoter: Frank J. Russo
Archived: Audio
■ **SET LIST**
See July 20, 1990.

■ Paul sang most songs during this show in a lower register, again due to the injury he had suffered on October 10. Gene admonished the crowd for their lack of enthusiasm, reminding them that Paul was performing with broken ribs.

Bruce briefly played "Oh Susannah" prior to "I Want You."

OCTOBER 26, 1990

Worcester, Massachusetts
The Centrum
Opening Acts: Winger, Slaughter
Attendance: 10,569   Capacity: 10,569
Promoter: Frank J. Russo
Archived: Audio
■ **SET LIST**
See July 20, 1990.

OCTOBER 27, 1990

New Haven, Connecticut
New Haven Veterans Memorial Coliseum
Opening Acts: Winger, Slaughter
Attendance: 6,363   Capacity: 7,000
Promoter: Metropolitan Entertainment
Archived: Video
■ **SET LIST**
See July 20, 1990.

■ This concert had been rescheduled from July 5.

OCTOBER 28, 1990 CANCELED

Baltimore, Maryland
Baltimore Arena
Opening Acts: Winger, Slaughter

OCTOBER 30, 1990 KISS CANCELED

Wheeling, West Virginia
Wheeling Civic Center
Opening Acts: Winger, Slaughter
Attendance: 3,243   Capacity: 6,000
Promoters: Belkin Productions, Future Entertainment
■ KISS canceled, but the opening acts elected to perform.

OCTOBER 31, 1990 KISS CANCELED

Lexington, Kentucky
Lexington Center
Opening Acts: Winger, Slaughter
Attendance: 3,554   Capacity: 7,000
Promoter: Belkin Productions, Future Entertainment

■ Again, the opening acts chose to perform despite KISS's cancellation. The show had been moved from Rupp Arena to a smaller venue when it was rescheduled from July 17th.

NOVEMBER 1, 1990

Charleston, West Virginia
Charleston Civic Center
Opening Acts: Winger, Slaughter
Attendance: 6,693   Capacity: 10,000
Promoters: Belkin Production, Future Entertainment
Archived: Audio
■ **SET LIST**
See July 20, 1990.
■ This concert had been rescheduled from July 14.

Michael Lipton, writing for *The Charleston Gazette,* noted: "Stanley's stage movements did not appear to be hampered by his injuries. But backstage it was a different story. Four medical personnel, including two physical therapists and a chiropractor, administered heat massages and sonic treatments before the show. After the band's Grateful Dead-length set, Stanley was helped into the bus."

NOVEMBER 2, 1990

Augusta, Georgia
Augusta/Richmond County Civic Center
Opening Acts: Winger, Slaughter
Attendance: 3,809   Capacity: 9,000
Promoter: Brusco Barr Presents

NOVEMBER 3, 1990

Albany, Georgia
Albany James H. Gray Sr. Civic Center
Opening Acts: Winger, Slaughter
Attendance: 4,235   Capacity: 12,000
Promoter: Brusco Barr Presents

NOVEMBER 6, 1990

Columbus, Georgia
Columbus Municipal Auditorium
Opening Acts: Winger, Slaughter
Attendance: 3,754   Capacity: 4,400
Promoter: Brusco Barr Presents

NOVEMBER 7, 1990

Asheville, North Carolina
Asheville Civic Center
Opening Acts: Winger, Slaughter
Attendance: 6,427   Capacity: 6,427
Promoter: Cellar Door Concerts

NOVEMBER 8, 1990

Hershey, Pennsylvania
Hersheypark Arena
Opening Acts: Winger, Slaughter
Attendance: 8,000   Capacity: 8,000
Promoter: Concert Co. Presentations

Archived: Video
■ **SET LIST**
See July 20, 1990.

NOVEMBER 9, 1990

New York, New York
Madison Square Garden
Opening Acts: Winger, Slaughter
Attendance: 13,938   Capacity: 14,500
Promoter: Metropolitan Entertainment
Archived: Video
■ **SET LIST**
I Stole Your Love
Deuce
Heaven's On Fire
Crazy Crazy Nights
Black Diamond
Shout It Out Loud
Calling Dr. Love
I Was Made for Lovin' You
Rise to It
Fits Like a Glove
Hide Your Heart
Lick It Up
God of Thunder
Eric Carr Drum Solo - reprise
Forever
Cold Gin
Tears Are Falling
I Love It Loud
Love Gun
Detroit Rock City
I Want You
Rock and Roll All Nite

■ This was Eric Carr's final performance with KISS. It also marks the final occasion where "Crazy Crazy Nights," "Fits Like a Glove," "Hide Your Heart," and "Rise to It" were performed live.

For the final show of the tour the drainage pipe set piece was erected much higher than normal and pyro packs were installed on the ceiling of the venue above the audience. Also, "Strutter" was once again cut due to time constraints.

Gary Corbett: "Gene, of all people, actually brought me out on stage and introduced me to the audience for everyone to see."

Larry Mazer: "The unions are so heavy in Manhattan that you can hardly make money. MSG has become this revered stop, but it's not a money-making stop. Economically, it was the worst date on the tour, even though we sold it out. We had a big party afterwards at Charlie O's around the corner. It was a great night. I think the tour made over $1 million profit, so there was no reason to complain. I am very proud of that stage and tour. My only regret is that we didn't film Hot in the Shade. I would love to look at that again. The Hot in the Shade Tour was just magic."

CHAPTER 21

REVENGE TOUR

Number of Shows: 77
Start Date: April 23, 1992 - San Francisco, California
End Date: December 20, 1992 - Phoenix, Arizona
Countries: Canada, England, Scotland, U.S.A., Wales
Opening Acts: Danger, Danger; Faster Pussycat; Fortress; Great White; Jackyl; Shooting Gallery; Trixter; Vesuvius
Average Attendance: 5,029* (Does not include club dates.)

The Hot in the Shade Tour, with its return to vintage material and sheer live spectacle, had reconnected KISS with their past and their fans. And, as 1990 drew to a close, the band had entered the decade with a renewed sense of purpose.

1991 would unfold in stark contrast. There would be no new album and no new tour, just a sense of abject shock, emptiness, and eventual loss.

In March, drummer Eric Carr had been diagnosed with a cancerous tumor in the right atrium of his heart. "I was running a real high temperature and had non-stop coughing and headaches," Eric explained in an interview with Jon Epstein of *US Rocker.* "After about a week of putting up with this shit, I decided to go to the doctor. He did a chest X-ray, which was negative, but my heart cavity was greatly enlarged. He sent me to the cardiologist, and he diagnosed pericarditis, which is a buildup of fluid around the heart between the pericardium and the heart itself."

After receiving treatment, the pericarditis had abated. Eric continues: "The fluid was basically all gone at that point, so the pictures were really clear, that's when we found the tumor in the heart. It was attached somehow to my right atrium and it was being pulled in and out of the tricuspid valve as it opened and closed. So, we did all kinds of tests. They showed that there were these particles all over my lungs which we assumed were pieces of this thing that was swinging back and forth; it was getting shredded from the abuse of being pulled. So I started looking for a surgeon. Gene and Paul wanted me to come out to L.A. so I could be near the band, but I was kind of on borrowed time, so I went ahead and did the surgery in New York."

By April, Eric had recovered enough to participate in the recording of "God Gave Rock and Roll to You II," a refurbished take on an old Argent song for the *Bill & Ted's Bogus Journey* film soundtrack, which was released on July 9. Though Eric did not play drums, he did contrib-

ute background vocals to the song. It was the last official recording Eric made with KISS.

Though the doctors had removed the cancerous tissue during surgery on April 9, more tumors appeared in Eric's lungs in June. He began treatment for the tumors on June 9 and six weeks later, after completing four courses of chemotherapy, Eric was happily pronounced cancer-free. That same week he flew to Los Angeles, against Gene and Paul's growing concern for his health, to participate in the filming of the band's video for "God Gave Rock and Roll to You II," (which MTV world-premiered on August 12).

While in Los Angeles for the video shoot, a "cancer-free" party was given for Eric by his girlfriend Carrie Stevens. "The night before the party," Gary Corbett explains, "Gene and Paul called Bruce and told him that he couldn't go to the party because they weren't going. The following morning they were going to have a meeting to fire Eric because they didn't want to deal

CHRIS DORSCHUTZ

Paul Caravello, 1950–1991.

Eric Singer, somewhere on tour in America, 1992.

with the chance that he would get sick again. I told them, they could have a replacement guy on the road who could step in at a moment's notice, so how could they not give Eric the courtesy? If he gets sick, then there's somebody to step in. But to take it away from him because he might get sick is ridiculous."

With the video shoot completed, Eric returned to New York to continue his recovery. Throughout his tenure with KISS, Eric was always sensitive regarding the fact that he was not an original band member and perhaps this made him especially protective of his place in KISS. "Eric called me up," states Gary Corbett, "and he was really paranoid asking, 'Are they going to fire me?' I told him to recuperate, relax, and just get better." Eric's uncertainty persisted. Corbett continues, "He and Carrie went out to spend the day at Great Adventure and somehow he got word that they were going to fire him. He called me up: 'They're firing me! They're firing me!' Being in that band was his life; it meant everything to him. The only thing he cared about was being the drummer in KISS."

Although Gene and Paul were committed to moving forward, which at least by implication meant that Carr was to be replaced, to their credit, they hesitated when it came to firing Eric, and he was never officially fired. Throughout the latter half of the summer, the lack of communication between KISS and Eric left his status a hazy issue. It is apparent that his status was not clearly articulated or even understood by either party. Eric continued to assume that he was a member of KISS, doing some interviews in mid-August and mailing autographs to inquiring fans while

KISS began to work in the studio with drummer Eric Singer in late August.

During the second week of September, Eric suffered the first of two brain hemorrhages. Eric was left partially paralyzed but he had not been robbed of his determination, and he resolved to recover quickly as he entered rehabilitation two weeks later. "It was horrible," remembers Corbett. "The family was not allowing KISS to know how Eric was doing, and they [KISS] weren't allowed in the hospital. They still had not officially fired him, because without Eric signing certain documents, he couldn't officially be let go from the band. That's why Eric's family gave such strict orders not to discuss his condition, because they thought that the band would find some legal precedent that would allow them to proceed without Eric's signature if he was physically unable to sign it, which he was. Without those documents, Eric was still covered by his health benefits and he was still getting his salary."

The issue became irrelevant when a second hemorrhage followed. Eric, weakened as he was from cancer treatments and the first hemorrhage, never recovered. On Sunday, November 24, 1991, Eric Carr passed away at the age of 41.

KISS's manager, Larry Mazer: "There was no sensitive way to deal with it. There was no way that anyone was going to come out of that looking good. There was no denying the fact that Eric [Carr] was not going to be able to do a tour. It just wasn't going to happen. We had no idea he was going to die, but we did know that he wasn't up to doing a tour. A decision had to be made to move on, and there was no good way of dealing with it."

As early as October 8, KISS had made the decision that Eric Singer would do the next tour with them and that Eric Carr's status would be left unresolved pending his recovery from the hemorrhage. Ultimately, Lonn Friend, in a segment that had been taped prior to Eric Carr's passing, reported that Eric Singer was KISS's new drummer on Saturday, November 30 during *Headbangers Ball*. Singer's first public appearance as a member of KISS came when he appeared at the NAMM Convention on January 17, 1992.

Eric Singer first became acquainted with the world of KISS when he toured as a member of Paul Stanley's solo band in 1989. Additionally, he had helped Paul on his demos for *Hot in the Shade*. Some of the drum tracks from those demos, such as those on "Forever," ended up on the album. Bruce Kulick relates, "I certainly spent a lot of time with Eric before he joined the band explaining how everything worked with Paul and Gene, so he had a little heads-up. It was a tragic thing losing Eric Carr before, and I wanted as smooth a transition as possible."

If *Hot in the Shade* had been KISS's first step in returning to their less pop-driven roots, *Revenge* was the emphatic completion of that journey. Bob Ezrin returned to produce his third album for the band, and *Revenge* was recorded at a half-dozen studios starting in late summer and continuing through the fall of 1991. While Eric Carr was ailing, the band hired Eric Singer—at that point, still gigging with Alice Cooper—for two weeks to record some of the drum tracks for the album. The initial plan was to record *Revenge* in two parts with the hopes that Eric

Carr would be able to return to do the second half. After it became apparent that Carr was in no condition to record, Eric Singer was brought back to add additional drum work to the album. *Revenge* was eventually released on May 19, 1992 and debuted at #6 on the *Billboard* charts, but it sank quickly, barely limping to Gold status on July 20 before disappearing altogether.

Larry Mazer: "The answer to KISS's flagging popularity was that KISS had become a pop band. And as much as 'Forever' helped, it hurt them a bit because it made them a pop band. To solve that, I insisted that they bring back Bob Ezrin and then demanded that the first single be a Gene Simmons song.

"I knew what the problem was from day one, and I made my acceptance to manage them contingent upon fixing this one problem, which was that the Prince of Darkness was not in the mix. By that I mean, for all intents and purposes, Gene Simmons was a sideman. If you look at the entire non-makeup era, there was nothing released as a single by Gene Simmons. The last single from Gene had been 'I Love It Loud.' He was managing Liza Minelli; he had Simmons Records; he was making these terrible movies. I made it a condition that he had to drop Liza, drop Simmons Records, drop the movies, and be back in KISS. So, the first single released from *Revenge* was 'Unholy,' which was a Gene Simmons song. My attitude was that the kids wanted Gene."

Gene's transformation from sideman to frontman came through with a resounding vengeance. The video for "Unholy" showed Gene with a ratty goatee, unkempt straggles of black hair and a physical presence that was far more dark and demonic than anything he had portrayed since abandoning his demon persona in 1983. The video world-premiered during *Headbangers Ball* on April 18.

As aggressive as Gene was with his appearance and the direction of his songwriting, he was contrite and at times completely self-deprecating in interviews. He frequently took himself to task harshly for his lack of commitment to the band over most of the previous decade. He publicly announced he had freed himself of his other creative duties and was back to being a member of KISS, 24 hours a day, seven days a week.

In contrast to the previous outing, the Revenge Tour began before the album was even released. KISS embarked on a 13-date club tour in the U.S. and Canada in April, which was quickly followed by a brief, eight-date tour of the U.K. in venues that were often not much larger. For the shows in the U.K., KISS used a slightly refined version of the Hot in the Shade Tour staging. "It wasn't that the Revenge Tour stage was not ready," states Mazer, "it's just that we loved the Hot in the Shade stage and wanted to use it again." At the shows in the U.K., Gene's fire-breathing act returned to "Firehouse," and Paul began breaking guitars again at the end of the show during "Rock and Roll All Nite," though by the time KISS returned to the States, the guitar-breaking routine had been dropped.

Gary Corbett returned to provide keyboards for the North American club dates and the brief tour of the U.K., but he departed soon after and was replaced by Santa Cruz native Derek Sherin-

ian, who had already performed alongside Singer on two Alice Cooper tours. Derek eventually gained some notoriety as a member of the progressive metal band Dream Theater.

APRIL 23, 1992

San Francisco, California
The Stone
Opening Act: Shooting Gallery
Attendance: 751   Capacity: 751
Promoter: California Concerts
Archived: Audio

■ **SET LIST**

Love Gun
Deuce
Heaven's On Fire
Parasite
Shout It Out Loud
Strutter
Calling Dr. Love
I Was Made for Lovin' You
100,000 Years
Unholy
Take It Off
God of Thunder
Lick It Up
Firehouse
Tears Are Falling
I Love It Loud
I Stole Your Love
Cold Gin
Detroit Rock City
I Want You
God Gave Rock 'N' Roll to You II
Rock and Roll All Nite

■ This was Eric Singer's first concert with KISS. "100,000 Years" and "Parasite" were performed live for the first time since 1976.

APRIL 25, 1992

West Hollywood, California
Doug Weston's World Famous Troubadour
Opening Act: Shooting Gallery
Attendance: 410   Capacity: 410
Promoter: Avalon Attractions
Archived: Audio, Partial Video

■ **SET LIST**
See April 23, 1992.

■ MTV personality Rikki Rachtman flew in to tape a special KISS edition of *Headbangers Ball*, which later aired on May 9. In what was a fairly unusual move, the MTV crew was allowed to tape a large portion of the show.

APRIL 26, 1992

West Hollywood, California
Doug Weston's World Famous Troubadour
Opening Act: Shooting Gallery
Attendance: 410   Capacity: 410
Promoter: Avalon Attractions
Archived: Audio

■ **SET LIST**

Love Gun
Deuce
Heaven's On Fire
Parasite
Shout It Out Loud
Strutter
Calling Dr. Love
I Was Made for Lovin' You
Unholy
100,000 Years
Take It Off
God of Thunder
Lick It Up

Firehouse
Tears Are Falling
I Love It Loud
I Stole Your Love
Cold Gin
Detroit Rock City
I Want You
God Gave Rock 'N' Roll to You II
Rock and Roll All Nite

APRIL 27, 1992

Tempe (Phoenix), Arizona
After the Goldrush
Opening Act: Shooting Gallery
Attendance: 1,000   Capacity: 1,000
Promoter: Evening Star Productions
Archived: Audio

■ **SET LIST**
See April 26, 1992.

APRIL 29, 1992

Houston, Texas
Backstage
Opening Act: Shooting Gallery
Attendance: 500   Capacity: 500
Promoter: Pace Concerts

■ As was common for most shows on the club tour, the band held a pre-show meet-and-greet at their hotel.

At the same time KISS was performing in Houston, their former drummer Peter Criss was gigging at a dinner theater in nearby Webster, Texas with his band Criss, forcing KISS fans to make the difficult decision of which show to attend.

When Eric Singer joined KISS in 1992, there is no doubt he felt he was moving up in the world. But as you can tell from this marquee in Houston, it wasn't necessarily that big of a step. At least KISS sold out.

APRIL 30, 1992

Dallas, Texas
Dallas City Limits
Opening Act: Shooting Gallery
Attendance: 500   Capacity: 500
Promoter: Pace Concerts
Archived: Audio

■ **SET LIST**
See April 26, 1992.

■ Gene and Eric were interviewed on the Dallas-based syndicated radio channel Z-Rock during the afternoon.

Lifelong KISS fan and Dallas-based attorney Kevin Gladden had a noteworthy encounter with Paul and Gene. Gladden relates: "The day after the Dallas show, KISS had an early morning flight so I went down to their hotel in hopes of seeing them before they left. When I walked in, Paul was sitting in the lobby reading a newspaper. He seemed very tired, but when I mentioned that I'd just seen Peter in concert, he perked up pretty fast and said, 'Sit down, I wanna hear ALL about this.' So, I told him about Peter's tour bus losing a wheel while driving to Houston and how a seemingly intoxicated 47 year-old Peter had introduced himself as being 37 to a female friend of mine. Paul just sat there shaking his head as I explained that Peter couldn't remember the words to "Hard Luck Woman." That's when I whipped out the concert ticket that had billed Peter as 'KISS Founder Peter Criss.' I'll never forget Paul turning around and telling Gene 'Check this out—KISS Founder Peter Criss!' Gene came over and Paul insisted that I repeat to Gene all the stories I'd just told him. They both seemed quite interested in what was going on with Peter. Neither seemed a bit surprised about the things they were hearing, but they both appeared to be at least a little disappointed. It didn't register with me until years later why; they were already thinking about the future."

MAY 2, 1992

Atlanta, Georgia
Center Stage
Opening Act: Shooting Gallery
Attendance: 1,000   Capacity: 1,000
Promoters: Concert/Southern Promotions
Archived: Video

■ SET LIST

Love Gun
Deuce
Heaven's On Fire
Parasite
Shout It Out Loud
Strutter
Calling Dr Love
I Was Made for Lovin' You
Unholy
100,000 Years
Take It Off
God of Thunder
Lick It Up
Firehouse
Tears Are Falling
I Love It Loud
I Stole Your Love
Cold Gin
Detroit Rock City
I Want You
God Gave Rock 'N' Roll to You II
Rock and Roll All Nite

MAY 4, 1992

Baltimore, Maryland
Hammerjacks
Opening Act: Shooting Gallery
Attendance: 1,500   Capacity: 1,500
Promoter: In-house
Archived: Audio

■ SET LIST

Love Gun
Deuce
Heaven's On Fire
Parasite
Shout It Out Loud
Strutter
Calling Dr Love
I Was Made for Lovin' You
Unholy
100,000 Years
Take It Off
God of Thunder
[Lick It Up]

Firehouse
Tears Are Falling
I Love It Loud
I Stole Your Love
Cold Gin
Detroit Rock City
I Want You
God Gave Rock 'N' Roll to You II
Rock and Roll All Nite

■ May 4 was declared "KISS Day" in Baltimore, and the mayor presented the keys to the city to the band.

MAY 5, 1992

Philadelphia, Pennsylvania
The Trocadero
Opening Act: Shooting Gallery
Attendance: 1,100   Capacity: 1,100
Promoter: Electric Factory Concerts
Archived: Video

■ SET LIST

See April 26, 1992.

■ The band played "Oh Susannah" prior to "I Want You."

MAY 6, 1992

Toronto, Ontario, Canada
The Phoenix Theatre
Opening Act: Shooting Gallery
Attendance: 1,000   Capacity: 1,000
Promoter: Concert Promotions Int'l
Archived: Video

■ SET LIST

See April 26, 1992.

MAY 8, 1992

Boston, Massachusetts
Avalon Ballroom
Opening Act: Shooting Gallery
Attendance: 1,350   Capacity: 1,350
Promoter: Don Law Presents
Archived: Audio, Partial Video

■ SET LIST

See April 26, 1992.

MAY 9, 1992

New York, New York
The Ritz
Opening Act: Shooting Gallery
Attendance: 2,500   Capacity: 2,500
Promoter: Metropolitan Entertainment
Archived: Video

■ SET LIST

See April 26, 1992.

■ The show sold out in 90 seconds; it was the fastest sellout in venue history. Although it shared the name "The Ritz," this club was not the same Ritz at which the band had performed in August 1988.

MAY 10, 1992

Brooklyn, New York
The Warehouse
Opening Act: Shooting Gallery
Attendance: 800   Capacity: 800
Promoter: Ken Krite
Archived: Audio

■ SET LIST

See April 26, 1992.

MAY 16, 1992

Glasgow, Scotland
Scottish Exhibition & Conference Centre
Opening Act: Danger, Danger
Capacity: 5,000
Promoter: MCP

Archived: Video

■ SET LIST

I Stole Your Love
Deuce
Heaven's On Fire
Parasite
Shout It Out Loud
Strutter
Calling Dr. Love
I Was Made for Lovin' You
Unholy
100,000 Years
Take It Off
God of Thunder
Lick It Up
Firehouse
Tears Are Falling
I Love It Loud
Love Gun
Cold Gin
Detroit Rock City
I Want You
God Gave Rock 'N' Roll to You II
Rock and Roll All Nite

MAY 17, 1992

Whitley Bay, England
Whitley Bay Ice Rink
Opening Act: Danger, Danger
Capacity: 3,000
Promoter: MCP
Archived: Video

■ SET LIST

See May 16, 1992.

MAY 18, 1992

Sheffield, England
Sheffield Arena
Opening Act: Danger, Danger
Capacity: 6,000
Promoter: MCP
Archived: Video

■ SET LIST

See May 16, 1992.

MAY 20, 1992

Cardiff, Wales
Welsh National Ice-Rink
Opening Act: Danger, Danger
Attendance: 4,000   Capacity: 4,000
Promoter: MCP
Archived: Audio, Video

■ SET LIST

See May 16, 1992.

■ KISS did an in-store during the afternoon at the Cardiff HMV and the following day in the London HMV.

MAY 21, 1992

London, England
Wembley Arena
Opening Act: Danger, Danger
Capacity: 11,000
Promoter: MCP
Archived: Video

■ SET LIST

I Stole Your Love
Deuce
Heaven's On Fire
Parasite
Shout It Out Loud
Strutter
Calling Dr. Love
I Was Made for Lovin' You
Unholy
100,000 Years
Take It Off

KISS onstage during their brief tour of Europe in May 1992.

God of Thunder
Firehouse
Tears Are Falling
I Love It Loud
Love Gun
Cold Gin
Detroit Rock City
I Want You
God Gave Rock 'N' Roll to You II
Rock and Roll All Nite

■ KISS made a brief appearance at an unofficial U.K. KISS Convention in London at the England-Astoria Theatre.

MAY 22, 1992

London, England
Wembley Arena
Opening Act: Danger, Danger
Capacity: 11,000
Promoter: MCP

MAY 24, 1992

Plymouth, England
Plymouth Pavilions
Opening Act: Danger, Danger
Capacity: 3,010
Promoter: MCP
Archived: Audio

■ SET LIST
See May 16, 1992.

MAY 25, 1992

Birmingham, England

National Exhibition Centre
Opening Act: Danger, Danger
Capacity: 5,649
Promoter: MCP
Archived: Audio

■ SET LIST
See May 16, 1992.

■ During the show, Paul announced, "Eric is backstage taking a piss . . . why don't you call him? ERIC . . . ERIC . . . ERIC . . ." and the crowd joined him. "I don't think he hears you." When Singer finally reappeared, Paul asked, "Did you have a good piss, Eric?"

MAY 26, 1992

Birmingham, England
National Exhibition Centre
Opening Act: Danger, Danger
Capacity: 5,649
Promoter: MCP
Archived: Audio, Partial Video

■ SET LIST
See May 16, 1992.

■ This marked the final performances of "I Stole Your Love," "Calling Dr. Love," "I Was Made for Lovin' You," and "God of Thunder" on the Revenge Tour. This show is also noteworthy as this is the final time that KISS opened with "I Stole Your Love."

For several days after the Birmingham show, KISS embarked on a promotional tour of Europe. Their most notable appearance occurred on May 29 in Hilversum, The Netherlands when the band lip-synched "Unholy" and "God Gave Rock 'N' Roll to You II" for the TV show *Countdown*.

KISS returned from Europe and continued to promote *Revenge* while gearing up for an arena tour of North America. Gene, Paul, and Eric appeared on the syndicated live radio show *Rockline*, on June 15 and the video for "I Just Wanna," world premiered on *Hangin' With MTV* the following day. The third video from Revenge, "Domino," soon followed with an August 8 world premiere during *Headbangers Ball*. In October, a fourth video, "Every Time I Look at You," was also released.

On the domestic front, Gene and Shannon Tweed welcomed their second child to the world when Tweed gave birth to a daughter, Sophie, on July 6. Later in the month, on July 26, Paul was married to Pamela Bowen, an actress whose credits include small roles on *Cheers* and *Beverly Hills, 90210*.

The North American leg of the Revenge Tour was initially scheduled to begin in Tulsa, Oklahoma and heavy promotion had been done for the gig, with both July 31 and August 1 mentioned as the start date for the tour. Nonetheless, the tour was pushed back nearly two months. In late September, the band took up residence at Lehigh University's Stabler Arena in Bethlehem,

Pennsylvania where production rehearsals were held prior to the first show of the tour.

Staging for this leg of the tour was once again designed by Robert Roth and constructed by Tait Towers. Larry Mazer: "The initial designs had the stage looking like this post-apocalyptic wasteland with guard towers and cars buried in the stage. But it costed out way too high. So, we're sitting there in a meeting in my office in Los Angeles, and it again came down to what was in the center of the stage. I think Paul said, 'Why not the Statue of Liberty?' So, we designed this Statue of Liberty stage prop where the face of the statue would blow off and a skull would be revealed beneath. The actual set piece was a disaster; some nights it would work, others it would only work halfway. Other stage props were so big that we couldn't use them most of the time. There just wasn't the same vibe on that tour."

KISS stuck with the set list formula that had been so successful for them on the Hot in the Shade Tour: a lengthy set weighted heavily in favor of vintage KISS material and a few 1980s hits. From *Revenge*, "Unholy," "I Just Wanna," "Domino," and "God Gave Rock 'N' Roll to You II" were performed nightly, with "Take It Off" included regularly as well. Among the 1970s songs in the set, which numbered as many as 15 for some shows, were "Hotter Than Hell," "Parasite," and "Watchin' You," all pulled from *Hotter Than Hell*, an album which had not been represented in any live KISS performance since 1979. Surprisingly, "Creatures of the Night" was brought back and even put in the opening slot just as it had been in the early 1980s.

Most nights, the production also included the use of strippers during "Take It Off." "That started at the first show in Bethlehem," states Mazer. "The house production manager for [promoter] Tom Makoul had a girlfriend who was a stripper, and they thought it would be a great idea to have a stripper on stage during 'Take It Off,' so they included it in Bethlehem. Then it became a ritual in each city for our production manager, Tim Rozner, to do a search of local strip joints. He'd bring down 20 girls or so, and Gene and Paul would pick three or four of them to appear onstage every night. After a while, there were three girls who enjoyed it so much that they stayed on board for over a month. All they asked was that they could ride on the tour bus. They didn't want to get paid. They didn't get a per diem at all."

Despite the many attempts Mazer and KISS had made to cater to the fans' wishes, the Revenge Tour was a disappointment, averaging just over 5,000 people per show at the arena gigs. Shows were canceled during the tour due to a lack of ticket sales, and the entire tour itself ended prematurely just before the Christmas holidays. The next leg of the tour was scheduled to begin in Texas in early January 1993, but the attendance figures were so poor in most markets that the dates never came to fruition.

In what has been interpreted as a knee-jerk reaction to "corporate rock," KISS, along with virtually every other hard rock/heavy metal band from the 1980s, found themselves disowned by the music-buying public, and replaced by a seem-ingly never-ending horde of supposedly earnest garage bands. At the bottom of another inevitable cycle, KISS found themselves outdated, again. To that end, the club tour KISS had done in the spring didn't help matters any, as in the minds of the general public it sent the signal that KISS had been relegated to playing in clubs, rather than choosing to play them.

The fact that KISS decided to tour arenas in 1992 was at the very least commendable, though turnouts were eerily reminiscent of those the band had drawn a decade before. The band was a sinking ship, and if they didn't know it when they began the tour, they certainly did before they returned home on December 21.

Note: During this leg of the tour, "I Want You" was lengthened rather considerably to include the following:

- A short guitar solo by Bruce.

- A short drum solo by Eric Singer that was usually followed by his rendition of "Oh Susannah" on harmonica. Later in the tour, the band would occasionally perform "Oh Susannah" a second time after Eric's harmonica solo. A longer (but still short by KISS standards) drum solo was also performed.

- The usual call-and-response bit between Paul and the audience was included in the mix, and Paul would also perform similar call-and-response bits separately with Eric and Bruce.

SEPTEMBER 30, 1992

Bethlehem (Allentown), Pennsylvania
Stabler Arena
No Opening Act
Archived: Audio, Partial Video

■ SET LIST

Creatures of the Night
I Just Wanna
Unholy
Heaven's On Fire
Domino
I Want You
Forever
War Machine
Lick It Up
Detroit Rock City
God Gave Rock 'N' Roll to You II
Love Gun
Star Spangled Banner

■ This was a partial dress rehearsal attended by record company employees and VIPs. Paul and Eric taped an interview for MTV, who also video-taped highlights of the rehearsal.

OCTOBER 1, 1992

Bethlehem (Allentown), Pennsylvania
Stabler Arena
Opening Acts: Faster Pussycat, Trixter
Attendance: 3,069   Capacity: 5,729
Promoter: Makoul Productions
Archived: Video

■ SET LIST

Creatures of the Night
Deuce
I Just Wanna
Unholy
Parasite
Strutter
Heaven's On Fire
Christine Sixteen
Domino
Watchin' You
Hotter Than Hell
Firehouse
I Want You
Forever
War Machine

CURT GOOCH

Bruce and Gene during the debut concert on the U.S. arena leg of 1992's Revenge Tour.

100,000 Years
Rock and Roll All Nite
Lick It Up
Take It Off
Cold Gin
Tears Are Falling
I Love It Loud
Detroit Rock City
Shout It Out Loud
God Gave Rock 'N' Roll to You II
Love Gun
Star Spangled Banner

■ This was the first performance of "Christine Sixteen" since 1979. It was also the first time that "Watchin' You" had been performed live since 1976.

OCTOBER 2, 1992

Binghamton, New York
Broome Co. Veterans Memorial Arena
Opening Acts: Faster Pussycat, Trixter
Capacity: 7,200
Promoter: Magic City Productions
Archived: Video

■ SET LIST

Creatures of the Night
Deuce
I Just Wanna
Unholy
Parasite
Heaven's On Fire
Christine Sixteen
Domino
Watchin' You
Hotter Than Hell
Firehouse
I Want You
Forever
War Machine
Rock and Roll All Nite
Lick It Up
Take It Off
Cold Gin
Tears Are Falling
I Love It Loud
Detroit Rock City
Shout It Out Loud
God Gave Rock 'N' Roll to You II
Love Gun
Star Spangled Banner

OCTOBER 3, 1992

Toronto, Ontario, Canada
Maple Leaf Gardens
Opening Acts: Faster Pussycat, Trixter
Attendance: 8,255   Capacity: 10,200
Promoter: Concert Promotions Int'l
Archived: Video

■ SET LIST

See October 2, 1992.

■ KISS went down to the MuchMusic studios to do a live interview on *Start Me Up.* They also made an in-store appearance at a Toronto HMV record store.

OCTOBER 5, 1992

Montréal, Quebec, Canada
Forum de Montréal
Opening Acts: Faster Pussycat, Trixter
Attendance: 4,500   Capacity: 12,085
Promoter: Donald K. Donald
Archived: Video

■ SET LIST

See October 2, 1992.

■ A small mishap occurred at the end of Gene's

fire-breathing act, as Gene's bass tech, Dave "Romeo" Bonilla, explains: "Gene threw his fire-breathing sword at the square box like he always did, but it hit the side and bounced off into the barricade."

OCTOBER 6, 1992

Portland, Maine
Cumberland County Civic Center
Opening Acts: Faster Pussycat, Trixter
Attendance: 4,500   Capacity: 9,150
Promoter: Don Law Presents
Archived: Audio

■ SET LIST

Creatures of the Night
Deuce
I Just Wanna
Unholy
Parasite
Heaven's On Fire
Christine Sixteen
Domino
[Watchin' You]
[Hotter Than Hell]
Firehouse
I Want You
Forever
War Machine
Rock and Roll All Nite
Lick It Up
Take It Off
Cold Gin
Tears Are Falling
I Love It Loud
Detroit Rock City
Shout It Out Loud
God Gave Rock 'N' Roll to You II
[Love Gun]
[Star Spangled Banner]

■ Dave Bonilla: "Whenever we played Maine, we would play this joke on Gene. He hates lobsters, they look like big cockroaches to him, so every time we would play a gig in Maine, when Gene would go back out for the encore, there would be a big lobster tail on his mic stand. He wouldn't even go near it."

OCTOBER 8, 1992

Worcester, Massachusetts
The Centrum
Opening Acts: Faster Pussycat, Trixter
Attendance: 7,199   Capacity: 9,289
Promoter: Don Law Presents
Archived: Video, Super 8mm

■ SET LIST

See October 2, 1992.

■ Paul informed the audience, "You know we made a decision this afternoon that we're gonna record *KISS Alive III.*" Paul's wife was in the photo pit videotaping portions of the show.

OCTOBER 9, 1992

East Rutherford, New Jersey
Brendan Byrne Arena
Opening Acts: Faster Pussycat, Trixter
Attendance: 8,557   Capacity: 14,943
Promoter: Metropolitan Entertainment
Archived: Audio

■ SET LIST

See October 2, 1992.

OCTOBER 10, 1992

Philadelphia, Pennsylvania
The Spectrum
Opening Acts: Faster Pussycat, Trixter

Attendance: 5,375   Capacity: 14,170
Promoter: Electric Factory Concerts
Archived: Video

■ SET LIST

Creatures of the Night
Deuce
I Just Wanna
Unholy
Parasite
Heaven's On Fire
Christine Sixteen
Domino
Watchin' You
Hotter Than Hell
Firehouse
I Want You
Forever
War Machine
Rock and Roll All Nite
Lick It Up
Take It Off
Cold Gin
Tears Are Falling
I Love It Loud
Detroit Rock City
Shout It Out Loud
God Gave Rock 'N' Roll to You II
[Star Spangled Banner]

OCTOBER 11, 1992

Uniondale, New York
Nassau Veterans Memorial Coliseum
Opening Acts: Faster Pussycat, Trixter
Attendance: 5,735   Capacity: 13,291
Promoter: Metropolitan Entertainment
Archived: Video

■ SET LIST

Creatures of the Night
Deuce
I Just Wanna
Unholy
Parasite
Heaven's On Fire
Christine Sixteen
Domino
Watchin' You
Hotter Than Hell
Firehouse
I Want You
Forever
War Machine
Rock and Roll All Nite
Lick It Up
Take It Off
Cold Gin
Tears Are Falling
I Love It Loud
Detroit Rock City
Shout It Out Loud
God Gave Rock 'N' Roll to You II
[Love Gun]
[Star Spangled Banner]

■ This is the last known performance of "Christine Sixteen" on the Revenge Tour.

OCTOBER 13, 1992

Hershey, Pennsylvania
Hersheypark Arena
Opening Acts: Faster Pussycat, Trixter
Attendance: 3,449   Capacity: 6,120
Promoter: DiCesare-Engler Productions

OCTOBER 14, 1992

Charleston, West Virginia
Charleston Civic Center
Opening Acts: Faster Pussycat, Trixter

Attendance: 3,982   Capacity: 3,982
Promoter: Belkin Productions

OCTOBER 16, 1992

Pittsburgh, Pennsylvania
Civic Arena
Opening Acts: Faster Pussycat, Trixter
Attendance: 6,646   Capacity: 11,000
Promoter: DiCesare-Engler Productions
Archived: Audio

■ SET LIST

Creatures of the Night
Deuce
I Just Wanna
Unholy
Parasite
Heaven's On Fire
Domino
Watchin' You
Hotter Than Hell
Firehouse
I Want You
Forever
War Machine
Rock and Roll All Nite
Lick It Up
Take It Off
Cold Gin
I Love It Loud
Detroit Rock City
Shout It Out Loud
God Gave Rock 'N' Roll to You II
Love Gun
Star Spangled Banner

OCTOBER 17, 1992

Roanoke, Virginia
Roanoke Civic Center
Opening Acts: Faster Pussycat, Trixter
Attendance: 4,698   Capacity: 7,000
Promoter: Cellar Door Concerts

OCTOBER 18, 1992

Landover (Washington, D.C.), Maryland
Capital Centre
Opening Acts: Faster Pussycat, Trixter
Capacity: 15,002
Promoter: Music Centre Productions
Archived: Audio

■ SET LIST

See October 16, 1992.

OCTOBER 20, 1992

Lexington, Kentucky
Rupp Arena
Opening Acts: Faster Pussycat, Trixter
Attendance: 3,042   Capacity: 6,000
Promoters: Future Entertainment, Belkin Productions

OCTOBER 21, 1992

Bristol, Tennessee
Viking Hall Civic Center @ Tennessee High School
Opening Acts: Faster Pussycat, Trixter
Attendance: 2,528   Capacity: 5,898
Promoter: Sunshine Promotions

■ This show was originally scheduled for Johnson City.

OCTOBER 22, 1992   POSTPONED

Knoxville, Tennessee
Knoxville Civic Coliseum
Opening Acts: Faster Pussycat, Trixter
Capacity: 10,000
Promoter: Sunshine Promotions

■ This show was postponed until November 7.

OCTOBER 23, 1992

Charlotte, North Carolina
Charlotte Coliseum
Opening Acts: Faster Pussycat, Trixter
Attendance: 4,739   Capacity: 9,949
Promoter: C & C Entertainment
Archived: Video

■ SET LIST

See October 16, 1992.

■ Revenge tourbooks were first sold at this show.

OCTOBER 24, 1992

Fayetteville, North Carolina
Cumberland County Memorial Arena
Opening Acts: Faster Pussycat, Trixter
Capacity: 6,300
Promoter: C & C Entertainment

OCTOBER 25, 1992

Columbia, South Carolina
Carolina Coliseum
Opening Acts: Faster Pussycat, Trixter
Capacity: 12,000
Promoter: C & C Entertainment

OCTOBER 27, 1992   CANCELED

Asheville, North Carolina
Asheville Civic Center Auditorium
Opening Acts: Faster Pussycat, Trixter
Capacity: 7,600
Promoter: C & C Entertainment

OCTOBER 29, 1992

Daytona Beach, Florida
Ocean Center
Opening Acts: Faster Pussycat, Trixter, Fortress
Attendance: 2,948   Capacity: 9,000
Promoters: Cellar Door Concerts
Archived: Video

■ SET LIST

See October 16, 1992.

■ Local act Fortress was added to the bill at the last moment.

OCTOBER 30, 1992

Tampa, Florida
USF Sundome
Opening Acts: Faster Pussycat, Trixter
Attendance: 3,502   Capacity: 8,100
Promoter: Cellar Door Concerts
Archived: Audio, Partial Video

■ SET LIST

See October 20, 1992.

OCTOBER 31, 1992

Miami, Florida
Miami Arena
Opening Acts: Faster Pussycat, Trixter
Attendance: 3,140   Capacity: 10,500
Promoter: Cellar Door Concerts
Archived: Video

■ SET LIST

See October 16, 1992.

■ This was Faster Pussycat's last show on the Revenge Tour, and, as a prank, KISS's crew littered Faster Pussycat's dressing room with several 50-pound bags of dog food and taped McDonald's applications to the mirrors. Derek Sherinian continues the story, "Paul was against the last night tradition of messing with the head-line act and he made it clear to all the warm-up bands. Faster Pussycat got dropped (from their record label) towards the end of the leg and I think their bass player was quitting. So there was

this 'who gives a fuck?' attitude. They decided to come out in drag on 'Take It Off.' Gene and Paul were flabbergasted that these people had the audacity to come on their stage. Gene reamed the stage manager. He was saying 'I don't give a fuck if you have to shoot 'em, no one gets on this stage.'"

NOVEMBER 3, 1992

Greenville, South Carolina
Greenville Memorial Auditorium
Opening Acts: Jackyl, Trixter
Capacity: 7,000
Promoter: C & C Entertainment

NOVEMBER 5, 1992

Atlanta, Georgia
The Omni
Opening Acts: Great White, Trixter
Capacity: 17,300
Promoter: Cellar Door Concerts
Archived: Audio

■ SET LIST

See October 16, 1992.

NOVEMBER 6, 1992

Nashville, Tennessee
Nashville Municipal Auditorium
Opening Acts: Great White, Trixter
Attendance: 6,173   Capacity: 6,912
Promoters: Steve Howser, Pace Concerts
Archived: Audio

■ SET LIST

Creatures of the Night
Deuce
I Just Wanna
Unholy
Heaven's On Fire
Parasite
Domino
Watchin' You
Hotter Than Hell
Firehouse
I Want You
Forever
War Machine
Rock and Roll All Nite
Lick It Up
I Love It Loud
Take It Off
Cold Gin
Detroit Rock City
Shout It Out Loud
God Gave Rock 'N' Roll to You II
Love Gun
Star Spangled Banner

NOVEMBER 7, 1992

Knoxville, Tennessee
Knoxville Civic Coliseum
Opening Acts: Great White, Trixter
Attendance: 3,950   Capacity: 10,000
Promoter: Sunshine Promotions
Archived: Partial Audio

■ SET LIST

[Creatures of the Night]
[Deuce]
[I Just Wanna]
[Unholy]
[Parasite]
[Heaven's On Fire]
[Domino]
[Watchin' You]
Hotter Than Hell
Firehouse

CHRIS DORSCHUTZ

I Want You
Forever
War Machine
Rock and Roll All Nite
Lick It Up
Take It Off
Cold Gin
I Love It Loud
Detroit Rock City
[Shout It Out Loud]
[God Gave Rock 'N' Roll to You II]
[Love Gun]
[Star Spangled Banner]

NOVEMBER 8, 1992

Huntsville, Alabama
Von Braun Civic Center
Opening Acts: Great White, Trixter
Attendance: 3,872   Capacity: 8,000
Promoter: New Era Promotions
Archived: Audio
■ **SET LIST**
See October 16, 1992.

NOVEMBER 10, 1992

Jackson, Mississippi   CANCELED
Jackson Coliseum
Opening Acts: Great White, Trixter

NOVEMBER 10, 1992

St. Joseph, Missouri
St. Joseph Civic Arena
Opening Acts: Great White, Trixter
Attendance: 3,713   Capacity: 7,382
Promoter: Steve Litman Productions
■ During KISS's first-ever concert in St. Joseph, which was put on sale only a couple of weeks prior to the date of the show, Paul was too sick to sing most of his vocals. Bruce Kulick explains: "Gene sang some of Paul's songs and it was a total disaster. It was a short set, then Gene sang the songs an octave lower—the ones he thought he could pull off—it was terrible. There was really terrible weather, and obviously Paul was sick. We should have canceled."

The following morning, Paul flew to New York to see a specialist to seek treatment.

NOVEMBER 12, 1992

Memphis, Tennessee   **KISS CANCELED**
Mid-South Coliseum
Opening Acts: Great White, Trixter
Attendance: 9,955   Capacity: 9,955
Promoter: Mid-South Concerts
■ With Paul receiving medical treatment in New York, KISS was forced to back out of one of the only sold-out shows on the tour. Despite KISS's absence, the opening bands did perform.

NOVEMBER 13, 1992

St. Louis, Missouri
The Arena
Opening Acts: Great White, Trixter
Attendance: 6,505   Capacity: 12,000
Promoter: Contemporary Productions
Archived: Audio
■ **SET LIST**
See October 16, 1992.
■ Producer Eddie Kramer was in attendance to observe KISS's show for the upcoming recording of *Alive III.*

NOVEMBER 14, 1992

Ames, Iowa
Hilton Coliseum
Opening Acts: Great White, Trixter
Attendance: 6,716   Capacity: 10,244
Promoter: Contemporary Productions
Archived: Audio
■ **SET LIST**
[Creatures of the Night]
[Deuce]
[I Just Wanna]
Unholy
Parasite
Heaven's On Fire
Domino
Watchin' You
Hotter Than Hell
Firehouse
I Want You
Forever
War Machine
Rock and Roll All Nite
Lick It Up
Take It Off
Cold Gin
I Love It Loud
Detroit Rock City
Shout It Out Loud
God Gave Rock 'N' Roll to You II
Love Gun
Star Spangled Banner

■ This was the final performance of "Cold Gin" on the tour.

NOVEMBER 15, 1992

Cedar Rapids, Iowa
Five Seasons Center
Opening Acts: Great White, Trixter
Attendance: 5,069   Capacity: 10,000
Promoter: JAM Productions
Archived: Video

■ SET LIST
Creatures of the Night
Deuce
I Just Wanna
Unholy
Parasite
Heaven's On Fire
Domino
Watchin' You
Hotter Than Hell
Firehouse
I Want You
Forever
War Machine
Rock and Roll All Nite
Lick It Up
Take It Off
Strutter
I Love It Loud
Detroit Rock City
Shout It Out Loud
God Gave Rock 'N' Roll to You II
Love Gun
Star Spangled Banner

■ Pyro caught the venue ceiling on fire during the final encore. This was the first appearance of "Strutter" on the Revenge Tour.

NOVEMBER 17, 1992

Kalamazoo, Michigan
Wings Stadium
Opening Acts: Great White, Trixter
Attendance: 3,970   Capacity: 8,113
Promoter: Cellar Door Concerts
Archived: Audio

■ SET LIST
See November 15, 1992.

NOVEMBER 18, 1992

Fort Wayne, Indiana
Allen Co. War Memorial Coliseum
Opening Acts: Great White, Trixter
Attendance: 4,745   Capacity: 5,000
Promoter: Sunshine Promotions
Archived: Audio

■ SET LIST
See November 15, 1992.

NOVEMBER 19, 1992   CANCELED

Columbus, Ohio
Battelle Hall @ Ohio Center
Opening Acts: Great White, Trixter
Promoter: Belkin Productions

NOVEMBER 20, 1992

Evansville, Indiana
Roberts Municipal Stadium
Opening Acts: Great White, Trixter
Attendance: 5,158   Capacity: 7,000
Promoter: Sunshine Promotions
Archived: Audio

■ SET LIST
Creatures of the Night
Deuce
I Just Wanna
Unholy

Parasite
Heaven's On Fire
Domino
Watchin' You
Hotter Than Hell
Firehouse
I Want You
Forever
War Machine
Rock and Roll All Nite
Lick It Up
Strutter
I Love It Loud
Detroit Rock City
Shout It Out Loud
God Gave Rock 'N' Roll to You II
Love Gun
Star Spangled Banner

■ "Take It Off" was dropped from the set list at this show.

NOVEMBER 21, 1992

Chicago, Illinois
University of Illinois-Chicago Pavilion
Opening Acts: Great White, Trixter
Attendance: 5,123   Capacity: 8,545
Promoters: JAM Productions, Majic Productions
Archived: Audio

■ SET LIST
Creatures of the Night
Deuce
I Just Wanna
Unholy
Parasite
Heaven's On Fire
Domino
Watchin' You
Hotter Than Hell
Firehouse
I Want You
Forever
War Machine
Rock and Roll All Nite
Lick It Up
Take It Off
Strutter
I Love It Loud
Detroit Rock City
Shout It Out Loud
God Gave Rock 'N' Roll to You II
Love Gun
Star Spangled Banner

NOVEMBER 22, 1992

Toledo, Ohio
John F. Savage Hall
Opening Acts: Great White, Trixter
Attendance: 3,166   Capacity: 9,918
Promoter: Belkin Productions
Archived: Video

■ SET LIST
See November 15, 1992.

■ This concert was originally scheduled for the Toledo Sports Arena.

NOVEMBER 24, 1992

Springfield, Illinois
Prairie Capital Convention Center
Opening Acts: Great White, Trixter
Attendance: 3,011   Capacity: 8,746
Promoter: JAM Productions
Archived: Video

■ SET LIST
Creatures of the Night
Deuce
I Just Wanna

Unholy
Parasite
Heaven's On Fire
Domino
[Watchin' You]
[Hotter Than Hell]
Firehouse
I Want You
Forever
War Machine
Rock and Roll All Nite
Lick It Up
[Take It Off]
[Strutter]
I Love It Loud
Detroit Rock City
Shout It Out Loud
God Gave Rock 'N' Roll to You II
Love Gun
Star Spangled Banner

NOVEMBER 25, 1992

Dayton, Ohio
Ervin J. Nutter Center
Opening Acts: Great White, Trixter
Attendance: 5,514   Capacity: 11,000
Promoter: Belkin Productions

NOVEMBER 27, 1992

Auburn Hills (Detroit), Michigan
The Palace of Auburn Hills
Opening Acts: Great White, Trixter
Attendance: 9,270   Capacity: 9,270
Promoter: Belkin Productions
Archived: Audio, Film, Video

■ SET LIST
See November 15, 1992.

■ Eddie Kramer was on hand to record the show for *Alive III*. As a precaution, at the band's sound check Kramer recorded KISS performing the first part of their show up through "Firehouse." The remaining portions of KISS's show were performed and recorded at sound check at the next two shows.

This show was archived by three different crews. An audio recording was made for *Alive III*. The show was also videotaped by The Palace's in-house video crew, which broadcast a live feed of the event throughout the venue, and another camera crew captured the concert on film for later use in the *KISS Konfidential* home video.

NOVEMBER 28, 1992

Indianapolis, Indiana
Market Square Arena
Opening Acts: Great White, Trixter
Attendance: 8,061   Capacity: 9,500
Promoter: Sunshine Promotions
Archived: Audio, Video

■ SET LIST
See November 15, 1992.

■ This show was recorded for *Alive III*. Video cameras were stationed at various positions around the stage to capture insert shots for *KISS Konfidential*.

NOVEMBER 29, 1992

Richfield (Cleveland), Ohio
The Coliseum Theatre
Opening Acts: Great White, Trixter
Attendance: 8,976   Capacity: 12,598
Promoter: Belkin Productions
Archived: Audio, Video

Creatures of the Night
Deuce
I Just Wanna
Unholy
Parasite
Heaven's On Fire
Domino
Watchin' You
Hotter Than Hell
Firehouse
I Want You
Forever
War Machine
Rock and Roll All Nite
Lick It Up
Take It Off
Strutter
Tears Are Falling
I Love It Loud
Detroit Rock City
Shout It Out Loud
God Gave Rock 'N' Roll to You II
Love Gun
Star Spangled Banner

■ This was the last of three consecutive shows recorded for *Alive III*. Footage for use in *KISS Konfidential* was also shot at this show.

"Tears Are Falling" was added to the set for possible inclusion on *Alive III*. Paul set up the song by announcing, "If we don't get it right tonight, it ain't going on the album." This was the final performance of "Tears Are Falling" on the Revenge Tour.

NOVEMBER 30, 1992

Milwaukee, Wisconsin
Bradley Center
Opening Acts: Great White, Trixter
Capacity: 18,000
Promoter: Cellar Door Concerts
Archived: Audio

■ SET LIST

Creatures of the Night
Deuce
I Just Wanna
Unholy
Parasite
Heaven's On Fire
Domino
[Watchin' You]
[Hotter Than Hell]
Firehouse
I Want You
Forever
War Machine
Rock and Roll All Nite
Lick It Up
Take It Off
[Strutter]
I Love It Loud
Detroit Rock City
Shout It Out Loud
God Gave Rock 'N' Roll to You II

Love Gun
Star Spangled Banner

DECEMBER 2, 1992   CANCELED

Green Bay, Wisconsin
Brown County Veterans Memorial Arena
Opening Acts: Great White, Trixter
■ This concert was canceled and moved to Madison, Wisconsin.

DECEMBER 2, 1992

Madison, Wisconsin
Dane County Expo Center Coliseum
Opening Acts: Great White, Trixter
Attendance: 2,174   Capacity: 2,174
Promoter: Belkin Productions

DECEMBER 3, 1992

St. Paul, Minnesota
St. Paul Civic Center
Opening Acts: Great White, Trixter
Attendance: 9,000   Capacity: 14,923
Promoter: Rose Productions
Archived: Audio

■ SET LIST

See November 15, 1992.

DECEMBER 4, 1992

Sioux Falls, South Dakota
Sioux Falls Arena
Opening Acts: Great White, Trixter
Capacity: 8,000

Promoter: Steve Litman Productions

DECEMBER 5, 1992

Fargo, North Dakota **TEMP HOLD DATE**
Civic Memorial Auditorium
Opening Acts: Great White, Trixter

DECEMBER 6, 1992

Denver, Colorado
McNichols Sports Arena
Opening Acts: Great White, Trixter
Capacity: 12,128
Promoter: Feyline Presents

DECEMBER 7, 1992

Casper, Wyoming **CANCELED**
Casper Events Center
Opening Acts: Great White, Trixter

DECEMBER 8, 1992

Salt Lake City, Utah
Delta Center
Opening Acts: Great White, Trixter
Capacity: 16,000
Promoter: United Concerts

DECEMBER 9, 1992

Boise, Idaho
BSU Pavilion
Opening Acts: Great White, Trixter
Attendance: 3,394   Capacity: 8,500
Promoter: United Concerts

DECEMBER 10, 1992

Portland, Oregon
Memorial Coliseum
Opening Acts: Great White, Trixter
Capacity: 9,231
Promoter: Bauer/Kinnear Enterprises

DECEMBER 11, 1992

Vancouver, British Columbia, Canada
Pacific Coliseum
Opening Acts: Great White, Trixter
Capacity: 17,613
Promoter: Perryscope Concert Productions
Archived: Audio
■ **SET LIST**
See November 15, 1992.

DECEMBER 13, 1992

Spokane, Washington **CANCELED**
Spokane Coliseum
Opening Acts: Great White, Trixter
Capacity: 8,000
Promoter: Bauer/Kinnear Enterprises
■ This gig was canceled several days in advance due to the fact that only 1,500 tickets had been sold.

DECEMBER 14, 1992

Seattle, Washington
Seattle Center Arena
Opening Acts: Great White, Trixter
Capacity: 9,258
Promoter: Perryscope Concert Productions
Archived: Audio
■ **SET LIST**
See November 15, 1992.
■ The concert was originally scheduled for the Seattle Center Coliseum, but was moved to a smaller venue due to a lack of ticket sales.

Management for opening act Great White penned a letter to Patrick McDonald of *The Seattle Times* on December 23 regarding some offensive comments both he and Gene Simmons allegedly made in a December 11 article which they felt disparaged Great White.

DECEMBER 16, 1992

Sacramento, California
ARCO Arena
Opening Acts: Great White, Trixter
Capacity: 13,500
Promoter: Bill Graham Presents
Archived: Video
■ **SET LIST**
See November 20, 1992.
■ "Take It Off" was not performed in Sacramento or at the December 19 show in San Bernardino.

Derek Sherinian: "At ARCO Arena there were just no people there. In his song raps, Paul would usually say, 'People on the left, let me hear you! People on the right, let me hear you!' In Sacramento, Paul said, 'Oris, (the soundman) let me hear you!' because there was no one around."

DECEMBER 18, 1992

Oakland, California
Oakland-Alameda County Coliseum Arena
Opening Acts: Great White, Trixter
Capacity: 15,000
Promoter: Bill Graham Presents
Archived: Video
■ **SET LIST**
See November 15, 1992.
■ KISS fans' other favorite band, the Grateful Dead, had played at the same venue for seven nights prior to the KISS concert. Making for an interesting mix, several Deadheads hung around hoping to stir up some "extra business" from the KISS crowd.

DECEMBER 19, 1992

San Bernardino, California
Orange Show Pavilion
Opening Acts: Trixter, Vesuvius
Capacity: 6,000
Promoter: Positive Attractions
Archived: Video
■ **SET LIST**
See November 20, 1992.
■ The Statue of Liberty prop couldn't fit into the venue and was not used at this show. Additionally, "Take It Off" was absent from the set again. This was KISS's only Southern California appearance on the arena tour.

DECEMBER 20, 1992

Phoenix, Arizona
America West Arena
Opening Acts: Great White, Trixter
Attendance: 3,741   Capacity: 6,700
Promoter: Evening Star Productions
Archived: Audio, Partial Video
■ **SET LIST**
See November 15, 1992.
■ To help mask the astonishing emptiness in the house (which had a true capacity of more than 18,000) a fog machine was set up at the soundboard.

There was talk among the band members of including "Black Diamond" in the set with Eric Singer performing lead vocals. But, when Singer came down with the flu (and had a bucket next to his kit during the show, just in case), the idea was scrapped.

This was Derek Sherinian's last concert with KISS, and both "Hotter Than Hell" and "I Just Wanna" were performed live for the final time.

CHAPTER 22

1993 - 1995

Number of Shows: 31
Start Date: May 20, 1993 - Los Angeles, California
End Date: February 14, 1995 - Sydney, Australia
Countries: Argentina, Australia, Brazil, Chile, Japan, Mexico, U.S.A.
Opening Acts: Angra; Black Sabbath; Dr. Sin; Fleetwood Mac; Gatos Sucios; Hermetica; I Mother Earth; Lita Ford; Logos; Mother Station; Open Skyz; Pat Travers Band; The Poor; Raimundos; Screamin' Cheetah Wheelies; Slayer; Snake Dance; Stick; Suicidal Tendencies; Tumulto; Victimas del Dr. Cerebro; Viper

As 1993 began, KISS's popularity outside their hardcore fanbase was virtually nil; "arena rock" had fallen into disfavor with most music consumers, and the prospects for improving KISS's profile were very slim. Rather than expend tremendous energy and expense to capture the interest of these new fans, the band began to embrace the core of their fanbase. Over the course of the subsequent two years, KISS's efforts became increasingly focused on appeasing the needs and requests of the zealous core of fans which had sustained them through lean times before.

Aside from a February 25 acoustic performance on Howard Stern's radio show, KISS was a virtual nonentity for the first four months of 1993 before resurfacing in May to promote the release of *Alive III,* the band's first live album in nearly 16 years. The album's sales mimicked *Revenge,* quickly peaking (at #9 on the charts) only to see sales fall off very rapidly thereafter.

Several public appearances followed: May 18 saw Paul, Gene, and Bruce placing their handprints in cement as they were inducted into Hollywood's RockWalk; a May 20 appearance on *The Arsenio Hall Show* showcased live performances of "Deuce" and "Detroit Rock City"; and lastly were two appearances on *Headbangers Ball,* on May 29 and June 5.

Perhaps the most interesting of the band's glut of appearances aired on June 28 when the WWOR evening news in Secaucus, New Jersey broadcast a KISS segment that showed Paul and Gene visiting several historical KISS landmarks including a boarded-up Hotel Diplomat and the band's old rehearsal loft on Twenty-third Street.

On June 17, the band began a promotional tour in support of *Alive III.* The tour launched in Houston and concluded in Los Angeles nearly a month later on July 16. In some markets, part of the promotion included advertised meet-and-greets with fans who usually gained admittance by purchasing a one-cent stick-on pass.

Yet another home video, *KISS Konfidential,* was released on July 20. The video focused on the Revenge Tour and featured live footage of the band cut around their 1992 appearance in Auburn Hills as well as archival live footage.

ANDRES VIOLANTE/COURTESY OF GABRIEL RAVARINI & KISSFEVER

Los Angeles, California
Paramount Studios
Archived: Video
■ SET LIST
Detroit Rock City
Deuce
■ This was the taping for KISS's appearance for
The Arsenio Hall Show.

Burbank, California
Hilton and Convention Center
Promoter: Concrete Marketing
Archived: Video
■ SET LIST
King of the Night Time World
Take Me
Goin' Blind
Got to Choose
Rock Bottom
She
Makin' Love
Let Me Go, Rock 'n Roll
Parasite
■ On the day prior to the concert, KISS was
presented with a Lifetime Achievement Award
from Concrete Marketing and a press conference
followed.

This was KISS's only publicized show of the
year. The concert was part of "Foundations Forum
'93," an annual convention to promote hard rock
and heavy metal. Members of the music industry
were charged $50 to attend the three-day con-
vention, and KISS's set list was advertised as being
exclusively from the first few studio albums. This
was the first known performance of "Goin' Blind,"
though it had been played under its original title
"Little Lady" in 1973.

Rikki Rachtman interviewed Gene and Paul
for the September 18 episode of *Headbangers
Ball,* and live footage from the show was also
included in the broadcast.

The Hilton joined in the fun by issuing room
keys emblazoned with the KISS logo.

It should be noted that several other bands
performed throughout the three-day convention
and in various parts of the hotel. It is believed
that no other bands played in the same room as
KISS on September 11, hence there are no opening acts listed.

Albuquerque, New Mexico
Ramada Classic Ballroom
No Opening Act
Archived: Audio
■ SET LIST
Rock Bottom
Love Gun
Domino
I Was Made for Lovin' You
Cold Gin
Detroit Rock City
Forever
■ This was the wedding reception for Adrienne,
the daughter of the Coors Brewing Co. owner,
and her husband Steve. Charlton Heston pre-
sided as Master of Ceremonies, though the
bride's brother introduced KISS.

The Albuquerque Philharmonic Orchestra
performed with KISS during "Forever," which

was dedicated to the happy couple. Additionally,
the lyrics to "Domino" were toned-down for the
occasion.

Lake Buena Vista, Florida
West End Stage @ Pleasure Island
No Opening Act
Dick Clark Productions
Archived: Video
■ SET LIST
Detroit Rock City
Rock and Roll All Nite
Rock and Roll All Nite
Makin' Love
■ This was the taping of KISS's appearance for
Dick Clark's New Year's Rockin' Eve show.
Although it was recorded, "Detroit Rock City"
was never broadcast. Prior to "Makin' Love,"
Gene played part of "Unholy," and at the conclu-
sion of the taping, Paul performed an impromptu
rendition of the *Mickey Mouse Club* theme.

———————

By October 1993, KISS had severed ties with
manager Larry Mazer. "KISS was claiming that
the previous tour of Europe had lost a ton of
money," protests Mazer. "I disputed the claim and
they were adamant about renegotiating my deal
(presumably to recoup some of their losses) and
I told them that I wouldn't do that. That's when
the relationship ended. After that, I kept hearing
stories about Jess Hilsen. Next thing I knew, he
supposedly had disappeared off the face of the
earth, having absconded with tons of money."
Hilsen, who would maintain his relationship with
KISS through some point in 1994, eventually disappeared when a warrant for his arrest was issued
for his alleged failure to pay alimony and child support. A September 23, 1996 article in *Forbes* magazine indicated that Hilsen was allegedly a fugitive
and that his whereabouts were still unknown.

Mazer continues, "Later, at a convention in
Nashville, in 1995, I sat down with Gene and
Paul to discuss things. It was my contention that
the tour of Europe in 1992 had not lost money
but that Jess Hilsen had taken it, and he showed
them the tour at a loss to cover his tracks. It is
literally impossible for that tour to have lost the
amount of money they claimed it did."

At the beginning of 1994, KISS, now fully
managing their career, was no closer to being a
current force in the music industry than it had
been in 1993. But fortunately for KISS, a trend
was beginning to surface that was the perfect
vehicle to help them re-establish their presence.
As the decade of the '90s moved into its middle
years, 1970s pop culture was becoming increasingly in vogue, experiencing a long-lasting renaissance that arguably surpassed its original popularity. Never ones to bypass opportunity, KISS took
advantage on several fronts in 1994 and 1995.

The first of their efforts was *KISS My Ass
Classic KISS Regrooved,* an idea that involved
recruiting several current artists to record cover
versions of classic KISS songs for a KISS tribute
album. The band released the album through
PolyGram, thus cleverly accounting for another
record against their recording contract. The germ
of the idea first appeared in early 1993, as Larry
Mazer explains, "I had brought a little album

into Gene called *Hard to Believe,* which had
acts like Nirvana and Mudhoney performing
KISS songs. I told him: 'Isn't this great?' because
having current acts like that doing your material
really gives you some validity in certain circles.
He looked at it, and I could immediately see the
wheels begin to turn in his head and I thought,
'Uh oh.' That led to *KISS My Ass,* which I wasn't
really supportive of, and ultimately I left while
they were pulling the project together."

KISS My Ass was eventually released on June
21, 1994, though a limited red vinyl edition had
appeared in stores two weeks earlier. Featured
on the album were artists like Lenny Kravitz,
the Gin Blossoms, and Garth Brooks. To help
promote *KISS My Ass,* on July 13, KISS appeared
on *The Tonight Show with Jay Leno* with Garth
Brooks to perform "Hard Luck Woman." Paul
and Gene followed that up on July 26, by performing "Christine Sixteen" with the Gin Blossoms on the *Late Show with David Letterman.*
Earlier in the year, on March 17, Gene and
Paul had appeared in London to perform "Goin'
Blind" on *MTV's Most Wanted.*

Televison appearances aside, KISS performed
a total of 12 concerts during 1994: three one-off
shows in the U.S., followed by an eight-date tour
of South America and Mexico, and a fourth U.S.
one-off show in Phoenix in October.

The set lists for the shows were all quite similar, and without any new studio album to promote, a very heavy emphasis was placed on
1970s material once again.

The four one-off shows in the U.S. had a very
impromptu feel to them without much consis-
tency in production design. The first three shows
used almost no staging whatsoever outside of
whatever was brought in by the promoters. Surprisingly, for the fourth one-off show, in Phoenix,
KISS used most of the staging from the North
American leg of the Animalize Tour.

In Mexico and South America, KISS used a
scaled-back version of the Hot in the Shade stage.

Despite the loose vibe of the 1994 shows, the
band was exceptionally tight musically. Bruce
Kulick: "I thought that we were really good at
those shows, though I'm not sure what would
make those any different. Perhaps because we
weren't on tour, we blew off a lot of steam
during that one- show-per-month type of thing."

Villa Park (Chicago), Illinois
Odeum Sports and Exhibition Center
Opening Acts: I Mother Earth, Open Skyz, Screamin'
    Cheetah Wheelies, Stick
Attendance: 8,000   Capacity: 8,000
Promoter: WBLZ
Archived: Video
■ SET LIST
Deuce
Detroit Rock City
Calling Dr. Love
Strutter
Parasite
Got to Choose
Goin' Blind
Makin' Love
War Machine
Love Gun
I Love It Loud

I Stole Your Love
Black Diamond
Heaven's on Fire

■ This concert was part of an event called "Blaze Fest" which was organized by local radio station WBLZ "The Blaze." The station produced programs and handed out bumper stickers featuring the KISS logo to commemorate the event.

Eric Singer made his lead vocal debut during the performance of "Black Diamond" and Paul began breaking guitars on stage again at this gig.

Blaze Fest also included a David Lee Roth meet-and-greet elsewhere in the venue. Dave Ulrich was originally scheduled to open the show, but he did not perform.

APRIL 19, 1994

San Antonio, Texas
East Stage @ Joe & Harry Freeman Coliseum
Opening Acts: Lita Ford, Snake Dance
Attendance: 11,830   Capacity: 12,500
Promoter: San Antonio Jaycees
Archived: Video

■ SET LIST

Deuce
Detroit Rock City
Calling Dr. Love
Strutter
Parasite
Got to Choose
Goin' Blind
Lick It Up
I Stole Your Love
War Machine
Love Gun
Cold Gin
I Love it Loud
Makin' Love
Black Diamond
Heaven's On Fire

■ The East Stage was one of two stages set up in the Coliseum's parking lot.

This performance was part of the week-long "25th Anniversary Le Semana Alegre," held annually in San Antonio. Motörhead, Cheap Trick, Trapeze, Fem 2 Fem and even NKOTB (who had changed their name from New Kids On The Block) performed during other nights of the festival. Plastic cups commemorating the KISS concert were sold.

The guitar player in Lita Ford's band, John Lowery, would later go on to find success as a member of Marilyn Manson.

JULY 13, 1994

Burbank, California
Studio 3 @ NBC Studios
Archived: Video

■ SET LIST

Hard Luck Woman

■ This was the taping of KISS's appearance on *The Tonight Show with Jay Leno*. KISS performed as the back-up band for Garth Brooks, who sang lead vocals on "Hard Luck Woman."

JULY 30, 1994

Nashville, Tennessee
Riverfront Amphitheatre
Opening Acts: Fleetwood Mac, Pat Travers Band,
    Mother Station
Promoter: Pace Concerts Southeast
Archived: Video

■ SET LIST

Deuce
I Stole Your Love
Parasite
Domino
Got to Choose
Calling Dr. Love
Lick It Up
Strutter
She
Makin' Love
Goin' Blind

War Machine
Love Gun
I Love It Loud
Detroit Rock City
Black Diamond
Heaven's On Fire

This was Gibson Guitar's 100th Anniversary Concert and was held in conjunction with the annual Nashville NAMM Convention. Brother Cane was scheduled to perform after Mother Station, but they did not appear. As the name implies, the stage was built directly off of the Cumberland River, and a riverboat passed by during the concert giving patrons a free show. The big rumor of the day had Garth Brooks slated to appear with KISS, but the pairing never happened.

AUGUST 27, 1994

São Paulo, Brazil
Estádio do Pacaembu
Opening Acts: Black Sabbath, Slayer, Suicidal
    Tendencies, Viper, Raimundos, Dr. Sin, Angra
Attendance: 28,000   Capacity: 30,000
Archived: Video

■ SET LIST

Creatures of the Night
Deuce
Parasite
Unholy
I Stole Your Love
Cold Gin
Watchin' You
Firehouse
Got to Choose
Calling Dr. Love
Makin' Love
War Machine
Take It Off
Domino
Love Gun
Lick It Up
God of Thunder
I Love It Loud
Detroit Rock City
Black Diamond
Heaven's On Fire
[Rock and Roll All Nite]

■ This was the first of three Monsters of Rock concerts featuring KISS, Black Sabbath, and others. Philips, PolyGram's parent company, hosted a press conference for the band on August 25 at Maksoud Plaza.

Starting with this show and continuing through the February 14, 1995 concert in Sydney, Paul began lighting his guitar on fire before he smashed it.

MTV Argentina later broadcast an hour of the concert and the entire show was professionally archived.

AUGUST 28, 1994

São Paulo, Brazil
Programa Livra Studios
Archived: Video

■ SET LIST

Parasite

■ KISS taped a live performance of "Parasite" for the TV show *Programa Livra*.

SEPTEMBER 1, 1994

Santiago, Chile
Centro Cultural Estación Mapocho
Opening Acts: Black Sabbath, Slayer, Tumulto
Capacity: 12,000

Promoter: D.S. Medios Y Espectaculos S.S.
Archived: Video

■ **SET LIST**

Creatures of the Night
Deuce
Parasite
Unholy
I Stole Your Love
Cold Gin
Watchin' You
Firehouse
Calling Dr. Love
Makin' Love
War Machine
I Was Made for Lovin' You
I Want You
Domino
Love Gun
Lick It Up
God of Thunder
I Love It Loud
Detroit Rock City
Black Diamond
Heaven's On Fire
Rock and Roll All Nite

■ The second performance on the Monsters of Rock Tour featured a very scaled-back production. This concert was professionally archived on video, but was apparently never broadcast.

KISS flew into Chile on the evening of August 28. Prior to the show day, PolyGram Chile hosted a press conference for the band and KISS made an in-store appearance at a local record store.

The presence of both Slayer and Black Sabbath on the bill drew concern from local religious conservatives. To avoid the fallout caused by any controversy, KISS distanced themselves in the press from Black Sabbath.

SEPTEMBER 3, 1994

Buenos Aires, Argentina
Estadio Monumental de River Plate
Opening Acts: Black Sabbath, Slayer, Hermetica, Gatos Sucios
Attendance: 45,000   Capacity: 70,000
Promoter: Rock & Pop Int'l
Archived: Video

■ **SET LIST**

Creatures of the Night
Deuce
Parasite
Unholy
I Stole Your Love
Cold Gin
Watchin' You
Firehouse
I Want You
Calling Dr. Love
Makin' Love
War Machine
I Was Made for Lovin' You
Domino
Love Gun
Lick It Up
God of Thunder
I Love It Loud
Detroit Rock City
Black Diamond
Heaven's On Fire
Rock and Roll All Nite

■ Promoter Daniel Grinbak offered tickets at half price for those people wishing to exchange tickets from the three canceled Argentina concerts in 1983. Manowar was slated to appear on the bill prior to Slayer, but they canceled. This was the third and final Monsters of Rock concert.

60 minutes of this performance was broadcast on *The Big Ticket* over MuchMusic Argentina. Additionally, an audience member videotaped the entire concert.

SEPTEMBER 4, 1994

Buenos Aires, Argentina
Ritmo de la Noche Studios
Archived: Video

■ **SET LIST**

Heaven's On Fire
I Was Made for Lovin' You

■ KISS performed on television channel TELEFE for a show called *Ritmo de la Noche*.

SEPTEMBER 5, 1994

Buenos Aires, Argentina
Estadio Obras Sanitarias
No Opening Act
Attendance: 5,000   Capacity: 5,000
Promoter: Rock & Pop Int'l
Archived: Video

■ **SET LIST**

Creatures of the Night
Deuce
Parasite
Unholy
I Stole Your Love
Cold Gin
Watchin' You
Firehouse
I Want You
Calling Dr. Love
Makin' Love
Got to Choose
War Machine
I Was Made for Lovin' You
Domino
Love Gun
Lick It Up
God of Thunder
I Love It Loud
Detroit Rock City
Black Diamond
Heaven's On Fire
Rock and Roll All Nite

■ Paul played this show and the subsequent shows on the 8th and 15th with his hair in a ponytail.

SEPTEMBER 8, 1994

Ciudad de México, Mexico
Palacio de los Deportes
Opening Act: Victimas del Dr. Cerebro
Attendance: 14,789   Capacity: 16,500
Promoter: OCESA Presents
Archived: Audio

■ **SET LIST**

Creatures of the Night
Deuce
Parasite
Unholy
I Stole Your Love
Cold Gin
Watchin' You
Firehouse
I Was Made for Lovin' You
Calling Dr. Love
Makin' Love
La Bamba
War Machine
I Want You
Domino
Love Gun
Lick It Up
I Love It Loud

Detroit Rock City
Black Diamond
Heaven's On Fire
Rock and Roll All Nite

■ On the afternoon of the show, Paul and Eric appeared on a Mexican version of *Total Request Live*.

SEPTEMBER 14, 1994

Buenos Aires, Argentina
Estadio Obras Sanitarias
Opening Act: Logos
Attendance: 5,000   Capacity: 5,000
Promoter: Rock & Pop Int'l
Archived: Video

■ **SET LIST**

Love Gun
Deuce
Parasite
Unholy
100,000 Years
Cold Gin
Watchin' You
Firehouse
I Want You
I Was Made for Lovin' You
Calling Dr. Love
Makin' Love
Domino
Tears Are Falling
War Machine
Lick It Up
Forever
Creatures of the Night
I Love It Loud
Detroit Rock City
Black Diamond
Heaven's On Fire
Rock and Roll All Nite

SEPTEMBER 15, 1994

Buenos Aires, Argentina
Estadio Obras Sanitarias
Opening Act: Logos
Attendance: 5,000   Capacity: 5,000
Promoter: Rock & Pop Int'l
Archived: Audio, Partial Video

■ **SET LIST**

See September 14, 1994.

SEPTEMBER 16, 1994

Buenos Aires, Argentina
Estadio Obras Sanitarias
Opening Act: Logos
Attendance: 3,500   Capacity: 5,000
Promoter: Rock & Pop Int'l
Archived: Video

■ **SET LIST**

100,000 Years
Deuce
Strutter
Unholy
Cold Gin
Watchin' You
Firehouse
I Want You
I Was Made for Lovin' You
Calling Dr. Love
Makin' Love
Domino
Tears Are Falling
She
Lick It Up
Forever
Love Gun
I Love It Loud

Detroit Rock City
La Bamba
Black Diamond
Heaven's On Fire
Rock and Roll All Nite

■ This concert is unique, as it's the only time the band ever opened a performance with "100,000 Years."

OCTOBER 21, 1994

Phoenix, Arizona
Arizona Veterans Memorial Coliseum
No Opening Act
Attendance: 80% of capacity
Promoter: Evening Star Productions
Archived: Video

■ SET LIST

Creatures of the Night
Deuce
Parasite
Unholy
I Stole Your Love
Cold Gin
Watchin' You
Firehouse
I Was Made for Lovin' You
Calling Dr. Love
Makin' Love
Forever
Domino
I Want You
Love Gun
She
Lick It Up
I Love It Loud
Detroit Rock City
Black Diamond
Rock and Roll All Nite

■ The band used the U.S. Animalize Tour staging for this gig. As part of the Arizona State Fair, admission was free to those who purchased tickets to the fair, though an additional charge of $5 was added for those wishing to have reserved seating.

———————

In January 1995, after several more months of inactivity, KISS departed for tours of Japan and Australia.

A week prior to the start of the short Japanese tour, Japan had been ravaged by one of the worst earthquakes in its history. The earthquake, which was centered near Kobe, spawned massive conflagrations, with some sources estimating that over 300 fires and 500 deaths occurred. KISS recorded live versions of "Strutter" and "Rock Bottom" at a sound check before the January 30 concert in Tokyo for use on a KISS AID phone line set up to benefit victims of the earthquake. The boat carrying KISS's gear was docked in Osaka Harbor at the time of the earthquake, prompting concern that their gear had been lost.

The set list from the 1994 tour of South America was more-or-less retained for the tours of Japan and Australia, with one or two minor alterations such as the inclusion of "King of the Night Time World" in the show's opening slot. Additionally, for the concerts in Japan, KISS used the North American stage from the Animalize Tour and the KISS logo from Hot in the Shade was also featured in the production.

JANUARY 24, 1995

Osaka, Japan
Osaka Castle Hall

No Opening Act
Promoter: Udo Artists
Archived: Video

■ SET LIST

King of the Night Time World
Deuce
Shout It Out Loud
Parasite
Unholy
Creatures of the Night
Calling Dr. Love
Makin' Love
Tears Are Falling
Domino
I Was Made for Lovin' You
Watchin' You
Firehouse
I Want You
Love Gun
She
Lick It Up
Forever
I Love It Loud
Black Diamond
Detroit Rock City
Heaven's On Fire
God Gave Rock 'N' Roll to You II
Rock and Roll All Nite

■ Prior to "I Was Made for Lovin' You," brief sections of "C'mon and Love Me" and "Strutter" were performed. After "I Was Made for Lovin' You," Paul also played part of the "Sukiyaki Song."

A tourbook designed exclusively for the Japanese and Australian tours debuted at this gig.

JANUARY 26, 1995

Kitakushu (Fukuoka), Japan
Kyushu Koseinenkin Kaikan
No Opening Act
Promoter: Udo Artists
Archived: Audio

■ SET LIST

See January 24, 1995.

JANUARY 28, 1995

Nagoya, Japan
Nagoya Century Hall
No Opening Act
Promoter: Udo Artists
Archived: Video

■ SET LIST

King of the Night Time World
Deuce
Shout It Out Loud
Parasite
Unholy
Creatures of the Night
Calling Dr. Love
Makin' Love
Domino
I Was Made for Lovin' You
Watchin' You
Firehouse
I Want You
Love Gun
She
Lick It Up
Forever
I Love It Loud
Black Diamond
Detroit Rock City
Heaven's On Fire
God Gave Rock 'N' Roll to You II
Rock and Roll All Nite

■ During the middle of "I Want You" KISS briefly segued into the "Sukiyaki Song."

JANUARY 30, 1995

Tokyo, Japan
Nippon Budokan Hall
No Opening Act
Promoter: Udo Artists
Archived: Video

■ SET LIST

King of the Night Time World
Deuce
Shout It Out Loud
Parasite
Creatures of the Night
Calling Dr. Love
Makin' Love
Tears Are Falling
Domino
I Was Made for Lovin' You
Watchin' You
Firehouse
I Want You
Love Gun
She
Lick It Up
Forever
I Love It Loud
Black Diamond
Detroit Rock City
Heaven's On Fire
God Gave Rock 'N' Roll to You II
Rock and Roll All Nite

JANUARY 31, 1995

Tokyo, Japan
Nippon Budokan Hall
No Opening Act
Promoter: Udo Artists
Archived: Audio

■ SET LIST

See January 30, 1995.

———————

The tour of Australia, the band's first since 1980, was an alternating mix of large-venue electric shows and acoustic performances at conventions. (The acoustic performances will be discussed at length in the subsequent chapter.) For their more standard shows in Australia, the band once again opted to use a reduced version of the Hot in the Shade stage. Scaled production notwithstanding, KISS had considerable problems with the pyro effects during the Australian tour, and a pyrotechnician was fired after the Perth gig when most of the pyro effects were detonated off-cue.

The origins of the tour lay at the feet of Paul Drennan, the former editor of the Crazy Knights Fan Club in Australia. Drennan explains, "I work in the music industry and had lobbied for years to get promoters to consider bringing the band down to Australia. The fan club had conducted petition after petition, and I regularly published promoters' fax and phone numbers and I know that they received thousands of letters. And after a couple of aborted attempts in 1990 and again in 1993, I got a call from Michael Chugg at Frontier Touring to finally book some dates for early 1995 at the arena I worked at.

"Actually having worked on many tours with all of the promoters in Australia, I think that Frontier would agree that the 1995 KISS tour was one of the easiest and least-demanding of any shows they'd done. The band was so happy to be back in Australia after 15 years. Gene and Paul especially were excited.

"The day tickets went on sale, front-row tickets were given away to the best-dressed KISS fan—makeup, costume, whatever. We hired big screens at each of the venue box offices that morning, ran videos at each major ticket outlet, had sausage sizzles, etc.

"The media was very hot for them too; they were on the news as a major story each night. Their arrival in Perth from Japan was covered nationally. In Adelaide, the plane arrival was leaked out and there were about 600 fans waiting in the small terminal and the band were swamped, which they got a kick out of, especially as it made the papers the next day. After 15 years, there was still a huge demand for the band in this country. Local news covered absolutely everything. It was certainly more than most tours even today get. It was a very proud moment for the fans here to see this unfold."

FEBRUARY 4, 1995

Perth, Australia
Entertainment Centre
Opening Act: The Poor
Promoter: Frontier Touring
Archived: Audio

■ SET LIST

King of the Night Time World
Deuce
Shout It Out Loud
Parasite
Calling Dr. Love
Makin' Love
Tears Are Falling
Domino
Shandi
I Was Made for Lovin' You
Watchin' You
Firehouse
I Want You
Take It Off
Love Gun
She
Lick It Up
Forever
I Love It Loud
Black Diamond
Detroit Rock City
Heaven's On Fire
God Gave Rock 'N' Roll to You II
Rock and Roll All Nite

■ Paul Drennan: "When KISS arrived in Perth from Japan, each one of them had caught the flu. Gene was hit the worst, and I remember walking him into the meet-and-greet in Perth before the show and he looked so ill. He said to me he didn't know how he was going to do it that night. They didn't drop one song that night, and even though he was sweating like I've never seen him sweat, he pulled off an amazing show."

One of the more unusual aspects of the show was the performance of "Shandi," which had not been included in the band's set list since December 1980. Drennan elaborates, "The next day in the airport lounge, Gene walked up to me and asked what I thought of 'Shandi.' I explained that whilst I knew it wasn't a favorite of his, the Australian fans were into it. He wasn't convinced, and it didn't reappear for the rest of the tour, unfortunately."

FEBRUARY 6, 1995

Adelaide, Australia
Adelaide Entertainment Centre
Opening Act: The Poor
Attendance: 6,596   Capacity: 7,274
Promoter: Frontier Touring
Archived: Audio

■ SET LIST

King of the Night Time World
Deuce
Shout It Out Loud
Parasite
Unholy
Creatures of the Night
Calling Dr. Love
Makin' Love
Tears Are Falling
Domino
I Was Made for Lovin' You
Take It Off
Watchin' You
Firehouse
I Want You
Love Gun
She

Lick It Up
Forever
I Love It Loud
Black Diamond
Detroit Rock City
Heaven's On Fire
God Gave Rock 'N' Roll to You II
Rock and Roll All Nite

FEBRUARY 8, 1995

Melbourne, Australia
National Tennis Centre @ Flinders Park
Opening Act: The Poor
Attendance: Sold Out
Promoter: Frontier Touring
Archived: Audio

■ SET LIST

King of the Night Time World
Deuce
Shout It Out Loud
Unholy
Creatures of the Night
Calling Dr. Love
Makin' Love
Tears Are Falling
Domino

I Was Made for Lovin' You
Take It Off
Watchin' You
Firehouse
I Want You
Love Gun
[She]
[Lick It Up]
[Forever]
[I Love It Loud]
[Black Diamond]
[Detroit Rock City]
[Heaven's On Fire]
[God Gave Rock 'N' Roll to You II]
[Rock and Roll All Nite]

FEBRUARY 9, 1995

Melbourne, Australia
National Tennis Centre @ Flinders Park
Opening Act: The Poor
Promoter: Frontier Touring
Archived: Video
■ SET LIST
King of the Night Time World
Deuce
Shout It Out Loud

Unholy
Creatures of the Night
Calling Dr. Love
Makin' Love
Tears Are Falling
Domino
I Was Made for Lovin' You
Take It Off
Watchin' You
Firehouse
I Want You
Love Gun
She
Lick It Up
Forever
I Love It Loud
Black Diamond
Detroit Rock City
Heaven's On Fire
God Gave Rock 'N' Roll to You II
Rock and Roll All Nite
■ Due to Gene's lingering cold, "Parasite" was dropped from the set list at this show.

FEBRUARY 11, 1995

Brisbane, Australia

Entertainment Centre
Opening Act: The Poor
Promoter: Frontier Touring

FEBRUARY 13, 1995

Sydney, Australia
Entertainment Centre
Opening Act: The Poor
Promoter: Frontier Touring
Archived: Video
■ SET LIST
See February 9, 1995.

FEBRUARY 14, 1995

Sydney, Australia
Entertainment Centre
Opening Act: The Poor
Promoter: Frontier Touring
■ While no set list is currently available, this was likely the final live performance of "Creatures of the Night," "Domino," "Forever," "God Gave Rock 'N' Roll to You II," "I Want You," "Take It Off," "Tears Are Falling," and "Unholy."

KISS sets Australia ablaze, February 1995.

CHAPTER 23

CONVENTION TOUR

Number of Shows: 32
Start Date: February 3, 1995 - Perth, Australia
End Date: December 12, 1995 - Hollywood, California
Countries: Australia, Canada, U.S.A.
Opening/Tribute Bands: Alive!; Black Diamond; Cold Gin; Desstroyer; Dynissty; Gene's Addiction; Hotter Than Hell; Karissma; Rock 'n' Roll Over; Strutter; Unmasked; Wicked Lester

In the past, KISS had generally disdained the idea of dwelling on the enormous shadow that their 1970s' success cast, always quickly squelching reunion rumors, and purposefully focusing on their current material, which they naturally claimed was their best yet. Then, in 1990, and even more so in 1992 after the poor showing of the *Revenge* album and tour, KISS began to focus increasingly on their past in an attempt to appeal to their hardcore fanbase. The 1995 conventions would mark the height of KISS's efforts towards that end.

The 26 acoustic concerts KISS performed at their official conventions in 1995 comprise the most unusual tour in the band's history. At the conventions, KISS embraced the demands of their fanbase to such a degree that the events were arguably designed to the exclusion of anyone but the most zealous of KISS fans. The admission fee itself, a then-exorbitant $100, was as much a tactic to limit attendance and create a sense of exclusivity for the attendees as it was to generate revenue.

The sense of exclusivity started immediately with KISS laminates being issued in place of tickets. The ticketing concept was the brainchild of Tommy Thayer, former guitarist in Black 'N Blue and KISS cover band Cold Gin. Thayer, who had worked on the band's retrospective book *KISSTORY*, had been hired as tour manager for the conventions though he eventually became a jack-of-all-trades for the band, much like Fritz Postlethwaite had been in the 1970s.

KISS's conventions were typically held at hotels or convention centers, and while they were missing the amusement park rides and circus tents of 1979's KISS World concept, the multi-attraction, day-long events were the closest thing to that aborted extravaganza that KISS would ever produce. One of the feature attractions was a KISS museum where fans could view memorabilia from throughout the band's career. Among the many items ensconced in Plexiglas were some of the band's original costumes from the 1970s and '80s (including Eric Carr's abandoned Hawk outfit). The costumes and their accessories (the latter often being replicas of the original items) were displayed on mannequins whose faces were painted with KISS makeup applied by Paul Stanley and Tommy Thayer. Also on display were instruments that the band had used over the years, concert posters, stage schematics, a collection of magazine covers featuring KISS, and a host of other miscellaneous items.

Merchandise was another important facet of the events, as KISS's merchandise machine, mostly dormant over the past 15 years, was slowly beginning to operate again. By January 1995, KISS had signed an agreement with Sony Signatures to handle their merchandising. Sony initially expanded the assortment of KISS merchandise to include such items as Gold records and leather jackets. They also began to market several items featuring the original lineup, which often ironically included the then current lineup's autographs.

Competing with the official KISS merchandise available, independent dealers had tables of merchandise set up throughout the hallways and/or smaller rooms at the venues. Not only did the band allow the direct competition to peddle their merchandise at the conventions, the band's monitoring of the dealers' sales was occasionally so lax that bootleg CDs and videos were also sold at some of the conventions.

Inside the main room of the conventions—typically a large ballroom—slide and video shows would run throughout the day. At the North American conventions, both Bruce and Eric were given the main stage to do guitar and drum clinics, respectively. (In Australia, the clinics had been held in smaller antechambers of the hotels, if at all.) This would usually be followed by the performance of a KISS tribute band.

A question-and-answer session with KISS was the prelude to the highlight of the convention: a lengthy acoustic performance by the band. The performances were the antithesis of a typical KISS concert: for the duration of the sets Paul and Bruce used electro-acoustic guitars (though Gene used an electric bass), and, short of a vinyl banner or two, there was no production design whatsoever.

KISS had rehearsed a number of songs for their acoustic performances, but there was very little, if any, consistent order to the set list from show to show. The band took requests from the audience which, not surprisingly, were often for the oldest, most obscure songs in the KISS catalog, many of which had either never been performed live or had not been in a set list in 15–20 years.

After the epic acoustic sets, the band would do lengthy meet-and-greets with fans, signing autographs, chatting with the attendees, and often not departing for their hotel rooms for a minimum of 60 minutes.

NICO CICCARONE/ WWW.NICOSTRIKE.COM

The first conventions were scheduled for Japan and Australia in January and February 1995, where KISS's concerts in the two countries would alternate between conventions one day and full-blown arena shows the next. The conventions initially scheduled for Japan were never booked, presumably for logistical reasons, but the conventions in Australia and, with two exceptions, the performances in North America in the summer, went on as planned.

Paul Drennan played a significant role in organizing the Australian conventions for KISS. "When the dates were set," Drennan recalls, "Gene contacted me about working on the conventions with them after the promoter had recommended me. The concepts were very vague initially, other than that Gene was absolutely determined to make them worthwhile and worth the entry money. I remember in a conference call between the promoter, Gene, and myself that the promoter expressed the idea that 12 hours was possibly too long a day. Gene's response was, 'I'd rather people say it was too long than too short.'

"I was introduced over the phone to Tommy Thayer, and we started to formulate the run sheet for the day, between tribute bands, merchandise tables, Q & A sessions, and clinics. Gene at that point had no idea how long the acoustic sets would be, nor did he know how long they would sign for. We had many, many discussions on how to ensure that the majority of fans got to meet the band and get an autograph, from forming formal queues to what ultimately happened, which was everyone jockeying for position. It was decided to do that because if there was a queue and the band had done an hour of signing and needed to leave, no one would be seen as missing out.

"Backstage after the first unplugged show in Perth, the band was really excited, you could tell that they had a ball playing songs like 'Magic Touch' and others that, even if they couldn't finish them, they had hit on an idea that was fun for them and the fans."

KISS and Frontier Touring handled promotion for the conventions in Australia jointly. The entire run of North American conventions was booked by Gene and Tommy Thayer, which allowed KISS the opportunity to have total creative control over the events. And while specific attendance and revenue figures were never made public, the lack of ancillary businesses involved—namely promoters and booking agents—coupled with the small production expenses of the acoustic sets, certainly made this a very lucrative tour for KISS.

Roughly coinciding with the break between the Australian and North American legs of the tour, the Internet exploded from its status as an obscure government and scholastic network into a very public communications revolution. Two very prominent KISS Web sites appeared during this timeframe, first KISS OTAKU and soon after, KISS ASYLUM. The advent of the Internet, these two sites, and the USENET and AOL newsgroups in particular, allowed KISS fans access to information on the band on an almost instantaneous basis.

Due to their unorganized and almost totally impromptu nature, the set lists for the Convention Tour are difficult to archive. While there were many numbers that the band had obviously rehearsed and were played in their entirety, the convention performances were filled with attempts at dozens of songs. The attempts varied widely in terms of length and band/audience participation: some were performed by the entire band, some by only one member, while others were done with the audience or a lone audience member providing most of the vocals. In other instances, songs were represented by nothing more than a riff or a note or two. To help clarify which songs were performed in their entirety and which were merely attempted, we've developed the following notation:

1. In instances where two asterisks (**) appear, this means that less than (roughly) 20 seconds of the song was performed. This includes cases where a band member sang part of a verse, where a riff was played once or twice, or even something as brief as the opening few chords of a song.

2. Songs listed with a single asterisk (*) after their names were attempted, but not performed in their entirety. This indicates that a reasonable attempt was made to perform the song.

3. Songs listed by title without additional notation were played in their entirety, or very close to it. In some instances, such as with "Black Diamond," songs were purposefully performed with a shorter arrangement. In all such cases, the song is considered to be complete.

Also note that for the North American leg of the tour, the "archived" listing has been omitted from each concert. Every North American concert on the Convention Tour was privately archived on videotape since the band permitted the taping of the concerts to occur. Lastly, since KISS exclusively promoted all of the North American conventions, and jointly promoted the Australian conventions with Frontier Touring, the promoter listing has been eliminated altogether.

FEBRUARY 3, 1995

Perth, Australia
Hyatt Hotel
Tribute Band: Karissma
Archived: Audio
■ SET LIST
Strutter
Hard Luck Woman
Radioactive**
Shandi
Forever
Domino
Do You Love Me*
Lick It Up
Rock Bottom
Charisma**
I Still Love You
Cold Gin**
Hotel California**
Black Diamond
All the Way*
Sure Know Something**
Heaven's On Fire**
Detroit Rock City
Down on the Corner**
Let Me Know*
Magic Touch*
Every Time I Look at You**
Room Service**
God Gave Rock 'N' Roll to You II**

Nothin' to Lose
I Love It Loud
Got to Choose
■ On the day prior to the convention in Perth, KISS held a press conference at the Hyatt Hotel.

Thirty minutes of this show were broadcast on Australian radio station Triple J. Eric Singer sang lead vocals on "Nothin' to Lose" in Perth and would continue to do so throughout the tour.

FEBRUARY 5, 1995

Adelaide, Australia
Hilton Hotel
Tribute Band: Unmasked
Archived: Audio
■ SET LIST
Strutter
Domino
Shandi
La Bamba**
Goin' Blind
I Still Love You
Let Me Know*
Cold Gin**
Rock Bottom
Beth**
Fits Like a Glove**
I Love It Loud
Got to Choose
Magic Touch*
Nothin' to Lose**
Calling Dr. Love
Plaster Caster**
Forever
Larger Than Life**
All the Way*
Comin' Home*
Mr. Speed *
Take Me
A World Without Heroes
Just a Boy**
Charisma**
Do You Love Me*
Hotter Than Hell
Cold Gin
■ Paul Drennan: "The Australian conventions went on sale just after the arena shows, as we were still working through some issues in some hotels in terms of noise and liquor licensing. Thankfully, after the second convention, we made the events 'dry' after some drunk fans just could not shut up through the Q & A sessions and persisted in screaming 'I love you guys!!' or 'Gene, Gene, Gene...' non-stop."

FEBRUARY 7, 1995

Melbourne, Australia
Hilton Hotel
Tribute Band: Dynissty
Archived: Audio
■ SET LIST
Strutter
Goin' Blind
Shandi
Nowhere to Run**
Rock Bottom
Watchin' You**
I Was Made for Lovin' You**
I Still Love You
Plaster Caster**
Domino
Magic Touch**
I Love It Loud
Got to Choose

Christine Sixteen**
Black Diamond
Cold Gin**
Oh Susannah
Hard Luck Woman
C'mon and Love Me**
Magic Touch**
Love Gun**
I Was Made for Lovin' You**
A World Without Heroes
Just a Boy**
Take Me
Hide Your Heart**
Room Service*
Two Timer**
Do You Love Me*
Crazy Crazy Nights**
Unholy
Shout It Out Loud**
Spit**
Shout It Out Loud
Forever
Love Her All I Can*
Comin' Home**
Nothin' to Lose
When You Wish Upon a Star**
Comin' Home*
Flaming Youth*
Mr. Speed*
Parasite**
All American Man**
Move On**
Tonight You Belong to Me**
Strange Ways**
Lick It Up**
Rock and Roll All Nite**
Sure Know Something*
Lick It Up

FEBRUARY 10, 1995

Brisbane, Australia
Hilton Hotel
Tribute Band: Wicked Lester
Archived: Audio, Partial Video
■ SET LIST
Strutter
Goin' Blind
Got to Choose
C'mon and Love Me*
Hard Luck Woman
A World Without Heroes
Rock Bottom
Love Gun**
Black Diamond
Help!**
Shandi
Love Her All I Can*
Forever
Oh Susannah
Domino
I Still Love You**
I Stole Your Love
Nothin' to Lose
100,000 Years**
Room Service*
New York Groove*
Torpedo Girl**
I Want You**
Strange Ways**
I Want You

■ The tribute band that performed at this show obviously bore no relation to Paul and Gene's pre-KISS band of the same name.

FEBRUARY 12, 1995

Sydney, Australia
Hilton Hotel
No Tribute Band
Archived: Audio
■ SET LIST
Strutter
Goin' Blind
Hard Luck Woman
I Still Love You**
I Stole Your Love
I**
A World Without Heroes
Shandi
Take Me**
Plaster Caster
Take Me
All the Way**
Love Theme from KISS**
Room Service**
Spit*
Tonight You Belong to Me*
Sure Know Something**
Forever
Nothin' to Lose
C'mon and Love Me
2,000 Man*
Rock Bottom
Domino
Comin' Home**
Take It Off*
Comin' Home*
Got to Choose
Every Time I Look at You
Black Diamond

■ Dynissty was scheduled to be the tribute band at this convention, but they canceled.

JUNE 16, 1995

West Hollywood, California
Hard Rock Cafe
No Opening Act
■ SET LIST
Hard Luck Woman
Domino
Every Time I Look at You

■ On June 16, KISS held a press conference at the Hard Rock Cafe in West Hollywood to kick off the North American leg of the tour. Following the 12 P.M. press conference, KISS played a three-song acoustic set.

JUNE 17, 1995

Burbank, California
Hilton and Convention Center
Tribute Band: Cold Gin
■ SET LIST
Comin' Home
Rock Bottom
Plaster Caster
C'mon and Love Me
Domino
Do You Love Me
Let Me Know**
A World Without Heroes
Shandi
Goin' Blind
Got to Choose
All American Man**
See You Tonite
Goodbye
Hard Luck Woman
Love Theme From KISS**
Nothin' to Lose

Take Me
Calling Dr. Love
Almost Human**
Camptown Races**
Winchester Cathedral**
I Still Love You

■ Peter Criss initially asked Gene for permission to bring his daughter Jenilee to the event, and Gene generously offered to give them a limousine to the convention. But what was supposed to be a casual appearance turned into the highlight of the day. First, Peter did a Q & A session with Gerri Miller from Metal Edge. Then, during the acoustic set, Peter sang "Hard Luck Woman" and "Nothin' to Lose" with the band. As spontaneous as it may have appeared, Peter's performance was not a spur-of-the moment decision as Peter had rehearsed with the band earlier in the week.

For the press, Gene played up the fact that Eric Singer had suggested the idea of Peter joining KISS on stage. Bruce Kulick explains: "I think Gene liked to look at it that way just to ease the pain. It was very unfair to say: 'Our current drummer, Eric, asked Peter to come down.' That would be an oversimplification. Eric welcomed having those guys back, but he also never thought that Peter could do a reunion tour."

Also appearing and doing a brief Q & A session were former KISS producers Michael James Jackson and Kenny Kerner.

During KISS's Q & A session, a member of the audience asked if it was permissible to videotape the show. Surprisingly, the band said yes, but asked that any recordings made of the performance not be sold.

Beginning in Burbank, the end of "Do You Love Me" was heavily rearranged and now sounded much more akin to the version on Destroyer than KISS's 1970s live arrangement of the song had.

JUNE 18, 1995

San Francisco, California
Gift Center Pavilion
Tribute Bands: Cold Gin, Desstroyer
■ SET LIST
Magic Touch**
Comin' Home
Plaster Caster
Parasite**
Take Me
A World Without Heroes
Nowhere to Run*
C'mon and Love Me
Do You Love Me
We Can Work It Out**
See You Tonite
Got to Choose
100,000 Years**
God of Thunder**
Unholy **
Domino
Never On a Sunday**
Hard Luck Woman
Love Her All I Can**
Sure Know Something
Shout It Out Loud**
Goin' Blind
Only You**
Rock Bottom
God Gave Rock 'N' Roll to You II
Heaven's On Fire
Almost Human**

Rockin' in the USA**
Sure Know Something**
All the Way *
Room Service**
Goodbye
Nothin' to Lose
Black Diamond
Christine Sixteen**
Charisma**
Almost Human**
Anything for My Baby**
Room Service*
Under the Rose**
All Hell's Breakin' Loose**
Forever
Acrobat*
I Still Love You
She
Fits Like a Glove**
I Love It Loud

■ Much to the amusement of the crowd and his bandmates, Bruce got the show got off to a rousing start by taking the stage and then promptly disappearing to use the bathroom. Note: The "Only You" listed in the set list is the song made famous by The Platters, not the KISS song "Only You."

JUNE 20, 1995

Seattle, Washington
Seattle Center
Tribute Band: Gene's Addiction
■ SET LIST
All American Man**
Comin' Home
Mr. Speed*
Plaster Caster
Young and Wasted**
C'mon and Love Me**
Do You Love Me
Domino
Got to Choose
A World Without Heroes
C'mon and Love Me
Nothin' to Lose
I Want You
Goin' Blind
Almost Human**
Take Me
See You Tonite
Hard Luck Woman
Ladies in Waiting**
Christine Sixteen**
Black Diamond
War Machine/Sex Type Thing**
I Still Love You
Birthday**
Rock Bottom
Birthday**
Forever
All the Way**
Shandi*
Let Me Know**
Birthday**
Goodbye
I Love It Loud
Calling Dr. Love
God of Thunder* (country version)
Hotter Than Hell

■ Tribute band Gene's Addiction did not perform until after KISS finished their meet-and-greet. In this and all subsequent instances, when "War Machine/Sex Type Thing" is cited, the lyrics to Stone Temple Pilot's "Sex Type Thing" were sung over the music to "War Machine."

JUNE 22, 1995

Salt Lake City, Utah
Utah State Fairpark
Tribute Band: Alive!
■ SET LIST
Goin' Blind
Comin' Home
Almost Human**
A World Without Heroes
Rock Bottom
Domino
C'mon and Love Me
Plaster Caster
Do You Love Me
Sweet Pain**
Two Timer*
I Love It Loud
Hotter Than Hell
Firehouse
Nothin' to Lose
A Million to One**
I Still Love You
See You Tonite
God of Thunder* (country version)
Torpedo Girl**
Take Me**
Every Time I Look at You**
Hard Luck Woman
Take Me Away (Together As One)**
Goodbye
Love 'em and Leave 'em*
Love 'em and Leave 'em*
Christine Sixteen
Black Diamond
Let's Put the X in Sex*
100,000 Years
Unholy**
Got to Choose**
Detroit Rock City**
I Want You

■ Alive! performed after KISS's meet and greet.

JUNE 24, 1995

Las Vegas, Nevada
Sahara
Tribute Band: Cold Gin
■ SET LIST
Comin' Home
Got Love for Sale**
Plaster Caster
C'mon and Love Me**
A Million to One**
C'mon and Love Me
Domino
Sure Know Something
Magic Touch*
Do You Love Me
Parasite**
A World Without Heroes
Got to Choose**
Shandi
Then She Kissed Me**
Nothin' to Lose
Rock Bottom
Charisma**
Almost Human**
Charisma*
Let's Put the X in Sex*
See You Tonite
Love in Chains**
Take It Off**
I**
Move On**
Goodbye
I Was Made for Lovin' You **

Goin' Blind
All the Way*
Forever
Makin' Love
War Machine/Sex Type Thing**
Christine Sixteen
Let Me Know*
Hard Luck Woman
I Was Made for Lovin' You
Calling Dr. Love
100,000 Years
She
Black Diamond*
God of Thunder* (country version)
I Stole Your Love**
Got to Choose
Rock and Roll Hell*
Watchin' You**
Take Me

■ Paul brought his infant son Evan out on stage during the acoustic set.

JUNE 25, 1995

Phoenix, Arizona
Hyatt Regency Phoenix
Tribute Band: Alive!
■ SET LIST
Plaster Caster
Mr. Speed
Comin' Home
Larger Than Life**
Sure Know Something
A World Without Heroes
Flaming Youth**
Unholy**
C'mon and Love Me
Christine Sixteen
I Want You**
Parasite**(country version)
Hard Luck Woman
Nothin' to Lose
Got to Choose
Unholy**
God of Thunder* (country version)
Unholy**
Domino
Goodbye
God Gave Rock 'N' Roll to You II**
See You Tonite**
War Machine/Sex Type Thing**
See You Tonite
Rock Bottom
Love Theme from KISS**
Calling Dr. Love
Let's Put the X in Sex*
I Love It Loud
Do You Love Me
Black Diamond
I Want You
Goin' Blind
All the Way**
I Still Love You
All the Way*
King of the Night Time World
Heaven's On Fire
God Gave Rock 'N' Roll to You II
Rock and Roll All Nite

JULY 1, 1995   CANCELED

Houston, Texas
Hobby Airport Hilton
■ Ticket holders were told that their tickets would be honored at the Dallas convention on July 2nd. The band claimed logistical problems forced the cancellation of the convention.

JULY 2, 1995

Irving (Dallas), Texas
Dallas/Fort Worth Airport Marriot
Tribute Band: Black Diamond
■ SET LIST

C'mon and Love Me
Plaster Caster
Room Service*
Comin' Home
Goin' Blind
Do You Love Me
All American Man**
Smoke on the Water**
Domino
Hard Luck Woman
100,000 Years
Let's Put the X in Sex**
Sure Know Something
Larger Than Life*
See You Tonite
Nothin' to Lose
War Machine**
I**
A World Without Heroes
Let's Put the X in Sex*
God of Thunder**
Mr. Speed*
Take Me
God of Thunder* (country version)
Oh Susannah**
Sweet Home Alabama**
War Machine/Sex Type Thing**
Makin' Love
I**
Love Her All I Can*
Christine Sixteen
Forever
Calling Dr. Love**
I'm So Bad*
Calling Dr. Love
I Want You
Almost Human**
I Still Love You
Charisma**
Charisma**
Tonight You Belong to Me*
Black Diamond
Rock Bottom
All the Way*
She**
Shandi
Great Expectations**
Cold Gin*
Rock and Roll All Nite

■ The Paul in the tribute band Black Diamond was, oddly enough, managed by Paul Stanley himself. Jason McMaster of the band Dangerous Toys impressed the other audience members when he did a masterful job singing the end of "I Want You" during KISS's acoustic set.

JULY 4, 1995   CANCELED

New Orleans, Louisiana
Radisson
■ Like the canceled Houston convention, people holding tickets for the New Orleans convention were rerouted to Dallas.

JULY 6, 1995

Miami, Florida
Radisson Mart Plaza
Tribute Band: Hotter Than Hell
■ SET LIST

Comin' Home
Goin' Blind

Do You Love Me
Sure Know Something
Strutter
Plaster Caster
Let Me Know**
Got to Choose
All American Man**
Christine Sixteen
Hard Luck Woman
Domino
C'mon and Love Me
Just a Boy**
A World Without Heroes
Mr. Blackwell**
Room Service*
Take Me
Nothin' to Lose
Hotter Than Hell**
I Want You**
Rock Bottom
Heaven's On Fire**
See You Tonite**
Unholy**
See You Tonite
Larger Than Life*
I Still Love You
Lick It Up
Then She Kissed Me**
Unholy**
Calling Dr. Love
Cold Gin
Hide Your Heart
Nowhere to Run**
I Love It Loud
Rock and Roll All Nite

JULY 8, 1995

Atlanta, Georgia
Hilton/Towers
Tribute Band: Hotter Than Hell
■ SET LIST

Comin' Home
Let Me Go, Rock 'n Roll**
Goin' Blind
C'mon and Love Me
Calling Dr. Love
Nowhere to Run*
Do You Love Me
Domino
Sure Know Something
Anything for My Baby**
A World Without Heroes
Got to Choose**
Larger Than Life**
Got to Choose**
Nothin' to Lose
Got to Choose
Every Time I Look at You
Plaster Caster
Rock Bottom
Two Timer*
Black Diamond
100,000 Years**
Take Me Away (Together As One)*
Hard Luck Woman
Unholy**
Take It Off
100,000 Years
I Love It Loud
See You Tonite**
Goodbye
See You Tonite
I Still Love You
Christine Sixteen
Heaven's On Fire
Lick It Up

Rock and Roll All Nite
Cold Gin

■ To promote the convention, Gene and Paul were interviewed via satellite on the local TV program Good Morning Atlanta.

JULY 9, 1995

Nashville, Tennessee
Nashville Convention Center
Tribute Band: Hotter Than Hell
■ SET LIST

Rockin' in the USA**
Comin Home
Plaster Caster
Unholy**
Mr. Speed*
Domino**
Goin' Blind
Sure Know Something
Two Timer*
C'mon and Love Me
Fits Like a Glove**
See You Tonite**
Take Me
All the Way**
Nowhere to Run**
Domino
Do You Love Me
Down on the Corner**
She
Hard Luck Woman
Rock Bottom
Nothin' to Lose
Unholy**
A World Without Heroes
See You Tonite**
Calling Dr. Love
Shandi
See You Tonite
Got to Choose**
All American Man**
Got to Choose**
Let's Put the X in Sex*
God of Thunder* (country version)
Got to Choose
War Machine
I Still Love You
Christine Sixteen
Forever
Anything for My Baby**
Heaven's On Fire
100,000 Years**
Strutter
Lick It Up
Rock and Roll All Nite
I Love It Loud

JULY 11, 1995

St. Louis, Missouri
Airport Hilton
Tribute Band: Hotter Than Hell
■ SET LIST

Do You Love Me
Comin' Home
I**
A World Without Heroes
Let Me Know*
Take Me
Domino
Mr. Blackwell**
Rock Bottom
Mr. Speed*
Nothin' to Lose
Firehouse
Goin' Blind
Sure Know Something**

Hard Luck Woman
Plaster Caster
Sure Know Something
Calling Dr. Love
Mr. Blackwell**
Got to Choose
Love Her All I Can**
God of Thunder (country version)
Shandi
See You Tonite
Take Me Away (Together As One)**
Makin' Love
Christine Sixteen
Love Theme from KISS*
I Still Love You
Black Diamond
I Want You

JULY 12, 1995
St. Louis, Missouri
KSHE Cool Rock Café
No Opening Act
Promoter: KSHE
■ SET LIST
Hotter Than Hell
Hard Luck Woman

■ The day after the convention, the band did a short question-and-answer session for an on-air interview on KSHE, and then did a very brief acoustic set. An attendee reported that approximately 200 people attended the event.

JULY 13, 1995
Indianapolis, Indiana
Ramada Plaza
Tribute Band: Strutter
■ SET LIST
Comin' Home
Domino
C'mon and Love Me
Got to Choose
A World Without Heroes
Let Me Go, Rock 'n Roll*
Do You Love Me
Nothin' to Lose
Let's Put the X in Sex*
Calling Dr. Love
Rock Bottom
Two Timer*
Goin' Blind
Sure Know Something
Christine Sixteen
Hard Luck Woman
Mr. Speed*
Watchin' You**
See You Tonite
Goodbye
Tears Are Falling
God of Thunder* (country version)
Take Me
Plaster Caster
I Still Love You
Black Diamond
Heaven's On Fire
Lick It Up**
Watchin' You**
I Love It Loud
Detroit Rock City
Rock and Roll All Nite

■ KISS Army founder Bill Starkey, who was attending his first KISS show since 1978, was a surprise guest speaker and briefly joined the band onstage during their Q & A session.

JULY 15, 1995
Schaumburg (Chicago), Illinois
Hyatt Woodfield
Tribute Band: Strutter
Attendance: Sold Out
■ SET LIST
C'mon and Love Me
War Machine**
Comin' Home
Nothin' to Lose
Domino
Take Me
Mr. Blackwell**
Goin' Blind
Do You Love Me
Let Me Know*
Sure Know Something
Calling Dr. Love
I**
Room Service**
Love Her All I Can**
I**
Uh! All Night**
Plaster Caster
Heart of Chrome**
Hard Luck Woman
Take It Off**
Christine Sixteen**
A World Without Heroes
100,000 Years
Rock Bottom
Makin' Love
Cold Gin
Got to Choose
Christine Sixteen
I Still Love You
Spit*
God of Thunder* (country version)
Then She Kissed Me**
I Want You
Let's Put the X in Sex*
Firehouse**
See You Tonite*
Mr. Speed*
Love 'em and Leave 'em**
She
Heaven's On Fire
I Love It Loud
Lick It Up
Rock and Roll All Nite

■ The tribute band Strutter did not appear until the very end of the event. The truck carrying their staging was delayed and did not arrive in time for the band to go on as scheduled.

JULY 16, 1995
Bloomington (Minneapolis), Minnesota
Radisson South & Plaza
Tribute Band: Strutter
■ SET LIST
Comin' Home
Christine Sixteen
Take Me
A World Without Heroes
Shandi
Nothin' to Lose
Uh! All Night**
Do You Love Me
Domino
Got to Choose
Calling Dr. Love
Love Her All I Can*
Sure Know Something
Rock and Roll Hell*
Crazy Crazy Nights*

Mr. Speed**
Flaming Youth**
Mr. Speed*
Plaster Caster
Hard Luck Woman
Burn Bitch Burn*
Black Diamond
Rock Bottom
Hide Your Heart
God of Thunder* (country version)
Unholy*
C'mon and Love Me
Heart of Chrome*
Spit*
Goin' Blind
100,000 Years
I Still Love You
Heaven's On Fire
Cold Gin
I Love It Loud
Lick It Up
Rock and Roll All Nite

■ Strutter's performance was again delayed until the end of the convention.

JULY 22, 1995
Detroit, Michigan
Cobo Conference and Exhibition Center
Tribute Band: Alive!
■ SET LIST
Comin' Home
Plaster Caster
Take Me
Almost Human**
Anything for My Baby**
Goin' Blind
Nothin' to Lose
War Machine/Sex Type Thing**
Love Her All I Can**
Domino
Room Service*
Got to Choose
A World Without Heroes
Do You Love Me
All American Man*
Christine Sixteen
Hard Luck Woman
God Gave Rock 'N' Roll to You II**
Calling Dr. Love
C'mon and Love Me
Let's Put the X in Sex**
She
Bad Moon Rising**
God of Thunder* (country version)
Rock Bottom
Mr. Speed*
Spit*
Sure Know Something
Hide Your Heart*
Let's Put the X in Sex*
Domino**
Let's Put the X in Sex
I Still Love You
Heaven's On Fire
Lick It Up
I Love It Loud
Detroit Rock City
Rock and Roll All Nite**
Do You Love Me
Forever

■ This show was taped by Z-Rock radio for a future broadcast, but it never aired.

In what may have been the highlight of the tour, a nine-year old girl filled in on lead vocals for Paul during the final attempt at "Let's Put the

X in Sex" and did such an amazing job that she received a standing ovation. Later, her younger brother Patrick joined the band on stage and played drums during the second performance of "Do You Love Me," which also brought the crowd to its feet.

JULY 23, 1995

Cleveland, Ohio
Sheraton City Centre
Tribute Band: Strutter

■ SET LIST

Comin' Home
Goin' Blind
Nowhere to Run*
Sure Know Something
Spit*
Take It Off**
Nothin' to Lose
A World Without Heroes
Room Service**
Love Her All I Can*
Do You Love Me
Domino
Shandi
Rockin' in the USA**
Rip and Destroy**
Take Me
Kissin' Time*
Plaster Caster**
Calling Dr. Love
Got to Choose
Uh! All Night**
Strange Ways*
Shock Me**
Rock Bottom
God of Thunder* (country version)
See You Tonite
Mr. Speed**
Magic Touch*
Goodbye
Christine Sixteen**
She's So European**
Christine Sixteen
Hard Luck Woman
Let's Put the X in Sex**
I*
Let's Put the X in Sex
Mr. Speed**
C'mon and Love Me**
Watchin' You**
C'mon and Love Me
Plaster Caster
Just a Boy**
I Still Love You
All the Way*
Under the Rose**
100,000 Years
Heaven's On Fire
Lick It Up
Firehouse**
Cold Gin
Mr. Speed*
Rock and Roll All Nite
I Love It Loud
Detroit Rock City

■ A wedding took place during the convention; Gene gave away the bride.

JULY 25, 1995

Toronto, Ontario, Canada
Hilton International
Tribute Band: Alive!

■ SET LIST

Sure Know Something**
Rock Bottom

Plaster Caster
Comin' Home
Goin' Blind
Sure Know Something
Take Me
Domino
Do You Love Me
Sweet Pain*
C'mon and Love Me
Hide Your Heart
Burn Bitch Burn**
Let Me Know*
A World Without Heroes
Hard Luck Woman
Every Time I Look at You
God of Thunder**
Nothin' to Lose
Calling Dr. Love
God of Thunder* (country version)
A Million to One*
Tonight You Belong to Me*
See You Tonite**
Christine Sixteen
Got to Choose
Love 'em and Leave 'em*
Spit*
Room Service*
Take It Off**
Any Way You Want It
I**
100,000 Years
I Still Love You
Almost Human**
2,000 Man*
Love Gun
I*
I Want You
The Ocean**
Heaven's On Fire
I Love It Loud
Lick It Up

JULY 26, 1995

Montréal, Quebec, Canada
Musique Plus Studios
No Opening Act

■ SET LIST

Comin' Home
Goin' Blind
Hard Luck Woman
Nothin' to Lose
Every Time I Look at You

■ KISS taped a five-song acoustic performance for the Canadian TV show *Planéte Rock*.

JULY 27, 1995

Montréal, Quebec, Canada
Le Chateau Champlain
Tribute Band: Alive!

■ SET LIST

Comin' Home
C'mon and Love Me
Plaster Caster
Sure Know Something
Nothin' to Lose
A World Without Heroes
Do You Love Me
Domino
Shandi
Love Her All I Can*
Black Diamond
Christine Sixteen**
A Million to One**
Let's Put the X in Sex
Calling Dr. Love
God of Thunder* (country version)

Got to Choose
Spit*
Hard Luck Woman
I*
Take Me
Christine Sixteen
War Machine/Sex Type Thing**
Every Time I Look at You
Stop That Pigeon**
See You Tonite
Love Theme from KISS**
Watchin' You**
Rock Bottom
Almost Human*
I Was Made for Lovin' You*
Hava Nagila**
(Hungarian Folk song)
Goin' Blind
I Still Love You
Heaven's On Fire
A Million to One**
Lick It Up
I Love It Loud
Deuce
Rock and Roll All Nite

JULY 29, 1995

Boston, Massachusetts
Westin Copley Place
Tribute Band: Rock 'n' Roll Over

■ SET LIST

Comin' Home
Plaster Caster
Goin' Blind
Do You Love Me
Domino
Nothin' to Lose
Sure Know Something
Calling Dr. Love
Take Me
A World Without Heroes
Every Time I Look at You
All the Way*
Rock Bottom
Mr. Speed *
C'mon and Love Me
God of Thunder* (country version)
Shandi
She
Strutter
Hide Your Heart
Larger Than Life**
Spit *
Let Me Know*
I Still Love You
War Machine/Sex Type Thing**
Christine Sixteen
Hard Luck Woman
Heaven's On Fire
Cold Gin
Lick It Up
I Love it Loud
Rock and Roll All Nite

JULY 30, 1995

New York, New York
Roseland Ballroom
Tribute Band: Alive!

■ SET LIST

Comin' Home
Plaster Caster
Goin' Blind
Do You Love Me
Domino
Nothin' to Lose
Sure Know Something

Calling Dr. Love
Take Me
A World Without Heroes
Every Time I Look at You
Rock Bottom
Mr. Speed
C'mon and Love Me
Spit*
I Still Love You
God of Thunder* (country version)
Christine Sixteen
Love Theme from KISS*
See You Tonite
Tonight You Belong to Me*
Goodbye
100,000 Years
Two Timer*
Let Me Know*
Deuce**
Got to Choose
Hard Luck Woman
Heaven's On Fire
Lick It Up
I Love It Loud
The Ocean**
Hide Your Heart
Rock and Roll All Nite

■ With Peter Criss's appearance at the Burbank convention having been such a success, KISS initially invited both him and Ace to appear at the New York convention. Peter and Ace's bands were touring together and were committed to a previous engagement, so they did not accept the offer.

AUGUST 1, 1995

Monroeville (Pittsburgh), Pennsylvania
The Monroeville Expo Mart
Tribute Band: Alive!
■ SET LIST
Comin' Home
Plaster Caster
Do You Love Me
Goin' Blind
Black Diamond
Hide Your Heart
Domino
Sure Know Something
God of Thunder* (country version)
Strange Ways*
Let's Put the X in Sex**
Shock Me*
A World Without Heroes
Nothin' to Lose
Hard Luck Woman
Calling Dr. Love
Rock Bottom
Charisma*
Simple Type**
Let's Put the X in Sex**
C'mon and Love Me
Deuce**
Spit*
Take Me
All the Way*
Let's Put the X in Sex
I Was Made for Lovin' You**
War Machine/Sex Type Thing**
Got to Choose
Shandi
Unholy*

Under the Gun**
Rock and Roll Hell*
Mr. Speed
Christine Sixteen
Forever
Room Service*
I Stole Your Love
Heaven's On Fire
Cold Gin
Lick It Up
She's So European**
Rock and Roll All Nite
■ Eric Singer sang lead vocals on "Strange Ways" during the acoustic set.

AUGUST 4, 1995

New York, New York
Studio 6A @ NBC Television Studios
Attendance: 210   Capacity: 210
Promoter: NBC
■ SET LIST
Comin' Home
Domino
■ KISS performed two songs for their appearance on Late Night With Conan O'Brien.

AUGUST 9, 1995

New York, New York
Sony Studios
Promoter: MTV Networks
■ SET LIST
Comin' Home
Plaster Caster
Goin' Blind
Do You Love Me
Domino*
Domino*
Domino
Got to Choose
Sure Know Something
A World Without Heroes
Hard Luck Woman
Rock Bottom
See You Tonite**
See You Tonite*
See You Tonite**
See You Tonite
I Still Love You
Down on the Corner**
Comin' Home*
C'mon and Love Me**
Comin' Home
Plaster Caster
Do You Love Me
Every Time I Look at You
Every Time I Look at You
Every Time I Look at You
Spit**
Heaven's On Fire*
Spit*
C'mon and Love Me
God of Thunder* (country version)
2000 Man
2000 Man
Beth
Beth*
(Horse Racing Fanfare)
Beth
Nothin' to Lose
Rock and Roll All Nite
(Horse Racing Fanfare)
Louie Louie**
Rock and Roll All Nite*

Happy Trails**
Rock and Roll All Nite**
Three Blind Mice**
Rock and Roll All Nite
Rock and Roll All Nite

■ A week after the Convention Tour ended, KISS entered Sony Studios on August 9 to tape an episode of MTV Unplugged™. The episode was certainly noteworthy for being a ratings success, but more importantly, Ace Frehley and Peter Criss appeared at the taping to perform with the band. It was the first public performance by the four original members of KISS since December 16, 1979.

Ace and Peter performed "2,000 Man" and "Beth" with Paul and Gene before Bruce and Eric returned, and all six men performed "Nothin' to Lose" and "Rock and Roll All Nite." MTV premiered the special on October 31, while a different mix of the show was broadcast via the MTV Radio Network. Sadly, when Bruce and Eric returned to the stage they were met with a small but noticeable chorus of boos from the audience. Bruce Kulick comments, "I thought it was pretty rude. Some of the die-hards don't like Eric and I, that's just something I had to live with over the years. That was my last (full) gig with KISS."

DECEMBER 15, 1995

Hollywood, California
Hollywood Palladium
Attendance: Sold Out Capacity: 3,750
Promoter: KLOS-FM
Archived: Audio
■ SET LIST
Calling Dr. Love
Hard Luck Woman
White Christmas (a capella)
■ This was a special acoustic performance for the nationally syndicated Mark And Brian radio show and was broadcast live over KLOS. KTLA-TV also broadcast live from the event. This marked the 139th and final performance of the Bruce, Eric, Gene, and Paul lineup of KISS.

KISS was one of many performers at the event. Bob and Delores Hope, Spencer Davis, The Gap Band, Mel Torme, Skee-Lo, Gary Hoey, Matthew Sweet, Peter Frampton, Mark Bonilla and the Dragon Choir Band, and Psychic Rain also performed.

As 1995 drew to a close, fences between the original bandmembers had been on the mend for quite some time. Paul and Gene made a noticeable dedication to Ace and Peter on the KISS My Ass release in June 1994, something that would have been inconceivable for most of the past 15 years. Then, in July of that same year, at an unofficial KISS convention outside of Detroit where Peter Criss was the special guest, Paul and Gene, accompanied by law enforcement officials, made a surprise appearance to claim some costumes that had allegedly been stolen from the band. The following day, Peter, Gene, and Paul flew back to Los Angeles together and many long-festering issues were reportedly resolved during the flight and a subsequent dinner.

CHAPTER 24

ALIVE/WORLDWIDE TOUR

Number of Shows: 192
Start Date: June 15, 1996 - Laguna Hills, California
End Date: July 5, 1997 - Finsbury Park (London), England
Countries: Argentina, Austria, Australia, Belgium, Canada, Chile, Czech Republic, Denmark, England, Finland, France, Germany, Hungary, Italy, Japan, Mexico, The Netherlands, New Zealand, Norway, Spain, Sweden, Switzerland, U.S.A., Yugoslavia
Headlining Act: Ozzy Osbourne
Opening Acts: The 4th Floor; 311; Alice in Chains; Alkbottle; Biohazard; The Bogmen; Caroline's Spine; Channel Zero; CIV; Core22; Coyote Shivers; Custard; D Generation; Deftones; Die Ärtze; Dog Eat Dog; Econoline Crush; El Fantastico Hombre Bala; Everclear; The Exponents; The Fauves; Fear Factory; Fireballs; Fugees; Fungus; Garbage; Glueleg; Goldfinger; Hellacopters; The Hunger; Irigy Hónaljmirigy; Johnny Bravo; KORN; L7; Live; Lush; Malon; The Melvins; Moonspell; The Mutton Birds; Naked Lunch; Neneh Cherry; The Nixons; No Doubt; Non-Intentional Lifeform; Otto; Outhouse; Pantera; Paradise Lost; Passion Orange; Poe; Powerman 5000; Pushmonkey; Rage Against the Machine; Red 5; Red Hot Chili Peppers; Reef; Reel Big Fish; Royal Crown Revue; Satisfucktion; Sepultura; Sex Tiger; Sideburn; Silverchair; Skunk Anansie; Snout; Sponge; Stabbing Westward; Stage; The Straws; Sugar Ray; Thunder; Uncle Meat; V8; The Verve Pipe; Waltari; Warpigs; Zluty Pes

Average Attendance: 13,737* (Does not include the 9/4/96 appearance for MTV.)

Just fifteen days into the new year, a rumor began spreading rapidly throughout the KISS community. It was the same rumor fans had been hearing in one form or another since the summer of 1987.

First, *The Gossip Show* on E! ran a piece on it on January 22.

Three days later, MTV News aired a segment.

Then on January 29, 1996, on a cold winter afternoon in Chicago, DJ Lou Brutus badgered his 46-year-old guest for information on the air. Brutus groveled, demanded, and implored, but

the guest would not budge. Instead, he sang quietly: "Fairy tales can come true, it can happen to you . . ."

And with those words, the fuse was lit.

The foundation on which KISS's monumental 1996 reunion rested had nothing to do with Gene Simmons's faltering quote of "Young at Heart." Instead, the pieces of the reunion's foundation had been connecting over a period of years, sometimes accidentally, sometimes purposefully, all too rapidly come together over the waning months of 1995.

KISS had largely been in nostalgia mode for

several years, with their concerts, merchandise, and conventions focused on the past and not the present. After the August 1995 MTV taping, KISS, Ace, and Peter maintained their separate career paths, with KISS recording new material and Ace and Peter's two bands concluding their Bad Boys Tour together.

With the reunion concept on the table, it is perhaps appropriate that two businessmen from KISS's past played a major role in moving the reunion forward. In January 1996, Danny Goldberg, who had successfully paired with KISS

ANDREW ALLIN

in both the 1970s and 1980s, became CEO of the Mercury Records Group. Goldberg relates, "When I returned to Mercury, they did not have an amazing roster; there were only a few acts on the label that anyone had ever heard of and KISS was one of them. I met with them right away, and we solved the *Unplugged* problem by asking MTV if they would unblock the taping and also got the rights to put it out as an album. Then, I urged them to put the makeup back on. We had taken the makeup off and that worked, so I urged them to put it back on. They knew it was just a matter of time. They're very savvy about these cycles. They told me it was an idea that they'd been thinking about for the last two years . . . and then they went and did it."

Former Dynasty/Unmasked Road Manager George Sewitt, who was managing both Ace and Peter at the time, also played a significant role in bringing his clients back into the fold.

For the KISS reunion to reach its potential, an incredibly ambitious plan was required, as the task that lay ahead was not simply a matter of recreating what KISS was in 1977, but what the general public *thought* KISS was in 1977. Imagination always outpaces reality, and the reunion, in essence, became a quest to recreate a myth: there needed to be mystique, that old sense of larger-than-life, an enormous pop-culture presence, and that pseudo-comic book hero aura. And for this to happen, for 1977 to be reconstructed on a massive scale, an additional industry heavyweight was required. KISS needed a latter-day Peter Grant (Led Zeppelin's manager) to pilot the ship, and that's exactly what they got when Doc McGhee and his company McGhee Entertainment were hired. McGhee, who had very successfully managed the likes of the Scorpions, Bon Jovi, and Mötley Crüe, was an engaging but hard-nosed carnival barker with a brilliant talent for creating opportunity for his artists.

In Goldberg and McGhee, KISS had two major industry players who would relentlessly pursue creating the spectacle necessary to launch the reunion. Goldberg recalls, "Ginger Greagor and Ken Sunshine headed the promotions efforts. I brought Kenny in just to handle the media playing field. We wanted to involve the mainstream press and not just the music press." Goldberg arranged for the original four members to make an appearance—in full makeup and recreated Love Gun Tour costumes—during the *Grammys*TM on February 28. He continues, "We cut a deal with Mike Greene, and the appearance was seen by a billion people. Gene came offstage after this huge reaction by the crowd, and I was standing next to Lisa Robinson, who as a New York writer had always championed the CBGB's crowd, when Gene leans over her and says, 'You ain't gonna be able to see the Ramones do that.'"

McGhee and Goldberg shared an aggressive approach to promotions and, once initiated, the public presence of the reunited KISS did not dissipate. The Internet was a hype machine unlike anything previously available to KISS or their fans, and every move the band made spread throughout the online KISS community almost instantly. KISS quickly became a part of pop culture once again. This was no more apparent

than it was on May 22 when the entire KISS CD catalog was one of the big prizes in the final showcase on *The Price Is Right*.

On April 16, Conan O'Brien hosted the band's high-profile press conference to announce the Alive/Worldwide Tour. The press conference was held in front of a large contingent of music industry and mainstream press members on the U.S.S. Intrepid, a 1940s-era aircraft carrier anchored on the west side of Manhattan.

Any lingering doubt regarding public interest in the reunion tour was vanquished on April 20 when all tickets for the tour's debut show in Tiger Stadium (nearly 40,000 in total) were sold out in 47 minutes. Tickets to an additional ten shows (in eight markets) went on sale on May 11. All ten shows sold out almost instantly, with concerts in Cleveland and Chicago reportedly selling out in less than six minutes. Second shows were added in both cities and sold out in minutes as well; in less than a year, KISS had gone from playing conventions in front of hundreds, to selling over 100,000 tickets in a single day.

Hundreds of thousands of fans worldwide who had been pining for 1977 essentially got their wish, even if the reality of what they eventually saw proved different than what they may have envisioned. KISS in 1996–97 not only recreated their 1977–78 concert drawing power, they surpassed it. The reunion tour remains the band's largest ever in terms of number of shows and in average attendance. Scores of fans saw multiple shows, with some following KISS from show to show for extended periods of time.

Over the course of nearly 13 months, the tour averaged 13,737 people per show. Out of a total 192 concerts, KISS sold out 127 with most of the remainder nearly sold out. The band visited 24 countries, featured 77 different opening acts, archived over 400,000 feet of concert footage, and performed in front of over 2.5 million people. The first half of the tour was heralded as the number one tour of the year by the trifecta of touring industry periodicals: *Amusement Business, Performance,* and *Pollstar.* So pervasive was the band's success that even the comparatively conservative *Forbes* magazine featured a cover story on KISS.

Adding almost unnecessary hype to the equation, Mercury put together *You Wanted the Best, You Got the Best!!,* which was released on June 25. The album was a collection of live tunes with an interview conducted by Jay Leno concluding the disc.

Initially described as a modern rendering of their 1977 show, the set evolved to become what Tour/Production Manager Tim Rozner described at the time as "a rock and roll command center." The stage was designed by Rozner and Brian Hartley in conjunction with KISS. Additionally, an elaborate exhaust system was designed by Tom Reedy to extract all of the pyro smoke.

For the first time in KISS's career, video played an integral role in the band's concerts with a 12 x 20 foot video screen—centered below a lighted KISS logo—dominating the backline of the stage. San Francisco-based Nocturne Productions was hired to provide video

production for the tour. Bob Brigham of Nocturne explains: "Doc McGhee called us and said that he wanted to do something different; he didn't want to just do video projection. At the time, we had video cube walls made up of cubes which were 2 feet high by 3 feet wide and they had a video projector inside with a lenticular lens like a rear-projection TV. They were roughly six feet deep. Of course, Doc is famous for being cheap. So he decides that there are going to be no production rehearsals. And Doc never starts off in Paducah, Kentucky to break in the show, and then take it into the big city to debut it to the world, he starts off smoking. Instead, they sell out this show in Tiger Stadium, and our first look at the band was in a dress rehearsal the night before. It just looked amazing, because the screen really punched through the lights, and at the time, it was state of the art."

Ace also contributed a video effect to the production that was used in-between the main set and the encores wherein the four solo album covers would morph from one to another on the video screens.

The production design leaned towards the melodramatic even before the show itself began. The Who's "Won't Get Fooled Again" was used to cue the drop of an enormous black curtain emblazoned with the KISS logo. The curtain would unfurl from the lighting rig as the house engineer would raise the P.A.'s volume considerably for Roger Daltrey's legendary scream. The subtle undertones of the song's final lyric "Meet the new boss, same as the old boss" rang especially true.

Many of the requisite KISS production gimmicks were used: Paul smashing a guitar, Gene spitting blood, and Ace once again shooting rockets from his guitar, hitting pyro packs mounted in the lighting rig. However, beginning in September 1996, Ace's trick was embellished when a light was rigged to fall off the lighting rig and dangle via an electrical cord, giving the impression that the explosion of the bottle rocket had jarred the light loose from its mount. The trick was effective enough to fool a surprisingly large percentage of the crowd.

Both Gene and Paul "flew" during the production. At most concerts throughout the tour, Gene was lifted via cable up to a platform in the lighting rig where he would sing the first two verses and choruses of "God of Thunder" before being lowered back to the stage. Then, beginning on March 25, 1997, Paul would be raised above the audience at the beginning of "Love Gun" and then transported to a small platform near the soundboard where he would sing the remainder of the song.

Production rehearsals for the tour began in June at Van Nuys International Airport in California and continued at Cobo Arena in Detroit from June 21–25 before moving to Tiger Stadium on June 26.

Songs from all seven of KISS's 1974–1979 studio albums were performed on the tour, with *KISS* and *Destroyer* receiving the most emphasis. The result was a balanced mix of predictable songs such as "God of Thunder" or "Cold Gin," and material that had rarely been performed in

20 years like "Take Me" and "Rock Bottom." During performances of "New York Groove," KISS would alter the lyrics of the final chorus to reflect the city that they were currently in, e.g., "New York Groove" would become "Milwaukee Groove." Excerpts of Zeppelin's "Heartbreaker" would also occasionally be performed by Paul prior to "Watchin' You." Lastly, Australian crowds were treated to "Shandi," which Paul performed by himself prior to "Black Diamond."

Unless otherwise noted, every KISS concert from 1996 through 2001 was archived on Betacam SP videotape by Nocturne Productions. Accordingly, the "archived" listing has been removed.

Throughout the reunion era, Ace frequently included excerpts of classical pieces in his solos, such as Richard Strauss's "Also Sprach Zarathustra," Beethoven's Fifth Symphony, Isaac Albeniz's "Asturias," and on rare occasion, Mozart's Symphony No. 40. For space considerations, the specific instances are not mentioned.

JUNE 15, 1996

Laguna Hills, California
Irvine Meadows Amphitheatre
Opening Acts: Red Hot Chili Peppers, No Doubt, KORN, Everclear, Garbage, Goldfinger, The Verve Pipe, Fugees, Lush, 311
Attendance: 15,400   Capacity: 15,400
Promoter: KROQ
■ SET LIST
Deuce
Love Gun
Cold Gin
Calling Dr. Love
Firehouse
Shock Me
Ace Frehley Guitar Solo
Gene Simmons Bass Solo
100,000 Years
Detroit Rock City
Black Diamond
Rock and Roll All Nite

■ This was a one-off show for the KROQ 4th Annual Weenie Roast and was the first gig with the original lineup in makeup since December 16, 1979. It was also the first time any KISS line-up had performed in makeup since June 25, 1983. Miniature tourbooks were produced and given away at the door.

All acts were broadcast live over KROQ, except KISS. Additionally, MTV declared June 24 "KROQ Weenie Roast Day" and aired small clips from KISS's performance.

Giant Gene, Ace, Peter, and Paul balloons were inflated in the middle of Garbage's set atop the concession stand in the middle of the venue.

After the house lights dimmed for KISS's performance, a helicopter flew in from stage right and shone a spotlight down on the crowd, circling the audience several times before departing.

The video screens used at this performance were smaller than those used for the main part of the tour. BCC Video, rather than Nocturne Productions, handled video production for this show.

The show experienced some problems when Ace's smoking guitar effect did not work, and neither of the rockets he shot from his guitar hit their designated targets; the first flew out over the audience, and the second misfired into the ceiling on stage left. Later, during "100,000 Years," one of the flamethrowers accidentally set fire to the grand finale fireworks on stage left, causing the pyro to shoot off in several directions, including into the crowd itself.

Production problems aside, the sight and spectacle of the four original members of KISS on stage together overwhelmed any of the show's shortcomings. This concert was also unique in that Gene's solo segued into "100,000 Years" for the first and only time since June 1976.

JUNE 28, 1996

Detroit, Michigan
Tiger Stadium
Opening Acts: Alice In Chains, Sponge
Attendance: 39,867   Capacity: 39,867
Promoter: Brass Ring Productions
■ SET LIST
Deuce
King of the Night Time World
Do You Love Me
Calling Dr. Love
Cold Gin
Christine Sixteen
Love Gun
Shout It Out Loud
Watchin' You
Firehouse
2,000 Man

Strutter
Shock Me
Ace Frehley Guitar Solo
Rock Bottom
Gene Simmons Bass Solo
God of Thunder
Peter Criss Drum Solo - reprise
New York Groove
Let Me Go, Rock 'n Roll
100,000 Years
Rock and Roll All Nite
Detroit Rock City
Beth
Black Diamond

■ In some regards, this was the biggest show of the band's career, and while a handful of the band's concerts have seen larger crowds in attendance, KISS has rarely, if ever, surpassed the hype and spectacle of their June 28 performance at Tiger Stadium.

Be it print, radio, or television, the national and local media presence was overwhelming, eclipsing any other American show in KISS's history and perhaps equaled only during the band's 1980 tour of Australia.

Bruce Redoute and Lee Neaves, famous for their appearance on the back cover of *Alive!*, found their 15 minutes of fame rekindled in the heat of the surrounding hype. The *Detroit Free Press* established a hotline looking for "the two kids on the back of *Alive!*" As a by-product of the search, the local FOX news affiliate succeeded in finding an imposter claiming to be one of the two kids. The real Redoute and Neaves soon came forth and the newspaper ran a lengthy piece on the two KISS fans. Redoute wrote a letter to the mayor seeking the proclamation from the city for KISS. He succeeded in his efforts, though the band's tight schedule prohibited them from accepting the proclamation.

On the night of the show, the atmosphere on Trumbull Street in Detroit crackled with anticipation. Redoute and Neaves rolled out of a limousine at Tiger Stadium with a replica of their famous *Alive!* sign, but were lost in the tumult of excitement and thousands of fans milling about outside the venue. MuchMusic and MTV were both taping footage as were *Entertainment Tonight* and *American Journal*. Local radio stations were doing live remotes, though MTV's "Choose or Lose" bus—a pseudo-political venture by MTV to register younger voters—seemed out of place, but was nonetheless present. Small private planes circled above the stadium trailing banners promoting after-show events and recaps.

The band arrived in full makeup and costume via limo from The Ritz-Carlton in Dearborn, Michigan. Two helicopters circled the venue after the lights dimmed and finally, at 10:17 local time, KISS took the stage. The band performed for over 2 hours, sharing the sweltering heat with a swarm of moths.

Not surprisingly, the production and set were enormous. Pat Morrow of Nocturne Productions remembers, "Tiger Stadium was very tough; you had all of these elements coming together, a new production, and it was typical Doc McGhee, he takes everyone to the limits of their capabilities and their professionalism and makes the impossi-

ble seem easy. Imagine Doc trying to pull it off and the first gig is a huge stadium in the city of rock and roll: Detroit. He's caused more gray hairs and pre-mature baldness than anyone I know."

The end of the show was punctuated by a firework display, which featured 700 titanium salutes.

Crowd shots for the "Shout It Out Loud" video were filmed during the show; close-ups of the band had been shot during rehearsals the day before.

Stone Temple Pilots were originally scheduled as the opening act, but lead singer Scott Weiland was forced into drug rehab for heroin addiction and Alice In Chains were added to the bill in their place.

JUNE 30, 1996
Louisville, Kentucky
Freedom Hall
Opening Act: Alice In Chains
Attendance: 15,891   Capacity: 15,891
Promoter: Sunshine Promotions
■ SET LIST
Deuce
King of the Night Time World
Do You Love Me
Calling Dr. Love
Cold Gin
Love Gun
Shout It Out Loud
Watchin' You
Firehouse
Strutter
Shock Me
Ace Frehley Guitar Solo
Rock Bottom
Gene Simmons Bass Solo
God of Thunder
Peter Criss Drum Solo - reprise
New York Groove
Let Me Go, Rock 'n Roll
100,000 Years
Rock and Roll All Nite
Detroit Rock City
Beth
Black Diamond

■ After the Detroit gig, both "2,000 Man" and "Christine Sixteen" were dropped from the set. Much as he did in Detroit, Peter feigned crying at the end of "Beth." This is the last time he would attempt to do so during the tour.

Local radio station WTFX distributed KISS bumperstickers.

JULY 2, 1996
St. Louis, Missouri
Kiel Center
Opening Act: Alice In Chains
Attendance: 16,310   Capacity: 16,310
Promoter: Contemporary Productions
■ SET LIST
See June 30, 1996.

■ Radio station KSHE distributed bumperstickers featuring Sweet Meat (a pig who serves as the station's mascot) in Gene's makeup.

JULY 3, 1996
Kansas City, Missouri
Kemper Arena
Opening Act: Alice In Chains
Attendance: 13,226   Capacity: 13,226
Promoter: Contemporary Productions

■ SET LIST
See June 30, 1996.

■ Alice In Chains drummer Sean Kinney was booed when he sang a line from "Beth" during their set, a stunt he had pulled at each of the previous four shows. This was Alice In Chains' final gig ever.

JULY 5, 1996
Dallas, Texas
Reunion Arena
Opening Act: Pushmonkey
Attendance: 14,637   Capacity: 14,637
Promoter: Beaver Productions
■ SET LIST
See June 30, 1996.

■ A disco ball was added to the production for the intros to "Rock Bottom" and "Black Diamond."

JULY 6, 1996
Houston, Texas
The Summit
Opening Act: Pushmonkey
Attendance: 12,955   Capacity: 12,955
Promoter: Beaver Productions
■ SET LIST
Deuce
King of the Night Time World
Do You Love Me
Calling Dr. Love
Cold Gin
Love Gun
Shout It Out Loud
Watchin' You
Firehouse
Shock Me
Ace Frehley Guitar Solo
Strutter
Rock Bottom
Gene Simmons Bass Solo
God of Thunder
Peter Criss Drum Solo - reprise
New York Groove
Let Me Go, Rock 'n Roll
100,000 Years
Black Diamond
Detroit Rock City
Beth
Rock and Roll All Nite

■ "Black Diamond" was moved from the end of the show to the end of the main set list and "Rock and Roll All Nite" now closed out the encores.

JULY 7, 1996
San Antonio, Texas
AlamoDome
Opening Act: Pushmonkey
Attendance: 18,337   Capacity: 18,337
Promoter: Beaver Productions
■ SET LIST
See July 6, 1996.

■ A different intro was put in place for this show. After the house lights were turned off, interview footage of fans, shot earlier outside the venue, talking about how KISS changed their lives, was broadcast over the side video screens prior to the "You wanted the best . . ." intro. Paul could be seen shaking his head in displeasure through the curtain as KISS was waiting for the video to finish. Additionally, owing to the large size of the venue (which can seat in excess of 50,000), the amount of pyro that the band used was drastically increased.

A local radio station distributed KISS buttons.

JULY 9, 1996

New Orleans, Louisiana
Louisiana Superdome
Opening Act: The Melvins
Attendance: 16,308   Capacity: 16,308
Promoter: Beaver Productions

■ SET LIST

See July 6, 1996.

■ Plastic KISS cups were distributed after the show courtesy of local radio station WCKW.

JULY 10, 1996

Memphis, Tennessee
The Pyramid
Opening Act: The Melvins
Attendance: 16,807   Capacity: 16,807
Promoter: Mid-South Concerts

■ SET LIST

Deuce
King of the Night Time World
Do You Love Me
Calling Dr. Love
Cold Gin
Love Gun
Shout It Out Loud
Watchin' You
Firehouse
Shock Me
Ace Frehley Guitar Solo
Strutter
Rock Bottom
Gene Simmons Bass Solo
God of Thunder
Peter Criss Drum Solo - reprise
New York Groove
Let Me Go, Rock 'n Roll
100,000 Years
Black Diamond
Beth
Detroit Rock City
Rock and Roll All Nite

JULY 12, 1996

Moline, Illinois
The Mark of the Quad Cities
Opening Act: The Melvins
Attendance: 10,349   Capacity: 10,349
Promoter: JAM Productions

■ SET LIST

See July 6, 1996.

■ During "Firehouse," an audience member threw a homemade fire helmet on stage, which Paul promptly donned for a few moments. Later, during "100,000 Years," Paul became so tangled in microphone cable that he was forced to stand very still while singing the final verse for fear that he would fall over.

JULY 13, 1996

St. Paul, Minnesota
St. Paul Civic Center
Opening Act: The Melvins
Attendance: 14,313   Capacity: 14,313
Promoter: Rose Productions

■ SET LIST

Deuce
King of the Night Time World
Do You Love Me
Calling Dr. Love
Cold Gin
I Stole Your Love

Shout It Out Loud
Watchin' You
Firehouse
Shock Me
Ace Frehley Guitar Solo
Strutter
Rock Bottom
Gene Simmons Bass Solo
God of Thunder
Peter Criss Drum Solo - reprise
New York Groove
Love Gun
100,000 Years
Black Diamond
Detroit Rock City
Beth

Rock and Roll All Nite

■ "I Stole Your Love" was added to the show.

JULY 14, 1996

Rosemont (Chicago), Illinois
Rosemont Horizon
Opening Act: The Melvins
Attendance: 14,944   Capacity: 14,944
Promoter: JAM Productions

■ SET LIST

See July 13, 1996.

■ Beginning in Rosemont, venue T-shirts (which had previously been available only in Detroit and Dallas) became a consistent part of the merchandise.

The first known airing of the "Shout It Out Loud (Live)" video occurred on MTV in the early morning hours on July 16.

JULY 16, 1996

Rosemont (Chicago), Illinois
Rosemont Horizon
Opening Act: The Nixons
Attendance: 14,944   Capacity: 14,944
Promoter: JAM Productions

■ **SET LIST**
See July 13, 1996.

■ Ace was suffering from a bronchial infection and his performance was very sedate and sloppy. The following morning, local DJ Mancow harshly criticized Ace for his performance, prompting management to call the radio station to inform him of the details of Ace's illness.

As he had in the 1970s, Paul wore a lengthy feathered robe when the band came out for their curtain call. He ripped off the bottom part, which was attached to the upper half of the robe by Velcro, and threw it into the audience. This show marks the last known occasion upon which he did so.

JULY 17, 1996

Dayton, Ohio
Ervin J. Nutter Center
Opening Act: The Nixons
Attendance: 11,194   Capacity: 11,194
Promoter: Belkin Productions

■ **SET LIST**
See July 13, 1996.

JULY 19, 1996

Cleveland, Ohio
GUND Arena
Opening Act: The Nixons
Attendance 17,438   Capacity: 17,438
Promoter: Belkin Productions

■ **SET LIST**
See July 13, 1996.

■ Local media coverage for this gig was rampant, with one radio station running a 24-hour KISS marathon leading up to the show.

JULY 20, 1996

Cleveland, Ohio
GUND Arena
Opening Act: D Generation
Attendance 17,832   Capacity: 17,832
Promoter: Belkin Productions

■ **SET LIST**
See July 13, 1996.

■ Opening act D Generation made their presence known with a rousing set that saw the band throwing out T-shirts and garbage bags full of shredded paper to the audience. They were told to tone down their act after this show.

JULY 21, 1996

Pittsburgh, Pennsylvania
Civic Arena
Opening Act: The Nixons
Attendance: 12,355   Capacity: 12,355
Promoter: DiCesare-Engler Productions

■ **SET LIST**
See July 13, 1996.

■ The giant KISS balloons, fully repainted, appeared again for the first time since the Weenie Roast.

JULY 22, 1996

Pittsburgh, Pennsylvania
Civic Arena
Opening Act: D Generation
Attendance: 11,916   Capacity: 12,355
Promoter: DiCesare-Engler Productions

■ **SET LIST**
See July 13, 1996.

■ All four members of Metallica were in attendance and watched the show from the soundboard.

JULY 25, 1996

New York, New York
Madison Square Garden
Opening Act: D Generation
Attendance: 14,705   Capacity: 14,705
Promoter: Delsener-Slater Enterprises

■ **SET LIST**
See July 13, 1996.

■ KISS set a personal standard by selling out Madison Square Garden on four consecutive nights, besting their December 1977 string of three sellouts. Promoter Ron Delsener stated that had their schedule been able to accommodate it, the demand for tickets was high enough for seven shows.

The concerts were clearly an event: at the premiere Garden show, sky lights featuring transparencies of the KISS members' faces were set up on Seventh Avenue, and a host of celebrities were in attendance. Before the show, the audience cheered when Donald Trump entered the arena to watch the show with Marla Maples and Shannon Tweed. Bill Aucoin was also in attendance.

Paul appeared teary eyed and choked-up during "King of the Night Time World." At the end of "Beth," Peter, too, seemed overcome with emotion. He threw out blue roses at three of the 1996 MSG shows and dedicated the song to his late mother while looking and pointing skyward.

In addition to the usual T-shirts, an "I Was There—KISS, Madison Square Garden" T-shirt was sold, which featured the *Love Gun* artwork and a New York City skyline in the background.

JULY 26, 1996

New York, New York
Madison Square Garden
Opening Act: CIV
Attendance: 14,705   Capacity: 14,705
Promoter: Delsener-Slater Enterprises

■ **SET LIST**
See July 13, 1996.

■ Red flares were added inside of each flame-thrower during the pyro display in "100,000 Years." The effect lasted only one show. The confetti storm that usually accompanies "Rock and Roll All Nite" was absent.

Presumably taped on this night, Joel Siegel was on hand to walk KISS to the stage for a "Good Morning America" segment, which aired August 1.

JULY 27, 1996

New York, New York
Madison Square Garden
Opening Act: 311
Attendance: 14,705   Capacity: 14,705
Promoter: Delsener-Slater Enterprises

■ **SET LIST**
Deuce
King of the Night Time World
Do You Love Me
Calling Dr. Love
Cold Gin
Let Me Go, Rock 'n Roll
Shout It Out Loud
Watchin' You
Firehouse
Shock Me
Ace Frehley Guitar Solo
Strutter
Rock Bottom
Gene Simmons Bass Solo
God of Thunder
Peter Criss Drum Solo - reprise
New York Groove
Love Gun
100,000 Years
Black Diamond
Detroit Rock City
Beth
Rock and Roll All Nite

■ The four KISS balloons were set up inside the venue for this gig.

JULY 28, 1996

New York, New York
Madison Square Garden
Opening Act: The Nixons
Attendance: 14,705   Capacity: 14,705
Promoter: Delsener-Slater Enterprises

■ **SET LIST**
Deuce
King of the Night Time World
Do You Love Me
Calling Dr. Love
Cold Gin
Let Me Go, Rock 'n Roll
Shout It Out Loud
Watchin' You
Firehouse
Shock Me
Ace Frehley Guitar Solo
Strutter
Rock Bottom
Gene Simmons Bass Solo
God of Thunder
Peter Criss Drum Solo - reprise
New York Groove
Love Gun
100,000 Years
Black Diamond
Detroit Rock City
Rock and Roll All Nite

■ With the show running late, "Beth" was dropped from the set list in order to avoid paying extra union fees.

JULY 30, 1996

Boston, Massachusetts
Fleet Center
Opening Act: The Nixons
Attendance: 15,832   Capacity: 15,832
Promoter: Beaver Productions

■ **SET LIST**
See July 27, 1996.

JULY 31, 1996

Boston, Massachusetts
Fleet Center
Opening Act: D Generation
Attendance: 15,832   Capacity: 15,832
Promoter: Beaver Productions

Ace and Paul playing the intro to the rarely performed "Rock Bottom," at Madison Square Garden.

■ **SET LIST**
Deuce
King of the Night Time World
Do You Love Me
Calling Dr. Love
Cold Gin
Let Me Go, Rock 'n Roll
Shock Me
Ace Frehley Guitar Solo
Shout It Out Loud
Watchin' You
Firehouse
Strutter
Rock Bottom
Gene Simmons Bass Solo
God of Thunder
Peter Criss Drum Solo - reprise
New York Groove
Love Gun
100,000 Years
Black Diamond
Detroit Rock City
Beth
Rock and Roll All Nite
■ As Paul was introducing a "song from *Destroyer*"

(ostensibly "Shout It Out Loud"), Ace ran to the microphone and shouted "Shock Me!" and Peter immediately launched into the song. Frehley realized that he was going to do his featured solo with the wrong guitar, and Paul covered for him by singing the first two lines of the second verse, enabling Ace to switch guitars.

A VH1 camera crew was present to tape segments for the show *Route 96* which aired on August 23.

AUGUST 2, 1996

Quebec, Quebec, Canada
Colisée de Quebec
Opening Act: D Generation
Attendance: 8,304   Capacity: 11,885
Promoter: Donald K. Donald
■ **SET LIST**
See July 27, 1996.

AUGUST 3, 1996

Montréal, Quebec, Canada
Centre Molson
Opening Act: D Generation

Attendance: 12,879   Capacity: 14,665
Promoter: Donald K. Donald
■ **SET LIST**
See July 27, 1996.

AUGUST 5, 1996

Ottawa, Ontario, Canada
The Palladium
Opening Act: D Generation
Attendance: 13,101   Capacity: 14,900
Promoter: Bass Clef
■ **SET LIST**
See July 27, 1996.
■ When Paul threw his smashed guitar into the audience, someone other than its intended target grabbed it. Paul then asked the person who caught it to give the guitar back to him and, surprisingly, the fan obliged. Stanley then gave it to the intended recipient.

AUGUST 6, 1996

Toronto, Ontario, Canada
Toronto Skytent
Opening Act: D Generation

Attendance: 27,035   Capacity: 27,035
Promoter: Concert Promotions Int'l
■ **SET LIST**

Deuce
King of the Night Time World
Do You Love Me
Calling Dr. Love
Cold Gin
Let Me Go, Rock 'n Roll
Watchin' You
Firehouse
Shout It Out Loud
Shock Me
Ace Frehley Guitar Solo
Strutter
Rock Bottom
Gene Simmons Bass Solo
God of Thunder
Peter Criss Drum Solo - reprise
New York Groove
Love Gun
100,000 Years
Black Diamond
Detroit Rock City
Beth
Rock and Roll All Nite

AUGUST 8, 1996

Cincinnati, Ohio
Riverfront Coliseum
Opening Act: D Generation
Attendance: 12,920   Capacity: 12,920
Promoter: Sunshine Promotions
■ **SET LIST**

See August 6, 1996.
■ Over the course of their career, thousands of items have been thrown onstage during KISS's concerts, but perhaps none were as unusual as the prosthetic leg a fan threw onstage at this show. Paul picked up the leg and the black magic marker that had been thrown to the stage with it and signed the leg. Each member then signed the leg in turn before returning it to the audience member.

AUGUST 9, 1996

Indianapolis, Indiana
Market Square Arena
Opening Act: D Generation
Attendance: 14,931   Capacity: 14,931
Promoter: Sunshine Promotions
■ **SET LIST**

See August 6, 1996.

AUGUST 10, 1996

Milwaukee, Wisconsin
Bradley Center
Opening Act: D Generation
Attendance: 15,872   Capacity: 15,872
Promoter: Cellar Door Concerts
■ **SET LIST**

See August 6, 1996.
■ On August 16, Mercury Records issued a press release stating that Bruce Kulick and Eric Singer had officially severed ties with KISS. To this point, Paul and Gene had made no moves to remove Kulick and Singer from the picture, wisely hedging their bets should the reunion tour have been less successful than it was.

AUGUST 17, 1996

Leistershire, Donington, England
Donington Park
Co-headliner: Ozzy Osbourne
Opening Acts: Sepultura, Dog Eat Dog, Biohazard,

Paradise Lost, Fear Factory
Attendance: 80,000+
Promoter: Aimcarve Ltd.
■ **SET LIST**

Deuce
King of the Night Time World
Do You Love Me
Calling Dr. Love
Cold Gin
Let Me Go, Rock 'n Roll
Shout It Out Loud
Watchin' You
Firehouse
Shock Me
Ace Frehley Guitar Solo
Strutter
Gene Simmons Bass Solo
God of Thunder
Peter Criss Drum Solo - reprise
Love Gun
100,000 Years
Black Diamond
Detroit Rock City
Rock and Roll All Nite
■ "Beth" was not performed. MTV Europe taped a special edition of *Headbangers Ball* from Donington.

A special Donington '96 tourbook was produced.

AUGUST 21, 1996

Phoenix, Arizona
America West Arena
Opening Acts: Caroline's Spine, Stabbing Westward
Attendance: 14,185   Capacity: 14,185
Promoter: Evening Star Productions
■ **SET LIST**

See August 6, 1996.

AUGUST 23, 1996

Inglewood (Los Angeles), California
Great Western Forum
Opening Act: Stabbing Westward
Attendance: 13,639   Capacity: 13,639
Promoter: Avalon Attractions
■ **SET LIST**

See August 6, 1996.

AUGUST 24, 1996

Inglewood (Los Angeles), California
Great Western Forum
Opening Act: Stabbing Westward
Attendance: 13,639   Capacity: 13,639
Promoter: Avalon Attractions
■ **SET LIST**

See August 6, 1996.
■ This was the final performance of "Rock Bottom."

Eric Singer and Bruce Kulick were in attendance at the show, as was Jay Leno, who showed up backstage to tape several skits for *The Tonight Show*.

AUGUST 25, 1996

Inglewood (Los Angeles), California
Great Western Forum
Opening Act: Red 5
Attendance: 13,639   Capacity: 13,639
Promoter: Avalon Attractions
■ **SET LIST**

Deuce
King of the Night Time World
Do You Love Me
Calling Dr. Love
Cold Gin

Let Me Go, Rock 'n Roll
Shout It Out Loud
Watchin' You
Firehouse
I Stole Your Love
Shock Me
Ace Frehley Guitar Solo
Strutter
Gene Simmons Bass Solo
God of Thunder
Peter Criss Drum Solo - reprise
New York Groove
Love Gun
100,000 Years
Black Diamond
Detroit Rock City
Beth
Rock and Roll All Nite
■ The audience sang "Happy Birthday" to Gene prior to "Rock and Roll All Nite."

AUGUST 27, 1996

San Jose, California
San Jose Arena
Opening Act: Stabbing Westward
Attendance: 14,803   Capacity: 14,803
Promoter: Bill Graham Presents
■ **SET LIST**

See August 25, 1996.

AUGUST 28, 1996

Sacramento, California
ARCO Arena
Opening Act: Stabbing Westward
Attendance: 11,357   Capacity: 11,357
Promoter: Bill Graham Presents
■ **SET LIST**

See August 25, 1996.

AUGUST 30, 1996

Portland, Oregon
Rose Garden
Opening Act: Stabbing Westward
Attendance: 13,633   Capacity: 14,262
Promoter: MCA Concerts
■ **SET LIST**

Deuce
King of the Night Time World
Do You Love Me
Calling Dr. Love
Cold Gin
Let Me Go, Rock 'n Roll
Shout It Out Loud
Watchin' You
Firehouse
Strutter
Shock Me
Ace Frehley Guitar Solo
I Stole Your Love
Gene Simmons Bass Solo
God of Thunder
Peter Criss Drum Solo - reprise
New York Groove
Love Gun
100,000 Years
Black Diamond
Detroit Rock City
Beth
Rock and Roll All Nite

AUGUST 31, 1996

Tacoma, Washington
Tacoma Dome
Opening Act: Stabbing Westward
Attendance: 15,260   Capacity: 16,479

ANDREW ALLIN

Promoter: MCA Concerts

■ Pyro at the end of "Black Diamond" set the venue's ceiling on fire, and the show was halted for 30 minutes. Gene announced over the P.A. that KISS would return after the fire had been tended to.

SEPTEMBER 1, 1996

Spokane, Washington
Spokane Arena
Opening Act: Stabbing Westward
Attendance: 7,950   Capacity: 8,772
Promoter: MCA Concerts

SEPTEMBER 2, 1996

Vancouver, British Columbia, Canada
General Motors Place
Opening Act: Stabbing Westward
Attendance: 13,183   Capacity: 13,183
Promoter: Perryscope Concert Productions
■ **SET LIST**
See August 25, 1996.

SEPTEMBER 4, 1996   CANCELED

Boise, Idaho
BSU Pavilion
Promoter: Beaver Productions

■ This show was canceled when KISS opted to tape a performance for the *MTV Video Music Awards*. 5,000 tickets had been sold at the time of cancellation.

SEPTEMBER 4, 1996

Brooklyn, New York
Fulton Ferry Landing
No Opening Act
Attendance: 400+
Promoter: MTV Networks
■ **SET LIST**
Rock and Roll All Nite
New York Groove
Deuce
Calling Dr. Love
Love Gun

■ This was a live performance for the *MTV Video Music Awards*. This appearance came about when an MTV executive reneged on a promise to broadcast the *Week In Rock* live from Tiger Stadium. To make amends, MTV gave KISS the opportunity to perform for the *MTV Video Music Awards*.

SEPTEMBER 5, 1996

Salt Lake City, Utah
Delta Center
Opening Act: The Hunger
Attendance: 10,761   Capacity: 10,761
Promoter: United Concerts

SEPTEMBER 7, 1996

Denver, Colorado
McNichols Sports Arena
Opening Act: The Hunger
Attendance: 13,226   Capacity: 14,273
Promoter: Feyline Presents

SEPTEMBER 8, 1996

Denver, Colorado
McNichols Sports Arena
Opening Act: The Hunger
Attendance: 7,644   Capacity: 14,273
Promoter: Feyline Presents

SEPTEMBER 10, 1996

Valley Center (Wichita), Kansas
Britt Brown Arena @ Kansas Coliseum
Opening Act: The Hunger
Attendance: 9,205   Capacity: 9,666
Promoter: Contemporary Productions

SEPTEMBER 11, 1996

Oklahoma City, Oklahoma
Myriad Convention Center
Opening Act: The Hunger
Attendance: 9,423   Capacity: 10,343
Promoter: Contemporary Productions

SEPTEMBER 13, 1996

Tupelo, Mississippi
Tupelo Coliseum
Opening Act: The Hunger
Attendance: 7,969   Capacity: 7,969
Promoter: New Era Promotions
■ **SET LIST**
Deuce
King of the Night Time World
Do You Love Me
Calling Dr. Love
Cold Gin
Watchin' You
Firehouse
I Stole Your Love
Shock Me

Ace Frehley Guitar Solo
Let Me Go, Rock 'n Roll
Shout It Out Loud
Strutter
Gene Simmons Bass Solo
God of Thunder
Peter Criss Drum Solo - reprise
New York Groove
Love Gun
100,000 Years
Black Diamond
Detroit Rock City
Beth
Rock and Roll All Nite

■ Conservative religious protestors staged a boy-cott of the concert. In response, Paul announced to the crowd: "I know there are some people who didn't want us to come here. I want us to all pause in a moment of silence in prayer for these people. Dear God, please, in your infinite wisdom, keep us and protect us from the morons outside who don't know why we're here!" One report indicated that the band had been offered $300,000 to cancel their performance.

SEPTEMBER 14, 1996

Birmingham, Alabama
Birmingham-Jefferson Civic Center
Opening Act: The Hunger
Attendance: 13,913   Capacity: 18,357
Promoter: New Era Promotions
■ **SET LIST**
See September 13, 1996.

SEPTEMBER 15, 1996

Pensacola, Florida
The Pensacola Civic Center
Opening Act: The Hunger
Attendance: 8,146   Capacity: 8,146
Promoter: Beaver Productions
■ **SET LIST**
See September 13, 1996.

SEPTEMBER 17, 1996

Miami, Florida
Miami Arena
Opening Act: The Verve Pipe
Attendance: 10,992   Capacity: 10,992
Promoter: Cellar Door Concerts
■ **SET LIST**
See September 13, 1996.
■ A crew from MTV Latino was on-hand to tape footage for a two-hour KISS special, *Hora Prima*, which premiered on October 10 and included "Do You Love Me" from Miami.

SEPTEMBER 19, 1996

Jacksonville, Florida
Jacksonville Veterans Memorial Coliseum
Opening Act: The Verve Pipe
Attendance: 5,516   Capacity: 5,516
Promoter: Fantasma Productions
■ **SET LIST**
See September 13, 1996.

SEPTEMBER 20, 1996

St. Petersburg, Florida
Thunderdome
Opening Act: The Verve Pipe
Attendance: 14,328   Capacity: 14,328
Promoter: Cellar Door Concerts
■ **SET LIST**
See September 13, 1996.

After nearly 17 years, the Catman is back behind the kit on the Alive/Worldwide Tour.

SEPTEMBER 22, 1996

Orlando, Florida
Orlando Centroplex Arena
Opening Act: The Verve Pipe
Attendance: 11,755   Capacity: 11,755
Promoter: Cellar Door Concerts
■ **SET LIST**
See September 13, 1996.

SEPTEMBER 24, 1996

Charleston, South Carolina
North Charleston Coliseum
Opening Act: The Verve Pipe
Attendance: 6,276   Capacity: 10,000
Promoter: C & C Entertainment
■ **SET LIST**
See September 13, 1996.

SEPTEMBER 25, 1996

Columbia, South Carolina
Carolina Coliseum
Opening Act: The Verve Pipe
Attendance: 9,034   Capacity: 9,034
Promoter: C & C Entertainment
■ **SET LIST**
See September 13, 1996.
■ Gene fell and broke his bass during "Detroit Rock City."

SEPTEMBER 27, 1996

Charlotte, North Carolina
Charlotte Coliseum
Opening Act: The Verve Pipe
Attendance: 18,593   Capacity: 18,593
Promoter: C & C Entertainment
■ **SET LIST**
See September 13, 1996.

SEPTEMBER 28, 1996

Greensboro, North Carolina
Greensboro Coliseum
Opening Act: The Verve Pipe
Attendance: 16,100   Capacity: 16,100
Promoter: C & C Entertainment
■ **SET LIST**
See September 13, 1996.
■ The attendance figure was announced as the highest ever recorded at the venue.

SEPTEMBER 29, 1996

Knoxville, Tennessee
Thompson-Boling Arena
Opening Act: The Verve Pipe
Attendance: 13,500   Capacity: 13,500
Promoter: Mid-South Concerts
■ **SET LIST**
See September 13, 1996.

OCTOBER 1, 1996

Atlanta, Georgia
The Omni
Opening Act: The Verve Pipe
Attendance: 13,168   Capacity: 13,168
Promoter: Concert/Southern Promotions
■ **SET LIST**
See September 13, 1996.
■ This concert was videotaped for a television broadcast in Japan. Additionally, tape of "Rock and Roll All Nite" was used for broadcast on *Dick Clark's New Year's Rockin' Eve*. Paul even went so far as to say "Happy New Years' Eve," and balloons were dropped over the main floor for the taping.

OCTOBER 2, 1996

Atlanta, Georgia
The Omni
Opening Act: The Bogmen
Attendance: 10,360   Capacity: 13,168
Promoter: Concert/Southern Promotions

■ SET LIST
See September 13, 1996.

OCTOBER 4, 1996

Roanoke, Virginia
Roanoke Civic Center
Opening Act: The Bogmen
Attendance: 8,226   Capacity: 8,226
Promoter: Cellar Door Concerts

■ SET LIST
See September 13, 1996.

■ Again, due to technical difficulties, "Beth" was dropped from the set.

OCTOBER 5, 1996

Hampton, Virginia
Hampton Coliseum
Opening Act: The Bogmen
Attendance: 9,276   Capacity: 9,276
Promoter: Cellar Door Concerts

■ SET LIST
See September 13, 1996.

OCTOBER 6, 1996

Landover (Washington, D.C.), Maryland
USAir Arena
Opening Act: The Bogmen
Attendance: 11,984   Capacity: 11,984
Promoter: Cellar Door Concerts

■ SET LIST
See September 13, 1996.

■ A new version of the Alive/Worldwide tour-book with eight extra pages was sold for the first time at this show.

OCTOBER 7, 1996

Landover (Washington, D.C.), Maryland
USAir Arena
Opening Act: Deftones
Attendance: 11,984   Capacity: 11,984
Promoter: Cellar Door Concerts

■ SET LIST
See September 13, 1996.

OCTOBER 8, 1996

Philadelphia, Pennsylvania
CoreStates Center
Opening Act: The Bogmen
Attendance: 14,903   Capacity: 14,903
Promoter: Electric Factory Concerts

■ SET LIST
See September 13, 1996.

OCTOBER 9, 1996

Philadelphia, Pennsylvania
CoreStates Center
Opening Act: Deftones
Attendance: 14,903   Capacity: 14,903
Promoter: Electric Factory Concerts

■ SET LIST
See September 13, 1996.

OCTOBER 11, 1996

Philadelphia, Pennsylvania
CoreStates Center
Opening Act: Coyote Shivers
Attendance: 9,152   Capacity: 14,903
Promoter: Electric Factory Concerts

■ SET LIST
See September 13, 1996.

OCTOBER 12, 1996

Albany, New York
Knickerbocker Arena
Opening Act: Deftones
Attendance: 13,038   Capacity: 13,038
Promoter: Magic City Productions

■ SET LIST
See September 13, 1996.

OCTOBER 13, 1996

Buffalo, New York
Marine Midland Arena
Opening Act: Deftones
Attendance: 14,142   Capacity: 14,142
Promoter: Magic City Productions

■ SET LIST
See September 13, 1996.

OCTOBER 15, 1996

Indianapolis, Indiana
Market Square Arena
Opening Act: Deftones
Attendance: 13,164   Capacity: 13,164
Promoter: Sunshine Promotions

■ SET LIST
See September 13, 1996.

■ This was the final live performance of "Strutter."

OCTOBER 16, 1996

Auburn Hills (Detroit), Michigan
The Palace of Auburn Hills
Opening Act: Coyote Shivers
Attendance: 13,633   Capacity: 13,633
Promoters: Belkin Productions, Cellar Door North Central

■ SET LIST
Detroit Rock City
King of the Night Time World
Do You Love Me
Calling Dr. Love
Cold Gin
Watchin' You
Firehouse
I Stole Your Love
Shock Me
Ace Frehley Guitar Solo
Let Me Go, Rock 'n Roll
Shout It Out Loud
Take Me
Gene Simmons Bass Solo
God of Thunder
Peter Criss Drum Solo - reprise
New York Groove
Love Gun
100,000 Years
Black Diamond
Deuce
Beth
Rock and Roll All Nite

■ "Take Me" replaced "Strutter" in the set list and the band opened the show with "Detroit Rock City."

OCTOBER 17, 1996

Auburn Hills (Detroit), Michigan
The Palace of Auburn Hills
Opening Act: Deftones
Attendance: 13,633   Capacity: 13,633
Promoters: Belkin Productions, Cellar Door North Central

■ SET LIST
Deuce
King of the Night Time World
Do You Love Me
Calling Dr. Love
Cold Gin
Watchin' You
Firehouse
I Stole Your Love
Shock Me
Ace Frehley Guitar Solo
Let Me Go, Rock 'n Roll
Shout It Out Loud
Take Me
Gene Simmons Bass Solo
God of Thunder
Peter Criss Guitar Solo - reprise
New York Groove
Love Gun
100,000 Years
Black Diamond
Detroit Rock City
Beth
Rock and Roll All Nite

OCTOBER 18, 1996

Lexington, Kentucky
Rupp Arena
Opening Act: Deftones
Attendance: 11,740   Capacity: 14,000
Promoters: Sunshine Promotions, Belkin Productions

■ SET LIST
See October 17, 1996.

OCTOBER 20, 1996

Cleveland, Ohio
GUND Arena
Opening Act: Deftones
Attendance: 17,037   Capacity: 17,037
Promoter: Belkin Productions

■ SET LIST
See October 17, 1996.

OCTOBER 21, 1996

Rosemont (Chicago), Illinois
Rosemont Horizon
Opening Act: Deftones
Attendance: 13,315   Capacity: 13,315
Promoter: JAM Productions

■ SET LIST
See October 17, 1996.

OCTOBER 23, 1996

Omaha, Nebraska
Omaha Civic Auditorium
Opening Act: Royal Crown Revue
Attendance: 10,666   Capacity: 10,666
Promoter: Beaver Productions

■ SET LIST
See October 17, 1996.

■ Attendance for the two Omaha shows set a box office record.

OCTOBER 24, 1996

Omaha, Nebraska
Omaha Civic Auditorium
Opening Act: Royal Crown Revue
Attendance: 10,666   Capacity: 10,666
Promoter: Beaver Productions

■ SET LIST
See October 17, 1996.

OCTOBER 26, 1996

Las Cruces, New Mexico
Pan American Center

Opening Act: Caroline's Spine
Attendance: 8,297   Capacity: 10,661
Promoter: Evening Star Productions
■ **SET LIST**
See October 17, 1996.

■ One fan in the front row had covered his face and head (which was mostly bald) with black and white greasepaint using a design that looked more like a Holstein cow than any member of KISS. Before "Detroit Rock City," his image was put up on the main video screen; when Ace saw him, he and the rest of the band burst into such uncontained laughter that the show was paused briefly.

OCTOBER 27, 1996
Albuquerque, New Mexico
Tingley Coliseum
Opening Act: Caroline's Spine
Attendance: 10,001   Capacity: 11,500
Promoter: Evening Star Productions
■ **SET LIST**
See October 17, 1996.

■ The originally scheduled opening act, Fluffy, did not perform and was replaced by Caroline's Spine.

OCTOBER 29, 1996
San Diego, California
San Diego Sports Arena
Opening Act: Caroline's Spine
Attendance: 9,872   Capacity: 10,778
Promoter: Bill Silva Presents
■ **SET LIST**
See October 17, 1996.

OCTOBER 31, 1996
Laguna Hills, California
Irvine Meadows Amphitheatre
Opening Act: Poe
Attendance: 13,485   Capacity: 15,416
Promoter: Avalon Attractions
■ **SET LIST**
See October 17, 1996.

■ At both the October 31 and November 1 shows, as Paul was giving one of his cliché raps about the selection of women in the audience, Peter did a double-take when he looked back and saw an extreme close-up of his daughter Jenilee on the video screens.

NOVEMBER 1, 1996
Laguna Hills, California
Irvine Meadows Amphitheatre
Opening Act: Reel Big Fish
Attendance: 9,065   Capacity: 15,416
Promoter: Avalon Attractions
■ **SET LIST**
Deuce
King of the Night Time World
Do You Love Me
Calling Dr. Love
Cold Gin
C'mon and Love Me
Firehouse
I Stole Your Love
2,000 Man
Ace Frehley Guitar Solo
Let Me Go, Rock 'n Roll
Shout It Out Loud
Take Me
Gene Simmons Bass Solo
God of Thunder
Peter Criss Drum Solo - reprise

New York Groove
Love Gun
100,000 Years
Black Diamond
Detroit Rock City
Beth
Rock and Roll All Nite

■ Both "C'mon and Love Me" and "2,000 Man" were added to the set list. "Take Me" was performed for the final time.

NOVEMBER 2, 1996
Las Vegas, Nevada
MGM Grand Garden Arena
Opening Act: Caroline's Spine
Attendance: 13,030   Capacity: 13,030
Promoter: Evening Star Productions
■ **SET LIST**
Deuce
King of the Night Time World
Do You Love Me
Calling Dr. Love
Cold Gin
C'mon and Love Me
Firehouse
I Stole Your Love
2,000 Man
Ace Frehley Guitar Solo
Let Me Go, Rock 'n Roll
Shout It Out Loud
Watchin' You
Gene Simmons Bass Solo
God of Thunder
Peter Criss Drum Solo - reprise
New York Groove
Love Gun
100,000 Years
Black Diamond
Detroit Rock City
Beth
Rock and Roll All Nite

■ Backstage, Gene accidentally spilled a soda on Annette Funicello, who was there to watch her sons' band Caroline's Spine.

NOVEMBER 5, 1996
Austin, Texas
Frank C. Erwin, Jr., Special Events Center
Opening Act: Johnny Bravo
Attendance: 7,929   Capacity: 13,506
Promoter: Pace Concerts

NOVEMBER 6, 1996
Lafayette, Louisiana
Cajundome
Opening Act: Johnny Bravo
Attendance: 6,703   Capacity: 10,000
Promoter: Beaver Productions
■ **SET LIST**
See Novemeber 2, 1996.

NOVEMBER 8, 1996
Shreveport, Louisiana
Hirsch Memorial Coliseum
Opening Act: Johnny Bravo
Attendance: 7,232   Capacity: 8,000
Promoter: Beaver Productions
■ **SET LIST**
Deuce
King of the Night Time World
Do You Love Me
Calling Dr. Love
Cold Gin
C'mon and Love Me
Firehouse
I Stole Your Love

Shock Me
Ace Frehley Guitar Solo
Let Me Go, Rock 'n Roll
Shout It Out Loud
Watchin' You
Gene Simmons Bass Solo
God of Thunder
Peter Criss Drum Solo - reprise
New York Groove
Love Gun
100,000 Years
Black Diamond
Detroit Rock City
Beth
Rock and Roll All Nite

NOVEMBER 9, 1996
Little Rock, Arkansas
T.H. Barton Coliseum
Opening Act: Johnny Bravo
Attendance: 9,200   Capacity: 9,200
Promoter: Mid-South Concerts
■ **SET LIST**
See November 8, 1996.

NOVEMBER 10, 1996
Dallas, Texas
Reunion Arena
Opening Act: Johnny Bravo
Attendance: 11,545   Capacity: 12,000
Promoter: Beaver Productions
■ **SET LIST**
See November 8, 1996.

■ Much to the delight of the band members, four female fans in the front row began making out with each other. One fan stripped completely naked and had actually thrown most of her clothes on the stage. She was awarded with a prototype KISS tie-dye T-shirt and Paul's smashed guitar. Because Paul's in-laws were at the show, the entire episode was never broadcast over the video monitors.

NOVEMBER 20, 1996
Birmingham, England
National Exhibition Centre
Opening Act: The Verve Pipe
Attendance: 11,500   Capacity: 12,000
Promoter: MCP
■ **SET LIST**
Deuce
King of the Night Time World
Do You Love Me
Calling Dr. Love
Cold Gin
C'mon and Love Me
Firehouse
I Stole Your Love
Shock Me
Ace Frehley Guitar Solo
Let Me Go, Rock 'n Roll
Shout It Out Loud
Watchin' You
Gene Simmons Bass Solo
God of Thunder
Peter Criss Drum Solo - reprise
New York Groove
Love Gun
100,000 Years
Black Diamond
Detroit Rock City
I Was Made for Lovin' You
Rock and Roll All Nite

■ "Beth" was not performed at the first three European shows.

NOVEMBER 21, 1996

Manchester, England
Nynex Arena
Opening Act: The Verve Pipe
Attendance: 8,000   Capacity: 21,000
Promoter: MCP
■ **SET LIST**
See November 20, 1996.

NOVEMBER 25, 1996

London, England
Wembley Arena
Opening Act: The Verve Pipe
Attendance: 11,000   Capacity: 12,000
Promoter: MCP
■ **SET LIST**
Deuce
King of the Night Time World
Do You Love Me
Calling Dr. Love
Cold Gin
Watchin' You
Firehouse
I Stole Your Love
Shock Me
Ace Frehley Guitar Solo
Let Me Go, Rock 'n Roll
Shout It Out Loud
I Was Made for Lovin' You
C'mon and Love Me
Gene Simmons Bass Solo
God of Thunder
Peter Criss Drum Solo - reprise
New York Groove
Love Gun
100,000 Years
Black Diamond
Detroit Rock City
Rock and Roll All Nite

NOVEMBER 28, 1996   POSTPONED

Barcelona, Spain
Palau Val D'Hebron - Sports Palais
Opening Act: The Verve Pipe
Capacity: 10,000
Promoter: Gay & Company
■ The show was postponed due to a French truckers' strike, and rescheduled for June 30, 1997.

NOVEMBER 29, 1996   POSTPONED

Zaragoza, Spain
Sala Multiusos
Opening Act: The Verve Pipe
Capacity: 10,000
Promoter: Gay & Company
■ Due to the French truckers' strike, this concert was rescheduled for June 24, 1997.

DECEMBER 1, 1996

Bruxelles, Belgium
Vorst Nationaal
Opening Act: The Verve Pipe
Attendance: 8,000   Capacity: 8,000
Promoter: Sound & Vision
■ **SET LIST**
Deuce
King of the Night Time World
Do You Love Me
Calling Dr. Love
Cold Gin
Watchin' You
Firehouse
I Stole Your Love
Shock Me
Ace Frehley Guitar Solo

RONNIE GREEN

Let Me Go, Rock 'n Roll
Shout It Out Loud
I Was Made for Lovin' You
C'mon and Love Me
Gene Simmons Bass Solo
God of Thunder
Peter Criss Drum Solo - reprise
New York Groove
Love Gun
100,000 Years
Black Diamond
Detroit Rock City
Beth
Rock and Roll All Nite

DECEMBER 2, 1996

Paris, France
Le Zenith
Opening Act: The Verve Pipe
Attendance: 6,289   Capacity: 6,289
Promoter: Gerard Drouot Productions

DECEMBER 4, 1996

Berlin, Germany
Deutschlandhalle
Opening Acts: Die Ärtze, The Verve Pipe
Attendance: 10,000   Capacity: 10,000
Promoter: Marek Lieberberg

DECEMBER 6, 1996

Stockholm, Sweden
Stockholm Globe Arena
Opening Act: The Verve Pipe
Attendance: 13,500   Capacity: 13,500
Promoter: EMA Telstar
■ **SET LIST**
See December 1, 1996.
■ The band reportedly sold out both shows in Sweden in less than 60 minutes. The demand for tickets was so overwhelming that on December 3, EMA Telstar put tickets on sale for a June 14, 1997 KISS concert in Stockholm and sold 33,000 tickets in under four hours.

DECEMBER 7, 1996

Göteborg, Sweden
Scandinavium
Opening Act: The Verve Pipe
Attendance: 11,791   Capacity: 11,791
Promoter: EMA Telstar
■ **SET LIST**
See December 1, 1996.

DECEMBER 8, 1996

Oslo, Norway

Spektrum
Opening Act: The Verve Pipe
Attendance: 9,200   Capacity: 9,200
Promoter: EMA Telstar
■ **SET LIST**
See December 1, 1996.
■ Paul sang a line from Sister Sledge's "We Are Family" during the breakdown in "Rock and Roll All Nite."

DECEMBER 10, 1996

Rotterdam, The Netherlands
Sportspaleis Aho'y
Opening Act: The Verve Pipe
Attendance: 4,500   Capacity: 4,500
Promoter: Mojo Concerts
■ **SET LIST**
See December 1, 1996.

DECEMBER 11, 1996

Frankfurt a.M., Germany
Festhalle
Opening Acts: Die Ärtze, The Verve Pipe
Attendance: 13,500   Capacity: 13,500
Promoter: Marek Lieberberg
■ **SET LIST**
See December 1, 1996.

DECEMBER 12, 1996

Oberhausen, Germany
Oberhausen Arena
Opening Acts: Die Ärtze, The Verve Pipe
Attendance: 12,500   Capacity: 12,500
Promoter: Marek Lieberberg
■ **SET LIST**
See December 1, 1996.
■ MTV Europe broadcast a half-hour long, KISS-produced special entitled *The Second Coming*, (not to be confused with the home video of the same name), which later aired in local markets in Europe and North America where KISS was to be performing.

DECEMBER 14, 1996

Praha, Czech Republic
Sportovní Hala
Opening Act: The Verve Pipe
Attendance: 15,000   Capacity: 15,000
Promoter: Interkoncerts
■ **SET LIST**
See December 1, 1996.

DECEMBER 15, 1996

Praha, Czech Republic
Sportovní Hala
Opening Act: The Verve Pipe
Attendance: 15,000   Capacity: 15,000
Promoter: Interkoncerts
■ **SET LIST**
See December 1, 1996.
■ Gene did not fly at either show in the Czech Republic as the venue was not tall enough to accommodate the flying rig.

DECEMBER 16, 1996

Wien, Austria
Libro Music Hall
Opening Act: The Verve Pipe
Capacity: 4,300
Promoter: Artists Marketing

DECEMBER 18, 1996

Milano, Italy
Palatrusardi
Opening Act: The Verve Pipe

Attendance: 8,000   Capacity: 8,000
Promoter: Barley Arts Promotions
■ **SET LIST**
See December 1, 1996.

DECEMBER 19, 1996

Zürich, Switzerland
Hallenstadion
Opening Acts: Die Ärtze, The Verve Pipe
Attendance: 12,000   Capacity: 12,000
Promoter: Good News Agency
■ **SET LIST**
See December 1, 1996.

DECEMBER 20, 1996

Stuttgart, Germany
Schleyerhalle
Opening Acts: Die Ärtze, The Verve Pipe
Capacity: 12,000
Promoter: Marek Lieberberg
■ **SET LIST**
See December 1, 1996.

DECEMBER 21, 1996

Dortmund, Germany
Westfalenhalle
Opening Act: Die Ärtze
Capacity: 13,000
Promoter: Good News Agency
■ After KISS had concluded "Shout It Out Loud," the audience kept singing the chorus over and over, prompting the band to start playing part of the song again.

DECEMBER 28, 1996

Worcester, Massachusetts
The Centrum
Opening Act: The 4th Floor
Attendance: 12,244   Capacity: 12,244
Promoter: Beaver Productions
■ **SET LIST**
Deuce
C'mon and Love Me
Let Me Go, Rock 'n Roll
Do You Love Me
Firehouse
Watchin' You
Shock Me
Ace Frehley Guitar Solo
Calling Dr. Love
Shout It Out Loud
I Stole Your Love
Cold Gin
King of the Night Time World
New York Groove
Love Gun
Gene Simmons Bass Solo
God of Thunder
Peter Criss Drum Solo - reprise
100,000 Years
Black Diamond
Detroit Rock City
Beth
Rock and Roll All Nite

DECEMBER 29, 1996

Uniondale, New York
Nassau Veterans Memorial Coliseum
Opening Act: The 4th Floor
Attendance: 13,972   Capacity: 14,550
Promoter: Delsener-Slater Enterprises
■ **SET LIST**
Deuce
I Stole Your Love
Let Me Go, Rock 'n Roll
Do You Love Me

Firehouse
Watchin' You
Shock Me
Ace Frehley Guitar Solo
Calling Dr. Love
Shout It Out Loud
C'mon and Love Me
Cold Gin
King of the Night Time World
Love Gun
Gene Simmons Bass Solo
God of Thunder
Peter Criss Drum Solo - reprise
New York Groove
100,000 Years
Black Diamond
Detroit Rock City
Beth
Rock and Roll All Nite

DECEMBER 30, 1996

Hartford, Connecticut
Hartford Civic Center
Opening Act: The 4th Floor
Attendance: 12,291   Capacity: 12,291
Promoter: Metropolitan Entertainment
■ **SET LIST**
See December 29, 1996.

DECEMBER 31, 1996

East Rutherford, New Jersey
Continental Airlines Arena
Opening Act: The 4th Floor
Attendance: 13,253   Capacity: 15,310
Promoter: Delsener-Slater Enterprises
■ **SET LIST**
Deuce
King of the Night Time World
Let Me Go, Rock 'n Roll
Do You Love Me
Firehouse
Watchin' You
Shock Me
Ace Frehley Guitar Solo
Calling Dr. Love
Shout It Out Loud
C'mon and Love Me
Cold Gin
I Stole Your Love
Love Gun
Gene Simmons Bass Solo
God of Thunder
Peter Criss Drum Solo - reprise
New York Groove
100,000 Years
Black Diamond
Detroit Rock City
Beth
Rock and Roll All Nite
■ Portions of the show were broadcast live on the 25th Anniversary broadcast of *Dick Clark's New Year's Rockin' Eve*. KISS balloons were dropped during "Rock and Roll All Nite."

JANUARY 18, 1997

Tokyo, Japan
Tokyodome
No Opening Act
Attendance: 46,000   Capacity: 46,000
Promoter: Udo Artists
■ **SET LIST**
See December 29, 1996.
■ Large KISS Army banners were hung on both sides of the stage. KISS's show began at 5:00 P.M.

and concussion bombs. There was no confetti shower at the end of the show, however.

NELSON MARÉ

JANUARY 22, 1997

Osaka, Japan
Osaka Castle Hall
No Opening Act
Capacity: 8,500
Promoter: Udo Artists

■ SET LIST

Deuce
King of the Night Time World
Let Me Go, Rock 'n Roll
Do You Love Me
Firehouse
C'mon and Love Me
Shock Me
Ace Frehley Guitar Solo
Shout It Out Loud
I Was Made for Lovin' You
Cold Gin
I Stole Your Love
Love Gun
Gene Simmons Bass Solo
God of Thunder
Peter Criss Drum Solo - reprise
New York Groove
100,000 Years
Detroit Rock City
Black Diamond
Beth
Rock and Roll All Nite

■ Due to a throat infection, Gene only sang lead vocals on the first verse of "Deuce" and shared them with Paul on "God of Thunder." Paul, Peter, and Ace handled the remainder of his lead vocals. Both "Calling Dr. Love" and "Watchin' You" were dropped from the set for the night.

Before "Let Me Go, Rock 'n Roll," Paul led the audience by humming "Ue wo mui te arukou," more commonly known to those outside of Japan as the "Sukiyaki Song."

JANUARY 24, 1997

Fukuoka, Japan
Kokusai Center
No Opening Act
Capacity: 5,900
Promoter: Udo Artists

■ SET LIST

See December 29, 1996.
■ Before "Watchin You," Paul played a few notes of "I Want You."

JANUARY 25, 1997

Hiroshima, Japan
Hiroshima Sun Plaza
No Opening Act
Capacity: 4,200
Promoter: Udo Artists

■ SET LIST

Deuce
King of the Night Time World
Let Me Go, Rock 'n Roll
Do You Love Me
Firehouse
C'mon and Love Me
Shock Me
Ace Frehley Guitar Solo
Shout It Out Loud
I Was Made for Lovin' You
Cold Gin
I Stole Your Love
Love Gun

JANUARY 20, 1997

Nagoya, Japan
Rainbow Hall
No Opening Act
Capacity: 7,000
Promoter: Udo Artists

■ SET LIST

See December 29, 1996.
■ Prior to "New York Groove," the audience sang "Happy Birthday" to Paul.

JANUARY 21, 1997

Osaka, Japan
Osaka Castle Hall
No Opening Act
Capacity: 8,500
Promoter: Udo Artists

■ SET LIST

See December 29, 1996.
■ Though Japanese fire laws are very strict, for its Osaka gigs KISS was able to use flamethrowers

Gene Simmons Bass Solo
God of Thunder
Peter Criss Drum Solo - reprise
New York Groove
100,000 Years
Black Diamond
Detroit Rock City
Beth
Rock and Roll All Nite

■ KISS T-shirts reading "KISS sets Hiroshima on fire" were recalled for fear of offending people.

"Watchin' You" and "Calling Dr. Love" were again dropped from the set.

JANUARY 31, 1997
Auckland, New Zealand
Auckland Supertop
Opening Act: The Exponents
Attendance: 8,000   Capacity: 8,000
Promoter: Frontier Touring
■ SET LIST
Deuce
King of the Night Time World
Let Me Go, Rock 'n Roll
Do You Love Me
Firehouse
Watchin' You
Shock Me
Ace Frehley Guitar Solo
Calling Dr. Love
Shout It Out Loud
I Was Made for Lovin' You
Cold Gin
I Stole Your Love
Love Gun
Gene Simmons Bass Solo
God of Thunder
Peter Criss Drum Solo - reprise
New York Groove
100,000 Years
Shandi
Black Diamond
Detroit Rock City
Beth
Rock and Roll All Nite

FEBRUARY 3, 1997
Brisbane, Australia
Entertainment Centre
Opening Act: Custard
Capacity: 12,000
Promoter: Frontier Touring
■ SET LIST
See January 31, 1997.

FEBRUARY 5, 1997
Sydney, Australia
Entertainment Center
Opening Act: Fireballs
Attendance: 12,000   Capacity: 12,000
Promoter: Frontier Touring
■ SET LIST
See January 31, 1997.
■ Ace played part of "Fractured Mirror" during his solo.

FEBRUARY 6, 1997
Sydney, Australia
Entertainment Center
Opening Act: Fireballs
Attendance: 12,000   Capacity: 12,000
Promoter: Frontier Touring
■ SET LIST
See January 31, 1997.

■ Ace and Paul were stranded in mid-air for over ten minutes when their cherrypicker would not retract. One of the stacks of Marshall amps was lowered, and the cherrypicker swung around over the stage, though both Frehley and Stanley had to jump the remaining eight feet to the stage floor.

FEBRUARY 9, 1997
Perth, Australia
Burswood Dome
Opening Act: Non-Intentional Lifeform
Attendance: 16,000   Capacity: 17,500
Promoter: Frontier Touring
■ SET LIST
See January 31, 1997.

FEBRUARY 11, 1997
Adelaide, Australia
Adelaide Memorial Drive
Opening Act: Fireballs
Attendance: 14,000   Capacity: 14,000
Promoter: Frontier Touring
■ SET LIST
See January 31, 1997.

FEBRUARY 13, 1997
Melbourne, Australia
National Tennis Centre @ Melbourne Park
Opening Act: Fireballs
Promoter: Frontier Touring
■ SET LIST
See January 31, 1997.

FEBRUARY 14, 1997
Melbourne, Australia
National Tennis Centre @ Melbourne Park
Opening Act: The Fauves
Promoter: Frontier Touring
■ SET LIST
See January 31, 1997.

FEBRUARY 15, 1997
Melbourne, Australia
National Tennis Centre @ Melbourne Park
Opening Act: Snout
Promoter: Frontier Touring
■ SET LIST
Deuce
King of the Night Time World
Let Me Go, Rock 'n Roll
Do You Love Me
Firehouse
Watchin' You
Shock Me
Ace Frehley Guitar Solo
Calling Dr. Love
Shout It Out Loud
I Was Made for Lovin' You
Cold Gin
C'mon and Love Me
Love Gun
Gene Simmons Bass Solo
God of Thunder
Peter Criss Drum Solo - reprise
2,000 Man
100,000 Years
Shandi
Black Diamond
Detroit Rock City
Beth
Rock and Roll All Nite

MARCH 7, 1997
Ciudad de México, Mexico
Palacio de los Deportes

Opening Act: Pantera
Attendance: 18,600   Capacity: 18,600
Promoter: OCESA Presents
■ SET LIST
Deuce
King of the Night Time World
Let Me Go, Rock 'n Roll
Do You Love Me
Firehouse
Watchin' You
Shock Me
Ace Frehley Guitar Solo
Calling Dr. Love
Shout It Out Loud
I Was Made for Lovin' You
Cold Gin
C'mon and Love Me
Love Gun
Gene Simmons Bass Solo
God of Thunder
Peter Criss Drum Solo - reprise
2,000 Man
100,000 Years
Black Diamond
Detroit Rock City
Beth
Rock and Roll All Nite
■ Part of "La Bamba" was played prior to "Black Diamond."

MARCH 8, 1997
Ciudad de México, Mexico
Palacio de los Deportes
Opening Act: Pantera
Attendance: 18,600   Capacity: 18,600
Promoter: OCESA Presents
■ SET LIST
See March 7, 1997.

MARCH 9, 1997
Ciudad de México, Mexico
Palacio de los Deportes
Opening Act: Pantera
Attendance: 18,600   Capacity: 18,600
Promoter: OCESA Presents
■ SET LIST
See March 7, 1997.

MARCH 11, 1997
Santiago, Chile
Velodrome del Estadio Nacional
Opening Act: Pantera
Attendance: 11,000   Capacity: 15,000
Promoter: D.S. Medios Y Espectaculos S.A.
■ SET LIST
See March 7, 1997.

MARCH 14, 1997
Buenos Aires, Argentina
Estadio Monumental de River Plate
Opening Acts: Pantera, V8, Malon
Attendance: 54,000   Capacity: 75,000
Promoter: Rock & Pop Int'l
■ SET LIST
See March 7, 1997.
■ The band played "La Bamba" prior to "Black Diamond."

RIFF was tentatively scheduled to appear on the bill but canceled.

MARCH 21, 1997
New Haven, Connecticut
New Haven Veterans Memorial Coliseum
Opening Act: Powerman 5000

Attendance: 6,679   Capacity: 6,900
Promoter: Metropolitan Entertainment
■ **SET LIST**
See March 7, 1997.

■ Paul sang the first verse and chorus of "Love Gun" without any musical accompaniment. He would continue to do this at most of the concerts on this leg of the tour. Additionally, Paul's flying effect was set up at this show and at the Springfield and Providence shows that followed, though it was not used at any of the three concerts.

On this leg, dubbed "The Lost Cities Tour," Paul frequently introduced "Shock Me" by referring to the Heaven's Gate cult whose members had recently committed mass suicide, ostensibly in an attempt to catch a ride on a UFO they believed was waiting for them in the tail of the Hale-Bopp comet.

MARCH 22, 1997
Springfield, Massachusetts
Springfield Civic Center
Opening Act: Powerman 5000
Attendance: 5,028   Capacity: 5,250
Promoter: Metropolitan Entertainment
■ **SET LIST**
See March 7, 1997.

MARCH 23, 1997
Providence, Rhode Island
Providence Civic Center
Opening Act: Powerman 5000
Attendance: 10,818   Capacity: 10,818
Promoter: Beaver Productions
■ **SET LIST**
See March 7, 1997.

MARCH 25, 1997
Portland, Maine
Cumberland County Civic Center
Opening Act: Powerman 5000
Attendance: 6,187   Capacity: 6,187
Promoter: Delsener-Slater Enterprises
■ **SET LIST**
See March 7, 1997.
■ Paul's flying effect made its concert debut.

MARCH 27, 1997
Wheeling, West Virginia
Wheeling Civic Center
Opening Act: Powerman 5000
Attendance: 6,454   Capacity: 6,950
Promoter: DiCesare-Engler Productions
■ **SET LIST**
See March 7, 1997.

MARCH 28, 1997
Hamilton, Ontario, Canada
Copps Coliseum
Opening Act: Glueleg
Attendance: 11,804   Capacity: 11,804
Promoter: Universal Concerts-Canada
■ **SET LIST**
Deuce
King of the Night Time World
Let Me Go, Rock 'n Roll
Do You Love Me
Firehouse
Watchin' You
Shock Me
Ace Frehley Guitar Solo
Calling Dr. Love
Shout It Out Loud
Cold Gin
Love Gun
C'mon and Love Me
I Was Made for Lovin' You
Gene Simmons Bass Solo
God of Thunder
Peter Criss Drum Solo - reprise
New York Groove
100,000 Years
Black Diamond
Detroit Rock City
Beth
Rock and Roll All Nite

MARCH 29, 1997
University Park, Pennsylvania
Bryce Jordan Center
Opening Act: Powerman 5000
Attendance: 11,872   Capacity: 11,872
Promoter: DiCesare-Engler Productions
■ **SET LIST**
March 28, 1997.

MARCH 31, 1997
Charleston, West Virginia
Charleston Civic Center
Opening Act: Powerman 5000
Attendance: 10,435   Capacity: 10,435
Promoter: Belkin Productions
■ **SET LIST**
March 28, 1997.

APRIL 1, 1997
Baltimore, Maryland
Baltimore Arena
Opening Act: Powerman 5000
Attendance: 7,234   Capacity: 9,489
Promoter: Cellar Door Concerts
■ **SET LIST**
See March 28, 1997.
■ After "Black Diamond," the band returned to the stage, whereupon Paul announced, "This tour has been great, we thank you, but this is the last show we will ever play together. Good night and thank you." He ran back to the microphone a few seconds later and yelled, "April Fools!"

APRIL 2, 1997
Richmond, Virginia
Richmond Coliseum
Opening Act: Powerman 5000
Attendance: 6,927   Capacity: 8,751
Promoter: C & C Entertainment
■ **SET LIST**
See March 28, 1997.

APRIL 4, 1997
Chapel Hill (Raleigh), North Carolina
Dean E. Smith Center
Opening Act: Powerman 5000
Attendance: 10,061   Capacity: 12,422
Promoter: C & C Entertainment
■ **SET LIST**
See March 28, 1997.

APRIL 5, 1997
Columbus, Georgia
Columbus Civic Center
Opening Act: Powerman 5000
Attendance: 6,207   Capacity: 7,112
Promoter: Concert/Southern Promotions
■ **SET LIST**
Deuce
King of the Night Time World
Let Me Go, Rock 'n Roll

Do You Love Me
Firehouse
Watchin' You
Shock Me
Ace Frehley Guitar Solo
Calling Dr. Love
Shout It Out Loud
Cold Gin
Love Gun
C'mon and Love Me
I Was Made for Lovin' You
Gene Simmons Bass Solo
God of Thunder
New York Groove
100,000 Years
Paul Stanley Guitar Solo
Black Diamond
Detroit Rock City
Rock and Roll All Nite

■ Peter Criss did not perform at this show, reportedly due to problems with bursitis and tendonitis of the shoulder and lower back. His drum tech, Ed Kanon, replaced him and wore full makeup and costume. After "King of the Night Time World," Paul announced to the audience that "Peter Criss is feeling a little sick tonight. He's back at the hotel, but we've got Eddie Kanon, his best friend, on drums tonight and we are going to kick your ass tonight!" "Beth" was dropped from the set list, as was the drum solo in "God of Thunder." Paul sang all lead vocals on "Black Diamond."

The irony in all of this is that Columbus, Georgia was the very first market in which "Beth" first got airplay in 1976.

APRIL 6, 1997
Nashville, Tennessee
Nashville Arena
Opening Act: Powerman 5000
Attendance: 15,267   Capacity: 15,267
Promoters: Pace Concerts, Cellar Door Concerts
■ **SET LIST**
See March 28, 1997.
■ Attendance at the concert established a venue record.

APRIL 8, 1997
Evansville, Indiana
Roberts Municipal Stadium
Opening Act: Outhouse
Attendance: 8,601   Capacity: 8,601
Promoter: Sunshine Promotions
■ **SET LIST**
See March 28, 1997.
■ Yet another greatest hits collection, *Greatest KISS* was released in the U.S. on April 8. The album had initially been released in Australia on November 11, 1996 with a different track listing.

APRIL 9, 1997
Fort Wayne, Indiana
Allen Co. War Memorial Coliseum
Opening Act: Outhouse
Attendance: 7,522   Capacity: 7,522
Promoter: Sunshine Promotions
■ **SET LIST**
See March 28, 1997.

APRIL 10, 1997
Grand Rapids, Michigan
Van Andel Arena
Opening Act: Outhouse

Attendance: 11,574   Capacity: 11,574
Promoters: Cellar Door Concerts, Belkin Productions

■ SET LIST
See March 28, 1997.

■ During Ace's solo, one of the rockets on the back of his guitar fired prematurely into the floor before ricocheting into the audience.

APRIL 12, 1997

Toledo, Ohio
John F. Savage Hall
Opening Act: Outhouse
Attendance: 8,689   Capacity: 8,689
Promoter: Belkin Productions

■ SET LIST
See March 28, 1997.

APRIL 13, 1997

Peoria, Illinois
Carver Arena @ Peoria Civic Center
Opening Act: Outhouse
Attendance: 9,202   Capacity: 9,202
Promoters: JAM Productions, Jay Goldberg

■ SET LIST
See March 28, 1997.

■ Bill Cosby was performing in the theater section of the Civic Center at the same time KISS was appearing at Carver Arena.

APRIL 15, 1997

St. Louis, Missouri
Kiel Center
Opening Act: Outhouse
Attendance: 11,184   Capacity: 13,184
Promoter: Contemporary Productions

■ SET LIST
See March 28, 1997.

■ KSHE distributed window decals featuring the *Rock and Roll Over* artwork, with Gene being replaced by Sweet Meat wearing Gene's makeup.

APRIL 16, 1997

Topeka, Kansas
Landon Arena @ Kansas ExpoCentre
Opening Act: Outhouse
Attendance: 5,953   Capacity: 8,500
Promoter: Contemporary Productions

■ SET LIST
See March 28, 1997.

APRIL 18, 1997

Sioux Falls, South Dakota
Sioux Falls Arena
Opening Act: Outhouse
Attendance: 6,404   Capacity: 6,404
Promoter: Steve Litman Productions

■ SET LIST
See March 28, 1997.

APRIL 19, 1997

Ames, Iowa
Hilton Coliseum
Opening Act: Outhouse
Attendance: 11,823   Capacity: 12,600
Promoter: Contemporary Productions

■ SET LIST
See March 28, 1997.

APRIL 20, 1997

Cedar Rapids, Iowa
Five Seasons Center
Opening Act: Outhouse
Attendance: 9,084   Capacity: 9,084
Promoter: JAM Productions

■ SET LIST
See March 28, 1997.

APRIL 22, 1997

St. Paul, Minnesota
St. Paul Civic Center
Opening Act: Outhouse
Attendance: 13,817   Capacity: 13,817
Promoter: Rose Productions

■ SET LIST
See March 28, 1997.

APRIL 23, 1997

Madison, Wisconsin
Dane County Expo Center Coliseum
Opening Act: Outhouse
Attendance: 8,233   Capacity: 8,233
Promoter: Belkin Productions

■ SET LIST
See March 28, 1997.

APRIL 25, 1997

Mankato, Minnesota
Mankato Civic Center
Opening Act: Outhouse
Attendance: 6,829   Capacity: 6,829
Promoter: Rose Productions

■ SET LIST
See March 28, 1997.

APRIL 26, 1997

Fargo, North Dakota
Fargodome
Opening Act: Outhouse
Attendance: 12,990   Capacity: 12,990
Promoter: Beaver Productions

■ SET LIST
See March 28, 1997.

■ The entire upper Midwest region of the United States and lower portions of Central Canada had been ravaged by floods during the weeks prior to KISS's concerts in the area. Revenue from KISS specialty T-shirts (reading: "We Will Survive") at the Fargo, Bismarck (April 27), and Winnipeg (April 29 & 30) shows went to a flood-victim relief fund.

APRIL 27, 1997

Bismarck, North Dakota
Bismarck Civic Center
Opening Act: Outhouse
Attendance: 7,941   Capacity: 7,941
Promoter: Beaver Productions

■ SET LIST
See March 28, 1997.

APRIL 29, 1997

Winnipeg, Manitoba, Canada
Winnipeg Arena
Opening Act: Econoline Crush
Attendance: 10,736   Capacity: 10,736
Promoter: Universal Concerts-Canada

■ SET LIST
See March 28, 1997.

■ This concert sold out in less than an hour.

APRIL 30, 1997

Winnipeg, Manitoba, Canada
Winnipeg Arena
Opening Act: Econoline Crush
Attendance: 7,986   Capacity: 10,736
Promoter: Universal Concerts-Canada

■ SET LIST
See March 28, 1997.

MAY 1, 1997

Saskatoon, Saskatchewan, Canada
Saskatchewan Place
Opening Act: Econoline Crush
Attendance: 12,604   Capacity: 12,604
Promoter: Universal Concerts-Canada

■ SET LIST
See March 28, 1997.

MAY 2, 1997

Edmonton, Alberta, Canada
Edmonton Coliseum
Opening Act: Econoline Crush
Attendance: 13,052   Capacity: 13,052
Promoter: Universal Concerts-Canada

■ SET LIST
See March 28, 1997.

MAY 3, 1997

Calgary, Alberta, Canada
Canadian Air Saddledome
Opening Act: Econoline Crush
Attendance: 12,929   Capacity: 12,929
Promoter: Universal Concerts-Canada

■ SET LIST
See March 28, 1997.

MAY 5, 1997

Seattle, Washington
KeyArena @ Seattle Center
Opening Act: Sugar Ray
Attendance: 7,217   Capacity: 7,217
Promoter: Universal Concerts

■ After his blood-spitting routine, a very exuberant Gene smeared fake blood all over his chest and crotch.

Local radio station KISW distributed "KISW Army" temporary tattoos.

MAY 6, 1997

Vancouver, British Columbia, Canada
General Motors Place
Opening Act: Econoline Crush
Attendance: 9,033   Capacity: 11,900
Promoter: Universal Concerts-Canada

■ SET LIST
Deuce
King of the Night Time World
Let Me Go, Rock 'n Roll
Do You Love Me
Firehouse
Watchin' You
Shock Me
Ace Frehley Guitar Solo
Calling Dr. Love
Shout It Out Loud
Love Gun
Cold Gin
I Was Made for Lovin' You
Gene Simmons Bass Solo
God of Thunder
Peter Criss Drum Solo - reprise
New York Groove
100,000 Years
Black Diamond
Detroit Rock City
Beth
Rock and Roll All Nite

MAY 7, 1997   CANCELED

Yakima, Washington
Yakima Valley Sundome
Opening Act: Sugar Ray
Promoter: Beaver Productions

■ The Yakima show as well as the Reno and Daly City shows (on May 9 and 10, respectively) were all canceled, in part due to production concerns about KISS's May 16 appearance at the "Rock im Park" festival in Germany.

MAY 9, 1997
Reno, Nevada **CANCELED**
Lawlor Events Center
Opening Act: Sugar Ray
Promoter: Evening Star Productions

MAY 10, 1997
Daly City (San Francisco), California
Cow Palace **CANCELED**
Opening Act: Sugar Ray
Promoter: Bill Graham Presents

MAY 16, 1997
Nürnburg, Germany
Frankenstadion
Opening Acts: Die Ärtze, Live, Neneh Cherry, Silverchair, Reef, Otto
Attendance: 40,000+
Promoter: Marek Lieberberg
■ **SET LIST**
Deuce
King of the Night Time World
Let Me Go, Rock 'n Roll
Do You Love Me
Firehouse
Watchin' You
Shock Me
Ace Frehley Guitar Solo

Calling Dr. Love
Shout It Out Loud
Love Gun
Cold Gin
I Was Made for Lovin' You
Gene Simmons Bass Solo
God of Thunder
Peter Criss Drum Solo - reprise
New York Groove
100,000 Years
Black Diamond
Detroit Rock City
Beth
Rock and Roll All Nite
■ This concert was part of the annual "Rock im Park" festival.
   On May 14 in Budapest, KISS (minus Ace) held a press conference at the Kiscelli Museum to announce the start of the European tour.

MAY 18, 1997
Eifel, Germany
Nürburgring
Opening Acts: Die Ärtze, Live, Neneh Cherry, Silverchair, Reef, The Mutton Birds, Otto
Attendance: 115,000
Promoter: Marek Lieberberg
■ **SET LIST**
See May 16, 1997.
■ The gig was part of the "Rock am Ring" festival. Thunder and rain were present throughout and threatened to cancel the event. The show went on, but as a safety precaution, Paul did not fly.

Much like the outdoor shows in Laguna Hills and Detroit, a helicopter flew over the crowd prior to the beginning of the show.
   Several songs were broadcast live on MTV Europe, and an additional half-hour of footage was aired on the channel on May 24 and 25 during the "Rock am Ring" weekend. Then, in August, a 60-minute version of the concert was broadcast throughout Europe.

MAY 21, 1997
Berlin, Germany
Waldbühne
Opening Act: Otto
Attendance: 16,000   Capacity: 24,000
Promoter: Marek Lieberberg
■ **SET LIST**
See May 16, 1997.
■ The concert was held outdoors and was once again plagued by rain.
   The opening act was a German comedian named Otto.

MAY 22, 1997
Leipzig, Germany
Messegelände
Opening Act: Die Ärtze
Attendance: 9,000
Promoter: Marek Lieberberg
■ **SET LIST**
See May 16, 1997.
■ The concert was originally scheduled for a large outdoor venue called Festwiese.

MAY 24, 1997

Hamburg, Germany
Trarennbahn Stadium
Opening Act: Die Ärtze
Attendance: 30,000   Capacity: 30,000
Promoter: Marek Lieberberg
■ **SET LIST**
See May 16, 1997.

MAY 26, 1997   CANCELED

Warszawa, Poland
Stadion Gwardi

MAY 29, 1997

Wels, Austria
Messegelände
Opening Acts: Alkbottle, Naked Lunch, Moonspell, Sex
   Tiger
Attendance: 8,000   Capacity: 15,000
Promoter: Artists Marketing
■ **SET LIST**
See May 16, 1997.

MAY 31, 1997

Imst, Austria
Skiarena Imst
Opening Acts: Alkbottle, Naked Lunch, Moonspell, Sex
   Tiger
Attendance: 4,000   Capacity: 8,500
Promoter: Artist Marketing
■ **SET LIST**
See May 16, 1997.
■ The concert took place in an open-air venue
at a ski resort. On a hill near the venue, "Jesus
Loves KISS" was written in flames that burned
throughout the show.

JUNE 1, 1997

Zürich, Switzerland
Hallenstadion
Opening Act: Sideburn
Attendance: 9,500   Capacity: 12,000
Promoters: Marco Guntensperger, Good News Agency
■ **SET LIST**
See May 16, 1997.

JUNE 4, 1997

Beograd, Yugoslavia
Sajan Arean Beograd Hala
Opening Acts: Die Ärtze, Moonspell
Capacity: 20,000
Promoter: Artists Marketing
■ **SET LIST**
See May 16, 1997.

JUNE 5, 1997

Budapest, Hungary
Petöfi Csarnok
Opening Acts: Warpigs, Irigy Hónaljmirigy
Attendance: 4,000+
Promoter: Multimedia Concerts
■ **SET LIST**
See May 16, 1997.
■ Originally scheduled for Margitszigeti Stadion
(capacity 20,800), the show was moved to a
smaller venue due to lack of ticket sales.

JUNE 7, 1997

Praha, Czech Republic
Fotbalovy Stadion Juliska
Opening Acts: Satisfucktion, Stage, Zluty Pes, Waltari
Attendance: 30,000   Capacity: 30,000
Promoter: Interkoncerts
■ **SET LIST**
See May 16, 1997.

JUNE 10, 1997

Ghent, Belgium
Flanders Expo
Opening Act: Uncle Meat
Attendance: 9,000   Capacity: 11,000
Promoters: Rock Torhout, Werchter
■ **SET LIST**
See May 16, 1997.

JUNE 11, 1997

Utrecht, The Netherlands
Prins van Oranjehal
Opening Act: Channel Zero
Attendance: 16,000   Capacity: 17,500
Promoter: Mojo Concerts
■ **SET LIST**
See May 16, 1997.
■ After "Let Me Go, Rock 'n Roll," the concert
was stopped for 45 minutes because fans were
being crushed against the stage barrier.

JUNE 14, 1997

Stockholm, Sweden
Olympic Stadion
Opening Acts: Hellacopters, Fungus
Attendance: 32,500   Capacity: 32,500
Promoter: EMA Telstar
■ **SET LIST**
See May 16, 1997.
■ Entombed was scheduled as an opening act for
both Stockholm shows, but they did not appear
at either gig.

JUNE 15, 1997

Stockholm, Sweden
Olympic Stadion
Opening Acts: Hellacopters, Fungus
Attendance: 35,500   Capacity: 35,500
Promoter: EMA Telstar
■ **SET LIST**
Deuce
King of the Night Time World
Let Me Go, Rock 'n Roll
Do You Love Me
Firehouse
Watchin' You
Shock Me
Ace Frehley Guitar Solo
Calling Dr. Love
Shout It Out Loud
Love Gun
Cold Gin
C'mon and Love Me
I Was Made for Lovin' You
Gene Simmons Bass Solo
God of Thunder
Peter Criss Drum Solo - reprise
New York Groove
100,000 Years
Black Diamond
Detroit Rock City
Beth
Rock and Roll All Nite

JUNE 17, 1997

Helsingfors, Finland
Hartwall Areena
Opening Act: Hellacopters
Attendance: 13,200   Capacity: 13,200
Promoter: EMA Telstar
■ **SET LIST**
See May 16, 1997.
■ An unofficial KISS expo complete with a wed-
ding ceremony was held at the venue on the day
of the concert.

JUNE 19, 1997

Oslo, Norway
Spektrum
Opening Act: Hellacopters
Attendance: 9,500   Capacity: 9,500
Promoter: EMA Telstar
■ **SET LIST**
See May 16, 1997.
■ The concert was originally scheduled for Valle
Hovin, a 50,000-seat outdoor venue.

JUNE 21, 1997

Valby (København), Denmark
Valby Idrætspark
Opening Acts: The Straws, Passion Orange
Attendance: 16,000   Capacity: 25,000
Promoter: DKB Concert Promotion
■ **SET LIST**
See May 16, 1997.
■ This was an outdoor show, and it rained heav-
ily throughout the concert. The McFarlane KISS
action figures made their debut at merchandise
stands.

JUNE 24, 1997

Zaragoza, Spain
Principa Felipe
Opening Act: El Fantastico Hombre Bala
Attendance: 7,500   Capacity: 7,500
Promoter: Gay & Company
■ **SET LIST**
See May 16, 1997.
■ Paul sang "La Bamba," "Guantanamera," and
"Una Paloma Blanca" before the intro to "Black
Diamond." There were no platforms or risers
used for any of the three Spanish shows.
   The concert was originally scheduled for
November 28, 1996 and the venue was changed
twice.

JUNE 25, 1997

Madrid, Spain
Sportspalace
Opening Act: El Fantastico Hombre Bala
Attendance: 9,000   Capacity: 10,000
Promoter: Gay & Company
■ **SET LIST**
Deuce
King of the Night Time World
Let Me Go, Rock 'n Roll
Do You Love Me
Firehouse
Shock Me
Ace Frehley Guitar Solo
Calling Dr. Love
Shout It Out Loud
Love Gun
Cold Gin
I Was Made for Lovin' You
Gene Simmons Bass Solo
God of Thunder
Peter Criss Drum Solo - reprise
New York Groove
100,000 Years
Black Diamond
Detroit Rock City
Beth
Rock and Roll All Nite

JUNE 28, 1997   CANCELED

Lisboa, Portugal
Cascais Hall
Capacity: 10,000
Promoter: Tournee LDA

JUNE 30, 1997

Barcelona, Spain
Palau Val D'Hebron - Sports Palais
Opening Act: El Fantastico Hombre Bala
Attendance: 6,000   Capacity: 8,000
Promoter: Gay & Company
■ SET LIST
See May 16, 1997.
■ This show was originally scheduled for November 27, 1996.

JULY 2, 1997

Genève, Switzerland
Geneva Arena
Opening Act: Core22
Attendance: 9,000   Capacity: 10,000
Promoter: Volume Agency
■ SET LIST
See May 16, 1997.

JULY 5, 1997

Finsbury Park (London), England
Finsbury Park

Opening Acts: Rage Against the Machine, Skunk
    Anansie, Thunder, L7
Attendance: 12,000   Capacity: 30,000
Promoter: MCP
■ SET LIST
See May 16, 1997.
■ Paul dedicated "Rock and Roll All Nite" to Doc McGhee and his brother Jim. He also soaked his guitar in lighter fluid and set it ablaze at the end of the show. This was the final live performance of "New York Groove" and "Watchin' You."

To promote the final show of the tour, KISS did a press conference at a wax museum in Picadilly Circus. Selected memorabilia from the KISS Convention Tour was on display for several days before the show.

The band would go on to release a 124-minute documentary of the overwhelmingly successful Alive/Worldwide Tour titled *The Second Coming.* The home video, which shipped Gold, was released November 24, 1998.

Springfield, Massachusetts, March 22, 1997, with KISS's classic hydraulic platforms absent from the production.

CHAPTER 25

PSYCHO CIRCUS TOUR

Number of Shows: 62
Start Date: October 31, 1998 - Los Angeles, California
End Date: January 3, 2000 - Anchorage, Alaska
Countries: Argentina, Austria, Belgium, Brazil, Canada, Czech Republic, England, Finland, France, Germany, Italy, Mexico, The Netherlands, Norway, Sweden, U.S.A.
Opening Acts: Big Wreck; Bionic; Buck Cherry; Caroline's Spine; Econoline Crush; Everclear; John Hayes Project; Junkbox; Lit; Los Villanos; Natural Born Hippies; Nickelback; Ozone Monday; PUYA; Rammstein; Smashing Pumpkins
Average Attendance: 12,826* (Does not include any of the three one-off performances after 4/24/99.)

KISS's reunion tour had been an overwhelming success, but with it a familiar pattern began to appear. Exactly as they had in that 1977–78 era of spoiled riches, when the opportunity to over-merchandise presented itself, KISS jumped at the chance. During the remainder of 1997 and into 1998, Sony Signatures expanded the selection of KISS merchandise exponentially—making available such ridiculous items as inflatable chairs, pool cues, mini-blinds, and an entire line of golf accessories—so thoroughly saturating the marketplace that it is a wonder they weren't crushed by the irony of committing the exact

same mistake that befell them 20 years earlier. Fortunately, the general tendency towards over-merchandizing that existed within in the industry helped to minimize the negative impact for the band.

KISS's reunion-tour press conference on the U.S.S. Intrepid had been a genuine event covered heavily by both music and mainstream press. The Psycho Circus press conference on September 21 at Mann's Chinese Theatre, however, foreshadowed the waning interest that defined the forthcoming tour. While KISS gamely attempted to maintain their usual sense of hype by arriving at the press

conference in a custom-made KISS Dodge Prowler and world-premiering the 3D video for "Psycho Circus," the novelty of the Alive/Worldwide Tour had clearly dwindled and some of the fanbase was becoming disinterested.

The following day, Mercury released *Psycho Circus*. The fact that this was KISS's first studio album with its original lineup in 19 years naturally generated a lot of initial interest, but the hype was fleeting. "The Grateful Dead were the biggest touring act in America for years," offers Danny Goldberg, "and their records never went Gold. Touring now is a different business, and with acts

like KISS, people are paying money for the privilege of seeing live an act that has affected them over a period of ten or 20 years and they want to hear the old songs. If you do what Carlos Santana did and actually have contemporary hits, you'll sell a lot of records. If you're putting out albums that only get played on the heritage rock stations, you'll maybe sell 100,000 or 200,000 records, but you will not be competitive with people who have legitimate hits. Nor will you be competitive with the teenage demographic, because if you're KISS, your audience is adults, and adults do not have the aggressiveness when it comes to buying new albums that teenagers do."

With a new album to promote, KISS quickly took to the road with a new production in tow. There were several new features present, including for the first time the use of two lighted KISS logos. However, most prominent among the tour's new features was the inclusion of 3D effects in the video production. Nocturne's Bob Brigham explains, "Doc called me in April 1998 and [Nocturne Productions co-founder] Pat Morrow and I flew down to Doc's house. He said he wanted to do a tour with 3D video. Pat said, 'Are you out of your mind? Nobody does 3D video. This is bullshit and if it was any good, don't you think Michael Jackson would be doing it?' Doc told him, 'I don't care. Gene and I have told the world that we're doing it and we're doing 3D video.'

"We started talking to 3D people, and Doc was finding a lot of them in L.A., and what we were going after was Stereoscopic 3D. That is where you use the 3D glasses with polarized lenses, where one lens lets light in, and the other blocks it. Two separate reels create the image on the screens: an A reel and a B reel. They are being played off laserdisc players with SMPTE time code locked in together; we called them 'Left Eye' and 'Right Eye.' If you take the glasses off and look at the image, it would look shifted, like it's out of focus. When you put the glasses on you have 3D." In addition to previously-recorded 3D footage, a cameraman was on hand to feed live 3D shots to the video screens.

Another effective change to the set was made to Peter's drum riser. Dating back to 1973, Peter's drum riser had risen by some means of hydraulic lift from underneath. For the Psycho Circus Tour, the drum riser was lifted from above by winches in the lighting rig. As the riser lifted up, fog machines and lights on the riser's undercarriage gave the effect that the riser was flying, with the fog appearing to propel the riser upwards, forwards, and side to side. Ace also added an effect to his repertoire through the addition of a small pyrotechnic device, which alternately spun clockwise and counterclockwise, emitting a shower of sparks from the headstock of his guitar.

KISS abandoned the replica Love Gun costumes and now donned replicas of the outfits used on the Destroyer and Rock and Roll Over Tours, though in this instance all four band members wore belts as part of their costumes, reportedly at the insistence of Doc McGhee.

A large portion of the set list from the Alive/ Worldwide Tour was still in place during the Psycho Circus Tour, though the band did add three songs from the new album: "Psycho Circus," "Within," and Ace's "Into the Void."

Attendance was down from the reunion tour, most notably in North America, where the nightly figures slipped over 21 percent to 10,737 over a conspicuously short 34-date tour. A relatively strong showing in Europe and some impressive turnouts in Central and South America inflated the tour's average attendance to over 12,800 per show. But given the context of the touring industry, which was experiencing similar downturns across the board, KISS's attendance figures were still robust. The disappointment in the tour stemmed largely from unrealistic expectations. Much like the Dynasty Tour paled in comparison to the Alive II Tour, the Psycho Circus outing was a relative letdown and could not escape from the towering shadow cast by the Alive/Worldwide Tour.

The band scored a major publicity coup when FOX-TV broadcast three KISS-themed programs over the course of two days. The sci-fi drama *Millennium* aired on October 30 and featured the band performing "Psycho Circus." Each band member also had small roles in the episode. KISS hosted *Mad TV* the next night, which was immediately followed by the half-hour special *KISS LIVE The Ultimate Halloween Party,* during which "Psycho Circus" and "Let Me Go, Rock 'n Roll" ("Shout It Out Loud" was substituted for West Coast viewers) were broadcast live from Dodger Stadium.

During the break between the North American and European legs of the tour, KISS again appeared on FOX-TV, this time on January 31 during the official pre-game show for Super Bowl XXXIII. The band lip-synched to a recently recorded version of "Rock and Roll All Nite" in front of a sold-out crowd of 74,803 at Miami's Pro Player Stadium.

Note: throughout the tour the length and content of Paul's introduction to "Black Diamond" would vary, when Paul would occasionally include an audience participation section in the intro. While these intros could arguably qualify as guitar solos, we have chosen not to list them as such.

OCTOBER 30, 1998

Los Angeles, California
Dodger Stadium
■ SET LIST
Psycho Circus
Shout It Out Loud
[Let Me Go, Rock 'n Roll]
[Shock Me]
[Do You Love Me]
[Calling Dr. Love]
[Firehouse]
[Cold Gin]
She
Peter Criss Drum Solo
I Was Made for Lovin' You
Into the Void
Ace Frehley Guitar Solo
Love Gun
Within
100,000 Years
King of the Night Time World
Gene Simmons Bass Solo
God of Thunder
Deuce
Detroit Rock City
Beth
Black Diamond
Rock and Roll All Nite
■ This was a partial dress rehearsal attended by record company employees and VIPs. Bruce Kulick was in attendance at the rehearsal and at the concert the following night.

Circus-act performers were scheduled to perform before the shows throughout the tour. When they could not reach an agreement with KISS, it was decided just prior to the October 30 rehearsal that they would not be traveling with the band. They did, however, perform at the Halloween show.

OCTOBER 31, 1998

Los Angeles, California
Dodger Stadium
Opening Act: Smashing Pumpkins
Attendance: 32,019   Capacity: 40,000
Promoters: Avalon Attractions, KROQ
■ SET LIST
Psycho Circus
Shout It Out Loud
Let Me Go, Rock 'n Roll
Shock Me
Do You Love Me
Calling Dr. Love
Firehouse
Cold Gin
Nothin' to Lose
She
Peter Criss Drum Solo

I Was Made for Lovin' You
Into the Void
Ace Frehley Guitar Solo
Love Gun
Within
100,000 Years
King of the Night Time World
Gene Simmons Bass Solo
God of Thunder
Deuce
Detroit Rock City
Beth
Black Diamond
Rock and Roll All Nite
■ Both "Nothin' to Lose" and "She" were performed and then dropped for the remainder of the tour. KISS used the 1977-era arrangement for "Nothin' to Lose" with Paul and Peter providing counterpoint, call-and-response vocals to Gene during the verses of the song.

The majority of the merchandise at Dodger Stadium was exclusive to the performance, including a $1,500 bottle of wine and a special version of the tourbook. The concert was broadcast live over the radio via The Album Network and over the Internet courtesy of Pepsi. Reportedly, KISS had pre-recorded the entire concert as a safety measure for the radio broadcast in case there were difficulties with the live transmission.

Full-page, 3D-ads, complete with free 3D-glasses, were taken out to promote the show. To help boost attendance, after the initial sales of tickets promoters began offering tickets at a two-for-one discount and eventually gave many tickets away for free.

NOVEMBER 12, 1998

Boston, Massachusetts
Fleet Center
Opening Act: Econoline Crush
Attendance: 12,500   Capacity: 12,500
Promoter: Beaver Productions
■ SET LIST
Psycho Circus
Shout It Out Loud
Deuce
Do You Love Me
Let Me Go, Rock 'n Roll
Shock Me
Within
Firehouse
Calling Dr. Love
Makin' Love
Cold Gin
King of the Night Time World
Into the Void
Ace Frehley Guitar Solo
100,000 Years
Gene Simmons Bass Solo
God of Thunder
Peter Criss Drum Solo
I Was Made for Lovin' You
Love Gun
Detroit Rock City
Beth
Black Diamond
Rock and Roll All Nite
■ Tickets for the first Boston concert were put on sale only 18 days prior to the date of the concert, an unusually short lead time for the first show of a tour.

NOVEMBER 13, 1998

Boston, Massachusetts
Fleet Center
Opening Act: Econoline Crush
Attendance: 7,220   Capacity: 12,500
Promoter: Beaver Productions
■ SET LIST
Psycho Circus
Shout It Out Loud
Deuce
Do You Love Me
Firehouse
Shock Me
Let Me Go, Rock 'n Roll
Cold Gin
Calling Dr. Love
Into the Void
Ace Frehley Guitar Solo
Makin' Love
Gene Simmons Bass Solo
God of Thunder
100,000 Years
Within
Peter Criss Drum Solo
I Was Made for Lovin' You
King of the Night Time World
Love Gun
Rock and Roll All Nite
Beth
Detroit Rock City
Black Diamond
■ Concerts on the early portion of the tour ended with the video screens displaying an advertisement promoting a contest to win the Dodge Prowler KISS car.

NOVEMBER 15, 1998

Albany, New York
Pepsi Arena
Opening Act: Econoline Crush
Attendance: 7,239   Capacity: 13,268
Promoter: Magic City Productions
■ SET LIST
See November 13, 1998.

NOVEMBER 16, 1998

Portland, Maine
Cumberland County Civic Center
Opening Act: Econoline Crush
Attendance: 6,699   Capacity: 7,000
Promoter: Beaver Productions
■ SET LIST
See November 13, 1998.

NOVEMBER 18, 1998

University Park, Pennsylvania
Bryce Jordan Center
Opening Act: Econoline Crush
Attendance: 6,274   Capacity: 10,400
Promoter: DiCesare-Engler Productions
■ SET LIST
Psycho Circus
Shout It Out Loud
Deuce
Do You Love Me
Firehouse
Shock Me
Let Me Go, Rock 'n Roll
Cold Gin
Calling Dr. Love
Into the Void
Ace Frehley Guitar Solo
Makin' Love
Gene Simmons Bass Solo
God of Thunder

King of the Night Time World
Within
Peter Criss Drum Solo
I Was Made for Lovin' You
100,000 Years
Love Gun
Rock and Roll All Nite
Beth
Detroit Rock City
Black Diamond

NOVEMBER 19, 1998

Washington, D.C.
MCI Center
Opening Act: Econoline Crush
Attendance: 13,952   Capacity: 17,000

Promoter: Cellar Door Concerts
■ **SET LIST**
See November 18, 1998.
■ When Paul brought out his faux guitar at the end of the set, he accidentally dropped it before he could smash it as he usually did. The guitar broke into pieces when it hit the stage. To cover for the mishap, Paul took the body of the broken guitar and banged it against Peter's drum riser several times, breaking it even further.

NOVEMBER 21, 1998

Philadelphia, Pennsylvania
First Union Spectrum
Opening Act: Econoline Crush

Attendance: 12,927   Capacity: 15,690
Promoter: Electric Factory Concerts
■ **SET LIST**
See November 18, 1998.

NOVEMBER 22, 1998

East Rutherford, New Jersey
Continental Airlines Arena
Opening Act: Ozone Monday
Attendance: 14,858   Capacity: 14,858
Promoter: Delsener-Slater Enterprises
■ **SET LIST**
Psycho Circus
Shout It Out Loud
Deuce
Do You Love Me
Firehouse
Shock Me
Let Me Go, Rock 'n Roll
Cold Gin
Calling Dr. Love
Into the Void
Ace Frehley Guitar Solo
Makin' Love
Gene Simmons Bass Solo
God of Thunder
Within
Peter Criss Drum Solo
I Was Made for Lovin' You
King of the Night Time World
100,000 Years
Love Gun
Rock and Roll All Nite
Beth
Detroit Rock City
Black Diamond

NOVEMBER 23, 1998

Manhattan, New York
Madison Square Garden
Opening Act: Econoline Crush
Attendance: 15,173   Capacity: 15,173
Promoter: Delsener-Slater Enterprises
■ **SET LIST**
See November 23, 1998.
■ On the afternoon prior to the show, KISS (sans makeup) dropped by WNEW to make an appearance on *The Opie & Anthony Show*.
"Makin' Love" was performed for the final time on the Psycho Circus Tour at this show.

NOVEMBER 25, 1998

Hartford, Connecticut
Hartford Civic Center
Opening Act: Econoline Crush
Attendance: 7,715   Capacity: 11,809
Promoter: Delsener-Slater Enterprises
■ **SET LIST**
Psycho Circus
Shout It Out Loud
Deuce
Do You Love Me
Firehouse
Shock Me
Let Me Go, Rock 'n Roll
Cold Gin
Calling Dr. Love
Into the Void
Ace Frehley Guitar Solo
King of the Night Time World
Gene Simmons Bass Solo
God of Thunder
Within
Peter Criss Drum Solo
I Was Made for Lovin' You
Love Gun

100,000 Years
Rock and Roll All Nite
Beth
Detroit Rock City
Black Diamond

NOVEMBER 27, 1998

Uniondale, New York
Nassau Veterans Memorial Coliseum
Opening Act: Econoline Crush
Attendance: 12,773   Capacity: 14,007
Promoter: Delsener-Slater Enterprises
■ **SET LIST**
Psycho Circus
Shout It Out Loud
Deuce
Do You Love Me
Firehouse
Shock Me
Let Me Go, Rock 'n Roll
Calling Dr. Love
Into the Void
Ace Frehley Guitar Solo
King of the Night Time World
Gene Simmons Bass Solo
God of Thunder
Within
Peter Criss Drum Solo
Cold Gin
Love Gun
100,000 Years
Rock and Roll All Nite
Beth
Detroit Rock City
Black Diamond
■ KISS briefly segued into "New York Groove" prior to "Detroit Rock City."

NOVEMBER 28, 1998

Rochester, New York
BlueCross Arena at the War Memorial
Opening Act: Econoline Crush
Attendance: 5,477   Capacity: 6,000
Promoter: Metropolitan Entertainment
■ **SET LIST**
See November 27, 1998.

NOVEMBER 29, 1998

Buffalo, New York
Marine Midland Arena
Opening Act: Econoline Crush
Attendance: 8,318   Capacity: 14,594
Promoter: Magic City Productions
■ **SET LIST**
See November 27, 1998.

DECEMBER 1, 1998

Montréal, Quebec, Canada
Centre Molson
Opening Act: Bionic
Attendance: 11,728   Capacity: 13,294
Promoters: Donald K. Donald, Universal Concerts
■ **SET LIST**
See November 27, 1998

DECEMBER 2, 1998

Toronto, Ontario, Canada
Toronto Skytent
Opening Act: Econoline Crush
Attendance: 15,608   Capacity: 15,608
Promoters: Donald K. Donald, Universal Concerts
■ **SET LIST**
See November 27, 1998.
■ The following day, KISS entered Copps Coliseum in Hamilton, Ontario, where they filmed lip-synched concert segments for the movie

Detroit Rock City. For the filming, which took place before a crowd of over 3,000, the band used replicas of the Love Gun Tour stage and costumes. The film shoot had originally been scheduled for November 6 at the Sports Arena in Los Angeles.

DECEMBER 4, 1998

Pittsburgh, Pennsylvania
Civic Arena
Opening Act: Econoline Crush
Attendance: 11,681   Capacity: 13,954
Promoter: DiCesare-Engler Productions
■ **SET LIST**
See November 27, 1998.

DECEMBER 5, 1998

Columbus, Ohio
Value City Arena at the Jerome Schottenstein Center
Opening Act: Econoline Crush
Attendance: 12,039   Capacity: 12,039
Promoter: Belkin Productions
■ **SET LIST**
See November 27, 1998.
■ Gene did his bloodspitting routine on the stage floor, as usual. Then, after he ascended to the platform in the lighting rig, more blood rained

down upon the attendees in the first several rows through a hole that had been made in Gene's platform. Roadies walked through the crowd and handed out towels to people who had been covered by the fake blood. With the exception of "Beth," Peter did not sing during the concert; Paul sang lead vocals on "Black Diamond."
The concert was announced as the first sellout in the venue's history.

DECEMBER 6, 1998

Cleveland, Ohio
GUND Arena
Opening Act: Econoline Crush
Attendance: 15,729   Capacity: 20,750
Promoter: Belkin Productions
■ **SET LIST**
See November 27, 1998.
■ The show was originally advertised for December 7.

DECEMBER 8, 1998

Charleston, West Virginia
Charleston Civic Center
Opening Act: Econoline Crush
Attendance: 5,121   Capacity: 13,500
Promoter: Belkin Productions

■ **SET LIST**
See November 27, 1998.

DECEMBER 9, 1998

Lexington, Kentucky
Rupp Arena
Opening Act: Econoline Crush
Attendance: 7,780   Capacity: 20,000
Promoter: Belkin Productions
■ **SET LIST**
See November 27, 1998.
■ Gene experienced technical difficulties with his ear monitors, which forced Paul to cover the lead vocals on the second verse of "Let Me Go, Rock 'n Roll."

DECEMBER 11, 1998

Dayton, Ohio
Ervin J. Nutter Center
Opening Act: Econoline Crush
Attendance: 8,877   Capacity: 11,754
Promoter: Belkin Productions
■ **SET LIST**
See November 27, 1998.
■ A pyro effect in "Rock and Roll All Nite" caught a lamp in the lighting rig on fire. The fire burned for several minutes, prompting Peter to mention it at the beginning of "Beth."

DECEMBER 12, 1998

Terre Haute, Indiana
Hulman Center
Opening Act: Econoline Crush
Attendance: 4,696   Capacity: 8,671
Promoter: Sunshine Promotions
■ **SET LIST**
See November 27, 1998.
■ This concert was recorded for a six-track EP titled *Live*. The limited-edition EP was released in Europe on February 22 as a bonus CD to *Psycho Circus*.

DECEMBER 13, 1998

Indianapolis, Indiana
Market Square Arena
Opening Act: Econoline Crush
Attendance: 9,805   Capacity: 14,908
Promoter: Sunshine Promotions
■ **SET LIST**
Psycho Circus
Shout It Out Loud
Deuce
Calling Dr. Love
Firehouse
Do You Love Me
Let Me Go, Rock 'n Roll
Shock Me
King of the Night Time World
Into the Void
Ace Frehley Guitar Solo
Gene Simmons Bass Solo
God of Thunder
Within
Peter Criss Drum Solo
Love Gun
Cold Gin
100,000 Years
Rock and Roll All Nite
Beth
Black Diamond
■ Most likely due to time constraints, "Detroit Rock City" was not included in the set list, and Paul's normally lengthy intro to "Black Diamond" was omitted as well.
This concert was also recorded for *Live*.

DECEMBER 15, 1998

Minneapolis, Minnesota
Target Center
Opening Act: Econoline Crush
Attendance: 11,978   Capacity: 19,500
Promoter: Rose Productions
■ **SET LIST**
See November 27, 1998.
■ Proceeds from the concert went to the Clean Water Fund.

DECEMBER 16, 1998

Omaha, Nebraska
Omaha Civic Auditorium
Opening Act: Econoline Crush
Attendance: 10,419   Capacity: 10,419
Promoter: Beaver Productions
■ **SET LIST**
See November 27, 1998.
■ The motor that lifts Gene to his lighting rig platform burned out during sound check. Gene's flying effect did not return until the December 31 gig in Auburn Hills.
After "Psycho Circus," Paul had security pull a seven-year-old fan out of the front row when he was elbowed in the nose. The band let the young fan watch the show from the side of the stage and later met with him.

DECEMBER 18, 1998

Rockford, Illinois
MetroCentre
Opening Act: Econoline Crush
Attendance: 5,344   Capacity: 7,000
Promoter: JAM Productions

DECEMBER 19, 1998

Cedar Rapids, Iowa
Five Seasons Center
Opening Act: Econoline Crush
Attendance: 7,861   Capacity: 8,939
Promoter: JAM Productions
■ **SET LIST**
Psycho Circus
Shout It Out Loud
Deuce
Do You Love Me
Firehouse
Shock Me
Let Me Go, Rock 'n Roll
Calling Dr. Love
Into The Void
Ace Frehley Guitar Solo
King of the Night Time World
Gene Simmons Bass Solo
God of Thunder
Within
Peter Criss Drum Solo
Cold Gin
Love Gun
100,000 Years
Rock and Roll All Nite
Beth
Detroit Rock City
Black Diamond

DECEMBER 20, 1998

Milwaukee, Wisconsin
Bradley Center
Opening Act: Econoline Crush
Attendance: 12,000   Capacity: 18,000
Promoter: Cellar Door Concerts
■ **SET LIST**
See December 19, 1998.

DECEMBER 27, 1998

Madison, Wisconsin
Dane County Expo Center Coliseum
Opening Act: Caroline's Spine
Attendance: 5,500   Capacity: 8,800
Promoter: Belkin Productions
■ **SET LIST**
See December 19, 1998.
■ Paul did not fly during the show, and the video screens were not in use.

DECEMBER 29, 1998

Rosemont (Chicago), Illinois
Rosemont Horizon
Opening Act: Caroline's Spine
Attendance: 10,774   Capacity: 12,100
Promoter: JAM Productions
■ **SET LIST**
See December 19, 1998.
■ This show was originally advertised for December 28. Paul's flying rig was stranded by a severe snowstorm, and a different flying scaffold was used for both the Chicago and Grand Rapids shows.

DECEMBER 30, 1998

Grand Rapids, Michigan
Van Andel Arena
Opening Act: Caroline's Spine
Attendance: 7,834   Capacity: 12,790
Promoters: Belkin Productions, Cellar Door Concerts
■ **SET LIST**
See December 19, 1998.

DECEMBER 31, 1998

Auburn Hills (Detroit), Michigan
The Palace of Auburn Hills
Opening Act: Caroline's Spine
Attendance: 14,431   Capacity: 14,431
Promoters: Belkin Productions, Cellar Door Concerts
■ **SET LIST**
Psycho Circus
Shout It Out Loud
Deuce
Do You Love Me
Firehouse
Shock Me
Let Me Go, Rock 'n Roll
Calling Dr. Love
Into The Void
Ace Frehley Guitar Solo
King of the Night Time World
Gene Simmons Bass Solo
God of Thunder
Within
Peter Criss Drum Solo
Cold Gin
Love Gun
100,000 Years
Rock and Roll All Nite
Beth
Black Diamond
Detroit Rock City
■ This gig was originally booked for the Pontiac Silverdome.

JANUARY 2, 1999

Nashville, Tennessee
Nashville Arena
Opening Act: Ozone Monday
Attendance: 12,692   Capacity: 15,570
Promoter: Pace Concerts
■ **SET LIST**
See December 19, 1998.
■ A VH1 crew was on hand to tape footage for a

short-lived show called *Rock Candy*, which later premiered on April 5.

JANUARY 29, 1999

Sunrise (Fort Lauderdale), Florida
National Car Rental Center **CANCELED**
Promoter: American Concerts

■ This concert was postponed on January 4. The promoter hoped to reschedule the concert for KISS's next tour and consequently the show was not officially canceled until January of 2000.

FEBRUARY 26, 1999

Helsingfors, Finland
Hartwall Areena
Opening Act: Buck Cherry
Attendance: 10,000   Capacity: 12,000
Promoter: EMA Telstar

■ **SET LIST**

Psycho Circus
Shout It Out Loud
Deuce
Do You Love Me
Firehouse
Shock Me
Calling Dr. Love
Let Me Go, Rock 'n Roll
Into The Void
Ace Frehley Guitar Solo
King of the Night Time World
Gene Simmons Bass Solo
God of Thunder
Within
Peter Criss Drum Solo
Cold Gin
Love Gun
100,000 Years
I Was Made for Lovin' You
Rock and Roll All Nite
Beth
Detroit Rock City
Black Diamond

■ Backyard Babies were originally announced as the opening act for the entire European leg, but they did not perform on the tour.

Prior to leaving for Europe, Paul had surgery on his left knee, which required him to wear a large, black knee-brace for all remaining concerts on the tour.

FEBRUARY 28, 1999

Oslo, Norway
Spektrum
Opening Act: Buck Cherry
Attendance: 8,000   Capacity: 8,000
Promoter: EMA Telstar

■ **SET LIST**

See February 26, 1999.

MARCH 2, 1999

Stockholm, Sweden
Stockholm Globe Arena
Opening Act: Buck Cherry
Attendance: 11,921   Capacity: 11,921
Promoter: EMA Telstar

■ **SET LIST**

Psycho Circus
Shout It Out Loud
Deuce
Do You Love Me
Firehouse
Shock Me
Let Me Go, Rock 'n Roll
Calling Dr. Love
Into The Void
Ace Frehley Guitar Solo
King of the Night Time World
Gene Simmons Bass Solo
God of Thunder
Within
Peter Criss Drum Solo
Cold Gin
Love Gun
100,000 Years
I Was Made for Lovin' You
Rock and Roll All Nite
Beth
Detroit Rock City
Black Diamond

MARCH 3, 1999

Stockholm, Sweden
Stockholm Globe Arena
Opening Act: Buck Cherry
Attendance: 12,343   Capacity: 12,343
Promoter: EMA Telstar

■ **SET LIST**

See March 2, 1999.

■ Bruce Kulick, who was appearing at a series of unofficial European KISS expos, was in attendance at this show. He also attended the Utrecht show on March 13.

MARCH 4, 1999

Göteborg, Sweden
Scandinavium
Opening Act: Buck Cherry
Attendance: 9,749   Capacity: 9,871
Promoter: EMA Telstar

■ **SET LIST**

Detroit Rock City
Psycho Circus
Shout It Out Loud
Deuce
Do You Love Me
Firehouse
Shock Me
Let Me Go, Rock 'n Roll
Calling Dr. Love
Into The Void
Ace Frehley Guitar Solo
King of the Night Time World
Gene Simmons Bass Solo
God of Thunder
Within
Peter Criss Drum Solo
Cold Gin
Love Gun
100,000 Years
Rock and Roll All Nite
Beth
I Was Made for Lovin' You
Black Diamond

■ KISS opened their set with "Detroit Rock City."

MARCH 5, 1999

Göteborg, Sweden
Scandinavium
Opening Act: Buck Cherry
Attendance: 9,871   Capacity: 9,871
Promoter: EMA Telstar

■ **SET LIST**

Psycho Circus
Shout It Out Loud
Deuce
Do You Love Me
Firehouse
Shock Me
Let Me Go, Rock 'n Roll
Calling Dr. Love
Into The Void
Ace Frehley Guitar Solo
King of the Night Time World
Gene Simmons Bass Solo
God of Thunder
Within
Peter Criss Drum Solo
Cold Gin
Love Gun
100,000 Years
I Was Made for Lovin' You
Rock and Roll All Nite
Beth
Detroit Rock City
Black Diamond

■ "Cold Gin" was dropped from the set after this show.

In what was definitely one of the lighter moments on the Psycho Circus Tour, Paul and Gene engaged in a water fight throughout the show, each dousing the other during various lead vocal parts. Finally, during "Rock and Roll All Nite," Paul walked over with a mouthful of water and stood only inches from Gene's face. Gene nervously sang the first verse of the song before Paul unloaded the entire mouthful of water in Gene's face.

MARCH 7, 1999

Berlin, Germany
Velodrome
Opening Act: Buck Cherry
Promoter: Marek Lieberberg

■ **SET LIST**

Psycho Circus
Shout It Out Loud
Deuce
Do You Love Me
Firehouse
Shock Me
Let Me Go, Rock 'n Roll
Calling Dr. Love
Into The Void
Ace Frehley Guitar Solo
King of the Night Time World
Gene Simmons Bass Solo
God of Thunder
Within
Peter Criss Drum Solo
I Was Made for Lovin' You
Love Gun
100,000 Years
Rock and Roll All Nite
Beth
Detroit Rock City
Black Diamond

■ Prior to "Rock and Roll All Nite," Paul sang "Deutschland, Deutschland, uber alles . . . " which, due to its affiliation with Adolf Hitler, is a forbidden part of the German national anthem. Realizing Paul's error, Gene quickly interrupted Paul, but a chorus of boos still issued from the crowd.

MARCH 8, 1999

Köln, Germany
Köln Arena
Opening Act: Buck Cherry
Attendance: 14,000
Promoter: Marek Lieberberg

■ **SET LIST**

See March 7, 1999.

MARCH 9, 1999

Frankfurt a.M., Germany
Festhalle
Opening Act: Buck Cherry
Attendance: nearly sold out
Promoter: Marek Lieberberg
■ SET LIST
See March 7, 1999.

MARCH 11, 1999

Erfurt, Germany
Messehalle
Opening Act: Buck Cherry
Attendance: 4,000
Promoter: Marek Lieberberg
■ SET LIST
See March 7, 1999.

■ While kidding around on stage, Paul asked Ace if he spoke German. Ace then replied, "Ja, Ja, Deutschland, Deutschland uber alles," thus committing the exact same mistake Paul had committed at the Berlin show.

MARCH 12, 1999

Bremen, Germany
Stadthalle
Opening Act: Buck Cherry
Attendance: 10,500   Capacity: 10,500
Promoter: Marek Lieberberg
■ SET LIST
See March 7, 1999.

■ The fire marshal prohibited use of all pyro effects. KISS obliged his wishes until "Black Diamond," when they unloaded the entire show's compliment of pyrotechnics, creating one of the most impressive displays of fire and sound seen at any KISS concert.

MARCH 13, 1999

Utrecht, The Netherlands
Prins van Oranjehal
Opening Act: Buck Cherry
Attendance: 14,300
Promoter: Mojo Concerts
■ SET LIST
See March 7, 1999.

MARCH 15, 1999

Milano, Italy
FilaForum
Opening Act: Buck Cherry
Attendance: 11,750   Capacity: 11,750
Promoter: Barley Arts Promotions
■ SET LIST
See March 7, 1999.

MARCH 17, 1999

Wien, Austria
Stadthalle
Opening Act: Buck Cherry
Attendance: 7,000
Promoter: Artists Marketing
■ SET LIST
See March 7, 1999.

MARCH 18, 1999

Praha, Czech Republic
Sportovní Hala
Opening Act: Buck Cherry
Attendance: 12,000+ (sold out)
Promoter: Interkoncerts
■ SET LIST
See March 7, 1999.

MARCH 19, 1999

München, Germany
Olympiahalle @ Olympiapark München
Opening Act: Buck Cherry
Attendance: 10,000 (sold out)
Promoter: Marek Lieberberg
■ SET LIST
See March 7, 1999.

MARCH 20, 1999

Stuttgart, Germany
Hanns-Martin Schleyer Halle
Opening Act: Buck Cherry
Capacity: 12,000
Promoter: Marek Lieberberg
■ SET LIST
See March 7, 1999.

■ This show was originally advertised for March 21.

MARCH 22, 1999

Bercy (Paris), France
Palais Omnisports de Paris-Bercy
Opening Act: Buck Cherry
Capacity: 16,500
Promoter: Gerard Drouot Productions
■ SET LIST
See March 7, 1999.

MARCH 23, 1999

Bruxelles, Belgium
Vorst Nationaal
Opening Act: Buck Cherry
Attendance: 6,491   Capacity: 8,000
Promoter: Sound & Vision
■ SET LIST
See March 7, 1999.

MARCH 25, 1999

London, England
Wembley Arena
Opening Act: Buck Cherry
Promoter: MCP
■ SET LIST
See March 7, 1999.

■ This was opening act Buck Cherry's last show on the tour. Shortly after this gig, they changed the spelling of their name to Buckcherry.

Keith Nelson of Buckcherry: "I couldn't believe the amount of chicks that were willing to get naked for those guys. The whole KISS experience was really cool. It was a good lesson on how a bunch of professional guys go out there and create it every night. We hung out with them a little bit, and Paul even let me play his signature model Washburn on stage one night."

MARCH 27, 1999

Dortmund, Germany
Westfalenhalle
Opening Act: John Hayes Project
Promoter: Marek Lieberberg
■ SET LIST
See March 7, 1999.

MARCH 28, 1999

Kiel, Germany
Ostseehalle
Opening Act: Natural Born Hippies
Promoter: Marek Lieberberg
■ SET LIST
See March 7, 1999.

APRIL 1 & 2, 1999

CANCELED

Moscow, Russia
Luzniki Stadion
Capacity: 100,000
Promoter: Moscovit-Concert
■ These shows were canceled on March 28 when N.A.T.O. air strikes in nearby Kosovo had soured relations between Russia and the U.S. The State Department could not guarantee the band's safety, so the three Russian concerts (April 1st and 2nd in Moscow, and April 4th in St. Petersburg) were canceled.

APRIL 4, 1999

CANCELED

St. Petersburg, Russia
DK Lensoveta
Promoter: Moscovit-Concert

APRIL 10, 1999

Buenos Aires, Argentina
Estadio Monumental de River Plate
Opening Acts: Rammstein, Los Villanos
Attendance: 35,000
Promoter: Rock & Pop Int'l
■ SET LIST
See March 7, 1999.

■ Originally scheduled for Velez Sarsfield Stadium, the venue was changed on March 4 when it was realized that a soccer match had been scheduled at the stadium for the same day.

On May 1, Volver TV broadcast the entire concert on the show *Puerta V.*

APRIL 13, 1999

CANCELED

Santiago, Chile
Centro Cultural Estacion Mapocho
Opening Act: Rammstein
Promoter: D.S. Medios Y Espectaculos S.A.
■ The concert was canceled on April 5. Over 8,000 tickets had been sold at the time of cancellation.

APRIL 15, 1999

CANCELED

Montevideo, Uruguay
Stadio Centenario
Opening Act: Rammstein
■ This performance was canceled on March 4.

APRIL 15, 1999

Porto Alegre, Brazil
Jockey Club Brasil
Opening Act: Rammstein
Attendance: 30,000
Promoter: OPINIAO
■ This concert was scheduled for a venue called Estádio Beira-rio, but was moved to Jockey Club Brasil on March 25.

APRIL 17, 1999

São Paulo, Brazil
Autodromo de Interlagos
Opening Act: Rammstein
Attendance: 53,000+
Promoter: OPINIAO

APRIL 21, 1999

San Juan, Puerto Rico
Coliseo Roberto Clemente
Opening Act: PUYA
Promoter: Larry Stein
■ Prior to "Black Diamond," Paul sang parts of "La Bamba" and "Guantanamera." The concert was originally advertised for Hiram Botham Stadium.

APRIL 24, 1999

Ciudad de México, Mexico
Foro Sol
Opening Act: Rammstein
Attendance: 44,831   Capacity: 44,831
Promoter: OCESA Presents

■ SET LIST

Psycho Circus
Shout It Out Loud
Deuce
Do You Love Me
Firehouse
Shock Me
Let Me Go, Rock 'n Roll
Calling Dr. Love
Into The Void
Ace Frehley Guitar Solo
King of the Night Time World
Gene Simmons Bass Solo
God of Thunder
I Was Made for Lovin' You
Within
Peter Criss Drum Solo
Love Gun
100,000 Years
Rock and Roll All Nite
Beth
Detroit Rock City
Black Diamond

■ The band did parts of "La Bamba" and "Guantanamera" prior to "Rock and Roll All Nite."

After the show, Paul cut his hair short and then flew to Toronto the following day to begin rehearsals for a successful run as the Phantom, in the musical "Phantom of the Opera."

———————

During the fall of 1999, KISS made a series of public appearances, which were followed by two one-off concerts, the first in Vancouver on New Year's Eve and the second in Alaska three days later. But the band's most notable move came

with the release of *Detroit Rock City*, a movie steeped in 1970s nostalgia and focusing on the adventures of four teenagers trying desperately to attend a sold-out KISS concert in Detroit in 1978. The soundtrack for the movie, which included a new KISS song, "Nothing Can Keep Me From You," was released on August 3, with the movie following ten days later. To help promote the film, KISS held a premiere party on August 9 in Westwood, California where the band performed a brief live set. The film opened to very disappointing box office returns and quickly disappeared from theatres. During that same busy week, on August 11, KISS received a star on the Hollywood Walk of Fame.

KISS's next public appearance of note came on August 23, at the MGM Grand Garden Arena in Las Vegas for the live broadcast of "WCW Monday Nitro." A wrestler named The Demon,

who wore Gene's make-up during his wrestling appearances, made his WCW debut and KISS lip-synched "God of Thunder" to help promote the event.

Then on October 29, KISS took part in a big event called "Pixelon's i-Bash '99," again in Las Vegas, at the MGM Grand Theme Park. The show was broadcast on PAX-TV the following day. Other industry icons such as The Who, Faith Hill, and Tony Bennett performed, though all of the other bands' sets were live performances while KISS merely lip-synched "Shout It Out Loud," "Love Gun," "God of Thunder," and "Rock and Roll All Nite." Initially, the choice to lip-synch the performance may have reflected poorly upon KISS, but in a strange twist of fate it may have been perfectly appropriate: Pixelon was a complete fraud. The company was founded by David Stanley under the alias Michael Fenne and the company's claim was to have developed streaming media software that would allow TV-quality video feeds on the Internet. Fenne was found to have raised over $35 million from private investors ($12 million of which went towards the Las Vegas event), but with the software nothing but a sham, he had no way to repay his creditors and surrendered to police in April 2000. A final note of irony is that Fenne had offered many of the "i-Bash" entertainers payment in the form of now worthless Pixelon stock.

AUGUST 9, 1999

Westwood (Los Angeles), California
Parking Lot @ UCLA Campus
Opening Act: Everclear (w. Robin Zander and Rick Nielsen)
Attendance: 1,300
Promoter: New Line Cinema
■ SET LIST
Detroit Rock City
Shout It Out Loud
Cold Gin
Rock and Roll All Nite

■ This was the premiere party for "Detroit Rock City" and guests could attend by invitation only. Robin Zander and Rick Nielsen of Cheap Trick performed "Surrender" with Everclear. VH1 aired a half-hour special from the event on August 11.

DECEMBER 31, 1999

Vancouver, British Columbia, Canada
BC Place Concert Bowl
Opening Acts: Big Wreck, Lit, Nickelback
Attendance: 12,933   Capacity: 15,000
Promoter: House of Blues Canada
■ SET LIST
Psycho Circus
Shout It Out Loud
Deuce
Heaven's On Fire
Shock Me
Firehouse

Do You Love Me
Let Me Go, Rock 'n Roll
2,000 Man
Cold Gin
Gene Simmons Bass Solo
God of Thunder
Peter Criss Drum Solo - reprise
Lick It Up
I Love It Loud
100,000 Years
Love Gun
Forever
Black Diamond
Detroit Rock City
Into the Void
Ace Frehley Guitar Solo
Beth
Rock and Roll All Nite

■ An *Alive IV* "I Was There" T-shirt was sold at the event, and it was publicly advertised that *Alive IV* was to be recorded at the show. Statements made later by the band claimed that only some of the source material for the album was recorded in Vancouver.

JANUARY 3, 2000

Anchorage, Alaska
George M. Sullivan Sports Arena
Opening Act: Junkbox
Attendance: 8,000   Capacity: 8,000
Promoter: Goldenvoice
■ SET LIST
Psycho Circus
Shout It Out Loud
Deuce
Heaven's On Fire
Shock Me
Firehouse
Do You Love Me
Let Me Go, Rock 'n Roll
Into the Void
Ace Frehley Guitar Solo
Cold Gin
Gene Simmons Bass Solo
God of Thunder
Peter Criss Drum Solo - reprise
Lick It Up
I Love It Loud
100,000 Years
Love Gun
Forever
Black Diamond
Detroit Rock City
2,000 Man
Beth
Rock and Roll All Nite

■ This show was not professionally archived on videotape as no video production was used in the show.

For this gig, KISS scaled back the lighting and staging dramatically. Nothing more than speaker cabinets, a drum riser, the KISS logo from the Alive/Worldwide press conference, and the KISS Army banners flanking the far sides of the P.A. were used.

CHAPTER 26

THE FAREWELL TOUR

Number of Shows: 142
Start Date: March 11, 2000 - Phoenix, Arizona
End Date: March 5, 2002 - Trelawny (Rio Bueno), Jamaica
Countries: Australia, Canada, Japan, Jamaica, U.S.A.
Opening Acts: American Pearl; The Beautiful People; Ginger; Kings of the Sun; Neve; Ted Nugent; The Screaming Jets; Serial Joe; Skid Row
Average Attendance: 10,329* (Does not include Jamaican show.)

The Alive/Worldwide Tour's dizzying success had left the Psycho Circus Tour in a no-win situation, laying a foundation of ridiculous expectations that no tour could meet. Disregarding KISS's inability to recreate the success of Alive/Worldwide, a combination of factors had conspired to make the Psycho Circus Tour somewhat of a failure. The band had clearly over-extended their merchandise assortment, the novelty of the reunion had faded, and with the lack of a magic ingredient such as a hit single, the tour had little power to draw outside the core of KISS's fanbase. The audience dwindled, and the tour became an exercise in diminished returns.

The parallels to the great drop in popularity KISS experienced in 1979–80 are apparent, but a critical difference remained. In both cases, KISS needed something to rekindle excitement outside their core fanbase. In 1979–80, the band failed to find a solution and their popularity and draw-ing power plummeted, sending them into a tailspin and a five-year-long recovery. Faced with the same downward slide in 2000, KISS played the card that had been up their collective sleeve for several years. With two simple words, "Farewell Tour," the band immediately created the sense of urgent interest that exists for all blockbuster tours. It was quick, it was easy, it was inevitable, and it was the perfect solution.

And so, on Valentine's Day 2000, KISS taped an early morning interview with VH1 to announce their forthcoming Farewell Tour. VH1 Music News broadcast the event later that afternoon.

One of several interviews taped via satellite that morning has become a particular favorite among fans. *FOX & Friends'* Brian Kilmeade accidentally offended the band members when he asked if the upcoming tour was going to be called "Jews in Space." Kilmeade was left to defend himself from the band's "What, are you on drugs?" reaction by stating that he had read it on the Internet. Ironically, Kilmeade was correct in his assertion, as Gene had jokingly called the tour "Jews in Space" in a previous interview. When it finally aired on July 18, Kilmeade's co-anchors, E.D. Donahey and Steve Doocy, and special guest Leeza Gibbons, mocked Kilmeade by posing as panel of judges and sarcastically rating the interview with scorecards.

KISS was very fortunate to have VH1 sign on as The Farewell Tour's official sponsor. The tour also benefited from VH1's debut of *The Daily One* on March 6. The short-lived show, which was designed to be a VH1 version of MTV's *TRL,* covered the KISS tour almost daily. Beyond that, the cable network greatly contributed to the tour's initial success by allowing fans to purchase tickets from their web site, moving a reported 70,000 tickets before they had gone on sale at traditional outlets.

Staging for the tour was new, as was some of the production, though KISS retained the replica Destroyer costumes from the Psycho Circus Tour. The design of the set was an effective blend of the Love Gun and Alive/Worldwide stages. Four stacks of amplifiers ran along the length of the stage and were set up one behind the other in ascending, successive fashion. The two, lighted KISS logos returned and were perched immediately above the uppermost stack of amplifiers, giving the entire assembly a sense of imposing height and depth missing from the previous two tours' stages. Peter's drum riser sat in the center of the rows of amps and was flanked by two staircases. The replica Love Gun tapestry beneath Peter's kit also returned, as did the hydraulic lifts for the end of the show.

A large video screen was again a feature part of the staging and Nocturne Productions returned to provide video production. Bob Brigham shares some details: "For The Farewell Tour, we used an LED screen. The main screen was 14' x 25' and we were using side projectors as well. There were four hard cameras: two 55:1 lenses from the front of the house at the mix position, then two hand-held cameras in the pit, one assigned to Gene, one to Paul and they'd take turns covering Ace. Additionally, Peter had two POV cameras on him, a pan-and-tilt near the hi-hat, and the other camera was near his ride cymbal."

The 3D effects from the Psycho Circus Tour were abolished and several new video features were developed in their place. A video retrospective of the band that typically ran during "Do You Love Me" and animated graphics during "Detroit Rock City" were exclusive to the tour. Also added were animated graphics for "Psycho Circus," which were pulled from a PC game titled "KISS Psycho Circus: The Nightmare Child," and for "2,000 Man," whose graphics were borrowed from a series of Web-based animated episodes titled *KISS Immortals*.

The choice of venues was unique among KISS tours with an inordinately high number of amphitheatre appearances occurring. The high percentage of outdoor concerts was the result of the 1998 formation of the SFX Music Group, a national conglomerate of high-profile promoters. SFX, which has since merged with Clear Channel Communications, owns and operates many amphitheatres around the country, and KISS performed nearly three-dozen concerts in such venues during the North American leg of the tour alone.

Attendance was initially excellent, with some markets even surpassing the figures established on the Alive/Worldwide Tour. In several instances, KISS made initial farewell performances only to return to the same city later. These follow-up concerts typically came with the billing "Final Encore Performance." As the tour progressed, however, the numbers began to plunge from an average of 11,953 per night on the tour's first 20 shows to only 6,637 per concert for the final 20 gigs of the North American leg.

Not surprisingly, many of the same songs from the Alive/Worldwide and Psycho Circus Tours were still in place in the set list. However, for the first time, the original line-up of KISS

performed material that was recorded after Peter and Ace's initial departures in the early 1980s: "I Love It Loud," "Lick It Up," and "Heaven's On Fire" were all added to the show. Paul's intro to "Black Diamond" was expanded and at most shows in North America included parts of "I Still Love You." By the Japanese and Australian legs, the intro had been expanded further and usually included a medley of song excerpts, among them "Hard Luck Woman," "I Want You," and "Shandi."

Ace also added medleys to the mix and over the first three months of the tour he would sporadically include riffs of songs in his featured solo. Most of the material (such as "Rip It Out," "Snowblind," and "Hard Times") had never been performed live by KISS. Later, at two performances in September, and then again in Japan and Australia, KISS added a medley to their encores.

During the final shows of the North American leg of the tour, Peter wore a teardrop as part of his makeup. "They were in a contract fight," recalls John Bestwick of Nocturne Productions. "That's what the tear in his makeup was about. At that point, they had been negotiating for about three months and twice a week they would get together with their lawyers. It finally came to a head. The tour was supposed to continue on for another five weeks after those early October dates, but at that point, it was 'OK, seven more shows, my contract is done and I'm finished.' Legally, his contract was actually up at some point in Pennsylvania (September 27 in University Park), but he did the final seven shows."

———————

For the North American shows where Paul performed parts of songs (such as "Forever" or "I Still Love You") in his "Black Diamond" intro, these songs are listed in the set list proper with an asterisk (*).

Information on the medleys that Ace occasionally included in his solo is provided when known.

MARCH 11, 2000

Phoenix, Arizona
Blockbuster Desert Sky Pavilion
Opening Act: Ted Nugent
Attendance: 14,584   Capacity: 19,586
Promoters: SFX Music Group, Evening Star Productions, In-house
■ **SET LIST**
Detroit Rock City
Shout It Out Loud
Heaven's On Fire
Deuce
Calling Dr. Love
Shock Me
Psycho Circus
Firehouse
Do You Love Me
Let Me Go, Rock 'n Roll
Into the Void
Ace Frehley Guitar Solo
Cold Gin
Gene Simmons Bass Solo
God of Thunder
Lick It Up
I Love It Loud
100,000 Years
Love Gun
Black Diamond

I Stole Your Love
Beth
Rock and Roll All Nite
■ Ace's father, Carl Frehley, passed away earlier in the week, prompting concern that Ace would not be able to perform in Phoenix due to funeral commitments. The concern proved unfounded, though Ace did depart early from the filming of the TV commercial for Pepsi, which was shot on March 10 during production rehearsals at the venue in Phoenix. The commercial premiered on March 26 during the *Academy Awards* TM broadcast.

A nine-minute retrospective film was shown on the video screens prior to the start of the show in both Phoenix and Tucson.

Initially, KISS started their shows with all four members descending from the lighting rig on a platform. Upon reaching the stage floor, they would take their positions to start the opening number. This intro was altered almost immediately so that Peter began the show behind his kit and Ace, Gene, and Paul descended to the stage while performing "Detroit Rock City."

A VH1 special called *Opening Night Live* was broadcast from the event. VH1 also cybercast part of the show from their web site.

MARCH 12, 2000

Tucson, Arizona
Tucson Convention Center
Opening Act: Ted Nugent
Attendance: 8,220   Capacity: 8,220
Promoters: Evening Star Productions
■ **SET LIST**
Detroit Rock City
Shout It Out Loud
Deuce
Heaven's On Fire
Calling Dr. Love
Shock Me
Psycho Circus
Firehouse
Do You Love Me
Let Me Go, Rock 'n Roll
Into the Void
Ace Frehley Guitar Solo (Hard Times, She, Torpedo Girl)
Cold Gin
Gene Simmons Bass Solo
God of Thunder
Lick It Up
I Love It Loud
100,000 Years
Love Gun
Forever*
Black Diamond
I Stole Your Love
Beth
Rock and Roll All Nite
■ Skid Row was scheduled to open the show; however, their lead singer missed his flight to Tucson and could not arrive in time to do the gig. Paul played the first verse and chorus of "Forever" during the intro to "Black Diamond."

MARCH 14, 2000

Las Cruces, New Mexico
Pan American Center
Opening Acts: Ted Nugent, Skid Row
Attendance: 10,051   Capacity: 10,051
Promoter: Evening Star Productions

GREG DEAN

Detroit Rock City
Shout It Out Loud
Deuce
Heaven's On Fire
I Love It Loud
Firehouse
Shock Me
Psycho Circus
Calling Dr. Love
Let Me Go, Rock 'n Roll
Do You Love Me
Into the Void
Ace Frehley Guitar Solo (Hard Times, Almost Human, She)
Cold Gin
Gene Simmons Bass Solo
God of Thunder
Lick It Up
100,000 Years
Love Gun
Black Diamond
I Was Made for Lovin' You
Beth
Rock and Roll All Nite

■ Beginning with this show, an edited version of the retrospective video that had previously played before the show was now screened during "Do You Love Me."

MARCH 17, 2000

Las Vegas, Nevada
Mandalay Bay Events Center
Opening Acts: Ted Nugent, Skid Row
Attendance: 9,296   Capacity: 9,296
Promoter: Evening Star Productions

■ SET LIST
Detroit Rock City
Shout It Out Loud
Deuce
I Love It Loud
Shock Me
Firehouse
Do You Love Me
Calling Dr. Love
Psycho Circus
Heaven's On Fire
Let Me Go, Rock 'n Roll
2,000 Man
Ace Frehley Guitar Solo (Hard Times, Parasite, She)
Lick It Up
Gene Simmons Bass Solo
God of Thunder
Cold Gin
100,000 Years
Love Gun
Black Diamond
Beth
I Stole Your Love
Rock and Roll All Nite

MARCH 18, 2000

Anaheim, California
Arrowhead Pond
Opening Acts: Ted Nugent, Skid Row
Attendance: 14,009   Capacity: 14,009
Promoter: Nederlander Organization

■ SET LIST
Detroit Rock City
Shout It Out Loud
Deuce
I Love It Loud
Shock Me
Firehouse
Do You Love Me
Calling Dr. Love
Psycho Circus
Heaven's On Fire
Let Me Go, Rock 'n Roll
2,000 Man
Ace Frehley Guitar Solo (Hard Times, Parasite, She)
Lick It Up
Gene Simmons Bass Solo
God of Thunder
Cold Gin
100,000 Years
Love Gun
Black Diamond
Beth
Rock and Roll All Nite

■ Peter dedicated his performance of "Beth" to his daughter.

While descending from the lighting rig during "God of Thunder," Gene was stranded several feet above the stage. Crew members ran out to assist him and placed the box into which he normally threw his firebreathing sword underneath him while they freed him from his harness. Paul covered for him by finishing the vocals to the song.

Gene's opportunity to return the favor occurred during "Love Gun" when Paul became stranded about ten rows into the audience while flying out to his platform. As the crew went out into the audience to help get Paul back to the stage, Gene sang (though ad-libbed is a more accurate term) the song up to the solo. After hanging over the audience for several minutes, a visibly exhausted Paul arrived back onstage.

To add insult to injury, when the band went to restart "Love Gun," Paul's guitar would not work. His guitar tech then ran out, took the malfunctioning guitar and, naturally, forgot to bring him a replacement.

Not surprisingly, when the show reached its finale, the hydraulic platforms failed to work.

MARCH 19, 2000

San Diego, California
San Diego Sports Arena
Opening Acts: Ted Nugent, Skid Row
Attendance: 10,818   Capacity: 12,085
Promoter: SFX Music Group

■ SET LIST

Detroit Rock City
Deuce
Shout It Out Loud
I Love It Loud
Shock Me
Firehouse
Do You Love Me
Calling Dr. Love
Psycho Circus
Heaven's On Fire
Let Me Go, Rock 'n Roll
2,000 Man
Ace Frehley Guitar Solo (Hard Times, Parasite, Snowblind)
Lick It Up
Gene Simmons Bass Solo
God of Thunder
Cold Gin
100,000 Years
Love Gun
Black Diamond
Beth
Rock and Roll All Nite

MARCH 21, 2000

Bakersfield, California
Bakersfield Centennial Garden
Opening Acts: Ted Nugent, Skid Row
Attendance: 9,343   Capacity: 9,343
Promoter: Nederlander Organization

■ SET LIST

See March 19, 2000.

■ The motor on the mechanism that transported Paul to his platform in the audience was broken. The crew pulled the wire through the pulleys and transported Paul manually.

MARCH 23, 2000

Oakland, California
Oakland Arena
Opening Acts: Ted Nugent, Skid Row
Attendance: 14,494   Capacity: 15,585
Promoter: SFX Music Group

■ SET LIST

See March 19, 2000.

■ The show was marred by tragedy when a member of the audience plunged to his death. 36-year-old Shawn Stubblefield tumbled from a retaining wall in the upper tier of the Oakland Arena and was pronounced dead on arrival at Highland Hospital.

MARCH 25, 2000

Reno, Nevada
Lawlor Events Center
Opening Acts: Ted Nugent, Skid Row
Attendance: 9,935   Capacity: 10,465
Promoter: SFX Music Group

■ SET LIST

See March 19, 2000. Ace's Medley: Parasite, Hard Times, Snowblind

MARCH 27, 2000

West Valley City (Salt Lake City), Utah
The E Center of West Valley City
Opening Acts: Ted Nugent, Skid Row
Attendance: 9,573   Capacity: 9,573
Promoters: Evening Star Productions, United Concerts

■ SET LIST

See March 19, 2000. Ace's Medley: Hard Times, Parasite, Snowblind, New York Groove

MARCH 28, 2000

Denver, Colorado
Pepsi Center
Opening Acts: Ted Nugent, Skid Row
Attendance: 15,287   Capacity: 17,000
Promoter: United Concerts

■ SET LIST

See March 19, 2000. Ace's Medley: Parasite, Snowblind, New York Groove, Hard Times

MARCH 29, 2000

Lubbock, Texas
United Spirit Arena
Opening Acts: Ted Nugent, Skid Row
Attendance: 11,529   Capacity: 13,000
Promoter: Stardate Productions

■ SET LIST

See March 19, 2000.

■ When Gene landed on his platform in the lighting rig, he broke the mike stand and was forced to hold the microphone in his hand while he sang "God of Thunder." Paul helped sing several lines of the song.

MARCH 31, 2000

San Antonio, Texas
AlamoDome
Opening Acts: Ted Nugent, Skid Row
Attendance: 20,760   Capacity: 20,760
Promoter: Beaver Productions

■ SET LIST

See March 19, 2000. Ace's Medley: Rocket Ride, She, Snowblind, Parasite, New York Groove

APRIL 1, 2000

Spring (Houston), Texas
Cynthia Woods Mitchell Pavilion
Opening Acts: Ted Nugent, Skid Row
Attendance: 12,908   Capacity: 12,917
Promoters: In-house, SFX Music Group

■ SET LIST

See March 19, 2000.

■ Ace accidentally knocked over a stack of amplifiers during the intro to "Cold Gin."

APRIL 2, 2000

Dallas, Texas
Starplex Amphitheatre
Opening Acts: Ted Nugent, Skid Row
Attendance: 18,135   Capacity: 18,135
Promoter: House of Blues Concerts

■ SET LIST

Detroit Rock City
Deuce
Shout It Out Loud
I Love It Loud
Shock Me
Firehouse
Do You Love Me
Calling Dr. Love
Psycho Circus
Heaven's On Fire
Let Me Go, Rock 'n Roll
2,000 Man
Ace Frehley Guitar Solo (New York Groove, Snowblind, Strange Ways, Parasite, Hard Times)
Lick It Up
Gene Simmons Bass Solo
God of Thunder
Cold Gin
100,000 Years
Peter Criss Drum Solo - reprise
Love Gun
Black Diamond
Beth
Rock and Roll All Nite

■ Peter's drum break in "100,000 Years" was lengthened to a mini-solo.

APRIL 4, 2000

Oklahoma City, Oklahoma
Myriad Arena
Opening Acts: Ted Nugent, Skid Row
Attendance: 12,533   Capacity: 12,533
Promoter: Beaver Productions

■ SET LIST

See April 2, 2000. Ace's Medley: Parasite, New York Groove, Ozone, Snowblind, Hard Times

APRIL 5, 2000

North Little Rock, Arkansas
Alltel Arena
Opening Acts: Ted Nugent, Skid Row
Attendance: 10,080   Capacity: 12,500
Promoter: Beaver Productions

■ SET LIST

Detroit Rock City
Deuce
Shout It Out Loud
I Love It Loud
Shock Me
Firehouse
Do You Love Me
Calling Dr. Love
Psycho Circus
Heaven's On Fire
Let Me Go, Rock 'n Roll
2,000 Man
Ace Frehley Guitar Solo (Parasite, Hard Times, New York Groove, Snowblind)
Lick It Up
Gene Simmons Bass Solo
God of Thunder
Cold Gin
100,000 Years
Peter Criss Drum Solo - reprise
Love Gun
Black Diamond
Rock and Roll All Nite

■ "Beth" was not performed at this gig, and Paul sang lead vocals on "Black Diamond." A local radio station reported that Peter was rushed to the hospital immediately following the show.

APRIL 6, 2000

Pensacola, Florida
The Pensacola Civic Center
Opening Acts: Ted Nugent, Skid Row
Attendance: 7,226   Capacity: 7,226
Promoter: Beaver Productions

■ SET LIST
See April 2, 2000. Ace's Medley: Parasite, Snowblind, New York Groove, Hard Times

APRIL 8, 2000

West Palm Beach, Florida
Mars Music Amphitheatre
Opening Acts: Ted Nugent, Skid Row
Attendance: 14,031   Capacity: 18,000
Promoter: Fantasma Productions

■ SET LIST
See April 2, 2000.

APRIL 9, 2000

Estero (Fort Myers), Florida
TECO Arena
Opening Acts: Ted Nugent, Skid Row
Attendance: 6,257   Capacity: 6,257
Promoter: Fantasma Productions

■ SET LIST
Detroit Rock City
Deuce
Shout It Out Loud
I Love It Loud
Shock Me
Firehouse
Do You Love Me
Calling Dr. Love
Psycho Circus
Heaven's On Fire
Let Me Go, Rock 'n Roll
2,000 Man
Ace Frehley Guitar Solo
Lick It Up
Gene Simmons Bass Solo
God of Thunder
Cold Gin
100,000 Years
Peter Criss Drum Solo - reprise
Love Gun
I Still Love You*
Black Diamond
Beth
Rock and Roll All Nite

■ Paul added the first verse and chorus of "I Still Love You" to his "Black Diamond" intro at this show. With rare exception, he would include portions of the song throughout the rest of the tour.

There were several production problems present within the performance: Gene made three unsuccessful attempts to fly, which were followed by Paul attempting to fly to his stage only to be stranded above the third row. Finally, one of the flamethrowers scorched a strand of lights on the lighting rig and caused them to smolder.

APRIL 11, 2000

Orlando, Florida
TD Waterhouse Centre
Opening Acts: Ted Nugent, Skid Row
Attendance: 10,428   Capacity: 12,437
Promoter: SFX Music Group

■ SET LIST
See April 9, 2000.

■ Beginning with this show, Peter's riser began the show fully raised and descended in synch with Ace, Gene, and Paul.

APRIL 12, 2000

Tampa, Florida
Ice Palace
Opening Acts: Ted Nugent (w. Pat Travers), Skid Row
Attendance: 12,245   Capacity: 14,033
Promoters: Cellar Door Concerts, SFX Music Group

■ SET LIST
See April 9, 2000.

APRIL 14, 2000

Birmingham, Alabama
Birmingham-Jefferson Civic Center
Opening Acts: Ted Nugent (w. Damon Johnson), Skid Row
Attendance: 13,628   Capacity: 13, 628
Promoter: New Era Promotions

■ SET LIST
See April 9, 2000.

APRIL 15, 2000

Atlanta, Georgia
Philips Arena
Opening Acts: Ted Nugent (w. Derek St. Holmes), Skid Row
Attendance: 14,495   Capacity: 14,495
Promoters: Alex Cooley, Peter Conlon, SFX Music Group

■ SET LIST
See April 9, 2000.

APRIL 16, 2000

New Orleans, Louisiana
New Orleans Arena
Opening Acts: Ted Nugent, Skid Row
Attendance: 13,565   Capacity: 13,565
Promoter: Beaver Productions

■ SET LIST
See April 9, 2000.

APRIL 18, 2000

Columbia, South Carolina
Carolina Coliseum
Opening Acts: Ted Nugent, Skid Row
Attendance: 8,798   Capacity: 9,227
Promoter: C & C Entertainment

■ SET LIST
See April 9, 2000.

APRIL 20, 2000

Charlotte, North Carolina
New Charlotte Coliseum
Opening Acts: Ted Nugent, Skid Row
Attendance: 15,886   Capacity: 15,886
Promoter: C & C Entertainment

■ SET LIST
See April 9, 2000. Ace's Medley: New York Groove, Hard Times

APRIL 21, 2000

Greenville, South Carolina
Bi-Lo Center
Opening Acts: Ted Nugent, Skid Row
Attendance: 12,049   Capacity: 12,049
Promoter: C & C Entertainment

■ SET LIST
See April 9, 2000.

■ John Bestwick of Nocturne: "At the end of each show, we put up a thank-you to whatever town we were in. And as testament to being a roadie and getting off the bus and not knowing what town you're in, I put up "Greenfield" instead of "Greenville." I thought, 'Well, this is just going to slip by the wayside.' And about 15 minutes after the show ended, I get a call from Gene Simmons from the limo. 'I understand that the wrong city

got put up on the wall.' I said, 'Gene it was barely up there at all.' I actually went back and looked at the video the next day, and it was up there for about 36 frames, which is a second and a half. I realized I had mis-programmed it, and as I saw the thing come sweeping up to the front of the screen, I killed it. The local newspaper picked up on it, and it was turned into this enormous story. It ended up being picked up by a local news station, and then on the Internet. Subsequently, the band wrote a letter to the newspaper and they all four signed it, and the newspaper printed it. They received thousands of emails requesting to see the letter signed by the band. They posted the letter on the Internet, and that blew it even further out of proportion.

"I took a huge amount of shit for that during the rest of the tour; it became an ongoing joke for us. When we got to Australia, I would put 'field' on the end of every city at soundcheck: 'KISS thanks Adelaide-field.' I lived in fear for every night after that. I was asking everyone in the crew how to spell ' New Jersey.' I was carrying a little pocket atlas with me. It became pretty funny."

APRIL 22, 2000

Greensboro, North Carolina
Greensboro Coliseum
Opening Acts: Ted Nugent, Skid Row
Attendance: 17,685   Capacity: 17,685
Promoter: C & C Entertainment

■ SET LIST
See April 9, 2000. Ace's Medley: Hard Times

APRIL 24, 2000

Chattanooga, Tennessee
The McKenzie Arena
Opening Acts: Ted Nugent, Skid Row
Attendance: 6,658   Capacity: 11,500
Promoters: Alex Cooley, Peter Conlon, SFX Music Group

■ SET LIST
See April 9, 2000.

APRIL 25, 2000

Memphis, Tennessee
The Pyramid
Opening Acts: Ted Nugent, Skid Row
Attendance: 14,259   Capacity: 14,259
Promoter: Beaver Productions

■ SET LIST
See April 9, 2000. Ace's Medley: Hard Times, New York Groove, Parasite

■ For the first of several times on the tour, Ace lost his place in "Shock Me" and began performing the guitar solo at the start of the second verse. A bemused Paul started singing the lyrics to the second verse, and Ace soon recognized his error.

APRIL 28, 2000

Antioch (Nashville), Tennessee
AmSouth Amphitheatre
Opening Acts: Ted Nugent, Skid Row
Attendance: 16,503   Capacity: 17,000
Promoter: SFX Music Group

■ SET LIST
See April 9, 2000.

APRIL 29, 2000

Louisville, Kentucky
Freedom Hall

Opening Acts: Ted Nugent, Skid Row
Attendance: 14,467   Capacity: 14,868
Promoter: SFX Music Group
■ **SET LIST**
See April 9, 2000.

APRIL 30, 2000

Knoxville, Tennessee
Thompson-Boling Arena
Opening Acts: Ted Nugent, Skid Row
Attendance: 13,040   Capacity: 13,040
Promoter: Beaver Productions
■ **SET LIST**
See April 9, 2000. Ace's Medley: Almost Human, Hard
    Times

MAY 2, 2000

Charleston, West Virginia
Charleston Civic Center
Opening Acts: Ted Nugent, Skid Row
Attendance: 7,711   Capacity: 10,000
Promoter: Belkin Productions
■ **SET LIST**
See April 9, 2000.

MAY 3, 2000

Roanoke, Virginia
Roanoke Civic Center
Opening Acts: Ted Nugent, Skid Row
Attendance: 7,178   Capacity: 9,000
Promoter: Beaver Productions
■ **SET LIST**
See April 9, 2000. Ace's Medley: Hard Times, Parasite,
    New York Groove

MAY 5, 2000

Cleveland, Ohio

GUND Arena
Opening Acts: Ted Nugent, Skid Row
Attendance: 26,698   Capacity: 17,500
Promoter: Belkin Productions
■ **SET LIST**
See April 9, 2000.
■ The attendance figure reflects combined atten-
dance for both the May 5 and 6 shows in Cleve-
land.

MAY 6, 2000

Cleveland, Ohio
GUND Arena
Opening Acts: Ted Nugent, Skid Row
Capacity: 17,500
Promoter: Belkin Productions
■ **SET LIST**
See April 9, 2000.
■ Ace added a third rocket to his solo, shooting
the first two at confetti-filled bags in the lighting
rig, with the third and final one shot out over the
crowd.

MAY 7, 2000

Grand Rapids, Michigan
Van Andel Arena
Opening Acts: Ted Nugent, Skid Row
Attendance: 11,791   Capacity: 12,240
Promoter: SFX Music Group
■ **SET LIST**
See April 9, 2000.

MAY 9, 2000

Toledo, Ohio
John F. Savage Hall
Opening Acts: Ted Nugent, Skid Row
Attendance: 6,143   Capacity: 8,794

Promoter: Belkin Productions
■ **SET LIST**
See April 9, 2000.
■ Paul did not fly.

MAY 11, 2000

Rosemont (Chicago), Illinois
Allstate Arena
Opening Acts: Ted Nugent, Skid Row
Attendance: 11,475   Capacity: 11,475
Promoter: JAM Productions
■ **SET LIST**
See April 9, 2000.
■ The concert was cybercast live on Pepsi's web
site. Beginning with this show, Ace began using
guitar picks that were customized for the city in
which the band was performing.

MAY 12, 2000

Rosemont (Chicago), Illinois
Allstate Arena
Opening Acts: Ted Nugent, Skid Row
Attendance: 11,475   Capacity: 11,475
Promoter: JAM Productions
■ **SET LIST**
See April 9, 2000.

MAY 13, 2000

Columbus, Ohio
Polaris Amphitheater
Opening Acts: Ted Nugent, Skid Row
Attendance: 16,869   Capacity: 16,869
Promoter: Belkin Productions
■ Severe winds were prevalent throughout the
show and forced the crew to take down the large
KISS Army banners.

GREG DEAN

MAY 15, 2000

Peoria, Illinois
Carver Arena @ Peoria Civic Center
Opening Acts: Ted Nugent, Skid Row
Attendance: 9,132   Capacity: 9,132
Promoters: JAM Productions, Jay Goldberg
■ **SET LIST**
Detroit Rock City
Deuce
Shout It Out Loud
I Love It Loud
Shock Me
Firehouse
Do You Love Me
Calling Dr. Love
Heaven's On Fire
Let Me Go, Rock 'n Roll
2,000 Man
Ace Frehley Guitar Solo
Psycho Circus
Lick It Up
Gene Simmons Bass Solo

God of Thunder
Cold Gin
100,000 Years
Peter Criss Drum Solo - reprise
Love Gun
I Still Love You*
Black Diamond
Beth
Rock and Roll All Nite

MAY 16, 2000

Moline, Illinois
The Mark of the Quad Cities
Opening Acts: Ted Nugent, Skid Row
Attendance: 11,548   Capacity: 11,548
Promoter: JAM Productions
■ **SET LIST**
See May 15, 2000.

MAY 18, 2000

Minneapolis, Minnesota
Target Center
Opening Acts: Ted Nugent, Skid Row

Attendance: 14,031   Capacity: 15,281
Promoter: Rose Productions
■ **SET LIST**
See May 15, 2000.
■ The show was originally scheduled for May 17, but was pushed back one night when severe weather in Chicago prevented KISS from flying into Minneapolis.

MAY 19, 2000

Milwaukee, Wisconsin
Marcus Amphitheatre
Opening Acts: Ted Nugent, Skid Row
Attendance: 17,172   Capacity: 22,828
Promoter: SFX Music Group
■ **SET LIST**
See May 15, 2000.
■ Bob Brigham of Nocturne: "We were experiencing power problems at the venue. During KISS's show, the video screen was turning on and off. We're back there trying to get it running, but everything we tried wasn't working because we were getting power spikes from the building. There was a processor on the LED screen with a surge protector so that when you have a drop-off of power, it clips and shuts itself off. When it feels power return, it turns back on, the end result is that the screen flickers and turns off. After the show, Doc goes nuclear; he fires me and fires Nocturne. I told him that there was always a logical answer to everything. He told me that he was docking us $115,000 for this and fuck you and so on. It turned out that it was just a bad power source in Milwaukee.

"What made the Milwaukee show more interesting was that because Milwaukee is so close, Gene was driven up from Chicago in a Town Car. I was privileged to drive up with Gene. After the mishap, I had to drive back from Milwaukee in the car with Gene, a guest of his, and the tour driver Paco Zimmer. Now, they are waiting in a Town Car for 25 minutes for me to get out of a meeting with Doc. I get in the car, and he says, 'Mr. Brigham, I'm going to make a statement. Then, you're going to respond to my statement. I'll go first. Tonight, it was 50 degrees. I froze my ass off out there. 20,000 fans did not get to see us do our show. I realize that all the cool stuff I did, no one responded to it. Do you know why, Mr. Brigham?' I said, 'Yes, Gene, because nobody saw it.' 'Yes, that's the correct answer. Nobody saw all my cool shit, thus they didn't go nuts. What do you have to say?' 'Well, we still don't have answers as to what went wrong. We're bringing in more parts and I guarantee we are going to have something in place that insures that this will not happen again. I am sorry your show was fucked, and I'm sorry we're a part of it.' 'Right answer. Now, let's talk about women.'

"As we were driving back down I-94 to Chicago, Gene got the munchies. We stopped at this little gas station, and I started talking to this rough-and-tumble truck-driver type guy with a KISS hat on. I said, 'Did you go to the show tonight?' He said, 'Oh yeah. That's my 29th KISS show.' I asked him, 'What did you think of the show?' He said, 'I've never seen the band better. That's the best KISS show I've ever seen.' 'Really? Would you do me a favor? I'm traveling with a friend of mine, and he's kind of having a bad night, would you go over and tell him how much you liked it?' So, he walks over and he goes, 'Hey bud, were you at the show tonight?' Gene says, 'Yes, I was there. You might say that.' 'Well, that's the best KISS show that I've ever seen in my life. I loved it.' Gene: "Really? You really enjoyed it?' The guy began stuttering: 'Wait a minute!' Gene ended up signing 10 autographs for him and his family and when Gene got back in the car all was forgiven."

Another casualty of mechanical malfunction was Paul's flying rig, which also did not work at this gig.

MAY 20, 2000
Noblesville (Indianapolis), Indiana
Deer Creek Music Center
Opening Acts: Ted Nugent, Skid Row
Attendance: 22,633   Capacity: 24,210
Promoter: SFX Music Group
■ SET LIST
See May 15, 2000.

MAY 22, 2000
Cincinnati, Ohio
Riverbend Music Center
Opening Acts: Ted Nugent, Skid Row
Attendance: 11,209   Capacity: 20,474
Promoter: SFX Music Group
■ SET LIST
See May 15, 2000.
■ KISS's use of pyrotechnics was scaled back due to the height of the venue.

MAY 24, 2000
Auburn Hills (Detroit), Michigan
The Palace of Auburn Hills
Opening Acts: Ted Nugent, Skid Row
Attendance: 13,476   Capacity: 13,476
Promoter: SFX Music Group
■ SET LIST
See May 15, 2000.

MAY 25, 2000
Auburn Hills (Detroit), Michigan
The Palace of Auburn Hills
Opening Acts: Ted Nugent, Skid Row
Attendance: 13,476   Capacity: 13,476
Promoter: SFX Music Group
■ SET LIST
See May 15, 2000.

MAY 26, 2000
Burgettstown (Pittsburgh), Pennsylvania
Post-Gazette Pavilion at Star Lake
Opening Acts: Ted Nugent, Skid Row
Attendance: 14,946   Capacity: 23,212
Promoter: SFX Music Group
■ SET LIST
See May 15, 2000.

JUNE 6, 2000
Richmond, Virginia
Richmond Coliseum
Opening Acts: Ted Nugent, Skid Row
Attendance: 7,744   Capacity: 9,000
Promoter: Beaver Production
■ SET LIST
See May 15, 2000.
■ In somewhat of a strange move, Paul flew out to his mini-stage, performed "Love Gun," and continued to play the first part of "I Still Love You" and the intro to "Black Diamond" before flying back to the stage as Peter began singing.

JUNE 8, 2000   POSTPONED
Syracuse, New York
War Memorial at Oncenter
Opening Acts: Ted Nugent, Skid Row
Promoters: Metropolitan Entertainment, SFX Music Group
■ Reportedly, the venue was too small for the production and the show was rescheduled for a larger venue, the Carrier Dome, on September 16. Ironically, that show was moved back to the War Memorial when ticket sales were sluggish.

JUNE 9, 2000
Wantagh, New York
Jones Beach Amphitheatre
Opening Acts: Ted Nugent, Skid Row
Attendance: 14,110   Capacity: 14,110
Promoter: SFX Music Group
■ SET LIST
See May 15, 2000. Ace medley: Hard Times, Parasite, New York Groove
■ Paul again did "Love Gun," "I Still Love You," and the "Black Diamond" intro from his mini-stage.

CBS-TV's The Early Show taped a segment on KISS, which aired on July 17.

Kyra Sedgwick and Kevin Bacon were in attendance. On April 11, Gene had made a cameo appearance in an episode of Sedgwick's short-lived sitcom Talk To Me. Actor/Musician Kevin Bacon: "My son is the biggest KISS fan. So, KISS is a very important part of our life right now. His room is covered with KISS memorabilia."

JUNE 10, 2000
Wantagh, New York
Jones Beach Amphitheatre
Opening Acts: Ted Nugent, Skid Row
Attendance: 9,422   Capacity: 14,110
Promoter: SFX Music Group
■ SET LIST
Detroit Rock City
Deuce
Shout It Out Loud
I Love It Loud
Shock Me
Firehouse
Do You Love Me
Calling Dr. Love
Heaven's On Fire
Let Me Go. Rock 'n Roll
2,000 Man
Ace Frehley Guitar Solo (Hard Times, Parasite, New York Groove)
Psycho Circus
Lick It Up
Gene Simmons Bass Solo
God of Thunder
Cold Gin
Peter Criss Drum Solo - reprise
Love Gun
I Still Love You*
100,000 Years
Black Diamond
Beth
Rock and Roll All Nite
■ This is the last known time that Ace included a medley in his solo.

Paul performed "Love Gun" and "I Still Love You" from his solo stage. Paul then flew back as the band launched into "100,000 Years."

JUNE 12, 2000
Mansfield, Massachusetts

Tweeter Center for the Performing Arts
Opening Acts: Ted Nugent, Skid Row
Attendance: 8,898   Capacity: 8,898
Promoter: SFX Music Group
■ SET LIST
See May 15, 2000.
■ Production was scaled back at both Mansfield shows due to the small size of the venue.

JUNE 13, 2000
Mansfield, Massachusetts
Tweeter Center for the Performing Arts
Opening Acts: Ted Nugent, Skid Row
Attendance: 8,898   Capacity: 8,898
Promoter: SFX Music Group
■ SET LIST
See May 15, 2000.
■ Ace and Paul reportedly got into a short verbal spat before "2,000 Man" as Frehley left the stage to change guitars.

JUNE 15, 2000
Portland, Maine
Cumberland County Civic Center
Opening Acts: Ted Nugent, Skid Row
Attendance: 8,288   Capacity: 8,288
Promoter: Beaver Productions
■ SET LIST
See May 15, 2000.

JUNE 16, 2000
Camden (Philadelphia), New Jersey
Blockbuster-Sony Music Entertainment Centre
Opening Acts: Ted Nugent, Skid Row
Attendance: 14,174   Capacity: 24,697
Promoter: SFX Music Group
■ SET LIST
See May 15, 2000.

JUNE 19, 2000
Erie, Pennsylvania
Lewis J. Tullio Arena @ Erie Civic Center
Opening Acts: Ted Nugent, Skid Row
Attendance: 6,796   Capacity: 6,796
Promoter: Belkin Productions
■ SET LIST
See May 15, 2000.

JUNE 20, 2000
Albany, New York
Saratoga Performing Arts Center
Opening Acts: Ted Nugent, Skid Row
Attendance: 9,427   Capacity: 20,000
■ SET LIST
See May 15, 2000.

JUNE 22, 2000
Montréal, Quebec, Canada
Centre Molson
Opening Acts: Ted Nugent, Skid Row
Attendance: 12,246   Capacity: 12,246
Promoter: House of Blues Canada
■ SET LIST
See May 15, 2000.

JUNE 23, 2000
Toronto, Ontario, Canada
Air Canada Centre
Opening Acts: Ted Nugent, Skid Row
Attendance: 15,675 Capacity: 15,675
Promoter: House of Blues Canada
■ SET LIST
See May 15, 2000.

JUNE 24, 2000
Buffalo, New York
HSBC Arena

Opening Acts: Ted Nugent, Skid Row
Attendance: 12,163   Capacity: 12,163
Promoters: Metropolitan Entertainment, SFX Music
  Group
■ SET LIST
See May 15, 2000.

■ On June 24 and 25, KISS, Greg Manning Auctions and Butterfields auctioned over $1.6 million of KISS memorabilia from Paul and Gene's personal collections. The dozens of auctioned lots included items such as original costumes, instruments, wardrobe cases, album cover artwork, posters, and other miscellany.

JUNE 27, 2000

East Rutherford, New Jersey
Continental Airlines Arena
Opening Acts: Ted Nugent, Skid Row
Attendance: 27,910   Capacity: 15,000
Promoters: Metropolitan Entertainment, SFX Music
  Group
■ SET LIST
See May 15, 2000.

■ The attendance figure reflects the combined attendance numbers for the June 27 and 28 concerts.

John Bestwick: "NHK came over and shot an HD show with six cameras, and we took that show and added additional footage from the concert tour to pull off a live pay-per-view.

"I would edit the pay-per-view in the hotels after the gigs, and we wouldn't get back to the hotels until about 12 to 2 A.M., depending upon how far away we were. [Skid Row guitarist] Dave Sabo had a Pro Tools system and I loaded up Final Cut Pro on it, and that's how we offlined the pay-per-view. Since it was his system, he wanted to be there and he and I would edit until 5 or 6. Then I'd get up at 11 A.M. and edit until 2 P.M. That went on for about five weeks. We edited it originally in widescreen. Then the day we delivered it to Showtime, they told us they weren't going to take it that way. So we had to have the show converted and it really spoiled a lot of it."

Television station NHK BS-2 in Japan aired a high definition broadcast of 12 songs from this show on September 7 during *That's Music From New York*.

JUNE 28, 2000

East Rutherford, New Jersey
Continental Airlines Arena
Opening Acts: Ted Nugent, Skid Row
Capacity: 15,000
Promoters: Metropolitan Entertainment, SFX Music
  Group
■ SET LIST
See May 15, 2000.

JUNE 30, 2000

Raleigh, North Carolina
Alltel Pavilion at Walnut Creek
Opening Acts: Ted Nugent, Skid Row
Attendance: 10,385   Capacity: 20,119
Promoter: SFX Music Group
■ SET LIST
See May 15, 2000.

JULY 1, 2000

Bristow (Washington, D.C.), Virginia
Nissan Pavilion @ Stone Ridge
Opening Acts: Ted Nugent, Skid Row

Attendance: 13,842   Capacity: 22,485
Promoter: SFX Music Group
■ SET LIST
See May 15, 2000.

JULY 2, 2000

Virginia Beach (Norfolk), Virginia
GTE Virginia Beach Amphitheatre
Opening Acts: Ted Nugent, Skid Row
Attendance: 11,762   Capacity: 19,932
Promoter: SFX Music Group
■ SET LIST
See May 15, 2000.

JULY 5, 2000

Hershey, Pennsylvania
Hersheypark Arena
Opening Acts: Ted Nugent
Attendance: 18,232   Capacity: 28,824
Promoters: Electric Factory Concerts, SFX Music Group
■ SET LIST
See May 15, 2000.

■ Skid Row was scheduled to perform, but canceled.

JULY 7, 2000

Scranton, Pennsylvania
Coors Light Amphitheatre at Montage Mountain
Opening Acts: Ted Nugent, Skid Row
Attendance: 15,119   Capacity: 16,000
Promoter: Metropolitan Entertainment
■ SET LIST
See May 15, 2000.

JULY 8, 2000

Hartford, Connecticut
Meadows Music Theater
Opening Acts: Ted Nugent, Skid Row
Attendance: 12,506   Capacity: 24,570
Promoter: SFX Music Group
■ SET LIST
See May 15, 2000.

JULY 11, 2000

Madison, Wisconsin
Kohl Center
Opening Acts: Ted Nugent, Skid Row
Attendance: 6,259   Capacity: 13,838
Promoters: Belkin Productions, Frank Productions
■ SET LIST
See May 15, 2000.

■ This is the last known occasion on the tour where Peter performed a drum solo in "100,000 Years."

JULY 13, 2000

Minneapolis, Minnesota
Target Center
Opening Acts: Ted Nugent, Skid Row
Attendance: 9,241   Capacity: 12,650
Promoter: Rose Productions
■ SET LIST
Detroit Rock City
Deuce
Shout It Out Loud
I Love It Loud
Shock Me
Firehouse
Do You Love Me
Calling Dr. Love
Heaven's On Fire
Let Me Go, Rock 'n Roll
2,000 Man
Ace Frehley Guitar Solo
Psycho Circus
Lick It Up

Gene Simmons Bass Solo
God of Thunder
Cold Gin
100,000 Years
Love Gun
I Still Love You*
Black Diamond
Beth
Rock and Roll All Nite

JULY 14, 2000

Fargo, North Dakota
Fargodome
Opening Acts: Ted Nugent, Skid Row
Attendance: 8,549   Capacity: 12,000
Promoter: Beaver Productions
■ SET LIST
See July 13, 2000.

JULY 16, 2000

Winnipeg, Manitoba, Canada
Winnipeg Arena
Opening Acts: Ted Nugent, Skid Row
Attendance: 10,772   Capacity: 11,506
Promoter: House of Blues Canada
■ SET LIST
See July 13, 2000.

JULY 17, 2000

Saskatoon, Saskatchewan, Canada
Saskatchewan Place
Opening Acts: Ted Nugent, Skid Row
Attendance: 7,272   Capacity: 12,258
Promoter: House of Blues Canada
■ SET LIST
See July 13, 2000.

JULY 19, 2000

Calgary, Alberta, Canada
Canadian Air Saddledome
Opening Acts: Ted Nugent, Skid Row
Attendance: 13,264   Capacity: 13,264
Promoter: House of Blues Canada
■ SET LIST
See July 13, 2000.

JULY 20, 2000

Edmonton, Alberta, Canada
Skyreach Centre
Opening Acts: Ted Nugent, Skid Row
Attendance: 13,074   Capacity: 13,074
Promoter: House of Blues Canada
■ SET LIST
See July 13, 2000.

■ The Skyreach Centre was running on reserve power, due to severe storms and flooding in the area, which caused extensive power outages.

JULY 22, 2000

George, Washington
Gorge Amphitheatre
Opening Acts: Ted Nugent, Skid Row
Attendance: 17,676   Capacity: 20,000
Promoter: House of Blues Concerts
■ SET LIST
July 13, 2000.

JULY 24, 2000

Portland, Oregon
Rose Garden
Opening Acts: Ted Nugent, Skid Row
Attendance: 6,667   Capacity: 21,000
■ SET LIST
July 13, 2000.

JULY 26, 2000

Nampa (Boise), Idaho

Idaho Center Arena
Opening Acts: Ted Nugent, Skid Row
Attendance: 6,412   Capacity: 9,000
■ SET LIST
See July 13, 2000.

JULY 28, 2000
Mountain View (San Jose), California
Shoreline Amphitheatre @ Mountain View
Opening Acts: Ted Nugent, American Pearl
Attendance: 4,755   Capacity: 20,000
■ SET LIST
See July 13, 2000.
■ Skid Row did not perform at this show (or any of the four subsequent shows) due to a prior commitment.

JULY 29, 2000
Marysville (Sacramento), California
Sacramento Valley Amphitheatre
Opening Acts: Ted Nugent, American Pearl
Attendance: 6,043   Capacity: 18,000
■ SET LIST
See July 13, 2000.

JULY 30, 2000
Concord (San Francisco), California
Chronicle Pavilion @ Concord
Opening Acts: Ted Nugent, Neve
Attendance: 4,729   Capacity: 12,500
■ SET LIST
See July 13, 2000.

AUGUST 1, 2000
Fresno, California
Selland Arena @ Fresno Convention Center
Opening Acts: Ted Nugent, Neve
Attendance: 6,380   Capacity: 8,000
■ SET LIST
See July 13, 2000.

AUGUST 2, 2000
Las Vegas, Nevada
Mandalay Bay Events Center
Opening Acts: Ted Nugent, Neve
Attendance: 6,731   Capacity: 8,675
Promoter: Evening Star Productions
■ SET LIST
See July 13, 2000.

AUGUST 11, 2000
Laguna Hills, California
Verizon Wireless Amphitheatre
Opening Acts: Ted Nugent, Skid Row
Attendance: 6,363   Capacity: 15,416
■ SET LIST
See July 13, 2000.
■ Audiences had already seen one reunion show where a band member did not perform, and this night they nearly saw a second. Nocturne's Bob Brigham relates: "We were coming off a break in the tour and Ace was supposed to get on a plane and come out to the West Coast on a Wednesday. Ace was grumbling that a Doberman bit his wife's dog in the neck, broke its neck and killed it. So, he didn't make his flight. Thursday, he didn't make his flight. So, finally they are going nuts, 'What do we do?' They were now down to Friday's flight, and the plan, when and if Ace missed this flight, was to have Tommy Thayer, who has his own Ace outfit, be in makeup so the show can go on. Tommy was suited up and ready to go. Ace arrived at the airport, but they had an added problem because his plane was late. They had a helicopter waiting for him on

the runway. He went right from the commercial aircraft to a helicopter, flew down to Irvine Meadows and we held the show about half an hour later."

AUGUST 12, 2000
Devore (San Bernardino), California
Glen Helen Blockbuster Pavilion
Opening Acts: Ted Nugent, Skid Row
Attendance: 13,807   Capacity: 65,000
■ SET LIST
See July 13, 2000.

AUGUST 14, 2000
Englewood (Denver), Colorado
Fiddler's Green Amphitheatre
Opening Acts: Ted Nugent, Skid Row
Attendance: 6,198   Capacity: 16,815
Promoter: House of Blues Concerts
■ SET LIST
See July 13, 2000.

AUGUST 15, 2000
Albuquerque, New Mexico
Tingley Coliseum
Opening Acts: Ted Nugent, Skid Row
Attendance: 5,550   Capacity: 11,775
■ SET LIST
See July 13, 2000.

AUGUST 17, 2000
Austin, Texas
Frank C. Erwin, Jr., Special Events Center
Opening Acts: Ted Nugent, Skid Row
Attendance: 7,445   Capacity: 11,000
Promoter: Beaver Productions
■ SET LIST
See July 13, 2000.

AUGUST 18, 2000
Lafayette, Louisiana
Cajundome
Opening Acts: Ted Nugent, Skid Row
Attendance: 8,632   Capacity: 10,000
Promoter: Beaver Productions
■ SET LIST
See July 13, 2000.

AUGUST 19, 2000
Jackson, Mississippi
Mississippi Coliseum
Opening Acts: Ted Nugent, Skid Row
Attendance: 7,624   Capacity: 9,500
Promoter: Beaver Productions
■ SET LIST
See July 13, 2000.
■ Ace Frehley of KISS, shot?
It happened as John Bestwick of Nocturne relates: "KISS was staying in Dallas while we were doing some shows across the Midwest. Ace has friends there, and they were shooting rifles one afternoon at some guy's house. Ace had a misfire and ended up getting a slash on his wrist that was a couple of inches long, and he had a piece of shell stuck in his chest. He got some bandages, and he went back to the hotel and saw Danny Francis, the security guy, and had a couple of drinks. He didn't tell anyone what's happened. He went to his room, and his girlfriend at the time called him about 8 P.M. or so. He had a few drinks and he was laying in bed talking to her. He said he's tired and didn't feel so good, and told her to call him later.
"He went to sleep, and she called him back about midnight, and he's rambling on, 'I don't

feel good. I have a headache. I've been bleeding. I got shot this afternoon.' He just rolled this all together. She totally freaked out, hung up, and called the hotel and got ahold of somebody downstairs and said, 'Ace is in his room, he's been shot, and we don't know what's going on.' The concierge called the police and an ambulance and then called Danny Francis. Danny got Doc, and then the two of them were pounding on Ace's room, trying to get him to answer the door. They got someone to open the door, and it had one of those latches on it so you can only open the door about two inches. They looked in, and all they saw were Ace's feet on his bed, one shoe off, one shoe on. Apparently, a SWAT team showed up and they locked down the entire hotel, thinking that there is some shooter inside. They went up and stormed his room and he sat up in bed when they come kicking through the door: 'What the hell is going on here?' 'We heard you were shot.' 'Oh, I had a little misfire this afternoon. I got a little cut on my hand.' The SWAT team guys are asking: 'Who is this guy?' It's Ace Frehley from KISS. 'Really?! Wow! We're big fans.' They were taking pictures with him and what not.
"They took Ace to the hospital to get him checked out, and he got a couple of stitches in his hand. They X-rayed him and found a small shell fragment in his chest, which they took out and put a bandage on him. The next day Doc did a little press release stating that Ace was injured in a shooting."

AUGUST 21, 2000
Biloxi, Mississippi
Mississippi Coast Coliseum
Opening Acts: Ted Nugent, Skid Row
Attendance: 4,219   Capacity: 15,000
■ SET LIST
See July 13, 2000.

AUGUST 22, 2000
Spring (Houston), Texas
Cynthia Woods Mitchell Pavilion
Opening Acts: Skid Row, The Beautiful People
Attendance: 9,236   Capacity: 12,651
Promoters: SFX Music Group, In-house
■ SET LIST
See July 13, 2000.
■ KISS returned to Houston for a second time on The Farewell Tour due in part to a successful petition organized by local radio station KLOL.
Houston's Hispanic community had taken exception to some remarks Ted Nugent had made about non-English-speaking immigrants during his previous performance in Houston on April 1. Nugent refused to tone down his commentary, so the venue banned him from performing.

AUGUST 23, 2000
Fort Worth, Texas
Fort Worth Convention Center
Opening Acts: Ted Nugent, Skid Row
Attendance: 7,049   Capacity: 10,000
■ SET LIST
See July 13, 2000.
■ Eric Singer was in attendance.

AUGUST 25, 2000
Bonner Springs (Kansas City), Kansas
Sandstone Amphitheatre

Opening Acts: Ted Nugent, Skid Row
Attendance: 11,512   Capacity: 18,000
Promoter: SFX Music Group
■ **SET LIST**
See July 13, 2000.

AUGUST 26, 2000

Maryland Heights (St. Louis), Missouri
Riverport Amphitheatre
Opening Acts: Ted Nugent, Skid Row
Attendance: 11,719   Capacity: 21,000
Promoter: SFX Music Group
■ **SET LIST**
See July 13, 2000.

■ The show was plagued by sweltering heat and typical late-August St. Louis humidity. Ace did the encores wearing a black T-shirt with "KISS" spelled out in rhinestones on it.

AUGUST 28, 2000

Wichita, Kansas
Britt Brown Arena @ Kansas Coliseum
Opening Acts: Ted Nugent, Skid Row
Attendance: 6,688   Capacity: 9,500
Promoter: Beaver Productions
■ **SET LIST**
See July 13, 2000.

AUGUST 29, 2000

Omaha, Nebraska
Omaha Civic Auditorium
Opening Acts: Ted Nugent, Skid Row
Attendance: 8,876   Capacity: 10,000
Promoter: Beaver Productions
■ **SET LIST**
See July 13, 2000.

AUGUST 30, 2000

Ames, Iowa
Hilton Coliseum
Opening Acts: Ted Nugent, Skid Row
Attendance: 5,926   Capacity: 12,520
Promoter: SFX Music Group
■ **SET LIST**
See July 13, 2000.

SEPTEMBER 1, 2000

Carbondale, Illinois
SIU Arena
Opening Acts: Ted Nugent, Skid Row
Attendance: 6,200   Capacity: 8,829
Promoter: JAM Productions
■ **SET LIST**
See July 13, 2000.

■ The P.A. system cut out several times during the concert.

SEPTEMBER 2, 2000

Cedar Rapids, Iowa
Five Seasons Center
Opening Acts: Ted Nugent, Skid Row
Attendance: 6,361   Capacity 8,769
Promoter: JAM Productions
■ **SET LIST**
See July 13, 2000.

SEPTEMBER 5, 2000

Rockford, Illinois
MetroCentre
Opening Acts: Ted Nugent, Skid Row
Attendance: 3,868   Capacity: 5,445
Promoter: JAM Productions
■ **SET LIST**
See July 13, 2000.

Ace in St. Louis, performing without a costume top in the sweltering August heat.

SEPTEMBER 6, 2000

East Lansing, Michigan
Jack Breslin Student Events Center
Opening Acts: Skid Row, The Beautiful People
Attendance: 4,792   Capacity: 14,500
Promoter: Belkin Productions
■ **SET LIST**
See July 13, 2000.

SEPTEMBER 8, 2000

Lexington, Kentucky
Rupp Arena
Opening Acts: Ted Nugent, Skid Row
Attendance: 6,762   Capacity: 16,500
Promoter: Belkin Productions
■ **SET LIST**
See July 13, 2000.

SEPTEMBER 9, 2000

Indianapolis, Indiana
Conseco Fieldhouse
Opening Acts: Ted Nugent, Skid Row
Attendance: 8,819   Capacity: 15,086
Promoters: SFX Music Group, Sunshine Promotions
■ **SET LIST**
See July 13, 2000.

SEPTEMBER 10, 2000

Evansville, Indiana
Roberts Municipal Stadium
Opening Acts: Ted Nugent, Skid Row
Attendance: 4,581   Capacity: 12,912
Promoters: SFX Music Group, Sunshine Promotions
■ **SET LIST**
See July 13, 2000.

SEPTEMBER 12, 2000

Clarkston (Detroit), Michigan
Pine Knob Music Theatre
Opening Acts: Skid Row, The Beautiful People
Attendance: 13,456   Capacity: 15,274
Promoters: Palace Sports & Entertainment, Belkin
     Productions, Cellar Door Concerts, SFX Music Group
■ SET LIST
See July 13, 2000.
■ Footage from this show was sent to VH1 for use on the KISS episode of *FanClub*.

SEPTEMBER 13, 2000

Dayton, Ohio
Ervin J. Nutter Center
Opening Acts: Ted Nugent, Skid Row
Attendance: 6,994   Capacity: 11,500
Promoter: Belkin Productions
■ SET LIST
See July 13, 2000.
■ Paul mentioned to the audience, "This is gonna look so good on our Showtime special," in reference to the insert shots that were being shot for the pay-per-view broadcast.

SEPTEMBER 15, 2000

Binghamton, New York
Broome Co. Veterans Memorial Auditorium
Opening Acts: Ted Nugent, Skid Row
Attendance: 3,228   Capacity: 6,800
■ SET LIST
See July 13, 2000.
Medley: I Was Made for Lovin' You, C'mon and Love
     Me, New York Groove, Hotter Than Hell, Parasite,
     Room Service, Watchin' You (Medley performed
     prior to "Rock and Roll All Nite.")

SEPTEMBER 16, 2000

Syracuse, New York
War Memorial at Oncenter
Opening Acts: Ted Nugent, Skid Row
Attendance: 5,938   Capacity: 7,500
■ SET LIST
See July 13, 2000.
Medley: Makin' Love, Parasite, She, Hard Luck Woman,
     Love Her All I Can, New York Groove (Medley
     performed prior to "Rock and Roll All Nite.")
■ On August 19, it was announced that the KISS concert in Syracuse was moved from the Carrier Dome to the War Memorial.

SEPTEMBER 18, 2000

Providence, Rhode Island
Providence Civic Center
Opening Acts: Ted Nugent, Skid Row
Attendance: 8,241   Capacity: 10,500
Promoter: Beaver Productions
■ SET LIST
See July 13, 2000.
■ Ted Nugent dedicated his show to Peter Criss, who had added a small teardrop to his makeup. He would include the teardrop as part of his makeup for all 11 remaining shows in which he participated on the tour.

SEPTEMBER 20, 2000

Quebec, Quebec, Canada
Colisée Pepsi
Opening Acts: Skid Row, Serial Joe
Attendance: 6,804   Capacity: 7,500
Promoter: House of Blues Canada
■ SET LIST
Detroit Rock City
Deuce
Shout It Out Loud

Peter in Providence, on September 18, 2000, with a newly added teardrop in his makeup.

I Love It Loud
Shock Me
Firehouse
Do You Love Me
Calling Dr. Love
Heaven's On Fire
Let Me Go, Rock 'n Roll
2,000 Man
Ace Frehley Guitar Solo
Psycho Circus
Lick It Up
Gene Simmons Bass Solo
God of Thunder
Cold Gin
100,000 Years
Love Gun
I Still Love You*
Black Diamond
Beth
I Was Made for Lovin' You
Rock and Roll All Nite

SEPTEMBER 21, 2000

Kanata (Ottawa), Ontario, Canada
Corel Centre
Opening Acts: Skid Row, Serial Joe
Attendance: 7,396   Capacity: 9,000
Promoter: House of Blues Concerts
■ SET LIST
See September 20, 2000.

SEPTEMBER 23, 2000

Hamilton, Ontario, Canada
Copps Coliseum
Opening Acts: Skid Row, Serial Joe
Attendance: 8,328   Capacity: 9,000
Promoter: House of Blues Canada
■ SET LIST
See July 13, 2000.

SEPTEMBER 24, 2000   **CANCELED**

Lake Placid, New York
Olympic Center
Opening Act: Skid Row

Promoter: Magic City Productions
- The show was canceled on September 18 due to poor ticket sales.

SEPTEMBER 26, 2000
Trenton, New Jersey
Sovereign Bank Arena at Mercer County
Opening Act: Skid Row
Attendance: 5,079   Capacity: 6,250
Promoters: Metropolitan Entertainment, SFX Music
    Group, Electric Factory Concerts
■ SET LIST
See July 13, 2000.

SEPTEMBER 27, 2000
University Park, Pennsylvania
Bryce Jordan Center
Opening Act: Skid Row
Attendance: 5,253   Capacity: 10,400
Promoters: In-house, Arena Network
■ SET LIST
See July 13, 2000.
- This was the last show Peter Criss was contracted to do.

SEPTEMBER 29, 2000
Columbus, Ohio
Nationwide Arena
Opening Act: Skid Row
Attendance: 6,187   Capacity: 8,500
Promoter: Belkin Productions
■ SET LIST
See July 13, 2000.
- Several fans who attended this concert departed believing that they had just witnessed the final KISS concert, as Paul announced, "this is the final night of the tour." Additionally, when Peter came out to do 'Beth' he said, "This is the last time I'm singing this. So this comes from my heart to you guys."

John Bestwick: "He [Peter] wasn't bluffing, it was honestly a case where they didn't know if they'd finish the tour. They thought they may have to cancel the last couple of shows. I don't think anyone in their heart thought Peter would pull the plug on shows that had already been sold, but it was possible, and there was talk that they'd pack the stuff up and send everyone home."

SEPTEMBER 30, 2000
Tinley Park (Chicago), Illinois
New World Music Theatre
Opening Act: Skid Row
Attendance: 6,771   Capacity: 30,000
Promoter: JAM Productions
■ SET LIST
See July 13, 2000.
- The customized KISS Dodge Prowler was on display at the venue.

OCTOBER 1, 2000
Champaign, Illinois
Assembly Hall
Opening Act: Skid Row
Attendance: 4,371   Capacity: 7,500
Promoter: JAM Productions
■ SET LIST
See July 13, 2000.

OCTOBER 3, 2000
Uncasville, Connecticut
Uncas Pavilion @ Mohegan Sun Casino
Opening Act: Skid Row
Attendance: 3,162   Capacity: 3,162
■ SET LIST
See July 13, 2000.
- Sal Governale, better known as "Sal the Stockbroker" for his frequent appearances on Howard Stern's radio show, was sitting in the front row making facial gestures at Gene, who instructed the security staff to tell Governale to cease his antics. When security approached him for the third time, Governale opted to leave the concert and was escorted out of the building. The entire event was played up on Howard Stern's show the following morning.

Due to the size of the venue, only one KISS sign—centered behind the drums—was used.

OCTOBER 4, 2000
Columbia (Washington, D.C.), Maryland
Merriweather Post Pavilion
Opening Act: Skid Row
Attendance: 4,369   Capacity: 15,274
- "2,000 Man" was not performed.

OCTOBER 6, 2000
Charlotte, North Carolina
New Charlotte Coliseum
Opening Act: Skid Row
Attendance: 9,116   Capacity: 9,958
Promoter: C & C Entertainment
■ SET LIST
See July 13, 2000.
- While he was performing "Beth," a fan threw a bouquet of blue roses onstage to Peter. The flowers were favorites of Peter's mother, who had passed away several years prior, and Peter had thrown blue roses into the crowd during "Beth" at KISS's Madison Square Garden appearances in July 1996. Peter appeared quite touched by the gesture and struggled to thank the fan while singing at the same time.

Prior to "Rock and Roll All Nite," another fan lifted an artificial leg on stage, and all the band members autographed it.

OCTOBER 7, 2000
Charleston, South Carolina
North Charleston Coliseum
Opening Act: Skid Row
Attendance: 7,888   Capacity: 8,652
Promoter: C & C Entertainment
■ SET LIST
See July 13, 2000.
Medley: Secret Agent Man, James Bond Theme, Wild
    Thing, Then She Kissed Me, She, Parasite
- As of this writing, this was Peter's final concert with KISS, and the final live performances of "Beth" and "2,000 Man." At the end of the show, Peter trashed his drum kit, throwing pieces of it all over the stage. Criss had also hired a photographer to come out on stage, much to the disapproval of Gene and Paul.

Gene and Paul left without saying goodbye to Ace and Peter, who were in a separate dressing room.

Also on October 7, *The Last KISS*, a 90-minute concert featuring highlights from the band's June 28 concert in East Rutherford, New Jersey, premiered on pay-per-view via Showtime Event Television.

October 7, 2000 in Charleston, South Carolina; Peter's final moment in KISS. It appears that shoving a floor tom up Gene's ass really is gratifying.

On September 15, 2000, KISS announced Japanese tour dates for The Farewell Tour. The on-sale date was scheduled for September 30 and the shows were announced as follows:

November 13: Hiroshima, Sun Plaza Hall
November 15: Osaka, Osaka Castle Hall
November 16: Osaka, Osaka Castle Hall
November 17: Nagoya, Rainbow Hall
November 19: Tokyo, Tokyodome
November 20: Yokohama, Yokohama Arena

However, on September 21, Udo Artists issued a statement that KISS had postponed their tour of Japan due to "scheduling circumstances."

After several months of relative silence, KISS dropped a bombshell. On January 31, an announcement was made on the band's official web site that Eric Singer had rejoined KISS to complete the band's world tour. Peter Criss was not mentioned in the announcement. In a joint statement, Stanley, Simmons, and Frehley remarked, "Eric has been a member of our family, and his drumming and singing have been the cornerstone of past KISS tours. We are stoked that we can bring our ultimate spectacle to KISS fans worldwide." Peter released his own statement, soon thereafter: "It is unfortunate Gene and Paul chose to terminate their association with me for the Japan and Australia tour dates. I am healthy and will truly miss performing." Peter's lawyer confirmed that a breakdown in contract negotiations had led to Peter's departure.

KISS made their first appearance with the new lineup on the *Today Show* in Australia on February 27. There was no thought of designing a new identity for Eric, and he performed all the remaining shows on the tour (to date) wearing Criss's costume and cat makeup. "The whole vibe was very different with Eric there," offers John Bestwick. "The stress level was reduced 20 percent from what it was when they were traveling here in the States. Peter is a nice guy in his own right, but they've been together for 30 years and they have their own inter-communal fights that they perpetuate. It was a love–hate thing with Peter. He'd say, 'These fucking guys. I love to play with them, but I just can't fucking handle them.' There were days when it was OK; then there were days when it was hellacious and they couldn't seem to get it all together. But from a musical standpoint, with Eric in place it was a much stronger show than those we were seeing in the States."

Staging and production remained the same for the Australian and Japanese dates as it had in North America, though two small props were added to the show. Beginning with the initial show in Japan, Paul used a pneumatic cannon to shoot balled-up T-shirts into the crowd during "100,000 Years." This prop was dropped after the second gig in Melbourne, reportedly due to insurance concerns. A flaming drumsticks effect, which was featured during Eric's drum solo, was added for the Australian shows.

Eric Singer becomes the third man to wear the Cat makeup, returning to KISS after a five-year absence.

MARCH 9, 2001

Yokohama, Japan
Yokohama Arena
No Opening Act
Promoter: Udo Artists
■ SET LIST
Detroit Rock City
Deuce
Shout It Out Loud
Talk To Me
I Love It Loud
Firehouse
Do You Love Me
Calling Dr. Love
Heaven's On Fire
Let Me Go, Rock 'n Roll
Shock Me
Ace Frehley Guitar Solo
Psycho Circus
Lick It Up
Gene Simmons Bass Solo
God of Thunder
Eric Singer Drum Solo - reprise
Cold Gin
100,000 Years
Love Gun
I Still Love You*
Black Diamond
I Was Made for Lovin' You
Rock and Roll All Nite

A single show in Yokohama was originally scheduled for March 14, but KISS's appearance was changed to two shows on March 9 and 10.

"Talk to Me" was added to the set list for the first time since December 1980.

MARCH 10, 2001

Yokohama, Japan
Yokohama Arena
No Opening Act
Attendance: Sold Out
Promoter: Udo Artists
■ SET LIST
See March 9, 2001.

MARCH 13, 2001

Tokyo, Japan
Tokyodome
No Opening Act
Attendance: 41,895
Promoter: Udo Artists
■ SET LIST
See March 9, 2001.
■ The giant KISS balloons were set up on both sides of the stage.

MARCH 16, 2001

Fukuoka, Japan
Kokusai Center
No Opening Act
Attendance: 5,559
Promoter: Udo Artists
■ SET LIST
See March 9, 2001.

MARCH 18, 2001

Nagoya, Japan
Rainbow Hall
No Opening Act
Attendance: 6,875
Promoter: Udo Artists
■ SET LIST
Detroit Rock City
Deuce
Shout It Out Loud
Talk To Me
I Love It Loud
Firehouse
Do You Love Me
Calling Dr. Love
Heaven's On Fire
Let Me Go, Rock 'n Roll
Shock Me
Ace Frehley Guitar Solo
Psycho Circus
Lick It Up

Gene Simmons Bass Solo
God of Thunder
Eric Singer Drum Solo - reprise
Cold Gin
100,000 Years
Love Gun
I Still Love You*
Black Diamond
I Was Made for Lovin' You
Medley: Got to Choose, Parasite, She, Makin' Love
Rock and Roll All Nite

MARCH 21, 2001

Osaka, Japan
Osaka Castle Hall
No Opening Act
Attendance: 8,500   Capacity: 8,500
Promoter: Udo Artists
■ SET LIST
See March 18, 2001.
Paul's Medley: Forever, I Still Love You
Medley: Hotter Than Hell, She, Parasite

MARCH 22, 2001

Osaka, Japan
Osaka Castle Hall
No Opening Act
Attendance: 8,500   Capacity: 8,500
Promoter: Udo Artists
■ SET LIST
See March 18, 2001.
Paul's Medley: I Want You, I Still Love You
Medley: Got to Choose, Parasite, She, Makin' Love

MARCH 29, 2001

Perth, Australia
Burswood Dome
Opening Act: The Screaming Jets
Attendance: 9,000   Capacity: 15,000
Promoter: The International Touring Company
■ SET LIST
Detroit Rock City
Deuce
Shout It Out Loud
Talk to Me
I Love It Loud
Firehouse
Do You Love Me
Calling Dr. Love
Heaven's On Fire
Let Me Go, Rock 'n Roll
Shock Me
Ace Frehley Guitar Solo
Psycho Circus
Lick It Up
Gene Simmons Bass Solo
God of Thunder
Eric Singer Drum Solo - reprise
Cold Gin
100,000 Years
Love Gun
Paul Stanley Medley: I Want You, I Still Love You,
    Shandi
Black Diamond
I Was Made for Lovin' You
Medley: Parasite, She, Makin' Love
Rock and Roll All Nite

APRIL 1, 2001

Adelaide, Australia
Adelaide Entertainment Centre
Opening Act: The Screaming Jets
Attendance: 6,635
Promoter: The International Touring Company
■ SET LIST
See March 29, 2001
Paul's Medley: I Still Love You, Hard Luck Woman,

Paul in Australia, 2001, holding the short-lived T-shirt gun prop.

Shandi
Medley: 2,000 Man, New York Groove, Parasite,
    Makin' Love, She
■ On February 16, this show was moved from its original venue, Hindmarsh Stadium, to the Adelaide Entertainment Centre. Potential for poor weather as well as lack of pre-production time due to a soccer match were the alleged reasons for the change of venue.

APRIL 3, 2001

Melbourne, Australia
Rod Laver Arena @ Melbourne Park
Opening Act: The Screaming Jets
Attendance: 9,112
Promoter: The International Touring Company
■ SET LIST
See March 29, 2001.
Paul's Medley: I Still Love You, Shandi
Medley: Parasite, Makin' Love, New York Groove, She,
    Got to Choose

APRIL 4, 2001

Melbourne, Australia
Rod Laver Arena @ Melbourne Park
Opening Act: The Screaming Jets
Attendance: 10,882
Promoter: The International Touring Company
■ SET LIST
See March 29, 2001.
Paul's Medley: Hard Luck Woman, Shandi
Medley: New York Groove, She, Makin' Love, Parasite

APRIL 5, 2001

Melbourne, Australia
Rod Laver Arena @ Melbourne Park
Opening Act: The Screaming Jets
Attendance: 6,922
Promoter: The International Touring Company
■ SET LIST
See March 29, 2001.
Paul's Medley: I Still Love You, Forever, Hard Luck
    Woman, Shandi

Medley: Goin' Blind, Parasite, New York Groove, Strutter, She, Rocket Ride, Mr. Speed
■ This third and final Melbourne show was added to the itinerary on February 21.

APRIL 7, 2001
Sydney, Australia
The Superdome
Opening Act: The Screaming Jets
Attendance: 19,841
Promoter: The International Touring Company
■ **SET LIST**
See March 29, 2001.
Paul's Medley: I Still Love You, Hard Luck Woman, Forever
Medley: New York Groove, Parasite, She, Makin' Love
■ The attendance figure reflects the combined attendance at the April 7 and 8 shows in Sydney.

APRIL 8, 2001
Sydney, Australia
The Superdome
Opening Act: The Screaming Jets
Promoter: The International Touring Company
■ **SET LIST**
See March 29, 2001.
Paul's Medley: I Still Love You, Hard Luck Woman, Shandi
No Medley

APRIL 13, 2001
Gold Coast, Australia
Carrara Stadium
Opening Act: The Screaming Jets, Kings of the Sun, Ginger
Attendance: 11,984

Promoter: The International Touring Company
■ **SET LIST**
See March 29, 2001.
Paul's Medley: Shandi, Hard Luck Woman
Medley: Parasite, New York Groove, She, Makin' Love, Strutter

---

OCTOBER 21, 2001
Washington, D.C.   **KISS CANCELED**
RFK Stadium
Other Acts on the Bill: Michael Jackson, Mariah Carey, *NSYNC, Destiny's Child, Usher, Rod Stewart, Aerosmith, Backstreet Boys, Ricky Martin, Train, P. Diddy, Goo Goo Dolls, Aaron Carter, James Brown, Al Green, Carole King, Huey Lewis, Bette Midler, and others
Promoter: Clear Channel Communications
■ On October 11, KISS confirmed that they would take part in the "United We Stand—What More Can We Give?" concert in RFK Stadium. The event was organized to raise money for the recovery efforts related to the September 11 terrorist attacks. A day later, KISS announced that they would not be appearing at the event because Paul Stanley was suffering from a hip ailment that prohibited him from performing.

Several months later, KISS reemerged to do two public performances in February 2002. The first appearance took place on February 5, where Gene, Paul, Ace, and Eric performed "Shout It Out Loud," "Lick It Up," "God of Thunder," "Love Gun," and "Rock and Roll All Nite" at the Roseland Ballroom in Manhattan, for what

was the most unusual KISS promotional appearance in years: the Spring 2002 Lane Bryant fashion show. The performance featured live vocals over pre-recorded music. The plus-size women's designer cybercast the event the following day via their website.

Then, on February 24 from a mobile stage in Rice-Eccles Stadium in Salt Lake City, KISS performed "Rock and Roll All Nite" in front of an estimated global audience of 3 billion people at the closing ceremonies of the Winter Olympics.

MARCH 6, 2002
Trelawny (Rio Bueno), Jamaica
Grand Lido Braco
Attendance: 500+
■ This gig was a private function held at Grand Lido Braco, a clothing-optional resort in the West Indies. KISS's lineup was comprised of Gene Simmons, Paul Stanley, and Eric Singer along with tour manager/ex-KISS tribute band member Tommy Thayer replacing Ace Frehley, who declined to attend as he was reportedly overseeing the construction of his recording studio. The details of the event and the identity of its host remain shrouded in secrecy, though many of the attendees were of Russian descent with the host rumored to be an investment banking tycoon. It is known, however, that KISS performed a full-scale show on an area of the 85-acre property that the resort staff casually calls "The Football Field," which is simply a cordoned-off section of the resort's nine-hole golf course.

While it seems to run counter to the secrecy surrounding this event, KISS's performance was apparently recorded for use on *Alive IV*.

In early Spring, KISS, again with Tommy Thayer as Ace's "Spaceman" character, made two promotional appearances. The first was a series of commercials taped on March 21 and 22 to promote the syndication of FOX-TV's *That 70s Show,* which included a lip-synched performance of "Rock and Roll All Nite." Then, on April 19 KISS taped "Detroit Rock City" (with live lead vocals and canned music) for an appearance on *Dick Clark's American Bandstand 50th Anniversary* special, which premiered May 3 on ABC-TV.

———————

By all appearances, Peter Criss's departure from KISS is permanent, with the possible exception being the final KISS show. And while his parting was due to irreconcilable contract issues, Criss has not commented publicly on his current status with KISS, while Gene has publicly maintained that Peter remains part of the group.

It is impossible to determine whether or not Ace will choose to be included in future KISS projects. Frehley, who is no longer under contract to the band, now simply accepts or declines the band's offers to join them for various appearances, although he has publicly stated that he will no longer maintain his involvement with the group.

The Farewell Tour itself remains equally unresolved, with no official end to the tour having occurred. In May 2001, it appeared as if a European leg for the tour was nearing confirmation with one date, September 12, in Wien, Austria, officially announced on the venue's website. Tickets never went on sale, and no further dates were announced.

Shrugging off the specter of the always uncertain future, KISS's legacy seems destined to endure, the 1996–97 Alive/Worldwide Tour having emphatically recaptured the band's place as icons in the world of pop culture. And despite their inability or unwillingness to bring The Farewell Tour to a satisfying conclusion, KISS's legacy is one to be proud of.

Perhaps KISS is just doing what they do best anyway. Always leave your audience wanting more . . .

NICO CICCARONE/WWW.NICOSTRIKE.C[...]

KISS in Gold Coast, Australia, April 13, 2001.

APPENDICES

**Total Number of KISS Performances
(January 30, 1973 – March 6, 2002)**

1810

**Number of Shows Headlined/
Co-Headlined**

1714

Number of Shows Opened

96

**Number and Percentage of Shows
Performed by Each KISS Member:**

Gene Simmons	1810 (100%)
Paul Stanley	1810 (100%)
Ace Frehley	1059 (58.5%)
Peter Criss	1003 (55.4%)
Eric Carr	653 (36.1%)
Bruce Kulick	602 (33.3%)
Eric Singer	155 (8.6%)
Vinnie Vincent	148 (8.2%)
Mark St. John	3 (0.2%)
Eddie Kanon	1 (0.05%)
Tommy Thayer	1 (0.05%)

**Top 10 Opening Acts
by Number of Performances**

1. Ted Nugent	170 shows
2. Skid Row	118 shows
3. Slaughter	111 shows
4. Queensrÿche	56 shows
Trixter	56 shows
5. Rush	51 shows
6. Faster Pussycat	47 shows
7. W.A.S.P.	45 shows
8. Winger	39 shows
9. Vandenberg	37 shows

Top 20 Most Frequently Played Venues

1. Madison Square Garden	13 shows
2. Roberts Municipal Stadium	13 shows
3. Cobo Arena	12 shows
4. The Daisy	12 shows
5. Market Square Arena	12 shows
6. Nippon Budokan Hall	12 shows
7. Omaha Civic Auditorium	12 shows
8. The Coliseum	12 shows
9. Civic Arena	11 shows
10. Providence Civic Center	11 shows
11. Alex Cooley's Electric Ballroom	10 shows
12. Allen Co. War
Memorial Coliseum	10 shows
13. Carolina Coliseum	10 shows
14. Charleston Civic Center	10 shows
15. Charlotte Coliseum	10 shows
16. Kiel Auditorium	10 shows
17. Knoxville Civic Coliseum	10 shows
18. The Omni	10 shows
19. San Diego Sports Arena	10 shows
20. Wembley Arena	10 shows

**Top 10 Most Frequently Played Cities
(Including suburbs)**

1. Los Angeles	48 shows
2. Manhattan/Brooklyn/Queens	45 shows
3. Detroit	34 shows
4. Atlanta	26 shows
5. Chicago	26 shows
6. Cleveland	22 shows
7. Philadelphia	21 shows
8. Indianapolis	20 shows
St. Louis	20 shows
9. Minneapolis/St. Paul	19 shows
10. San Francisco/Oakland	19 shows

Top 10 Largest Crowds

1. Rio de Janeiro, Brazil	June 18, 1983	137,000+
2. Eifel, Germany	May 18, 1997	115,000+
3. Donington, England	August 20, 1988	97,535
4. Donington, England	August 17, 1996	80,000+
5. São Paulo, Brazil	June 25, 1983	65,000+
6. Buenos Aires, Argentina	March 14, 1997	54,000+
7. São Paulo, Brazil	April 17, 1999	53,000+
8. Tokyo, Japan	January 18, 1997	46,000+
9. Buenos Aires, Argentina	September 3, 1994	45,000+
10. Melbourne, Australia	November 18, 1980	45,000+

**Top 5 Most Attended
Headlining Tours (per show)**

1. Unmasked	16,442*
2. Alive/Worldwide	13,737
3. Alive II	13,550
4. Psycho Circus	12,826
5. Destroyer	11,073

*This is based upon a very limited number of attendance figures. If the remaining figures from the tour were available the tour's average attendance would likely drop precipitously.

**Top 5 Least Attended
Headlining Tours (per show)**

1. Revenge	5,029
2. Lick It Up	5,052
3. Creatures of the Night	5,313
4. Crazy Nights	5,691
5. Asylum	6,181

Gigs Where KISS Did Two Performances

3/25/74	Washington, D.C.
4/21/74	Charlotte, North Carolina
9/14/74	Toronto, Ontario
1/9/75	Vancouver, British Columbia
3/19/75	Northampton, Pennsylvania
3/21/75	New York, New York
5/29/75	Las Vegas, Nevada
7/20/75	Davenport, Iowa
10/4/75	Passaic, New Jersey
2/6/76	St. Paul, Minnesota
4/2/77	Tokyo, Japan

Top 10 Promoters

1. Belkin Productions	129 shows
2. Sunshine Promotions	77 shows
3. Cellar Door Concerts	70 shows
4. Mama Concert
Productions (MCP)	61 shows
5. Beaver Productions	53 shows
6. JAM Productions	46 shows
7. Udo Artists	39 shows
SFX Music Group	39 shows
8. Contemporary Productions	38 shows
9. Donald K. Donald	35 shows
10. Stardate Productions	35 shows

**Demon Flambé: Gigs Where Gene Set
Himself On Fire**

12/31/73	New York, New York
7/13/74	Tampa, Florida
5/29/75	Las Vegas, Nevada
12/18/75	Waterbury, Connecticut
2/24/76	Inglewood, California
4/22/76	Ottawa, Ontario
12/5/76	Mobile, Alabama
12/12/76	Lakeland, Florida
8/27/77	Inglewood, California
1/25/84	Denver, Colorado
2/26/84	Hampton, Virginia
3/9/84	New York, New York
12/8/85	Austin, Texas

Songs Used as Opening Numbers

Creatures of the Night
Detroit Rock City
Deuce
I Stole Your Love
I've Had Enough (Into the Fire)
King of the Mountain
King of the Night Time World
Love Gun
Nothin' to Lose
100,000 Years
Psycho Circus
Rock Bottom

First and Last Known Dates of Performances of KISS Songs

For all subsequent lists involving songs, the material performed at KISS's 1995 Conventions has not been included. Also not included are any partial performances of songs (or medleys), or any material that was performed live by KISS but was not written and recorded by the band, e.g., The Who's "Won't Get Fooled Again." Cover songs that were officially recorded by KISS, such as "God Gave Rock 'N' Roll to You II" are included, however.

Regarding the first and last known dates of performance for individual songs, in most cases, these dates are verified. However, in some instances,

assumptions have been made when we felt there was enough evidence to justify it. For example, there is no known tape of the first concert of the Love Gun Tour in Halifax on July 8, 1977. However, the existing set lists for that tour are almost entirely identical, so it is a safe assumption to state that "Shock Me," for instance, was first performed live at that show.
*Although both "Two Timer" and "Tomorrow and Tonight" were released on live albums and obviously made to appear as if they were performed live, there is no evidence whatsoever that either was ever included in any of KISS's performances.

Song	First Known Date of Performance	Last Known Date of Performance
100,000 Years	6/16/73	4/13/01
2,000 Man	6/15/79	10/7/00
Acrobat	6/16/73	4/18/74
All Hell's Breakin' Loose	1/8/84	3/17/84
Any Way You Slice It	11/29/85	11/29/85
Bang Bang You	11/13/87	10/3/88
Beth	11/24/76	10/7/00
Betrayed	4/14/90	4/25/90
Black Diamond	1/30/73	4/13/01
Burn Bitch Burn	9/30/84	9/30/84
Calling Dr.Love	7/8/77	4/13/01
Christine Sixteen	7/8/77	6/28/96
C'mon and Love Me	3/19/75	6/15/97
Cold Gin	8/17/73	4/13/01
Crazy Crazy Nights	11/13/87	11/9/90
Creatures of the Night	12/29/82	2/14/95
Detroit Rock City	5/13/76	4/13/01
Deuce	1/30/73	4/13/01
Do You Love Me	7/3/76	4/13/01
Domino	9/30/92	2/14/95
Exciter	10/11/83	3/7/84
Firehouse	1/30/73	4/13/01
Fits Like a Glove	10/11/83	11/9/90
Flaming Youth	3/26/76	7/18/76
Forever	3/11/90	2/14/95
Get All You Can Take	9/30/84	9/30/84
Gimme More	10/11/83	3/17/84
God Gave Rock 'N' Roll to You II	4/23/92	2/14/95
God of Thunder	4/24/76	4/13/01
Goin' Blind (aka Little Lady)	1/30/73	7/30/94
Got to Choose	10/17/74	9/5/94
Hard Luck Woman	11/24/76	12/4/76
Heaven's On Fire	9/30/84	4/13/01
Hell or High Water	11/13/87	12/31/87
Hide Your Heart	4/14/90	11/9/90
Hooligan	7/8/77	9/5/77
Hotter Than Hell	1/31/75	12/20/92
I Just Wanna	9/30/92	12/20/92
I Love It Loud	12/29/82	4/13/01
I Still Love You	12/29/82	3/27/86
I Stole Your Love	7/8/77	3/17/00
I Want You	11/24/76	2/14/95
I Was Made for Lovin' You	6/15/79	4/13/01
Into the Void	10/30/98	3/14/00
Is That You?	7/25/80	12/3/80
I've Had Enough (Into the Fire)	9/30/84	11/18/84
Keep Me Comin'	12/29/82	12/30/82
Keep Me Waiting	1/30/73	1/30/73
King of the Mountain	11/29/85	4/2/86
King of the Night Time World	7/3/76	4/24/99
Kissin' Time	5/24/74	5/28/74
Ladies in Waiting	11/15/75	1/25/76
Ladies Room	11/24/76	5/19/78
Let Me Go, Rock 'n Roll (aka Baby, Let Me Go)	1/30/73	4/13/01
Let Me Know	6/16/73	6/21/75
Lick It Up	10/11/83	4/13/01
Life in the Woods	1/30/73	9/1/73
Little Caesar	4/14/90	5/3/90
Love 'em and Leave 'em	11/24/76	11/24/76
Love Gun	7/8/77	4/13/01
Love Her All I Can	1/30/73	1/30/73
Mainline	11/28/74	11/28/74
Makin' Love	11/24/76	11/23/98
Move On	6/15/79	12/16/79
New York Groove	6/15/79	7/5/97
No, No, No	11/13/87	10/3/88
Nothin' to Lose	6/16/73	10/31/98
Parasite	10/17/74	2/6/95
Psycho Circus	10/30/98	4/13/01
Radioactive	6/15/79	7/13/79
Reason to Live	11/13/87	10/3/88
Rise to It	4/14/90	11/9/90
Rock and Roll All Nite	5/10/75	4/13/01
Rock and Roll Hell	12/29/82	12/31/82
Rock Bottom	5/6/75	8/26/96
Room Service	4/19/75	5/6/75
Shandi	11/8/80	2/4/95
She	1/30/73	10/31/98
Shock Me	7/8/77	4/13/01
Shout It Out Loud	3/11/76	4/13/01
Simple Type	1/30/73	8/25/73
Strange Ways	1/7/75	1/9/75
Strutter	6/16/73	10/15/96
Sweet Pain	7/3/76	7/3/76
Take It Off	4/23/92	2/14/95
Take Me	11/24/76	11/1/96
Talk to Me	7/25/80	4/13/01
Tears Are Falling	11/29/85	2/14/95
Thrills in the Night	12/4/84	12/14/84
Tossin' and Turnin'	6/15/79	7/18/79¡
Uh! All Night	11/29/85	4/12/86
Under the Gun	9/30/84	6/9/90
Unholy	4/23/92	2/14/95
War Machine	12/29/82	9/15/94
Watchin' You	1/30/73	7/5/97
When Your Walls Come Down	11/13/87	11/23/87
Within	10/30/98	4/24/99
Young and Wasted	10/11/83	2/2/86
You're All That I Want	7/25/80	9/11/80

Alphabetical List of Acts Who Headlined Over KISS (45) (Includes Co-headliners)

Acts	# of Shows
10cc	1
Aerosmith	2
Argent	3
Billy Preston	1
Black Oak Arkansas	6
Black Sabbath	4
Blue Öyster Cult	14
The Brats	3
David Lee Roth	2
Dr. John	1
The "All New" Fleetwood Mac	1
Foghat	1
Golden Earring	2
Hunter-Ronson	1
Iggy & the Stooges	1
Iron Maiden	5
Isis	2
James Gang	1
Jo Jo Gunne	1
Johnny Winter	1
Kathi McDonald	2
Manfred Mann's Earth Band	12
Marshall Tucker Band	1
Nazareth	4
New York Dolls	5
Ozark Mountain Daredevils	1
Ozzy Osbourne	1
Queen Elizabeth featuring Wayne County	1
Quicksilver Messenger Service	4
Rare Earth	2
Redbone	2
Renaissance	1
REO Speedwagon	2
Rory Gallagher	3
Rush	3
Savoy Brown	16
Silverhead	1
Suzi Quatro	2
Teenage Lust	1
Uriah Heep	2
War	1
Whitesnake	1
Wild Honey	2
Wishbone Ash	3
ZZ Top	8

Alphabetical List of Acts Who Opened for KISS (375)

Act	Number of Shows	Act	Number of Shows	Act	Number of Shows
The 4th Floor	4	Deftones	9	Heaven	12
13th Floor	1	Desstroyer	1	Heavy Metal Kids	6
.38 Special	2	Detective	16	Heavy Pettin'	8
311	2	The Detroit Dogs	2	Helix	34
AC/DC	5	Diamond Reo	2	Hellacopters	4
Accept	15	Dictators	6	Helloween	3
Albatross	1	Die Ärtze	11	Hermetica	1
Alice in Chains	4	Dirty Looks	3	Herva Doce	1
Alive!	7	The Dixie Dregs	1	Hickock	1
Alkbottle	2	Dog Eat Dog	1	Highfever	1
American Pearl	2	Dokken	7	Hoa Bihn	1
Angra	1	Double Yellow Line	1	Hot Lucy	1
Anthrax	25	Downtown Bruno	1	Hotter Than Hell	4
Artful Dodger	16	Dr. Hook & the Medicine Show	3	Hotz	1
Arosa	1	Dr. Sin	1	The Hunger	8
ASTIGAFA	1	Dynissty	1	Hydra	6
Atlanta Rhythm Section	7	Earth Quake	1	I Mother Earth	1
Axe	6	Easy Stream	1	If	1
Back Street Crawler	1	Econoline Crush	32	Irigy Hónaljmirigy	1
Balaam & the Angel	1	Edda	1	Iron Maiden	24
Ballin' Jack	2	Eddie Boy Band	1	Isis	1
Barbarossa	2	El Fantastico Hombre Bala	3	Island	1
The Beautiful People	3	Electromagnets	1	J. Geils Band	1
Big Wreck	1	Eli	2	Jackdaw	1
Biohazard	1	Ethos	2	Jackyl	1
Bionic	1	Everclear	2	James Gang	4
Black 'N Blue	24	The Exponents	1	James Montgomery Band	4
Black Diamond	1	Eyes	8	Jessie Bolt	1
Black Sabbath	3	Fallen Angel	1	Jo Jo Gunne	2
Black Sheep	5	Fancy	2	Joe	1
Blackfoot	3	Fantasy	1	Joe Lynn Turner	1
Bloontz	1	Faster Pussycat	47	John Cougar & the Zone	7
Blue Öyster Cult	5	Fat Chance	10	John Hammond	1
Bob Seger & the Silver Bullet Band	34	The Fauves	1	Johnny Bravo	5
Booga Booga	1	Fear Factory	1	Jon Butcher Axis	1
The Bogmen	5	Finch	1	John Hayes Project	1
Bon Jovi	27	Fireballs	4	Johnny & Edgar Winter	1
Bow Wow	15	Flaming Youth	2	Journey	5
Boz Scaggs	1	Fleetwood Mac	1	Judas Priest	15
Breathless	11	Flight	1	Junkbox	1
Brian Auger's Oblivion Express	1	The Flock	3	Kansas	1
Brownsville Station	2	Fludd	3	Karissma	1
Buck Cherry	20	Flying Saucer	1	Kenny Kramer	1
Camel	3	Foringjarnir	1	King Kobra	27
Cannonball	1	Fortress	1	Kings of the Sun	17
Caroline's Spine	9	Fugees	1	Kix	1
Channel Zero	1	Fungus	2	KORN	1
Chastain	1	Garbage	1	Krokus	17
Cheap Trick	29	Gary Wright	3	L7	1
Chris Jagger	1	Gatos Sucios	1	(Lakeland String Quartet)	1
City Slicker	2	Gene's Addiction	1	Legs Diamond	3
CIV	1	Ginger	1	Les Variations	1
Climax Blues Band	1	Girl	3	The Leslie West Band	5
Clowns	1	Glueleg	1	Lit	1
Cockney Rebel	1	Goldfinger	1	Lita Ford	1
Cold Gin	3	The Good Rats	1	Little Caesar	20
Conqueror Worm	1	Graham Parker & the Rumour	1	Little Feat	1
Core22	1	Great White	35	Live	2
Coyote Shivers	2	Guns N' Roses	1	Logos	3
Custard	1	Hammerhead	1	Los Villanos	1
D Generation	11	Hammersmith	8	Loverboy	1
Danger, Danger	28	Harvest	1	Luger	1
Dare Force	1	Head East	1	Lush	1
David Lee Roth	2	Headpins	4	M-S Funk	1
Defectors	1	Heartsfield	1	Malon	1
				Man	1

Act	Number of Shows	Act	Number of Shows	Act	Number of Shows	Act	Number of Shows
Mantis	1	Pezband	1	Scream	1	Target	1
Max Onion	2	Piper	8	Screamin' Cheetah Wheelies	1	Techtones	2
Megadeth	1	Planets	1	The Screaming Jets	8	Ted Nugent	170
The Melvins	5	Plasmatics	22	Sentinel	1	Ted Nugent & the	
Mercury	1	Poe	1	Sepultura	1	Amboy Dukes	1
Michael Fennelly	1	Point Blank	15	Serial Joe	3	Testament	2
Michael Stanley Band	1	The Poor	7	Sex Tiger	2	Thee Image	1
Mike Quatro	2	Powerman 5000	12	Shake City	1	Thin Lizzy	1
Mojo Boogie Band	1	Pure Prairie League	1	The Shoes	1	Third Rail	1
Molly Hatchet	1	Pushmonkey	3	Shooting Gallery	13	Thunder	1
Montrose	10	PUYA	1	Sideburn	1	Thunderhead	1
Mood Jga Jga	1	Queensrÿche	56	Silverchair	2	Tigres de Oro	4
Moon Pie	1	Rage Against the Machine	1	Silverhead	2	Tom Petty and the	
Moonspell	3	Rags	2	Skid Row	118	Heartbreakers	1
Mother Station	1	Raimundos	1	Skunk Anansie	1	Tongue	1
Mötley Crüe	7	The Raisin Band	1	Skyhook	1	Trapeze	1
Mott	15	Rammstein	4	Skyscraper	1	Treat	1
Mountain Smoke	1	The Raspberries	1	Slade	4	Trixter	56
Mushroom	1	Rebillot Quartet	1	Slaughter	111	The Tubes	1
The Mutton Birds	1	The Red & the Black	1	Slayer	3	Tumulto	1
Naked Lunch	2	Red 5	1	Smack Dab	1	UFO	2
Nantucket	8	Red Hot Chili Peppers	1	Smashing Pumpkins	1	Uncle Meat	1
Natural Born Hippies	1	Redbone	1	Smokehouse	2	Unmasked	1
Natural Gas	1	Reef	2	Snake Dance	1	Uriah Heep	33
Nazareth	2	Reel Big Fish	1	Snout	1	V8	1
Neil Merryweather &		REO Speedwagon	4	Sponge	1	Vandenberg	37
Space Rangers	1	Riot	24	Stabbing Westward	9	The Verve Pipe	29
Neneh Cherry	2	Ritual	2	Stage	1	Vesuvius	1
Neve	3	The Road Crew	1	Stampeders	4	Victimas del Dr. Cerebro	1
New England	22	Rock 'n' Roll Over	1	Starz	1	Viper	1
Nickelback	1	The Rockats	1	Status Quo	2	Vitale's Madman	2
Night Ranger	14	Rockets	29	Steelover	1	Vixen	8
The Nixons	6	Ronny Legg	1	Stick	1	W.A.S.P.	45
No Doubt	1	Rory Gallagher	2	Stone Wall	1	Waltari	1
Non-Intentional Lifeform	1	Ross	1	The Straws	1	Warpigs	1
Open Skyz	1	Royal Air Force	1	Stray	4	White Lion	18
Otto	3	Royal Crown Revue	2	Street Punk	1	Whiteface	1
Outhouse	15	Rush	51	Strutter	4	Why On Earth	1
Outlaws	5	Salem Witchcraft	2	Stu Daye	1	Wicked Lester	1
Ozone Monday	2	The Sam Hurrie Band	2	Styx	16	Winger	39
Pantera	5	Sammy Hagar	3	Sugar Ray	1	Wizzard	1
Paradise Lost	1	Saraya	1	Suicidal Tendencies	1	Yesterday & Today	1
Passion Orange	1	Satisfucktion	1	Sweet	1	Zebra	1
Passport	2	Savoy Brown	2	Sweetwater	1	Zluty Pes	1
Pat Travers Band	5	Scorpions	4	T. Rex	1		

Comprehensive List of Performances (1810 Total)

ARGENTINA (8)

Buenos Aires (8)

9/3/94	Estadio Monumental de River Plate
9/4/94	Estudios Alberto Olmedo
9/5/94	Estadio Obras Sanitarias
9/14/94	Estadio Obras Sanitarias
9/15/94	Estadio Obras Sanitarias
9/16/94	Estadio Obras Sanitarias
3/14/97	Estadio Monumental de River Plate
4/10/99	Estadio Monumental de River Plate

AUSTRALIA (37)

Adelaide (5)

11/18/80	Adelaide Oval
2/5/95	Hilton Hotel
2/6/95	Adelaide Entertainment Centre
2/11/97	Adelaide Memorial Drive
4/1/01	Adelaide Entertainment Centre

Brisbane (4)

11/25/80	Lang Park
2/10/95	Hilton Hotel
2/11/95	Entertainment Centre
2/3/97	Entertainment Centre

Gold Coast (1)

4/13/01	Carrara Stadium

Melbourne (10)

11/15/80	Victorian Football League Park
2/7/95	Hilton Hotel
2/8/95	National Tennis Centre @ Flinders Park
2/9/95	National Tennis Centre @ Flinders Park
2/13/97	National Tennis Centre @ Melbourne Park
2/14/97	National Tennis Centre @ Melbourne Park
2/15/97	National Tennis Centre @ Melbourne Park
4/3/01	Rod Laver Arena @ Melbourne Park
4/4/01	Rod Laver Arena @ Melbourne Park
4/5/01	Rod Laver Arena @ Melbourne Park

Perth (8)

11/8/80	Entertainment Centre
11/9/80	Entertainment Centre
11/10/80	Entertainment Centre
11/11/80	Entertainment Centre
2/3/95	Hyatt Hotel
2/4/95	Entertainment Centre
2/9/97	Burswood Dome
3/29/01	Burswood Dome

Sydney (9)
11/21/80 Sydney Showground
11/22/80 Sydney Showground
2/12/95 Hilton Hotel
2/13/95 Entertainment Centre
2/14/95 Entertainment Centre
2/5/97 Entertainment Centre
2/6/97 Entertainment Centre
4/7/01 The Superdome
4/8/01 The Superdome

AUSTRIA (7)

Graz (1)
11/9/83 Liedenan Stadthalle

Imst (1)
5/31/97 Skiarena Imst

Linz (1)
11/7/83 Stadthalle

Wels (1)
5/29/97 Messegelände

Wien (3)
11/8/83 Stadthalle
12/16/96 Libro Music Hall
3/17/99 Stadthalle

BELGIUM (7)

Bruxelles (5)
9/21/80 Vorst Nationaal
11/13/83 Vorst Nationaal
11/3/84 Vorst Nationaal
12/1/96 Vorst Nationaal
3/23/99 Vorst Nationaal

Ghent (1)
6/10/97 Flanders Expo

Kortrijk (1)
6/6/76 Ontmoetingscentrum

BRAZIL (7)

Belo Horizonte (1)
6/21/83 Estádio do Mineirão

Porto Alegre (1)
4/15/99 Jockey Club Brasil

Rio De Janeiro (1)
6/18/83 Maracaña Stadium

São Paulo (4)
6/25/83 Estádio do Morumbi
8/27/94 Estádio do Pacaembu
8/28/94 Estudios Programa Livre
4/17/99 Autodromo de Interlagos

CANADA (100)

Calgary (7)
2/6/74 Student Gymnasium @ Southern
Alberta Institute of Technology
5/20/74 Foothills Arena @ University of
Calgary
7/31/77 Corral Arena
3/3/85 Corral Arena
3/9/88 Olympic Saddledome
5/3/97 Canadian Air Saddledome
7/19/00 Canadian Air Saddledome

Edmonton (8)
2/5/74 Dinwoodie Lounge @ University of
Alberta
5/17/74 Kinsmen Fieldhouse
7/27/77 Edmonton Coliseum
7/29/77 Edmonton Coliseum
3/1/85 Kinsmen Fieldhouse
3/8/88 Edmonton Coliseum
5/2/97 Edmonton Coliseum
7/20/00 Skyreach Centre

Halifax (2)
4/19/76 Halifax Forum
7/8/77 Halifax Forum

Hamilton (3)
10/12/90 Copps Coliseum
3/28/97 Copps Coliseum
9/23/00 Copps Coliseum

Kitchener (3)
9/13/74 Sir Wilfred Laurier Theatre
4/23/76 Memorial Auditorium
7/16/77 Memorial Auditorium

Lethbridge (4)
5/19/74 Lethbridge Exhibition Pavilion
1/7/75 Lethbridge Exhibition Pavilion
7/28/77 Canada Games Sportsplex
3/2/85 Canada Games Sportsplex

London (5)
7/25/74 Centennial Hall
12/22/74 London Arena
4/24/76 London Gardens
7/18/77 London Gardens
10/13/90 London Gardens

Moncton (2)
4/18/76 Moncton Coliseum
7/9/77 Moncton Coliseum

Montréal (12)
4/21/76 Forum de Montréal
7/12/77 Forum de Montréal
8/6/79 Forum de Montréal
1/13/83 Forum de Montréal
3/13/84 Forum de Montréal
10/19/90 Forum de Montréal
10/5/92 Forum de Montréal
7/26/95 Musique Plus Studios
7/27/95 Le Chateau Champlain
8/3/96 Centre Molson
12/1/98 Centre Molson
6/22/00 Centre Molson

Ottawa (6)
4/22/76 Ottawa Civic Centre
7/14/77 Ottawa Civic Centre
1/15/83 Ottawa Civic Centre
10/18/90 Ottawa Civic Centre
8/5/96 The Palladium
9/21/00 Corel Centre

Quebec (4)
1/12/83 Colisée de Quebec
3/12/84 Colisée de Quebec
8/2/96 Colisée de Quebec
9/20/00 Colisée Pepsi

Regina (2)
8/2/77 Regina Agridome @ Regina
Exhibition Park

3/7/85 Regina Agridome @ Regina
Exhibition Park

Saskatoon (3)
5/18/74 Saskatoon Arena
5/1/97 Saskatchewan Place
7/17/00 Saskatchewan Place

Sudbury (1)
7/19/77 Sudbury Arena

Toronto (17)
6/15/74 Massey Hall
9/14/74 Victory Theatre (two shows)
4/26/76 Maple Leaf Gardens
9/6/76 Varsity Stadium
8/4/79 Maple Leaf Gardens
1/14/83 Maple Leaf Gardens
3/15/84 Maple Leaf Gardens
4/8/86 Maple Leaf Gardens
12/10/87 Maple Leaf Gardens
6/15/90 C.N.E. Stadium
5/6/92 The Phoenix Theatre
10/3/92 Maple Leaf Gardens
7/25/95 Hilton International
8/6/96 Toronto Skytent
12/2/98 Toronto Skytent
6/23/00 Air Canada Centre

Vancouver (12)
5/28/74 The Gardens
1/9/75 Commodore Ballroom (2 shows)
7/24/77 Pacific Coliseum
11/19/79 Pacific Coliseum
2/27/85 Pacific Coliseum
3/11/88 Pacific Coliseum
9/6/90 Pacific Coliseum
12/11/92 Pacific Coliseum
9/2/96 General Motors Place
5/6/97 General Motors Place
12/31/99 BC Place Concert Bowl

Winnipeg (9)
2/8/74 Tache Hall Auditorium @ University
of Manitoba
5/16/74 Manitoba Centennial Concert Hall
4/28/76 Winnipeg Arena
7/21/77 Winnipeg Arena
3/9/85 Winnipeg Arena
3/5/88 Winnipeg Arena
4/29/97 Winnipeg Arena
4/30/97 Winnipeg Arena
7/16/00 Winnipeg Arena

CHILE (2)

Santiago (2)
9/1/94 Centro Cultural Estación Mapocho
3/11/97 Velodrome del Estadio Nacional

CZECH REPUBLIC (4)

Praha (4)
12/14/96 Sportovní Hala
12/15/96 Sportovní Hala
6/7/97 Fotbalovy Stadion Juliska
3/18/99 Sportovní Hala

DENMARK (7)

Århus (1)
11/17/83 Vejlby-Risskov Hallen

Hillerød (1)
11/21/83 Frederiksborg Hallen

København (5)
5/29/76   Falkoner Teatret
10/11/80 Brøndby Hallen
10/21/84 Falkoner Centret
9/15/88   K.B. Hallen
6/21/97   Valby Idrætspark

ENGLAND (46)

Birmingham (6)
5/14/76   The Odeon Theatre
9/26/88   National Exhibition Centre
9/27/88   National Exhibition Centre
5/25/92   National Exhibition Centre
5/26/92   National Exhibition Centre
11/20/96 National Exhibition Centre

Bradford (1)
9/28/88   St. George's Concert Hall

Brighton (1)
9/30/84   The Brighton Centre

Chester (1)
9/6/80   Deeside Leisure Centre

Ipswich (1)
10/11/84 Gaumont Hall

Leeds (2)
10/21/83 Queens Hall
10/13/84 Queens Hall

Leicester (2)
10/24/83 De Montfort Hall
10/10/84 De Montfort Hall

Leistershire (2)
8/20/88   Donington Park
8/17/96   Donington Park

London (14)
5/15/76   Hammersmith Odeon Theatre
5/16/76   Hammersmith Odeon Theatre
9/8/80   Wembley Arena
9/9/80   Wembley Arena
10/23/83 Wembley Arena
10/14/84 Wembley Arena
10/15/84 Wembley Arena
8/16/88   Marquee
9/24/88   Wembley Arena
9/25/88   Wembley Arena
5/21/92   Wembley Arena
11/25/96 Wembley Arena
7/5/97   Finsbury Park
3/25/99   Wembley Arena

Manchester (3)
5/13/76   Free Trade Hall
10/4/84   Apollo Theatre
11/21/96 Nynex Arena

Newcastle (4)
10/29/83 City Hall
10/7/84   City Hall
10/8/84   City Hall
9/29/88   City Hall

Plymouth (1)
5/24/92   Plymouth Pavilions

Poole (1)
10/25/83 Leisure Centre

Sheffield (1)
5/18/92   Sheffield Arena

Southampton (1)
10/1/84   Gaumont Theatre

St. Austell (1)
10/2/84   Cornwall Coliseum

Stafford (3)
9/5/80   Bingley Hall
10/22/83 New Bingley Hall
10/12/84 New Bingley Hall

Whitley Bay (1)
5/17/92   Whitley Bay Ice Rink

FINLAND (5)

Helsingfors (4)
11/23/83 Icehalle
9/19/88   Icehalle
6/17/97   Hartwall Areena
2/26/99   Hartwall Areena

Oulu (1)
11/25/83 Icehalle

FRANCE (13)

Avignon (1)
9/23/80   Parc des Expositions

Clermont-Ferrand (1)
10/19/83 Maison des Sports

Lille (1)
11/12/83 Foire Internationale

Lyon (1)
9/24/80   Palais des Sports

Paris (8)
5/22/76   Olympia Theatre
9/27/80   Le Bourget Exhibition Centre
10/16/80 Le Hippodrome de Pantin
10/31/83 Espace Ballard
11/5/84   Le Zenith
9/13/88   Le Zenith
12/2/96   Le Zenith
3/22/99   Palais Omnisports de Paris-Bercy

Toulouse (1)
10/18/83 Palais des Sports

GERMANY/WEST GERMANY (48)

Berlin (3)
12/4/96   Deutschlandhalle
5/21/97   Waldbühne
3/7/99   Velodrome

Bochum (1)
8/28/88   Ruhr Stadion

Bremen (2)
10/1/80   Stadthalle
3/12/99   Stadthalle

Dortmund (3)
9/15/80   Westfalenhalle
12/21/96 Westfalenhalle
3/27/99   Westfalenhalle

Düsseldorf (3)
5/19/76   Philipshalle
9/12/80   Philipshalle
10/30/84 Philipshalle

Eifel (1)
5/18/97   Nürburgring

Erfurt (1)
3/11/99   Messehalle

Essen (1)
11/11/83 Grughalle

Frankfurt A.M. (6)
5/24/76   Stadthalle
9/13/80   Rebstokgelände
11/1/83   Stadthalle
10/17/84 Stadthalle
12/11/96 Festhalle
3/9/99   Festhalle

Hamburg (2)
10/4/80   Ernst-Merck Halle
5/24/97   Trarennbahn Stadium

Hannover (2)
10/2/80   Niedersachsenhalle
10/29/84 Stadium Sporthalle

Kassel (1)
9/20/80   Eissporthalle

Kiel (1)
3/28/99   Ostseehalle

Köln (2)
9/30/80   Sporthalle
3/8/99   Köln Arena

Leipzig (1)
5/22/97   Messegelände

Mannheim (2)
5/18/76   Saalbau Rosengarten
10/31/84 Friedrich-Ebert-Halle

München (5)
6/3/76   Circus Krone
9/18/80   Olympiahalle @ Olympiapark
          München
11/2/83   Löwenbraükeller
10/18/84 Circus Krone
3/19/99   Olympiahalle @ Olympiapark
          München

Nürnberg (5)
6/4/76   M.T.V. Gründighalle
9/11/80   Hessehalle
11/6/83   Hammerleinhalle
10/19/84 Hammerleinhalle
5/16/97   Frankenstadion

Oberhausen (1)
12/12/96 Oberhausen Arena

Schweinfurt (1)
8/27/88   Mainwiesen

Stuttgart (4)
9/17/80   Sindelfingen Messehalle

11/4/83   Sindelfingen Messehalle
12/20/96   Schleyerhalle
3/20/99   Schleyerhalle

HUNGARY (2)

Budapest (2)
9/2/88   Kisstadion Lelàtò
6/5/97   Petöfi Csarnok

ICELAND (1)

Reykjavík (1)
8/30/88   Rei∂höllin

ITALY (6)

Genova (1)
8/31/80   Palasport

Milano (3)
9/2/80   Motovelodromo Vigorelli
12/18/96   Palatrusardi
3/15/99   FilaForum

Modena (1)
9/10/88   Festa Della Unità

Roma (1)
8/29/80   Castel Sant'Angelo

JAMAICA (1)

Trelawny
3/6/02   Grand Lido Braco

JAPAN (39)

Fukuoka (4)
3/30/77   Kyuden Taiiku-Kan
1/26/95   Kyushu Koseinenkin Kaikan
1/24/97   Fukuoka Kokusai Center
3/16/01   Kokusai Center

Hiroshima (1)
1/25/97   Hiroshima Sun Plaza

Kyoto (1)
3/26/77   Kyoto Kaikan

Nagoya (5)
3/28/77   Aichi-Ken Taiiku-Kan
4/16/88   Civic Assembly Hall
1/28/95   Nagoya Century Hall
1/20/97   Rainbow Hall
3/18/01   Rainbow Hall

Osaka (9)
3/24/77   Osaka Kosei Nenkin Hall
3/25/77   Osaka Kosei Nenkin Hall
3/29/77   Royal Festival Hall
4/18/88   Royal Festival Hall
1/24/95   Osaka Castle Hall
1/21/97   Osaka Castle Hall
1/22/97   Osaka Castle Hall
3/21/01   Osaka Castle Hall
3/22/01   Osaka Castle Hall

Tokyo (16)
4/1/77   Nippon Budokan Hall
4/2/77   Nippon Budokan Hall (two shows)
4/4/77   Nippon Budokan Hall
3/28/78   Nippon Budokan Hall

3/29/78   Nippon Budokan Hall
3/31/78   Nippon Budokan Hall
4/1/78   Nippon Budokan Hall
4/2/78   Nippon Budokan Hall
4/21/88   Nippon Budokan Hall
4/22/88   Nippon Budokan Hall
4/24/88   Yoyogi Olympic Pool
1/30/95   Nippon Budokan Hall
1/31/95   Nippon Budokan Hall
1/18/97   Tokyodome
3/13/01   Tokyodome

Yokohama (3)
4/20/88   Bunka Taiikukan
3/9/01   Yokohama Arena
3/10/01   Yokohama Arena

MEXICO (5)

Ciudad De México (5)
9/8/94   Palacio de los Deportes
3/7/97   Palacio de los Deportes
3/8/97   Palacio de los Deportes
3/9/97   Palacio de los Deportes
4/24/99   Foro Sol

THE NETHERLANDS (7)

Amsterdam (1)
5/23/76   RAI Congrescentrum-Amsterdam

Leiden (1)
10/5/80   Groenoordhal

Rotterdam (1)
12/10/96   Sportpaleis Aho'y

Tilburg (1)
9/4/88   Willem II Stadium

Utrecht (2)
6/11/97   Prins van Oranjehal
3/13/99   Prins van Oranjehal

Zwolle (1)
11/4/84   Ijsselhal

NEW ZEALAND (3)

Auckland (2)
12/3/80   Western Springs Stadium
1/31/97   Auckland Supertop

Wellington (1)
11/30/80   Athletic Park

NORTHERN IRELAND (1)

Belfast (1)
10/3/88   King's Hall

NORWAY (6)

Drammen (2)
10/13/80   Drammenshallen
10/22/84   Drammenshallen

Lilleström (1)
9/21/88   Skedmohallen

Oslo (3)
12/8/96   Spektrum
6/19/97   Spektrum
2/28/99   Spektrum

PORTUGAL (1)

Lisboa (1)
10/11/83   Sports Palais

SCOTLAND (7)

Edinburgh (4)
10/28/83   Playhouse Theatre
10/6/84   Playhouse Theatre
10/1/88   Playhouse Theatre
10/2/88   Playhouse Theatre

Glasgow (3)
10/27/83   Apollo Theatre
10/5/84   Apollo Theatre
5/16/92   Scottish Exhibition & Conference
             Centre

SPAIN (7)

Barcelona (2)
10/16/83   Estadio Deportes de Juventud
6/30/97   Palau Val D'Hebron - Sports Palais

Madrid (3)
10/13/83   Pabellon del Real Madrid
10/14/83   Pabellon del Real Madrid
6/25/97   Sportspalace

San Sebastian (1)
10/15/83   Velodromo de Anotea

Zaragoza (1)
6/24/97   Principa Felipe

SWEDEN (21)

Göteborg (8)
5/26/76   Scandinavium
10/10/80   Scandinavium
11/18/83   Scandinavium
10/27/84   Scandinavium
9/16/88   Frölundaborg
12/7/96   Scandinavium
3/4/99   Scandinavium
3/5/99   Scandinavium

Lund (2)
5/30/76   Olympen
10/24/84   Olympen

Malmö (1)
11/20/83   Ishallen

Stockholm (10)
5/28/76   Stora Scenen @ Gröna Lund in Tivoli
             Gardens
10/9/80   Eriksdalshalle
11/19/83   Hovet
10/26/84   Hovet
9/17/88   Hovet
12/6/96   Stockholm Globe Arena
6/14/97   Olympic Stadion
6/15/97   Olympic Stadion
3/2/99   Stockholm Globe Arena
3/3/99   Stockholm Globe Arena

SWITZERLAND (8)

Bâle (2)
9/28/80   Sporthalle St. Jakob
11/3/83   Sporthalle St. Jakob

Genève (1)
7/2/97   Geneva Arena

Lausanne (2)
11/15/83   Halle des Festes
11/1/84   Palais De Beauleiu, Halle 18

Zürich (3)
6/2/76   Volkshaus
12/19/96   Hallenstadion
6/1/97   Hallenstadion

UNITED STATES OF AMERICA (1402)

ALABAMA (25)

Birmingham (12)
7/14/74   Municipal Auditorium
10/22/75   Municipal Auditorium
7/23/76   Rickwood Field
3/3/77   Birmingham-Jefferson Civic Center
12/29/77   Birmingham-Jefferson Civic Center
8/16/79   Birmingham-Jefferson Civic Center
1/28/83   Boutwell Auditorium
1/6/84   Boutwell Auditorium
1/18/85   Boutwell Auditorium
8/7/90   Oak Mountain Amphitheatre
9/14/96   Birmingham-Jefferson Civic Center
4/14/00   Birmingham-Jefferson Civic Center

Dothan (1)
12/3/75   Dothan Civic Center

Huntsville (7)
3/11/76   Von Braun Civic Center
12/7/76   Von Braun Civic Center
12/14/79   Von Braun Civic Center
1/27/83   Von Braun Civic Center
1/17/85   Von Braun Civic Center
8/16/90   Von Braun Civic Center
11/8/92   Von Braun Civic Center

Jacksonville (1)
10/1/74   Leone Cole Auditorium @ Jacksonville State University

Mobile (3)
3/13/76   Expo Hall @ Mobile Municipal Auditorium
12/5/76   Mobile Municipal Auditorium
8/20/79   Mobile Municipal Auditorium

Montgomery (1)
10/26/75   Garrett Coliseum

ALASKA (3)

Anchorage (2)
6/2/74   Sundowner Drive-In Theatre
1/3/00   George M. Sullivan Sports Arena

Fairbanks (1)
6/4/74   Baker Field House

ARIZONA (17)

Phoenix (14)
8/17/76   Tempe Stadium
8/22/77   Arizona Veterans Memorial Coliseum
11/10/79   Arizona Veterans Memorial Coliseum
3/28/83   Arizona Veterans Memorial Coliseum
2/6/85   Arizona Veterans Memorial Coliseum
2/9/86   Arizona Veterans Memorial Coliseum
3/25/88   Compton Terrace
9/16/90   Arizona Veterans Memorial Coliseum
4/27/92   After the Goldrush
12/20/92   America West Arena
10/21/94   Arizona Veterans Memorial Coliseum
6/25/95   Hyatt Regency Phoenix
8/21/96   America West Arena
3/11/00   Blockbuster Desert Sky Pavilion

Tucson (3)
8/21/77   Tucson Community Center
2/2/86   McKale Memorial Center
3/12/00   Tucson Convention Center

ARKANSAS (8)

Little Rock (6)
8/4/76   T.H. Barton Coliseum
11/29/85   T.H. Barton Coliseum
2/21/88   T.H. Barton Coliseum
8/24/90   T.H. Barton Coliseum
11/9/96   T.H. Barton Coliseum
4/5/00   Alltel Arena

Pine Bluff (2)
10/14/79   Pine Bluff Convention Center
2/11/83   Pine Bluff Convention Center

CALIFORNIA (102)

Bakersfield (3)
2/2/84   Bakersfield Civic Auditorium
2/21/85   Bakersfield Civic Auditorium
3/21/00   Bakersfield Centennial Garden

Fresno (6)
1/26/75   Selland Arena @ Fresno Convention Center
6/6/75   Warnors Theatre @ Warnors Center for the Performing Arts
8/17/77   Selland Arena @ Fresno Convention Center
11/27/79   Selland Arena @ Fresno Convention Center
1/29/84   Selland Arena @ Fresno Convention Center
8/1/00   Selland Arena @ Fresno Convention Center

Los Angeles (48)
2/17/74   Long Beach Auditorium
2/18/74   Los Angeles Room @ Century Plaza Hotel
2/21/74   Aquarius Theatre
5/31/74   Long Beach Auditorium
1/17/75   Long Beach Arena
2/1/75   Santa Monica Civic Auditorium
4/1/75   NBC Studios
5/30/75   Shrine Auditorium
5/31/75   Long Beach Arena
2/23/76   The Forum
2/24/76   The Forum
8/20/76   Anaheim Stadium
8/26/77   The Forum
8/27/77   The Forum
8/28/77   The Forum
5/19/78   Magic Mountain Amusement Park
11/6/79   Anaheim Convention Center
11/7/79   The Forum
1/15/82   ABC Studios
3/26/83   Irvine Meadows Amphitheatre
3/27/83   Universal Amphitheatre
1/27/84   Long Beach Arena
2/17/85   Long Beach Arena
2/18/85   Long Beach Arena
2/11/86   The Forum
8/8/87   Grand Olympic Auditorium
3/26/88   Pacific Amphitheatre
4/25/90   Chuck Landis' Country Club
9/14/90   Long Beach Arena
4/25/92   Doug Weston's World Famous Troubadour
4/26/92   Doug Weston's World Famous Troubadour
5/20/93   Paramount Studios
9/11/93   Hilton and Convention Center
6/16/95   Hard Rock Cafe
7/13/94   Studio 3 @ NBC Studios
6/17/95   Hilton and Convention Center
12/15/95   Hollywood Palladium
6/15/96   Irvine Meadows Amphitheatre
8/23/96   Great Western Forum
8/24/96   Great Western Forum
8/25/96   Great Western Forum
10/31/96   Irvine Meadows Amphitheatre
11/1/96   Irvine Meadows Amphitheatre
10/30/98   Dodger Stadium (rehearsal)
10/31/98   Dodger Stadium
8/9/99   Parking Lot @ UCLA Campus
3/18/00   Arrowhead Pond
8/11/00   Verizon Wireless Amphitheatre

Sacramento (7)
2/24/85   Sacramento Memorial Auditorium
2/5/86   Sacramento Memorial Auditorium
3/28/88   ARCO Arena
9/12/90   California Expo Amphitheatre
12/16/92   ARCO Arena
8/28/96   ARCO Arena
7/29/00   Sacramento Valley Amphitheatre

San Bernardino (7)
1/18/75   Swing Auditorium
2/26/76   Swing Auditorium
2/3/84   Orange Show Pavilion
2/20/85   Orange Show Pavilion
2/8/86   Orange Show Pavilion
12/19/92   Orange Show Pavilion
8/12/00   Glen Helen Blockbuster Pavilion

San Diego (12)
5/30/74   San Diego Sports Arena
1/19/75   Golden Hall @ Convention & Performing Arts Center
6/7/75   Civic Theatre
2/27/76   San Diego Sports Arena
8/19/77   San Diego Sports Arena
11/29/79   San Diego Sports Arena
2/22/85   San Diego Sports Arena
2/10/86   San Diego Sports Arena
4/1/88   San Diego Sports Arena
9/15/90   San Diego Sports Arena
10/29/96   San Diego Sports Arena

3/19/00   San Diego Sports Arena

San Francisco/Oakland (19)
6/1/74   Winterland
1/31/75   Winterland
6/1/75   Winterland
8/22/76   Oakland-Alameda County Coliseum Arena
8/16/77   Cow Palace
11/25/79 Cow Palace
4/3/83   San Francisco Civic Auditorium
2/1/84   Berkeley Community Theatre
2/9/85   Henry J. Kaiser Auditorium
2/4/86   Cow Palace
3/30/88   San Francisco Civic Auditorium
9/13/90   Concord Pavilion
4/23/92   The Stone
12/18/92 Oakland-Alameda County Coliseum Arena
6/18/95   Gift Center Pavilion
8/27/96   San Jose Arena
3/23/00   Oakland-Alameda County Coliseum Arena
7/28/00   Shoreline Amphitheatre @ Mountain View
7/30/00   Chronicle Pavilion @ Concord

COLORADO (12)

Denver (12)
1/15/77   McNichols Sports Arena
11/17/77 McNichols Sports Arena
11/4/79   McNichols Sports Arena
1/25/84   University of Denver Ice Arena
2/19/86   McNichols Sports Arena
3/23/88   McNichols Sports Arena
8/31/90   Red Rocks Amphitheatre
12/6/92   McNichols Sports Arena
9/7/96   McNichols Sports Arena
9/8/96   McNichols Sports Arena
3/28/00   Pepsi Center
8/14/00   Fiddler's Green Amphitheatre

CONNECTICUT (15)

Hartford (4)
2/16/77   Hartford Civic Center
12/30/96 Hartford Civic Center
11/25/98 Hartford Civic Center
7/8/00   Meadows Music Theater

New Haven (9)
12/18/76 New Haven Veterans Memorial Coliseum
1/28/78   New Haven Veterans Memorial Coliseum
9/3/79   New Haven Veterans Memorial Coliseum
3/1/84   New Haven Veterans Memorial Coliseum
11/24/84 New Haven Veterans Memorial Coliseum
12/21/85 New Haven Veterans Memorial Coliseum
12/19/87 New Haven Veterans Memorial Coliseum
10/27/90 New Haven Veterans Memorial Coliseum
3/21/97   New Haven Veterans Memorial Coliseum

Uncasville (1)
10/3/00   Uncas Pavilion @ Mohegan Sun Casino

Waterbury (1)
12/18/75 Palace Theatre

FLORIDA (53)

Daytona Beach (1)
10/29/92 Ocean Center

Fort Myers (2)
1/9/86   Lee County Arena
4/9/00   TECO Arena

Jacksonville (7)
12/6/75   Jacksonville Veterans Memorial Coliseum
12/10/76 Jacksonville Veterans Memorial Coliseum
12/31/83 Jacksonville Veterans Memorial Coliseum
1/10/86   Jacksonville Veterans Memorial Coliseum
2/14/88   Jacksonville Veterans Memorial Coliseum
8/1/90   Jacksonville Veterans Memorial Coliseum
9/19/96   Jacksonville Veterans Memorial Coliseum

Lakeland (5)
3/20/76   Lakeland Civic Center
12/12/76 Lakeland Civic Center
6/15/79   Lakeland Civic Center
2/4/83   Lakeland Civic Center
12/29/83 Lakeland Civic Center

Miami (12)
3/21/76   Miami Jai-Alai Fronton
12/11/76 The Sportatorium
1/3/78   The Sportatorium
6/17/79   The Sportatorium
12/30/83 The Sportatorium
1/11/85   Sunrise Musical Theatre
1/12/85   Sunrise Musical Theatre
2/12/88   The Sportatorium
8/3/90   Miami Arena
10/31/92 Miami Arena
7/6/95   Radisson Mart Plaza
9/17/96   Miami Arena

Orlando (7)
7/12/74   Orlando Jai-Alai Fronton
10/19/75 Orlando Sports Stadium
1/10/85   Orlando Sports Stadium
8/2/90   Orlando Centroplex Arena
12/12/93 Pleasure Island
9/22/96   Orlando Centroplex Arena
4/11/00   TD Waterhouse Centre

Pensacola (4)
1/21/85   The Pensacola Civic Center
11/14/87 The Pensacola Civic Center
9/15/96   The Pensacola Civic Center
4/6/00   The Pensacola Civic Center

Tallahassee (1)
1/1/84   Tallahassee-Leon Co. Civic Center

Tampa/St. Petersburg (10)
7/13/74   Curtis Hixon Convention Hall
7/5/75   Florida State Fairgrounds
10/20/75 Bayfront Center Arena
1/13/85   Bayfront Center Arena
1/7/86   USF Sundome
2/13/88   Bayfront Center Arena
8/4/90   USF Sundome
10/30/92 USF Sundome
9/20/96   Thunderdome
4/12/00   Ice Palace

West Palm Beach (4)
7/11/74   West Palm Beach Auditorium
2/3/83   West Palm Beach Auditorium
1/8/86   West Palm Beach Auditorium
4/8/00   Mars Music Amphitheatre

GEORGIA (38)

Albany (1)
11/3/90   Albany James H. Gray Sr. Civic Center

Atlanta (26)
6/19/74   Alex Cooley's Electric Ballroom
6/20/74   Alex Cooley's Electric Ballroom
6/21/74   Alex Cooley's Electric Ballroom
6/22/74   Alex Cooley's Electric Ballroom
7/17/74   Alex Cooley's Electric Ballroom
7/18/74   Alex Cooley's Electric Ballroom
9/18/74   Alex Cooley's Electric Ballroom
9/19/74   Alex Cooley's Electric Ballroom
9/20/74   Alex Cooley's Electric Ballroom
9/21/74   Alex Cooley's Electric Ballroom
11/23/74 Alexander Memorial Coliseum
12/5/75   The Omni
8/29/76   Altanta/Fulton County Stadium
12/30/77 The Omni
6/30/79   The Omni
12/26/83 The Omni
1/9/85   The Omni
12/31/85 The Omni
2/10/88   The Omni
7/20/90   Lakewood Amphitheatre
5/2/92   Center Stage
11/5/92   The Omni
7/8/95   Hilton/Towers
10/1/96   The Omni
10/2/96   The Omni
4/15/00   Philips Arena

Augusta (3)
12/28/83 Augusta/Richmond County Civic Center
12/30/85 Augusta/Richmond County Civic Center
11/2/90   Augusta/Richmond County Civic Center

Columbus (5)
12/2/75   Columbus Municipal Auditorium
11/30/76 Columbus Municipal Auditorium
2/15/88   Columbus Municipal Auditorium
11/6/90   Columbus Municipal Auditorium
4/5/97   Columbus Civic Center

Macon (1)
12/8/76   Macon Auditorium

Savannah (2)
11/24/76 Civic Center
6/19/79 Civic Center

HAWAII (1)

Honolulu (1)
2/29/76 Neal S. Blaisdell Memorial Center
Arena

IDAHO (3)

Boise (3)
9/3/90 BSU Pavilion
12/9/92 BSU Pavilion
7/26/00 Idaho Center Arena

ILLINOIS (50)

Carbondale (3)
3/22/86 SIU Arena
9/28/90 SIU Arena
9/1/00 SIU Arena

Champaign (1)
10/1/00 Assembly Hall

Chicago (26)
4/19/74 Aragon Ballroom
11/2/74 Herman L. Rider Memorial
Gymnasium @ Maine Township
High School West
11/8/74 Aragon Ballroom
2/21/75 Aragon Ballroom
4/19/75 Fremd High School Gymnasium
5/8/75 John F. Kennedy Gymnasium @
Lewis University
11/22/75 International Amphitheatre
5/4/76 River Trails Middle School
Gymnasium
1/22/77 Chicago Stadium
1/15/78 Chicago Stadium
1/16/78 Chicago Stadium
9/22/79 Chicago Amphitheatre
2/15/84 University of Illinois-Chicago Pavilion
1/17/86 University of Illinois-Chicago Pavilion
1/8/88 University of Illinois-Chicago Pavilion
6/3/90 New World Music Theatre
11/21/92 University of Illinois-Chicago Pavilion
4/2/94 Odeum Sports and Exhibition Center
7/15/95 Hyatt Woodfield
7/14/96 Rosemont Horizon
7/16/96 Rosemont Horizon
10/21/96 Rosemont Horizon
12/29/98 Rosemont Horizon
5/11/00 Allstate Arena
5/12/00 Allstate Arena
9/30/00 New World Music Theatre

Dekalb (1)
4/8/74 University Center Ballroom @
Northern Illinois University

Moline (2)
7/12/96 The Mark of the Quad Cities
5/16/00 The Mark of the Quad Cities

Normal (1)
4/12/75 ISU Union & Auditorium

Pekin (1)
8/17/75 Pekin Community High School (East
Campus) Stadium

Peoria (5)
12/17/84 Carver Arena @ Peoria Civic Center
3/3/88 Carver Arena @ Peoria Civic Center
5/30/90 Carver Arena @ Peoria Civic Center
4/13/97 Carver Arena @ Peoria Civic Center
5/15/00 Carver Arena @ Peoria Civic Center

Rockford (5)
11/15/75 National Guard Armory-Rockford
12/31/82 MetroCentre
1/22/86 MetroCentre
12/18/98 MetroCentre
9/5/00 MetroCentre

Springfield (5)
12/30/74 National Guard Armory
2/25/83 Prairie Capitol Convention Center
3/8/86 Prairie Capital Convention Center
12/6/87 Prairie Capital Convention Center
11/24/92 Prairie Capital Convention Center

INDIANA (64)

Evansville (15)
9/29/74 Roberts Municipal Stadium
12/8/74 Roberts Municipal Stadium
12/31/74 Evansville Coliseum
11/23/75 Roberts Municipal Stadium
8/6/76 Roberts Municipal Stadium
1/23/78 Roberts Municipal Stadium
9/20/79 Roberts Municipal Stadium
3/17/84 Roberts Municipal Stadium
12/5/84 Roberts Municipal Stadium
3/25/86 Roberts Municipal Stadium
12/30/87 Roberts Municipal Stadium
5/31/90 Mesker Music Theatre
11/20/92 Roberts Municipal Stadium
4/8/97 Roberts Municipal Stadium
9/10/00 Roberts Municipal Stadium

Fort Wayne (10)
12/27/74 Allen Co. War Memorial Coliseum
4/11/76 Allen Co. War Memorial Coliseum
1/24/77 Allen Co. War Memorial Coliseum
9/18/79 Allen Co. War Memorial Coliseum
12/7/84 Allen Co. War Memorial Coliseum
3/20/86 Allen Co. War Memorial Coliseum
12/26/87 Allen Co. War Memorial Coliseum
5/20/90 Fort Wayne Expo Center
11/18/92 Allen Co. War Memorial Coliseum
4/9/97 Allen Co. War Memorial Coliseum

Hammond (2)
10/18/74 The Parthenon Theatre
3/30/86 Civic Center

Indianapolis (20)
8/3/74 Indianapolis Convention Center
12/28/74 Indianapolis Convention Center
4/22/75 Indianapolis Convention Center
8/28/75 Indianapolis Convention Center
8/2/76 Market Square Arena
12/11/77 Market Square Arena
8/10/79 Market Square Arena
2/24/83 Market Square Arena
2/16/84 Market Square Arena
12/2/84 Market Square Arena
1/16/86 Market Square Arena
12/27/87 Market Square Arena
6/8/90 Deer Creek Music Center

11/28/92 Market Square Arena
7/13/95 Ramada Plaza
8/9/96 Market Square Arena
10/15/96 Market Square Arena
12/13/98 Market Square Arena
5/20/00 Deer Creek Music Center
9/9/00 Conseco Fieldhouse

La Porte (1)
12/18/74 National Guard Armory

Merrillville (1)
3/2/88 Star Plaza Theatre

Peru (1)
10/31/74 Circus Center Building

Schererville (1)
2/22/75 The Omni 41

South Bend (5)
8/4/74 Morris Civic Auditorium
12/29/74 Morris Civic Auditorium
12/28/75 Morris Civic Auditorium
9/1/76 Joyce Athletic & Convocation Center
Arena
3/23/85 Joyce Athletic & Convocation Center
Arena

Terre Haute (8)
11/21/75 Hulman Civic University Center
1/25/77 Hulman Civic University Center
1/1/83 Hulman Civic University Center
12/6/84 Hulman Center
3/23/86 Hulman Center
2/18/88 Hulman Center
5/17/90 Hulman Center
12/12/98 Hulman Center

IOWA (33)

Ames (3)
11/14/92 Hilton Coliseum
4/19/97 Hilton Coliseum
8/30/00 Hilton Coliseum

Burlington (1)
4/17/75 Memorial Auditorium

Cedar Rapids (9)
11/21/74 Veterans Memorial Coliseum
10/10/79 Five Seasons Center
12/18/84 Five Seasons Center
3/18/86 Five Seasons Center
5/23/90 Five Seasons Center
11/15/92 Five Seasons Center
4/20/97 Five Seasons Center
12/19/98 Five Seasons Center
9/2/00 Five Seasons Center

Davenport (4)
12/10/74 Palmer Alumni Auditorium @
Palmer College of Chiropractic
7/20/75 RKO Orpheum Theatre (2 shows)
11/28/87 Palmer Alumni Auditorium @
Palmer College of Chiropractic

Des Moines (7)
1/21/77 Veterans Memorial Auditorium
11/29/77 Veterans Memorial Auditorium
10/4/79 Veterans Memorial Auditorium
3/17/85 Veterans Memorial Auditorium

3/16/86   Veterans Memorial Auditorium
12/4/87   Veterans Memorial Auditorium
6/2/90   Veterans Memorial Auditorium

Dubuque (4)
2/16/83   Dubuque Five Flags Center
2/11/84   Dubuque Five Flags Center
2/19/88   Dubuque Five Flags Center
9/30/90   Dubuque Five Flags Center

Sioux City (4)
12/30/82   Sioux City Municipal Auditorium
2/8/84   Sioux City Municipal Auditorium
3/17/86   Sioux City Municipal Auditorium
10/7/90   Sioux City Municipal Auditorium

Waterloo (1)
2/10/77   McElroy Auditorium

KANSAS (12)

Salina (2)
3/9/86   Bicentennial Center
8/26/90   Bicentennial Center

Topeka (3)
11/26/87   Landon Arena @ Kansas ExpoCentre
10/6/90   Landon Arena @ Kansas ExpoCentre
4/16/97   Landon Arena @ Kansas ExpoCentre

Wichita (7)
1/9/77   Henry J. Levitt Arena
12/6/77   Henry J. Levitt Arena
10/12/79   Britt Brown Arena @ Kansas Coliseum
11/23/87   Britt Brown Arena @ Kansas Coliseum
5/9/90   Britt Brown Arena @ Kansas Coliseum
9/10/96   Britt Brown Arena @ Kansas Coliseum
8/28/00   Britt Brown Arena @ Kansas Coliseum

KENTUCKY (21)

Bowling Green (1)
12/6/74   Van Meter Auditorium @ Western Kentucky University

Lexington (8)
3/5/77   Rupp Arena
1/18/78   Rupp Arena
7/16/79   Rupp Arena
1/6/83   Rupp Arena
10/20/92   Rupp Arena
10/18/96   Rupp Arena
12/9/98   Rupp Arena
9/8/00   Rupp Arena

Louisville (11)
4/14/74   Beggar's Banquet
4/21/75   Louisville Memorial Auditorium
12/27/75   Louisville Gardens
9/8/76   Freedom Hall
12/12/77   Freedom Hall
9/16/79   Freedom Hall
12/15/84   Commonwealth Convention Center
12/12/85   Freedom Hall
12/29/87   Freedom Hall
6/30/96   Freedom Hall
4/29/00   Freedom Hall

Owensboro (1)
8/27/75   Sportscenter

LOUISIANA (23)

Baton Rouge (3)
7/16/74   Independence Hall
12/27/77   Riverside Centroplex
8/18/79   Riverside Centroplex

Lafayette (3)
12/6/85   Cajundome
11/6/96   Cajundome
8/18/00   Cajundome

Lake Charles (2)
12/6/79   Benton Memorial Coliseum
11/17/87   Lake Charles Civic Center

New Orleans (9)
3/12/76   A Warehouse
12/4/76   Municipal Auditorium
2/14/83   Louisiana Superdome
1/8/84   Kiefer UNO Lakefront Arena
1/15/85   Kiefer UNO Lakefront Arena
3/2/86   Kiefer UNO Lakefront Arena
2/23/88   Kiefer UNO Lakefront Arena
7/9/96   Louisiana Superdome
4/16/00   New Orleans Arena

Shreveport (6)
8/10/76   Hirsch Memorial Coliseum
12/8/79   Hirsch Memorial Coliseum
3/19/83   Hirsch Memorial Coliseum
3/1/86   Hirsch Memorial Coliseum
8/18/90   Hirsch Memorial Coliseum
11/8/96   Hirsch Memorial Coliseum

MAINE (11)

Augusta (1)
12/30/76   Augusta Civic Center

Bangor (1)
4/16/76   Municipal Auditorium

Portland (9)
7/28/79   Cumberland County Civic Center
1/21/83   Cumberland County Civic Center
12/13/87   Cumberland County Civic Center
7/6/90   Seashore Performing Arts Center
10/25/90   Cumberland County Civic Center
10/6/92   Cumberland County Civic Center
3/25/97   Cumberland County Civic Center
11/16/98   Cumberland County Civic Center
6/15/00   Cumberland County Civic Center

MARYLAND (8)

Baltimore (8)
3/24/74   Painter's Mill Music Fair
8/2/75   Baltimore Civic Center
7/13/76   Baltimore Civic Center
2/28/84   Baltimore Civic Center
11/27/84   Baltimore Civic Center
4/10/86   Baltimore Arena
5/4/92   Hammerjacks
4/1/97   Baltimore Arena

MASSACHUSETTS (30)

Boston (9)
5/11/75   Orpheum Theatre

8/14/75   Orpheum Theatre
12/14/75   Orpheum Theatre
5/8/92   Avalon Ballroom
7/29/95   Westin Copley Place
7/30/96   Fleet Center
7/31/96   Fleet Center
11/12/98   Fleet Center
11/13/98   Fleet Center

Mansfield (3)
6/29/90   Great Woods Center for the Performing Arts Amphitheatre
6/12/00   Tweeter Center for the Performing Arts
6/13/00   Tweeter Center for the Performing Arts

South Yarmouth (1)
7/11/76   Cape Cod Coliseum

Springfield (9)
3/28/76   Springfield Civic Center
9/12/76   Springfield Civic Center
1/27/78   Springfield Civic Center
9/5/79   Springfield Civic Center
3/28/85   Springfield Civic Center
4/6/86   Springfield Civic Center
1/28/88   Springfield Civic Center
7/3/90   Springfield Civic Center
3/22/97   Springfield Civic Center

Worcester (8)
1/22/83   The Centrum
2/24/84   The Centrum
11/23/84   The Centrum
12/20/85   The Centrum
1/27/88   The Centrum
10/26/90   The Centrum
10/8/92   The Centrum
12/28/96   The Centrum

MICHIGAN (73)

Battle Creek (1)
3/26/86   Kellogg Center Arena

Cadillac (1)
10/9/75   Cadillac High School Auditorium

Detroit (34)
4/7/74   Michigan Palace
4/12/74   Michigan Palace
4/13/74   Michigan Palace
5/12/74   Benjamin F. Yack Arena
5/14/74   Fraser Hockeyland Arena
9/28/74   Michigan Palace
12/20/74   Michigan Palace
12/21/74   Michigan Palace
5/16/75   Cobo Arena
1/25/76   Cobo Arena
1/26/76   Cobo Arena
1/27/76   Cobo Arena
1/27/77   Cobo Arena
1/28/77   Cobo Arena
1/29/77   Cobo Arena
1/20/78   Olympia
1/21/78   Olympia
7/13/79   Pontiac Mini-Dome
2/23/83   Cobo Arena
2/18/84   Cobo Arena
12/8/84   Cobo Arena

12/14/85	Cobo Arena
1/17/88	Cobo Arena
5/18/90	The Palace of Auburn Hills
10/14/90	The Palace of Auburn Hills
11/27/92	The Palace of Auburn Hills
7/22/95	Cobo Conference and Exhibition Center
6/28/96	Tiger Stadium
10/16/96	The Palace of Auburn Hills
10/17/96	The Palace of Auburn Hills
12/31/98	The Palace of Auburn Hills
5/24/00	The Palace of Auburn Hills
5/25/00	The Palace of Auburn Hills
9/12/00	Pine Knob Music Theatre

Flint (6)
4/4/74	Nordic Arena
6/12/74	I.M.A. Sports Arena
12/12/74	I.M.A. Sports Arena
4/4/75	Nordic Arena
11/16/75	I.M.A. Sports Arena
11/17/75	I.M.A. Sports Arena

Grand Rapids (5)
5/2/74	Thunder Chicken
10/17/74	Thunder Chicken
4/10/97	Van Andel Arena
12/30/98	Van Andel Arena
5/7/00	Van Andel Arena

Jackson (1)
6/18/75	Sports Arena

Kalamazoo (3)
10/7/75	Herbert Reed Field House @ Western Michigan University
10/15/90	Wings Stadium
11/17/92	Wings Stadium

Lansing (5)
10/21/74	The Brewery
10/22/74	The Brewery
4/29/75	Metro Ice Arena
3/22/85	Lansing Civic Center
9/6/00	Breslin Center

Marquette (3)
3/20/85	Lakeview Arena
1/5/88	Lakeview Arena
10/4/90	Lakeview Arena

Mt. Pleasant (1)
1/30/76	Rose Arena

Muskegon (3)
8/16/75	L.C. Walker Arena
1/11/88	L.C. Walker Arena
6/13/90	L.C. Walker Arena

Port Huron (2)
11/18/75	McMorran Place
3/7/86	McMorran Place

Saginaw (8)
11/10/74	Delta College Gymnasium
8/15/75	Wendler Arena @ Saginaw Civic Center
1/7/83	Wendler Arena @ Saginaw Civic Center
2/17/84	Wendler Arena @ Saginaw Civic Center
12/11/84	Wendler Arena @ Saginaw Civic Center
3/6/86	Wendler Arena @ Saginaw Civic Center
1/12/88	Wendler Arena @ Saginaw Civic Center
5/15/90	Wendler Arena @ Saginaw Civic Center

MINNESOTA (28)

Duluth (6)
11/3/74	Duluth Arena Auditorium
1/18/77	Duluth Arena Auditorium
10/6/79	Duluth Arena Auditorium
3/13/85	Duluth Arena Auditorium
3/13/86	Duluth Arena Auditorium
5/27/90	DECC

Mankato (1)
4/25/97	Mankato Civic Center

Minneapolis/St. Paul (19)
5/19/75	St. Paul Civic Center Theater
2/6/76	St. Paul Civic Center Theater (2 shows)
2/6/77	Metropolitan Sports Center
12/2/77	St. Paul Civic Center
9/28/79	Metropolitan Sports Center
2/18/83	Metropolitan Sports Center
2/12/84	Metropolitan Sports Center
12/29/84	St. Paul Civic Center
1/21/86	St. Paul Civic Center
12/1/87	St. Paul Civic Center
5/25/90	Metropolitan Sports Center
12/3/92	St. Paul Civic Center
7/16/95	Radisson South & Plaza
7/13/96	St. Paul Civic Center
4/22/97	St. Paul Civic Center
12/15/98	Target Center
5/18/00	Target Center
7/13/00	Target Center

Rochester (2)
12/2/87	Mayo Civic Center
10/5/90	Mayo Civic Center

MISSISSIPPI (12)

Biloxi (6)
12/12/79	Mississippi Coast Coliseum
3/18/83	Mississippi Coast Coliseum
1/9/84	Mississippi Coast Coliseum
1/16/85	Mississippi Coast Coliseum
8/19/90	Mississippi Coast Coliseum
8/21/00	Mississippi Coast Coliseum

Jackson (5)
12/3/76	Mississippi Coliseum
12/10/79	Mississippi Coliseum
11/13/87	Mississippi Coliseum
8/17/90	Mississippi Coliseum
8/19/00	Mississippi Coliseum

Tupelo (1)
9/13/96	Tupelo Coliseum

MISSOURI (36)

Cape Girardeau (1)
5/22/90	Show Me Center

Columbia (1)
9/25/90	The Hearns Center

Kansas City (Missouri & Kansas) (12)
4/13/75	Soldier's & Sailor's Memorial Hall
7/26/76	Municipal Auditorium
2/9/77	Kemper Arena
11/27/77	Kemper Arena
9/30/79	Municipal Auditorium
3/1/83	Municipal Auditorium
12/26/84	Municipal Auditorium
1/25/86	Municipal Auditorium
2/20/88	Municipal Auditorium
5/12/90	Sandstone Amphitheatre
7/3/96	Kemper Arena
8/25/00	Sandstone Amphitheatre

Springfield (1)
9/24/90	John Q. Hammons Student Center

St. Joseph (1)
11/10/92	St. Joseph Civic Arena

St. Louis (20)
3/31/74	Forest Park
5/3/74	Ambassador Theatre
11/7/74	Kiel Auditorium
2/20/75	Kiel Auditorium
11/1/75	Kiel Auditorium
7/28/76	Kiel Auditorium
7/29/76	Kiel Auditorium
12/7/77	The Checkerdome
10/2/79	The Checkerdome
2/27/83	Kiel Auditorium
12/4/84	Kiel Auditorium
1/23/86	Kiel Auditorium
1/9/88	Kiel Auditorium
6/1/90	Kiel Auditorium
11/13/92	The Arena
7/11/95	Airport Hilton
7/12/95	KSHE Cool Rock Café
7/2/96	Kiel Center
4/15/97	Kiel Center
8/26/00	Riverport Amphitheatre

MONTANA (3)

Billings (2)
8/7/77	Metra
8/29/90	Metra Park

Missoula (1)
2/16/76	Harry Adams Fieldhouse

NEBRASKA (15)

Lincoln (4)
3/6/76	Pershing Auditorium
1/20/77	Pershing Auditorium
12/27/84	Pershing Auditorium
9/26/90	Pershing Auditorium

Omaha (11)
2/8/77	Omaha Civic Auditorium
11/30/77	Omaha Civic Auditorium
10/8/79	Omaha Civic Auditorium
2/9/84	Omaha Civic Auditorium
1/24/86	Omaha Civic Auditorium
11/27/87	Omaha Civic Auditorium
5/10/90	Omaha Civic Auditorium
10/23/96	Omaha Civic Auditorium
10/24/96	Omaha Civic Audtiorium

12/16/98 Omaha Civic Auditorium
8/29/00   Omaha Civic Auditorium

NEVADA (13)

Las Vegas (11)
5/29/75   Space Center @ Sahara (2 shows)
4/1/83   Aladdin Theatre for the Performing Arts
1/28/84   Thomas & Mack Center
2/7/85   Aladdin Theatre for the Performing Arts
2/7/86   Thomas & Mack Center
4/2/88   Thomas & Mack Center
6/24/95   Sahara
11/2/96   MGM Grand Garden Arena
3/17/00   Mandalay Bay Events Center
8/2/00   Mandalay Bay Events Center

Reno (2)
1/31/84   Lawlor Events Center
3/25/00   Lawlor Events Center

NEW HAMPSHIRE (1)

North Swanzey (1)
7/4/88   Cheshire Fairgrounds

NEW JERSEY (22)

Asbury Park (5)
3/29/74   Sunshine In Concert Hall
6/17/74   Sunshine In Concert Hall
11/16/74 Sunshine In Concert Hall
6/25/75   Convention Hall
4/14/90   The Stone Pony

East Rutherford (9)
3/29/85   Brendan Byrne Arena
4/11/86   Brendan Byrne Arena
12/20/87 Brendan Byrne Arena
6/30/90   Brendan Byrne Arena
10/9/92   Brendan Byrne Arena
12/31/96 Continental Airlines Arena
11/22/98 Continental Airlines Arena
6/27/00   Continental Airlines Arena
6/28/00   Continental Airlines Arena

Jersey City (1)
7/10/76   Roosevelt Stadium

Passaic (5)
4/27/74   Capitol Theatre
5/9/74   The Joint in the Woods
10/25/74 Capitol Theatre
10/4/75   Capitol Theatre (2 shows)

Trenton (1)
9/26/00   Sovereign Bank Arena at Mercer County

Wildwood (1)
7/23/75   Wildwoods Convention Center

NEW MEXICO (8)

Albuquerque (6)
1/11/77   Tingley Coliseum
12/1/79   Tingley Coliseum
1/22/84   Tingley Coliseum
9/18/93   Ramada Classic Ballroom
10/27/96 Tingley Coliseum
8/15/00   Tingley Coliseum

Las Cruces (2)
10/26/96 Pan American Center
3/14/00   Pan American Center

NEW YORK (115)

Albany (5)
8/9/75   Palace Theatre
7/7/90   Knickerbocker Arena
10/12/96 Knickerbocker Arena
11/15/98 Pepsi Arena
6/20/00   Saratoga Performing Arts Center

Amityville (12)
3/9/73   The Daisy
3/10/73   The Daisy
4/13/73   The Daisy
4/14/73   The Daisy
6/8/73   The Daisy
6/9/73   The Daisy
6/15/73   The Daisy
6/16/73   The Daisy
8/17/73   The Daisy
8/18/73   The Daisy
8/24/73   The Daisy
8/25/73   The Daisy

Binghamton (6)
12/19/75 Broome Co. Veterans Memorial Arena
3/7/84   Broome Co. Veterans Memorial Arena
11/29/84 Broome Co. Veterans Memorial Arena
6/22/90   Broome Co. Veterans Memorial Arena
10/2/92   Broome Co. Veterans Memorial Arena
9/15/00   Broome Co. Veterans Memorial Arena

Buffalo (8)
12/15/76 Veterans Memorial Auditorium
1/25/78   Veterans Memorial Auditorium
8/8/79   Veterans Memorial Auditorium
11/18/84 Veterans Memorial Auditorium
1/24/88   Veterans Memorial Auditorium
10/13/96 Marine Midland Arena
11/29/98 Marine Midland Arena
6/24/00   HSBC Arena

Glens Falls (4)
1/16/83   Glens Falls Civic Center
11/16/84 Glens Falls Civic Center
12/19/85 Glens Falls Civic Center
12/11/87 Glens Falls Civic Center

Hempstead (1)
8/23/75   Calderone Concert Hall

Manhattan/Brooklyn/Queens (45)
1/30/73   Coventry
1/31/73   Coventry
2/1/73   Coventry
5/4/73   Bleecker Street Loft, Eighth Floor
5/26/73   Lamont Hall @ Lamont-Doherty Earth Observatory
6/1/73   Bleecker Street Loft, Eighth Floor
7/13/73   The Crystal Room @ Hotel Diplomat
8/10/73   The Crystal Room @ Hotel Diplomat
8/31/73   Coventry

9/1/73   Coventry
12/21/73 Coventry
12/22/73 Coventry
12/31/73 Academy of Music
1/8/74   Bill Graham's Fillmore East
1/26/74   Academy of Music
3/23/74   Academy of Music
3/21/75   Beacon Theatre (2 shows)
7/1/75   Capitol Theatre (Port Chester)
5/1/76   The Americana
10/1/76   Puglia
2/18/77   Madison Square Garden
12/14/77 Madison Square Garden
12/15/77 Madison Square Garden
12/16/77 Madison Square Garden
7/24/79   Madison Square Garden
7/25/79   Madison Square Garden
7/25/80   Palladium
3/9/84   Radio City Music Hall
3/10/84   Radio City Music Hall
12/16/85 Madison Square Garden
8/12/88   The Ritz
8/13/88   The Ritz
11/9/90   Madison Square Garden
5/9/92   The Ritz
5/10/92   The Warehouse
7/30/95   Roseland Ballroom
8/4/95   Studio 6A @ NBC Television Studios
8/9/95   Sony Studios
7/25/96   Madison Square Garden
7/26/96   Madison Square Garden
7/27/96   Madison Square Garden
7/28/96   Madison Square Garden
9/4/96   Fulton Ferry Landing
11/23/98 Madison Square Garden

Middletown (1)
6/17/90   Orange County Fair Speedway

Niagara Falls (1)
4/14/76   Niagara Falls Convention & Civic Center Arena

Poughkeepsie (4)
3/8/84   Mid-Hudson Civic Center
11/28/84 Mid-Hudson Civic Center
4/4/86   Mid-Hudson Civic Center
1/26/88   Mid-Hudson Civic Center

Rochester (6)
10/5/75   The Dome Center
1/20/83   Rochester Community War Memorial
11/17/84 Rochester Community War Memorial
4/7/86   Rochester Community War Memorial
1/30/88   Rochester Community War Memorial
11/28/98 Blue Cross Arena at the War Memorial

Syracuse (8)
10/2/75   Onondaga County War Memorial
12/12/75 Onondaga County War Memorial
12/16/76 Onondaga County War Memorial
1/18/83   Onondaga County War Memorial
11/20/84 Onondaga County War Memorial
12/16/87 Onondaga County War Memorial
6/16/90   Cayuga County Fairgrounds

9/16/00   War Memorial at Oncenter

Uniondale (9)
12/31/75 Nassau Veterans Memorial Coliseum
2/21/77   Nassau Veterans Memorial Coliseum
9/1/79   Nassau Veterans Memorial Coliseum
11/26/84 Nassau Veterans Memorial Coliseum
1/29/88   Nassau Veterans Memorial Coliseum
6/28/90   Nassau Veterans Memorial Coliseum
10/11/92 Nassau Veterans Memorial Coliseum
12/29/96 Nassau Veterans Memorial Coliseum
11/27/98 Nassau Veterans Memorial Coliseum

Utica (3)
4/13/76   Memorial Auditorium
4/2/86   Memorial Auditorium
1/22/88   Memorial Auditorium

Wantagh (2)
6/9/00   Jones Beach Amphitheatre
6/10/00   Jones Beach Amphitheatre

NORTH CAROLINA (43)

Asheville (6)
12/1/74   Asheville Civic Center
6/27/75   Asheville Civic Center
11/28/75 Asheville Civic Center
3/1/77   Asheville Civic Center
6/28/79   Asheville Civic Center
11/7/90   Asheville Civic Center

Charlotte (16)
4/21/74   Flashes (2 shows)
11/28/74 Charlotte Coliseum
4/25/75   Charlotte Park Center Auditorium
11/29/75 Charlotte Park Center Auditorium
11/25/76 Charlotte Coliseum
1/5/78   Charlotte Coliseum
6/24/79   Charlotte Coliseum
1/6/85   Charlotte Coliseum
12/28/85 Charlotte Coliseum
2/7/88   Charlotte Coliseum
7/25/90   Charlotte Coliseum
10/23/92 Charlotte Coliseum
9/27/96   Charlotte Coliseum
4/20/00   New Charlotte Coliseum
10/6/00   New Charlotte Coliseum

Fayetteville (9)
7/19/74   Cumberland County Memorial Arena
11/30/74 Cumberland County Memorial Arena
4/26/75   Cumberland County Memorial Arena
11/27/75 Cumberland County Memorial Arena
12/27/76 Cumberland County Memorial Arena
1/5/85   Cumberland County Memorial Arena
2/6/88   Cumberland County Memorial Arena
7/28/90   Cumberland County Memorial Arena
10/24/92 Cumberland County Memorial Arena

Greensboro (9)
9/12/75   Greensboro Coliseum
8/27/76   Greensboro Coliseum
12/31/77 Greensboro Coliseum
7/3/79   Greensboro Coliseum
12/29/85 Greensboro Coliseum
2/5/88   Greensboro Coliseum
7/27/90   Greensboro Coliseum
9/28/96   Greensboro Coliseum
4/22/00   Greensboro Coliseum

Raleigh (3)
11/27/76 J.S. Dorton Arena @ North Carolina State Fairgrounds
4/4/97   Dean E. Smith Center
6/30/00   Alltel Pavilion at Walnut Creek

NORTH DAKOTA (12)

Bismarck (5)
2/12/77   Bismarck Civic Center
12/29/82 Bismarck Civic Center
3/11/85   Bismarck Civic Center
10/2/90   Bismarck Civic Center
4/27/97   Bismarck Civic Center

Fargo (3)
5/26/90   Red River Valley Speedway
4/26/97   Fargodome
7/14/00   Fargodome

Grand Forks (2)
1/17/77   University of North Dakota Fieldhouse
3/10/85   University of North Dakota Fieldhouse

Jamestown (1)
3/14/86   Jamestown Civic Center

Minot (1)
11/12/74 Minot Municipal Auditorium

OHIO (72)

Ada (1)
5/9/75   King Horn Convocation Center @ Ohio Northern University

Akron (1)
4/8/75   Akron Civic Theatre

Cincinnati (8)
9/10/76   Riverfront Coliseum
1/10/78   Riverfront Coliseum
9/14/79   Riverfront Coliseum
3/24/85   Cincinnati Gardens
3/21/86   Cincinnati Gardens
6/12/90   Cincinnati Gardens
8/8/96   Riverfront Coliseum
5/22/00   Riverbend Music Center

Cleveland (22)
4/1/74   The Agora
6/14/74   Allen Theatre
6/21/75   Music Hall
2/1/76   The Coliseum
9/3/76   The Coliseum
1/8/78   The Coliseum
7/18/79   The Coliseum
7/19/79   The Coliseum
2/22/83   The Coliseum Theatre
2/22/84   The Coliseum Theatre
12/14/84 The Coliseum Theatre
12/11/85 The Coliseum Theatre
1/15/88   The Coliseum
6/9/90   The Coliseum
11/29/92 The Coliseum Theatre
7/23/95   Sheraton City Centre
7/19/96   GUND Arena
7/20/96   GUND Arena
10/20/96 GUND Arena
12/6/98   GUND Arena
5/5/00   GUND Arena
5/6/00   GUND Arena

Columbus (13)
4/3/74   The Agora
10/30/74 The Agora
4/30/75   Veterans Memorial Auditorium
10/11/75 Veterans Memorial Auditorium
3/6/77   St. John Arena
2/19/84   Battelle Hall @ Ohio Center
12/12/84 Battelle Hall @ Ohio Center
3/29/86   Battelle Hall @ Ohio Center
1/13/88   Battelle Hall @ Ohio Center
6/6/90   Battelle Hall @ Ohio Center
12/5/98   Value City Arena at the Jerome Schottenstein Center
5/13/00   Polaris Amphitheater
9/29/00   Nationwide Arena

Dayton (13)
4/11/75   The Palace Theatre
1/31/76   Hara Arena
8/8/76   Hara Arena
1/9/83   University of Dayton Arena
2/21/84   Hara Arena
12/13/84 Hara Arena
12/13/85 Hara Arena
12/31/87 Hara Arena
6/7/90   Hara Arena
11/25/92 Ervin J. Nutter Center
7/17/96   Ervin J. Nutter Center
12/11/98 Ervin J. Nutter Center
9/13/00   Ervin J. Nutter Center

Toledo (13)
10/19/74 Renaissance Valentine Theatre
3/28/75   Sports Arena
11/12/75 Sports Arena
7/31/76   Sports Arena
12/16/79 Sports Arena
1/8/83   Sports Arena
3/25/85   Sports Arena
3/28/86   Sports Arena
12/7/87   Sports Arena
5/19/90   Sports Arena
11/22/92 John F. Savage Hall
4/12/97   John F. Savage Hall
5/9/00   John F. Savage Hall

Youngstown (1)
10/27/74 Tomorrow

OKLAHOMA (18)

Norman/Oklahoma City (10)
3/4/76   Civic Center Music Hall
1/7/77   Lloyd Noble Center
11/15/77 Myriad Convention Center
10/17/79 Lloyd Noble Center
3/21/83   Lloyd Noble Center
2/21/86   Lloyd Noble Center
11/25/87 Lloyd Noble Center

8/25/90 Myriad Convention Center
9/11/96 Myriad Convention Center
4/4/00 Myriad Arena

Tulsa (8)
6/13/75 Tulsa Fairgrounds Pavilion
3/8/76 Tulsa Assembly Center
1/6/77 Tulsa Assembly Center
11/26/77 Tulsa Assembly Center
10/29/79 Tulsa Assembly Center
2/22/86 Expo Square Pavilion
11/24/87 Expo Square Pavilion
5/8/90 Expo Square Pavilion

OREGON (16)

Medford (3)
1/11/75 National Guard Armory
5/23/75 National Guard Armory
3/13/88 Jackson County Expo Park

Portland (13)
5/24/74 Paramount Northwest Theatre
1/10/75 Paramount Northwest Theatre
5/24/75 Paramount Northwest Theatre
5/26/75 Paramount Northwest Theatre
2/11/76 Memorial Coliseum
8/13/77 Memorial Coliseum
2/14/85 Memorial Coliseum
2/13/86 Memorial Coliseum
3/14/88 Memorial Coliseum
9/9/90 Memorial Coliseum
12/10/92 Memorial Coliseum
8/30/96 Rose Garden
7/24/00 Rose Garden

PENNSYLVANIA (70)

Allentown (8)
3/19/75 Roxy Theatre (2 shows)
10/6/75 Memorial Hall
11/15/84 Stabler Arena
4/1/86 Stabler Arena
6/27/90 Allentown Fairgrounds Grandstand
9/30/92 Stabler Arena (rehearsal)
10/1/92 Stabler Arena

Erie (7)
4/9/75 Erie County Fieldhouse
1/23/76 Erie County Fieldhouse
3/5/84 Lewis J. Tullio Arena @ Erie Civic Center
3/27/86 Lewis J. Tullio Arena @ Erie Civic Center
12/9/87 Lewis J. Tullio Arena @ Erie Civic Center
10/16/90 Lewis J. Tullio Arena @ Erie Civic Center
6/19/00 Lewis J. Tullio Arena @ Erie Civic Center

Harrisburg (3)
8/25/75 Farm Show Arena
3/26/76 Farm Show Arena
7/8/90 City Island Sports Complex

Hershey (3)
11/8/90 Hersheypark Arena
10/13/92 Hersheypark Arena
7/5/00 Hersheypark Arena

Johnstown (4)
5/17/75 Cambria County War Memorial Arena
3/25/76 Cambria County War Memorial Arena
1/23/88 Cambria County War Memorial Arena
10/10/90 Cambria County War Memorial Arena

Lock Haven (1)
9/15/74 Thomas Field House

Philadelphia (21)
3/22/74 Valley Forge Music Fair
4/29/74 KYW-TV Studios
5/3/75 Tower Theater
10/3/75 Tower Theater
3/24/76 Philadelphia Civic Center
12/21/76 The Spectrum
12/22/77 The Spectrum
1/30/78 The Spectrum
9/7/79 The Spectrum
3/3/84 Tower Theater
11/25/84 The Spectrum
12/17/85 The Spectrum
12/18/87 The Spectrum
6/26/90 The Spectrum
5/5/92 The Trocadero
10/10/92 The Spectrum
10/8/96 CoreStates Center
10/9/96 CoreStates Center
10/11/96 CoreStates Center
11/21/98 First Union Spectrum
6/16/00 Blockbuster-Sony Music Entertainment Centre

Pittsburgh (16)
4/15/75 Stanley Theatre
12/20/75 Civic Arena
9/4/76 Civic Arena
1/13/78 Civic Arena
7/21/79 Civic Arena
3/4/84 Stanley Theatre
3/26/85 Civic Arena
4/12/86 Civic Arena
1/16/88 Civic Arena
6/23/90 Coca-Cola Star Lake Amphitheatre
10/16/92 Civic Arena
8/1/95 The Monroeville Expo Mart
7/21/96 Civic Arena
7/22/96 Civic Arena
12/4/98 Civic Arena
5/26/00 Post-Gazette Pavilion at Star Lake

Scranton (1)
7/7/00 Coors Light Amphitheatre at Montage Mountain

University Park (3)
3/29/97 Bryce Jordan Center
11/18/98 Bryce Jordan Center
9/27/00 Bryce Jordan Center

Wilkes-Barre (3)
9/16/74 Paramount Theatre
12/23/74 Paramount Theatre
9/14/75 King's College Gymnasium

PUERTO RICO (2)

San Juan (2)
1/12/86 Coliseo Roberto Clemente
4/21/99 Coliseo Roberto Clemente

RHODE ISLAND (12)

Providence (12)
8/8/75 Providence Civic Center
12/29/75 Providence Civic Center
1/1/77 Providence Civic Center
2/2/78 Providence Civic Center
2/3/78 Providence Civic Center
7/31/79 Providence Civic Center
8/1/79 Providence Civic Center
12/22/85 Providence Civic Center
12/12/87 Providence Civic Center
6/20/90 Providence Civic Center
3/23/97 Providence Civic Center
9/18/00 Providence Civic Center

SOUTH CAROLINA (22)

Charleston (3)
11/29/74 Charleston Municipal Auditorium
9/24/96 North Charleston Coliseum
10/7/00 North Charleston Coliseum

Columbia (10)
7/6/76 Carolina Coliseum
2/27/77 Carolina Coliseum
1/6/78 Carolina Coliseum
6/22/79 Carolina Coliseum
12/27/85 Carolina Coliseum
2/16/88 Carolina Coliseum
7/24/90 Carolina Coliseum
10/25/92 Carolina Coliseum
9/25/96 Carolina Coliseum
4/18/00 Carolina Coliseum

Greenville (9)
11/27/74 Greenville Memorial Auditorium
6/28/75 Greenville Memorial Auditorium
11/28/76 Greenville Memorial Auditorium
6/26/79 Greenville Memorial Auditorium
1/3/85 Greenville Memorial Auditorium
2/3/88 Greenville Memorial Auditorium
7/26/90 Greenville Memorial Auditorium
11/3/92 Greenville Memorial Auditorium
4/21/00 Bi-Lo Center

SOUTH DAKOTA (7)

Rapid City (3)
8/8/77 Rushmore Plaza Civic Center
3/19/88 Rushmore Plaza Civic Center
8/28/90 Rushmore Plaza Civic Center

Sioux Falls (4)
2/19/83 Sioux Falls Arena
5/11/90 Sioux Falls Arena
12/4/92 Sioux Falls Arena
4/18/97 Sioux Falls Arena

TENNESSEE (54)

Bristol (1)
10/21/92 Viking Hall Civic Center @ Tennessee High School

Chattanooga (3)
9/10/75 Soldiers' and Sailors' Memorial Auditorium

1/29/83 UTC Arena
4/24/00 The McKenzie Arena

Johnson City (7)
4/24/75 Freedom Hall Civic Center @
         Science Hill High School
7/19/76 Freedom Hall Civic Center @
         Science Hill High School
2/26/77 Freedom Hall Civic Center @
         Science Hill High School
1/4/85 Freedom Hall Civic Center @
         Science Hill High School
1/3/86 Freedom Hall Civic Center @
         Science Hill High School
1/1/88 Freedom Hall Civic Center @
         Science Hill High School
7/18/90 Freedom Hall Civic Center @
         Science Hill High School

Knoxville (12)
9/11/75 Knoxville Civic Coliseum
7/15/76 Knoxville Civic Coliseum
9/12/79 Knoxville Civic Coliseum
2/1/83 Knoxville Civic Coliseum
1/10/84 Knoxville Civic Coliseum
1/8/85 Knoxville Civic Coliseum
1/4/86 Knoxville Civic Coliseum
1/2/88 Knoxville Civic Coliseum
7/19/90 Knoxville Civic Coliseum
11/7/92 Knoxville Civic Coliseum
9/29/96 Thompson-Boling Arena
4/30/00 Thompson-Boling Arena

Memphis (13)
4/17/74 Lafayette's Music Room
4/18/74 Lafayette's Music Room
3/14/76 Auditorium North Hall
12/2/76 Mid-South Coliseum
12/9/77 Mid-South Coliseum
8/12/79 Mid-South Coliseum
1/7/84 Mid-South Coliseum
1/22/85 Mid-South Coliseum
12/1/85 Mid-South Coliseum
11/15/87 Mid-South Coliseum
8/8/90 Mid-South Coliseum
7/10/96 The Pyramid
4/25/00 The Pyramid

Nashville (17)
4/15/74 Muther's Music Emporium
4/16/74 Muther's Music Emporium
10/30/75 Nashville Municipal Auditorium
7/21/76 Nashville Municipal Auditorium
8/14/79 Nashville Municipal Auditorium
1/30/83 Nashville Municipal Auditorium
1/11/84 Nashville Municipal Auditorium
1/19/85 Nashville Municipal Auditorium
11/30/85 Nashville Municipal Auditorium
2/9/88 Nashville Municipal Auditorium
7/21/90 Coca-Cola Starwood Amphitheatre
11/6/92 Nashville Municipal Auditorium
7/30/94 Riverfront Amphitheatre
7/9/95 Nashville Convention Center
4/6/97 Nashville Arena
1/2/99 Nashville Arena
4/28/00 AmSouth Amphitheatre

TEXAS (95)

Abilene (5)
1/5/77 Taylor County Coliseum
11/19/77 Taylor County Coliseum
10/27/79 Taylor County Coliseum
1/25/85 Taylor County Coliseum
2/27/86 Taylor County Coliseum

Amarillo (4)
1/10/77 The Amarillo Civic Center
12/3/79 The Amarillo Civic Center
3/22/83 The Amarillo Civic Center
2/4/85 The Amarillo Civic Center
9/22/90 The Amarillo Civic Center

Austin (8)
6/14/75 City Coliseum
1/16/84 City Coliseum
1/26/85 Frank C. Erwin, Jr. Special Events
         Center
12/8/85 Frank C. Erwin, Jr. Special Events
         Center
2/26/88 Frank C. Erwin, Jr. Special Events
         Center
5/6/90 Frank C. Erwin, Jr. Special Events
         Center
11/5/96 Frank C. Erwin, Jr. Special Events
         Center
8/17/00 Frank C. Erwin, Jr. Special Events
         Center

Beaumont (3)
11/7/75 McDonald Gym @ Lamar University
3/13/83 Beaumont Civic Center
2/26/86 Beaumont Civic Center

Belton (1)
11/20/87 Bell County Expo Center

Corpus Christi (6)
6/15/75 Memorial Coliseum
3/14/83 Memorial Coliseum
1/19/84 Memorial Coliseum
1/27/85 Memorial Coliseum
2/24/86 Memorial Coliseum
11/18/87 Memorial Coliseum

Dallas/Fort Worth (19)
11/8/75 Texas Hall @ University of Texas-
         Arlington
8/11/76 Tarrant County Convention Center
9/4/77 Tarrant County Convention Center
9/5/77 Tarrant County Convention Center
10/23/79 Tarrant County Convention Center
3/9/83 Dallas County Convention Center
         Arena
1/13/84 Dallas County Convention Center
         Arena
1/29/85 Reunion Arena
12/4/85 Reunion Arena
2/28/86 Tarrant County Convention Center
2/27/88 Tarrant County Convention Center
5/5/90 Starplex Amphitheatre
9/21/90 Tarrant County Convention Center
4/30/92 Dallas City Limits
7/2/95 Dallas/Fort Worth Airport Marriot
7/5/96 Reunion Arena
11/10/96 Reunion Arena
4/2/00 Starplex Amphitheatre
8/23/00 Fort Worth Convention Center

El Paso (5)
8/15/76 El Paso County Coliseum
3/23/83 El Paso County Coliseum
1/21/84 El Paso County Coliseum
2/5/85 Special Events Center
9/19/90 Special Events Center

Galveston (1)
3/11/90 West Beach Pocket Park #1

Houston (16)
10/4/74 Music Hall
11/9/75 Sam Houston Coliseum
8/13/76 The Summit
9/1/77 The Summit
9/2/77 The Summit
10/21/79 The Summit
3/10/83 Sam Houston Coliseum
1/18/84 Sam Houston Coliseum
1/31/85 Sam Houston Coliseum
12/7/85 Sam Houston Coliseum
2/24/88 The Summit
8/21/90 The Summit
4/29/92 Backstage
7/6/96 The Summit
4/1/00 Cynthia Woods Mitchell Pavilion
8/22/00 Cynthia Woods Mitchell Pavilion

Lubbock (7)
11/20/77 Lubbock Municipal Coliseum
10/31/79 Lubbock Municipal Coliseum
1/24/85 Lubbock Municipal Coliseum
11/21/87 Lubbock Municipal Coliseum
5/3/90 Lubbock Municipal Coliseum
         (rehearsal)
5/4/90 Lubbock Municipal Coliseum
3/29/00 United Spirit Arena

Midland (1)
11/2/79 Al G. Langford Chaparral Center

Odessa (3)
1/23/84 Ector County Coliseum
2/3/85 Ector County Coliseum
9/20/90 Ector County Coliseum

San Angelo (1)
1/17/84 San Angelo Coliseum

San Antonio (13)
11/6/75 Municipal Auditorium
11/22/77 Joe & Harry Freeman Coliseum
11/23/77 Joe & Harry Freeman Coliseum
10/19/79 HemisFair Arena @ Henry B.
         Gonzalez Convention Center
3/11/83 HemisFair Arena @ Henry B.
         Gonzalez Convention Center
1/14/84 HemisFair Arena @ Henry B.
         Gonzalez Convention Center
1/30/85 HemisFair Arena @ Henry B.
         Gonzalez Convention Center
12/3/85 HemisFair Arena @ Henry B.
         Gonzalez Convention Center
2/25/88 HemisFair Arena @ Henry B.
         Gonzalez Convention Center
8/22/90 Joe & Harry Freeman Coliseum
4/19/94 Parking Lot - East Stage @ Joe &
         Harry Freeman Coliseum
7/7/96 AlamoDome
3/31/00 AlamoDome

Waco (2)
2/1/85   Convention Center
2/23/86   Convention Center

UTAH (12)

Salt Lake City (12)
2/9/76   Terrace Ballroom
1/13/77   O. Thayne Accord Arena @ Salt
           Palace Center
8/4/77   O. Thayne Accord Arena @ Salt
           Palace Center
2/5/84   O. Thayne Accord Arena @ Salt
           Palace Center
2/11/85   O. Thayne Accord Arena @ Salt
           Palace Center
2/17/86   O. Thayne Accord Arena @ Salt
           Palace Center
3/21/88   O. Thayne Accord Arena @ Salt
           Palace Center
9/1/90   SaltAir Resort Main Pavilion
12/8/92   Delta Center
6/22/95   Utah State Fairpark
9/5/96   Delta Center
3/27/00   The E Center of West Valley City

VIRGINIA (24)

Hampton (4)
3/7/77   Hampton Coliseum
7/5/79   Hampton Coliseum
2/26/84   Hampton Coliseum
10/5/96   Hampton Coliseum

Norfolk (7)
9/13/75   The Scope
7/3/76   The Scope
1/25/83   The Scope
1/14/86   The Scope
1/20/88   The Scope
7/13/90   The Scope
7/2/00   GTE Virginia Beach Amphitheatre

Richmond (6)
4/27/75   Mosque Theatre
12/21/75   Richmond Coliseum
7/8/76   Richmond Coliseum
7/12/90   Richmond Coliseum
4/2/97   Richmond Coliseum
6/6/00   Richmond Coliseum

Roanoke (7)
6/20/75   Salem-Roanoke County Civic Center
12/28/76   Roanoke Civic Center
7/10/79   Roanoke Civic Center
7/11/90   Roanoke Civic Center
10/17/92   Roanoke Civic Center
10/4/96   Roanoke Civic Center
5/3/00   Roanoke Civic Center

WASHINGTON (24)

George (1)
7/22/00   Gorge Amphitheatre

Seattle (15)
5/25/74   Paramount Northwest Theatre
1/12/75   Paramount Northwest Theatre
5/25/75   Paramount Northwest Theatre
2/13/76   Paramount Northwest Theatre
2/14/76   Paramount Northwest Theatre

8/12/77   Seattle Center Coliseum
11/21/79   Seattle Center Coliseum
2/13/85   Seattle Center Arena
2/14/86   Seattle Center Coliseum
3/17/88   Seattle Center Coliseum
9/7/90   Seattle Center Coliseum
12/14/92   Seattle Center Arena
6/20/95   Seattle Center
8/31/96   Tacoma Dome
5/5/97   KeyArena @ Seattle Center

Spokane (8)
5/26/74   John F. Kennedy Pavilion @ Gonzaga
           University
5/27/75   Spokane Coliseum
2/12/76   Spokane Coliseum
8/11/77   Spokane Coliseum
2/26/85   Spokane Coliseum
3/15/88   Spokane Coliseum
9/8/90   Spokane Coliseum
9/1/96   Spokane Arena

WASHINGTON, D.C. (18)
3/25/74   The Bayou (2 shows)
4/6/75   G.W. Lisner Auditorium
5/10/75   Capital Centre
11/30/75   Capital Centre
12/19/76   Capital Centre
12/19/77   Capital Centre
12/20/77   Capital Centre
7/7/79   Capital Centre
7/8/79   Capital Centre
2/1/88   Capital Centre
7/10/90   The Patriot Center
10/18/92   Capital Centre
10/6/96   USAir Arena
10/7/96   USAir Arena
11/19/98   MCI Center
7/1/00   Nissan Pavilion at Stone Ridge
10/4/00   Merriweather Post Pavilion

WEST VIRGINIA (14)

Charleston (10)
6/22/75   Charleston Civic Center
7/17/76   Charleston Civic Center
1/4/83   Charleston Civic Center
1/15/86   Charleston Civic Center
1/18/88   Charleston Civic Center
11/1/90   Charleston Civic Center
10/14/92   Charleston Civic Center
3/31/97   Charleston Civic Center
12/8/98   Charleston Civic Center
5/2/00   Charleston Civic Center

Huntington (3)
11/26/75   Veterans Memorial Field House
1/11/78   Huntington Civic Center
9/10/79   Huntington Civic Center

Wheeling (1)
3/27/97   Wheeling Civic Center

WISCONSIN (35)

East Troy (1)
9/29/90   Alpine Valley Music Theatre

Green Bay (5)
2/3/77   Brown County Veterans Memorial
           Arena

2/14/84   Brown County Veterans Memorial
           Arena
3/5/86   Brown County Veterans Memorial
           Arena
1/6/88   Brown County Veterans Memorial
           Arena
5/28/90   Brown County Veterans Memorial
           Arena

Kenosha (1)
3/27/75   Kenosha Ice Arena

La Crosse (5)
12/13/74   Mary E. Sawyer Auditorium
11/3/75   Mary E. Sawyer Auditorium
2/20/83   Mary E. Sawyer Auditorium @ La
           Crosse Center
3/15/85   Mary E. Sawyer Auditorium @ La
           Crosse Center
3/12/86   Mary E. Sawyer Auditorium @ La
           Crosse Center

Madison (10)
2/5/76   Dane County Expo Center Coliseum
2/4/77   Dane County Expo Center Coliseum
12/3/77   Dane County Expo Center Coliseum
9/26/79   Dane County Expo Center Coliseum
3/19/85   Dane County Expo Center Coliseum
3/1/88   Dane County Expo Center Coliseum
12/2/92   Dane County Expo Center Coliseum
4/23/97   Dane County Expo Center Coliseum
12/27/98   Dane County Expo Center Coliseum
7/11/00   Kohl Center

Milwaukee (13)
5/6/75   Riverside Theater
2/4/76   Milwaukee Auditorium
2/1/77   Milwaukee Auditorium
2/2/77   Milwaukee Auditorium
9/24/79   Milwaukee Arena
2/10/84   Milwaukee Auditorium
12/30/84   Mecca Auditorium
1/20/86   Mecca Auditorium
1/7/88   Mecca Arena
11/30/92   Bradley Center
8/10/96   Bradley Center
12/20/98   Bradley Center
5/19/00   Marcus Amphitheatre

WYOMING (1)

Casper (1)
3/20/88   Casper Events Center

WALES (1)

Cardiff (1)
5/20/92   Welsh National Ice-Rink

YUGOSLAVIA (1)

Beograd (1)
6/4/97   Sajan Arean Beograd Hala